. . . .

THE EMBODIMENT
OF REASON

E THE MBODIMENT OF REASON

Kant on Spirit,
Generation, and
Community

Susan Meld Shell

THE UNIVERSITY OF CHICAGO PRESS
CHICAGO AND LONDON

Susan Meld Shell is associate professor of political science at Boston College.

The University of Chicago Press, Chicago 60637
The University of Chicago Press, Ltd., London

© 1996 by The University of Chicago
All rights reserved. Published 1996
Printed in the United States of America

05   04   03   02   01   00   99   98   97   96   1   2   3   4   5

ISBN 0-226-75215-1 (cloth)
ISBN 0-226-75217-8 (paper)

Library of Congress Cataloging-in-Publication Data

Shell, Susan Meld, 1948–
     The embodiment of reason : Kant on spirit, generation, and
community / Susan Meld Shell.
         p.   cm.
     Includes bibliographical references and index.
     1. Kant, Immanuel, 1724–1804.   I. Title.
B2798.S5   1996.
193—dc20   95-47170
                                                        CIP

⊗ The paper used in this publication meets the minimum requirements of the American National Standard for Information Sciences—Permanence of Paper for Printed Library Materials, ANSI Z39.48-1984.

Contents

Acknowledgments

Of the many who helped me while I worked on this study, I owe particular thanks to Ronald Beiner, William James Booth, Charles Griswold, Peter Fenves, Robert Fishman, William Galston, Michael Gillespie, Joseph Knippenberg, Joan Landes, Harvey C. Mansfield, Jr., Arthur Melzer, Michael O'Donovan-Anderson, Clifford Orwin, Thomas Pangle, Steven Smith, Patrick Riley, Tom Rockmore, Nancy Rosenblum, Nathan Tarcov, Richard Velkley, Hent de Vries, Jules Vuillemin, Samuel Weber, Howard Williams, and Bernard Yack. I would also like to thank John Tryneski and others at the University of Chicago Press for their timely and knowledgeable assistance through all phases of the publishing process, and to an anonymous reader for very helpful comments on the manuscript.

An early version of chapter 3, now thoroughly revised, appeared in *Kant and Political Philosophy* (1993), edited by Ronald Beiner and William James Booth. An earlier version of chapter 4 appeared under the title "Kant's Political Cosmology" in *Essays on Kant's Political Philosophy,* edited by Howard Lloyd Williams (©1992 by Susan Shell). A shorter version of chapter 7 appeared as "Kant's Idea of History," in *History and the Idea of Progress,* edited by Arthur M. Melzer, Jerry Weinberger, and M. Richard Zinman (©1995 by Cornell University; used by permission of the publisher, Cornell University Press).

I began the study as a postdoctoral fellow at McMaster University, whose interest and support I gratefully acknowledge. My colleagues and students at Boston College have been a continuing source of stimulation and encouragement, Michael Clarke, Susan Collins, Lorna Knott, Michael Ehrmantraut, Michael Foley, Claus Freyinger, Michael Grenke, Louis Hunt, and Christopher Kukk deserving special mention. I should also like to thank the National Endowment for the Humanities, the Bunting Institute of Radcliffe College, and the Lynde and Harry Bradley Foundation for their very generous support of various stages of the project.

My deepest debt is to my husband, Marc Shell, and our children, Hanna and Jacob. To them this book is dedicated.

1 Introduction

Metaphysics is therefore also the fulfillment of all culture of
human reason.
                    Kant, *Critique of Pure Reason* (A/850 = B/878)

[Kant], for fear of obstructing the circulation of the blood, . . .
never would wear garters; yet, as he found it difficult to keep
up his stockings without them, he had invented for himself a
most elaborate substitute. . . . In a little pocket, somewhat
smaller than a watch pocket, but occupying pretty nearly the
same situation as a watch pocket, on each thigh, there was
placed a small box, something like a watch case, but smaller.
Into this box was introduced a watch spring in a wheel, round
about which wheel was wound an elastic cord, for regulating
the force of which there was a separate contrivance. To the two
ends of this cord were attached hooks, which hooks were
carried through a small aperture in the pockets, and so, passing
down the inner and outer side of the thigh, caught hold of
two loops which were fixed on the off side and the near side of
each stocking. As might be expected, so complex an apparatus
was liable, like the Ptolemaic system of the heavens, to
occasional derangements.
                    Thomas De Quincey, *The Last Days of Immanuel Kant*

The following study examines Kant's insight into the perplexity intrinsic
to our awareness of ourselves as worldly or embodied beings, a perplexity
heightened by modern notions of nature and the human subject. Attention
to this insight reveals an intellectual career more unified in its fundamental
concerns than has generally been recognized; and it makes possible a
deeper understanding of Kant's relation to later intellectual movements,
whose insights he anticipates and in some important ways surpasses. Addi-
tionally, and not least, it brings to light the image of an extraordinarily
focused human being, for whom philosophizing and living at its most mun-
dane converged to a remarkable degree. Kant's greatness lies, at least in
part, in a singularity of purpose — a self-imposed attentiveness — by which,
in aiming to found philosophy as a systematic science, he also, and not

1

incidentally, expressed and fashioned his own character. In the course of Kant and Herder's bitter polemic over ideas of history, Herder accused his former teacher of trying to give spiritual birth to himself. More positively and accurately assayed, Kant's systematizing efforts go together with — and in a nontrivial sense constitute — a lifelong self-experiment. To this extent, Kant's life can be (and was, evidently, by him) regarded as a "masterpiece." In overstepping, then, the usual boundaries between textual and biographical analysis, I claim special warrant — one justified, I hope, by the results.

In 1747, at the age of twenty-two, Kant put forward a novel definition of the world, to whose "definition" or "explanation" (*Erklärung*), he added, no one before him had paid adequate attention (*Acht*). Kant's life work, it is the burden of my study to suggest, *is* that elucidation, or, at the very least, an example of unprecedented respect for it. Viewed either way, Kant's life work fulfills his early promise and with it the conditions of originality he initially sets himself. Viewed either way (as an *Erklärung* of the world in which we find ourselves, or as unprecedented *Achten* with regard to it), Kant's efforts during the course of an unusually long and extraordinarily productive career exhibit a unity that is both singular and singularly important philosophically and historically. The following chapters aim both to uncover that unity and to help clarify its significance.

One obstacle to such a project is the distinction Kant himself draws between his later, "critical" works and those written prior to the *Inaugural Dissertation* of 1770. While this distinction is clearly crucial to an understanding of Kant's final system (or efforts to arrive at one), the latter is, as I will try to show, best understood not as a radical rejection of all that comes before, but as a solution to problems that often reveal themselves most clearly in earlier works.

The unity of Kant's work is especially evident, as I also aim to show, in its articulating points of juncture — worldly negotiations of which Kant's *Erklärung* is the earliest and most fundamental. That self-awareness is and perhaps must be mediated by a community of bodies (not least one's own) implies both our distinctness from the world and our engagement within it, a double bind in which we find ourselves and whose dissolution (envisioned as transcendence or as merger) we both desire and fear. From this worldly negotiation arise other notions, of which "spirit" is emblematic, that both elaborate upon Kant's early insight and, in crucial ways, transform it.

Kant appropriates, to a new conception of nature or worldly totality, a typically modern understanding of complex wholes as reciprocally rather than hierarchically informed. In Kant's earliest work, this appropriation is fueled by an effort to transcend the natural commerce it would comprehend, a commerce whose fluidity calls into question the substantiality of the individual soul as traditionally conceived. Kant's sense of urgency in this regard is abetted by a particularly acute sensitivity to the tenuousness (and uncanny reversibility) of his own bodily boundaries, a sensitivity that is bound up with his own avowed tendencies toward "hypochondria" and consequently heightened awareness of the peculiarity of "healthy" consciousness. It is this tendency to hypochondria, which Kant locates midway between soundness of mind and madness, that, as much as anything, alerted him (as I will claim) to the need for — and possibility of — a definition of the limits of human consciousness.

From the beginning, Kant's concept of the world as a "commercium," or reciprocally interactive community of substances, struggles with the problem that complex unity or wholeness so conceived entails. For how can a substance be changed or affected by other substances (as "commercium" implies) and yet remain, qua substance, unchangeable or permanent (as substantiality seems to require)? This problem led Leibniz to deny the real (as opposed to ideal) community of substances. Unable to reconcile metaphysical substantiality with the spatiotemporal interaction that we perceive, he chose ultimately to interpret the latter as a confused appearance of the former. Kant, for reasons to be discussed below, refused — however much Leibniz's thought in other ways appealed to him — to follow his predecessor in this reduction of outer to inner perception. Without a principle of necessity governing the mutual relations of substances, we would be unable to distinguish (as he insists we can) between knowledge and fantasy. The actual world would be reduced to a mere combination of thoughts (and an arbitrary one at that). It is the palpable mutual recalcitrance of bodies — both others and our own — that furnishes the immediate basis for this necessity and thus rouses the mind from Leibniz's beguiling but ultimately nightmarish dreamworld. Bodily compression is for Kant, at least in his early work, a kind of ultimate fact — a register of the presence to the mind of something other than or "outside" itself — which no amount of Leibnizian "internalization" can explain away.

Given the intractability of this outer dimension, another sort of solution to the problem of worldly community presented itself to Kant, one that he believed could do justice to the actuality of the world-whole (as Leibniz's account ultimately does not) without compromising the substantial integrity of the elements that comprise it. The key to this reconciliation lies in Kant's peculiar conception of creation as the spatiotemporal unfolding of God's originating idea. Adapting the rationalist definition of worldly perfection as a maximization of unity and diversity, Kant keys the ontological integrity of each worldly element to an inner essence identified with God's purpose in creating it. The world so modeled is a "perfect machine" whose parts mutually interact according to each part's own inward design. As such, the world can be fully comprehended only by God, who grasps — immediately, as it were — each part both in its inner uniqueness and in its outer relation to the whole. For human understanding, bound up with the rest of creation in the nexus of space and time, comprehension is inevitably partial and, at best, progressive, except to the extent that some means avail of transcending generation (the natural unfolding of creation) and thus participating in immediate community with the divine.

Kant's boldness in this attempt is underscored by the language in which he chose to cast his early *Universal Natural History and Theory of the Heavens* (1755). That language, which translates the workman/artifact metaphor of Pope's *Essay on Man* into erotic (and sexual) terms, abolishes the distinction (as does Kant's later conception of the "technique of nature") between "making," or *technai;* and "generation." God the creator is also the quintessential *genitor,* with the additional provision that as creator ex nihilo he *makes* matter, rather than, in the manner of Plato's demiurge, merely informing it. God's omnipotence and omnisufficiency are revealed neither in his stirring and shaping of a matter eternally present, nor in his immediate deliverance of a world already formed, but rather in initiating a matter capable of organizing itself. Creation is the child of a single parent, or — to be more precise — its embryo, since it, like the infant in utero, progressively evolves, without ever (this side of eternity, or birth out of the world of becoming) arriving at its final form. But Kant's prevailing image of nature is not that of a child but of a mother, herself infinitely productive of individuals and species, yet regulated in her fertility by God's inseminating scheme. In the crucible of nature's fluxions, which (unlike Leibniz's monadic ladder of perfection) guarantees only the survival of species, (human) individuality is continually at risk. That the various elemental kinds (both material and biological) are irreplaceable Kant is prepared to insist, without, however, granting individuals a similar assurance as to their necessary place within the natural order. The result is an image of nature that is alternately attractive and repulsive, uplifting and degrading. Indeed, given the essentially compromising status — from the standpoint of the individual — of natural generation, the human soul is forced, if it would evade the plantlike torpor to which it is otherwise prone, to resist, above all, the procreative drive in favor of a nobler principle of philosophic or contemplative attraction.

When Rousseau, in the 1760s, pricked the bubble of Kant's metaphysical enchantment, he broke in on a romance that was already troubled. Rousseau would not have affected Kant so powerfully (an effect to which Kant himself testifies) if their thought had not shared a profound affinity. Both Kant and Rousseau recognized the problem posed by modern science for traditional conceptions of the soul. Traditionally, the soul was understood as substance—a complex whole governed by reason as its informing part. For Rousseau, the collapse of natural hierarchy (or a rational principle within nature) dictated by modern science implied the collapse of reason itself as a dependable governor of the soul. (Indeed, reason for Rousseau becomes the principle cause or symptom of the soul's derangement, and only secondarily and ambiguously, an agent of curative deliverance.) Instead of reason, Rousseau looked to the simplicity of prereflective, prerational consciousness as the most humanly relevant example of unity of form in nature. All of his celebrated ideals, from domestic love, to citizen virtue, to philosophic reverie, take their bearings from this exemplary model, which they seek, more or less adequately, to recover, and—to the extent that they enhance the "sentiment of existence" that is the source of man's natural happiness—expand. In *Emile,* the work of Rousseau with which Kant seems to have been most taken and whose impact can be most easily measured, Rousseau emphasizes education to moral virtue as the means of reforming the soul in the face of the deforming corruptions of contemporary society. The virtue he describes, however, is not the parochial virtue of the Spartan and Roman citizen (stressed in the *Social Contract* and other, overtly political works) but one that arises from Emile's love for and consequent ideal participation in a general will embracing humanity at large. This stress on the universal and on a virtue stemming from conscious overcoming of natural drives (rather than, as with the Spartan citizen, from unconscious habituation to the mores of one's particular society) was to have particular significance for Kant's new understanding of worldly community as a morally (rather than metaphysically) intelligible whole.

Rousseau, in short, enables Kant to translate the implicitly moral model that inspired his early metaphysical efforts into explicitly moral terms. The divine schema that eludes man's theoretical grasp becomes accessible in and through a new moral ideal inspired by Rousseau's conception of the general will. Not cognition but virtuous self-mastery becomes man's badge of honor—one that lifts him beyond nature's abysmal fluctuations into direct community with the divine or holy will. At the heart of this moral economy lies human freedom—not the ambiguous, not to say monstrous, indeterminacy that defines the human in Kant's *Universal Natural History*—but a freedom that consists in both making and submitting to universal law. As a power of original causation, moral will (albeit viewed from a practical point of view) borrows something of the aura of divine creation. Equally importantly, as a force that is simultaneously individual and universal, it short-circuits the progressive realization of totality, whose comprehension Kant's earlier cosmology vainly attempted.

Such a redirection of erotic impetus, however, requires a kind of metaphysical exorcism—an exercise in physical and spiritual deflation. Such is

the effect of Kant's *Dreams of a Spirit Seer,* the first work to set forth boundary keeping as the central task of theoretical philosophy, the better to preserve the purity of Kant's new moral ideal from contamination by the sensible. In so doing, *Dreams,* which is perhaps the wittiest piece that Kant
ever wrote, definitively explodes Kant's old approach to the problem of
self-definition. The model of interactive community between mind and
body — a model that Kant had previously assumed without being able adequately to explain — gives way before a series of burlesque figurative rever-
sals. Within the limits prescribed for healthy human reason, spirit is indistinguishable from gas, and the intelligible world as metaphysically
conceived, from the windy enthusiasms of the mad. The boundary between matter and spirit is not coextensive with the bodily membrane that
separates inner consciousness from its outer relations with the corporeal
world. For the body is not an infinitely compressible spherical circumference, as Kant's earlier *Physical Monadology* suggests, but a "plant with its
stomach for a foot" — a wormlike tube whose carapace against the outer
world simultaneously channels it within. In a word, the "inwardness" that
the body manages to confine is entirely relative to one's perspective and
has nothing to do with absolute inwardness, formerly identified with the
"spirit" of the substantial soul and now associated by Kant with moral
personality. At the same time, *Dreams* allows Kant to conduct a sort of
thought experiment which brings home to him the necessity of representing in time and space any world that is not conceived in purely moral terms
(a first step toward his later discovery that the world we know is one only
of appearances).

Kant's turn toward democracy and human rights is the political expression of this metaphysical and moral revolution. Man's existence is justified
(and in this sense given a sufficient ground or reason) not by the ennobling
reason of a few but by the moral freedom and dignity of all. At the same
time, moral community, at the level of concrete institutions, is envisioned
by Kant, especially in those works that bear the immediate imprint of
Rousseau's thought, as explicitly male. The morality of feeling that Kant
had earlier briefly espoused is now dismissed as chimerical and, at the same
time, effeminate. To be governed by the force of attraction, however beautiful its object, is to remain the sport of nature. Still, without the susceptibility to others that is expressed, above all, by sexual need, humanity would
have remained in its primitive condition of mutual isolation. It is, as Rousseau revealed, the idealization of man's natural sexual need that lays the
psychological groundwork for his moral self-transcendence. Women, more
artful than men and also closer to nature, are to be men's educators if not
quite their equals. Thrown out with a pitchfork by the ideal of freedom,
nature returns as culture (or "cultivation"), with its peculiarly "feminine"
blurring of the boundaries between reason and unreason.

The upshot is a new way out of the "labyrinth of nature"—one that replaces nature's "leading strings" with the "guiding thread" of an idea—an idea that is not "given" or received, as with traditional models of contemplation, but (like Kant's early conception of the schema of creation) spontaneously projected by the mind (albeit one that need no longer be divine). The meaning of enlightenment shifts in emphasis from discovering or making light to coming of age. Enlightenment is above all a declaration of human independence. And yet the liberating act that severs us irrevocably from nature is also said by Kant to fulfill nature's highest purpose. Nature's "step-motherly" status is a function not of her cruelty (as common folktales might have it) but, quite literally, of the potential lack of any genuine affinity between man and nature. If freedom means, preeminently, the capacity to begin anew, enlightened man can indeed be thought of as the new Adam, parentless (or at least motherless). The *Rechtstaat,* or the intelligible world externally conceived, is described by Kant as a new "womb," where all the inlaid human talents and dispositions squandered by nature can at last find the nurture that will permit them fully to develop. The discrepancy between our natural and our rational entelechies—an indeterminacy that Kant observed to characterize our peculiarity as a species long before Rousseau brought the fact home to him—Kant now addresses by presenting (or calling for) an "idea" of human history.

At the same time, Kant's moralization of the intelligible world opens a path to his critical explanation of experience. Partly on the basis of that moralization, Kant renounces his former effort to conceive the world theoretically as a community of ontologically distinct, inwardly determined substances. This generally overlooked consideration sets in a clearer light, as I argue below, Kant's "transcendental idealism"—a doctrine whose meaning has proved notoriously puzzling to scholars. To state that argument briefly: so long as the objects of our knowledge are taken for things in themselves, there is no way other than moral to understand how one thing can stand in necessary but nonlogical connection with another thing. Transcendental idealism, or the doctrine that we have knowledge of appearances only, recommends itself to Kant primarily through its ability to furnish an answer to the otherwise theoretically unanswerable question of how commerce among substances (and with it human knowledge of the world) is possible.

Having explained how worldly knowledge, or experience, is possible, Kant turns to the question of how organic life—and with it man, the being in whom the possibility of his own worldly knowledge somehow lies—itself is possible, a question that proves both intractable and peculiarly and especially enlightening. In his *Lectures on the History of Philosophy,* Hegel wondered particularly at Kant's unwillingness to pursue the implications of his understanding of organic life, which Kant associated — tentatively — with political organizations such as the American constitution, without further developing the connection. Kant's reticence here is linked to the same respect and concern for individuality that underlies his biological reserve. There are some mysteries, if truly enlightened community is to be secured, that must be left in the dark, above all that out of which humanity itself emerges. The relation between the idea of reason and the progression of culture, a relation Hegel claims to fully comprehend, retains in Kant a remembrance of and reverence for the biblical creation. In the end, Kant's thought (like the perfected man that he describes in his early reflections on Rousseau) is poised upon the hair's breadth of this moderating reverence.

My general purpose, in seeking to expose the consistency of Kant's lifelong enterprise, is to help lay bare some of the forgotten questions which much of later German thought — including, but not limited to, the philosophy of history — intends, explicitly or implicitly, to answer. Much that passes these days for a critique of "Western metaphysics" as a whole is, I think, part of the legacy of this forgotten set of questions. Many of those who are most critically set on overturning metaphysics tend (uncritically, and perhaps unwittingly) to take Kant's word for what metaphysics *is*. It is partly with a view to understanding the dimensions of that contemporary debate, then, that this study of Kant's thought is undertaken. Whether and to what degree the fruits of Kant's thought are idiosyncratic to his own soul may have urgent, if ironic, import for today's vehement assault upon the universal in the name of "difference." For what seems to be and what is truly universal may well diverge in ways unacknowledged by today's intellectual Horatios. The central difficulty with the new historicist attack upon philosophy may well be that it is insufficiently historical.

Beyond such theoretical debates, however, lies the question of Kant's practical significance; and here Kant's unparalleled effort to reconcile the competing demands of freedom and communal belonging has immediate contemporary bearing. Contrary to the belief of some, individuality is not *opposed* to community in Kant's original formulation, but a mediation, however tenuous, of one and many. The conception of the civil constitution, which Kant put forward as an alternative to the classical regime, divorces, in a particularly modern way, the action of informing from the activity of ruling and thus lays the basis for an egalitarian conception of the political whole, a conception whose possibility classical thought ultimately denied.

From Fichte and Hegel to Marx, from Nietzsche and Heidegger to the so-called postmodernists, Kant's heirs, however much they otherwise disagree, share in rejecting the primacy of the moral law, a rejection partly linked to their common failure to appreciate the problem to which, for Kant, the moral law responds. As a result of this rejection, the idea of free-dom is loosened from its primary Kantian association with moral imput-ability; instead, it becomes identified with efficacy, with self-overcoming, with being before death, in short, with any number of *fragments* of Kant's originating insight. The disastrous political consequences of this loosening seem, at the close of the twentieth century, tragically obvious. The follow-ing chapters are thus intended not only to disclose, in ways that have not previously been fully explored, the peculiar "humanity" of Kant, but also to help reveal the comprehensive understanding on which a genuinely Kantian politics rests. It is my hope thus to contribute, however modestly, to current revivals of the liberal spirit.

2 Anticipations of Community: Kant and the *True Estimation of Living Forces*

Kant's earliest published work, *Thoughts on the True Estimation of Living Forces* (1747),[1] was written when he was twenty-two and still a student at the University of Königsberg. Ambitiously sweeping in its claims, the essay aims to settle the long-standing dispute between the Leibnizians and the Cartesians over the true measure of living force.[2]

The work was not a great success among Kant's contemporaries. (Lessing quipped maliciously that in attempting to measure living force Kant failed accurately to estimate his own.) Indeed, compared with Euler's *Mechanica sive motus scientia* (1736) or D'Alembert's *Essai de dynamique* (1743), Kant's effort, from the perspective of classical mechanics, was for the most part obsolete.[3] Irving Polonoff goes so far as to suggest that the controversy over living force was already a settled and forgotten issue in the important intellectual centers of Europe and that Kant's very interest in the question is therefore a sign of his provincial backwardness.[4]

The evident flaws of Kant's most youthful work have prevented it from receiving the attention it deserves.[5] For despite these flaws, the work holds considerable interest, and not only as the youthful manifesto of intellectual independence and self-confidence that Ernst Cassirer sees in it,[6] nor as an exercise in reconciliation — precociously suggestive from the perspective of his later thought — for which it has also been recognized. Beyond its youthful exuberance and effort to mediate between opposing schools, Kant's earliest publication is revealing of concerns that occupied him for the remainder of his life.

Kant's peculiar conception of the mind-body relation stands at the heart of these concerns. Leibniz translated the Cartesian distinction between extension and thought into one between the apparent realm of bodies in space and the inner reality of perceiving substances (his so-called monads) to which such appearances ultimately reduce. For Leibniz, space is "imaginary," and the physical relations that it accommodates are merely "well-founded phenomena." Only monads — their indestructibility assured by their lack of extension — are ultimately real. Kant's innovation lies in his simultaneous agreement with Leibniz as to the "internal" character of substance, and disagreement as to the reducibility of the outer relations of bodies in space to inwardness alone. Here, and throughout his life, Kant is unflagging in his rejection of "preestablished harmony" as an adequate theory of our relation to the world. Leibniz's substances are windowless mirrors of the universe; Kant's have open windows, if not doors. The immediate implications of this uncanny inner openness will be discussed below, especially as regards Kant's earliest efforts to account for worldly knowledge.

To deal with *Living Forces* with any thoroughness is beyond the scope of this chapter. It would require, among other things, a discussion of many minor as well as major themes and controversies of late seventeenth-century and early eighteenth-century science. Our task here is less that of the antiquarian than of the salvager: to extract from the wreckage of Kant's maiden voyage (to adopt the nautical metaphor that Kant himself so favored) some of the elements that constitute the work's genuine—but heretofore largely neglected—legacy.

I. Kant on "Forces of Bodies in General"

Living Forces opens with some "metaphysical concepts" that bear on "the force of bodies in general" (I:17). Leibniz, according to Kant, was right to measure force by its effect, that is, its ability to overcome obstacles (in line with the general metaphysical principle that "the effect is always equal to the cause"). His followers err, however, in identifying this force with *vis motrix,* or the motion of bodies, rather than activity. Kant thus agrees with Leibniz that force must be measured by its effect but disagrees about what this effect fundamentally consists of. Where Leibniz's followers equate that effect with motion, Kant identifies it with "activity," or the alternation of a substance's inner state. Against the visible phenomenon of motion, Kant opposes the deeper reality of inner change.

Leibniz, according to Kant, was the first modern thinker to disassociate force and motion. Prior to Leibniz, bodies at rest were thought to be devoid of force, a thesis disputed only by Aristotle, who claimed to discover in his "dark [*dunkele*] entelechy" the secret of bodily activity. All other thinkers, looking "no further than the senses teach," regarded force as something communicated to bodies from outside. Leibniz thus "deserves the thanks of human reason" for recognizing that bodies have an essential force that belongs to them prior even to extension (I:17).[7]

Leibniz's followers, however, attempt to define this force more definitely as "moving force" (*vis motrix*), on the grounds that "one never sees it bring forth anything other than motion." To Leibniz's followers, pressure (for example) is to be understood as a striving toward motion, and force is exercised only when that motion becomes actual. By their account, an object pressing on the surface upon which it rests does not act but instead strives to move. For Kant, however, the pressing body truly acts. To make *vis motrix* (rather than activity) the cause of motion is like the Schoolman's trick of identifying *vis calorifica* as the cause of heat (I:18). Having accepted Leibniz's teaching on the essential character of force in general, his followers deny it in the case where activity and motion are most tellingly divorced. But motion and activity, Kant counters, are related only indirectly: a body has motion "in an especial degree" precisely by virtue of the fact that "infinitely small opposition is made to it," and thus it "hardly acts."[8]

UTILIZATION AND ENDURANCE

Kant explains the relation between activity and motion in the following terms:

> Consider substance A whose force is determined to act outside itself (i.e., to change the inner state of other substances). Such a substance, in the first instant of its effort, either finds an object that endures [*erduldet*] its entire force, or it does not. If all substances met with the first alternative, we would be unacquainted with motion, and would therefore not designate it as bodily force. If, on the other hand, substance A cannot immediately utilize [*anwenden*] its entire force, it will only utilize a part of it. It cannot, however, remain inactive with the remainder. It must act with its entire force, for if it were not entirely utilized it would cease to be called a force. Since we do not encounter the consequence of such a practice [that is, immediate expenditure of force] in the world's coexisting states, we have to find them in the second measuring of the same, i.e., in the successive series of things. The body thus utilizes its force, not all at once but little by little. In the succeeding moments, however, it cannot act upon the same substance that it originally acted upon, for that substance suffered only a part of A's force, it being incapable of accepting the other part. But substance C, which it affects in the second moment, must have an entirely different relation of place and location vis à vis A as does B, which it previously effected; for otherwise there would be no reason [*Grund*] why A did not originally effect C at the same time as B. . . . A therefore changes its location inasmuch as it successively acts. (I:19)

Kant agrees that force is measured by its effect. Unlike Leibniz and his followers, however, he equates this effect with activity, understood not as visible motion but as the alteration of another substance's inner state. Motion, on Kant's account, is the "outer phenomenon" of force, which every substance seeks to exercise or expend by altering the inner state of other substances. If substances could expend their force immediately there would be no motion and no space (and presumably no time). Motion is thus not the *effect* of activity (as both Leibniz and his followers generally held), but the outer appearance that accompanies striving to act. That there *is* motion indicates our world to be of such a kind that substances strive to act, that is, expend their forces bit by bit rather than immediately. Space, for its part, is the consequence of this succession—another way of saying that body A could not expend its force entirely on body B and went on to body C. The bizarre upshot of Kant's portrayal is a world of substances striving to expend themselves but unable to do so immediately due to the inability of other substances to receive or "suffer" (*erdulden*) that expenditure. Motion and space are entirely the consequence of this indefinitely (or infinitely) deferred consummation.

Leibniz's treatment of space rested on his view that substances do not genuinely interact but merely play out their own internal scripts in such a way that each substance mirrors the whole from its own point of view. Space, on Leibniz's understanding, is an "imaginary" manifestation of physical relations that are themselves merely *phenomena bene fundata*—appearances grounded in the ultimate, nonphysical reality of substances that harmonize without interacting. Kant agrees with Leibniz as to the phenomenal character of motion and the derivative character of space yet denies that in the last analysis, substance acts alone. A substance might expend its force immediately upon other substances, whose relation to it would necessarily be one of absolute sufferance or passivity. The phenomenon of motion, however, indicates that in our world, substances expend their force or act only in relation to the partial sufferance of other substances.

For Leibniz, activity and passivity are ultimately internal to substance, which plays out its part without any real relation to other substances. For Kant, on the contrary, expenditure of force and sufferance are a two-way street, a fact that definitively overturns Leibniz's model of monadic solitude. On Leibniz's account, the relative and ultimately imaginary status of space and time follows from the fact that substances don't really affect one another. On Kant's account, our sheer awareness of space and time (however relative and ultimately derivative their status) depends upon, and thus reveals, the fact that substances *do* mutually affect one another.

The novelty (and for some empirically minded scholars, the perversity) of Kant's approach thus lies in his attempt to reconcile the seemingly unreconcilable: on the one hand, he insists, with Leibniz, on the interiority of substance and its priority to extension; on the other hand, he insists, with Descartes and Newton, that bodies actually expend their force upon other bodies.[9]

ACTIVITY, PRESSURE, AND THE REPRESENTING SOUL

Kant attributes our tendency to identify force with motion (rather than, in the primary instance, pressure) to the fact that we do not clearly become aware of (*gewahr werden*) what a body does when it acts in a state of rest. As a result, we think ahead to the motion that would occur if the obstacle holding it in place were removed. Because we are not sure

> what a body does when it acts in the state of rest, we always call to mind the motion that would follow if one were to remove the obstacle. This suffices to supply one with an external characteristic of what goes on in the body and cannot be seen. But commonly the motion is regarded as that which the force does if it breaks loose [*recht losbricht*], and as its only consequence. This is a slight departure from the true way of thinking, and easily corrected; and we must not think it an error of any consequence. It is indeed [*in der That*] of consequence, but not in mechanics and natural philosophy. For [on account of this error] it is difficult in metaphysics to represent how matter can be in such a state as to in any genuinely [*in der That*] active [*wirksame*] manner (that is, through physical influence) bring about representations in the soul of man. What, it is said, can matter do beside causing motions? All its force can at most displace/derange [*verrücken*] the soul from its position. How can the force, which can only give rise to motions, generate representations and ideas? The latter are a kind of thing so different than the former that it is inconceivable how one should be the source of the other. (I:19–20)

Kant holds as a principle advantage of his theory its ability to explain the material production of ideas — to make "representable" (to use his own language) the power of matter to bring forth representations in the soul.[10] (Kant thus offers — if his language is taken literally — a representation of representation itself.)[11] His theory accounts not only for the outward manifestations of force: it also uncovers the site at which outer and inner meet, the seat of the generation (*Erzeugung*) of ideas. Physical influence between body and soul[12] is no more (or less) mysterious than the invisible but real activity exemplified by pressure (or activity without motion) generally.[13] Mutual influence between body and soul functions both as a fact — whose metaphysical basis Kant's theory of force aims to define — and as a prototype that makes such force (whose effect is otherwise hidden from the senses) uniquely accessible.

Kant's theory also dispels the similar difficulties that arise concerning the ability of the soul to set matter in motion. Such difficulties disappear "if one reckons force, not in terms of motion, but in terms of influences on other substances — influences one cannot determine more precisely." Then the question "can the soul cause motions?" becomes the question "can its essential force be determined to an outwardly directed action [*Wirkung*]?" — that is to say "is it capable of acting outside itself upon other beings and bringing about changes?" So long as one admits that the soul has a position (*in einem Orte ist*), the question is easily answered: for (as Kant has shown above) the concept of position, when analyzed, signifies the action of substances upon each other (I:20–21). Once one admits that the soul has a position in space, "the complete triumph" of the physical-influence school is thus assured.

In this way it also becomes "easy to conceive" the contrary paradoxical assertion — that is, to explain how "it is possible that matter, which one imagines [*von der man doch in der Einbildung steht*] as being unable to cause anything but motions, impresses certain representations and images [*Bilder*] on the soul."

> For matter which is set [*gesetzt*] in motion affects [*wirkt in*] every-thing that is spatially connected to it, thus also the soul. That is to say, it alters the soul's inner state insofar as it relates to the external. Now the entire inner state of the soul is nothing other than the combination [*Zusammenfassung*] of all its representations and concepts, and insofar as this inner state is related to the external it is called the *status repraesentativus universi*. Thus matter, by means of the force that it has in its motion, alters the state of the soul by which it represents the world. In this way one conceives [*begreift*] how matter can impress representations in the soul. (I:21)

Knowledge is not a perception wholly internal to the soul (as Leibniz claimed), a representation independent of and without real relation to the world it represents. On the contrary, the soul represents the world only insofar as it is in a position to be affected by the world, that is, is part of the world it represents. The world's actuality (*Wirklichkeit*) or presence to the mind is inseparable from its effectuality (*Wirksamkeit*). The upshot of this insight into the true basis or ground of knowledge is a new under-standing, or *Erklärung*,[14] of the world — one that is by Kant's account alto-gether novel.

KANT'S *ERKLÄRUNG* OF THE WORLD

Solitary Substances and Multiple Worlds

Kant claims to be the first to "give sufficient attention to the explanation [*Erklärung*] of the world" (I:22). His explanation rests on two preliminary theses: first, "that a thing can actually exist and yet be present nowhere in the world"; second, "that it is true in the strict metaphysical sense that more than one world can exist."

The first thesis follows from the fact that to exist, and to stand in actual connection with other beings, are entirely different things. A self-sufficient being, by way of example, contains the "source of all its own determina-tions" and hence "does not stand in any relation, necessary to its own existence, with any other being." Substances can therefore exist and yet be present nowhere in the world.

From this "paradoxical thesis" there follows a second, "no less wonderful," and which "capture[s] the understanding, so to speak, against its will" (I:22). According to this second thesis — opposed by both the Leibnizian and the Aristotelian schools — more than one world can exist.

> Because we cannot say that something is a part of a whole if it does not stand in any connection with the other parts . . . , and since the world is a being [*Wesen*] that is actually composited [*wirklich zusammen gesetzt*], it follows that a substance that is connected with nothing in the world does not in any way belong to the world, though it may be something in thought. (I:22)

When several such beings are mutually related they constitute their "own quite special world," entirely distinct from this one. It follows that there can be many worlds, between whose respective members there is no connection. What is taught in the lecture halls of philosophy (*Weltweisheit*) is therefore incorrect, it being possible "that God has created many millions of worlds, taking (world) in its proper metaphysical meaning." The error of the philosophers, who teach in their schools that only one world can exist, arises from their failure to pay enough respect (*Acht*) to "the explanation of the world" (*Erklärung von der Welt*), by whose definition (*Definition*) only that can be reckoned as belonging to a world which stands in an actual connection with the (other) members (I:22–23).[15]

Kant's reference to the schools touches not only Aristotle and his scholastic legacy but also Leibniz, whose claim that this is the best of all possible worlds implicitly assumes that only one world can exist. For Leibniz, out of the many worlds possible (but not mutually), God in his goodness brought into existence that which is the best, by which Leibniz means "having the most reality," or alternatively, having the greatest amount of diversity consistent with the greatest degree of simplicity. Leibniz's famous "theodicy" justifies the evil in the world on the grounds that since our world is the best possible, any change would bring about a greater evil. His theodicy thus assumes that beings intrinsically possible (that is, thinkable without contradiction) may not be jointly possible, hence, that in creating the world God's will was limited by the prior condition of what Leibniz calls "compossibility." In affirming that a plurality of worlds can exist, Kant implicitly rejects the basis of Leibniz's theodicy.[16]

Kant and Leibniz on Imaginary Unities

Kant's claims regarding solitary substances and multiple worlds are linked by his fundamental *Erklärung* of the world as an "actually composited being [*wirklich zusammen gesetztes Wesen*]" — an actual union, in other words, as distinguished from an imaginary one.

> One cannot say that something is part of a whole if it does not stand in any connection [*Verbindung*] with the other parts (for then there would be no difference to be found [*würde zu finden sein*] between an actual union and an imagined one [*unter einer wirklichen Vereinigung und unter einer eingebildeten*]). (I:22)

That we indeed find there to be such a difference Kant here assumes, without stating precisely how we know this or come to recognize the difference when we see it.

The contrast with Leibniz here is both striking and instructive. In his treatise *On the Way to Distinguish Real from Imaginary Phenomena*, Leibniz argues "that the most powerful proof of the reality of phenomena (a proof that is, indeed, sufficient by itself) is success in predicting future phenomena from those that are past and present." Well-founded phenomena are distinguished (for example, from dreams or fantasies) by their interconnectedness as attestable by a variety of experiments. A dream that passed such tests would be indistinguishable from what is real: "Even if this whole life were said to be nothing but a dream, and the visible world only a phantasm, I should call this dream or this phantasm real enough, if we were never deceived by it when we make good use of reason."[17] Although it is not impossible, metaphysically speaking, that there is a consecutive dream lasting as long as a man's lifetime, this would be as contrary to reason, according to Leibniz, as the fiction that a book could be formed by throwing down type at random.[18]

The distinction between real appearances and dreams or fantasies is thus one that Leibniz draws on essentially practical grounds.[19] We cannot ultimately be sure that our perceptions are not a lifelong deception, just as we cannot be sure that there exist beings other than ourselves and God. But since nothing would change for us were this the case, its possibility is effectively irrelevant.

Leibniz draws another distinction germane to Kant's purpose, that between a mere "aggregate" and a genuine unity, the latter of which always has its foundation in a simple substance. Leibniz's argument takes its point of departure (interestingly enough) from the relation between the body and the soul:

> In my opinion, our body in itself (setting aside the soul), or the *Cadaver*, can be called *one* substance only by a wrong use of terms, like a machine or a heap of stones, which are only beings by aggregation; for regular or irregular arrangement has nothing to do

with unity of substance. . . . I hold that a marble pavement is probably only like a heap of stones, and thus cannot pass for only one substance, but is a collection of several. For suppose there are two stones — for example, the diamond of the Grand Duke and that of the Great Mogul — we might give them both, in respect of their value, one and the same collective name, and we might say that they are one pair of diamonds, although they are actually far distant from one another. But it will not be said that these diamonds compose one substance. Now more or less make no difference here. Accordingly, if we bring them nearer one another, and even make them touch one another, they will be none the more united in substance; and although, after they had been brought into contact, we were to join to them some other body in such a way as to prevent them separating again — for instance if we were to set them in one ring — all *that* would make of them is what is called *unum per accidens*. For it is by accident that they are compelled to share in the same motion. I hold then that a marble pavement is not one concrete [*accompli*] substance, any more than would be the water of a pond with all the fish it holds, or than a flock of sheep, in which the sheep should be supposed to be so bound together that they could only walk in step, and that one could not be touched without all the others crying out. There would be as much difference between a substance and such a being as between a man and a community. . . . which are moral beings and in which there is something imaginary and created by our minds. Unity of substance requires an indivisible and naturally indestructible concrete being, since the notion of such a being includes all that is ever to happen to it.[20]

The prototype of unity for Leibniz is the (human) soul, whose "containment" of its past, present, and future states contrasts with the spurious unity of the body. The soul does not depend upon the body, which is ultimately merely a confused reflection of the principle, intrinsic to the soul, that generates the soul's own inner states.[21] "Big with its future," the soul is assured of its continuing identity through (an eternity of) time. It follows that unity has nothing to do with extension or the composition of parts: what is put together (either naturally or by the mind) can be decomposed. Only the intensive unity of consciousness, in which identity and manifoldness are inseparably joined, is genuinely real.

Individual substances (or monads) are thus the only genuine unities. The (seemingly) composited wholes that we encounter in experience are either "accidental" (as is the case with two diamonds joined in a ring) or "imaginary" (as is the case with a military or scholastic community). What is required for genuine unity is that the being in question be "indivisible and naturally indestructible," which can never be the case where parts are compelled to move together "by accident." Reciprocal motion (like that of a machine, or a flock of sheep, each of which cry out when one is touched) is not enough to transform a mere aggregate or heap (like the cadaver) into a genuine unity (like the soul).

It follows from this that well-founded phenomena taken in their entirety do not constitute a genuine unity. Such a conclusion, however, tends to undercut the basis of Leibniz's distinction between a well-founded appearance and a fantasy. It is the reliability of the interconnection of such appearances, after all, that serves as the principle test of their "reality." And yet it now seems that any such connection does not differ in kind from that of a mere aggregate, resting either on "imagination" or on "accident."

It would seem to follow that the world is not, on Leibniz's understanding, a genuine unity.[22] Phenomenally speaking, its parts may move together (like the flock of sheep who all cry out when one is touched); and metaphysically, its substances are joined together in the mind of God. But neither of these facts satisfies his strict criteria for unity *ens se*. The metaphysical possibility that only I and God might exist (without this changing anything for me) suggests the tenuousness of Leibniz's worldly bond. It is not just that the connection between monads exists only in the mind of God, but that nothing "intrinsic" to any monad binds it to the rest, at least not in any way that we can securely ascertain.

If the world is a unity in a more telling sense, it is only due to the limiting condition of compossibility, which establishes a relation between the things that constitute the world prior to and independent of God's will. Apart from this limiting condition, nothing would unite existing beings other than the arbitrary fact that God chose to create them. Without the prior condition of compossibility, the sum of existing beings would resemble—indeed be indistinguishable from—an accidental or imagined unity in the Leibnizian sense. The sum of all existent beings would no more constitute a genuine unity—a unity in itself—than does the thought connecting the diamond of the Great Mogul with the diamond of the Grand Duke.[23]

Efficacy (*Wirksamkeit*) and Actuality (*Wirklichkeit*)

Kant's understanding of the world as an "actually composited being" allows him to avoid this troubling result, without making the claim—which he will later show to be equally problematic—that God is "limited" by the prior condition of compossibility.[24] It does so by grounding worldly unity in a lawful necessity intrinsic to the world (rather than, in the Leibnizian manner, to a consideration that is extrinsic to God's will).[25] The world's status as an actual rather than imagined union lies not in any limiting condition or necessity imposed on divine creativity, but in the mutual activity or essential force (itself grounded in God's creative act) by virtue of which things mutually affect one another.

Kant's *Erklärung* presents the world as a "composite unity," that is, a unity with parts (the possibility of which Leibniz implicitly denies). What makes it a unity is not its lack of parts (as with Leibniz's monads) but the "lawful" connection by which its parts are interbound. Leibniz had denied complex entities the status of true unities on the grounds that such entities are in principle "divisible,"—that is, that their parts are not linked by "necessity" but only accidentally and/or by the imagination. For Leibniz, then, only monads are true unities, or unities "by necessity." Kant responds to Leibniz's objection with a necessity of a different sort—not a necessity arising from the concept of a substance as such, but one that obtains for, and only for, those substances that are members of a given world. In place of Leibniz's necessity of logic, in other words, Kant substitutes (something like or akin to) the necessity of law. Such lawlike necessity is not absolute (that is, valid for all substances) but applies only to those substances that constitute a world through their shared mode or principle of reciprocal activity.[26]

The Paradox of Worldly Knowledge

The actuality (*Wirklichkeit*) of a world is inseparable for Kant from the mutual activity of its parts—their capacity to mutually effect one another's inner states. To distinguish between an actual and an imaginary whole is to acknowledge this active connection. But how is this connection to be represented and thereby recognized? The mere thought of such connection will not do (for then an imaginary whole, whose "parts" are merely connected in thought, and a real whole would again be indistinguishable).

Kant's *Erklärung* of the world is thus intrinsically paradoxical. A world is a being that is *actually* composed (not merely composed in thought), that is, a being whose parts really "work upon" each other or interact. But every representation is held together in thought. Kant thinks the world as precisely that sort of union that is not (merely) held together in thought (for such a conceptual unity is, by definition, imagined and not actual). He is thus left with the paradoxical thought or definition of a world as a created thing to which, intrinsically, no (human) thought or definition can be adequate.

This difficulty will emerge in full force in Kant's *Universal Natural History* (1755). The concept or representation of the world is (uniquely) inseparable from its actuality.[27] To *think* the world it will thus prove necessary to (re)*create* (or actually composite) it, as that later work will ambitiously (!) attempt to do.

Imagination and the Three-Dimensionality of Space

Whereas all worlds are governed by a principle or law of mutual action, the *content* of that law, as Kant suggests, varies with each particular world. It is this content, he further speculates, that determines the particular dimensionality of that world. Although the ground of the three-dimensionality of our space "is still unknown," Kant guesses that it arises "from the fact that substances in the existing world so act upon one another that the strength of the effect holds inversely as the square of the distances" (I:23–24).

Force is not the phenomenal correlate of substantial activity (as Leibniz claimed); it *is* that activity, at least insofar as substance is worldly. Force, however, "cannot be thought apart from a certain law that reveals itself in the mode of its action" (I:24).

In our own world, this mode of action is governed by the inverse square law (or law of universal gravitational attraction), "according to which substances, by dint of their essential forces, seek to unite themselves," and from which arises the three-dimensionality of space.[28] But the specific *content* of this law (and its accompanying number of spatial dimensions) is ultimately arbitrary, God having it in his power to have chosen a different principle (for example, the inverse cube law), from which a different number of dimensions would have arisen:[29]

> The impossibility, which we observe in ourselves, of representing a space of more than three dimensions seems to me to be due to the fact that our soul receives impressions from without according to the law of the inverse square of the distances, and because its nature is so constituted that it not only suffers, but also acts outside itself in this way. (I:24–25)

Anticipating (by almost forty years) his critical treatment of space and time as "forms of intuition," Kant suggests that our knowledge of the world is conditioned by the specific nature of our receptive faculty, a nature that is in no way necessary to a rational soul as such.[30] The fit between our specific mental constitution and the world it represents is here linked to his assumption (later abandoned) that the soul has a location in space and thus is "present in the world" in the same way that body is.

The upshot is a distinction between reason and imagination that is foreign to consciousness as Leibniz conceived it. The otherwise puzzling "impossibility" (*Unding*) of our "representing in imagination" (I:23) a space with more than three dimensions rests on the "arbitrary" fact that God made our world this way rather than another (and gave us minds suitable for imagining it) (I:24). The impossibility that we "observe in ourselves" of representing a space of greater than three dimensions is an impossibility for imagination (not reason). Like the inverse square law, which can only be known empirically (rather than on the basis of reason alone), it suggests a cognitive dualism foreign to Leibniz and upon which Kant's later critical distinction between concept and intuition will build.

Kant thus points in a few introductory pages of his earliest work to the central chasm of human knowledge, to whose articulation he will devote much of the remainder of his life — the engulfing relation between reason and the "given." On the one hand, there are the absolute necessities that we share with all other rational souls as such; on the other, there is the lawful or contingent necessity determined by our interaction in and with the world. Whether the soul's identity ultimately resides wholly in the first sort of necessity, or whether, and in what way, it is implicated in the second, becomes a defining theme of Kant's later thought. For the present, it is enough to note Kant's suggestion that the knowing soul — for all its longing to escape material entanglements — may be inextricably confined to and by bodily space.

II. Kant on the True Estimation of Living Forces

KANT AND LEIBNIZ ON DEAD AND LIVING FORCE

In the *Specimum dynamicum,* Leibniz distinguishes between dead and living force in the following terms:

> Force is . . . of two kinds: The one elementary, which I also call *dead* force, because motion does not yet exist in it but only a solicitation to motion, such as that of . . . a stone in a sling even while it is still held by the string; the other is ordinary force combined with actual motion, which I call *living* force [*vis viva*].[31]

Living force (or actual motion) arises when dead force is "vivified" by the removal of impediments (as with the stone when the sling is taken away). Force is measured, according to Leibniz, by its *effect,* by which he means

> not any effect whatever but that for which force is expended or consumed and which may therefore be called *violent.* The force which a heavy body exercises in moving along a perfectly horizontal plane is not of this kind, because, however far such an effect is prolonged, it always retains the same force, and though we use the same principle in calculating this effect also, which we may call *harmless,* we [here] exclude it from consideration.[32]

Living force can thus also be understood as the integral of dead force over time — a "composition" of the infinite number of moments in which dead force is exhibited. Such entities, to be sure, are not "found in nature as such" but are merely "means of making accurate calculations of an abstract kind."³³ For time, like motion, "taken in an exact sense, never exists," a whole not existing "if it has no co-existing parts."³⁴

The ultimate thrust of Leibniz's account of force is to deny, in a manner consistent with the principle of the equality of action and reaction, that any substance ever genuinely effects another substance. When two bodies collide, the force initially exhibited by each body is, on Leibniz's account, redirected "internally" upon the elements that compose it. In the mechanics of Descartes, a moving body that meets one at rest is deemed the cause or agent of the latter's subsequent motion. By Leibniz's reasoning, on the contrary, it is ultimately meaningless to speak of one body giving motion to another. If two bodies of equal mass collide, it does not matter which is "moving" and which "at rest." Each will receive an equal effect, caused not by the other body but "from its own elasticity, brought about by the motion which is already in it."

> [E]very passion of a body is spontaneous or arises from an internal force, though upon an external occasion. . . . Repercussion and repulsion . . . arise from elasticity within the body itself, or from the motion of an ethereal fluid matter which permeates it, and so from an internal force existing within it.³⁵

Leibniz, then, denies interaction on both the phenomenal and the metaphysical level: his physical assumption of the perfect elasticity of bodies corresponds to his metaphysical claim that substances or "monads," the ultimate realities, do not interact but undergo change brought about by their own internal principle of development.³⁶

Kant appropriates Leibniz's distinction between dead and living force, but with significant changes in keeping with Kant's claim that substances genuinely interact. He associates *dead* force, not with an elementary force intrinsic to matter, but with the "violent" motion imparted to a body from an outside source (as with an object pushed by hand across a flat surface). Kant associates *living* force, on the other hand, not with "violent" motion but the sort of motion he calls "free" (as with a projectile hurtling through space).³⁷ Accordingly, Kant divides all motion into two sorts:

> The first has the property . . . of maintaining itself and enduring for an infinitely long period, as long as it encounters no obstacles. The second is the enduring effect of a constant imparted force, an effect that derives only from an external force, and which does not need an obstacle to nullify it, but rather disappears as soon as that external force ceases to be maintained. (I:28)

Kant identifies "living" force not, as for Leibniz, with violent motion in which force is "consumed," but with the sort of motion that Leibniz deems "harmless" and therefore (for purposes of estimating force) uninteresting.

Agreeing with Leibniz that force is to be measured by its effect, Kant trans-
poses the site of that effect from that of outer motion to that of inward
"utilization" and "sufferance." The sign of a living force is not motion over
time (as with Leibniz) but freedom — the ability of a body to sustain its
motion indefinitely, that is, until it encounters (and acts upon) an obstacle.

The crucial distinction for Kant is not a "mathematical" one between a
moment of infinitely short duration and a longer period of time (as with
Leibniz), but a "metaphysical" one between striving to act and enduring
the effects of another body's striving. Motion brought about by living force
has its source within the moving body itself; motion brought about dead
pressure (*todten Drucke*) has a source external to the moving body.

On the basis of this metaphysical distinction, Kant offers a preliminary
answer to the question of whether force is proportional to velocity alone
(mv) or to the square of the velocity (mv²). Where free motion is involved,
the force involved is measured according to the square of the velocity. The
reason is as follows:

> If a body in free motion were to course through infinitely subtle
> space, its force should be measured according to the sum of all
> effects that it brings about in an eternity of time. For if this aggre-
> gate were not equal to the entire force, one would need, in order
> to find a sum equal in intensity to the entire force, a period of
> time longer than infinity, which is absurd. If one now compares
> two bodies A and B, where A has a velocity of 2 and B of 1, then
> A, from the beginning of its motion through eternity, will press
> the infinitely small particles [*Massen*] of space through which it
> passes, with twice the velocity of B. But A will also cover twice as
> much space as B. (I:29)

As a result, the total effect brought about by A will be four times the effect
of B; hence, force is proportional to the square of the velocity (mv²).[38]

Dead pressure, on the other hand, is proportional to velocity alone (mv).
Kant's explanation turns on the fact that in this case the body acted upon
has only to nullify the "velocity that a body uses to change its location,"
without regard to the "strength with which it endeavors to maintain this
force" (I:30).[39]

Kant's conception of a substance "striving to maintain its striving" is not
only anthropomorphic (a feature arguably shared by the physics of Hobbes
and Leibniz, to name only a few of Kant's competitors) but also curiously
involuted. "Free" motion stems from an "inner endeavor" to endeavor, a
striving that is supposed to multiply geometrically the force exerted with
velocity alone.

Kant's conception — an approximate equivalent of inertia in the Newtonian sense — has the effect (lacking in Newton) of giving unimpeded mo-

tion a sort of positive value reminiscent of Aristotle's distinction between the natural tendency of a body toward its proper place, and the "violent" motion that can impede that tendency. This contrasts with the Leibnizian position earlier discussed, in which living force is associated with violent, as opposed to harmless, motion. For Leibniz all motion is ultimately reducible to a "striving to change" on the part of individual monads, with action and sufferance ultimately reducible to a relation between form and matter likewise intrinsic to individual monads. Kant, on the contrary, differentiates between internally grounded striving and striving imparted from without—the crucial factor being the ability of a substance, in the former case, to "determine" itself, that is, to actively maintain its own inner state rather than succumbing to determination from without.

Kant does not, however, share Aristotle's view of motion as arising from a being's tendency to seek its proper place. What Kantian substance rather seeks is to utilize its force in the overcoming of resistance, a utilization that—this side of eternity at least—is in principle inexhaustible.

It is thus rhetorically opportune of Kant to turn, in ending part 1, to the "exertion" (*Bemühung*) of the philosopher himself, "whose only recompense, after a laborious undertaking, is to be able finally to content himself [*sich beruhigen*] with a properly grounded science [*recht gründlichen Wissenschaft*]" (I:31). When he will cross the threshold of such science, however, is not possible to say. He must therefore not misjudge his strength, nor hide defects in his discoveries he is in no condition (*Stand*) to remedy. Nor should he put the delight caused by the fantasy (*Einbildung*) of such a science before the true uses of knowledge. "Understanding is much inclined to applause, and it is certainly very difficult to hold it back in this regard for long." Still, "one should finally restrain oneself in this way, in order to sacrifice to a grounded knowledge everything that a widely ranging/rambling one has in itself of what's charming [*was eine weitläuftige Reizendes an sich hat*]."

Kant's curious coda warns of the ease of confusing the *aim* of philosophic knowledge with its vain and tranquilizing image. Imitating the substance he has described, he puts utility and industry before the seductive charm of rest.[40] Reason is intrinsically at risk (and in need of constraint); for it cannot labor without an end in mind, an end whose false appearance brings delight and by which it will be tempted—to its downfall—to wander vainly.[41]

LEIBNIZ'S ERROR

Parts 2 and 3 discuss the notion of living force in greater detail. In part 2, Kant takes up a number of competing theories, with that of Leibniz receiving the bulk of the attention. His main criticism of Leibniz stems from the latter's (alleged) failure to provide a qualitative basis for distinguishing between dead and living force, a distinction that is crucial, as we have seen, to Kant's understanding of activity, and thus of worldhood generally.

Leibniz associates living force with *any* motion of more than momentary duration. He thus fails, according to Kant, to take into account the fact that motion can endure and yet express dead force alone. For example, a ball that moves across a flat surface only so long as it is pushed exhibits no living force however long its "bound" motion may continue. The crucial difference between dead and living force does not lie in the quantitative distinction between an indeterminately small and a definite (or finite) lapse of time, but in the qualitative difference between motion that is "impressed from outside" and motion whose source is internal to the body itself. Substances display "living force" when they increase their motion beyond the amount that is initially communicated by an outward source, not just when (as Leibniz implies) their motion lasts longer than a moment.

Kant agrees with Leibniz that living force expresses the ultimate metaphysical reality of body but differs in insisting that the difference between living and dead force must be established on metaphysical rather than mathematical grounds.[42] So long as one remains with mathematics (and the purely external properties of body that mathematics addresses), the Cartesian measure of force is the only valid one. Kant's criticism of Leibniz thus has the dual purpose of both vindicating the Leibnizians and the Cartesians within their proper spheres, and of establishing the boundary between inner essence and outer appearance that makes their mutual vindication possible.[43]

But if living force is not just the quantitative composition of an infinite number of increments of dead force (as Leibniz claimed), how *does* it arise, and in what sense is it susceptible to estimation? The answer lies in Kant's novel notion of "intension."

"INTENSION" AND THE QUANTIFICATION OF SUBSTANCE

Kant identifies "intension"[44] with "the striving to maintain motion" without which the resistance by which force is measured would "have nothing to cancel":

> Motion is the outer phenomenon of force; the striving to maintain this motion, however, is the basis [*Basis*] of activity [*Activität*]; and velocity indicates how many times one must take it [that is, by what amount one must multiply it] in order to have the entire force. Hereafter we will call [that striving] intension. Thus force is equal to velocity times intension. (I:141)

If a body's force is such that it strives to maintain its motion only for an instant, then intension is effectively the same irrespective of the velocity, and quantity of force is controlled by velocity alone (mv). In such a case, intension is like a point, and force (in this case equivalent to velocity) a line (I:142–43). If, on the other hand, the force contains sufficient striving in itself to maintain motion at a given velocity without external help, it is of a kind different and "infinitely more perfect" than the first. In this latter case, intension is like a line, and force a plane (I:143).

The examples of the planets and other bodies that exhibit free motion (that is, maintain their own motion unless they encounter resistance) testify to the existence in the world of living force. No necessity, however, requires that there be such a thing as free motion, nor that bodies inwardly produce such a striving and force that does not come from anything external (I:149). Living force is thus not a necessary property of a body's outer aspect (a property reachable by mathematics alone), but something hypothetical and contingent, requiring the testimony of experience and the grounding of metaphysics (I:152).

The interval in time between the moment at which a body exhibits only dead force and the moment at which it achieves living force Kant calls "vivification."[45] For any given body vivification begins at a certain determinate velocity (and not before) and is fully achieved at a higher determinate velocity. Thus each body has what amounts to its own signature — certain minimal and maximal degrees of velocity, determined by its "natural constitution," between which its inner force comes progressively alive (I:159–60).

The notion of intension, Kant believes, allows him to reconcile the qualitative difference between dead and living force with the principle of continuity and thus succeed where Leibniz failed. Leibniz could not explain how a body "that at point A has a dead force should have an infinitely greater living force when it moves an imperceptibly small distance from A" (I:38). "Intension" provides the missing key. As a body approaches closer to point A, its intension changes in degree but not in kind.[46] When intension is indeterminately small, the external forces impinging on a body produce the outward signs typical of dead force. When it is "vivified" (by reaching a determinate velocity) and becomes "definite," the body exhibits the free motion indicative of living force.

For Leibniz the quantity of movement (mv) is to the quantity of living force (mv^2) as the imaginary or modal is to the physical or real. But this reality is an absolute merely of the "second order." It does not itself have the quality of inwardness that Leibniz reserves to monads proper.[47] The points of force that constitute the reality of body are not themselves monadic entities but merely their "appearance."

For Kant, by way of contrast, substance (insofar as it is worldly) is inherently dual. Every substance strives to maintain its motion (a striving, to be sure, that only becomes measurable when it is "vivified"). But such striving has meaning only insofar as it is related to — and countered by — the opposing striving of other substances.

Kant's notion of intension internalizes physical quantity (which Leibniz associated with appearances), bringing it within the boundaries of the representing soul. For Leibniz, substance is to appearance as quality is to quantity;[48] for Kant, quantity and quality inwardly comingle.[49] "Intension" thus not only anticipates Kant's critical conception of "intensive quantity" but also suggests in a preliminary fashion Kant's ultimate strategy for resolving the question of community between body and soul.

It is easy to criticize Kant's notion of intension — an obviously inferior alternative, from the viewpoint of classical mechanics, to the Newtonian conception of inertia — just as it is easy to criticize his "solution" to the controversy over living force generally. Still, for all its manifest difficulties and confusions, the approach provisionally and haltingly sketched out in *Living Forces* was to bear greater fruit than its contemporary critics could have guessed.

III. Conclusion

Kant's account of living force, advanced with such assurance and bravado by the twenty-two-year-old author, met with little approval and was soon abandoned. Aspects of the argument, however, were to prove more enduring. One such vital element consists in Kant's linking of physical influence (his support for which was in itself by no means novel) with what Kant refers to, without undue modesty, as an *Erklärung* of the world. Mutual influence between substances — and in particular, between body and soul — is for Kant at once the unifying connection by which the world as a whole is actualized and the mode by which its actuality is made manifest to representing consciousness. In combining worldly actuality and mutual activity in this way, Kant strikes a fundamental blow against Leibniz's theodicy and the doctrine of compossibility on which it rests. If a world's principle of unity applies to it, and conceivably, it alone, more than one world can exist (just as, for Leibniz, more than one monad can exist). But if many, indeed, an infinite number of worlds can exist (each of them conceivably inhabited by rational beings), we seem no longer to have any reason to believe that the world we inhabit is the best, especially where the possibility lies open that we might have been placed in another world — or, indeed, no world at all.

Kant leaves the spelling out of such moral implications for later works. What he is here most concerned to suggest is the cognitive dualism (flatly at odds with the claims of the Leibnizian-Wolffian school) that such a view of worldly unity entails. For Kant, worlds in general share a common structure or form of connectedness whose particular matter or content, peculiar to each world, is only revealed to a being belonging to that world and therefore subject to its law. What is necessarily true about worlds in general, or for all rational beings, is thus contrasted with what is true only contingently or on the basis of God's will, and therefore valid only for the inhabitants of a particular world. In the case of our world, the principle of connection is the so-called inverse square law—utterly contingent on God's will, from Kant's point of view, hence discoverable neither mathematically nor metaphysically but only through experience. This law is related—somewhat mysteriously—to the fact that we find it impossible to imagine a space of more than three dimensions, despite the fact that reason alone adduces nothing against such spaces. The highest science of geometry for a finite being would lie in mastering these multiple spaces, though Kant leaves it open whether human beings, or only beings more perfect than ourselves, would be suited to the task. In all of this, one sees not only the first indications of an intellectual division of labor that will culminate in Kant's distinctions between sensibility and understanding and between the synthetic and the analytic a priori. More importantly, one observes in its earliest form something of the problematic out of which those later distinctions arise. Kant's epistemological concerns, as we will see, are not sui generis but reflect Kant's lifelong interest in the relation between the body and the mind.

Kant's *Erklärung* suggests another difficulty which will have consequences of considerable significance for his later thought (and for later German Idealists as well): Kant's understanding of a world raises the problem of the relation between knower and known in a unique way. Any mental representation differs, as representation, from the object represented. (Our thought or representation of a tree is not the tree.) And yet truth is traditionally said to lie in a certain harmony or adequation between our representation and what it represents, as if the latter's essential form, to use the scholastic metaphor (with which Kant's account of physical influx shows him to still be vaguely in agreement), flew into and literally impressed itself upon the soul. Kant's definition of a world as an "actually composited union," however, is curiously ill-adapted to this traditional model of knowledge. For the essential form of a world consists precisely in the actuality of its composition, that is, the mutual activity among its parts in which its unity consists. To *think* such a unity, however, is merely to composite things (its would-be parts) in thought, hence *not* to represent just that which *distinguishes* a world from a merely ideal or imaginary union and thus constitutes a world's specific or defining feature. This conceptual difficulty will dog Kant's next major works, and will, along with the incipient cognitive dualism mentioned above, play a defining role in his evolving understanding of community over the course of the next two decades.

Finally, there is Kant's novel account of essential force, which, while intended to diffuse the mystery surrounding the relation between body and soul, succeeds only in rendering it the more uncanny. For Leibniz, substance is to the dynamic interplay of force as reality is to appearance. Leibniz preserves the unity of individual substance in the face of this dynamic interplay by, in the final analysis, reducing the interplay of force to pre-established harmony, and the outwardness of corporeal space to the inwardness of consciousness. Kant, on the contrary, insists both on the unity of individual substance (of which the human soul is prototypical) *and* on the irreducibility of outwardness to inwardness. The fundamental insight that emerges from *Living Forces* is thus Kant's (paradoxical) understanding of the human mind as an inner unity that is somehow open to the external, that is, as a monad with windows (not just mirrors) if not doors.[50] Kant's later critical insistence on the indispensability of "outer" experience to the unity of consciousness is thus prefigured in Kant's earliest work.

In *Living Forces* Kant sets up the embodied soul (that is, the mind located in space) as the model of worldly substance generally. We can distinguish between real and imaginary unions (just what Leibniz ultimately denies) only because we ourselves are divided between thought (which allows us to think or conceive of a worldly law in general) and experience (which reveals its specific "mode of activity"), that is, only because we are creatures of both reason (which reaches beyond the world) and imagination (which locates us within it).

To the degree, however, that worldly recognition implies such a division of the mind, our "position" in the world remains unsettled. Kant will return to the question in the *Universal Natural History,* in which he undertakes to comprehend the universe by — so to speak — ideally recreating it. For the present it is enough to note Kant's crucial reliance, in this his earliest "*Erklärung* of the world," on the problematic nexus of body and soul — the vexed site at which intension and extension meet.

3 Commerce and Community in Kant's Early Thought

I. Introduction

KNOWLEDGE AND EMBODIMENT

Kant's rejection of monadic isolation is part of the enduring legacy of *Living Forces:* all knowing finite substances are implicated in an outer world. This conjunction of mental inwardness and worldly outwardness, however, is complicated by a peculiar sort of switch: the knowing soul is "in" the world, and to this extent "outside," even as the "outer" world as known somehow is or comes to be "inside" the soul. To know the world, the soul must be part of or present in the outer world, even as it represents or makes the world inwardly present to itself. (Leibniz's denial of this fact placed him in the untenable position of being unable to distinguish between knowledge and fantasy.) In short, *Living Forces* already gives striking evidence of Kant's lifelong concern with the "boundaries" of consciousness.[1]

But the solutions offered in *Living Forces* are hardly satisfying. For one thing, the soul's "position" in the world is simply assumed, without adequate attention to the difficulties entailed by the attendant doctrine of "physical influence" between body and soul. For another, the basis of the interactive bond that joins one worldly substance with another remains highly problematic. Still, Kant comes away from the exercise with a model of embodied substance from which subsequent works will draw, one that seems to make singularly accessible the relation between parts and whole by which worldhood is defined.

The years following the publication of *Living Forces* were highly productive ones for Kant. In 1754 he published two short essays on the rotation and the physical aging of the earth. The following year brought the *Universal Natural History and Theory of the Heavens,* along with the Latin essays *Succinct Exposition of Some Meditations on Fire* and *New Elucidation of the First Principles of Metaphysical Knowledge,* which qualified him for a teaching post at the University of Königsberg. In 1756 Kant published several essays on earthquakes (occasioned by the great earthquake in Lisbon), an essay on wind, and the *Physical Monadology* (part 1 of the uncompleted *Metaphysicae cum geometria iunctae usus in philosophia naturali* [The use in natural philosophy of metaphysics combined with geometry]). During this period, Kant assumed a series of tutorial posts, which evidently provided him with ample opportunity to think and write. It seems highly likely that both the *Universal Natural History*[2] and the *New Elucidation* (the two works that form the subject of the present chapter) were drafted at least in part while Kant belonged to one of these cultivated households.[3]

THE AMBIVALENCE OF ATTRACTION

When one reflects on the difference between the *Universal Natural History* and his earlier worldly *Erklärung,* one is struck by the emphasis the later essay places on Newtonian attraction as the principle by which, for Kant, the universe is centered. Just as the sun's attractive force, by Newton's lights, makes possible the planetary system, so, by analogy, the cosmic center of attraction unites the stars and galaxies into a cosmic whole. The universal principle of attraction (and central *Senkungspunkt* that it suggests) is thus crucial to Kant's new approach to the cosmos as a "systematic constitution."

Attraction, however, plays an ambiguous as well as crucial role. Kant's systematic point of support (or *Unterstützungspunkt*) is also a sinkhole (or *Senkungspunkt*), which would swallow up the universe were there not present a second force to counterbalance the first. (As we will see, the status of that counterforce, which Kant also associates — not always consistently — with "repulsion," "impetus," and "dissipation" remains doubtful.)[4]

Whatever the scientific merits of Kant's theory of repulsion, the "sinkhole" of attraction has a power and resonance that transcend the physical. If the mind must somehow be present in the world that it represents, then it too is subject to attraction's downward drag. Moreover, if — as Kant maintains — the material center of the universe is a sort of crucible from which organized matter continually emerges and into which it continually returns, our susceptibility to the force of physical attraction becomes the badge of our own bodily mortality.[5] As embodied beings we are drawn toward the cosmic sinkhole that is both womb and tomb — the universal site of birth and death, and hence both literally and figuratively the site at which reason and unreason "collide."

But we are saved from this anxious fate by the model of divine knowing in relation to which reason measures itself. The perfect or divine mind knows the world without being part of it. It is thus immune to the downward drag by which embodied minds are necessarily encumbered. By increasing the clarity and distinctness of our knowledge — by ascending to ever more general concepts and ideas — we grasp more and more with equal effort. In this way we continually approach (though never reach) the

standard set by divine perfection, in which knowing and creating ultimately merge.[6]

We are hindered in that approach, however, by the very worldly participation that on Kant's account makes (our) knowledge possible. Hence
Kant's heroic efforts (*per impossibile*) in the *Universal Natural History* to
grasp the universe in its totality. A metaphysical Theseus, Kant follows the
thread (*Faden*) of analogy out of the labyrinth at whose dizzying center
reason and unreason monstrously conjoin.[7] Approaching totality by means
of ever more comprehensive concepts and images, the mind draws closer
philosophically to the higher, spiritual center of the universe and thus establishes its mastery over the lower, or natural center of attraction. The
difficulty is that in thus transcending (or abandoning) the evidence of the
senses, reason risks leaving the track that distinguishes knowledge from
fantasy. This difficulty, indeed, may account for what has struck many readers as a disturbing rhetorical unevenness on Kant's part—a tendency to
insist on the certainty of his position, even as he admits, almost in the same
breath, to its excessive boldness. Kant ultimately characterizes his account
as a kind of "permissible" poetry (not decisively distinguishable, I will suggest, from the "arbitrary fictions" [*wilkürliche Erdichterungen*] of Thomas
Wright). In the end, Kant's cosmic history seems to be "speculative" (*ver-
mutlich*) or "conjectural" (*mutmaβlich*) in the most literal sense: an act of
courage or boldness (*Mut*) in which the spirit "swings itself upward" by
the force of its own impetuosity.

LAW, COMMUNITY, AND THE DIVINE IDEA

The stated goal of the *Universal Natural History* is to account for the constitution and mechanical origin of the universe by means of Newtonian principles. Such a project was, of course, not altogether novel. Newton, out of
piety or prudence, refrained from giving a mechanical explanation of the
origin of the solar system, preferring to attribute the location of the planets
to the immediate agency of God. Descartes, on the other hand (taking his
cue from Lucretius), did begin work on a mechanical history of the universe.[8] And yet when Kant at the beginning of his *Universal Natural History*
echoes Descartes by boldly stating, "give me matter and I will build a world
from it,"[9] he is by his own account attempting something new: namely, a
mechanical cosmogony that is friendly rather than indifferent or hostile to
the existence of God.

Kant, of course, was not the first to attempt such a mediation. His great
predecessor Leibniz, for example, had given an account of the universe in
which the ultimate cause or ground of things lies in the "optimizing" will
of God. God wills the best world possible. Things happen as they do, and

the world is as it is because God's will is not omnipotent but must defer to a prior standard of compossibility. At the same time, to make this reconciliation work, Leibniz is forced to argue that mechanical causation is merely a well-founded appearance, or *phenomenon bene fundatum,* which does not involve true interaction.

The difficulty with Leibniz's ingenious doctrine, from Kant's standpoint, is its subversion of what we (or at any rate he) means by worldly knowledge. Kant's earlier work linked our ability to distinguish between knowledge and fantasy to the status of the world as a genuine whole, that is, a unity with parts (the possibility of which Leibniz ultimately denied). Kant now develops that clue by expanding his interpretation of Newton's laws of motion as a world-informing principle of interactivity, a regulated intercourse that he refers to—interestingly enough—as a *commercium.*[10] Where ancient and medieval thought look to the regime, governed hierarchically by a ruling part, for their image of the cosmos, Kant's model calls to mind the reciprocal equality of civil or market society. The form of worldly community for Kant lies not in a ruling part but in the submission of each part to the same, reciprocally determining law.[11] Kant's cosmic "constitution" is thus closer to the liberal model of society than to a regime or "constitution" in the classical (or medieval) sense.[12] His theory of substantival commerce enables him to explain the action of the world upon our soul (and vice versa), while at the same time preserving the distinction between body and mind.

The exchanges of matter leave soul-substances intact, but only if we assume a divine schema or idea on which the possibility of worldly interaction among substances ultimately depends. Nature's lawfulness proves to be unthinkable (as we will see) apart from nature's insemination by God's germinal "idea." Kant's history bears the traces of a cosmic struggle between spiritual (male) and material (female) principles of generation—between the order of a material world bounded and informed by reason and the monstrous disorder of a (presumptively) self-sufficient nature. Kant's seminal idea puts down the threat of motherly omnipotence.[13] (As we will also see, however, Kant's model of spiritual procreation leaves the natural expression of man's "potency" in an embarrassing position—one in which "performance" is paradoxically "unmanly.")

To fully comprehend the lawfulness of nature is to understand God's plan. The difficulty is that such an idea is, in the final analysis, inaccessible to man. What God's schema comprehends immediately becomes available to us historically, hence, bit by bit or partially, an incrementalism that, for reasons already suggested, inevitably falls short. Kant therefore supplements his patient call for perpetual progress with an impetuous appeal to immediate transcendence, a contemplative berth beyond worldly space and time from which to contemplate the whole. Such release, however, remains intrinsically paradoxical, since it can only succeed by voiding the worldly bond and thus vitiating the boundary between knowledge and fantasy. Spiritual detachment is ultimately brought down by the need for — and inescapability of — worldly attachment.

In what follows I will attempt to trace the wavering course of Kant's ambiguous spiritual ascent. Failure to find satisfaction in the world is for Kant both a badge of honor and a token of inadequacy. It is only insofar as he begins to see in man's worldly exposure — his strange inner openness — an alternative center and reference point that some of these difficulties begin to resolve themselves. Kant's heroic appeal to the "higher attraction" of reason is ultimately doomed to failure. Man can escape the labyrinth of nature only by recognizing and being guided by his own "monstrousness."

II. Kant's *New Elucidation*

Metaphysics and cosmology define the double route of Kant's would-be spiritual ascent. Speaking generally, the *New Elucidation* devotes itself to a conceptual account of the divine idea (and our capacity to grasp it), while the *Universal Natural History* narrates the unfolding of that idea in worldly space and time. Despite its ambition, the *New Elucidation* is an incomplete and in some ways halting work — less of a whole, rhetorically speaking, than its cosmological counterpart. Kant's account of the first principles of metaphysical knowledge is as much concerned with the constraints imposed on created intellects (including, of course, his own) as with the creative fount of existence. The point is not to know the divine idea directly, but to acquire an idea, so to speak, of that idea — a copy or ectype of that which is available only to the "archetypal" mind of God.

REASONING AND THE ABSOLUTE NECESSITY OF GOD

The core of Kant's argument rests on a revised understanding of the so-called principle of sufficient reason. In its original, Leibnizian form the principle of sufficient reason asserts that for everything existent there is a sufficient cause or ground (*ratio*). Leibniz's metaphysical system rested on two fundamental principles: the law of sufficient reason and the law of noncontradiction. The latter furnishes the principle of truths "of reason" known a priori; the former that of truths "of fact" known by experience, or a posteriori. In the case of truths known a priori (for example, a triangle has 180 degrees), the opposite is logically impossible. In the case of truths known a posteriori (for example, Caesar crossed the Rubicon), the opposite is not logically impossible. Thus the necessity that connects the subject and predicate cannot be known immediately (by man) but only successively, by way of experience. The ultimate reason or ground of a posteriori truth lies in the will of God, and specifically, in his well-motivated choice to create this, the best world possible. Thus, for Leibniz, possibility precedes actuality. Out of an infinity of possible worlds, God chose to create the best. He could not have chosen to create a triangle of less or more than 180 degrees, but he could have chosen to create a (nonoptimal) world that would have lacked a Rubicon-crossing Caesar.

Thus all contingent truths, for Leibniz, have their ground in the principle of sufficient reason. Wolff, on the other hand, was inclined to collapse Leibniz's two principles into one, making identity or noncontradiction the principle of all human knowledge as such.[14] On this understanding, the difference that Leibniz maintained between the metaphysical (or a priori) and the historical tended to blur: hence Wolff's ubiquitous "geometric" proofs proceeding from "clear and distinct" definitions.

Kant signals his departure from both philosophic strains by denying the primacy of the principle of noncontradiction ("That is true the opposite of which is false"), substituting in its stead what he calls "the double principle of identity" ("Whatever is, is"; and "Whatever is not, is not") (I:389; [61]).

Those who take the principle of contradiction to be primary, Kant claims, misunderstand the fundamental character of all reasoning (*ratiocinatio*), which ultimately comes down to uncovering (or asserting and denying) an identity between a subject and a predicate. God, to whom all lies immediately in view, has, therefore, "no need of reasoning": "Indeed, since all things lie open to his view with total clarity, one and the same act of representation sets before his intellect which things are compatible and which are not, nor does he have any need for analysis which an obscuring ignorance requires of our intelligence" (I:391; 64).[15]

A "reason," according to Kant, is that which "determines" a subject with regard to its (possible) predicates. Reasons determine either antecedently (in which case they constitute the ground or reason for something coming into being or existing in a certain way), or they determine consequently (in which case they constitute the ground or reason of our knowing something). Consequently determining reasons, in other words, constitute the evidence that determines our knowledge, that is, fixes our choice among opposing predicates that are, prior to that evidence, indeterminate with respect to knowledge. (Before we have evidence of what color a particular swan is, its whiteness and its nonwhiteness are, so far as our knowledge is concerned, equally possible.)

God constitutes the one exception to Kant's "principle of determining reason" thus understood. God cannot have an antecedent reason for existing; but no being has its ground in itself (for then ground and grounded would absurdly be one);[16] hence God is groundless—he simply *exists*. God is the only being "in which existence is prior to . . . or identical with possibility." As the totality of all realities [*omnitudo realitatis*], God is that without which possibility is itself impossible (I:396; 72).[17] As soon as you deny his existence, the very concept of possibility vanishes (I:395–96; 71–72). Hence, God is absolutely necessary; his nonexistence is unthinkable.

Without the "collection" in God's mind of all realities in their mutual connection, possibility—which implies a thing's contingency or dependence on something other than itself—would not be an issue.[18] The difference between God's intellect, which grasps these relations immediately and therefore "has no need of reasoning," and our own lies in the fact that in God's mind, the union in question is "real," whereas the union we conceive is merely "ideal." "Form for yourself," says Kant,

> the concept of some being . . . in which there is a totality of reality. . . . Given this concept, existence also has to be attributed to this being. . . . But if all those realities are only *conceived* as united together, then the existence of that being is also an existence only in ideas [*idealiter . . . non realiter*]. (I:394; [70]; emphasis added)

In arguing for the "absolute necessity" of God's existence, Kant distinguishes a ground or reason for knowing and a ground or reason for existence: our concept of God as the totality of all realities grounds our knowledge that he exists, an existence that is itself, as Kant insists, ungrounded.

But this difference itself rests on the implicit distinction Kant draws between our concept of God as the totality of all realities (that is, as one in or before whom all realities are immediately present) and our *own conception* of such a union. *Accordingly, we cannot make the world's possibility intelligible to ourselves.* Our concept of the world is saved from paradox (if not outright contradiction) by the thought (arguably no less paradoxical) that God's nonexistence is unthinkable (I:394; 69).

THE NONTHINKABILITY OF ADAM'S FATHER

Kant's insistence on God's groundlessness leads him to dispute Wolff's claim that God (like every other being) has a sufficient ground. A being grounded in nothing, Wolff argued, would have nothing as its ground—absurdly turning nothing into something. Kant objects that such a being, in Wolff's formulation, is like the first man, a man without a father. Suppose, Kant stipulates, the first man was not begotten (*genitum*) by a father:

> Then there would be nothing which had begotten him, and he would therefore have been begotten by nothing. Since this is contradictory, it must be admitted that he was begotten by some-

thing. It is not difficult to escape from the fallacy of this argument. If he has not been begotten, then nothing has begotten him. That is, he who would be thought to have begotten him is nothing, *a non-entity* [emphasis added]. This is indeed as certain as certain can be [*certissimum*], but if the proposition is turned around back to front, it allies itself with the worst distortion of sense [*sed prae-postere conversa proposito pessime detortum nanciscitur sensum*]. (I:398; [75])

To say that nothing is God's ground is no more to turn nothing into something than to say no one is Adam's father is to turn no one into someone. Still, Kant might have responded to Wolff's fallacy with any number of other, and simpler, examples (for example, to say that "no one bought a certain house" is not to say that the house was actually purchased—that is, by "no one"). And yet, Kant's resort to superlatives, and redundant ones at that, suggests that something peculiar is at stake. What is it, precisely, that makes the nonexistence of the first man's begetter "most certain" and its existence the "worst distortion of sense"?[19] Is there some way that Kant's example is particularly apt?

Comparison of the passage to the section immediately preceding it suggests that the example is not casually chosen. Kant would, after all, agree that the first man (like any being other than God) must have an antecedent cause. If the first man was not begotten, then he who would be thought to have begotten him is (by the terms of Kant's reasoning in the passage quoted) a nonentity. It follows not only that God did not beget the first man, but also that merely to think of God begetting him is to think of God as a nonentity. But this is precisely what Kant's earlier claim concerning God as the source of all possibility expressly and emphatically ruled out. The thought that the source of all possibility does not exist is itself (supposed to be) impossible. And yet it is precisely toward such a thought that Kant's example points us. One is stopped only by (thinking) the distinction between God's creation of the first man and the begetting of all subsequent men by their (human) fathers. What could be regarded as the most fundamental claim of Kant's *New Elucidation*—that God's nonexistence is unthinkable—rests here on our thinking the distinction between God's creation of Adam and Adam's begetting of his sons, that is, between divine and human modes of propagation.

The nonbegetting of Adam, merits a (hyperbolic) "certissimum," I would hazard, because the assimilation of divine and human modes of propagation is as unthinkable as the nonexistence of God. At the same time, the conceptually problematic status of "certissimum"—a status that Kant almost immediately flags (I:400; 79)—suggests that specifying the difference between divine creation and natural generation is no easy matter. It is to this very specification, as we will see, that Kant's *Universal Natural History* largely devotes itself.

FREEDOM AND DETERMINACY

Crusius had objected to the principle of determining reason on the grounds that it is incompatible with freedom of the will and hence destructive of morality. Kant responds with his first published consideration of the compatibility of moral freedom with determinism (a determinism that here assumes the form of Stoic "fate") (I:399; 76). Partly anticipating his more famous, critical resolution of the problem, Kant argues that freedom and determinism are compatible, so long as the determination in question is internal to the will.

By these lights, even God's act of creation is "determined", not in a way that implies that God is externally constrained, but in the sense that another would be unfitting or unworthy (*indignum*):[20]

> In God the act of creating the world is not wavering [*ambiguum*][21] but is determined with such certainty that an opposite [way of creating it] would be unworthy of God, that is, plainly incompetent [*competere plane non possit*]. . . . Yet God's action is not less free because it is determined by reasons which, as certainly inclining his will, include motives of his own infinite intelligence, and which do not originate in some blind/dark [*caeca*] efficacy of nature. (I:400; [79])[22]

The determinacy of creation is the warrant of God's competence or lack of ambiguity. To be free, in a Godly sense, is to be absolutely unwavering. Kant's primary understanding of freedom, then, links it with steadfastness. To be free in a more general and less exalted sense is to be "self-determined" (though not, as in Kant's later moral thought, "autonomous"). In the case of men's free acts, then, opposite actions are excluded, not by anything "external to the desires and spontaneous inclinations of the subject." Instead, "In the very inclining of his wishes and desires, in so far as he gladly [*lubenter*] submits to the enticement of his representations [*representationum*], his actions are determined by a fixed law in a nexus[23] most certain and yet voluntary."

The distinction between physical and moral actions is not a matter of determinacy versus indifference, but of determinacy's source, the "mark" of free action being its determination through the motives of the intellect (that is, "one's own" reasons) rather than through the "external solicitations" that determine the behavior of animals (I:400; [79]). The power to perform action is determined "only through the inclination of pleasure towards the enticements of things offered by our [inner] representations of what pleases" (I:401; 80). To will is to be pleased to do (*lubuit*) that to which the object of our representation attracts us. What "determines" the will is thus the strength of the attraction relative to that which might otherwise have pleased us. Kant leans on the Latin *lubit* (literally "it is pleasing"), with its blurring of the active and the passive. To want or desire is to suffer a sort of inner compulsion.

All action of the will is thus determinate, even when the conscious mind seems to be wavering in uncertainty. This conclusion, however, raises the moral difficulty that evil action seems inculpable: how can one be blamed for action to which one is somehow forced? Kant's answer takes the form of a dialogue between a defender of the "freedom of indifference" and an upholder of determinate reason capable of responding to that moral charge. At issue is the reconcilability of a determinism reminiscent of Stoic fate with the requirements of imputability.[24]

The moral determinist's reply looks both to the nature of the attraction and to the will's own power to resist "illicit pleasure." Freedom is determination according to the representation of the good (what is best) (I:402; 82). Yet those not so determined are to be blamed; for "when sinners delight in what they do, it is perfectly equitable that they pay the penalty for their illicit pleasure" (I:404; 86).[25] In an effort to explain how, if freedom is determination according to the representation of the good, evil can be culpable, Kant appeals to the sinner's sense that he succumbed to pleasure where he might, with "strenuous effort," have resisted (I:405; 87). He who drinks, games, and makes "offerings to Venus" does not do so unwillingly but by an "innermost principle of the will" that is marked with the "baseness" of the objects to which he is attracted.

Here, as in his later moral thought, Kant associates freedom, not with a *lack* of determinacy, but with determination stemming from an *inward* source. If what "attracted [*invitant*] did not determine [one]" (I:402; [83]), the will would lack all fixity, and the blame for all things would devolve on God:

> In setting himself to create the primordial state of the universe, God started a series which includes, in a fixed nexus of reasons intimately bound together, some things that are moral evils. . . . But from this it does not follow that God can be reproached as the author of morally evil actions. If, as with machines, intelligent beings held a passive attitude towards those things which impel toward determinations and changes, the ultimate blame . . . would indeed fall upon God. . . . But things which happen through the will of beings endowed with intelligence and the spontaneous power of self-determination obviously proceed from a sound inner principle, from conscious impulses, and from the choice of one or another alternative according to their free power

of choice. Hence though the state of things is established in some manner before the occurrence of free acts, however much that intelligent being may be enslaved in such a nexus of circumstance that it is absolutely certain that moral evils will result from it. . . . yet this future is determined by reasons among which the voluntary direction of actions upon what is base is the pivot. (I:404; [85–86])

The ultimate source of such determination, however, remains unclear. To be determined is, on the one hand, to make up one's mind or choose between the path of vice and virtue. Determination, on this account, implies a will active on its own behalf. To be determined is, on the other hand, to yield to the representation that most pleases us or to which we are most attracted (I:401; 80). Determination on this account implies a will passively succumbing to the greater force. Kant's dissatisfaction with the latter theory (and the Wolffian/Baumgartean model on which it rests) is suggested by Kant's final appeal to the power of the will to "resist" attraction of the baser sort and thereby be "reclaimed" for the good, that is, to determine rather than be determined by the force of attraction. What Kant has yet to resolve is whether the ultimate ground of choice lies in the object that "entices" the will or in the principle that leads one to yield to or resist the enticement.[26] This ambivalence on Kant's part concerning the ultimate status of attraction will have special importance when we turn to the *Universal Natural History.*

ABSTRACTION, OR THE POWER OF TURNING ONE'S ATTENTION

The *illusion* of indeterminacy of the will arises, according to Kant, from the fact that we feel ourselves to be the authors of the representations which contain the motives for choice:

The natural force of desire, inherent in the human mind, directs itself not only to objects but also to furnishing the intellect with various representations. In so far as we feel that we are ourselves the authors of the representations which contain the motives for choice in a given case, so that we are able either to attend to them, suspend our attention, or turn our attention in another direction, we are conscious of being able not only to strive towards the objects in conformity with our desire but also to change those objective reasons themselves in a variety of ways and as we please. We therefore can scarcely refrain from supposing that the application of our will is exempt from all law and lacking in fixed determination. But suppose that we make an effort to arrive at a correct understanding of the fact that the inclination of the attention tends towards this combination of representations rather than another. Since grounds attract us in a certain direction, we shall, in order at least to test our freedom, turn our attention in the opposite direction, and thus make it preponderant so that the desire *is directed thus and not otherwise.* In this way, we shall easily persuade ourselves that determining grounds must certainly be present. (I:403; [84])

Kant's complicated argument speaks to, but also leaves obscure, the relation between attraction and the will's spontaneous activity. Specifically, it leaves unresolved whether the ground of choice (or "objective reason") lies in the objects/representations themselves or in us as "authors" of our representations, an authorship we sense on the basis of our consciousness of a power to attend or not as we may please (*lubitum*). Attention tends toward an eliciting representation of which the mind, by virtue of its power over attention, is itself (or feels itself to be) the source.[27] (That "attention" and "tend" have a common Latin root, *tendo,* meaning "to stretch towards, aim at," does not lessen the obscurity.) Kant finds it sufficient here to establish that (in either case) a determinate tendency of attention is secured: even if we change our representation for the sole purpose of "testing our freedom," a fixed tending of attention results. Hence, freedom of the will and indeterminacy or indifference of the will are not (as Kant's opponent insists) equivalent.

The more far-ranging question of whether the soul is actively or passively engaged when it attends is implicitly addressed in the next section, in which Kant attempts to reconcile the principle of conservation (that is, the thesis that "the amount of absolute reality in the world . . . neither increases nor decreases") with the possibility of "spiritual" progress.[28] The totality of all realities is as unchanging as God Himself. Human intellection, on the other hand, is a progressive or timely activity, perpetually approaching, by a turning and concomitant withdrawal of the mind's attention, what God apprehends in an immediate concatenation.

No doubt the infinite perception of the whole universe which is always internally present to the soul, albeit only obscurely, already contains within itself whatever reality must be in those thoughts that are afterwards to be illumined with greater light. The mind, then, by merely turning its attention later on to such thoughts and withdrawing to an equal degree from others, and shedding a more intense [*intensiori*] light on the former, daily obtains greater knowledge. It does not, of course, extend the range of absolute reality (in fact, the matter [*materiale*] of all ideas, derived from their connection with the universe, remains the same), but the formal aspect [*formale*], which consists in the combination of notions and the application of attention either to their difference or to their agreement, certainly undergoes a variety of changes. (I:408; [92])

By moving via its power over attention from the particular to the general, the soul is able to increase its formal range without altering the total quantity of the "reality" thereby embraced. (God, who does not need to "abstract and combine" universal notions in this way, stands both at the upper limit of this scale and altogether beyond it.) The soul is both passive and active, albeit in a way that is not yet clearly differentiated from a higher, spiritual "receptivity" to God. This unresolved tension resurfaces in the *Universal Natural History,* with catastrophic consequences we will soon have occasion to examine.

SUCCESSION AND COEXISTENCE

Part 3 of the *New Elucidation* draws out the implications of the contrast between the intellects of God and man.

According to the "principle of succession," "Substances are capable of change only to the extent that they are connected with other substances, their reciprocal dependence determining the mutual change of state" (I:410; 96). A simple substance, exempt from all "external nexus," is immutable. Substances cannot change "internally" (hence cannot undergo successive states) unless their "external" relation to other substances also changes ("motion" being the "appearance" of this change).[29]

The proof, according to Kant, follows from the principle of determining reason in the following way. A substance that undergoes a succession of states is characterized by opposing determinations or predicates. (For example, a man changes from being happy to being sad; an apple changes from being green to being red.) A ground or reason, however, determines a predicate by excluding its opposite. (The "ground" of the apple's being red "excludes" its being not red, or green.) Hence any "internal" determination of a substance will exclude its opposite. The opposing determinations implicit in time or succession must, then, derive from a source external to the substance.

The dependence of time on the real interconnection of substances refutes, according to Kant, Leibniz's claim that single substances change continuously through an "internal principle of activity." The change registered in inner sense testifies to the "real existence of bodies," overturning the foundations of preestablished harmony (I:411; 98). (Kant's first "refutation of idealism"—like the later, more famous version—moves from the changes of which the mind is aware in "inner sense" to the necessary existence of things external to the mind.) It also implies an "indissoluble connection [*nexum*]" with matter to which the human soul, in carrying out "its internal functions of thought," is bound.[30]

According to the second principle (of "coexistence"), "Finite substances are unrelated by their existence alone, and in no way maintained in com-merce [*commercio*] except insofar as they are sustained in a state of harmony [*mutuis respectibus conformatae*] by the common [*communi*] principle of their existence — that is, the divine intellect" (I:412–13; [100]). The proof is this: Individual substances, which do not cause each other's existence, have an existence that can be understood independently of all other sub-stances. That substances are indeed related (that "everything is found in universal mutual nexus") can therefore not be understood on the basis of their existence alone, nor even on that of their common origin in God, but only on the basis of a divine idea that establishes their reciprocal connec-tion or correlation. In short, the universal nexus that we "find" implies a schema or plan of the divine mind (or so implies, if such a nexus is to be "understood"). By virtue of that schema, the divine intellect not only "gives existence to things but also established their mutual relations by conceiving their existences as correlated." To this "concept of the divine idea," and to it alone, "the universal commerce of all things" is therefore to be ascribed (I:413; [101]).

What is required to make worldly nexus "understandable" is a divine schema that "conceives" substances, not only in their individual existence but also in their co-relation. The world is "not possible to conceive" apart from the divine idea (I:414; [103]), that is, apart from a concept that we ourselves cannot conceive.

Commerce and Community

Everything thus hinges on the "reality" of worldly commerce understood as something separate from and in addition to the individual "reality" of its members — commerce, that is to say, "through true efficient causes" (see I:415; [105]). And yet what, if the ground of worldly commerce is the mind of God, distinguishes that unity from the preestablished harmony of Leibniz? What, in the final analysis, makes Kant's world more or other than an ideal or imaginary whole? The answer evidently lies in Kant's insistence on the externality of worldly consciousness, that is, in his refusal to con-ceive the relatedness of substances as, in the Leibnizian manner, a function of their inwardness alone. Kant steers a narrow course between preestab-lished harmony (with its assimilation of all reality within the boundaries of the individual) and physical influx "vulgarly conceived" (which implies a transfer of reality from one substance to another, thus breaching individual boundaries). Kant's basic insight into the irreducible otherness of knowl-edge, in other words, leads him to insist on the "reality" of worldly com-merce, which preserves the "inwardness" of substances even as it accounts for their "outward" participation in a greater whole (I:415; [103]).

Accordingly, the divine idea at once assimilates and differentiates the inner and outer realms. One substance determines another

> not through its internal characteristics but only in virtue of the nexus by which such substances are held together [*colligantur*] in the idea of an infinite being. Consequently, whatever determinations and changes are found in them always refer to what is external; physical influx is thereby excluded; and there exists a universal *harmony* of things. But this does not beget [*progignitur*] the *pre-established* harmony of *Leibniz*, which is properly *consensus* among substances, not their mutual inter*dependence*. For God does not employ through technical artifice a series of neatly constructed reasons adapted to the agreement [*conspirationem;* literally, "breathing together"] of substances; nor is there an ever special divine influx, i.e., commerce among substances through *Malebranchean occasional causes.* [For] . . . the divine action has no need to be determined in a variety of ways to accommodate circumstances. There is rather a real action of substances that occurs among them, or commerce through truly efficient causes, because the same principle that set up the existence of things brings it about that they are bound by this law, and so their mutual involvement is established through those determinations which belong to the origin of their existence. (I:415; [104])

Like Malebranche and Leibniz, Kant refers the world's connectedness to the sustaining agency of God. What *distinguishes* Kant's referral is his insistence on the singularity and *instantaneousness* of God's grounding act. Where Leibniz conceives God's intellect in terms of a "series" of elegant reasons, where Malebranche conceives God's acts as determined as the "occasion" arises, Kant conceives both intellect and act in an indivisible and instantaneous production, an "efficacious representation" (I:414; 102) in which thought and act are one.

To this originating moment of creation Kant refers an otherwise irresolvable tension between the unity of the universe and its multiplicity. God is the totality or completion of what confronts us as an endless task of attending to ever more inclusive similarities and differences. The superiority of Kant's theory lies, as he puts it, in its disclosure or illumination (*aperiens*)[31] of "the very origin of the reciprocal nexus of things" (I:416; [105]).[32] What it cannot do is to disclose this origin in a way that is available to man (or any other "reasoning" being). Everything thus rests on the idea of a "schema" that is in principle inaccessible to (human) reason.[33] If, as Kant implies, worldly connection necessarily involves "efficacy," his description of God's creative thought-act as an "efficacious representation" (*efficaci repraesentatione*) seems question-begging. His resort to the divine schema has the effect of resolving "outside" of time a problem that cannot be solved within it—the problem, namely, of how substances can be both ontologically distinct and mutually dependent, both "in themselves" and "in relation to" (or for) each other.[34] But precisely by escaping time, the divine schema evades human intellection. Kant's fundamental insight into the embodied character of human knowledge is thus threatened by the very model of divine reason that is supposed to ground it. The perfection of reason spells the end of reasoning.

III. *Universal Natural History*

If the *New Elucidation* looks forward hopefully to an "abundant harvest" of future knowledge (I:416; 105), the *Universal Natural History* may well represent its first fruit. Certainly no work by Kant has more images of fertility (as befits a book on the creation of the universe). As we will see, however, nature's fecundity is by no means unambiguous for Kant, repelling even as it fascinates. The relation between procreation and creation is a key theme of Kant's argument. Kant's personification of nature as female and God as male suggests, indeed, a sort of contest between motherly and fatherly principles of generation, with mother (or nature) always eager to swallow up again the children to which she gives rise, and father (or God) sustaining yet elusive.

"EPICURUS IN THE MIDST OF CHRISTENDOM"

Kant seeks from the outset to uncover the systematic (*das Systematische*) that binds up the members of infinite creation (I:221; 81). Such a project, he acknowledges, is likely to arouse unfavorable prejudice (*Vorurteil*),[35] both for its difficulty and for its apparent hostility to religion. Yet he ventures, on the basis of a slight conjecture (*Vermutung*), to undertake the dangerous journey, as a result of which he can now see "new lands."[36] He would not have undertaken the journey, he insists, without prior security about the duties of religion; and yet he also admits to a continuing uneasiness over the clouds that seemed implicitly to hide a monster (*Ungeheuer*). Only in the course of the journey have these clouds dispersed and the splendor of the highest being broken forth. Despite his claims of assurance, Kant's effort required an initial act of faith or courage (*Mut*). It is thus no wonder if weaker minds find Kant's plan repulsive (*anstößig*). To undertake the journey, it seems, one must overcome a (weak-minded) sense of horror for the sake of a higher, if unseen, goal (I:221–22; [81]).

If the order and beauty of the world structure were only the effect of matter abandoned (*überlassen*) to the laws of motion, if the blind (*blinde*) mechanism of nature could produce such perfection out of chaos, then nature would be "self-sufficient" (*sich selbst genugsam*), and an important proof of God's existence would be sapped of strength (*entkräftet*).³⁷ "Epicurus [would] live again in the midst of Christendom," and the clear light of faith would be trampled underfoot by an unholy philosophy (I:222; [82]).

In fact, however, this order and beauty serve to confirm God's existence, inasmuch as they cannot be understood to arise other than as a consequence of God's "highest plan." Kant's own plan loses its unholiness, and his confidence (*Zuversicht*) rises to undaunted serenity (*unerschrockenen Gelassenheit*) on the basis of this higher plan, of which his own is to be a faithful (if artificial) copy. ("Give me matter," Kant cries, "and I will build a world of it!" (I:230; [88]). Indeed, the ease with which Kant's own "schema" generates an image of the world (thus replicating the divine original) is itself tendered as confirming evidence (I:226; 85).

The basic juridical thrust of Kant's argument³⁸ is thus as follows: against pious believers in God's special providence and free-thinking upholders of the universal laws of motion, Kant urges a third way, one that finds God not in the special but the universal. The very susceptibility of matter to common laws implies a common origin in an infinite understanding: "if the natures of things were in themselves and independently necessary what an astonishing accident [*Ungefähr*], or rather, what an impossibility, that they should so go together in their natural strivings exactly as if a superior wise choice had so united them" (I:225; [84]). Is it possible that

> many things, each with a nature independent of the others, should so exactly determine one another as to yield a well ordered whole? And if this latter is the case does it not give undeniable proof of the community [*Gemeinschaft*] of their first origin, which must be an all-sufficient, highest understanding, in which the natures of things were projected for united ends? (I:227–28; [86])

It is this *planful* coordination, rather than any particular action (such the supposed arrangement of the cooling breezes of Jamaica for human benefit) that bespeaks God's presence.³⁹ In keeping with the image of creation as an infinitely artful mechanism, the laws of motion are only understandable in terms of the united purposes of an infinite intelligence. In offering, given matter, to "build a world of it," Kant echoes Descartes rather than Epicurus.⁴⁰

The superiority of Kant's account over that of the ancient materialists lies in its discovery of an intrinsically lawful order where the ancients saw only "blind" or "causeless" chance. Accordingly, Kant attributes the deflection of matter from its primal fall to an original "force of repulsion" (*Zurückstoßungskraft*) coordinate with—and no less compelling than—the Newtonian force of attraction. (This repulsive force is associated with "tossing force" [*schießende Kraft*] or impetus [*Schwungskraft*] and plays a crucial role, both physically and spiritually, in the elaboration of Kant's system.) Epicurus's appeal to chance to account for the "swerving" (*clinamen*) of the atoms is a fatal false step from the "path of truth" that leads ultimately to the "abyss" (*Abgrund*) of deriving "reason from unreason" — Kant's characterization of the Lucretian effort to account for life on the basis of the nonliving. It is the lawful — hence "essential" or inward rather than "foreign" character — of this order that finally answers Epicurus and saves reason from unreason (I:227–28; 86). A willing subject, nature is internally compelled "by her own disposition." Nature's beauty lies in her free yet binding unity, sign of her legitimate (or unforced) submission to the purposes of the divine intellect (I:223, 226, 228; 82, 85, 86).

And yet the gap between matter and intelligence, unreason and reason on which Kant insists itself presents a difficulty: the laws of attraction (and repulsion) that explain the material world do not seem able to account for life, let alone higher intelligence. Kant, who is ready to recreate the material world, wonders whether, "given matter, [he] can show how [even] a caterpillar is generated."[41] What gives him pause is our ignorance of the "true disposition" of the living thing and the development of the manifoldness within it, which bespeaks nature's "secret art."[42] The complexity of the simplest animal or plant is greater than that of material nature as a whole, whose mechanical causes can thus be known more easily. In its susceptibility to the law of attraction, matter reveals a simplicity that lends itself to human comprehension. Despite its enormity, material nature is more attuned to our mental capacities than as near a thing as our own living bodies. Kant's attempt to comprehend the whole thus admits of an initial deformity — or incompleteness. Our own place in the whole is less easily grasped than that of the comets and planets. Whether this (necessary) gap does not defeat Kant's purpose (which is, after all, to understand the material whole in its relation to the intellectual or spiritual) is a question that is here left hanging.

Still, in a final appeal to the fairness of his readers and to dissuade them from dismissing his hypotheses as a mere "philosophic dream," Kant promises to forego all "arbitrary fictions" (*willkürliche Erdichtungen*), relying only on the "certain" laws of attraction and (somewhat more problematically) repulsion to animate his re-creation. To this plea he adds the caveat that certain arguments claim greater certainty and precision than others and should so be judged. Where, in the latter sections of the essay, rigor fails, a seductive (*reizend*) (I:235; [92]) agreeableness and pleasure may succeed in carrying the reader along.

KANT'S GALACTIC REVOLUTION

Part 1, "On the Systematic Constitution of the Fixed Stars," starts with an observation available to "anyone who views the starry heavens on a clear night"[43] — that luminous streak called the Milky Way (*Milchstraße*) whose configuration indicates that the fixed stars (or "firmament") are not fixed at all, that is, that they are not placed on the hollow sphere of the heavens (as traditionally held) but "disperse themselves orbitally around a central point." Kant finds it curious (*es ist zu bewundern*) that no one prior to the astronomer Thomas Wright saw that what appeared to the ancients as a band encircling the earth is in fact a disc, made up of orbiting solar stars, of which the earth is itself a (minute) part.[44] Kant credits Wright with giving him "the first prompting" to regard the fixed stars, "not as a dispersed swarm (*zerstreutes Gewimmel*) without visible order," but as a visible system analogous to that of the sun (I:231; [88]). The Milky Way newly configured as a centered orb is the starting point of Kant's effort to advance beyond the limits previously set to man's curiosity (*Wissbegierde*).[45]

Kant's new configuration has the affect of reestablishing the connection — severed with the destruction, by the new astronomy, of the traditional celestial canopy — between earth and stars. The infinite reach of Newtonian gravitation allows Kant to penetrate the constitution of the galaxy, held together, like the planetary system to which it is analogous, by the force of attraction exerted from the center outward. Gravity or attraction toward the center is thus the ruling principle of the stellar constitution. Yet gravity unimpeded would eventually draw all into a single lump were there not a second, no less primal force of repulsion, by which attracted bodies are deflected horizontally from their downward course. Together, these two forces constitute a universal system of orbital motions destined (*geschickt*) for an imperishable duration (I:250; 104).

Kant's attempt to demonstrate that the "fixed" stars are in fact moving is the literal anticipation (and equivalent) of his later, figurative "Copernican Revolution." Here, as later, appearances are deceiving. If the fixed stars seem to confirm their name, this may be, Kant argues, because they move too slowly and at too great a distance to be readily observed on earth. However, recent technical improvements in the instruments of observation, combined with analogy, support (*unterstützen*) the stimulating (*reizend*) hope that the disparate reports of ancient and modern astronomers may be connected in a coherent history of stellar motion (I:253; [106]).

The most arousing (*reizend*) feature of Kant's doctrine, however, is its "sublime representation" (*erhabene Vorstellung*) of the "plan of creation" (I:253; [106]). If the distant nebulous stars may be taken to be other milky ways (rather than, as with the author of the *Astrotheology*, holes through which the heavenly fire shines),[46] a "prospect [*Aussicht*] opens up" upon the "infinite field of creation" and offers a "representation [*Vorstellung*] of God's work that is commensurate with the infinity of its great creator [*Werkmeister*]" (I:255; [108]). A reversal of the traditional and/or mystical view of the heavenly clouds as apertures or openings to the fire of heaven provides both a picture and outlook that measures the "immeasurable." (Kant sensibly adds, in an argument repeated and modified in the *Critique of Judgment,* that such a plan [*Entwurf*] can also usefully guide empirical observation.) Kant's original "Copernican turn" itself turns on a reversal of foreground and background, inward and outward. At once echoing and reversing the topos of sun and clouds by which Kant earlier sought to assuage the reader's (and his own) uncertainty, the heavenly fire (or monster?) does not break through the clouds (*nebula*), whose constitutional solidity reflects the "enlightened [*erleuchteten*] insights" of Maupertuis rather than the "imaginings" of the *Astrotheology.*

From this prospect, one sees "the first members of a progressive relation," and "the first part of this infinite progression already permits to be known what should be conjectured [*vermuten*] about the whole." Here "is no end but the abyss of a true immeasurability," one in which all human capability "sinks" even when it is "lifted up [*erhoben*] by the science of number." "The wisdom, goodness, power that has manifested itself is infinite, and even in the same measure, fruitful and active [*geschäftig*]; the plan of their revelation must therefore be, as they are, infinite and without limit" (I:256; [108]). In short, the plan of creation as a progressive unfolding is both measurable and immeasurable, both conformable to man's capacity and beyond it. As such, the plan both sinks the mind (as into an abyss) and lifts it up, beyond the science of number, to presume (*vermuten*) about the whole. Creation is immeasurable and yet — to the extent that it reveals His plan — commensurate with God. This fact domesticates the wild infinity of chaos, promising a new order in motion to replace the older faith in an unyielding firmament.

At the same time, however, that worldly plan harbors a fundamental ambiguity that works its way through the remainder of the essay, an ambiguity deriving from the plan's dual character as both mirror and window, a picture of and outlook on the whole. In its capacity as representation it copies or reflects what in its capacity as prospect it looks out on or anticipates. Kant's plan both is and is not identical to that of God; is and is not, that is to say, outside the space and beyond the time in which that plan is realized. This tension is nowhere more acute than in Kant's discussion of the "origins" of the universe.

COMMERCE AND COSMOGONY

Part 2 of the *Universal Natural History* delves more deeply into the emergence of both planetary and stellar constitutions from the original cosmic "state of nature" (I:259; 111).[47] Kant's first task is to show that gravity (pace Newton) does not require an interfering God. Newton, Kant suggests, mistakenly attributed the maintenance of the solar system to the immediate action of God because he could find no material cause for the "community" of planetary influence. (The Cartesians, on the other hand, rejecting gravity, attribute planetary motion to the material community provided by the celestial ether.) Kant means to make good Newton's deficiency by reconciling the material community with gravitational action at a distance.

Accordingly, Kant posits an "original state of nature"[48] — a first moment in which matter, resolved into its "elementary groundstuff [*Grundstoff*]," is dispersed throughout infinite space in the simplest arrangement that could "follow upon nothing." This dispersal would bring everything to an immediate standstill (from which the world as we know it could never have evolved) but for the *diversity in the kinds* [Gattungen] *of elements* (Kant's emphasis), which contributes to the regulating (*Regelung*) of nature and the shaping (*Bildung*) of the chaos (I:263; [114]).

In Kant's version of Epicurean chaos, order arises neither from "chance" nor from the continual intervention of God, but from a matter "that essentially contains the principles of its own motion." Accordingly, Kant's point of historical departure is that first moment in which matter was infinitely and equally distributed throughout space, that is, that "state of nature" in which "nothing had yet formed," or rather in which "nature, immediately bordering with creation, was as raw, as unformed as possible."

But such a state — "the very simplest that can follow upon nothing" — would not be formless, matter already displaying in its elemental properties the "mark" of perfection that follows from its "origin in the eternal idea of the divine intelligence." Such marks, seemingly "sketched out" (*entworfen*) at random, prompt matter to perfect itself. Nature is thus both passive or receptive (that is, of the "character" impressed upon it by the divine understanding) and active with respect to her own historical evolution.

The puzzling question of matter's heterogeneity — a key issue dividing Newton and Leibniz — is resolved in the veiled figure of a nature that carries (or is made pregnant by?) the projective sketch (*Entwurf*) of God. Through this figure, Kant reconciles the absolute unity of matter (as subject to universal law) with its infinite division into distinct kinds. Nature's temporal "self-organization" presupposes its origin in and formation by an atemporal God. In short, Kant replaces both the awkward Newtonian separation of matter and motion, and their equally unsatisfying Leibnizian assimilation "in the realm of appearance," with a conception of natural fertility — of a matter *essentially* endowed with motion and life. At the same time, the *principle* of life must ultimately be derived from a source extrinsic to the body that it vivifies. A truly self-subsistent nature — a material mother uncoupled from a spiritual father — is for Kant (as we will see) quite literally unthinkable.

Out of this diversity organized motion begins, as rarer matter, impelled by the force of attraction, sinks toward that which is denser. To account, however, for the fact that some matter is halted in its descent to the center of attraction, Kant posits a second force of "repulsion," owing to which masses deflect each other in their downward path, thus moving sideward according to the principle of "least reciprocal action."[49] This second force (a Kantian innovation) is especially associated with the effluence (*Ausfluß*) of "strongly smelling bodies," the elasticity of vapors (*Dünste*), and the expansion of "all spiritous/spiritual matters" (*geistigen Materien*), that is, with the tendency of bodies to disperse themselves through mutual aversion (I:265; [115]).[50]

The resulting "constitution," in which bodies "hinder one another's [free] motion as little as possible," calls to mind Kant's later descriptions of the perfect juridical condition, which also reconciles stability and motion through the free but lawful action of individual bodies.[51] In the former case, it is the balance between the forces of sinking (*Senkenden*) and sideways impetus, or swinging (*Schwungskraft*), that maintains each body in "free circular motion" at the height at which it "hovers" (*schwebt*). Stability results, in other words, from the equation of the attractive force exerted on each body from the center, and the repellent "least reciprocal action" by which bodies move each other sideways. Those particles, on the other hand, that "cannot freely maintain themselves," sink downward to the center of attraction (I:266; [116]).[52] The upshot is the growth, out of a so to speak infinitely small germ [*Keim*], of a large solar mass, about which smaller bodies orbit at a distance in inverse proportion to their densities.

WHOLENESS AND INFINITY

Section 7 of part 2, "on creation in the whole circumference [*Umfang*] of its infinity," follows the "thread of analogy" from planetary systems and galaxies to(ward) the universe in its entirety. By positing a point in the universe of greatest density or attractive force, Kant claims to extend his understanding from the solar system to an "infinity" of worlds. By taking his bearings from this cosmic sinkhole — this navel of the universe — the whole of creation seems to fall within his reach (I:265; 115. I:306–7; 148–49).

The results of Kant's attempt, however, are at best inconclusive. His grasp, along with the support on which it rests, is fragile and ultimately illusive, as Kant himself (as we will see) rhetorically concedes. The universal "object of attraction" is both *Unterstützungspunkt* and *Senkungspunkt,* both steadying ground and dizzying abyss. Accordingly, Kant's vision of the whole is alternately attractive and repulsive: the center will and will not hold.

Worth and Worthiness

What both "moves" and "astonishes" in Kant's model of the universe is, he claims, the submission of infinite diversity to a single "universal rule" (I:306; [148]). Kant's effort to understand the world as an absolute (and not merely relative) reconciliation of unity and diversity (or as a plenitude as full as God himself, the *ens realisimum*) gives rise to difficulties that Leibniz did not have to face. For Kant and Leibniz alike, the ground or reason why anything exists is ultimately a matter of its "worthiness" or value.[53] To be is to be worthy of creation, to merit existence in God's eyes. Leibniz identifies this merit with the principle of sufficient reason: the world in part and as a whole exists because God is "inclined" though not necessitated to create the best. Kant, on the contrary, links the world's worthiness with its *Allergeschicklichkeit* — its aptness or craftsmanship: the world deserves to exist because, and to the extent that, it "befits" its creator, that is, is like unto God himself.[54] But the metaphor of *technai* or production, with its implicit distinction between idea and product, provides a way out of the pantheistic labyrinth to which Kant's definition of perfection otherwise seems inexorably to lead. The difference, for Kant, between God and the world hinges on the contrast between the instantaneousness of God's idea or sketch (*Entwurf*) and its temporal projection, between creation as the immediate *source* of space and time, and creation as an endless temporal and spatial unfolding[55] (see I:314; 154). (It was upon this relation, we recall from the *New Elucidation*, that Kant staked his opposition to the doctrines of occasionalism and preestablished harmony.)

But *technai* or craftsmanship is not the only trope to which Kant turns in describing the relation between God and Creation: "It would be absurd [*ungereimt*] to think to posit divinity in effectuality [*Wirksamkeit*] with an infinitely small part of its creative means [*Vermögens*], and to close up [*verschließen*] its infinite force, the treasure of a true immeasurability of natures and worlds, in an eternal lack of exercise" (I:309; [151]).

To think of the universe as less than infinite is to posit an enfeebled God. It is "necessary" (or at least more "decent" (*anständig*)) to represent nature's essence (*Inbegriff*) as it should be — a witness to that power which no yardstick (*Maßstab*) can measure. Our knowledge of the "reason" why things are as they are is tied to our own sense of decency (or discomfort) over the question of God's potency.

God's means are actualized only by being spent. This plenitude is tempered, however, by nature's more doleful economy. Temporalized, God's liberality becomes nature's squandering (*Verschwendung*). Created things bear the "mark" of their own worthlessness (*Eitelkeit*) and must "pay their levy to impermanence." Worldly existence is thus is rooted in a dual economy—one associated, as we will see in what follows, with the uplifting endurance of the spirit, the other with the endless fluctuations of an abasing matter.

Nature's *Beständigkeit* and the Center of Creation

Kant's completion of his cosmic story (and concomitant "swing" from part to whole) begins with his assumption of a central point of "most uncommon attraction" (*ungemeinste Attraction*), a point able to compel (*nöthigen*) all other systems, comprehended (*begriffene*) around it in a prodigious (*ungeheuren*) sphere (I:307; [149]).

Attraction thus initially emerges as the all-penetrating source and basis of Kant's cosmic constitution (I:308; [150]). Attraction is "as widely distributed a property of matter as co-existence." Or more exactly, "attraction is that universal connection that unites the parts of nature into one space." As the "original source of motion" that is anterior to motion and needs no foreign cause, it cannot be stopped by any obstacle, because "it works upon matter in its deepest inwardness [*Innerste*], without any push, even in the universal stillness of nature." It is thus the "source of systematic connection" and the lasting constancy (*Beständigkeit*) that secures its membership from downfall (*Verfall*) (I:308–9; [150]).

And yet, as if to call into question the very constancy that he has just asserted, Kant now wonders if the world will ever end (I:309; 150). The true guarantee of the world's endurance is not attraction (as Kant had just implied) but the fact that a world capable of perishing would not deserve existence. (Unlike individual creatures, creation as a whole has a sure claim on immortality.)

Kant's argument is simple: a finite creation would be unworthy of an infinite creator.[56] A limited creation absurdly implies a self-limiting God. In the place of such a "closing up" of unused treasure, Kant proposes the model of an "inexhaustible" creation, a flowing forth of ever-increasing wealth. The image of a hoarding God gives way to a more generous divine economy. What is ever newly created, however, is not the "matter" of the universe but its form. Matter (like space) is "actually infinite" from the beginning (*von Anbeginn*), whereas the order or "formation" of the universe, an order that subsists in the "relations" of matter, temporally unfolds itself "in unforced sequence" (I:310; [152]).

The relation between God and the world is thus resolved in the figure of creation as both immediate and unending. Time is the field in which the possible (or "all that can exist") is actualized. But this infinite actuality is itself already contained, germinally as it were, in the universal laws "implanted" in a matter coextensive with infinite space. God's "communal plan" immediately comprehends the full unfolding of the universe, even as it sets that unfolding on its way.

It is this plan that in the last analysis sustains the universe against the centralized collapse into which the force of attraction, over "long periods," would otherwise draw it.

> Will then that systematic connection, that we have weighted before in all parts, also pertain to the whole, and attraction and repulsion [*fliehenden Kraft*] bind together in a single system the entire universe, the all of nature? I say yes; for . . . [otherwise, given the infinity of the chain of members] even the smallest displacement in the universe would bring about its downfall . . . nor could its parts be kept safe from the collapse with which their inner reciprocal attraction [*innere Wechselanziehung*] continually threatens them. (I:310–11; [152])

A world constitution that cannot sustain itself without a miracle (*Wunder*) lacks the steadiness (*Beständigkeit*) that "mark[s] God's choice" — a choice one also more decently (*weit anständiger*) hits upon by portraying the universe systematically. A dispersed (*zerstreuetes*) swarm of lesser systems would rush in an unopposed tendency (*Hang*) toward destruction were there not established "a certain relational arrangement against a universal center," which thereby functions as a kind of cosmic pivot (*Stützpunkt*).

God's upholding act of creation finds its natural counterpart (and rival) in the material center that as universal "Unterstützungspunkt" literally supports the universe even as, in its capacity as "universal sinking point" (*allgemeiner Mittelpunkt der Senkung der ganzen Natur*), it threatens to destroy it. (What distinguishes a sinkhole from a fulcrum is, of course, the presence of resistance.)

From this "clot [*Klumpen*] of most exceptional attraction," comprehending (*begreifen*) in its sphere all that "eternity will bring forth," nature "[makes] her start" (I:311; [152]). (And on its basis Kant also claims to comprehend [*begreifen*] the whole [I:312; 153].) Initially the claim is somewhat doubtful: Kant admits that in "infinite space no point can have the privilege of being called center." Still, he argues, there must in the beginning have existed, somewhere in the universe, a particle of greatest density. Representation of this center brings "silent satisfaction," one that raises man's spirit "to the noblest astonishment" — but only if one gives up Kant's initial assumption of matter distributed evenly throughout in favor of one conforming to the "law" according to which dispersion (*Zerstreuung*) increases with distance from the center (I:312; [153]).

This crucial step constitutes a kind of new beginning, one that vivifies nature by projecting — consonant with God's presence — a perpetually expanding boundary between inner order and outer chaos. Could we but step over this boundary (within which we ourselves dwell) we would see

> how the infinite space of the divine presence, in which is to be met the stock [*Vorrath*] of all possible natural formations, is buried [*begraben*] in a silent night of matter, to serve for stuff for worlds to be generated in the future, and to bring them into motion by mainsprings that begin this motion with a weak stirring, whereby the immeasurability of this desolate space ought still to be enlivened. (I:313; [154])

The enlivening womb of cosmic generation is equally a tomb of darkness, uplifting only by virtue of a God by Whom all is laid out in advance.

If through a "bold [*kühne*] representation" one could "hold eternity together, so to speak, in a single concept," one would see the entirety of space filled with world-orders and creation as completed (I:314; [154]). Such comprehension is dissolved, however, by the asymmetry of past and future: the finitude of past time measured against the infinity of time to come means that the finished (hence comprehensible) region of the universe is always infinitely smaller than the region that remains in chaos. Beyond the expanding boundary of cosmic progress nature maintains an infinite if ever-receding wildness.

This wildness is domesticated, however, by the prospect of order to come; Kant's "pleasurable imagining" of nature in the "raw" (*roh*) is bold without being blameworthy because its purpose is to anticipate her future beauty (I:315; [155]). The ensuing map (*Karte*) of infinity may be unprovable, hinting at a project that seems "destined to remain forever hidden from human understanding." But it is saved from the charge of being a mere fantasy (*Hirngespinst*) by the vital thread or fathom (*Faden*) of analogy.[57]

The "most plausible ground" supporting (*unterstützen*) this analogy is, peculiarly enough, the threat—albeit hypothetical—of nature's inconstancy.

> If one assumes that creation is not stable [*beständig*] in itself, in as much as against the universal striving of attraction, effective through all its parts, it sets no equally thoroughgoing determination that can sufficiently resist the tendency of the former toward disorder and destruction, if it has not distributed orbital forces [*Schwungskräfte*], that in their connection with the centralizing inclination stipulate [*festsetzen*] a systematic constitution—if one makes this assumption, one is then compelled to accept that the entire world-all has a central point [*Mittelpunkt*], one that holds together all its parts in allied relation, and from the entire inner

concept [*Inbegriff*] of nature makes up a single system. (I:316; [156])

This "seminal" *Inbegriff* holds the key to nature's *Beständigkeit* — and with it the (precarious) status of the center of attraction as fulcrum rather than abyss. The only conceivable principle of such a system, according to Kant, is one that distributes matter outward from the center, according to the law of increasing dissipation (*Zerstreuung*). Earlier this dissipation was associated with the rawness and disorder of the outer reaches over against the orderliness of those closer to the center. The inherent perishableness of everything created, however, changes the sense of the comparison. The inner regions of the universe are merely organized sooner, giving way to disorder as further regions become organized in turn. The initial impression of a scale of value radiating outward from the center is thus reversed: the expanding circle of order now bears a chaos in its wake.

Taking into account the "inescapable inclination" (*Hang*) of each world-structure to "go under" (*Untergang*), Kant's "full hypothesis" projects the expanding circle of order as a kind of wave action, chaos receding from its outer limit even as it advances from within.

> The entire affair [*Stück*] of nature that we know, even if it is only an atom with respect to that which remains hidden above or below our horizon, confirms this fruitfulness of nature, which is limitless, because it is nothing other than the exercise of divine omnipotence. Innumerable animals and plants are daily destroyed, and are a sacrifice to transiency [*Vergänglichkeit*]; but nature, through an inexhaustible power of generation, brings forth no fewer somewhere else, and fills out the emptiness. Considerable pieces [*Stücke*] of the surface of the earth that we inhabit are buried [*begraben*] again by the sea, from which a favorable period had pulled them out; but in other places nature completes the lack and brings forth other regions that the depths of the waters had hidden, in order to expand over them new riches of her fruitfulness. In such a way, worlds and world orders pass away, and are swallowed up in the abyss of eternity; yet creation is always busy raising up new formations in other celestial regions, and repairing [*ergänzen*] the loss with profit. (I:317; [157])

But why, if nature's wealth is limitless, must things go under? The answer is that all that comes to be (in time, that is) must pass away. "All that is finite, that has a beginning and origin [*Ursprung*] has upon it the mark of its limited nature" and "must come to an end." This rule applies even to a world order, whose constancy (*Beständigkeit*) seems to verge on the infinite, and yet which must (as Newton showed) eventually wear down.

We should not bemoan such decay, however, as a true loss to nature, whose *Beständigkeit* consists in the exchange itself.

> She shows her riches in a kind of prodigality [*Verschwendung*] which, while some parts pay tribute to transitoriness, maintains itself undamaged through innumerable new generations in the entire extent of her perfection. What an innumerable amount of flowers and insects perish during every cold day; but how little are they missed, even though they are the splendid artifacts of nature, and evidence of divine omnipotence; in another place this loss [*Abgang*] is compensated with surplus [*Überfluß*]. Nor is man, who seems to be the masterpiece [*Meisterstück*] of creation, exempted from this law. Nature shows that she is just as rich, just as inexhaustible in bringing forth the most excellent among the creatures as with the least treasured [*Geringschätzigsten*], and that even their going under is a necessary shading in the manifoldness of her suns, because their production costs her nothing. The harmful effects of polluted air, earthquakes and floods sweep whole nations from the earth's surface; but it does not appear that nature thereby suffers a loss [*Nachteil*]. In this way whole worlds and systems leave the stage, after they have played their role. The infinity of creation is great enough to view itself in relation to a world or a milky way of worlds the same way that one looks upon a flower or an insect in comparison with the earth. Thus while nature decks out eternity with changing scenes, God remains busy in an unceasing creation, shaping the tools for the formation of still greater worlds. (I:318; [158])

Kant holds out as most befitting (*anständig*) to the wealth of nature, our habituation to these terrible revolutions (*erschreckliche Umstürzungen*) as being her customary ways. We best stand up to nature's overturnings, it seems, by imitating her indifference. Individuals go under, but nature maintains herself in the exchange or "play" (*Schauspiel*) by which they come and go. The rule that "all that is finite or begins must pass away" exempts the universe itself, whose ordering circumference expands outward to infinity. The finite region of decay is always smaller than the infinite field of future generation; thus nature's economy not only breaks even but also turns an ever-growing profit.

The decency (*Anständigkeit*) of Kant's theory is increased, he adds, by the (divine) law governing nature's ever-expanding fruitfulness: at the outer boundary of her generation she is ever young and her "breedings [*Zeugungen*] newly fruitful," while at the inner boundary she is always aging (I:319; [159]). Order fills in the gap between menopause and menarche, as it were.[58] (As such, the organized world anticipates Kant's later rendition of the drama of man, spatially and temporally bounded between birth and death, yet also somehow capable of limitless progress.)

This respectability (*Anständigkeit*) is crowned by a "final idea" as probable as it is befitting (*wohlanständig*), an idea through which "the satisfaction stimulated by the portrayal of nature's alterations" may be "lifted up [*erhoben*] to the highest grade of delight" (*Wohlgefallens*) (I:320; [160]). The idea for which we are bidden to "make room" transforms nature's decay into the site of her renewal: as the inner regions of the universe return to chaos, the stage is set for a renewal of life and an overcoming of the standstill of the world machine. So conceived, the universe continually expands outward into space even as, at its inner boundary, it perpetually repeats itself. Like the planetary system that emerges, phoenixlike, out of its solar death, whole galaxies will decay only to revivify.

The rule that all that has an origin must have an end exempts creation itself.[59] The spirit that contemplates this "phoenix of nature," however, is brought down (*versenken*) in astonishment rather than uplifted. The soul, it seems, cannot find sufficient satisfaction in perpetual transit. (What was to rise to the highest level of delight thus comes instead to nothing.)[60]

For satisfaction one must turn to an alternate source — that Being the light of whose intellect spreads over nature "as from a center."

> Oh happy, when among [*unter*] the tumult of the elements and the rubble/dreams[61] of nature [the soul] is always set on a height from which it can see the ravages, which the feebleness [*Hinfälligkeit*] of the things of the world brings about, rush by under its feet. A happiness, that reason dare not be bold [*sich erkühnen darf*] enough to wish for, revelation teaches us to hope for with conviction. When, therefore, the chains, which keep us tied to the vanity of creatures, fall away in the moment that is determined for the metamorphosis [*Verwandlung*] of our being, then will the immortal spirit, freed from dependency on finite things, find true happiness in community [*Gemeinschaft*] with the immortal being. (I:322; [161])

As material gives way to spiritual community, nature herself becomes newly satisfying and uplifting:

> All of nature, which has a harmonious relation with the delight [*Wohlgefallen*] of the divinity, can only fill with everlasting satisfaction that rational creature who finds himself united with the primordial source of all perfection. Seen from this center [*Mittelpunkt*] nature will show from all sides utter security [*lauter Sicherheit*] and fitness [*Wohlanständigkeit*]. (I:322; [161])

The changing scenes of nature cannot disturb the restful happiness of a creature who is once raised (*einmal erhoben ist*) to such a height, of which hope of immortality provides a sweet foretaste (I:322; 161).[62]

The wavering rise and fall of Kant's argument is momentarily arrested by the pious hope that puts a (temporary) end to reason's boldness. Revelation succeeds where reason fails, beautifying nature even as it raises the soul once and for all above the fray. But this uplifting revelation is itself verbally disarmed: the soul remains "under" (*unter*) the tumult that the spirit hopefully transcends.

"General Theory and History of the Sun"

A supplement (*Zugabe*) on the "general theory and history of the sun"[63] devotes itself to the unfinished business of the previous (and putatively all-inclusive) chapter.[64] The main puzzle to be solved is why the sun, or center of the planetary system (a condition Kant earlier associated with the densest matter), should be on fire (a condition he earlier associated with the most volatile matter). The sun, Kant concludes, is a mixture (*Vermengung*) of both heavy elements and light, the latter pulled down (*hinabgestürtzt*), owing to the languor (*Mattigkeit*) of their impulse (*Schwung*).[65] The sun's subsequent glow is born of this spiritous supplement, combined with the constant influx of thick nourishment from the sun's interior (*Innern*) (I:323–24; [162–63]).

The sun is, it seems, a sort of womb, enlivened by the volatile matter that is insufficiently impulsive to resist it. Kant presses on, however, to the stronger grounds of his conjectures. As a flaming body, the sun is not only hot but, "so to speak, self-effective"[66] — able, that is, to return to life rather than passively "exhausting itself" in the distributive community (*Gemeinschaft*) of matter (I:325; [163].

One reason is the great compression of the solar air, in which smoke clouds rise and fall in tar and brimstone rains, bringing new nourishment to the fire and causing winds so vehement that "imagination cannot represent them." If some region of the surface is choked off by vapors or the scarcity of nourishment, the air above cools off and contracts, making place for the neighboring region to expand proportionally.

The consequent depletion of air, however, raises a difficulty (*Hauptknot*) that can only be solved by penetrating beneath the surface: if the flaming body becomes choked, its violence turns against the interior, forcing deep chasms[67] to release the rekindling air enclosed in their caves (*Höhlen*). Fed from these caves, the sun's fire is self-renewing, if (Kant adds) one "posits [*setzt*] in her bowels" (*Eingeweide*) — through a "freedom not forbidden in an object so unknown" — matter "inexhaustibly productive" of air (I:326; [164–65]).[68]

Literally breathing from her own bowels, the sun is the ultimate emblem of natural self-sufficiency (albeit one implicitly violated by Kant's own rhetorical liberties). As such she is also the exemplar par excellence of maternal self-sufficiency, one that requires only the most vestigial of supplements — in this case the volatile matter that is too lacking in impulse to resist her

downward attraction. (Kant later speaks of the *Vermengung* of the Chaos
as itself providing the seeds [*Samen*] of renewal.)

Portrayed by the imaginative power that Kant would have "more closely
represent it," the sun is simultaneously beautiful and abhorrent:

> thick vapors which put out the fire and which through the power
> of winds rise and form dark clouds which in fiery showers storm
> down again and as burning streams gush from the heights of the
> firm solar land into the flaming valleys; the crash of elements, the
> debris of burnt out matter, and nature ringing with the destruc-
> tion, nature which, even with the most loathsome [*abscheulichs-
> ten*][69] condition of her disarrangements [*Zerrüttungen*], brings
> about the beauty of the world and the utility of the creatures.
> (I:327–28; [165–66])

His treatment of the sun would bear all the marks of what Kant later
calls the dynamical sublime (*Erhab*), were its wavering between attraction
and repulsion finally resolved in favor and by virtue of a (higher) principle
of uplifting (*erhaben*) attraction.[70] In his *Universal Natural History* the vertiginous physical center of attraction (which requires the counterforce of
repulsion to prevent individual bodies from merging with the central core)
contrasts with the divine center of attraction, which—"equidistant" from
all points—preserves rather than threatens individual existence. The contrast between the threatening attraction that governs the physical universe
(and calls forth—in us at least—a countervailing repulsion) and an individually substantiating attraction directly associated with (divine) reason
anticipates Kant's critical analysis of the sublime.[71]

What is especially disturbing in this conjunction of terror and enjoyment
is the idea that beauty and utility depend (given nature's self-sufficiency)
on what is "most loathsome." The appeal of a nature so abominably
founded is, to say the least, ambiguous.

It is therefore with evident relief that Kant follows the thread of analogy
from the solar and galactic middlepoints to the conjectural center of the
universe.[72]

> Concerning what may be the constitution of this fundamental
> piece of the entire creation, and what may be found there, we will
> leave to Mr. Wright of Durham to determine, he who with fanati-
> cal inspiration [*Begeisterung*] lifted up on this happy place, as if on
> the throne of all of nature, a forceful being of a divine sort, with
> spiritual powers of attraction and repulsion, which, being effective
> in an infinite sphere around itself, would draw all virtue to itself
> but repel back vice. (I:329; [166])

Kant's dismissal of Wright is rooted, in part, in unease over the boldness
of his own speculations:

We do not want let loose the reins to the boldness [*Kühnheit*] of our own conjectures, to which we have perhaps already permitted too much, to the point of arbitrary fictions [*Erdichtungen*]. The Godhead is everywhere equally present in the infinity of world space; everywhere, where there are natures capable of swinging themselves upward [*empor schwingen*], over the dependency of the creatures, to community with the highest being, there is he equally near. The entire creation is penetrated by his forces, but only one who knows how to free himself from the creatures, who is noble enough to perceive that the highest degree of happiness is alone to be sought in the enjoyment of this source of perfection, that one alone is capable of finding himself nearer to this true reference point of all excellence than anything else in the entirety of nature. (I:329–30; [167])

The abominable "sinking point" of nature gives way to a spiritual center that is at last truly uplifted/ing. Kant's objection to Wright thus also stems from the conflation — not to say collision — of these natural and spiritual centers. When Kant later conjectures (without succumbing to Wright's "enthusiasm") about the relation between these two points of reference, he will invert Wright's rank order, locating "the worst and most imperfect species [*Gattungen*] of thinking nature" in the "deepest abasement" of the universal sinking point, where intelligence in all shades of diminution at last loses itself entirely, while beings of increasing intelligence inhabit regions at an ever-increasing distance from the center. If there "should be a law" distributing the dwelling places of rational beings, it will place the lowest species (*Gattung*) here at that "communal" center (which is also the beginning of the spirit world's species/races [*Geschlecht*]) (I:330–31; [167–68]).

Nature's innermost center is also the "outermost limit" of intelligent being. Like birth itself, it is the "beginning" (*Anfang*) in which reason and unreason "collide" (*zusammenstoßen*). Spiritual perfection thus has an outermost limit (at the beginning) but no end. Rational beings are projected from their obliterating site of origin, saved (like Kant himself) by the ever-lengthening thread of infinity or open-ended progress, there being no degree of perfection above which rational beings "cannot be further uplifted." In this way spiritual perfection can ascend ever higher, gradually approaching "the goal of the highest excellence [*Trefflichkeit*] — namely the Divinity — without ever being able to reach it" (I:331; [168]).

God thus serves a function analogous to that played, in Kant's critical treatment of the sublime, by the (autoerotic) power of reason.[73] What remains unclear is the precise status of this uplifting *Anständigkeit*. For to the extent that the "upward swing" of nobility is itself propelled by natural repulsion, it remains part of the very economy it would escape (a difficulty reflected in Kant's telling allusions to the *geistigen Materien* that lack sufficient *Schwung* to resist the sun's [or nature's] downward drag). And yet all that distinguishes Kant's own uplifting representation of the Divinity from the "Begeisterungen" of Wright lies in the latter's "unlawful" (hence repellent?) conflation of the spiritual and material centers of attraction.

DEFICIENCY AND ABUNDANCE

Nature's "beauty" and "excellence," Kant now tells us, justify reason's "indignation" over the "bold madness" (*kühne Thorheit*) that would ascribe the constitution of the world to chance (I:331; [168]). (Anger, if nothing else, propels reason past the Epicurean abyss.) For that so many objectives should "come together in one end" would be "impossible" did that constitution not originate in the *Entwurf* of God. The remaining question is whether the divine plan was "implanted" in the highest laws of motion and laid down in the determinations of the eternal natures, or whether it is imposed on nature, as by a "foreign hand."

Although "an almost universal prejudice" speaks for the latter alternative, Kant restores to nature her ability to bring forth order without prejudice to the power of the divinity. The greater nature's regularity, the more evidence there is of God's "implanting" force, without which the reciprocal interaction of substances would lack its "principle of necessity" (I:332; [169]).[74]

Matter is freely subject, because it obeys laws that are internal to its nature. The true impiety lies in insisting on the special, rather than general, operation of God's laws — in maintaining, for instance, that the cooling breezes of Jamaica occur especially for man's benefit, rather than as the outcome of general mechanical principles. Such a philosophy turns all of nature into a miracle (*in Wunder verkehren*); thus placing God "in the machine," it obliterates the distinction between creator and creation. What is at stake is therefore not so much pious faith (which might be thought capable of otherwise defending itself) as the very distinction between God and nature. Nature, Kant is led (with greater *Anständigkeit* and *Richtigkeit*) to conclude, "if left to her universal properties, is fruitful with nothing but [*lauter*] beautiful and perfect fruits, that not only show harmony and excellence in themselves, but also with the entire extent of their being, with the needs of man, and with the glorification of the divine properties" (I:333; [170]).

Nature is beautiful, then, to the extent that she reveals, through the very exchanges of her mechanical laws, a purposive harmony that includes, but is not exhausted by, human ends. In light of such considerations, and in opposition to "lazy" (*träge*) philosophy (*Weltweisheit*) and "ungrounded" prejudice, Kant hopes to "ground on incontrovertible grounds" his own conviction in a worldly mechanics (I:334; [170]).

Kant's subsequent "proofs" look both to the regularity of the system (for example, the uniform direction of the planets) — a regularity that can be accounted for mechanically but is at odds with an appeal to "fitness" (*Wohlständigkeit*) since God's choice "would manifest itself with greater freedom in all sorts of deviations and differences" — and to the system's *ir*regularity, the less than perfectly precise determination of its relations. If God's wisest intention and greatest capacity were the immediate cause of such motions, he would have made a better (that is, a more exacting) job of it. Kant's theory is upheld, in short, by an appeal, both to the world's less than perfect uniformity and to its less than perfect variety. The *Bewegungsgrund* underlying nature's motions cannot be immediately traced to the motivating reason of God, because nature as we ourselves encounter her is less than absolutely perfect. Nature only fulfills her destiny over the infinite course of time; at any given time, therefore, she remains incomplete, and a closed book if we would try to decipher in her mark (*Merkmal*) the immediate sign of God's intention. It is for this reason that man must content himself with the *ratio cogniscendi,* the knowledge of consequences that the science of mechanics provides. The *ratio essendi, God's* reason for creating things, is only knowable *grosso modo* and by the (broken) thread of analogy.

The disutility of comets is a particular reproach to those who would explain natural phenomena on the basis of their purportedly beneficial qualities. Unable to maintain a steady orbit, comets are "deficiencies" (*Mängel*) of nature and "imperfect members of creation" — unsuitable either as habitats for rational beings or (contrary to conjecture) as solar nourishment (since most will not reach this end prior to the downfall [*Umsturz*] of the system). If one did not take into account nature's lawful development, such a marking (*Anmerkung*), however certain (*gewiβ*), would also be repulsive (*anstöβig*).

The surest proof of Kant's theory thus lies in its singular ability to maintain nature's attractiveness, by accommodating us to her otherwise repellent "deficiencies." Seen in this light, nature's lack (*Mangel*) becomes the sign of her overabundance:

> Only in a mechanical sort of explanation are the beauty of nature and the manifestation/revelation [*Offenbarung*] of omnipotence not a little glorified. Nature, who contains all possible stuff of manifoldness, stretches out her extent over begettings [*Gattungen*] from perfection to nothing, and her deficiencies themselves are a sign of superfluity, in which her essence [*Inbegriff*] is not exhausted. (I:338; [173–74])

Kant's theory uniquely transforms nature's otherwise repellent void into the "mark" of God's inscription. Nature's flux becomes God's currency. The ensuing ease (*Leichtigkeit*) and correctness (*Richtigkeit*) with which from these assumed principles (*Grundsätze*) all worldly phenomena are derived constitute the fulfillment (*Vollendung*) of Kant's conjecture (*Mutmaßung*)—his own speculative *Entwurf*—giving it a "value that is no longer arbitrary" (I:341; [176]).

This rhetorical apex, however, proves anticlimactic. The certainty of Kant's theory is "raised up to the highest peak of conviction" by a consideration of the mass and density of the planets in relation to their distance from the common center of sinking. The uniform density of each planet rules out God's immediate action, since in that case he would have more easily realized his purpose (that they should experience like effect from different quantities of light) by varying only their surface densities. Likewise, the increasing masses of the planets must be explained mechanically, since the alternative account in terms of God's special purpose—that is, the attraction of more moons to the outer planets for the convenience of their inhabitants—cannot explain why God did not simply increase these planets' interior density.[75]

Only those who lie deep in the fetters (*Fesseln*) of prejudice or who are utterly incapable of "swinging themselves upward" from the wasteland (*Wust*) of opinion can fail to be to be moved by so many demonstrations. One could thus believe that "no one except the feebleminded" could deny their truth, save for the harmony between the world structure and the utility of rational creatures, a harmony that "seems to have for its ground more than the mere universal laws of nature" (I:346; [180]). After surmounting every other obstacle, Kant's theory runs up against its own success: the "harmony" between nature and man that it enacts by making nature attractive to us.

This difficulty is answered by nature's inclusion—by virtue of her very plenitude—of the lacking and defective (*Abweichungen*). The same unlimited fruitfulness brings forth "the inhabited globes as well as the comets, the useful mountains and the harmful precipices, the habitable lands and the empty wastes, the virtues and the vices" (I:347; [181]). Nature's perfection paradoxically includes her imperfection.

Confronted with the universe he has (re)created, Kant cannot quite bring himself to call it good. Man's appreciation of the whole seems to require his displacement from nature's "tumult" to—or imaginative reconstruction of—the perspective of a God who is everywhere and therefore nowhere. And yet, if Kant cannot locate man *within* the whole—cannot, that is to say, show that man's purpose and the purpose of the universe intersect—his model of the whole in terms of a divine schema of harmonizing ends threatens to collapse. It becomes reasonable, then, to look for an alternative reference point—one from which man can survey the world without relinquishing his place within it.

Conjectural Certainty and the Arousal (*Reizen*) of Reason

Hence the conjectural appendix to the *Universal Natural History,* devoted to "a comparison" of "the inhabits of the various planets" (I:349; 182).[76] Man's unhappiness *can* be reconciled with the purposiveness of the whole, but only if we give up our geocentrism and view matters from an interplanetary perspective (I:346; 180). If man is of all creatures the one who "least achieves his purpose," this need not count against the splendor and perfection of the whole. What seems to man to be a defect is a "necessary shading" from a higher standpoint, one that takes into account the needs of other rational beings.[77]

The basis of that standpoint—that most literally cosmopolitan perspective—is a novel theory (to which Kant earlier alluded) that locates the dullest beings on Mercury, the brightest on Saturn. Just as matter radiates outward from the center according to the principle of decreasing density, so, Kant speculates, does spirit radiate outward according to the principle of increasing intelligence. This thesis, presented earlier in the essay as mere conjecture, is now more firmly grounded in what we know of man. Even though man's "inner makeup remains an unfathomed problem [*unerforschtes Problema*]," man can serve as a "ground and universal reference point": "whatever the infinite distance between the ability to think and the motion of matter, between the rational spirit and the body," it is "certain" that "man, who obtains all his concepts and representations through the impressions that the universe excites in his soul . . . is wholly dependent on the makeup of the matter to which the creator joined him" (I:355; [186]). The crux of Kant's knowledge of other rational beings thus turns on the "certainty" of the mind's bodily dependency.[78]

Of particular significance in this regard is our experience of thought as a laborious process and a related contempt for those unable or unwilling to make the effort. The root of this contempt, as we will see, lies in a peculiar (and in some sense perverse) opposition between mental and physical performance.

> In the measure in which [man's] body develops, the fitness of his thinking nature also obtains the corresponding degree of perfection, only reaching a steady [*gesetztes*] and manly [*männliches*] capacity when the fibers[79] of his tools [*Werkzeuge*] have delivered the strength and endurance which is the completion of their development.

Kant's implicit identification of intellectual and sexual maturity is, how-ever, immediately qualified. Those fitnesses develop early enough "which allow man [*Der Mensch*] to satisfy the needs to which he is subject through his dependence on external things." In some, however, "development stops at that level." "The capacity to combine abstract concepts, and to master the inclination of the passions through free application of understanding comes late, and in some not in an entire lifetime." In all human beings, Kant continues,

> [that capacity] is rather weak, and serves the lower forces over which it ought to rule, and in whose government consists the ex-cellence of man's nature. When one regards the nature of most men, man seems to be created as a plant, to draw in sap and grow, to propagate his kind [*Geschlecht*], and finally to grow old and die. Of all creatures he least achieves the end of his existence, because he consumes his more excellent fitnesses for such purposes as lower creatures achieve more securely and decently [*anständiger*] with less. He would indeed be the most contemptible of all, at least in the eyes of true wisdom, if the hope of the future did not lift him up, if there were not a period of full development in store for the forces shut up in him. (I:356; [187])

Man of all creatures seems least to realize his end because he alone lacks adequate time for the development of his higher capacities. (The prospect of an eternal life, or at the very least, perpetual progress, arises from the palpable discrepancy between physical and spiritual perfection, the former obtainable by the individual, the latter, as Kant will much later put it, only by the species.)[80]

Due to this (fatal) gap between sexual and intellectual maturity, human thought (or the "connection and comparison" of impressions) involves a perpetual struggle for (self-) mastery. The laboriousness and difficulty of thought arises not from the recalcitrance of matter as such (which is as much conduit as obstruction) but from a kind of temporal displacement — a discrepancy between man's natural and spiritual entelechies.[81]

> If one seeks the cause of the obstacles that keep human nature in such deep abasement, it will be found in the grossness of the mat-ter in which his spiritual part is sunk, in the inflexibility of the fibers and sluggishness [*Trägheit*] and immobility of the sap/fluid that should obey its stirrings. The nerves and fluids of his brain deliver to him only gross and unclear concepts, and because he cannot, in the inwardness of his faculty of thought, counterbal-ance sufficiently powerful representations against the enticements [*Reizungen*] of sensible perceptions: thus he is carried away by his passions, and confused and overwhelmed by the tumult of the elements that maintain his machine. The efforts of reason to rise

in opposition and to drive away this confusion through the light of judgment are like flashes of sunlight, when thick clouds continually interrupt and darken its serenity. (I:356; [187])

Freed from the tumult of the elements, the light of reason would break forth like a clear sun. As matters stand, however, man's soul is inescapably occluded:

The action of reflection and of representations clarified by reason is a fatiguing condition, in which the soul cannot set itself without opposition, and out of which the soul would, through the natural inclination of the bodily machine, soon fall back into the passive condition, in which sensory enticements [*Reizungen*] govern and determine all its actions. (I:357; [188–89])

This mental lethargy (*Trägheit*), itself a consequence of man's dependence on gross and rigid matter, is "the source of all error and depravity." Like the *flüchtige Materie* that fuel the solar fire, human reason lacks sufficient impetus to resist being drawn down toward the material center of attraction.

Through the difficulty connected with the effort to dissipate [*zerstreuen*] the fog of confused concepts, and to distinguish and separate the universal knowledge obtained through the comparison of ideas from the sensory impressions, one's thinking readily gives way to overhasty approval . . . of a view which, because of the lethargy of its nature and the resistance of matter can hardly be looked upon from another side.

Prejudice (*Vorurteil*), the enemy of judgment, is the fruit of such lethargy — an unwillingness to undertake the laborious process of comparison and combination by which alone the diversity of sensory impression can be divested of its confusion. (Kant's own cosmopolitan "comparison" is thus itself an act of cloud-dissipating enlightenment.)[82]

But the task is not a simple one: man is locked in battle with the very force on which his spiritual vitality depends. His spirit waxing and waning with "the liveliness of the body," he can no more wish to be rid of his material confinement than to exchange places with the inhabitant of another planet: the heat that draws spirit down also gives it life and animation. Translated to Venus, an Earthling, formed of stuff proportioned to earth's heat, would suffer "enormous motions and collapse" caused by the dissipation of its sap/fluids and the violent tension of its elastic fibers. A Venetian, on the other hand, built from more sluggish matter requiring greater heat, would grow cold and lifeless on a more distant planet, whose lesser heat sufficed for inhabitants made of finer stuff (I:558; [188–89]).[83]

The ambivalence of physical attraction gives rise to the anxiety of (im)-

potence. Spiritual abasement is inseparable from physical arousal. Spiritual virility both depends upon and struggles to resist the uncontrollable, "plant-like" rise and fall of sexual desire. Hence the profound ambiguity of men's physical performance, in which "elasticity" merges with "dissipation," and "firm endurance" with "thickness and rigidity."[84]

The inverse relation between spiritual and physical potency on which Kant here insists, points, I hazard to suggest, to a deeper problem, stemming from the seeming destruction, by the new science of Descartes, of the traditional distinction between efficient and material causation. According to that tradition, rooted in Aristotle, the male principle in generation corresponds to the efficient cause, which ensouls or concocts the material cause (or substance) provided by the female. On this account, the man's incorporeal spirit or pneuma (in the Stoic's materialist version, a mixture of air and fire) bestows sensitivity and reason upon the otherwise plantlike semen of the woman. Natural generation, by traditional lights, testifies to the superiority of male over female and reason over matter.[85]

The obliteration by the new science of the distinction between efficient and material causation tended to undermine this hierarchy, though not, it seems, without a lively effort on the part of many to save it.[86] Others, such as Leibniz, found means of avoiding the difficulty entirely. Leibniz, much taken with the discoveries of Leewenhoek's microscope as evidence of the ubiquity of life throughout the universe, affirmed both the necessity of embodiment and the impossibility of generation in any strict sense: every monad has existed since the beginning of creation and will continue to exist throughout eternity. What appears as death is merely a diminution of consciousness (that is, a kind of swoon) out of which the monad reawakens, much as a caterpillar becomes a butterfly.[87] For Kant, however, the matter is more complicated. His quantification of substance, as we saw in chapter 2, raises at least the possibility of the total obliteration of consciousness (diminution to zero), and with it the soul's passing out of existence. As he later puts it, in refuting Moses Mendelssohn's proof of the immortality of the soul, "consciousness has always a degree, which always allows of diminution." Thus "the supposed substance . . . may be changed into nothing; not indeed by dissolution, but by gradual loss (remissio) of its powers."[88] Simplicity (or lack of extended parts) does not assure immortality in the way that Leibniz thought. But the threat of contingency that adheres to the phenomenon of death applies even more radically to generation, with its abysmal suggestion of the emergence of reason out of unreason. The very act of generation—traditionally the emblem of man's rational, and formal, supremacy—threatens to dissolve into unregulated, and hence "loathsome," fecundity. Against this threat, only God's inseminating spirit (which assures, among other things, the eternity of biological species) is proof, while man's physical generative power descends to the level of the plants. The plantlike passivity traditionally associated with the female principle of generation infects, in Kant's account, the male principle as well, at least insofar as it remains within the nexus of the physical. It is not in generating, but in resisting generation for the sake of a higher sort of attraction, that man's spirit uplifts itself.

By a related process of reversal, the traditional preference for male heat (associated with the informing pneuma) over female cold (associated with the mere potentiality of substance) gives way, in Kant's presentation, to an eccentric (and ambiguous) preference for cold over heat — and this despite the association of the latter with what Kant regards as the requirements of life.[89]

Accordingly, man's *Senkungspunkt* again becomes an *Überstützungspunkt*: consideration of the cause of human abasement yields the following "universal concept" that "embraces all" (I:358; [189]). The grosser the bodily machine (the denser the matter, in other words, of which it is composed), the more sluggish the thought of the rational being dependent on it. The further a rational being is from the solar heat, the finer/more volatile is its bodily machine and the quicker its thought and more perfect its intelligence.

This now "more than probable conjecture" opens up a field for "agreeable speculation" about the higher natures — creatures whose spiritual insights arouse more vivid excitements (*Reizungen*) than do the seductions (*Anlockungen*) of their senses. Ruling and "setting under foot" the storm of passion, such creatures would, like a calm sea, quietly receive and reflect God's image (I:359–60; [189–90]). The habitat of such natures, moreover, would be suited to their needs (the more rapid transition between day and night, for example, suiting their quicker performance). (It is not, we are reminded, teleology as such that Kant here opposes, but only one prejudiced by anthropocentrism and geocentrism.)

All finally harmonizes (*stimmet alles überein*) to confirm the foregoing law. Distance from the sun is not (to counter Wright's harmony-destroying opinion) an evil but a good. The intensity of the effect of light and heat is not absolute, but relative to the density of matter that receives it; able to do more with less, the higher natures are also relatively immune to the sun's destructive force. "Decay and death" do not affect them "as they do us lower beings" (I:362; [192]). The same sluggishness (*Trägheit*) of matter that causes the debasement of the lower natures also brings about their tendency (*Hang*) for corruption (*Verderben*). The reason is this: the nourishing sap that makes living bodies grow eventually incorporates itself into their fibers, constricting the canals through which it ought to pass. When full growth is achieved, these vessels can no longer enlarge. Physical (and sexual) maturity is thus the harbinger of death, signaling the beginning of an eventually fatal constriction whereby the body's own mechanical drive, expended for its nourishment, gradually numbs and destroys (*zu Grunde richten*) the structure of the entire machine.[90]

From this entrapping cycle of growth and decay higher natures are relatively immune. Their greater "elasticity" secures them an endurance proportional to their spiritual perfection, in the same way that "the frailty of human life" has a correct relation to our "unworthiness" (I:363; [193]).

But Kant cannot leave off without returning to the objection with which his comparison began: a "natural doubt" that nature's purposiveness can be reconciled with the workings of "raw matter." This doubt is dissipated (*zerstreuen*) by a countering of nature's unbounded dissipation (*ungebundene Zerstreuung*) with her subservience to the divine idea. Nature's vortex gives way to a higher community of origin, where the single natures of things "form, so to speak, within themselves" a single system of mutual relation (I:364; [193]).

Thus is "the entire span of nature" connected in unbroken gradation that mutually relates all its members. Toward the center of the material system are spiritual beings "sunk" in such a torpor of physical grossness as to "border on unreason." At the outer edges are beings whose vaporous rarity "lifts them up" to greater freedom of action and enables their thought to approach the instantaneousness of divine comprehension. Between these two extremes, earthbound man occupies a "dangerous middle road" (I:366; [195]). Halfway between "wisdom and unreason," man is poised between the spiritual and physical centers of attraction. Man's perfection or end is thus uniquely indeterminate.[91] Neither effortlessly raised up to the splendor of the divine center nor guiltlessly sunk into the torpor of the material center, he alone[92] must not only struggle to achieve the dignity of which he is capable—he also must assume the blame for his own failure.

None of this, of course, detracts from the perfection of the whole. There *must* be some point in the universe at which the inversely proportional spiritual and material ladders cross. Here neither the spiritual nor the material forces of attraction are (fully) determinative, and neither rational nor physical desire fully authoritative. Man's freedom, however, does him no credit. Without the decisive victory of his higher nature, he is merely the defect or monster that nature in its plenitude also embraces.[93]

Man's spiritual victory over his own monstrousness, however, is achievable by few at best. Most men are content to "suck sap, propagate (*sein Geschlecht fortzusetzen*), grow old and die," bringing about indecently what lower creatures manage with greater efficiency and decorum. Given the vegetative languor to which his lower nature predisposes him, man's situation might well seem hopeless, were there no way to stimulate his higher desire.

It is the (thwarted) purpose of the *Universal Natural History,* I believe, to serve as such a stimulant. Kant's theory of the heavens is a sort of philosophical and spiritual aphrodisiac. If man is deflected from his higher path by its laboriousness, Kant's cosmic history shortcuts the task of uniting many into one and thus makes the journey relatively effortless. The achievement of his universal system is thus truly heroic — or would be, if he could say with certainty that the world that he has built *is* (or is like) the universe and is not merely a beguiling fantasy.

To entertain oneself with such representations may be permissible and even "upstanding" (*anständig*): it cannot, however, suffice. The human desire for knowledge (*Wißbegierde*) still "reaches out desirously after distant objects," seeking "in such dark knowledge to find light." Ignorance about what we are, and greater ignorance about what we may become, points to the possibility that death is not an end but merely a change in cosmic position, one that brings us closer to the objects that excite (*reizen*) our curiosity. Dissatisfied with this imaginative vision of perpetual progress, however, Kant adds one of immediate transcendence: "after vanity [*Eitelkeit*] has exacted its due from human nature, the immortal soul will swing itself up [*empor schwingen*] with a quick swing [*Schwunge*] above all that is finite, and establish its existence in a new relation to the whole of nature, one that springs from a closer connection with the highest being." From here on, "a more elevated nature, which has the source of happiness in itself, will no longer disperse itself [*sich zerstreuen*] among outer objects in order to find contentment." In this way, the *Inbegriff* of creation, "which has a necessary harmony for the delight [*Wohlgefallen*] of the highest being," must also have a necessary harmony with the delight of its own," moving them as well "with everlasting satisfaction."

"Hope of the future" propels man beyond nature's ambiguous largess:

> To one who has thus filled his spirit [*Gemüt*] with such considerations . . . the vision of the starry heavens on a still night gives a kind of pleasure that only noble souls can feel. In the universal quiet of nature and stillness of the senses the hidden knowledge capacity of the immortal spirit speaks an ineffable language, and yields undeveloped concepts that can be felt but not described.

Unhappy, then, the planet that could generate thinking creatures who "unmindful of the enticements [*Reizungen*] that such an object can arouse [*anlocken*], are held in service to vanity." And yet how happy the planet from which is opened up "a road to a nobility and happiness, a road lifted up infinitely higher than the advantages offered by the most exceptional equipment of nature" (I:367–68; [196]).

To perfect creation by delighting in it we must, paradoxical as it may seem, cease to be part of it. But in ceasing to be part of creation, we relinquish our claim to know it as actual.[94]

Thus we return to the problem with which we began—the problem of how the soul can both be in the world and make the world inwardly present to itself; of how to recognize the world as *actual* while comprehending it as *whole*. Kant can attempt the latter, it seems, only by abandoning the former.

And yet without success in *both* Kant cannot make the higher road compellingly attractive—cannot, that is to say, dispel the nagging doubt that philosophy's entrancing image of the whole is merely a beguiling fantasy. The beckoning goal of worldly contemplation is thus threatened by an undercurrent of repulsiveness. Like the physical sun, Kant's spiritual vision is occluded by a certain monstrousness. Yet it is precisely the *lack* of repulsiveness that is supposed to distinguish the spiritual goal of man's "higher nature" from the ambiguous natural goal of his "lower" one. Thus, in the end, Kant is left without a stable principle of value on which to base his own elevation beyond nature's dismal economy. In the end, the difference between spiritual and natural attraction threatens to collapse.

CONCLUSION: GENESIS AND GENERATION

As a wavering (and erotically inconclusive) attempt to comprehend the whole, Kant's *Universal Natural History* is ambiguous in the most literal sense. His effort takes the form, on the one hand, of a "mechanical" account of the formation of the heavens, an account whose novelty consists primarily in the opposition that it posits between an all-penetrating force of attraction and an equally crucial (although infinitely diffuse) impulse of repulsion, that is, a dualism *within* nature on which nature's organization is seen ultimately to depend. In making this attempt, Kant steers a middle course between a (pan)theism that brings God into the world, and an atheism that liberates the world from all need of God. The ultimate success of Kant's universal history thus hinges on an adequate definition of the relation between God and Creation, or between the all-encompassing immediacy of the divine idea and its progressive propagation through an infinity of space and time. Worldly genesis involves a sort of "epigenesis," a development of "germs" implanted in matter by God "in the beginning." Kant's juridical metaphor for the peculiar character of the worldly bond—matter's "uncoerced" submission to law—is thus grounded in a deeper allusion to the procreative act. Kant's portrayal of the laws of nature as both "internal" to nature itself *and* as deriving from an "external" source rests on an appeal to the character of procreation. To (partially) comprehend the whole is thus to (partially) comprehend the male and female generative roles.

One principle source of instability in his account stems from the essential ambiguity of those roles. Kant simultaneously locates the opposition between spirit and matter (or male and female) *between* God and Creation, and *within* Creation itself. Thus the curious role of so-called *geistige Materie* and other manifestations of the all-important, but elusive, *Schwungskraft* that not only offsets the dizzying *Senkungspunkt* of nature, but also empowers, rhetorically at least, the philosophic act itself. The spiritual nexus of mind and matter is inseparable from the problem, implicit in Kant's schema, of (male) eros generally. Kant's ambiguous ascent, both gradually, via the principle of continuity, and all at once, by a single impetuous leap, never entirely frees itself from the awful fear and possibility of collapse. A second aspect of Kant's history—openly speculative and deliberately reassuring—concerns the world of intelligences, in which we participate without the entangling complications that characterize our natural attachments. Here spiritual community replaces the community of matter, and a wholeness beyond space and time sustains the boundaries of individuality rather than, in the manner of nature's flux, perpetually threatening to dissolve them. As such Kant's spiritual community anticipates the basic structure of his later "noumenal realm": each an instance of parted unity that somehow transcends the temporal/spatial flux of nature. In each case, too, however, such unity is beyond the power of the human mind to represent as actual. Hence, Kant's ultimate inability, in the *Universal Natural History,* to secure the boundary between truth and poetry.[95]

Kant's effort to represent the world as a totality also founders on the continuing tension between the individual self-subsistence of its elements and their unity. His reconciliation of this tension takes the form of a double community: one consisting in the reciprocal relation of the elements, the other resting on each element's immediate relation to God.

To the extent that the two midpoints of Kant's system fail to mesh, the unity he seeks is not achieved. Immediate unity (in God) is at once the ground of nature's reciprocal community and its infinitely distant goal. Kant's effort to think the whole as a community of substances thus both requires the infinity of creation (as the "point," so to speak, where the parallel lines of absolute unity and infinite diversity meet) and is done in by it.[96] In the *Universal Natural History* this tension pervades the image or series of images by which Kant seeks to represent the universe—as both oscillating and expanding, progressing and eternally recurring.

At the same time, Kant's appraisal of the human situation suggests a third locus of community at a midpoint of creation that is neither wholly within nature (as is its physical center) nor wholly beyond nature (as is its spiritual center). Like all created spirits, man himself enacts the mysterious community of matter and spirit in which the unity of creation ultimately resides. What makes man unique (and uniquely wretched) in comparison with other spiritual/material beings is the peculiarly balanced reciprocity of matter and spirit within him. Man alone is undetermined, perched on a razor's edge between the predominance of spirit to which his higher nature draws him and the predominance of matter to which his lower nature drags him. Unable to escape the problem of his own (double) nature and the degradation it entails, man also enjoys a kind of privileged affinity with the whole that otherwise eludes him.

Thus Kant's unepicurean devotion — in a work that otherwise pays much homage to Epicurus — to the idea of immortality. The whole, according to Kant, is to be thought of as a community of reciprocal exchange or "commerce" among self-subsistent elements. The human soul, aware both of its susceptibility to flux and (however dimly) of its claim to immortality, is thus the prototype of the connection between permanence and flux by which the whole as such is constituted.

But the community of matter and spirit that defines the human soul remains a "problem." If the structure of the human soul reflects that of the whole, it does so precisely through its "noble" capacity "to swing itself, by means of a quick swing" above all that is finite. The redundancy of Kant's language suggests the unfounded character of what it describes. The "ground" of man's noble elevation is the attraction exercised by his vision of the world as a totality. But the vision remains fundamentally defective, and to this extent "repulsive." Kant's project, which calls upon man to be the part whose contemplation of the whole completes the whole thus falls prey to circularity. The whole cannot be grasped as whole until it is completed; but it cannot be completed until man grasps the whole. Hence the two paths between which Kant oscillates — the quick *Schwung* of liberating attraction and the infinitely long struggle towards absolute comprehension. But comprehension perpetually pursued is comprehension infinitely postponed.[97] The infinity that poses the difficulty also permits Kant to evade the difficulty.

In the end, Kant's *Universal Natural History* seems to value contemplation of the whole less than the "noble independence" that is evinced by one's desire for it, a preference that gives his account a peculiarly moral — one is tempted to say "Kantian" — flavor. If so, Kant's later self-confessed "turn," under Rousseau's tutelage, from the pursuit of mankind's honor achieved through speculative knowledge, to the defense of human rights, takes on new meaning.

Theory and practice are together for Kant from the beginning. Rousseau did not so much moralize Kant as redirect his moral concern from cosmic to human community and its more satisfying economy of intrinsic worth or "dignity." In such community Kant would later discover the true "intelligible world" — or the only one truly available to us — and with it compelling support at last for man's individual integrity within a larger whole. The physical economy of nature, alternately infinite and finite, gives way to the kingdom of ends and its moral economy of absolute worth. The dual points of attraction — both ground and abyss — that center Kant's early cosmology give way to the moral will as itself the final ground of human purposiveness and perfection.

But the notion of infinite totality, which Kant's early cosmology was meant to incite as well as regulate, never ceased to exercise its compelling charm. Suppressed as a theoretical "delusion" in Kant's critique of pure reason, it reemerged as a "regulative idea" in his doctrines of teleological and aesthetic judgment, politics and history. If Kant's early conception of metaphysical community partially models itself on civil or market society, his later idea of cosmopolitical community as the infinitely receding goal of history reflects, in turn, the displaced appeal of this ever-beckoning point of attraction.[98]

IV. Appendix: The *Physical Monadology*

In the following year (1756) Kant published part 1 (*Physical Monadology*) of what was apparently intended to be a longer work, *The Use in Natural Philosophy of Metaphysics Combined [iunctae] with Geometry*. In that work, Kant substantially revises the theory of body that he expounded nine years earlier in *Living Forces*. His general intention is to provide a theory of body that can meet the challenge posed by the contradictory claims of metaphysics and geometry concerning the infinite divisibility of space. One can, it seems, either have simple substances (as metaphysics asserts) or an infinitely divisible real space (as geometry asserts), but not both. Leibniz's way out of the difficulty was to disconnect space and substantiality entirely. Kant suggests a different route, one in which the simplicity of substance and the reality of an infinitely divisible space are reconciled without disjuncture, and metaphysics and geometry are thereby "married" (*connubio*) (I:480; [121]).

Kant's argument is roughly as follows: simple substance (or the monad) is that which does not consist of a plurality of parts (prop. 1). Bodies consist of monads (prop. 2). Bodies fill space, which is divisible ad infinitum (prop. 3). Monads are not only *in* space but also *fill* a space without detriment to their simplicity (prop. 5). Kant explains: the opinion dividing metaphysicians and geometers — that is, that an absolutely simple element cannot fill space without sacrificing its simplicity — is false. Since space is not a "substance" but "a phenomenon of certain external relations of substances," a relation of one and the same substance can be divided without detriment to its simplicity or unity: for "to find some plurality in a relation is not the same as to dismember [*divellere*] substance into parts" (I:480;

[122]). A monad does not "determine" its space by the plurality of its parts (for it has no parts) but by the "sphere of its activity, whereby it hinders things on both sides of it from any further mutual approach" (prop. 6).

Repulsion is the force by virtue of which monads resist such approach. But the contact or "immediate presence" of monads is not explicable on the basis of repulsion alone, for if particles only repelled one another, "there would be no connection into bodies," and "no volume would be fixed and circumscribed by definite limits" (prop. 10). Contact thus requires a countervailing force of attraction. It is the dynamic relation between these attractive and repulsive forces that determines a body's circumference and hence its determinate volume.

Kant posits, in addition, an inertial force of fixed magnitudes corresponding to the different elemental kinds, which permits him to explain the diversity of the elements without positing, in the Newtonian manner, the existence of a void.[99] According to the Newtonians, free motion is not possible in a completely filled medium.

> They accordingly suppose that the structure of the elements — which is maximally removed from human intelligence — fortuitously conform to our fancy [*pro lubitu confingitur*], and rashly conceive sometimes that the elements would have the structure of the thinnest bubbles, sometimes that of branching and twisting fibers, for with such assumptions one can think of matter as wonderfully distended, and of immense [*ingens*] space enveloping very little matter. (Prop. 12)[100]

Kant claims to be able to account for both motion and the variety of elements without appealing to the "fancy" of a matter "wonderfully distended" in empty space. (We will have reason to return in a later chapter to Kant's peculiar views on spatial constriction and distention.) In any event, the Newtonian view is untenable on its face, since the assumed fibrils and tenuous skins would eventually wear down, filling up the interstitial spaces and thereby bringing all motion to a halt.

In place of perfectly hard atoms in a void, Kant posits a space entirely filled by elements of varying degrees of inertial force or — what amounts here to the same thing — elasticity. As a consequence, elements are at once "completely impenetrable" and infinitely susceptible to the activity of other elements, a susceptibility they register in the compression of the circumference of their active sphere to a dimension approaching zero (I:487; 132).[101]

As the very name of Kant's work suggests, the *physical monadology* means to reconcile the seemingly conflicting views of Newton and Leibniz vis à vis matter and space. Kant wants to insist (with Newton) that substances occupy space, even as he claims (with Leibniz) that space is merely the

outer appearance of the inner changes that substances undergo. The key
to this "connubial" reconciliation lies in Kant's peculiar understanding of
compression (*compressio*) as a function of the dynamic relation between
forces of attraction and repulsion. Leibniz had also insisted (against Newton) upon the (infinite) elasticity of matter, making this one basis for his
argument against real interaction: when two bodies collide, each is merely
the occasion for the changes that the other undergoes independently and
on the basis of its own intrinsic passive force.[102] For Kant, on the contrary,
elasticity comes into play only with compression, that is, with the "felt"[103]
force of repulsion or impenetrability that registers the immediate presence
of something external and that constitutes "contact" in the "genuine sense"
(I:483; [127]).

Kant accounts for the volume or outer limits of a body, on the other
hand, in terms of the cancellation by its own force of attraction of its power
to repel. The limits of a body are thus defined by the self-canceling cessa-
tion of its repulsive reach, as the intensity of its repulsive force diminishes
from infinity (at its center) to a quantity exactly equal to its inherent power
to attract other bodies.

As a consequence of this reconfiguration, division of the space a substance occupies (because it lacks sufficient force fully to repel the counterforce exerted by a neighbor) does not impugn its inner simplicity and
unity. Space can be infinitely divided (and a substance's sphere of activity
infinitely restricted) without that substance being "dismembered" (*divellere,* literally, "to pluck or tear asunder"). However much its outer sphere
may be compressed, substance remains inviolable.

At the same time, this compressibility must run up against an inner limit
if the inviolable unity of substance is to be preserved. Because space can be
infinitely divided without ever arriving at this innermost, yet spatial, point
(where the force of repulsion or impenetrability is infinite), the unity and
permanence of the substance is never breached. Kant's marriage of geometry and metaphysics thus hinges on the notion of a limit to the outer compressibility of a substance, a point that is at once the innermost boundary
of a substance's outer sphere, and a conduit between substance's inner and
outer dimensions. Each substance acts by pressing upon the spheres of
other substances, even as it resists their encroachment onto its own.
Amidst the flux of force by which the boundaries of bodies are defined,
each substance can count on having room (however restricted) in which
to act:

> Since any forces spread out in space from a definite point are
> weakened as the distance from the point increases, the repulsive
> force of the given element will react more strongly to the other in
> proportion as the other approaches its center; and since the repel-
> ling force is finite at any given distance from the center of repul-

sion and increases in a definite proportion with the approach to this center, *it will necessarily be infinite at the central point itself; for these reasons it is evident that by no thinkable force can an element be penetrated in its interiority [penitus penetrari possi]*. (Prop. 13; emphasis added)

As a consequence, the danger posed by interaction to substantial perdurance is preemptively disarmed: elements remain inwardly immune to the dismemberment to which matter is outwardly subject.[104] Substance (to pursue the personifying tendency that Kant's language invites) avoids an obliterating inward penetration only by being constantly on guard. Simultaneously threatening and reassuring, compression is at once that which substance struggles by its nature to resist and that without which substance would lack worldly definition or "determinate volume."

A final note: Kant's new approach bypasses the awkward balancing act of the *Universal Natural History,* whose central drama each monad now individually enacts. With this recasting, moreover, goes a new sobriety of manner. Kant's warning in the preface to the *Physical Monadology* against too great a "freedom of conjecture," which strays from the shores of "the testimony of experience" into "deep seas," seems directed at his own former endeavors. Partly negating that warning, however, he immediately adds that by "setting out in this sound way," we can exhibit the "laws of nature but not the origin and causes of these laws." Those who

> hunt out the phenomena in this manner [that is, by hugging the shores of sensory testimony] are to that extent far removed from the deeper understanding of the first causes; nor will they attain a science of natural bodies any more than those who persuade themselves that by ascending the pinnacles of ever higher mountains, they will at last be able to reach out and touch the heavens with their hands. (I:475; [116])

The metaphysics that many say can be absent (*vacare*) from physics "is in fact its only prop [*adminiculo*], kindling light."

Bodies consist of parts. It is of no little importance to make it clear how they are compounded with one another, whether it is only by the copresence of their primitive parts or by the reciprocal opposition of their forces that they fill space. But how in this business is metaphysics to be reconciled with geometry, when it seems easier to mate (*iungi*) griffins with horses than transcendental philosophy with geometry (I:475; 116)?[105]

Mixtures of metaphysical substance and spatiotemporal matter, physical monads are the hybrids of that unlikely marriage. Kant seems to have solved at least part of the problem that grounded (in both senses of the term) his earlier philosophic flights. Yet despite his apparently fruitful insight into the "interior nature of bodies," he remains unsure how far beyond the shores of experience he can afford to venture. The boundaries of reason remain to be defined.

4   Kant's Moral Cosmology: Freedom and Desire in the *Remarks concerning "Observations on the Feeling of the Beautiful and the Sublime"*

I. Kant and Rousseau

A series of notes attached to Kant's own copy of his *Observations on the Feeling of the Beautiful and the Sublime* (1764) furnish a remarkable record of Kant's early reading of Rousseau and the preoccupations they engendered.[1] Scholars estimate its date of composition to be around 1765 — two years after Kant's initial reading of *Emile* — a time long enough to allow for protracted reflection, yet perhaps short enough to preserve the contours of Rousseau's immediate impact. (Kant was forty-one at the time and sixteen years away from publishing the first edition of the *Critique of Pure Reason*.)[2]

Two passages describe with special force Kant's estimation of Rousseau's importance: in the first, often quoted, passage Kant writes:

> I am by inclination an inquirer. I feel in its entirety a thirst for knowledge and a yearning restlessness to increase it, but also satisfaction in each forward step. There was a time when I thought that this alone could constitute the honor of mankind, and I despised the people, who know nothing. Rousseau set me right. This blind prejudice vanished. I learned to honor human beings and I would be more useless than the common worker if I did not believe that this view could give worth to all others to establish the rights of mankind. (XX:44)

The second, less often quoted passage makes Rousseau the Newton of the moral world:

> Newton was the first to see order and regularity bound up with great simplicity, where before him disorder and badly matched manifoldness were to be met with, whereas since then comets travel in geometric course. Rousseau was the first to discover under the manifoldness of the available shapes [*Gestalten*] of mankind man's deeply hidden nature and the concealed law according to which providence through its observation is justified. After Newton and Rousseau the objections of King Alfonso and the

> Manicheans are no longer valid, God is justified, and Pope's teaching is henceforth true. (XX:58–59)[3]

In the first place (to summarize crudely but not, I think, misleadingly), Rousseau democratizes pride; he teaches Kant to seek mankind's honor not in the knowledge that remains the privilege of the few (who try to approximate the perfection of the Divine Understanding), but in the rights that properly belong to all.

In the second place, Rousseau shows Kant the "hidden law" that governs and informs a moral world which—together with the physical world to which it is analogous—"justifies providence."

Kant's earlier philosophic accounts of the world-whole had foundered on the gap between the unity of the world and the limitless diversity of the elements comprising it. Reason's reach exceeded reason's grasp. Rousseau "justifies providence" by making the discrepancy between human power and desire a central theme of philosophy itself. Philosophy as imitation and approximation of divine wisdom is replaced by philosophy as therapy for the corrupted human condition. The failure of human reason to comprehend the world-whole as an infinite totality, the task Kant sets himself in his earlier writings, is one of kind rather than degree. And the wound—dissatisfaction with the human condition—is to be salved not by an inevitably inadequate displacement of perspective in which we seek to imitate (in the manner of Pope's *Essay on Man*) the standpoint of God, but head-on, through a closer reading of our own nature, that is, of the natural feelings (both moral and otherwise) that are our proper teachers.

Man cannot rationally comprehend the natural whole, but he can through feeling come to know that human part which is itself (or can become) a kind of whole. (Here is one springboard for the lofty ambition of the German Idealists, from Kant to Marx and beyond, to understand human affairs, or history, as *the* totality, that is, as a second and improved natural universe.)

Man's problem is not his "mediocrity"—his middling station within the hierarchy of being (as Kant had earlier argued)—but his apparent indeterminacy. Man seeks to comprehend the chain of being and finds it broken in himself. He seeks to but cannot orient himself in terms of a determinate place within the whole (as Kant's earlier work attempted to do) because he cannot grasp the whole as such, a grasp without which the classical ideal of "mediocrity" or the "mean," lacking any absolute reference, becomes a sort of "occult quality."[4] Man must seek his point of reference not in the greater whole to which his thought is inadequate, but in the lesser, human whole that Kant refers to as the "moral world."

Another passage of the *Remarks* puts the matter starkly: "Everything goes by us in a flux [*Flusse*], and the varying tastes and differing shapes of man make the whole game uncertain and delusive. Where do I find the fixed points of nature that man cannot displace, and which can give him marks [*Merkzeichen*] concerning the bank to which he should adhere?" (XX:46).

In his earlier *Observations on the Feeling of the Beautiful and the Sublime* (1764) Kant felt compelled to regard "the peculiarities of human nature" with the eyes of an "observer rather than a philosopher" (II:207). By revealing the deeply hidden nature that underlies the flux of human affairs, Rousseau indicates the principle of unity that governs the diversity and so permits Kant to regard man from a truly philosophic standpoint.[5]

Following Rousseau, Kant's primary definition of man is a negative one: man is "free" or "lawless" in the sense of being (or regarding himself as) outside the laws of motion that govern the world of matter. The question thus becomes how this freedom is to be rendered consistent with human "determinacy" — not, to be sure, in the sense in which physical objects are determined, but in the sense of having one's fixed place within a larger whole in which one's existence is not canceled but upheld. Human existence must discover a niche for itself between the Scylla of individual isolation and the Charybdis of submergence in the greater all.

Hence Kant's new metaphysical modesty, his "Socratic" and "procrastinating doubts"[6] concerning man's speculative powers, represent not so much an abandonment of his former metaphysical efforts to "comprehend the whole" as a bringing to the surface of their implicit human meaning. A "world" remains for Kant what it always was: a reciprocal community of self-subsistent elements. Only now the ground of this community is not the Divine Intellect (which creates each element both in its essential individuality and its intrinsic relatedness, via the laws of physical motion, to every other element), but a feeling immediately available to every member of the community as free and equal being.[7]

Finally, following Rousseau, Kant no longer regards the "wretchedness" of the human situation as natural and inevitable, a consequence of our station in the universe "halfway between reason and unreason,"[8] but as historical, a function of human choice and action. Happy in his natural condition, man is the cause of his current misery. But unlike Rousseau, Kant is also convinced that man can be the agent of his own salvation. If human misery is a historical disease, it is also one that is humanly curable. Moreover, the cure for human misery is not merely a return to nature but an elevation beyond it. Providence (or nature) is justified not only in the negative sense of being "off the hook," but also, as we will see, in the positive sense that man's freedom is the necessary vehicle of his perfection.

Both Newton and Rousseau bring rule-governed order and unity to a manifold formerly perceived as chaotic. But whereas the laws uncovered by Newton concern physical necessity, those uncovered by Rousseau concern principles of freedom—determinations of the indeterminate. The justification of providence is no longer to be sought interspecially, in the supposed gradations of perfection which make up the universe in its plenitude, but intraspecially, and specifically, within the human species. As man was formerly the stumbling block, so is he now the solution.[9] Man is both an element within the natural whole and a whole unto himself. Thus he is specifically discouraged from comparing himself with the inhabitants of other planets (as Kant's earlier *Universal Natural History* urges us to do). The physically and mentally rarefied Saturnians are no longer to be taken as models for our bootless emulation (XX:47). Our perfection lies rather in "rightly understanding what one must do to be a man [*Mensch*]" (XX:41). With interspecies comparison gone, the old curse of man—his middling station—is also removed. Man's place in the whole is now defined by his (unique) capacity for free will, along with his physical isolation on this planet.[10] Perfection lies not with an ethereal intelligence forever beyond us, but with the universally accessible ideas of freedom and equality.

The key to Kant's brave new (moral) world lies in the related ideas of equality and freedom by which men constitute themselves both as individuals and as members of an (ideal) community. Freedom, equality, and right have for Kant a complex interdependence. To begin with, freedom is an "idea" or, alternatively, a "feeling" which is intimately bound up with that capacity for self-consciousness which makes us "complete beings" and distinguishes us from all other creatures inhabiting the planet:

> An animal is not yet a complete being because it is not conscious of itself and its drives and inclinations may be resisted by another or not—it will sense the evil but it disappears the next instant and the animal knows nothing of its own existence. But that man himself should require no soul and have no will of his own, and that another soul should move my limbs [*Gliedmassen*], that is topsy-turvy and absurd. (XX:93)

Animals are governed by the laws of physical necessity. Man alone is free: aware of, and hence able to control, the drives that dictate unobserved the motions of other animals. Man's natural freedom from determination by instinct gives him a qualified purchase on the exchanges by which material beings in general arise and perish. The very necessity of nature's laws renders them predictable, to a creature of foresight, and hence to a certain extent manageable.

But this very freedom, so dear to ourselves, is perilous when we encounter it in others.

> Man is dependent on many outer things, be his state what it will. He constantly depends on some things through his needs and on

others through his desires, and though he may well be the manager of nature he is not its master. Therefore he must accommodate his will to nature; for nature will not accommodate itself to him according to his wishes. But what is far harder and more unnatural than this yoke of necessity is the subjection of a man under the will of another man. For one who is accustomed to enjoying the good of freedom there is no misfortune more dreadful [*erschrecklicher*] than to see himself subjected to a creature of his own kind who can compel him to do what he will. . . . Accordingly it takes long habituation to make the dreadful thought of servitude tolerable. (XX:91–92)

The willful activity that underlies human self-awareness has other consequences for human reason. Unlike Leibniz's monad, which conceptually "contains" all its (past, present, and future) states, the Kantian self is both complete and essentially open-ended. The primal prudential calculus — to act or not to act, to overcome or submit in order to realize some possible future state[11] — implies the ability to anticipate the future as a merely possible (rather than actual or given) condition. "The movement of matter follows a certain determinate rule, but those of men [*Menschen*] are without rule" (XX:93). If it is to be consistent with his survival, man's freedom from instinct must go together with an ability to foresee and plan for his own future.[12]

As in Kant's later critical treatment of the transcendental unity of consciousness, the completeness of human being involves the capacity to distinguish between the actual and the possible.[13] The unity of consciousness is not abstracted "*ex posteriori*" from the content of actual experience but grasped in advance as intrinsic to all possible experience (all experience, that is to say, that can be "mine").[14]

Man is boosted beyond the physical world by his qualified immunity to the necessary laws that regulate its motion. This is the negative sense in which man is free, that is, without rule. At the same time, this mutual freedom poses a danger to man that no animal faces. It is not merely his attachment to a body that renders man vulnerable. To be "complete" in the human sense is to be susceptible to injury that is more than bodily. An animal can be hurt, killed, or controlled by another. But only a human being is vulnerable to the "horror" of anticipated subjugation.

Subjection to another will is perilous because, unlike the resistance of brute nature, it is unpredictable, hence peculiarly dangerous. But more is involved here than physical danger (which animals also can suffer). Man's primary horror is not death (which he hardly knows), nor momentary opposition, but the "prospect" or anticipation of permanent subjugation to another will. Unlike Rousseau, Kant posits in man a natural fear of slavery.

Unity of soul for Kant is not merely the object of a nostalgic or ideal longing (as with Rousseau) but properly man's permanent possession, to be
defended along with—and prior to—life itself. The desire for self-
preservation is more than and prior to the fear of death.

> All other evils of nature are subject to fixed laws that man learns
> to recognize so as to choose how far he should attempt to master
> or give in to them. . . . But the will of another man is the effect of
> his own drives . . . and harmonizes only with his true or imagined
> welfare. Nothing if I was previously free can open up to me a
> more horrible [*greslicheren*] prospect of grief and despair than that
> my own future state should lie not in my own will but in that of
> another. . . . The motions of matter contain a certain determinate
> rule but those of men are without rule. (XX:92–93)

The problem with subjection to another will is in part, as noted above,
its unpredictability. Unlike that of nature, willful opposition cannot be
reckoned upon; thus it subverts the decision to resist or relent that is consistent, according to Kant, with man's natural tranquility. But unpredictability is not the whole of it. What makes man unpredictable is not primarily his cleverness, but rather the indeterminacy of his intention. (As for
Hobbes, the natural effect of inequalities in human intelligence is negligible.) If I could anticipate the ends of my enemy, I might anticipate his
means. But to the extent that his ends are "imaginary" they become truly
lawless. All willful action implies the imaginative anticipation of the good
toward which our will is directed. The primal horror for man turns his
capacity to anticipate the future against itself. To anticipate being enslaved
is to anticipate the unanticipatable.

The primal horror for uncorrupted man, whose own desires are limited
by his powers, is thus the "prospect" of subjection to the indeterminate or
limitless desires of others. In corrupted man, on the contrary, the force of
limitless desire is immediate. Indeed, corruption can be defined as the loss
of, and moral education as the attempt to reinstill, man's original revulsion
against desire liberated from the constraints of nature.

Kant locates the ground of this primary revulsion in man's sense of his own
right to rule himself; that is, in his "self-esteem" (*Selbstschätzung*) (XX:3,
8, 97, 102, 130). Self-esteem and the abhorrence of slavery that is its immediate expression are both natural to man and consistent, in their natural
state, with his natural sufficiency (or "simplicity") (XX:183). For Rousseau, pride (*amour propre*) implies dependence on the opinions of others
and thus represents a corruption of man's natural condition; with Kant, on
the contrary, it is coeval with human self-awareness and consistent with
man's natural independence and equality. Kant, in short, collapses Rousseau's distinction between natural self-love and unnatural self-esteem, be-

tween *amour de soi* and *amour propre*. Self-esteem is as natural to man as is rational self-awareness—a consciousness of one's "own" existence, as opposed to Rousseau's (mere) "sentiment of existence." Natural man is a unity, according to Rousseau, only because he is not yet rational. Kant differs from Rousseau in his ascription to natural man of conscious unity or completeness. Thus the "wholeness" that for Rousseau remains a perennial human problem coeval with the emergence of reflective reason is for Kant a foregone conclusion. For Kant subjection is a conceptual "absurdity" before it is a moral evil. Or to speak more precisely, its "contradictory" character is itself the firmest indication of its evil.

The problem, according to Kant, is not pride as such but pride inconsistent with the law of equality, that is, with the equal pride of others (XX:183). The natural expression of pride (at least for males) is not the desire to dominate but the fear of domination. Kant thus reads the structure of the general will—Rousseau's formula for reciprocal esteem *within* society—back into man's original condition. What Rousseau intended as a palliating substitute, given the irreversible emergence of *amour propre*, for man's natural independence, serves Kant as a key to uncovering the natural condition itself. Through the formula of the general will, self-esteem accomplishes a task that was, by the lights of Kant's earlier thought, humanly unfathomable. Like metaphysical substances, human beings are "inwardly" complete even as they participate reciprocally in a greater whole. Individual pride is self-sufficient and sui generis, even as it points to each man's membership in a universal (if ideal) community of wills. Kant's early metaphysical and cosmological attempts to understand the (natural) world as a reciprocal community of separate elements finds a new kind of resolution in that world's practical equivalent—the idea of a moral world as a reciprocal community of independent wills. For Kant, unlike Rousseau, individuality and community are thus together, ideally at least, from the beginning.

II. Kant's Sexual Politics

In one other important departure from Rousseau, Kant says nothing about man's evolution from a rudely solitary to a conjugal existence. There is no suggestion of man's natural sexual apathy in Kant, who flatly states that man has a "natural need" to acquire a wife (XX:163). Where Rousseau studied the emergence of society out of rudely natural, asocial elements, Kant presupposes an at least minimal level of society, one that includes both permanent sexual pairing and the sexual rivalry that Rousseau associates with the postnatural savage. The atoms from which Kant wishes to construct the moral world already contain a principle of (sexual) "attraction" propelling them toward unity. This tendency is offset, however, by an opposing tendency of men to "repel" one another, a tendency born of their inherent love of freedom and concomitant fear of domination. As he had earlier corrected Lucretius's history of the cosmos by eliminating the appeal to chance, so he now corrects Rousseau's history of civil inequality. In both cases, for Kant, the course of history is lawfully determined by a dynamic interplay between forces of attraction and repulsion—physical in the case of nature, psychological and moral in the case of man.[15]

In the simplicity of man's natural condition, men live dispersed and self-sufficient lives. Man's natural self-love does not lead him to invest any object (other than himself) with an exclusive interest inimical to the claims of others. He is happy (because his power is adequate to his need) and good, not in the sense of actively promoting the welfare of others, but in the negative sense of lacking any motive to do harm.

This self-sufficiency, however, is crucially qualified by men's conjugal requirements. As the only "naturally exclusive need," sex is different from men's other appetites. The objects of sexual need are nonexchangeable and so irreplaceable. Man has a natural choosiness about the object of his sexual desire that does not characterize his other natural urges.[16] These exclusive sexual claims give rise to a kind of Hobbesian *bellum omnium contra omnes,* and also to the earliest (and only strictly natural) sort of property (XX:74, 183 f.).

Woman, who lacks man's natural sufficiency, collaborates actively in this appropriation. Man needs woman to satisfy desire; woman needs man to live.[17] This natural inequality in the capacities of the two sexes lies at the basis of all the others. Whereas man's "need" for a woman is different from, and potentially opposed to, what he needs to preserve himself, woman's needs are one. Thus, "woman is closer to nature" (XX:50). Unlike male desire, that of woman never liberates itself entirely from crude necessity.[18] Unambiguously grounded in need, woman's sexual desire does not lend itself to the ideal sublimation of which male desire alone is capable.[19]

The relation between the sexes lies at the root of all subsequent changes in the human condition, changes culminating in the state of "luxury" (*Üppigkeit*) that is for Kant the emblem of our present corruption. Natural man, whose powers are adequate to his desires, lives in a state of "sufficiency." Luxurious man, on the contrary, is subject to desires whose satisfaction depends on the subjugation or control of others, desires to which his own powers can never be adequate, and which rest on an ultimately illusory conception of happiness.

The corrupt desires of social man (which Kant especially associates with the effeminate excesses of courtly life)[20] are in general reducible to two: the drive for external honor (or the limitless desire for preference over others) and greed (or the limitless desire for wealth at the expense of others) (XX:55, 130, 161, 163). The desires for limitless honor and wealth are both corruptions of an otherwise natural and healthy desire to preserve one's life and freedom, corruption brought about for the most part through sexual desire. Man's desire to possess a woman exclusively is opposed by woman's need to appeal to a wide audience, either to attract a mate or to replace him (XX:98). (Kant notes that widows — unlike widowers — always remarry [XX:75].) His desire to possess her requires that he in turn win her favor. Thus the desire to possess exclusively becomes the desire to be esteemed, first as a means of obtaining favor, then as a end in itself.

On the basis of this seemingly innocuous beginning, humanity has been gradually transformed, from a disbanded group of independent, self-sufficient isolates, to a corrupt society, a kind of civil madhouse in which delusion reigns and the misery of each depends upon the misery of all. From this condition of increasing luxury stem "suffering, class oppression and hatred, and wars" (XX:175).

The key to Kant's history of the corruption of the species lies in the relation between means and ends and the peculiar way in which woman's example to man subverts it. Woman's natural dependence on man produces in her a drive to please universally as the only means commensurate with her (limitless) insecurity. Woman would thus be the slave that man naturally fears to be were she not armed by nature with a capacity for "artful appearance," to which man for his part is peculiarly susceptible (XX:74, 137). Woman is thus a natural manipulator, whose arts of pleasing anticipate two other universal means which come to falsely substitute for final ends: honor and money.[21]

The inequality and injustice that characterize men's present state can thus all be traced to a mistaking of "appearance" for the thing itself. This mistaken substitution arises from a kind of "illusion" (*Wahn*) that rests on a confusion between opinion and reality and which gives what ought properly to be a means the status of a final end. The two basic vices of corrupted society — the pursuit of honor for its own sake and the pursuit of money for its own sake — share in this confusion. When the pursuits of honor and money cease to be means of preserving one's natural liberty or securing one's real enjoyment, they become "delusional."[22]

The root of this corrupting confusion of ends and means is primarily sexual.[23] Woman is compensated by nature for her inferior strength by her capacity (and desire) to please by appearing to be better than she is, and by the power of male imagination. Thus woman is naturally adept in the art of deceiving, that is, of manipulating man's proneness to esteem her more highly than she deserves (XX:174, 176). Man is subject to a certain gullibility, a capacity to be smitten by mere appearances, that woman lacks. Nature has balanced woman's weakness with regard to active capacity by giving man a compensating weakness in being "easily attached to appearance and easily deceived."[24] Thus "man is inclined to make great concepts of the object of his love and to feel equally his own unworthiness." Woman is more prosaic in her regard for her lover. As she fancies herself "worth courting" and readily believes herself able to command a man's heart, she is little inclined to imbue him with fantastic ideas of superiority (XX:176, 16, 69, 85, 108).

Among earlier, more warlike peoples such as the Spartans, whose women were held in subjection and isolated from male society (and among the modern English, whose social segregation of the sexes Kant praises), woman's natural artfulness had little occasion to express itself (XX:164). Thus manners remained "simpler" and "closer to nature." Contemporary society, on the other hand, is characterized by the "novel invention" that permits men and women to intermingle freely, and so gives fullest scope to the power of illusion (XX:188). The desire to please universally and love of ease that are woman's natural weapons become in society emasculating examples that teach men to be weak and foppish.

The "unnatural freedom of women" (XX:183) culminates in a regime of taste that goes hand in hand with political inequality (of men). "Where there are castles and great differences between men, everything is given over to taste" (XX:51). When morals are simple and all luxury is banned, men rule. When official business is placed in a few hands and most become idle, women abandon their simplicity and attain great influence over men (XX:188–89).[25] The corruption of contemporary society is thus coeval with woman's sexual tyranny.[26] The "law of nature" that mandates sexual exclusivity also makes the freedom of women "unnatural." The natural freedom of men is done in by that of women.

Not least, female tyranny is associated with various kinds of morbid religious and philosophic excess. Theology strives to contain men's unlimited and corrupted desires by arousing fearful (and illusory) images of eternal punishment, images that would be both impossible and unnecessary if men had remained in a state of natural simplicity.[27] Metaphysics, for its part, loses itself in longings both unnecessary and vain to reach a perfection that is beyond our power and so relinquishes what is truly its final end: the determination (*Bestimmung*) of man.[28]

III. Marriage and the Bounds of Taste

The restoration of man to the "circle nature has determined for him" thus becomes the proper function of philosophy. The goal is not a return to nature as such, but nature historically perfected; or perhaps more accurately, history perfected through recourse to the example of nature. Not simplicity alone, but what Kant calls "wise simplicity." The greatest perfection lies in a tranquility of soul accompanied not by lack of feeling (as experienced by natural man) but by fullness of feeling (which can only be experienced by artful or socialized man). Whereas happiness "without taste" consists in simplicity or sufficiency alone, happiness "with taste" consists in a "feelingful soul at rest" (XX:12). Whereas natural happiness is experienced in isolation, perfection presupposes society. Kant's task is thus to reconcile the equilibrium between power and desire associated with man's natural sufficiency, with the fullness of soul associated with taste and the emergence of "unnecessary pleasures."[29]

Kant's method finds its "touchstone" in two criteria by which the natural can be distinguished from the unnatural. One must ask, first, whether the matter pertains to that which cannot be "altered," and second, whether it is common (*gemein*) to all men or whether, on the contrary, it is for only a few, to the detriment and subjection of the rest (XX:35). The reform, or reeducation of social man thus takes its bearings from "nature" in a double sense: first, man must take his bearings from necessity; and second, man must be regulated by the idea of equality.[30]

One thing that "cannot be changed" is the existence of women, who are necessary for the perpetuation of the species, but who are also the primary cause of man's loss of natural simplicity: "The greatest obstacle preventing the return of the male sex to happy simplicity is the female sex" (XX:108).

As we have seen, woman poses a threat to man primarily through her capacity to "infatuate," that is, to awaken in him a desire for imaginary goods. Woman's dependence with regard to the necessities makes her a ready manipulator of man's desire for pleasure exceeding necessities. Thus her power over man is a function both of her weakness and his strength. Man is mastered by his very surplus of erotic energy. Where woman is attached to man by necessity, man is attached to woman through a kind of superfluity that expresses itself in the power of his imagination. Where the object of woman's desire is fixed by need, that of man is indeterminate. If free will was a characteristic of humanity in general, open-ended desire seems to be the specific characteristic of men. Woman's will is free in its choice of means, but its ends are more or less set by her natural condition of dependence. Man's will is free in a profounder and more disturbing sense. Naturally self-sufficient, his preservation is not so much served as threatened by desire. Happiness, according to Kant, lies in "the equilibrium of sensations" enjoyed by "the soul at rest" (XX:149). Sexual love disturbs this equilibrium in a particularly forceful way.

The "high ground" of happiness, according to Kant, lies not in the mere experience of agreeable sensations, but in a "consciousness of oneself in one's entire state." The equilibrium of sensations by which happiness is defined is a kind of "smooth surface" that strong passions and sensations can only serve to disturb. Natural man is spared this disturbance through his "insensibility" (XX:149). The task for man, whose passions have been stirred, of recovering this equilibrium is hindered, however, by the seductive amusements which constantly surround him in society: "all amuse-ments intoxicate, i.e., obstruct so that one does not sense the entire sum of happiness" (XX:154). The intoxicating pleasures of society, and in particular the society of women, rob men of the sense of happiness as "an entire sum" corresponding to their "consciousness of [themselves] in [their] entire state," that is, of their identity as self-consciously complete beings.

A primary concern of (Rousseauian) education is to correct this corruption of the natural relation between the sexes. Woman's unnatural tyranny must give way to the sexual "law of nature," which gives men exclusive possession of their wives. At the same time sexual chastity can no longer depend (as in the rude state of nature) on lack of opportunity. The relation between husband and wife must be able to hold its own in the face of society with all its seductive dangers.

Marriage, for Kant, accomplishes this goal by reconciling the tranquility experienced by natural man with the "fullness of feeling" only possible in social man. As such it depends upon, even as it limits and refines, the play of taste associated with modern society and its "free intermingling" of the sexes.

If the sexual inclination is the bane of man's historical existence, it is also of all inclinations "that which accepts the most ideal embellishment" (XX:137). Except for man's need for a wife, nature, as noted above, makes him self-sufficient. But nature is not sufficient for man's enjoyments. Man's need for a wife, that is, his sexual inclination, opens him up to enjoyments that exceed the bounds of strictly natural necessity. Man, unlike wo-man, could survive independently. Thus in the male sex, at least, self-preservation (and with it the sense of freedom) and sexual inclination are divided. What unites them is male imagination and the capacity and need of women to exploit it. Male desire possesses the tendency or capacity to project itself upon imaginary objects, particularly where immediate natural gratification is postponed or denied. Woman's coyness is her natural means of whetting men's appetite and thus rendering him dependent on her for his pleasures, as she is physically dependent on him for her needs. Thus the natural inequality of the sexes lays the foundation for man's discovery of unnatural or unnecessary pleasures, that is, his acquisition of "taste" (XX:124).[31]

Taste (*Geschmak*) for Kant is linked specifically with the "agreeable," that is, with "refined" as distinguished from "crude" pleasures, which are linked with natural need (*Nothdurft*) (XX:124–25). At the same time, the educated yet simple taste Kant prefers differs from the overly heightened delicacy associated with the excesses of corrupt society. In defining healthy taste Kant must walk a fine line between the crudeness of natural inclination and the foppish excess of unnatural extravagance.

The aesthetic standard to which Kant implicitly appeals in walking this line is the Wolffian formula for rational perfection: art improves nature (and appeals to taste) by bringing "manifoldness and unity into harmony." Physiologically, such harmonies serve as still points (*Ruhepunkte*) in the face of which the nerves can unite and sensibility be both lively and at ease.[32] Unlike the stillness of natural consciousness, which arose from "insensibility," the ease (*Bequemlichkeit*) of taste arises through a kind of heightened "tenderness" (*Zärtlichkeit*) of the nerves, one that permits them to respond in unison to the artful harmonization of unity and manifoldness. In short, art restores to consciousness its ease (*Bequemlichkeit*), not by repressing sensibility but by ordering it in accordance with the (natural) ideal of unity and manifoldness in harmony (XX:125). Properly directed, taste permits a self-sufficiency compatible with society and its "unnecessary pleasures" and thus allows for a simplicity that incorporates rather than opposing the "agreeable" (XX:149).

Ideals of taste divide themselves, depending on the relative weight assigned to diversity or unity, between the beautiful and the sublime. Taste thus contains within itself a principle of complementarity akin to that of marriage: where beauty is associated with novelty, diversity (or the manifold), and, speaking generally, the feminine, sublimity is associated with steadfastness, unity, and, speaking generally, the masculine. Kant adapts a formal standard of aesthetic perfection (derived in large part from Baumgarten and Wolff) to the requirements of domestic life. So transformed, marriage itself becomes a kind of aesthetic whole whose unity transcends the crude need that grounds the natural relation between the sexes. To put it another way, perfected domesticity replaces the natural inequality of the sexes and its destabilizing dynamic with a genuine unity in which the (species) identity of the sexes and their (gender) difference are somehow reconciled.

Establishment of sexual order *within* society thus represents a qualitative advance beyond rude nature. Marriage is a means not only to restoring man's natural completeness but also to establishing it on a higher plane. Marriage rightly construed makes possible not only the "completeness" of the person as individual, but also his or her "perfection" as member of a larger whole (XX:5, 62, 73, 87).[33]

Beyond the alternatives of female subjugation and female tyranny, Kant proposes one in which women rule domestically by inspiring men to virtue:

> When morals are simple and all luxury is banned, men rule. When official business is placed in a few hands and most become idle, women abandon their simplicity and attain great influence over

men. When women inspire men to virtue and Roman/romantic (*romanische*) respect,[34] then they rule men domestically through goodness. (XX:189)

Woman's capacity to rule men legitimately, like her capacity to tyrannize, is rooted in the (male) susceptibility to sexual infatuation through which nature counterbalances woman's physical weakness. Man's ability to idealize woman (or believe her to be better than she is) is thus inseparable from his proneness to illusion.

But the decisive step in the development of ideal taste arises from the emergence, out of the "free intermingling of the sexes," of "artful amorous longing":

> In the free intermingling of the sexes, which is a new invention, longing grows but also moral taste. One of the properties of this drive [*Trieb*] is that it lies at the basis [*Grunde*] of ideal attractions [*Reitzen*] but it always must be embossed [*getrieben*] as a kind of secret. From this stems a kind of coy decorum even in strong desires, without which these would become common and, finally, subject to surfeit [*Überdrusse*]. (XX:188–89)

The "artful unity of amorous inclination, ideal enjoyment and moral taste" requires that women mask their sexual need. In that way "woman's submission can appear to be either compelled or a sign of partiality" (XX:189), and man left uncertain about the basis of his "victory."[35] This appearance remains, however, one-sided. Woman's masked submission to sexual need is the occasion for man's qualified transcendence of need. Carnal pleasure, whose outstanding feature is its debilitating brevity, is transformed into ideal pleasure, whose outstanding feature is its steady (and invigorating) endurance over time (XX:126).[36]

Idealized sexual pleasure thus rests upon a deception (XX:48): the object of man's desire must herself appear to be sexually indifferent, the character of her submission indeterminate between rape and gracious preferment.[37]

What man takes pleasure in is the image of his beloved as a source both of carnal enjoyment and spiritual favor, that is, as both a physical and a spiritual center of attraction. The pain of sexual need is offset by the pleasure of spiritual substantiation. Thus woman assumes the dual role divided in Kant's earlier cosmology between the physical and spiritual or divine centers of attraction. In ideal love, man spans the gap left by the failure of Kant's earlier metaphysical attempts to comprehend the world as a physical and spiritual whole — or would, if it did not finally rest on the illusory image of woman as the source of value.

In fact woman does experience sexual need and is to this extent no "goddess" but a mere human being, whose carnal attractions, once consummated, are repulsive (XX:133). The difficulty of maintaining ideal love in marriage stems from its connection to the unstable cycle of carnal love between attraction and repulsion, that is, the immediate connection between rude sexual desire and satiety/disgust. Wives, to be sure, can offset this repulsion by inspiring "high esteem" through the fact (or appearance) of their virtuous mastery of physical desire. Innocent chastity can give way to virtuous chastity. The woman who is virtuously chaste, who (unlike the innocent maiden) knows all the pleasures of society and freely gives them up, is the most perfect woman (XX:185); the synthetic feeling of beauty and sublimity excited by a woman who thus unites both love and respect produces "the greatest impression that can befall the human heart" (XX:3).[38]

Most women, however, are not capable of true virtue; nor is true virtue in woman necessary for her to have the requisite effect of maintaining her husband's love. For this the appearance of virtue suffices. Even in its perfection, love of woman cannot distinguish between truth and appearance.

The ground of human worth is not a godlike (or goddesslike) point of attraction beyond the self (as Kant's earlier cosmology had claimed, and as romantic love pretends), but sui generis. True pride is self-grounded, nonrelative and yet universal, that is, obedient to the law of equality. The moral world is not governed by the laws of an alien God (as the theocracy of Judaism, which Kant chastises, claims) but by a principle of equality intrinsic to the human capacity for self-esteem (*Selbstschätzung*).

Thus in the end marriage remains an at best ambiguous and fragile bridge between the natural and the ideal. Everything beautiful and noble in love ultimately depends on raw sexual desire, to which it all too frequently degenerates (XX:76); "free enjoyment of lustful inclination and the unsuppressed discovery of its objects cancels everything ideal that can be spread over inclination" (XX:128). The ideal in beauty lies in the hope rather than the possession (XX:123). "This," according to Kant, "is why it is so difficult to maintain ideal pleasures in marriage. Except when the wife is ceded mastery" (XX:128).

Marriage is given over to the rule of female inclination and taste (XX:16), which can be trusted to keep interest alive through a kind of prudent coyness. Where friendship thrives in the presence of its object, love thrives in its absence. A clever wife compensates for this by making her favors scarce.[39]

But this solution to the problem poses a certain difficulty. On the one hand, Kant praises the marital state for its capacity to restore the mental tranquility disrupted by sexual desire; thus, "sexual inclination finds its rest only in marriage" (XX:154). On the other hand, this rest cannot depend upon or lead to satiety, which would abolish everything ideal in sexual love. Marriage, then, seems in the end less the "greatest perfection" he at one point calls it than an uneasy balance between attraction and repulsion, desire and surfeit. Even in marriage, ideal love is difficult if not impossible to sustain, particularly given women's loss of beauty with age (XX:125).

For this reason, perhaps (and perhaps also because of woman's tendency toward fickleness [XX:77]), Kant's ultimate view of marriage remains equivocal.[40] Thus, for example, he calls it "to some extent fortunate that marriage is onerous," for otherwise the population would increase and injustice become even more universal (XX:85). More to the point: "With women the drive for honor can only be satisfied through sexual union . . . because she must be pursued. With men, however, this is not necessary." Men, who are merely dragged through the business, can "resolve to remain bachelors" (XX:165). Perhaps most tellingly, Kant observes: "It is said that love of honor is the final weakness of the wise. I believe that insofar as wisdom is not of the sort that the ancients presupposed, love of woman is the final weakness of the wise" (XX:97).

The last obstacle to wisdom (or educated simplicity), then, is not the love of honor (which is compatible with independence, hence simplicity) but sexual desire, from whose distracting charms philosophy itself is not exempt:

> Correct knowledge of the world structure following Newton is perhaps the most beautiful product of inquisitive human reason. With regard to this Hume notes how easily the philosopher caught up in these delightful meditations, can be disturbed by a little brown maid, [just as] rulers are not moved to despise conquest by the smallness of the earth in comparison with the world-all. (XX:120)

The reference is obviously to Thales, whose fall into a pit while contemplating the heavens amused a serving maid. But in Kant's version of the story, it is the maid herself (and not her laughter or the fall) that the philosopher finds disturbing. The beauty of the world-structure all too easily succumbs to beauty in its human shape. "The cause is that although it is surely beautiful it is also unnatural to lose oneself outside the circle that heaven has here determined for us." It is the same "with sublime contemplations concerning the heavens of the blessed" (XX:120–21). The delights of contemplation cannot withstand the pull of sexual attraction. Sexual feeling, unlike pain, cannot be easily mastered by the understanding.[41]

Philosophy as Kant formerly conceived it aims too high.[42] Philosophy rightly conceived makes itself "useful" by "canceling harmful appearances." Metaphysics rightly conceived is thus the "science of the limits of human reason" (XX:181). The rapturous model of contemplation errs because it exceeds the circle of what is properly human, taking for truth what is at best uncertain, at worst a mere appearance or illusion.[43] Philosophy wrongly conceived is in this respect like sexual infatuation. By pricking the bubble of illusion in which "appearance" is taken for "the thing itself" (*Sache selbst*), philosophy's zetetic doubt performs a task analogous to sexual disenchantment.[44]

Philosophy rightly conceived thus offers an alternative to marriage as an antidote to male infatuation, an alternative route to tranquility of soul consistent with the existence of society. A philosophy based on "Socratic" doubt cancels only that which is "useless," while "useful" truths remain unaffected (XX:181). This "useful" metaphysics not only contributes to the moral struggle to establish the rights of man; it also makes possible a "tranquility of soul" that arises not from the absence of inclination but its mastery. Thus, whereas "appearance demands refinement and art," truth points to "simplicity and tranquility" (XX:181).

Kant indeed wonders whether such tranquility of soul might itself provide the foundation for the "totality of ethics": "Amusements and dissipations are in opposition to rest. The sexual inclination finds its rest only in marriage. To abuse others is disquieting to oneself. Affects in general cause unrest" (XX:154).

But Kant ends on a negative note: "it is unfortunate that through such a morality other men have no use . . . outside of the fact that it is already a great virtue to do no evil." Individual tranquility of soul fails to provide that positive connection with others that Kant associates with the physical (and sexual) forces of attraction (XX:154).[45] Philosophy alone, even when it is the negative philosophy of the ancients, is not enough.

IV. Moral Worldhood and the Dynamics of Illusion

Marriage and philosophy share the virtue of reestablishing (with lesser or greater success) the equilibrium between power and desire enjoyed by man in the rude state of nature. But tranquility alone is insufficient as a basis for moral worldhood, which implies a positive principle of unity among the individuals that comprise it. That positive connection is furnished by "moral feeling," which Kant defines as a feeling of pleasure or displeasure that involves us "through our being ourselves an active principle through freedom of good or evil" (XX:145).

Moral feeling is an immediate pleasure obtained through the active exercise of our own will (as distinguished from a mediate pleasure derived from our passive relation to an object). The immediacy of moral feeling is rooted in the sense of necessity or obligatoriness that it conveys: "obligation is a kind of moral need" (XX:127). Moreover, unlike responses to natural need, moral action is immediately good, hence not useful (XX:142; 163). As such, moral feeling reconciles the "necessity" that Kant associates with rude nature with the "transcendence of the merely useful" that he associates with taste. The will that is moved by moral feeling acts for the sake of a good that is not merely good for something else but necessary in itself (XX:150).

Moral feeling is immediate pleasure taken by the will in its capacity to be a cause of good or evil "in accordance with the law of equality." Since according to this law all count alike, moral feeling impels one to sacrifice for others only when their gain outweighs one's loss. In the state of rude equality, moral feeling has little effect, since there are few occasions on which my loss in helping others is outweighed by their gain (XX:9, 11, 36, 145).

At the same time, virtue, or the capacity to act out of moral feeling, requires "strength" (XX:104), that is, a surplus of power over (nonmoral) desire. Thus natural man has a much greater capacity to sacrifice for others on the basis of moral feeling than does civilized man (XX:173). In the rude state of nature, however, the very conditions that assure this capacity also assure that it will rarely be called upon. The limited character of desire makes for a universal self-sufficiency that precludes active benevolence (except toward one's natural inferiors — women and children — toward whom it therefore indicates a kind of "contempt" [XX:36]). To make a sacrifice for the sake of one's equals (or superiors) would be to give up more than they gain and thus to violate the law of equality by assigning their well-being a higher value than one's own (XX:36).

Corrupted or luxurious society, on the other hand, provides much occasion for moral sacrifice, while at the same time ruining man's strength. The awakening of limitless desire based on chimerical ideas of happiness destroys not only man's natural tranquility but also the (nonmoral) sufficiency required if moral feeling is to be effectual in him. If natural man has the power but not the occasion to be moved by moral feeling, social man has the occasion but not the power.

By restoring man to a condition of simplicity *within* society, the educational project outlined in the *Remarks* combines man's natural/moral strength with the social occasion for its exercise. As such his project is itself a kind of exercise in moral mechanics: "The question is whether, in order to move [*zu bewegen*] the affects of myself or others I should take my point of support [*Stützungspunkt*] from outside the world or within it. I answer that I find it in the state of nature, that is, in freedom" (XX:56).

Society restored to a condition of sufficiency is the realization of a moral world in which individuals are reciprocally united through the effectual force of moral feeling. The *Bewegungsgrund* of the moral world is thus analogous to the "moving force" that unifies the world of nature:

> The single naturally necessary good of a man in relation to the will of others is equality (freedom) and with respect to the whole

unity. Analogy: Repulsion through which a body fills its own space as all others fill their own. Attraction, whereby all parts bind themselves into one. . . . The natural instincts of active benevolence toward others consist in love toward the [female] sex and toward children. Benevolence toward other men [*Menschen*] is based purely in equality and unity. There is unity in a sovereign state but not equality. If equality is combined with unity there arises the perfect republic. (XX:165–66)[46]

As in his earlier *Universal Natural History* Kant assumes the role of world-builder or demiurge. But where he earlier sought, given matter, to create a hypothetical natural universe, he now seeks, given men, to realize an ideal moral world. Imitation of the divine creation thus gives way to a more practicable goal. The formula of unity in harmony with equality furnishes a kind of moral "law of motion" analogous to the physical laws of Newton.[47] But the "ground" of this reciprocal harmony is not divine intelligence (as in Kant's earlier physical cosmology) but "general will," understood as an immediate synthesis of the one and the many. It is this implicit universality that gives moral will its force: the "condition of virtue is powerful, hence only to be met with in the powerful condition of common being" (XX:104). The good will contains the merely singular as much as it contains the universal (XX:145). Will is "perfect to the extent that it is the greatest ground of the good in general according to laws of freedom." Moral feeling, in turn, is "feeling for this perfection" (XX:136–37).

Society restored to a condition of simplicity differs from the original simplicity of nature in that the rule of equality that there remained merely implicit is now consciously in force, in the sense that men adopt it as an explicit rule of conduct.[48] So conceived, the moral world brings into harmony the force of repulsion (that prevailed in the original condition of human dispersion) and the force of attraction (that prevailed under the political and sexual tyranny of corrupted society).

At the same time, the source of the will's goodness does not lie in its "utility." Accordingly, the "motive ground" of moral action is not mediate pleasure from some realized good (that is, the perfection or well-being of another), but rather immediate pleasure in "one's own causality." "To subordinate all to free will is the greatest perfection" (XX:144).[49]

Kant's insistence on immediate pleasure as the criterion of moral feeling, combined with his denial that men take immediate pleasure in the perfection or well-being of others, rule out both an aristocratic ethic based on imitation and a sentimental ethic based on the so-called natural instinct of benevolence:

> The ability to recognize something as a perfection in another does not mean that we feel pleasure in it. If however we have a feeling of pleasure in it, then we are moved to seek it and apply our forces

to it. The question is thus whether we feel immediate pleasure in the well-being of another or properly immediate pleasure only in the capacity of applying our force. If both are possible which is effectual? Experience teaches that in the simple state a man regards another's happiness with indifference. (XX:144)

An ethic based on imitation, which presumes that man is inspired to virtue by the example of others he regards as superior, violates the law of equality (except in the ambiguous case of ideal love, in which man is inspired to virtue by the example of woman, whom he [falsely] regards as his superior.) In his antipathy to an ethic of imitation and its anti-egalitarian, authoritarian assumptions, Kant goes so far as to give qualified approval of envy (*Neid*). Envy is merely the corrupted form of a praiseworthy self-regard. The cure for envy lies not in learning to take pleasure in the greater happiness and perfection of others, but in recognizing their chimerical character. "Envy ceases when I can wipe off the deceptive appearance of another's happiness and perfection" (XX:179).[50]

Kant also rejects the (more democratic) appeal to natural benevolence as a basis for morality. So long as men depend on things, the happiness of another cannot be immediately shared (XX:25). Universal love of the human race is thus a chimera that exposes one to self-deceiving longings for a goal one lacks both the power and the will to actualize (XX:25). High moral ideals rest as much on chimeras as does moral corruption (XX:22). Insofar as they are beyond human power, such ideals are "delusional," an example of "moral luxury," or "sentiment without effect" (XX:22, 172, 9). This moral luxury contrasts with the real, though limited, activities of simple men : "With luxury proliferates the fantasy of love of mankind while the capacity and the desire lessen. The simple man occupies himself only with those he can help" (XX:135).[51]

Kant contrasts the determinate character of obligation, or "selfishness in equilibrium," with the indeterminate duty of love or benevolence. Strict obligation consists in "my not doing to another more than I would let him do to me, and giving him all that is his. . . . If I promise him something I rob him if I do not fulfill a hope I have erected. If he is hungry and I do not help him I have violated no obligation" (XX:157).[52] Moral feeling in society has to do either with need (in which case it is obligation) or goes further (in which case it is sentiment) (XX:117). Whereas obligation is a kind of moral necessity, determined by the measure of reciprocal equality, benevolent sentiment easily degenerates into an ineffectual wish to do more than we have the power or will to accomplish. As a kind of "moral need," obligation is more effectual against selfish need than is benevolent sentiment, which tends to project ideals that are incompatible with man's natural condition (XX:173). As long as man depends on things, he cannot act without regard to self-interest. A good man is thus to be distinguished from a good rational being: the latter has no limit but its finitude; the former has much in himself to limit (XX:24).

Kant's rejection of "goodheartedness" as an essentially empty sentiment, devoid of genuine moral force, leads him to reject an ethic based on altruism, or the supposedly natural desire to benefit others. But an ethic based on egoism is also inadequate, even when it is the refined egoism of the ancient sages, with their ultimate appeal to "tranquility of soul." An ethic based on tranquility of soul goes very far. The trouble is that in the end "others have no use." The *Bewegungsgrund* that unifies Kant's moral world is neither altruism nor selfishness (XX:146). But what then is it?

In the end, this question isn't answered. The ethic sketched in the *Remarks* never unequivocally defines the central relation between happiness and moral goodness.[53] Morality undertaken for the sake of happiness cannot distinguish its *Bewegungsgrund* from nonmoral inclination; moral action undertaken without regard to personal happiness is an ideal beyond the reach of human nature. It seems as if moral feeling must either cease to be effectual in man, or cease to be moral.

What Kant appears to have in mind is something like the following: in man's current corrupted state, the moral drive is not sufficient (XX:9, 28, 98). A return to simplicity of taste will restore men's strength and with it their capacity for virtue (XX:19, 46, 48, 51, 186). For its part, virtue, as the ability to master inclination, provides the assurance of tranquility during one's entire state that Kant associates with true happiness (XX:149). "Virtue brings its own natural reward, not in the goods of luxury but in those pertaining to sufficiency" (XX:174). The greatest perfection, which lies in the subordination of "all to the free will" (XX:144), thus combines both assured happiness and complete moral goodness. "Freedom rightly understood (moral not metaphysical) is the highest principle of all virtue and also of all happiness" (XX:31). What remains to be established is their order of priority. But here Kant seems to be of two minds. On the one hand, several passages suggest that self-esteem hinges on the experience of self-sacrifice, and that the motive ground of morality therefore cannot be happiness.[54] True sacrifice, however, is incomprehensible, given Kant's ultimate appeal in the *Remarks* to moral feeling. To give something up in response to feeling—even moral feeling—is not a true sacrifice, but merely a prudent investment in a higher happiness (cf. XX:179–80). Without sacrifice, Kant cannot account for human self-esteem; with it he cannot account for moral action. As a result, he is driven to distinguish between "common" and "greater" duties, the latter of which entail "sacrifice" and "self-mortification," and which require "hope in an afterlife" as their *Bewegungsgrund* (XX:12).[55] In the end it is unclear whether the "tranquility of soul" that constitutes happiness is the condition of moral virtue or its consequence.

Remarks thus leaves us with two principles of world "unity," two forces of "attraction" whose relation remains unresolved: a "natural instinct of active benevolence" rooted in sexual desire (and inequality), and a noninstinctual benevolence associated with the free community of equals (XX:165–66). The first is "indeterminate" and destabilizing but also dynamic; the second is determinately bound up with the timeless concept of a perfected moral/political whole.[56]

The first principle serves as the basis of a drive toward union otherwise lacking in natural man, whose concernful regard for his own independence causes him, all things being equal, to "flee from" his fellows. If the initial self-subsistent equality of natural men resembles the elements of the physical universe in their primordial dispersion (as traced out in Kant's earlier natural cosmology), men's drive toward unity resembles the gravitational force owing to which world systems have evolved.

The second principle, on the other hand, is immediately bound up with the timeless idea of a "perfect republic." The physical world as a completed system (whose comprehension, as per the Divine Schema, Kant's earlier cosmology despaired finally of achieving) finds its moral/political equivalent in the idea of a moral/political whole that perfectly combines equality and unity. In such a system, men are united, not through their common subjection to a superior — if benign — sovereign, but through an immediate equilibrium between mutually repelling respect and mutually attracting (but asexual) love.[57]

The difficulty arises from the fact that the relation between these two principles of unity must be resolved if Kant is to maintain the status of the moral world as something other than a chimera. The moral world is a timeless idea that depends on the timely force of sexual attraction for its realization. Without the destabilizing power of this attractive force, man would never have emerged from the crude equilibrium of the original state of nature. The cause of man's corruption is thus the precondition of his higher perfection. And yet a gap remains between the moral love that unifies the moral world and the sexual love that points men toward it.

In sum, the human realm described in the *Remarks* is governed by two "motive grounds," two separate principles of motion.[58] The first, nonmoral principle is dynamic; the second, moral principle is static. The first arises out of the tension between sexual desire and men's primordial fear of domination; the second furnishes a timeless "law of equality" by which the independence of each individual is immediately bound up with his membership in the whole. One model is developmental or historical; the other rests upon the eternal idea of the perfect republic, or unity and equality in immediate harmony.

What is still lacking is an account of the relationship between these two principles of motion, that is, between moral and nonmoral feeling.[59] Without the unnatural expansion of sexual desire there is no history, and without history, no perfected moral world. But where is the guarantee that this dynamic development will in fact culminate in a community of self-sufficient citizens? Kant sometimes suggests a kind of self-regulating mechanism by which the greatest social excesses bring on their own destruction: debauchery ultimately depopulates, luxury ultimately impoverishes, the too-great freedom of women ultimately pricks the bubble of enchantment through which they tyrannize over men. Indeed, Kant goes so far as to suggest that it is in precisely such pivotal moments of "turning back" from excess to simplicity that man's perfection lies:

> Man in his perfection is not in a state of sufficiency; also not in a state of luxury; but rather in a return from the latter to the former. Strange [*Wunderlich*] disposition of human nature. This most perfect state rests upon a hair's breadth. The state of simple and original nature does not last long. The state of nature restored is more enduring but never as innocent. (XX:153)

Remarks reveals a Kant still struggling toward the "two world" theory that receives its final expression in the *Critiques*, in which the intelligible world is lifted decisively from its original speculative moorings to become the moral "kingdom of ends."[60] At the same time, the *Remarks* also shows the roots of his ongoing preoccupation with human history, here propelled by the dynamic interplay between the repulsive force of human freedom and the attractive force of human desire. In these same years, woman's cunning is replaced in Kant's thought by "the cunning of nature" as cyclical "return" gives way to progress and man's "a-social sociability" becomes the moving force of history.[61]

Kant's *Remarks* anticipates many of the elements of his mature moral doctrine: the categorical nature of obligation, the principle of universalization, the unconditional goodness of good willing, the special status of moral feeling as an immediate satisfaction; the distinction between true virtue and mere good-heartedness.

But the relation between the aesthetic (or cultural) and the moral is, arguably, never fully resolved. The "uncertain and delusive game" arising from the "flux" of human taste never decisively submits to the timeless order of the moral world. It would be going too far to suggest that Kant's efforts to integrate moral being and historical becoming foundered over his personal decision to remain a bachelor. At the same time, Kant's extended attention in the *Remarks* to the power and perils of sexual illusion sheds light upon his later critical "purity."[62] The gap, in his later thought, be-tween nature and reason as mediated imperfectly by history is identical to the gap between womankind, which must be characterized in terms of "nature's ends," and humankind generally, which can only be characterized in terms of the ends man chooses for himself. In keeping with his later promotion of notions of progress as vehicles of moral hope, Kant comes to look more favorably upon economic luxury and the female "refinement" of society.[63] To this extent, nature's "rich" sexual "economy," whose "admirable arrangements" aim at the preservation and cultivation of the species, becomes typical of providence generally.[64]

It is perhaps best to leave off on the Rousseauian note with which this chapter began. In a late work Kant returns to the question of Rousseauian education as a remedy for man's deviation from the "state of nature," a deviation he links to the gap between men's sexual and civil maturity: "Rousseau devoted three works to the damage done to our species by 1) leaving nature for *culture*, which weakened our forces 2) *becoming civilized*, which produced inequality and reciprocal oppression and 3) supposedly *becoming moral*, which involved unnatural education and distortion of our way of thinking."[65]

This comment, which could easily have been lifted from the *Remarks*, written more than thirty years earlier, is followed by the following pessimistic conclusion: "Since [man] needs, for his moral education, *good* men who must themselves have been educated for it, and since none of these are free from (innate or acquired) corruption, the problem of moral education for our *species* remains unsolved in principle and not merely in degree."[66]

It is therefore only from "providence" that man can anticipate the education of the human race as a "whole." By providence Kant "means precisely the same wisdom that we observe with admiration in the preservation of the species of organic natural beings, constantly working toward their destruction and yet always protecting them" (X:328; 189).

But this providential remedy for Rousseauian "hypochondria" (X:326; 187) over the human condition cannot be taken as Kant's final word. In a roughly contemporaneous letter to Schiller, Kant gives a radically different appraisal of nature's organic/sexual order:

> The organization of nature has always struck me as amazing and as a sort of chasm of thought; I mean, the idea that fertilization, in both realms of nature, always needs two sexes in order for the species to be propagated. After all, we don't want to believe that providence has chosen this arrangement, almost playfully, for the sake of variety. On the contrary, we have reason to believe that

propagation is not possible *in any other way*. This opens a prospect on what lies beyond the field of vision, out of which, however, we can unfortunately make nothing, as little as out of what Milton's angel told Adam about the creation: "Male light of distant suns mixes itself with female, for purposes unknown."[67]

Marriage is the prototype of the mysteriousness of creation. In the tension between nature's incomprehensible "chasm" and its providential sexual "economy" lies a clue to Kant's earlier philosophic struggles.

5   Dreams of a Spirit Seer

> If it were to occur to someone to linger for a while over the
> question: What exactly is this thing which, under the name of
> *spirit* [*eines Geistes*], people believe they understand so well, he
> would put all these know-it-alls in the most difficult position
> of embarrassment [*Verlegenheit*].
>
> (II:319; [307])

Kant's *Dreams of a Spirit Seer, Elucidated by Dreams of Metaphysics* (1766)
elaborates upon the theme of wise simplicity developed in the *Remarks*.
The essay is, nominally at least, a response to the Swedish visionary Eman-
uel Swedenborg, whose voluminous *Arcana* Kant had "purchased and
worse yet read." From the beginning, Kant justifies his study on the apparently frivolous subject of ghost sightings in terms of its "utility," that is, as
an effort to salvage some good from an otherwise useless expense of money
and effort. And indeed throughout the essay money and effort will serve
as standards by which he measures the utility of his chosen course. At the
same time, his intention to make good his loss professes his susceptibility
to disutility—susceptibility enough to make him spend the money and
read the book. The principle of utility will serve as the guiding thread of
his philosophy, enabling him to steer, as will soon be evident, an (almost)
impartial course between dogmatic inspiration and skeptical debunking.
Yet despite Kant's protestations, utility needs more than its own "reasonableness" to recommend it, as his own unreasonable curiosity already reveals (II:318; [306]). Thus from the beginning *Dreams* presents itself as
an exercise in self-catharsis.

But not only that. Impetuous friends have goaded Kant into examining
the veracity of "common tales" (*gemeine Erzählungen*). These, even more
than the shadowlands inhabited by dreamy philosophers, pose a puzzle. In
the limitless country of the dreamers, where houses may be built "ad libi-
tum," philosophers sketch the plans for which "hypochondriacal vapors,
wet-nurses' tales and wonders of the cloister" furnish the materials. The
reason for this "paradise of dreamers" is furnished by its evident utility, at
least for Holy Rome, which "possesses in this land profitable provinces"

since "the keys that open the gates of the other world open at the same time and sympathetically, the money chests of the present" (II:317; [305]).[1]

Thus utility explains, in its own way, the jurisdiction of a spirit world supported by "venerable" religious policy. The queerer matter is the provenance of seemingly useless common ghost tales. Between the testimony of reasonable and obdurate eyewitnesses and the inner resistance of his own unsurmountable doubt, the philosopher cuts a naive figure. Simplicity threatens to give way to simplemindedness (*Einfältigkeit*). The question of the ground of ghost tales thus replays the older debate between a science bent on establishing its universality and religious insistence on the possibility of miracles. To admit the veracity of a single tale would have "astonishing consequences."[2]

And yet no reason (*Grund*) presents itself that would altogether disprove them. (Unlike the appearance of miracles, they cannot be readily explained — and thus explained away — in terms of their political utility.)

To affirm the existence of ghosts and to deny it thus seem equally prejudicial. Yet Kant admits to a certain partiality: to avoid the prejudice of ungrounded skepticism he has allowed himself to be carried away by that of naive credulity. "Common report" must be given its due if only because common experience, as he will soon make clear, furnishes the only criterion by which dreaming can be distinguished from wakefulness.

I. "A Tangled Metaphysical Knot"
(*Ein verwickelter metaphysischer Knoten*)

The first, "dogmatic" part of the essay devotes itself to an account of what reason can offer by way of a theory of spirits. Chapter 1 begins with the admission that Kant does not know whether spirits exist or not, nor even what the term "spirit" means. The notion of "spirit" may be a concept abstracted from experience in the usual way (in which case spirits would be real); or it may be what Kant here calls a "surreptitious" concept, propagated "unconsciously" on the basis of "covert" inferences from experience (in which case "spirit" might refer to something imaginary). How then is "spirit" to be given a determinate meaning without begging the crucial ontological question? (How "really," as opposed to "nominally," define what may, after all, only be imaginary?) Kant finds an answer to this knotty problem (II:319; [307]) in common tales to which the term "spirit" is connected. Comparison of such "ghost tales" with common usage reveals consistently recurring characteristics that may allow access to the term's hidden meaning (II:321 n; [308 n]).

Kant begins with a thought experiment: imagine something "extended, compressible, and divisible," something that "fills" a certain space by resisting its occupation by something else and which would "undoubtedly" be called material. Now think, he says, of a simple being with reason. Would that thought, Kant asks, correspond to what is commonly meant by "spirit"? He says no (and here parts company with the "well-cleared [*gebähnten*]³ track of other philosophers"). A simple being *inwardly* endowed with reason might outwardly act like matter (a theory Kant worked out at greater length in his earlier *Physical Monadology*). Such a being would not be distinguishable by any recognizable mark from matter (which may, for all we know, be inwardly rational). *Retention* of the concept "spirit" therefore requires *elimination* of the mark by which matter is recognized, namely the repulsive force that allows it to "fill" space. Spirit must be understood in terms that relate it, if only negatively, to the outer relations of force by which matter is made known to us. Spirit is thus not only that which is inward (or "rational") but also that which, due to its perfect penetrability, takes no part in the community of reciprocal action and reaction which constitutes the system of physical nature.⁴ One can retain the concept of a spirit only by thinking of "[rational] beings who can be present even in a space filled with matter, thus beings who do not possess the quality of impenetrability, and who never constitute a solid whole, no matter how many you unite" (II:321; [309]).⁵

The immunity of spirits to the laws of impact means that they cannot come within the range of my senses and so cannot be known as real. Spirits are thus "unthinkable" in the sense that they cannot be conceived concretely. But that spirits are unthinkable for us does not imply that spirits are impossible.⁶

The possibility that such beings exist can therefore neither be confirmed nor denied (II:323; [311]). Such beings might even be capable of occupying space, so long as in doing so they offer no resistance to other bodies. Such beings would be *immediately active* in space without thereby *filling* it.

If the human soul is a spirit of this sort (which Kant admits is not yet proved), its relation to the human body can be understood as one of property or ownership (II:324; [312]). As in Kant's later *Doctrine of Right,* that body whose changes (*Veränderungen*) alter me is *my* body; likewise, its place is *my* place. Spirit, then, does not occupy a single organ of the body or even a minute part of one (as Descartes taught) but is in its entire body (or wherever it "senses" and so suffers). The spirit, in short, *is* wherever it feels itself to be vulnerable: "Where I feel, it is there that I *am*."⁷

Kant's reason for rejecting Descartes's identification of the soul with a *specific* portion of the body is as follows: if one were to locate the soul in a specific place, one could no longer distinguish it with certainty from the raw ground stuff of bodily natures (II:327; [314]). In that case the idea jokingly proposed by Leibniz "that we may be swallowing in our coffee atoms destined to become human lives" would "no longer be a laughing matter [*Gedanke zum Lachen*]." So conceived, the "thinking I" would share the common fate of all material natures of returning to the (Epicurean) chaos from which contingent combination momentarily drew them (II:327; [314]), a thought that lends a cannibalistic aftertaste to Leibniz's jest.

This abysmal thought should (Kant insists) awaken the wayward thinker who, led off "in a sort of dream," is inattentive to his own principles (*Grundsätze*). Kant brings the wayward reader back to himself with the thought of the soul's abysmal dissolution, an experience he implicitly compares to the nightmares of falling or being swallowed up by which sleepers are sometimes awakened.[8] It is, as Kant insists, "sometimes necessary to startle [*erschrecken*] a thinker who is on an improper path [*unrechtem Wege*] with the consequences, so that he is more attentive to the grounding principles by which he has allowed himself to be lead on, as in a dream." The thinking I's distinctiveness is marked by (if nothing else) the startling consequences of a false step that represents the merger of thought and matter (or pretends to).

Kant "inclines very much" toward asserting the existence of immaterial beings in the world and placing his own soul among them. The reason that so inclines him is "very obscure," he says, even to himself, and applies to the sentient being of animals: namely—an "inner capacity to determine oneself voluntarily" that he here identifies with the "principle of life." Life so understood differs essentially from mere matter, whose defining mark is the "filling [*Erfüllung*] of space by a necessary force limited by outer counteraction." The obscurity of life's inner force makes it unreasonable to demand conceptual knowledge of its various species. This does not, however, prevent Kant from distinguishing between the immaterial beings that contain the principle of animal life, and spirits proper, which (also) have reason.[9]

The "mysteriousness" of the community of soul and body, given soul's exemption from the compressing exchanges of matter, has a kind of natural (and to this extent comprehensible) incomprehensibility: since all our concepts of external action concern the relations of material bodies, it is no wonder that the relation of body and soul should be opaque to us. Kant's best surmise is that there is a spiritual essence present in the innermost core of matter, an essence that does not act upon the forces determining the outward relations of the elements but rather upon "the inner principle," and which thus furnishes the ground or reason of their external efficacy. The purely external relations of reciprocal force that make up the world of matter presuppose an unknowable inner ground that secures each substance's individual identity. Leibniz was right to identify this inner ground with representation (*vorstellen*), for consciousness or something like it is the only sort of inwardness of which we can form any true conception. At the same time, Kant denies to matter a genuine power of representation (*Vorstellungskraft*) on the grounds that a physical whole (composed of a number of material substances, individually capable of obscure representation) does not constitute a mental whole or "thinking unity" (*denkende Einheit*) (II:328 n; [315 n]). The principles of physical and mental unity diverge; what constitutes the joining necessity — what makes or breaks the bond between a spirit and a body — remains nature's mystery. At the same time, however, this mystery sustains at least the hope of spiritual life beyond the dissolution of the body. Without this disjunction between matter and spirit, we would be indistinguishable from the doomed atoms of Leibniz's coffee (a doom from whose recognition Leibniz was shielded by his denial of the reality of bodily interaction).

II. "A Mysterious Philosophic Fragment"

The "mysterious philosophic fragment" that follows as chapter 2 aims to divine this secret bond by establishing a link with spirits bypassing the community of matter (II:316; [329]). This divination Kant likens to a kind of twilight state midway between waking and sleeping: here attention turns from the mechanical causation associated with dead matter to the beings which contain the ground of life. That such grounds are possible and even likely is as much as reason can establish. How, and how far their influence extends cannot be known, precisely because they transcend the laws of physical causation.

But if (as seems likely) such immaterial natures exist, it is even more likely that they communicate immediately, it being less probable that they should communicate by means of corporeal objects so different from their own spiritual nature. Such a spiritual community would consist of self-determining beings existing "for themselves" and not merely (as is the case with the purely external community of matter) in relation to others. For such beings, the need to assume the conditions of space and time would disappear; the individual's experience of belonging to a world would not require (as is ordinarily the case for us) a consciousness of temporal succession. Immediately united, such beings would constitute an "intelligible world," its parts in "reciprocal connection and community" without corporeal mediation. This community would be "natural and indissoluble," the union of such beings with matter occurring accidentally, by particular divine provision.

The peculiar character of this heterogenous union underscores its mysteriousness. Kant would steer a reasonable course between the unappealing (but not impossible) alternatives of "hylozoism," which gives life to everything, and materialism, which takes all life away (II:330; [317]). He finds evidence of life (and against materialism) in the external perception of "free arbitrary movement," which indicates the presence of an "inner" force lacking in dead matter. This evidence counts against materialism without, however, undermining the possibility of hylozoism. Lack of voluntary external movement does not indicate the absence of life. Plants, for example, obtain nourishment (and have an inward principle of motion) without moving themselves externally. The difference between plant and animal is in any case a slippery one: if, as Boerhaave says, *the animal is a plant that has its roots* (internally) *in the stomach,*" it is equally the case that *"the plant is an animal that has its stomach* (externally) *in the root"* (II:330; 318).[10] Where life is concerned, the outer and the inner seem to be interchangeable.[11] The stomach is both the quintessential organ of inwardness and a "root" that sucks up nourishment from the external world. Kant's moebiuslike "play of concepts" disconcertingly recalls his earlier image of the coffee cup and its cannibalistic conflation of the inner and the outer. The organ of inwardness is also an abyss in which one fears to be swallowed up. Perhaps only through such assimilation of outwardness and inwardness is the otherwise inscrutable community of spirit and matter at all accessible.

So conceived, the immortality of the spirit, along with its participation in a heavenlike community, would be assured. Here, spatial and temporal distance, "the great cleft canceling all (corporeal) community," would disappear. Man is thus to be understood as an inhabitant of two worlds, one home permanent and eternal, the other limited to his temporary "personal union" with a body (II:332; [319]). Even if this is the case, however, it is not provable that man in this life communicates with the other world. It is likely that pure spirits would have no immediate experience of the material world (being unable to interact with it). Thus, they would influence (or literally "flow into") human souls, but with a sort of hermeneutic impermeability, since the ideas of embodied and disembodied spirits would "differ in kind" (II:333; [320–21]). Both sorts of spirits would reciprocally influence one another without understanding one another, there being no way to translate between their differing understandings of their (respective) worlds.

It is easy to see in Kant's sketch of intelligible worldhood the model for his later noumenal realm. To the noncorporeal inhabitants of such a world, knowledge of "things in themselves" would be self-knowledge of their own inner essence in its immediate community with all other essences. Such a world would be "intelligible" or fully accessible to reason. But it would only be accessible to a reason other than human. As a community of spiritual (rather than corporeal) beings, it would avoid the limiting conditions of spatiotemporality required by human perception. For us, intelligible worldhood remains an object of aesthetic, rather than metaphysical, contemplation. The "inner ground," vainly sought in Kant's earlier metaphysical musings, reemerges in the "beautiful" image of a systematic spiritual constitution (*Verfassung*). (Cosmo)politics (or the beautiful image of perfect justice) replaces cosmology as key to "cutting or unraveling" the metaphysical knot (II:333, 319; [320], [307]).

To support the pleasant supposition of such a spiritual constitution, Kant turns to the common human experience of inner conflict between egoism and altruism. The inner nature that is metaphysically opaque is morally visible, or at least palpable, in the feeling of this struggle between self-love and a kind of compulsive attraction toward the good of others. (Once again, what is most radically inward reveals itself by way of the external.) Kant associates this compulsion with the alien force exerted by the moral will of all, a will that finds expression in our inner experience of the "strong law of duty and weaker one of benevolence" (II:334–35; [322]). As in the *Remarks,* the physical world finds its spiritual equivalent in the moral one. Moral unity can thus be understood on the analogy of gravitational attraction, the so-called moral sense being a feeling for the dependence of the individual will upon the common will.[12] Unlike the mediated reciprocity of nature, in which individual beings continually arise and perish, that of the moral world permanently upholds and sustains its members, even as it unites them in a greater whole.

The appeal of this image of perfect justice may draw us toward (unwarranted) philosophic partiality. Moral satisfaction is a seductively potent charm (*Reiz*).

> All morality of actions can, in accordance with the order of nature, never have its complete effect in the bodily life of men, but it can have it in the spirit world in accordance with pneumatic laws. The true intentions, the secret motives of many endeavors, fruitless by impotency, the victory over self, or occasionally the hidden treachery in apparently good actions, are mostly lost as to their physical effect in the bodily state, but in the immaterial world they would have to be regarded as fruitful [*fruchtbare*] grounds . . . [in accordance with] the moral quality of free will. (II:336; [323])[13]

One is attracted to the idea of spiritual worldhood out of longing for justice. At the same time, the reader cannot help but sense that Kant's moral appeal here is displacing, without fully eradicating, an earlier, more "metaphysical" sort of longing. The idea of a spirit world is appealing because morally satisfying, but also (perhaps) because it cuts or unravels another sort of nodal entanglement. The knot that binds us to the whole is, like Kant's later "leading string," both source and hindrance.[14] In short, spiritual worldhood makes conceivable a kind of "being in the world" which overcomes the threat of individual dissolution that always accompanies Kant's descriptions of natural community. Unlike its natural (maternal) counterpart, moral activity's "fruitfulness" (*Fruchtbarkeit*) upholds rather than destroying individuals, whose integrity lies in their moral imputability or capacity to merit reward or punishment. The natural economy and its abysmal terrors give way to a moral one in which each member reckons securely on the basis of his own efforts.[15]

One's place in the spirit world would be the same, before and after one's (corporeal) death—past, present, and future constituting a continuous whole. Embodied spirits would experience in temporal terms their own timeless condition as moral beings. In this way, justice would be secured within the order of nature and without appeal to divine intervention (saving us from the embarrassment of imposing on an inscrutable God the dictates of our own moral need).

The rarity, for its part, of ghost sightings is easily accounted for by the impermeability of pure and embodied thought. What I think as human being is not remembered by me as spirit, and conversely, just as what I think when asleep is not remembered upon wakening. Such sleep-thought (as distinct from dreaming, which we experience according to Kant in a mixed state between sleep and wakefulness) may well be our clearest thought, since when we sleep we are free from the external stimulus of our bodies. But precisely because of the absence of bodily reference, we are unable when awake to recall our sleep-thought to consciousness as belonging to the same person (II:338 n; [325 n]). The body that obstructs our clarity is also the ground of (and barrier to) our personal identity. Kant chides philosophers who appeal to sleep for proof of the "reality of obscure ideas," for the obscurity we are conscious of occurs not during sleep (of whose thought content we are upon waking never conscious) but during the transition between sleeping and waking (when dreams and chimeras also occur). Our inability to connect our sleep-thought to the unity of self that characterizes waking consciousness is not a function of sleep-thought's relative obscurity but of the disappearance, in sleep, of the bodily (or objective) reference that sustains the unity of waking consciousness. As in Kant's later critical period, the experience of bodily sensation as "one's own" furnishes the objective referent on which unity of consciousness turns, at least so far as we are (wakefully) in a position to know.

Our inability to grasp the ground of consciousness, its ultimate reason or cause, means, however, that we cannot exclude the possibility that consciousness takes another, disembodied form, giving man a sort of "double personality." Inhabiting different worlds, the members of this double unit could influence each other only "symbolically," each expressing the other's thought in the (embodied or disembodied) manner of its own ideas, along the lines of poetic analogy. Man's spiritual thoughts, for example, might "stir up" in his embodied self analogous ideas, as when our own most abstract thoughts assume the garments of poetic imagery (II:339; [326]). So construed, metaphor would serve as a literal "translation" between separate worlds, even as geometers translate time into space by representing time as a line. Analogy (or relational, as opposed to qualitative, equivalence) can serve as a bridge between worlds because, as is already clear, all worlds for Kant, whatever their differing qualities, share a similar relational structure.

To such influx only the unusually (and pathologically) sensitive would be susceptible, experiencing this influence as a kind of delusion (II:340; [327]). Sufferers of such nervous imbalance would see chimeras and wild images, without perceiving the true spiritual source of their fantasies. Kant's spiritual hypothesis, with its great "pneumatic" republic, thus provides a convenient (though unverifiable) explanation for insanity. Like Tiresias, who paid for his prophetic gifts with blindness, those "gifted" with sight into the other world lose something of their intelligence in this one.[16]

III. "Antikabbala. A Fragment of Common Philosophy to Cancel Community with the Spirit World"

Kant's attempted disclosure or "opening up" (*Eröffnung*) of our relation to the spirit world gives way in the third chapter of part 1 to "cancellation" (*Aufhebung*). (It is, as such, a "cancellation" of his previous "cancellation.") Spiritual consciousness and dreaming, previously distinguished, are now equated. Quoting Aristotle (and Heraclitus), Kant observes, "When we are awake, we have a common world, but when we dream, everybody has his own." Wakefulness is thus the condition of community, while, conversely, those who (claim to) have their own worlds as good as dream. Community in this world, as measured by conformity to common sense, is the touchstone of right thinking, as contrasted with the "thin air" out of which philosophers construct their own imaginary worlds. But the times are turning against such airy projects. The success of mathematicians in mapping out the features of this common world permits Kant to prophesy that philosophers too may soon awaken completely (II:342; [329]).

Despite their affinity, the source of ghost seeing and philosophic fantasizing is not (quite) the same. To show why this is so, Kant draws attention to a distinction between ghost seeing and "dreaming while awake."[17] Such a day or waking dreamer knows that he dreams, because he remains aware of the distinction between his fantasies and the real, external sensations of his body. The body and its "externally" directed sense thus serves as a benchmark of objectivity, enabling the daydreamer to distinguish between images perceived (from without) and those that are merely concocted. In short, the objectivity of the daydreamer hinges on his ability to distinguish between "inner" and "outer," an ability that depends, in turn, on an ongoing relation with the body as both "one's own" and as a conduit to the

world beyond. Body is thus experienced both as separate from and inseparable from the self, that is, as a kind of inalienable "property" on whose
externality in relation to the mind the ongoing unity and identity of the
conscious self depends (II:343; [330]).

True spirit seers, by way of contrast, also experience their own inner
fantasies as real, projecting concocted images outward upon the world.
The peculiar delusion of ghost-seers is thus one of radical displacement.
Ghost-seers place outside themselves what ought to appear within. The
notion, taken from the science of optics, of "imaginary focus" provides the
model for a kind of material explanation for this curious misdirection.
Ghost-seeing is a sort of spiritualized "optical illusion" in which the vibrating nerve tissues accompanying our thought project lines that meet in an
imaginary focus outside rather than inside the brain. Drawing here on Descartes, Kant hypothesizes that thoughts are accompanied by certain "material ideas" — vibrations of the cranial nerves that copy the motion of sense
impression and whose "focus" corresponds to the location of the image
perceived (II:345; [332]).[18]

The illusion of ghost-sighting is only heightened by the vividness attaching to the attention drawn by an image so much outside its ordinary
place. The great "clarity" of the image is a sign not of its spiritual reality
(as Kant's previous chapter had hopefully suggested) but of a common
physiological phenomenon whereby any image much attended to seems
clearer and hence more real.

Pursuing his probabilities, Kant locates the source of ghost-seeing in a
combination of nervous disease and the follies suggested by a prejudiced
education. But while the properly educated would not succumb to visions,
reason alone cannot dissolve them, for they concern a disturbance of the
senses that precedes the judgment of reason. As such ghost-seeing represents an error of the sort that Rousseau's Savoyard Vicar discounted[19] and
which indicates the weakness of naive empiricism, with its reliance on the
"immediacy of the senses" as a sufficient touchstone of truth. Only the
truth of bodily awareness, not sense experience per se, can furnish an adequate criterion of reality; for the relation between mind and body is the
mysterious but undeniable prototype for all community, all articulated
unity between the world and the individuals that comprise it.[20]

Nevertheless, Kant ends his critique of visionaries with an appeal to the
judgment of nonseers, who will prefer a material explanation of the phenomenon in question to one based on dizzying speculation and idealism,
even one that admits the insanity of the dreamers. (Visionaries, who cannot be persuaded by reasons, exclude themselves from the community of
reasoners.) Exemplifying the preference he elsewhere claims for mechanical
over idealistic explanation, Kant mocks his earlier attempt to reconcile the
world of common sense with the possibility of spirits, an attempt that has

itself become an "embarrassment" (*Ungelegene*) (II:347; [335]. Such efforts now appear to be the product of a "bottomless (*bodenlos*) philosophy" that can be reconciled with anything and is therefore worth nothing.

The place for visionaries is relocated from the twilight zone between worlds to the hospital, where those whom Holy Rome once thought necessary to burn need only be purged. Kant's earlier spiritual "pneumatology" gives way to a more material sort of wind.[21] In this position (*Lage*) of things, there is no need "to excavate so far back as metaphysics to hunt up the secrets in the feverish brains of dreamers" (II:348; [336]). Physiology discloses another route to the bottom of things, rendering Kant's earlier effort to loosen/dissolve (*auflösen*) the metaphysical knot superfluous (or worse):

> The sharpsighted Hudibras could alone have solved [*auflösen*] the riddle for us; for according to his opinion, when hypochondriacal wind rages in the guts, its direction is indicated as follows: if it goes downwards, there occurs a f___ [*F–*]; *if it rises upwards it becomes an appearance [*Erscheinung*] or holy infusion [*Eingebung*]*.[22]

The ultimate weapon against the spiritualists is not reason but ridicule. Kant's allusion to Butler's satire — too raw for Kant's turn-of-the-century English translator[23] — not only ridicules the visionaries; it also deflates Kant's own spiritual pretensions. The charms of his previous metaphysical flight lose their appeal in a rapid scatological descent — an exercise in metaphysical detumescence. The final passage of the chapter is thus itself intended as a purgative. The purgation, however, modifies the medical procedure earlier recommended: instead of emptying the body to relieve the mind, Kant will empty the mind directly (he remains, to this extent, more idealist than materialist). The evacuation is accomplished by the reductive association of the spiritually attractive with the physically repulsive. Desire countered by embarrassing disgust, the object of Kant's earlier desire is stripped of its allure.

Or so Kant implies in the first paragraph of the following chapter: Kant's "theoretical conclusion." Returning to the theme of judgment, it appears that reason was in charge all along. The resort to ridicule was a weapon of prejudice used to counter prejudice. As with commercial scales, accuracy of judgment is best tested by letting merchandise and weights "change pans." Kant has ridiculed what he formerly found worthy of honor to cancel its attractiveness and thereby "purify" his soul. Anticipating Nietzsche's affective aesthetic, Kant plays with his own emotions to secure a tranquil mind "open to all reasons [*Gründe*]" (II:349; [336]). Permeable to reason, the mind stands ready to appropriate all that it finds genuinely instructive. Mental propriety forsakes its former exclusivity in favor of a kind of common ownership: "the judgment of one who refutes my reasons becomes my judgment," for weighed against the scale of self-love it is found to have greater substantial value (*Gehalt*). The trick is to exchange positions so that one views one's own judgment from "outside," the better to observe its "most secret causes."

The parallaxes that arise from such an effort are the price that must be paid to avoid the optical deception to which a single viewpoint is subject. Parallax is an apparent displacement of an object caused by a change in the position from which it is viewed; as such it is a kind of double vision (like that which he previously attributed to drunkards), albeit one that Kant willingly accepts to see through a more intractable sort of illusion.[24] Only in this way can one put in their "true places" concepts of the human power of knowledge. Like the astronomer who observes the stars from separate earthly positions to establish their true positions, a thinker ought to observe his own concepts from a double standpoint, at the same time making allowance for any consequent displacement of the object observed. In the case of Kant's own experiment in parallaxis, the cause of inaccuracy is one that he neither can nor wishes to remove, namely "hope of the future." Whereas ridicule (or the subjection of Kant's theory to the judgment of the skeptical) can remove his blind affection, it cannot shake this primal prejudice in its favor because it is one that all men share. Reason itself bears this hope inscribed upon one of its arms. Kant's exercise, which attempts to locate our concept of reason's power, is in the uncomfortably self-reflexive position of putting reason in the pan of its own scale. The problematic that underlies Kant's later critical project is thus anticipated here. But the problem is also diffused by a hope that assures against the static equilibrium to which reason might also be distressingly subject. Reason, it seems, cannot be strictly impartial, if only because it is partial to itself. And if, as earlier chapters have suggested, anticipation of the future is somehow endemic to human reason, then hope furnishes a reason to believe in ghosts however much the probabilities weigh against it.

But what exactly is hoped for? Do we hope to receive something from the future (for example, happiness), or is the future itself what is promised? Kant seems to mean the latter, for he goes on to attribute the common crediting of ghost stories to a widespread hope that we exist after death. This hope is the likely source both of the phantoms that appear to the wishful, especially at dusk, and of philosophic systems (including Kant's own) that base themselves on a presumed community with the spirit world. In the hope underlying Kant's pet opinion (*Lieblingsmeinung*), both ordinary person and philosopher find common "inclination," giving weight to what would otherwise be "empty air" (II:350–51; [337–38]). At the same time, the mysterious communion of body and mind proves to be a nonissue, so long as it is severed from the question of death. Neither the impulse to know for knowledge's sake, nor the seductive charm of cosmic justice, but the sheer desire to live on emerges as the secret engine of Kant's spiritual system-building. The playful topic for which he continues to half-apologize points to serious business.

The scale of judgment is thus left hanging in the balance, tipped, if at all, by what reason itself recognizes as a prejudice. The bold ignorance that denies the truth of individual ghost-sightings retains a queer (*wunderlich*) reservation about them taken altogether. As with teleological causation generally, whose inaccessibility to human reason is one of the essay's underlying themes, the whole is somehow (queerly) greater than the sum of its parts. This sense of oddness keeps Kant from taxing others to follow where he leads. Here the community of judgment to which he earlier appealed apparently dissolves at a point similar to that which will later separate the subjective community of reason from the subjective one of taste.

Kant has limited reason in order to make room for faith — in this case faith in the reality of a future life. As in his later critique of pure reason, theory assumes the task of staking out the boundaries of possible knowledge. Kant's theory of spirits exhausts all philosophical insight into them, so that in the future many things may be opined of spirits but never more known (II:351; 338). Theory, in short, knows a priori or in advance. It prophesies the future by uncovering the limits of the possible — not the limits of what can possibly exist, for here our ignorance of ultimate grounds obscures our vision, but the limits of what we can possibly know about existence. In the face of nature and its inexhaustible diversity, we can at least know exhaustively that the secret of life will always remain a mystery, since the ground of life is in principle excluded from the material community from which we draw the data of experience. Thus spirit can be thought only as the negation of what can be known. On such a footing, pneumatology (literally, "the science of wind") can make itself useful as a doctrine of man's necessary ignorance.[25]

Having said so, Kant now puts the "whole matter of spirits" (*ganze Materie von Geistern*) aside as settled/loosened (*abgemacht*) and complete, at the same time placing it far off: "in the future it doesn't concern [him] [*Sie geht mich künftig nichts mehr an*]" (II:352; [339]). Kant thus practices on himself the cure he elsewhere preaches for "hypochondriacal wind," willfully abstracting his attention as a matter of prudence (*Klugheit*) in the hope of applying his limited capacities to greater profit elsewhere. Prudence involves planning and thus hope or anticipation of the future. The essence of human (as opposed to divine) wisdom lies in maximizing the efficacy of finite forces over a finite time span.[26] "It is for the most part unsound to want to extend the tiny measure of one's forces over all [sorts of] windy [*windichte*] projects." Philosophy, business, and medicine follow a common counsel. In the end, Kant returns to the Rousseauian theme of utility, but with a businesslike twist: he would restrict his aspiration to his powers, not for the sake of the dreamy tranquility that Rousseau associates with living for the moment, but rather to husband his forces to maximize their future effect. Unlike that of Rousseau, Kantian wisdom is inseparable from the hope that necessarily attends all prudent investment.

IV. Ghost Stories

Surprisingly, however, Kant has more to say. The first, "dogmatic" part of his essay is followed by a second, "historical" (*historisch*) part, whose first chapter tells a tale (*Erzählung*) the truth of which readers are invited to accept or not as they may like. Kant thus assumes a kind of apathy or indifference that avoids the embarrassment (*Verlegenheit*) of philosophers caught between painful doubt and humiliating credulity. Those who purchase the appearance of wisdom by putting on airs are especially threatened by the reproach of yielding to common illusion; hence their scorn for things that equalize the wise and the ignorant by being incomprehensible to both of them (II:353; [340]).

It is thus no wonder that so many secretly harbor a belief in ghosts that they refuse to avow openly or publicly admit as a subject of respectable inquiry. Ghost stories (*Geistergeschichten*) are a hidden heresy against the fashionable opinion (or dogma) of the Enlightenment and its Academy. Kant's response is to tell his readers a tale (*Erzählung*) that is at the same time a spiritual history (*Geistgeschichte*), leaving the matter of its truth and/ or importance (like any good story teller) to the decision of the listener.

In keeping with this intention, Kant begins his tale in the well-worn formulas of fiction:

> there lives at Stockholm a certain Herr Schwedenberg,[27] a gentle-man of comfortable means and independent position [and who may therefore be the more presumed to seek no material gain from his endeavors]. For more than twenty years his whole occu-pation has been, as he himself says, to stand in closest intercourse with spirits and departed souls, to receive news from the other world, and in exchange give it news from this one, to write great volumes about his discoveries, and to travel at times to London to attend to their publication. (II:354; [341])

Kant's report on Swedenborg's credentials (*Creditiv*) takes the form of three stories that purport to offer this-worldly proof of his community with the spirit world (*Geistergemeinschaft*). The first story concerns the haut monde, that is, the testimony of a princess (supported by a diplomatic inquiry). The other stories rest on "common" hearsay. Of these, the first concerns the wife of a deceased envoy, whose hidden bill of receipt for a silver service Swedenborg is able to recover, enabling the wife to settle an outstanding bill with a goldsmith. The second concerns a distant fire on which Swedenborg reports while visiting the home of a merchant.

Kant's excuses his circulation of such (dubious) histories by comparing them with his own former spiritual philosophy: the dreams of Swedenborg are no worse than the pretenses of reason (tales drawn from metaphysical lotusland [*Schlaraffenland*]) (II:356; [343]). At the same time, his equation of the few and the many (united by their common ignorance) makes it clear that his own skepsis applies to skepticism itself. Academic skepticism is itself a kind of dogma, whose ground is to be located (like the territories of Holy Rome) in false pride. Kant's *Dreams* is not the skeptical diatribe against dogmatism it is often taken to be, but a first blossoming of the position he will come to describe as an alternative to dogmatism and skepticism alike. To put it another way, in the face of a battle between dogmatism and skepticism which is itself dogmatic (a battle all the more troubling since it is masked by hypocrisy and pretension), Kant offers as a remedy agnostic histories in which the line between truth and fiction is left deliberately indeterminate. "The boundaries of folly and understanding are marked so unknowably that one with difficulty walks along in one region without at times stepping slightly into the other." Kant's ingenuousness (*Treuherzigkeit*), which makes room[28] for such digressions even against reason's protests, is a remnant of family honor rather than an "heirloom" of natural stupidity. Kant's attraction to ghost stories is thus in part a sign of his democratic (hence familial) loyalties against the aristocratic pretensions of fashionably enlightened society. To believe in ghosts is to side with the common man — including Kant's own parents — whose credulity need not be linked with lack of innate intelligence. Reversing the feudal rhetoric of courtly pretension, common ghost-seeing (or believing) becomes a badge of both democratic sympathy and personal family honor.

But this defense of common understanding has a double edge. Kant will tell the queer (*wunderlich*) tale of Swedenborg's spiritual journey, leaving it to others with the money and time to undertake more worldly journeys to test his proofs against the test of eyewitness evidence (II:357; [344]). It is only distance, Kant suggests, or the money and time required to cover it, that stands in the way of his investigating these stories more thoroughly. If worldly communication were more adequate — if travel were easier — in the manner promoted by commerce and diplomacy, that distance could perhaps be rendered negligible. Thus Kant suggests a way in which the honor of common judgment, impugned by its "credulity," might be vindicated and restored. Kant's appeal to common judgment ultimately makes sense only if the community of reason becomes truly universal: only if this-worldly commerce makes it possible to test the stories of dreamers (for example, by enhanced methods of communication) before the witnesses pass on. Between the lines of Kant's simultaneous praise and ridicule of common understanding lies a veiled appeal to what he will in later works call history (*Geschichte*) as bridge between the natural and spiritual worlds, between rude simplicity and genuine enlightenment.[29]

V. Ecstatic Trips and Defective Fundaments

Kant begins his account of Swedenborg's substantive claims by addressing the potential misgivings of the careful reader. It may seem suspect that the history Kant is about to relate fits so well with Kant's own speculative "pneumatology." For as he "set the dogmatic part before the historic, and thus set reasons before experience," he may have given rise to the suspicion of underhanded dealing "by having the whole affair [*Geschichte*] in his head from the start" and then pretending to present nothing but abstract considerations, so that he might in the end present the unwary reader with the "pleasant surprise of confirmation by experience" (II:358; [344]). To this trick of the learned trade (against which he warns the naive reader) he adds another, linked to the same unresolved dilemma concerning the relation between abstract reasoning and experience. "For one must know that all knowledge has two ends by which one can grab it: one a priori, the other a posteriori." Seeking to connect them, some grab at the latter end, insisting that after beginning from experience one gradually ascends to higher and more general concepts. The difficulty with this approach is that one soon comes to a "why" that cannot be answered, a situation that is as honorable as that of a merchant who when presented with a bill of exchange for payment "replies in a friendly way that one should come back later." To avoid this embarrassment, other sharp-sighted men embrace the ruse of beginning at the other end, "at the far limits of metaphysics," only to find themselves nowhere: "of beginning I don't know where, and of coming out I know not whither." Proceeding from the "ground" and yet unable to link up with experience, such thinkers cannot orient themselves within the world of sense and so fail to find a place at all. It seems, indeed, as if the "atoms of Epicurus, after having fallen for an eternity, might sooner collide by chance and form a world" than that these most universal and abstract concepts might clarify experience.

Faced with the embarrassing alternatives of a departure from a metaphysical utopia that is literally "nowhere" and a perpetually deferred arrival, philosophers have taken the deceptive route "as if by common agreement" of working from separate ends and then secretly "squinting" at each other's results to assure that the "parallel lines" of their efforts meet at "the unthinkable."[30] What is in fact an innocent — if queer — coincidence between the results of Kant and the claims of Swedenborg calls to mind the twist or "clinamen" by which Epicurus (mistakenly) and later philosophers (deceptively) create false worlds. Cheating philosophers are like novelists who send their heroines to a distant place only to have them chance upon their lovers by a "lucky adventure"—writers who seem to leave everything to chance while in fact moving the machinery behind the scenes to achieve a happy ending (II:359; [345–46]). Against such intellectual chicanery, by which the many are fooled, Kant raises a voice of democratic protest that is at the same time an apology for his own brand of wisdom. The proof that Kant, though learned, is not one of the guilty lies both in his willingness to reveal their secrets and the ludicrousness of the testimony that seemingly confirms his theory.

If Swedenborg's visions seem to confirm Kant's earlier thoughts, it must either be that they contain more merit than a first glance reveals or that he has stumbled on the truth in the manner of poets who appear as prophets when events chance to bear out their ravings. Yet despite his efforts to distance himself from the fictive practices of others, Kant, by his very title, with its evocation of the language of romances, foists upon himself an ironic literary mantle. He would describe the "ecstatic" travels of his "hero" through the spirit world—a remote country indeed. Swedenborg's ecstatic journey puts him literally "outside," a radical displacement from the world and/or himself suggestive of erotic pleasure and mantic lunacy. At the same time, his ability to "fill his bottle" in "the lunar world" bespeaks a kind of economic sleight of hand. Where other authors earn credit for their big books with the "heedless expenditure" of their own reason, Swedenborg has managed to fill his own lunar bottle by drawing on the intellectual reserves of his audience (II:360; [346]). If expense of reason is the standard by which works are judged, his "big work" takes highest honors; for instead of merely expending his own reason, he has managed to consume the reason of others.

Despite this lunatic abridgment of the normal laws of intellectual expenditure and profit, Kant is himself taken with the remarkable correspondence between Swedenborg's "eyewitness" claims and reason's subtlest speculations—Kant's own "philosophic brainchild" (*philosophische Hirngeburt*). Kant attributes this apparent coincidence to the "rare play of the imagination" that leads some to see images of the Holy Family in a frosted windowpane, that is, to the faculty that leads us unwittingly to project upon natural formations images already in our mind. (That Kant elsewhere associates such perceptions with a philosophically privileged state of transition between sleeping and wakefulness should not go unremarked.) In this condition of imaginative "play" he admits to a kind of unwitting imitation of the deceptive practice previously described. Imaginative squinting at the facts (which in this case happen to be nonsense) may have twisted his perception of them. The joke, which must also serve as his rhetorical excuse, consists in the fact that in this case the coincidence is cause for embarrassment rather than self-congratulation.[31] In short, Kant has his own difficulty with the relation between the a priori and the a posteriori. How the two can come together (as they must if there is to be a philosophic account of man's place in the world) without our witting or unwitting connivance remains unclear. Kant's superiority to other philosophers lies not in his ability to solve the problem they all struggle with, but in his honesty — his "Socratic" willingness to admit his own ignorance even as he exposes that of others. The play of Kant's own imagination (to which *Dreams* gives unique — and uniquely witty — scope) is by no means in the clear. How is a thinker to be sure that the harmony he seeks and seems to find between the historical and the dogmatic, sense and reason, is not a figment of his brain? How distinguish the doctrines of philosophy from the romances of a poet, willing to do anything for laughs? Kant's almost manic wittiness in this section suggests, perhaps, both his own uneasiness over the writing of the big work he already planned and one cause of the delay in its completion: his inability to resolve the question of the relation between metaphysics and experience, or "how the soul is present in the world," as he puts it a roughly contemporaneous letter to Mendelssohn.[32]

Saving his own time and effort, Kant omits the details of Swedenborg's revelation and instead concentrates on the "audita and visa," or what Swedenborg professes to have seen with his own eyes and heard with his own ears, as both "the foundation [*Grund*] of all his other reveries [*Träumerei*]" and as pretty much in accord with the adventures of Kant's own "metaphysical airship" (*Luftschiff*) (II:360; [347]). Kant is struck by the plainness of Swedenborg's style (suggestive perhaps of a more artless version of Kant's own honesty); his stories and their connection seem to be based on his fanatical perceptiveness rather than the inventions of reason, indicating the rarer and more interesting phenomenon of a systematic delusion of the senses. Here, then, is one ready excuse for Kant's fascination: the deception of the senses, which "concerns the first fundament [*erste Fundament*]" of judgment, cannot, like deceptions of reason, be "willfully" guarded against through an effort to guide the powers of the mind and "restraint of an empty curiosity [*Vorwitz*]" (II:361; [347]). Anticipating the later "discipline" by which Kant critically restricts reason's dialectical propensities, his indictment of curiosity also suggests a deeper anxiety. The will can restrain wayward curiosity (and thus forestall the perpetually unanswered and unanswerable why?); but how can judgment guard against perversion in its very seat, a defect (*Unrichtigkeit*) equivalent to lunacy?[33]

Swedenborg's testimony boils down to the conviction that "*his insides have been opened up*" (*sein Innerstes aufgethan ist*) (Kant's emphasis) (II:361; [348]). This inner openness enables him to perceive the interior connection to the spirit world that other men share but cannot perceive. On this account, Swedenborg also distinguishes the outer from the inner memory, upon which the difference between the outer and the inner man is based. Outer memory belongs to us as members of the visible world. Inner memory preserves forever all the effects (including those caused by spirits) on inner sense. Swedenborg's privilege lies in the immediate availability to his consciousness of both sorts of memory, so that he already sees himself in this life in the company of spirits who for their part see him as a man. By virtue of his clarity of inner sense (concerning the otherwise obscure influences of spirits on the human soul), Swedenborg functions as a reciprocal medium between the spiritual and the material worlds, his gift lying in his access while still a man to the inner remembrance of the soul that constitutes the "book" of life.

As such, Swedenborg is a kind of two-way "oracle," translating between the immediate language of the spirits and the embodied language of living men, a faculty that enables him to travel throughout the universe without actually going anywhere (for example, by reading the thoughts of the inhabitants of distant planets). This displacement is possible because one's relative position in the spirit world differs radically from one's place in this one. In that spaceless world, proximity is a function of moral affinity rather than physical location. Thus the soul of an Indian may be next to another man in Europe, while persons dwelling corporeally in the same house may be spiritually very distant. Such genuinely elective affinities are at the same time the arms of cosmic justice: when one dies one simply becomes conscious of the company — good, bad, or indifferent — that, spiritually speaking, one already keeps (II:362–63; [348–49]).

Swedenborg claims to enact the fantasy of immediate community, of the abolition of physical distance, that Kant's earlier cosmology had toyed with. He is chimerically the stationary cosmopolite that Kant, the "world citizen" who never stirred from Königsberg, wished literally to be and would for all practical purposes become. Moreover, Swedenborg achieves this marvel by resolving, at least apparently, the puzzling relation between inward and outwardness to which Kant calls pointed attention in part 1 of his essay. There is no space in the Swedenborgian spirit world (like the Kantian spirit world earlier described and derided). Nevertheless (in deference to the fact that relations of community must *appear* spatially, even to spirits), spiritual community exists, according to Swedenborg, in a kind of "imaginary space." Indeed, his own perception of spirits in inner sense is projected by his mind into outer, albeit imaginary spatial form, much as the mentally infirm, in Kant's earlier discussion, project their inner visions outward. Community cannot be perceived — cannot be concretely grasped, even by spirits — apart from appearances in space. It is this implication of Swedenborg's perceptual delusion that Kant seems to find especially "important" (II:364; [351]).

The uniqueness of Swedenborg's perception lies not in the kinds of images he perceives but in the way he distinguishes between (and relates images to) the inner and the outer worlds. Swedenborg's ability to distinguish
between inner and outer sense hinges not, as for normal consciousness, on
the absence in the former and presence in the latter of a spatial component,
but rather on a distinction between "inner and outer memory," a distinction that proves to depend, in turn, on the difference between thoughts
that are eternally present (like a "completed book") and those that come
and go. To communicate spiritually (through the internal world) is to have
access to all that has every happened to inner sense and all that will ever
happen. To put it another way, Swedenborg replaces a distinction that
turns on the presence or absence of spatial reference, with one that turns
on the (temporal) difference between change and permanence.[34] He distinguishes between the outer and the inner not as we do, through a play
between inner and outer sense inseparable from embodiment, but directly.

It is therefore doubly deranging that Swedenborg imagines spirit as a
"body" in the most literal sense: a "great man" whose spiritual members
substantiate and give meaning to their material counterparts (II:365;
[352]. Buried within our knowledge of the material world lies a hidden
meaning that Swedenborg claims to be uniquely able to decipher. The key
to this mysterious language lies in the "sympathy" we experience within
ourselves between our soul and body. Just as the interworkings of our own
bodily members give indications of the various powers of the soul, so the
interworkings of the material community provide "signs" of the workings
of the spiritual whole that give it "form, activity and stability." Where
Kant's own pneumatology had suggested corporealization of the spiritual
as the basis of poetic figure (as when "red" stands for anger or "white" for
purity), Swedenborg literalizes the metaphor. Poetic figure becomes a
bodily "sign" that his open or outward inwardness makes him uniquely
capable of reading. This legible "inner meaning" constitutes, according to
Swedenborg, the kernel value (*Wert*) of all outward things. Indeed, these
outward things are themselves merely "appearances" (*Apparanz, Erschei-*
nungen) brought about by the mutual influence of spirits (II:364; [351]).
   In this image of the spirit world as greatest man (*maximus homo*), all
Swedenborg's reveries unite (II:365; [352]).[35] Each spirit finds himself "in
that place and in that apparent [*scheinbaren*] member" which accords with
his own organic function in the spiritual body. The question of "how the
soul is present in the world" (a question with which Kant was himself so
preoccupied) is answered by a mad appeal to the inner workings of the
heart or pancreas — to an image, in other words, "than which none is more
adventuresome or strange" (II:364; [352]). It is no wonder that Kant
found Swedenborg's lunacy simultaneously repulsive and attractive.

In this monstrous figure of a man (which Kant puts down to childish memory tricks) spatial relations are transposed into organic ones symbolizing the functional articulation of the spiritual community, even as our own bodies indicate (through inner sense) the functional articulation of our souls. This rendering in terms of inner (bodily) space of the "most intimate" community sets each spirit in a place that only appears to be in "immeasurable space" and which "never changes," because it is in fact only a determinate function of mutual relations and influences.[36]

In short, Swedenborg renders spiritual community visible by substituting inner for outer space (if our intimate sense of the workings of our bodies can be said to involve inner space). In this way, he figuratively swallows the world; everything without, including immeasurable space, becomes accessible within. As in Kant's earlier discussion of the stomach and the root, "opening one's insides" is ultimately indistinguishable from "bringing the outside in."

At this (pregnant) moment, and on the verge of discussing what he previously described as his "pet" interest, life after death, Kant stops short, owing both to fatigue (is he afraid to sleep?) and anxiety lest he cause some of his readers (figuratively) to abort: just as a collector of natural specimens displays both naturally formed and monstrous [*Mißgeburten*] objects of procreation, yet is careful in showing the latter "lest among the curious, there be pregnant [*schwangere*] persons who might receive a harmful impression," so Kant himself fears producing "moon-calves." In this case, however, the fear is offset by a juridical disclaimer: he has "warned readers in advance" and so cannot be burdened with the consequences. Absolving himself in this way from the weight of his readers' misbegotten pregnancies, Kant already signals the direction his own brand of spiritual displacement will later take — not from the outer to the inner worlds, but from the physical to the moral (II:366; [352–53]).[37]

In the end, Swedenborg's "private appearances" come to nothing, lacking as they do the corroboration of "living witnesses." A dreamer, his world is in principle one that cannot be shared by others. Kant would thus have "wasted his time" had he only intended to spare curious readers the need to purchase an expensive book, for they will regret having spent even this much effort only to be led back to the ignorance from which they started. In fact, however, Kant's real intention all along has been to pursue a different sort of dream. As his title already suggests, the true concern of his essay is metaphysics itself, with whom it is Kant's "fate to be in love [*verliebt zu sein*]" (II:368; [354]).

Metaphysics (who has been stingy in her favors toward Kant) offers two sorts of profit (*Vorteile*). The first, in which she usually deceives our "hopes," promises to satisfy desirous reason by revealing the "hidden properties of things": "The shades/shadows, like light wind and very similar to fleeting sleep, three times escaped the hand that vainly grasped toward them."[38]

The second sort of profit, more commensurate with human nature, consists in "setting boundaries for human reason" (and thus—if one extends Kant's metaphor—in modestly desisting from leading men on.) Such a "science of boundaries" would recognize whether "the tasks at hand are within the limits of human knowledge," determining "its relation to the concepts of experience upon which our judgment must always support itself." Metaphysics, in short, secures the "fundament" about which Kant earlier expressed no small anxiety.

In his insistence on the boundary-setting function of metaphysics and in his linking of that function to the dependence of human knowledge on "concepts of experience," Kant anticipates his famous critical stance. What remains emphatically "precritical" is his failure to resolve the problem of the relation between the a priori (or dogmatic) and the a posteriori (or historical). What is still lacking is any intimation of his later position concerning the categories (or a priori concepts of experience) and the a priori forms of intuition. Kant has yet to integrate his own empirical realism (or the notion that human knowledge requires data from sensible experience) with the transcendentalism that insists on the "ideality of space and time." Idealism (of which he accuses Swedenborg) remains for Kant a radical derangement rather than an answer and a cure. In its reconciliation of "idealism" and "realism," then, Kant's later, critical position will in some sense combine the two metaphysical tendencies here described—one modest and defensive, the other bent on "conquering" another world. Without an openness to this latter impulse, without the "ecstatic" and seductive intimation of a (possible) world beyond the bounds of sense, there can be no awareness of the "transcendental" limits of experience. As Hegel would later insist, recognition of a boundary presupposes a perspective or viewpoint beyond it.[39]

In *Dreams,* Kant remains content merely to suggest the boundaries, to an extent sufficient to spare the reader the trouble of seeking data from a "world other than the one in which he senses [*empfindet*]." In so doing, Kant has "wasted his time in order to gain it" and "deceived the reader in order to be of use to him" (II:368; [354]).[40] Returning to the theme of temporal and spatial economy, Kant defends his own learned fraud before the bar of human utility. Though he offers no new knowledge, he has destroyed the illusion that "inflates" (*aufblähet;* compare *blähen,* to cause wind) reason and "fills up the place in reason's narrow space" that wisdom and useful lower instruction (*Hinterweisung*) might occupy.

The "small country," "intimate knowledge" of whose borders Kant has just linked with the proper and/or proprietary concerns of metaphysics, is now associated with an intimate space indeed. Kant combats the inflationary charms of metaphysics gone awry with a fortitude ("Courage, gentlemen, I see land!") that is truly intestinal. In his figurative purgation of reason's "narrow space," the boundaries and borders under dispute are curiously reversed. The realm of contestable space by which he previously defined the (external) world of sense is figuratively rechanneled and absorbed into a kind of inner chamber, in which reason is called upon to resist (on pain of cramping) its own tendencies toward self-inflation (or engorgement) (*Überfüllung*).[41]

Nevertheless, the wearied reader is immediately brought back to earth (*Boden*). Where Kant once walked "with Demokritus, in empty space," he would now "fold his silky wings" and so return, it seems, to the wormish state that (like the serpent,[42] who was condemned to walk on his belly?) keeps to low ground. Once the "styptic"[43] power of self-knowledge contracts our wings, we should content ourselves with regarding that ground as the place to which we are assigned and so by "holding fast to utility" find satisfaction (II:368; [355]).

Thus self-knowledge implies acceptance of our wormlike condition (albeit as worms who dream of becoming butterflies). The deeroticizing and demystifying acceptance of our own bodily envelope and its confining, yet grounded, space proves crucial to our own mental health. But the difficulty of locating this space (and with it the hinge between the outer and inner worlds) remains. The problem of "how the soul is present in the world" is to this extent inseparable from Kant's own pneumatic metaphors. The alimentary/pulmonary canal, with its blurring of stomach and root, inner and outer space, is man reduced to his most wormlike. The only answer Kant is here prepared to give clings to "utility," or the prudent husbanding and investment of one's own (bodily) force.

VI. "Practical Conclusion"

Kant's "practical conclusion" returns to the sober, less figurative language of a moral tract. Where learnedness indulges curiosity, setting no limits to it other than impossibility, wisdom chooses among innumerable tasks only that which it is "laid upon humanity" to solve because it is a matter of genuine use. Thus vain science, chastened by experience (Kant's own?) comes round to a position of Socratic sufficiency. So long as an impossible knowledge is sought, the pleasure that accompanies the extension of knowledge will make it seem a duty, and deliberate contentedness will appear as foolish opposition to the ennoblement (*Veredelung*) of our nature. Still, science may finally arrive at "determining the limits set for it by human nature":

Questions about spiritual nature, freedom and predestination, and the future state, etc., initially bring into motion all the forces of understanding, and through their excellence draw men into the rivalry of speculation. . . . But should this investigation develop into a philosophy that judges its own proceedings, and that knows not merely objects alone, but objects in relation to human understanding, then the boundaries are drawn closer together, and marking stones are laid so that in future investigation can never digress outside its proper district. (II:369; [356])

In this way, the "limbus" of vain speculation is gradually driven out beyond the "horizon [*Gesichtskreise*] of man." A fully bounded space has no threatening fissures, no openings for human waywardness. The internal geography of the previous section is thus projected outward and (once again) reversed. What reason has to fear is not congestion but release, not balloonlike bloating but the empty air that bears balloons aloft. The internal wind of Kant's earlier discussion is now a phantom to be purged or expelled to some *intermundia* beyond the human orbit.

And indeed, it now appears that the radically internal and radically external are, to the extent that they are both inaccessible to human reason, interchangeable. What is "beyond the horizon of man" is precisely identical with the (inner) ground or cause of things. In relations of cause and effect, substance and action, philosophy can dissolve and simplify complex appearances. But when it comes to "fundamental relations," philosophy has no more business. *How* something can be a cause, or possess a force, cannot be understood by reason; *that* something is a cause or has a force must be taken from experience.

Yet experience makes this connection in a "non-arbitrary way," in (of all things) the felt action of mind on body. "I well know that thought and will move my body, but I can never reduce this appearance, as a simple experience, to another appearance through analysis [*Zergliederung;* literally, "dismemberment"]; thus I can recognize but not understand [*einsehen;* literally, see into] it" (II:370; [356]).

This exemplary experience of differentiated unity is the quintessential "synthesis" (the opposite of analysis or "dismemberment") upon which Kant's later thought will build. Embodied consciousness is the mysterious whole we recognize but whose foundation we cannot penetrate. "That my will moves my arm is not more intelligible to me than if somebody said to me that he could hold back the moon in its orbit."[44] The difference is that I experience one, "while the other has never come within the range of my sensation" (II:370; [356–57]). I recognize changes "in myself" of a kind other than that which makes up my concept of body (and is, presumably, not "in myself"). But whether this (inner) being might exist and think

without being connected to a body cannot be decided, since our only access to the nature of such a being is via (bodily) experience.

Concern with the question of the community of mind and matter thus
leads Kant back to a concern with immortality. Alluding to Socrates' example of bodily action in the *Phaedo,* Kant draws the apparently opposite
conclusion: all judgments concerning human immortality are fictions (*Erdichtungen*) less useful than the hypotheses of natural science.[45]

Such hypotheses are useful because they can be proven or disproven
given "time which brings experience." But experience must be more than
idiosyncratic. Where "pretended experiences cannot be subsumed under
laws of experience accepted by most men," it only goes to show irregularity
in the historical testimony of the senses (as in the case of ghost-seeing).

Proof of the soul's immortality, however, proves to be unnecessary as
well as impossible. Self-important philosophers pretend that such knowledge is required as a motive (*Bewegungsgrund*) for virtue on earth. But true
wisdom does not exceed the means at the command of everyman. The
subtlest speculations of scholars circle back to the conclusions of a quiet
and unprejudiced mind. The simplicity of the heart furnishes immediate
moral precepts that do not require us to "fix our machinery to the other
world" for the sake of moving man here (II:372; [358]). The moral translation of Kant's earlier "pneumatology" is a lasting residue, even after the
pneumatology itself dissolves. The ethico-democratic credo of righteous
nobility (which is both more in accord with human nature and morally
purer) bases expectation of the future on "the sentiment of a well disposed
soul" rather than basing its good conduct on expectation of a world to
come: "there probably has never lived an upright [*rechtschaffene*] soul who
was able to bear the thought that with death everything comes to an end,
and whose noble mind had not aspired to/raised up [*sich erhoben*] the hope
of the future." We lift ourselves up not on the wings of a false and idle
knowledge, but through a righteous willingness to labor. (II:373; 359)[46]

In his correspondence with Moses Mendelssohn, Kant called *Dreams* a
"volatile" (*flüchtig*) sketch,[47] composed while he was in a state of conflict
and printed[48] sheet by sheet in a way that made it difficult to anticipate the
argument in advance.[49] As such, *Dreams* is a work that, by Kant's own
admission, defies the unity of mind — the planful purposiveness — that can
be attributed to his other publications. In writing it Kant was of two (or
more) minds, at once in earnest and in jest. The ambiguity of tone that
Mendelssohn complained of Kant defended as the honest outgrowth of
his own lack of intellectual resolution.

Given these caveats, reading the essay is somewhat less like analyzing a conventional treatise, somewhat more like interpreting a dream. The vola- tility or flightiness of Kant's thought, which takes here an exceptionally witty turn, is striking in itself, suggesting what he will later call the "play of genius" more than the deliberate and ponderous course of reasoned judgment. In short, *Dreams* is as close as Kant ever got to publishing what he would call a work of art.

But it is not only (or particularly successful) art. *Dreams* is instead a sort of hybrid, whose unity derives neither from "nature speaking through genius" nor from supremely self-conscious reflection but from a problem that reaches to the heart of our communal experience. *Dreams* is the essay Kant wrote while he was struggling most explicitly with the problem of "how the soul is present in the world," that is, with the position of man himself. The body is a walking root through/by which the mind opens into and gains purchase on the world.

The inward projection of a "spirit world" is an attractive "fiction" that allows us to have our communal cake without being swallowed by it too. At the same time, however, Kant's many punning references to spirit's windy counterpart and/or equivalent suggests the disturbing reversibility of the boundaries he means to draw.[50] Mind defines itself, if at all, in the space (neither empty nor full) that distinguishes one sort of spirit from the another.

Here, then, is one source for the fundamental synthesis (as opposed to dismemberment) on which Kant will build; the "identity of identity and difference" that the German Idealists later take as their standard and goal has its seat in Kant's understanding of the duplicity of human conscious- ness, which both excludes the body and depends on it (so far as conscious- ness can tell) in the most intimate of ways. Kant responds by striving to replace nature's leading strings with self-imposed bonds, that is, by closing or driving out the empty spaces, release into which might make us ridicu- lous; in other words, by finding freedom in adherence to the law. The recurrent theme of ridicule against metaphysics' erotic pretensions is, as Kant admits, self-ridicule; not only a defense shield against the ridicule of others, but also a talisman to ward off seductive attractions that lead no- where and worse. The reduction of spirit to wind is erotic reverie in re- verse, in which self-induced disgust/nausea provides the deflationary cure. *Dreams,* in short, as Kant remarked to Mendelssohn, is a "cathartic."[51]

At the same time, Kant's anger with the inflated pretensions of meta- physics extends beyond himself to the profession of philosophers, who, being less honest lovers than himself, impose their vanity upon the gullible many. The plea for intellectual integrity thus combines with a moral/intel- lectual defense of the many against the overweening and ungrounded pride of the few. The resigned composure of the truly wise is almost indistin-

guishable from the virtue available to all honest men. The only difference
in value between wise and merely virtuous simplicity lies in the ability of
the former to see through sophisticated lies. It is this negative capacity
that makes metaphysics essential, as Kant told Mendelssohn, to the future
happiness of mankind.

In a Rousseauian vein that echoes his famous confession in the *Remarks,*
Kant insists on linking his own zetetic turn with a moral repositioning
(Rousseau "turned him round/set him right"). But the deeper source of
this double adjustment is, one suspects, the possibilities it made available
for community conceived as a purely substantiating (rather than equivo-
cally threatening) sort of whole. In moral community one escapes entirely
from the need to confront the disturbingly reversible boundaries that define our commerce in and with the material world. The ascetic price of this
escape (which Nietzsche was not the first to note) was one that Kant was
more than willing to pay, for reasons suggested above. But Kant has yet to
complete his moral flight. Before translation from the spirit to the moral
world can take effect, the dream of intelligible worldhood must be laid
definitively to rest. Only then will the relation between morality and obligation, on the one hand, and utility and prudence, on the other, fully
resolve itself.

6   Community in Theory and Practice

The role of the concept of community in Kant's critical thought has not, generally speaking, received the attention it deserves. In this chapter I consider that role anew, in light of the significance of community in Kant's thought as a whole. This inquiry will help clarify Kant's critical position and in particular the (frequently misunderstood) relation between his "transcendental idealism" and his "empirical realism." It will also bring to light themes unifying Kant's critical theory and practice that are often overlooked.

Rousseau, by Kant's own account, "set him upright/aright" by furnishing a new model of spiritual worldhood that is morally, rather than theoretically, accessible. The key to that new model is the concept of a community of free and equal wills, and hence a moral whole (the idea of the perfect republic) whose principle of morally necessary reciprocity defines each member both as an individual and as immediately united with the rest. This new, autoerotic "idea," projected by human reason out of its very freedom, supplanted Kant's earlier effort to approach the divine idea metaphysically — an effort undone by, among other things, its implicit spiritual (and erotic) passivity.

But Kant was not long content with the theoretical agnosticism that Rousseau counseled. A "great light," which dawned around 1769, seems to have requickened his speculative hopes. This new light — which centrally consists in his discovery of the ideality of time and space[1] — makes the world's possibility newly accessible to us, theoretically as well as morally, effectively opening the way to Kant's critical philosophy.[2]

I. Community and the Critical Philosophy

THE INAUGURAL DISSERTATION

The first work to appear after the dawning of that light was the *Inaugural Dissertation* (*On the Form and Principles of the Sensible and Intelligible World*). A world, it tells us, is a whole — a unity with parts — that is not itself part of larger whole. It is informed by a principle of reciprocal coordination, which alone satisfies the dual requirement that the matter(s) that make up the world be joined *necessarily* (for otherwise they would constitute a mere aggregate rather than a whole),[3] and that they retain separate (inward)

133

identities (for otherwise the unity in question would be simple rather than complex, or having parts).[4] Accordingly,

> if there happened to be certain wholes consisting of substances, and if these wholes were not bound to one another by any connection, the bringing of these wholes together, a process by means of which the mind forces the multiplicity into an ideal unity, would signify nothing more than a plurality of worlds held together by a single thought.

Real worldly unity, by contrast, implies a worldly "form," consisting of the "principle of the *possible influences* of the substances which constitute the world." Such a principle is not only necessary to the very possibility of "transient" influence among substances; it is also

> *essential* to a world, [and] . . . for that reason *immutable* and not subject to any change. And this is the case, first of all, on account of a *logical ground*. For any change presupposes the identity of the subject, whereas determinations succeed one another. . . . But, above all, the same result follows because of a *real ground*. For the nature of a world, being the first internal principle of each and every one of the variable determinations which belong to its state, cannot be opposed to itself. . . . Accordingly, in any world there is a certain constant and invariable form, which, as [its] perennial principle . . . , must be regarded as belonging to its nature. (II:390–91; 381)

Many, Kant admits, believe that such inquiry is unnecessary, for they take space and time — "given in themselves" — to be that in virtue of which the multiplicity of actual things relate together as a whole. Space and time, however (Kant is now convinced), are neither *rational* nor *objective* ideas of any connection, but rather "phenomena" that "bear witness to" without "exposing" a principle of universal connection.

The distinction in origin between sensible cognition (whose "paradigm" is geometry) and metaphysics (as the "organon" of everything pertaining to understanding) allows Kant to differentiate between the *insoluble problem of totality* understood as a completed infinite series and the *rational concept of totality* implicit in the notion of worldhood in general. He is thus able (at last) to extricate himself from the "thorny" question on which earlier efforts to represent totality — a totality implicit in the notion of a world — inevitably foundered (II:392; 382).[5] (Not incidentally, he is also able partly to resolve a related and for him equally long-standing problem concerning the relation between metaphysics and geometry.)[6]

Kant's recognition of the ideality and subjectivity of space and time, in other words, allows him to refer the universal connection of things — insofar as the world of appearances is concerned — to a ground that is human rather than divine. This does not, however, detract from the reality of said world inasmuch as the connection is characterized (in ways he has yet fully to work out) by the necessity of law.[7]

With respect to the intelligible world, one must immediately add, Kant is less forthcoming, if not in some ways downright misleading.[8] On the one hand, the form of any world is said to require a principle of possible interaction (or *commercium*) among a plurality of substances—a principle that cannot be given by their mere existence but must be referred (if the connection is to be "real" rather than merely "sympathetic") to their common cause or ground. In the case of the sensible world, that ground is evidently furnished by us. In the case of the intelligible world (the world of things in themselves), it is furnished by God. And yet Kant is remarkably vague on the question of whether we can have theoretical knowledge of God's existence.[9] It is tempting to conclude that already for Kant the (more) humanly relevant aspect of intelligible worldhood is not theoretical but moral.[10] In any case, Kant admits that we cannot conceive the form of a real (as opposed to sympathetic or harmonious) interaction among substances[11]—though this does not, Kant adds, rule out the full "acceptability" of *influxus physicus* (rightly understood) on other grounds.[12]

THE *CRITIQUE OF PURE REASON*

Generations of scholars have puzzled over Kant's claim to be both a "transcendental idealist" and an "empirical realist." Almost from the beginning, readers have tended to regard Kant's self-ascription as a kind of dilemma, only one of whose horns can be safely grabbed. Attention to community as an ongoing problem for Kant can shed helpful light—or so it is the burden of the following to suggest—on a claim that many regard as paradoxical at best, unintelligible at worst.

To state my argument briefly: Kant is able, by giving up on knowledge of things in themselves, to explain how real connection among substances (and with it, worldly knowledge or experience) is possible.[13] So long as one regards the objects of our knowledge as things in themselves (per Kant's own early efforts) there is no way (other than moral) to understand how one thing can stand in necessary but nonlogical relation to another: no way, in other words, to explain the "*fact*" (as he puts it in the essay on negative quantities) "*that because something is, something else is*" or "*because something is, something else is canceled* [*aufgehoben*]."[14] It is only when one understands objects as constituting a whole whose reciprocally binding principle is grounded in the mind that this problem of necessary connection (as the *Dissertation* already to some extent anticipates) can be overcome. But this in turn requires that the objects not be determined "in themselves" but only as "appearances," that is (and here the *Critique* breaks new ground), only in relation to all other objects that together constitute the totality of (one's own) possible experience.[15]

Kant's realism, in short, does not lie in an assertion of the independent existence of the objects of our knowledge but rather in his claim that we find ourselves in a world to whose lawful bonds we too are (therefore) subject. Indeed (contrary to the expectations of common sense), to insist upon the independent existence of the objects of our knowledge is precisely to rule out the possibility of our coexisting with them in any sort of knowable worldly connection.[16]

At the same time, Kant is at pains to show that this doctrine of appearances is not the crude idealism that treats the outer world as an epiphenomenon of inner perception. The inner transcendental ground to which he refers the necessity governing appearances lacks sensible content; hence his idealism avoids reducing outer thing to inner perception (a reduction that, as we have seen, he consistently resisted). Instead, he links real (or worldly) connectedness with the synthetic a priori functions of judgment, which, as the "Transcendental Deduction" attempts to show, is bound up with the transcendental unity of consciousness. In place of his early twofold distinction between inner perception and outer appearance, he asserts a threefold distinction between the phenomenal world, empirical consciousness (with its inclusion on equal terms of *both* outer and inner sense), and the transcendental self. Without that self, which here plays a role Kant once reserved to God, the determinate interplay of outwardness and inwardness that constitutes "experience" would not be possible.[17]

Kant thus means to accomplish two things: *first,* to show that realism (of the worldly sort that matters to him) entails idealism, albeit of a special kind; *second,* to distinguish his own realism-friendly idealism from the empirical or dogmatic idealism of Berkeley and Descartes. That second effort is especially evident in the second edition, in which Kant found himself compelled to respond to readers' confusion on this very point.[18]

In short, the existence of external objects (as appearances) is no less obvious than the existence of oneself, both following upon the "immediate witness of [one's] self-consciousness" (A/371).[19] Kant is a realist by "disposition" even before he is a realist by philosophical conviction.[20] The central problem for him is not to demonstrate that objects other than ourselves exist (something he never genuinely doubts) but to explain their real connection as parts of a world to which we knowingly belong. This key dimension of the first *Critique* is often lost sight of, even by those who read it mainly as a rejoinder to Hume. What is neglected in such discussions is the question of why Hume should have mattered so much to Kant. The answer is that Kant was already long preoccupied with the question of worldly necessity, whose problematic character Hume did not so much reveal as help Kant better understand.

Placing the *Critique of Pure Reason* in the context of Kant's lifelong concern with the problem of worldly knowledge not only puts one in a better position to understand the *Critique*'s general aim, it also helps reveal the importance of the concept of "community" to some of that work's key arguments. Specifically, worldly interaction, the relation between inner and outer sense, and the unifying function of transcendental synthesis stand together in a new and clearer light once it is recognized that all are instances of "community" in a variety of related senses.

The Analogies of Experience

General neglect of the importance of the role of community in the first *Critique* no doubt stems in part from Kant's own presentation. Community is thematically treated only in the relatively brief discussion of the Third Analogy, to which commentators tend, in Paul Guyer's words, to give "short shrift."[21] Furthermore, for readers unfamiliar with Kant's earlier work, the argument of the Third Analogy is especially (and needlessly) opaque.

Notions such as "reciprocal causation" and "reciprocal determination" strike many modern readers as anachronistic and/or hopelessly confused. Certainly, the role of the concept of community in the *Critique* — as compared with the *Inaugural Dissertation* — seems much reduced. In the *Dissertation,* community (or reciprocal interaction) figures as the formal principle of worldhood as such. In the *Critique,* by way of contrast, it shares with eleven other a priori categories the role of "making experience possible." As Guyer has argued, however, this appearance of diminished importance is deceiving. For one thing, "community" is not just any category, but a category of *relation;* it therefore reaches to the heart of the question of how *objective* experience is constituted. For a second, community is not just *any* category of relation, but, as Kant makes clear, their summary and culmination.[22]

The principle of the Analogies is: "Experience is possible only through the representation of a necessary connection of perceptions" (A/176 = B/218).[23] This principle can be usefully compared with those applicable to the "quantitative" category types that precede it, that is, the principles of intuition and perception, which respectively establish the extensive magnitude of all intuitions and the intensive magnitude of the "real that is an object of sensation" (A/116 = B/207).

Kant adds in a note:

> All combination (*conjunctio*) is either composition (*compositio*) or connection (*nexus*). The former is the synthesis of the manifold when its constituents do not necessarily belong to one another. For example, the two triangles into which a square is divided by

> its diagonal do not necessarily belong to one another. Such also is the synthesis of the *homogeneous* in everything which can be *mathematically* treated. This synthesis can itself be divided into that of *aggregation* and that of *coalition,* the former applying to *extensive* and the latter to *intensive* quantities. The second mode of combination (*nexus*) is the synthesis of the manifold so far as its constituents *necessarily belong to one another,* as, for example, the accident to some substance, or the effect to the cause. It is therefore synthesis of that which, though *heterogeneous,* is yet represented as combined *a priori.* (B/201 n)

The crucial element in that synthesis—which applies to what he tellingly calls "experience"—is the representation of constituents as heterogenous and yet "necessarily belonging together." This heterogenous kinship involves, in turn, both the *"physical* connection of the appearances with one another, and their *metaphysical* connection in the *a priori* faculty of knowledge."[24]

The argument of the Analogies is roughly as follows: experience—as distinguished from mere perception—involves the determination of objects in time. To be an object of experience, in other words, is to have a fixed temporal position vis à vis every other possible object of experience. Now time is the form of intuition that all our perceptions share. But the subjective succession in time of our perceptions cannot by itself determine such an objective temporal order of appearances. For that subjective sequence furnishes no criterion that would allow us to distinguish cases in which perception B follows necessarily upon perception A (in Kant's famous example, the perception of the boat downstream that follows on the perception of a boat upstream) from those in which the order of perception is indifferent—our perception of the house roof that can either follow or precede our perception of the door. In short, the subjective sequence of perceptions is by itself insufficient to determine the objective order of experience, which assigns each object a fixed temporal position. Without something to bind down our perceptions in this way, our awareness, Kant says, would be something less even than a dream.

The main task of the Analogies is to lay out the a priori principles which must (so to speak) be added to perception to make possible the "necessary connection of perceptions" required for experience. Experience here plays a role similar to that of worldly knowledge in the *New Elucidation:* both involve determinate relations of coexistence and succession that link the related entities "necessarily."

One obvious difference is that whereas Kant earlier sought that relation among substances in themselves, he now limits his inquiry to appearances. Thus, according to the First Analogy, the substance whose permanence experience assumes is to be construed, not as "thing in itself," but merely as a necessary correlate of succession and coexistence.

The Second Analogy addresses itself to the requirements of such determinate succession. That we are indeed able to distinguish objective sequences of events from the subjective sequence of our perceptions can only be owing to an a priori rule which establishes a relation of necessity such that perception A and perception B are judged irreversible. We experience a perception of a boat upstream followed by a perception of a boat downstream as an objective *event* only insofar as we connect them according to a rule that tells us that the perceptions *had* to happen in this order, a rule that therefore cannot derive from the perceptions themselves. Kant calls this rule the "principle of succession in time, in accordance with the Law of Causality."

According to that rule, "all alterations take place in conformity with the law of the connection of cause and effect" (B/232); or, according to what the first edition calls the "principle of production," "everything that happens, that is, begins to be, presupposes something upon which it follows according to a rule" (A/189). (The vexed question of whether Kant is entitled to proceed from necessary order of succession to cause and effect can, for purposes of the present discussion, be set aside.)

Which brings us to the Third Analogy, whose principle of coexistence, "in accordance with the law of reciprocity or community [*Wechselwirkung oder Gemeinschaft*]," states that "All substances, insofar as they can be perceived to coexist in space, are in thoroughgoing reciprocity" (A/211 = B/256–57).[25] Kant's basic argument here is, once again, that the temporal relation of objects cannot be established — given the necessity involved — on the basis of perception alone, but presupposes the employment of an a priori rule. In the case of temporal succession, the rule was that of causation. In the present case — coexistence — the rule is that of interactive reciprocity.

The question is how a succession of perceptions (and a plurality of perceptions can never, according to Kant, be simultaneous)[26] can give rise to knowledge of things as coexistent. It might seem from Kant's previous examples of the house and ship that *lack* of a rule binding down our perceptions in a particular order would suffice to establish that their respective objects coexist, as with the door and roof, which we can perceive in either order. In fact, however, regularity is as much a part of judgments of coexistence as of judgments of causal or objective succession. Like knowledge of an objective succession of things, knowledge of their objective coexistence presupposes a *rule,* which in this case establishes the necessary indifference (or "reciprocity") of the order of our perceptions, just as, in the case of succession, a rule established their necessary order. Without such a rule, we have merely an apprehension of alternating perceptions (roof . . . door

... door ... roof), an apprehension that can only reveal (*angeben*) that "one perception is in the subject when the other is not there, and vice versa," but not that "two objects are coexistent, that is, that if one object exists, the other also exists at the same time, and that this is necessarily the case, so that our perceptions can follow from each other reciprocally" ([A/211 = B/257]).

The crucial element involved in knowledge of things as coexistent is, then, a certain rule, independent of the perceptions themselves, according to which each determines and is determined by the other reciprocally. Hence there is required "a concept of understanding [*Verstandesbegriff*] of the reciprocal succession of the determinations of these externally coexistent things, in order to say that the reciprocal succession of perceptions is objectively grounded, and coexistence thereby represented as objective" (A/211 = B/257). Coexistence, in other words, cannot be represented without an a priori concept of the reciprocal determination of substances.[27] Such a relation between two substances, such that one contains the ground of the other's determinations, is called influence, and when it is mutual, community or reciprocal action (*Wechselwirkung*). Thus the coexistence of objects in space cannot be known, save on the presupposition of their reciprocal interaction; and this rule is in turn a condition of the possibility of things themselves as objects of experience (A/211 = B/258).

Kant can at last make unproblematic use of the concept of substantival interaction, because the entities in question are no longer "in themselves" but only "in appearance." There is thus no need to explain how a substance can "inwardly determine and be determined by" something other than itself; for the determinations in question are no longer (metaphysically) inward. The concept of substantival interaction (along with the principle of judgment with which it is associated) now provides the ground, once reserved to the humanly incomprehensible divine schema, for that "real relation" by virtue of which things "coexist," that is, are simultaneous members of a common world.

That this world is one of experience (or appearances) rather than things in themselves allows the real wholeness essential to a world to be humanly conceivable.[28] A world, as Kant defined it in the *Dissertation,* is a parted unity that is not itself a part. What makes our knowing the world seem problematic is that it involves (in the useful language of the *Dissertation*) not merely a *whole of representation* but a *representation of a whole* (II:390; 381).

But how are the necessitating links that distinguish a world from a mere aggregate to be presented or contained in thought? Logical or analytic entailment will not work. For from the mere concept of a substance that exists in isolation, nothing follows logically, or by conceptual necessity, with regard to any other substance. As Kant later puts it:

the category of community according to its possibility is not to be conceived at all through mere reason alone; thus the objective reality of this concept is not to be comprehended as possible without intuition and outside of space. For how is one to think it possible, given the existence of more than one substance, that from the existence of one to that of another something (as effect) should reciprocally be able to follow; so that because in one something exists there must also be something in the other which cannot be understood on the basis of the latter's existence alone? For this would require community, which is inconceivable (*nicht begrifflich*) among things each of which is, through its substance, entirely isolated. Thus Leibniz, in attributing community to the substances of the world, as thought through the understanding alone, made use of the mediation of a Godhead. For it rightly seemed to him inconceivable that community should arise from their existence alone.[29]

For Kant, by way of contrast, community is now entirely comprehensible (and without resorting to the mediation of a Godhead) because the substances in question are appearances informed a priori and synthetically:

> We can, however, make the possibility of community (of substances as appearances) entirely comprehensible [*faßlich*] to ourselves, if we represent them to ourselves in space and thus in outer intuition. For this already contains a priori in itself formal outer relations as conditions of the possibility of the real (in communal action and reaction). ([B/292–93])[30]

Our ability to grasp the possibility of a dynamical community of substances itself depends on the synthetic character of human cognition. In so claiming, Kant radically internalizes the line of worldly demarcation; the inner/outer boundary of his earlier work gives way to the twin dualities of form and matter on the one hand, thought and intuition on the other, dualities whose hidden root is as mysterious as the "epigenesis"—the sexual production of a living being—to which Kant metaphorically compares it.[31] In the averted gaze of that stabilizing removal, attempting to conceive the world ceases (somehow) to be dizzying.

"Community" of Mind and Matter: The "Paralogisms"

Physical Monadology presented matter as the phenomenal (or outer) aspect of simple substances in a relation of community (substances, in other words, reciprocally determining one another inwardly). On such an understanding, the mind's embodiment was seen to be a necessary—if strictly phenomenal—aspect of worldly consciousness. This understanding figured the position of the embodied mind as the point into which a substance's sphere of activity can be infinitely compressed without dismemberment. The critical philosophy reconfigures *within* appearance the distinction between inner and outer sense, while at the same time showing that this realm is no less *real* for being merely phenomenal.

In a section called "Paralogisms of Transcendental Psychology" Kant discusses community in the explicit context of the relation between matter and mind.[32] The "A" version proceeds approximately as follows: three "dialectical questions" concerning the community (*Gemeinschaft*) of body and soul constitute the true (*eigentlich*) goal of rational psychology. These questions are *first*, that of the possibility of community between soul and an organized body in the life of man; *second*, that of the beginning of this community, or the soul in and before human birth; *third*, that of the end of this community, or the soul during and after death (A/384).

All the difficulties that one believes one finds in these questions, difficulties that lead to dogmatic objections that lay false claims to deep insight, rest, however, on a mere illusion. Our concern with these difficulties (bound up as they are with life, birth, and death) gives way once we acknowledge that outer objects are only appearances.[33]

What gives rise to mind/matter community as a *question* is the (seeming) heterogeneity of mind (as inward) and matter (as spatially extended). In version A Kant's dissolution of that problem of heterogeneity takes the form of an insistence that the soul (as object of inner sense) and matter are both representations. The question of community is thus referred, from the heterogenous domains of soul and "substances of a different kind outside us," to the (homogenous) connection "of the representations of inner sense with the modifications of our outer sensibility." The vexed question of community between mind in matter is reduced, in other words, to that of "how [representations of inner and outer sense] can be so connected with each other according to settled laws that they hang together in one experience" ([A/386]). Once the appearances of inner and outer sense are recognized as "mere representations in experience," we "*find nothing that is contrary to sense and which makes strange* [befremdlich] *the community of both kinds of sense*" (emphasis added).

In refuting the doctrine of physical influx (the view of ordinary understanding) transcendental idealism also dispels the "strangeness" that otherwise besets the articulation, within consciousness, of inwardness and outwardness.

> The much discussed question of the community of the thinking and the extended, freed from everything merely imagined, comes then simply to this: *how in a thinking subject outer intuition,* namely that of space (with its filling in of shape and motion), *is possible.* And this is a question which no human being can possibly answer. ([A/393])

The natural but false problem of community of mind and matter—what Kant calls the *proton pseudos*[34] of ordinary understanding—is thus replaced by the unanswerable (but no longer estranging) question of outer sense, that is, of the intrinsic openness of human consciousness.

In the "B" version of the "Paralogisms," Kant's argument takes a slightly different course. The A version had shown itself liable to an overly idealist reading. In the B version Kant does not urge, as he did in A, the homogeneity of inner and outer appearances qua mental. Instead, he reminds us that the respective objects of inner and outer sense may, for all we know, be alike in kind, making the question of the community of mind and matter merely a special case of the general question (already resolved) of the community of substances (B/427–28).

What both versions share, with their referral of the supposed community of mind and matter to the articulation, *within* consciousness, of the subjective and the objective is not an answer to the (unanswerable) question of how community of mind and matter is possible, but, instead, a means of removing the uncanniness of our experience—its capacity to "make strange." At the same time, Kant admits that "long custom" makes it difficult to dispel all at once the difficulty that we have made for ourselves.

> [I]n the end the entire self-made difficulty comes down to this: how and by what cause the representations of our sensibility stand in such interconnection that those, which we call outer intuitions, can be represented according to empirical laws as objects outside us—a question that does not in the least contain the supposed difficulty of explaining the origin of our representations from quite foreign, effective sources to be found outside us. ([A/387])

The difficulty comes down, in other words, to an explanation of how experience is possible—a question that summarizes the mission of the *Critique* in general.[35] Kant's critical project thus emerges as, among other things, a grand effort to dispel the sense of estrangement to which "common understanding" is subject (and to which Kant was himself perhaps especially disposed).[36]

A further consequence of Kant's resolution of the erstwhile problem of the community of mind and matter is the removal of the topics of birth, life, and death from the purview of rational psychology (thus eliminating the latter's positive content and agenda). Hereafter rational psychology is to be regarded not as a science, but as a discipline, concerned not with the advancement of knowledge but the avoidance of transcendental illusion (B/421).[37] (It would, however, be premature to dismiss these topics from the critical arena entirely, as will be clear when we take up the *Critique of Judgment* in later chapters.)

The "Ideal of Reason"

The concept of community plays another important role in the *Critique,* albeit indirectly. The category of *community* finds its systematic counterpart (as per the Table of Judgments) in *disjunctive judgments of relation* (the general idea being that such judgments involve a certain "community" among known constituents such that they mutually exclude each other and yet determine a totality of true knowledge (A/74 = B/99).[38]

Accordingly, disjunctive judgments also correspond to the third and last of the "fundamental syllogisms," which Kant associates with the "transcendental ideas" of reason. These ideas are, respectively, that of the complete subject (the object of "psychology"), that of the complete series of conditions (the object of "cosmology"), and that of "the absolute *unity of the series of the condition of all objects of thought in general* (the object of "theology") (A/334 = B/391). In keeping with this plan, Kant's treatment of (the illusions of) rational psychology ("The Paralogisms") and cosmology ("The Antinomy")[39] is followed by a treatment of theology ("The Ideal of Pure Reason").

In an important sense this third and final section also concerns itself (like the first section) with substance and (like the second) with the world; for what is at issue is the critical equivalent of what Kant once called the divine schema: the total complex of realities (which we can only grasp successively, in time) immediate in—or, to take a less *Spinozistic* tack—thought and/or willed by God. In a discussion that hearkens back to his *New Elucidation* and *The One Possible Basis for a Demonstration of the Existence of God,* Kant sketches out a notion of God as the *ens realisimum,* the sum total and/or source of all possibility, and thus as the condition of the complete determination of each and every thing (A/573 = B/601).[40]

Kant's general argument can be put as follows. A reality, according to the traditional terminology he here adopts, is a positive affirmation about a thing: when I say "the cat is black," "blackness" is one of its realities. Now for every reality or positive determination of a thing there is a contrary negation ("the cat is not black"). Complete determination of a thing thus presupposes the totality of all possible realities (anything that might be true of anything), along with a list of affirmations and negations (predicates) through which each thing is exhaustively determined.

Now we, whose mode of cognition is discursive, can never cognitively determine a thing exhaustively, that is, know something (in the world) completely. Still, we can *think* such complete determination in the abstract, and it is that thought which brings us to the idea of God as *ens realisimum.*

But this thought of God does not entail God's existence or even his absolute possibility. Concerning his existence (and against all so-called ontological proofs) it is enough to say, Kant argues, that existence is not a predicate (that is, what he here calls a "reality"). Concerning God's possibility, there is certainly nothing, logically speaking, standing in the way. Nothing in the idea of an *ens realisimum* is logically contradictory. But to know that something is really—not just logically—possible, more is required than logical self-consistency. For us to know that God as *ens realisimum* is possible in the latter sense, we would have to know that the (temporal and spatial) *effects* of these realities are mutually (that is, really) compatible.[41] To know that God as *ens realisimum* is *not* really possible, on the other hand, we would have to know that these effects are *not* compatible, that is, that one would "necessarily cancel out" the other. Such compatibility or incompatibility, however, could in principle only be known by a divine intelligence, for such knowledge would require an immediate and complete intuition of the infinite complex of relations among all substances, relations that we can only grasp successively and partially. Hence, the absolute possibility of God as *ens realisimum* is (for us) neither provable nor disprovable.[42]

The idea of the sum total of all possible predicates of things—what traditional rationalist metaphysics hypostatizes as the *ens realisimum*—finds its legitimate theoretical expression, Kant claims, in the idea of nature understood as the sum total of all possible experience. The divine idea is thus brought down to earth in a way humanly usable, turning the *ens realisimum* into a mere regulative ideal—the *focus imaginarius,* as it were—of our efforts to expand our empirical knowledge (A/578–82 = B/606–10).[43]

But what has this to do with community? Or is the link between community and the ideal of reason just another example of that forced symmetry of which Kant is so often accused? In anticipation, perhaps, of that very objection, Kant admitted in the opening lines of the chapter that the ideal of reason "seems even farther removed from experience" than do the ideas of rational psychology and cosmology (A/568 = B/596). Hence we might well expect the connection between the category of community and the idea to which it corresponds to be less evident than was the case with the categories of substance and causality.[44]

Still, he insists, the connection is not fanciful. The *ens realisimum* is that in which the infinite particularity of things is reconciled with their absolute unity; it is, in other words, that which "grounds" the worldly commerce of substances.[45]

The *ens realisimum* is what we are led to think when we ask (as it is the nature of reason to do) how the totality of things, both individually and collectively, is possible. The ideal of reason is thus in an important sense the culmination of the other two transcendental Ideas: for it concerns the absolute unity, not just of the thinking subject, or of the series of conditions in appearance, but of the condition of all objects of thought in general. It concerns, in other words, the absolute ground of all relations as such (A/334 ff. = B/391 ff.; A/696 f. = B/724 f.).

II. Community in Practice

We saw in an earlier chapter how Rousseau's idea of the general will inspired Kant's revolutionary moralization of the "Platonic" metaphysical ideal. On the basis of that revolution, we become knowing members (at last) of the intelligible world on the basis of our recognition of a morally necessitating principle that unites all rational beings. Through our recognition (as duty) of that reciprocally necessitating law, the possibility of commerce among substances in themselves is finally comprehensible, albeit only practically.

This law—in the later, critical elaboration, which incorporates the notion of autonomy—makes a community of things in themselves *morally* conceivable through a link no less reciprocally necessitating for being individually "self-determined" and hence "inward" in the metaphysically relevant sense. By interpreting self-determination as moral authorship, it becomes possible to comprehend a commercium of beings that are "necessary" in the special (moral) sense of being irreplaceable by an equivalent.

The Groundwork of the Metaphysics of Morals

The notion of substantival community carries an explanatory force in Kant's moral thought that has generally been overlooked.[46] Much of Kantian ethics that is frequently dismissed as "empty formality," for example, appears in a new and more compelling light when the formal grounding of the will is understood as a partial solution to the old problem of worldly possibility. The notion of the will as both self-determining and determined by a universal law (a law equally valid for every other will) enables us to think of substances that are mutually related without ceasing to be "things in themselves"—a thought that is otherwise opaque to us. Seen in this light, the moral law furnishes the "formal" principle by virtue of which each will stands in a relation of mutual determination with every other will. In determining itself autonomously, the will simultaneously constitutes itself as a member of a universal community. To put it in more traditional terms, the will, or speaking more broadly, moral personality, does not have first its essential form and then its external relations; rather, the principle of its relatedness *is* its essential form, without this fact in any way diminishing its self-subsistent identity. So conceived, the idea of moral personality resolves, albeit in a practical way, the tension between individuality and universality that would be resolved theoretically had we cognitive access to the noumenal.

The *Groundwork of the Metaphysics of Morals*, published in 1785, elaborates on that theme. According to the *Groundwork*, "everything in nature works in accordance with laws. Only a rational being has the capacity to act according its *representation* of the law, i.e., according to principles; has, that is to say, a will" (IV:412; [80]). The will represents the law, not as object of theoretical cognition, but as a necessary ground of action. As such, the moral law furnishes what Leibniz's monadology failed to supply (and what the younger Kant sought in vain): a *grounded* account of the necessary or rule-governed character of the relationship *among* self-subsistent entities.

Kant's subsequent discussion of man (or any other rational being) as end in itself furnishes the "matter" that allows him to characterize the moral law, not only as universally binding, but also as determining the will "objectively."[47] By objectivity, Kant has in mind a necessary connection analogous to that which distinguishes our merely subjective perceptions from the objective experience we have in common. As ends in themselves, rational beings share directly or indirectly (as a matter of categorical necessity) in one another's ends. They share directly in one another's ends when those ends are materially the same. They share indirectly when they desist from using other rational beings as means alone.[48] The ensuing ideal (the so-called kingdom of ends) makes it possible to conceive "of a whole of all ends (a whole both of rational beings as ends in themselves and also of the personal ends that each may set before himself) in systematic connection" (IV:433; [101]). As such it is a moral analogue to what Kant once called divine schema of creation, that is, a nontemporal, nonspatial version of community *cum commercium*. Although we cannot (like God) immediately intuit the connection of substances as final purposes, we can be morally certain — through our representation of the moral law and the reciprocal system of ends and means that it invokes — of the possibility of commerce among substances understood as things in themselves.

Like natural necessity, which consists in the lawful relation of material bodies, practical necessity consists in the lawful relation of rational beings (IV:434; [102]). The difference is that the latter necessity binds individuals together not only externally (as with natural necessity) but also inwardly and essentially: "from the idea of the *dignity* of a rational being, who obeys no law other than the one it gives itself," reason relates the maxim of each will, both to itself and to every other will.

Dignity (*Würde*),[49] which Kant identifies with absolute (or "inner") value (*Wert*), as distinguished from value that is only relative (or "external"), furnishes reason with an immediate "practical motive." Values are inner causes of action. The crucial question, where man is concerned, is whether these causes are to be merely springs (*Triebfeder*) or genuine motives (*Bewegungsgründe*). All values are determined "by the law" (IV:436; 103). The question is, to which law do we submit? "The kingdom of ends is possible only through . . . self-imposed rules," while nature is possible "only through laws concerned with causes whose action is necessitated from without" (IV:438; [106]). If man were not worthy to be a member of the kingdom of ends "he would have to be regarded as subject merely to the law of nature — the law of his own needs" (IV:439; [106]). It is this need, indeed, that renders him fungible, where nature is concerned, that is, exchangeable for an equivalent. Man thus faces a choice: the external law of nature, which can only establish values that are relative; or the moral law, which establishes a value that is absolute. Since "all values are determined by the law," law-giving itself must have an "unconditioned, incomparable worth," and autonomy is thus the ground of worth (*Grund der Würde*) for every rational being (IV:436; 103). In choosing between heteronomy and autonomy, we insert ourselves in one or another of two radically different sorts of communal economy.[50]

Kant had long characterized substantival commerce as a reciprocal alteration (*Veränderung*) or exchange (*Wechsel*) of accidental states — an exchange, in other words, between subjects not themselves (ex)changed[51] (much as traders in a marketplace trade goods (or "properties") without themselves being traded).[52] This market metaphor is made explicit — and literalized — in Kant's moral rendering of the intelligible world[53] as an economy in which individuals reckon absolutely:[54]

> Everything in the kingdom of ends has either a *price* [*Preis*] or a *dignity* [*Würde*]. If something has a price, then something else can be put [*gesetzt*] in its place as an *equivalent* [*Äquivalent*].
>
> That which is lifted up [*erhaben ist*] above all price such that it allows of no equivalent, has a dignity. That which refers to universal human inclinations and needs has a *market price* [*Marktpreis*]. That which, even without presupposing a need, conforms to a certain taste, that is, a delight in the mere purposeless play of our mental forces, has an *affection price* [*Affectionspreis*]. But that which constitutes the only condition under which something can be an end in itself has not a merely relative value, that is a price, but an inner value, that is a *dignity.*
>
> Now morality is the only condition under which a rational being can be an end in himself; for only in this way is it possible to be a law-giving member of a kingdom of ends. Thus virtue [*Sittlichkeit*], and humanity to the extent that it is capable of it, is that which alone has dignity. Skill and diligence in work have a market price. Wit, lively imagination and humor have an affection price. But faithfulness in promises and kindness out of principle (not instinct) have an inner value. Absent these, neither nature nor art can set anything in their place. For their value does not consist of effects . . . but attitudes of mind [*Gesinnungen*], i.e., the maxims of the will. . . . This estimation gives us to know as a dig-

nity the value of such a kind of thinking [*Denkungsart*], and sets it infinitely above all price, with which it cannot be brought into reckoning and comparison without, so to speak, violating [*vergreifen*][55] its holiness. (IV:434–35; [102–3])

The quantitative "categories" of unity, multiplicity, and totality that Kant brings to bear in his exposition of the categorical imperative are therefore more than architectonic flourishes; for the analogy between the natural and moral realms is deeply embedded in the structure of reason itself. The form of the law expresses the universality of the will and thus its unity; the matter expresses the ends of the will in all their multiplicity; while the complete determination of all the will's maxims expresses the allness or totality of its system of ends.[56]

Each moral person is an end-setting being who is himself an absolute end, that is, a being that cannot be treated as a means only. To say that moral personality is priceless, that is, that it cannot be exchanged for any equivalent, is to posit a system of beings whose law-making, end-setting capacity (or freedom) is both the source of value and its limit.

The "metaphysics of morals" can thus provide what speculative metaphysics could not—a demonstration of the possibility of an intelligible world through insight (albeit of a merely practical kind) into the essence of things, that is to say, into that which "does not alter with their external relations."[57] Dignity is the practical analogue of absolute essence, a self-subsistent (*selbstständig*) value that, unlike the substance(s) of Kant's early speculative efforts, requires no extrinsic ontological grounding.[58] It is therefore not God as Creator whom Kant here invokes but God as Judge. The possibility of the intelligible world is established on moral, not ontological, grounds. Its reality does not depend upon the creative intellect of God but the collective will of all finite rational beings, who constitute the world's (potential) members. It is thus enough to know that "a kingdom of ends would actually come into existence" if the categorical imperative "were universally followed" (IV:84; [106]). The kingdom of ends, in other words, does not exist "but can be made actual by our conduct" through the practical idea of such a kingdom (IV:436 n; 104 n).[59]

THE *METAPHYSICS OF MORALS*, PART ONE: THE *DOCTRINE OF RIGHT* (*RECHTSLEHRE*)

As a system of external relations among substantial beings, Kant's conception of right (*Recht*) bears a striking structural resemblance to his earlier physical monadology (a resemblance born out by his comparison of the juridical system of coercion to the physical principle of action and reaction) (VI:233; 58). What wills (*Willküren*) and physical monads share is a capacity to affect and be affected by each other, a capacity that presupposes their spatial community (*communio*), and original community (*communio*) of land, respectively.

Private Right and the "Transcendental Deduction"

Kant's concept of right can be thought of as the external, formal aspect of intelligible worldhood (intelligible worldhood in, so to speak, its "appearance").[60] As such, it is a system of property (understood as the medium through which wills externally relate) at once individualistic and communitarian, defining as it does the external boundaries that another will cannot penetrate without doing me injury, and conversely. The immediate authorization, in the case of such injury, of a countervailing act of coercive repulsion is the "construction" that, as Kant notes, calls to mind the principle of action and reaction.

Where those boundaries are coextensive with the limits of my body, the relation between owner and owned is, on Kant's account, "*analytic.*" For to trespass my bodily boundary is necessarily (or so Kant here assumes) to affect me "inwardly." The right to possession of one's body is thus "innate."

A complication arises, however, in those cases in which I lay claim to objects that are *not* (or are not physically in contact with) my body. Such claims must be capable of justification; for were this not the case, certain intrinsically useful things would remain unownable (*res nullius*) and hence — juridically speaking — unusable. Kant's solution is a practical "deduction" of a right to property that is neither (part of) my body nor in my physical possession.[61] The accompanying *a priori synthesis* combines original community of land (*communio fundi originaria*) with a common or communal will (*gemeine Wille*) to appropriate it separately. The upshot is a system of dynamic relations among embodied wills, a system that reconciles motion (that is, the acquisition and exchange of external property) with equilibrium — both directly (or ethically) and externally — through a system of justified "coercion."

The juridical and transcendental deductions share the synthetic function of uniting a conceptual *commercium* with an intuitive (or material) *communio.* The transcendental and juridical deductions are, indeed, explicitly contrasted and compared at VI:249; 71. As Kant there makes clear, the object can be treated juridically as a thing in itself (rather than — as in the transcendental version — as an appearance) because the requisite relation of necessity between mind and object is furnished by *right* as "a pure practical *rational concept*" of will under laws of freedom."

Similarly, Kant's classification of juridical relations under the categorical headings of *substance, causality,* and *community* (*commercium*) calls attention to the functional similarities between the general or universal juridical will (*Gemeine Wille*) and the transcendental unity of apperception. The analogy between the transcendental and juridical a priori syntheses is made more explicit in a series of unpublished preliminary versions of Kant's published argument (the so-called *Vorarbeiten zum Privatrecht*); there, after submitting juridical possession to the twelve categories of understanding, Kant addresses the "schematism of acquisition" as "translation through common will [*gemeinschaftliche Willkühr*]," an idea that makes it possible to apply the concept of right to man considered as a sensible being whose property relations involve space and time (XXIII:298–300). Common possession of the soil is the first act of "apprehension" or "taking possession" (*Besitznehmung*), whose material correlate is my "presence in space" such that objects (in the first instance, the ground on which I am placed without my will) are in a position of use. Right thus presupposes (as the elaborations of Kant's *Vorarbeiten* variously insist) our common possession of the soil, a community (*communio*) that is itself the synthesis of the idea of a united will combined with the sheer facticity of our placement, willy-nilly, on the (surface of) the earth.[62]

Right is not an immediate relation to things (for example, the soil) but a "disjunctive-universal" relation to other human beings (XXIII:323). Right emerges, from the labored pages of the *Vorarbeiten*, as the (sole) means by which we gain collective intellectual control over the soil (*Boden*) and thus bring the sheer contingency of birth, that is, my "placement on the earth without my choice [*Willkür*]," under the authority of self-made law. Only through right do we secure a necessary intellectual relation to the soil, and by extension, all other outer things: without "outer mine and yours there could be no public laws to secure to each what is his own."[63] This ideal common possession fulfills a role formally equivalent to that of the community (*communio*) of space in the "Transcendental Deduction." The connection of wills and things without contradiction is "only possible in the idea of a common will [*gemeinschaftlichen Willkühr*] in which empirical possession is willed or constituted" (XXIII:309, 311).

Kant thus designates as "very analogous" right understood as an a priori synthetic law of freedom involving our relation to objects outside us, and that theoretical (that is, empirical) "realism" which critical philosophy directs against an errant "psychological idealism" (XXIII:310–11). Just as the latter involves recognition that we are not conscious of our own existence as empirically determined in time, apart from an apprehension (*Auffassung*) of a manifold outside us (in space),

> so also, without outer objects of the will, we could not become conscious of the possession of our own determinations and the inborn right of the use of ourselves; thus we can see that the right to serve ourselves by means of outer objects is a condition of the possibility of the inner use of our will, and that an a priori right with regard to outer objects must be assumed. (XXIII:310–11)[64]

Juridical community, in short, constitutes the purely "external" relations of a morally intelligible world. *Like* the transcendental concept of community to which it corresponds, juridical community "divides" the reality of substance and synthetically establishes a binding relation (characterized as "possession") between the inward and the outward. *Unlike* the transcendental concept of community, which applies "theoretically," but only to "appearances," the juridical concept is "intelligible," or applicable to "things in themselves" — intelligible, however, only in a practical sense.

As such, the juridical concept of community resolves a central problem of Kant's early cosmology: how to comprehend the division of substance into substances, a division implicit in our experience of the world's reality. That problem is theoretically soluble, according to Kant's critical doctrine, but only by relinquishing all claims to knowledge other than knowledge of appearances. Juridical community offers another sort of solution to the problem — a solution, moreover, that applies to things in themselves, without ceasing (like the "corpus mysticum" of a purely ethical commonwealth) to be accessible to human experience. (The key to that accessibility — the juncture of the natural and the rational in the person of the human sovereign — will be taken up shortly.) As such, juridical community is as close as we can come to exposing our position as embodied, rational beings.[65]

(Sexual) Commerce and Community

It might seem that, so far as *ius privatum* is concerned, the juridical deduction exhausts the meaning of "community property." Kant, however, also associates property with community in a special sense, that is, in regard to the rights exercised by and over persons within the household.

Kant's relational categories (*substance, causality, and community*) refer juridically to *"rights over things [ius reale]," "rights against a person [ius personale],"* and *"rights over a person akin to rights over a thing [ius realiter],"* respectively. Where *ius reale* and *ius personale* have clear precedent in Roman law, the right corresponding to the concept of "community" (*ius realiter*) is, as Kant admits, a "new phenomenon [*stella mirabilis*] in the judicial sky" (VI:358; [165]).

Community property in this special and novel sense finds its ultimate material and intellectual basis in the natural fact (and necessity) of sexual community (*commercium sexuale*). What is fundamentally at issue, in the case of ownership over a person as if he/she were a thing, is the legitimation of an act that — in the course of nature (*vaga libido*) — turns persons into "fungibles" (*res fungibiles*), not only in the sense of being economically exchangeable for some equivalent (as when the [homogenous] labor of one worker is equal in value to that of another, as Karl Marx will later put it), but also in the more literal sense of dissolving the bodily boundaries that determine us as (human) individuals.[66] Hence Kant's peculiar (and notorious) comparison of sexual intercourse to cannibalism. As an act that physically "consumes" another, intercourse literally turns human beings to meat.[67]

The only way to reconcile sexual intercourse with "humanity in our person" is by subjecting it in advance to the condition of *lawful* reciprocity, that is, marriage—an institution that establishes the juridical equality of each partner in his or her capacity as owner of the other.[68] But since a person "is an absolute unity," this effectively confers a right over the entire person.[69]

The primary function of marriage is neither procreation without sin (the traditional religious view) nor provision for the next generation (the Lockean view) but the (ideal) preservation of the parties involved in the course of their (real) submission to a process of individual decomposition necessary to man's preservation *as a species*. (The rights of spouses thus exceed that of a master over a servant, whose authority specifically excludes the power to consume (*verbrauchen*) [VI:283; 101].) Parental right, for its part, derives from the parental duty stemming from the (sexual) act that brings another into the world without his/her prior (!) consent. Sexual intercourse, one might conclude, represents at its most blatant the paradox intrinsic in the notion of man as a "species-being"—that is, of "humanity" as a species-character or perfection that can only be actualized collectively.[70]

Public (*öffentlich*) Right

There is, however, a more general way in which the concept of community impinges on juridical relations—community, that is to say, not just as coordinate with substance and causality, but also as *the principle* by which *any* world is necessarily informed. Juridical community in this larger "public" sense describes the condition under which something material can be noumenally one's own. As such, it externalizes in peculiarly human terms the relations of things in themselves—relations that are not otherwise intellectually accessible. The concept of right, in other words, makes intelligible community (or noumenal *commercium*) uniquely "comprehensible" to us as rational children of the earth. Hence the centrality of the republican "Idea" to the articulation of Kant's system as a whole, a centrality we will have later occasion to examine in detail.[71]

Something is externally mine when its use by another would cause me injury (*Läsion*), even when it is not in my physical possession (VI:249; 71). But I am justified in asserting my right over a thing only when I recognize an equivalent right in others, and conversely. Intelligible possession, then, presupposes a "civil condition," that is to say, a "collective general (common) and powerful will" (*collectiv allgemeiner [gemeinsamer] und machthabener Wille*) capable of guaranteeing the lawful relation of reciprocal restraint implicit in the juridical condition (VI:256; 77).[72]

Public right is thus the sum [*Inbegriff*] of laws that require a universal promulgation to bring forth a juridical condition, that is:

> a system of laws for a people [*Volk*], that is, for a multitude of men, or for a multitude of peoples, who, standing in reciprocal influence with respect to one another, need a rightful condition under a will uniting them, [in other words] a constitution (constitutio), in order to enjoy/share in [*theilhaftig zu werden*] what is according to right. This condition of individuals of a people in relation to one another is called civil (status civilis) and the whole in relation to its own members is called the state (civitas). On account of its form, as bound together through the common interest of all to be in a juridical condition, it is called the common wealth [*gemeine Wesen*, literally "common being" or "common thing," the literal translation of *res publica*]. (VI:311; [123])

The civil condition is that systematic form whereby a multitude of interacting individuals becomes a whole.[73] The *Volk* (gens) is thus the product of the existence of a state rather than (as the German language misleadingly suggests) its source (see VI:343; 150).[74] Inasmuch as the constitution's form is constituted by laws necessary a priori through which a multitude becomes a whole, it is "the form of the state in general" (VI:313; [125])[75] The constitution is thus the "state as [the Platonic] idea." One could almost call it *the* Platonic idea, or alternatively, the only organism (or lawfully contingent whole) whose form is humanly intelligible.[76]

Plato's idea of the perfect republic, suitably revised, is that of a

> constitution allowing *the greatest possible human freedom* in accordance with laws by which *the freedom of each is made to be consistent with that of all the others*. . . . But it is not only where human reason exhibits genuine causality, and where ideas are operative causes (of actions and their objects), namely, in the moral sphere, but *also in regard to nature itself, that Plato rightly discerns clear proofs of an origin from ideas* [emphasis added]. A plant, an animal, the orderly arrangement of the cosmos — presumably therefore the entire natural world — clearly show that they are possible only according to ideas. . . . But only the totality of the connection of things in the universe [*Weltall*] is completely adequate to the idea.

The constitution is the shared idea or norm by virtue of which what would otherwise remain a mere aggregate becomes a genuine whole (VI:323–24; 134).

The metaphor of the body politic is, of course, quite ancient; common medieval versions equated the king with the head, or alternatively the heart, as seat of the polity's soul.[77] Hobbes notoriously usurped the metaphor, transforming the polity into an artificial person — a mechanism rivaling the Leviathan and Behemoth created by God — with the king or sovereign serving as its will. Hobbes did not attempt to integrate (except for the founding moment of the civil compact) the individual wills of each subject with that of the sovereign, whose external control of the body politic resembled that of an operator working a machine.[78] Rousseau replaces the clockwork image with that of a living organism. This is not the place to examine Rousseau's new understanding of natural wholeness in detail. It must suffice to say that for Rousseau the old notion of body informed by soul gives way to a conception of life that is compatible with modern physical science and takes its bearings from the unity of consciousness. Rousseau, in other words, returns to an organic model of the state without the hierarchical trappings with which that model was traditionally associated. Rousseau's understanding of the political organism as a whole consisting of coequal parts seems to have struck Kant especially forcefully when he first encountered it in the early 1760s — a time when he was attempting to sort out his own relation to Platonic "ideas."

Like the polis as classically conceived, the Kantian state is informed by its constitution (or regime). Unlike ancient constitutions, however, which Aristotle classified according to the differing aims or aspirations of their ruling parts, Kant's constitution is the formal principle of juridical unity as such, the lawful connection whereby a multitude of individuals become coequal parts or members of a whole. Thus, whereas regimes, on Aristotle's reckoning, could be democratic, aristocratic, or monarchic (to name only the simplest types), all states, according to Kant, whatever their actual type of government, are *essentially* republican; for it is only by virtue of that principle of mutual coexistence among wills that there exists a *res publica*, a "common wealth" — or alternatively, a "shared reality" — at all.[79] This definition of the principle of the res publica as one of mutual coexistence highlights its association with the theoretical category of community as earlier discussed; for like that category, it involves a necessary connection among substances (wills), a connection whose basis is a sort of "shared reality."

Hence the aptness of Kant's characterization of the juridical and transcendental deductions as complementary "refutations of idealism." The juridical condition presupposes an original, common appropriation of the soil by virtue of which, the earth itself — the "substance" in relation to which all other objects of ownership are merely "accidents" — is systematically divided. As that which "makes it possible to have external things as one's own" (*Sachenrecht* or *ius reale*), the earth can itself be regarded as the substance of reality, that is, that which can be appropriated as a thing.[80]

The head of state (*Beherrscher*), who is to be regarded as the "supreme proprietor" of a country's territory, thus stands in, in an important respect, for the *ens realisimum* as earlier described.[81] For he performs the conceptually analogous function of including as attributes of his person the totality of all realities. Only insofar as one regards the head of state as supreme proprietor of the land, says Kant, can right proceed according to a "necessary formal principle of *division* [Eintheilung]" rather than empirically, or from part to whole, according to a "principle of *aggregation*" (VI:323–24; 133–34).[82]

To be sure, Kant immediately adds, this supreme proprietorship is (like the *ens realisimum*) only "an idea" to represent the ownership that belongs distributively to the people as a whole. The head of state thus owns both everything and nothing — everything, inasmuch as it assigns to each what is his; nothing, inasmuch as the head of state's personal ownership of the land would turn subjects into serfs or slaves.

A further clue to the peculiar nature of the *Beherrscher*'s role emerges from Kant's discussion of the special "horror" associated with the formal execution of a monarch. Of all the atrocities involved in the overthrowing of a king, assassination is not the worst, for it can be partly excused by the right of necessity, that is, the people's fear that should he remain alive he might regain his forces [*sich ermannen*].[83] But the formal execution (*Hinrichtung*) of a monarch

> grips with horror the soul filled with the idea of the rights of man, a horror one feels again and again, whenever one thinks of such a scene [*Auftritt*]. . . . How does one explain this feeling, which is not aesthetic (sympathy, an effect of imagination by which we put ourself in the place of the sufferer) but moral feeling resulting from the complete overturning of all concepts of right? (VI: 320 n; [131–32 n])

The basis of our horror, according to Kant, is this: that whereas the murder of a king is regarded only as an exception to the rule that a people makes its maxim (that is, the rule against murder), his formal *execution* (*förmliche Hinrichtung*) "must be regarded as the complete *overturning* [Umkehrung] of the principles of the relation between a sovereign and his people (in which the people, *which has only the sovereign's legislation to thank for its own existence* [emphasis added], makes itself his head [*Herrscher*])." Thus, whereas to do violence to the head of state is an act of "*parricide*," or the attempted "murder of the fatherland" (VI:320; [131]), his execution constitutes an act of civic "*suicide*," like "*a chasm that* without return [*Wiederkehr*] *swallows up everything* [Alles]" (VI:323; [132]).[84]

To execute the king is not only to destroy the state, but also to "unman" it, that is, to ruin not only the effective basis of its unity (for it is only by virtue of the *Beherrscher* that a people exists at all), but also its capacity for (re)generation (*Wiedererzeugung*). (If a new state arises, it is, as Kant later puts it, through "palingenesis," not "metamorphosis" [VI:340; 148]).

Hence the cosmological — and sexual — connotations of violent revolution. The *Beherrscher* is to the "organism" of the state (see [VI:315; 126]) as the Roman genius is to the family gens. To kill the head is like "committing patricide." To formally execute him is to turn the enlivening, form-giving principle of the state against itself. With the monarch's execution, the ground of all (juridical) possibilities gives way, as if nothingness were to swallow up the infinite (and infinitely potent) storehouse of the *ens realisimum*.[85]

The civic suicide involved in formal execution of a monarch is thus the juridical equivalent of that natural self-sufficiency that figured abysmally in Kant's early cosmologies. Popular execution of a reigning monarch is as "unthinkable" an act as a nature that usurps God's form-giving privilege.[86] It is no wonder if "formalities" pretending to the act produce abortions and monstrosities.

According to strict principles of justice, the head of state should not be a monarch (*rex*), whom Kant associates with the executive authority, but the head of a legislative body composed of every citizen qualified to vote. A citizen so qualifies by being "self-sufficient" in the sense of being able to live from his own wealth or capital (material or intellectual) rather than through the arrangements or by the direction of others.[87] Only those with independent wealth sufficient to so sustain themselves as individuals are in a position to be members of the "commonwealth."

Kant excludes women from active citizenship despite his proviso that nothing should stand in the way of passive citizens "working their way up" to active status. Evidently, Kant believed women to be disqualified by nature (VII:295; 78), a conclusion in keeping with the patriotic (as opposed to patriarchal) character of juridical authority, whose primary function (as Kant suggests) is to "beget upon the land" a "brotherhood of citizens." Kant's deduction of right, with its almost obsessive attention to the original "appropriation of the soil," preempts the material (or maternal) sort of autochthony whose celebration he found so disagreeable in Herder.[88]

Thus Kant's vexingly paradoxical formulations concerning the power of the ruler (who is both creature and creator),[89] along with his peculiar hostility toward violent revolution, can be partly explained by the ruler's metaphorical proximity to biological fatherhood,[90] with all the latter's spiritual ambiguity. The state is like a living organism, in which ideal form is brought to bear on and through matter itself.[91] To suspend that process "even for an instant" (that is, by violent revolution) is as deadly as that dreamless sleep which, Kant elsewhere speculates, would sever the vital connection in a living animal between mind and viscera.[92] Hope of perpetual progress toward a perfect constitution is the permissible and, indeed, necessary dream that facilitates the state's ongoing metamorphosis toward a condition (the only one in which the state "literally exists") in which the *spiritual* and *empirical* forms finally converge (VI:340; [148]).

It is no wonder, then, that one "filled with the idea of human rights" should find the formal execution of a head of state especially abhorrent. However justice loving (*rechtliebend*), human beings require a master, without whom there is no effectual connection among wills, and hence no real community other than a natural commerce that exposes them to mutual destruction (VI:312; [124]).[93]

THE *METAPHYSICS OF MORALS*, PART TWO: THE *DOCTRINE OF ETHICS* (*TUGENDLEHRE*)

The *Doctrine of Right* dealt with the formal condition of outer freedom (the conditions under which outer freedom is consistent with itself); the *Doctrine of Virtue* deals with the ends that it is our duty to have (VI:380; 186). It thus concerns a harmony not of outer means (alone) but (also) of inner ends.

Yet in defining this "kingdom of ends" or "corpus mysticum," Kant is as concerned with maintaining the distinctness and distinctiveness of individuals as with their unification. Thus the intelligible world is to be morally conceived (where duties toward others are concerned) not as a simple union but as a community informed by a dynamic balance between the twin forces of love (which draws men together) and respect (which keeps them at a distance):

> In speaking of laws of duty (not laws of nature) and, among these, of laws for men's external relations with one another, we consider ourselves in a moral (intelligible) world where, by analogy with the physical world, *attraction* and *repulsion* bind together rational beings (on earth). The principle of *mutual love* admonishes men constantly to *come closer* to one another; that of the *respect* they owe one another, to keep themselves *at a distance* from one another; and should one of these great moral forces fail, "then nothingness (immorality), with gaping throat, would drink up the whole kingdom of (moral) beings like a drop of water" (if I may use Haller's words, but in a different connection). (VI:449; 243–44)

Virtue no less than right takes its bearings from a (by now) familiar communal reciprocity of attraction and repulsion: not love alone, but also a certain (mutual) aloofness. Indeed, as the allusion to Haller suggests, of the two forces taken in isolation, attraction would seem to pose the greater danger; for repulsion without attraction would lead to infinite dispersion, *not* the abysmal collapse described in Haller's poem. (It was rule based on the principle of benevolence, we recall, that Kant called the "greatest tyranny thinkable.")

Kant's treatment of the "community of sympathy" shows a similar aversion to proximity-inducing love unmediated by a distancing respectfulness. The duty of love as it applies to humanity (or man "as an animal endowed with reason") is that of sympathy (*Mitgefühl, theilnehmende Empfindung*). There are, however, according to Kant, two sorts of sympathetic community, one free (*communio sentiendi liberalis*), the other unfree (*communio sentiendi illiberalis, servilis*). Whereas the former arises from a *will* to share (*mittheilen*) in others' feelings to strengthen one's own moral resolve, the latter implies a natural susceptibility akin to physical contagion. (Kant notes that compassion [*Mitleidenschaft*] is similar to "warmth or contagious diseases," which also "spread naturally among men living next to one another") (VI:456–57; [250]).

To share in the sufferings of another whom I cannot help is "to be infected with his pain (via imagination)";[94] but to bring more evil in the world cannot be a duty.[95] Kant nevertheless adds (almost as if he feared catching himself in an act of [feminine] cowardice) that one has a positive duty to cultivate fellow feeling[96] and "not to shun sick rooms" to avoid painful feelings one may not be able to resist.[97] Thus it was a sublime way of thinking that the Stoic ascribed to a wise man who sought a friend not to receive help but to give it, and when the help was unavailing, said "What is it to me?"[98]

Kant's thematic discussion of friendship, which concludes the main section of the *Doctrine of Virtue,* casts a certain shadow, however, on the dynamic balance of attraction and repulsion that informs the ethical community. Friendship, says Kant, is "the most intimate union [*die innigste Vereinigung*] of love and respect." But if friendship is to be perfect, this love and respect must be "reciprocal" and "equal." Here, however, there arises a series of difficulties:

> One easily sees that this [friendship] is an ideal of participation [*Theilnehmung*] and sympathizing [*Mittheilung*] in the wellbeing of the other through the moral good will uniting them. . . . But it is readily seen that friendship is only an idea (though a practically necessary one) and unattainable in practice, although striving for friendship . . . is a duty set by reason. . . . For in his relations with his neighbor how is it possible for a person to be certain whether one of the elements requisite to this duty (e.g., reciprocal benevolence) is *equal* in the disposition of each of the friends? Or, even more difficult, how can he tell what relation there is in the same

person between the feeling from one duty and that from another (the feeling from benevolence and that from respect?) And how can he be sure that if the *love* of one is stronger, he may not, just because of this, forfeit something of the other's *respect,* so that it will be difficult for both to bring love and respect subjectively into that equal balance required for friendship? For love can be regarded as attraction and respect as repulsion, and it the principle of love bids friends to draw closer, that of respect requires them to maintain a proper distance.[99]

The purely inward character of ethical community precludes the determinacy that characterized juridical interaction and presupposes, in human experience at any rate, susceptibility to outward coercion. In the face of this indeterminacy, Kant appears to favor (once again) repulsion over attraction. Hence his insistence on a "limitation on confidence [*Vertraulichkeit*]" along with a rule that "friends not be too familiar [*gemein*] with one another" (VI:469–70; [261]).

This insistence on a certain "pathos of distance"—even, and perhaps especially, within the bonds of friendship—provides a sort of anticipatory, democratic answer to Nietzsche's later animadversions against the "last men," who like "to rub against one another for warmth." Indeed, there is in Kant's and Nietzsche's common fastidiousness a curious aesthetic convergence; both are nauseously repelled by common intimacies—Nietzsche, in the name of "aristocracy," Kant in the name of a nobility consistent with equality.[100]

All the more reason, then, for Kant's "Appendix" on "the virtues of social intercourse [*Umgangstugenden*]," it being a duty "not to *isolate* oneself but to use one's moral perfections in exchange with others (officium commercii, sociabilitas)." Here, in public intercourse (in ways we will have further occasion to explore in chapter 8), is the appropriate setting for that "reciprocity" and "openness" to others, the cultivation of which is a duty. For here, the individual can be the "fixed center" (*Mittelpunkt*) of his principles and yet regard this circle drawn around him as "part of an all-inclusive circle" that constitutes the cosmopolitan mentality (*Gesinnung*). Such a community of agreeableness (*humanitas aesthetica et decorum*) is, it seems, the closest we can come "without leaving the world" to being parts of a noncoercive whole while remaining whole ourselves (VI:473–74; [265]).

7 Kant's Idea of History

Kant's use of history has long been a puzzle to scholars.[1] First and foremost, as an account that claims to discern rational purpose in history and describes a certain trajectory of (the condition of) the human species from worse to better, Kantian history seems to call into question the absolute infinite worth of each human individual, on which Kant also emphatically insists. For as he himself admitted, a progressive history (history with a happy ending, or history at least with a perpetually improving denouement) condemns those who are born earlier (through no fault of their own) to busy themselves for the advantage of their distant progeny. As Kant himself states,

> It remains strange [Kant's word, *befremdend,* also means astonishing or displeasing] that earlier generations seem to carry through their toilsome labor only for the sake of the later . . . [and that] only the latest of the generations should have the good fortune [*Glück*] to dwell in an edifice upon which a long series of their ancestors had labored without being permitted to partake of the fortune they had prepared. (VIII:20; 14)

It would seem, then, that a progressive history is fundamentally unfair or, in the words of Hannah Arendt, at odds with "human dignity."[2] For either it produces *moral* improvement (in which case it seems to undermine the radical moral freedom on which Kant also insists — the absolute obligation of every person, whatever his or her external circumstance, to do right), or it produces *physical* improvement (in which case it seems to treat those of us born earlier not as ends in ourselves but as mere means to the well-being of those to come), or it does both. Kant nevertheless claims that a progressive history, however "riddlesome," is also somehow "necessary."

The riddlesome necessity of a progressive history brings us to difficulty number two: in what sense it is possible to speak — given Kant's strict separation of the realm of nature (in which all is determined by the laws of *physics*) from the realm of freedom (in which all is governed by the *moral* law — of a philosophically salient pattern or direction to history in the first place. This difficulty is all the more pressing, given Kant's lifelong alertness to the power of nature to cancel any and all human plans. An errant asteroid, as he suggests in a late work, could destroy the world tomorrow.

Nothing we know about the world through science gives any assurance that humankind is nature's special darling. On the contrary, the geological evidence, in which Kant took an early and avid interest, suggests that our planet has undergone a series of devastating revolutions in which vast numbers of creatures—perhaps entire species—have been annihilated. In Kant's own philosophic youth, the Lisbon earthquake claimed the lives of 40,000, thus shattering, many say, the "Panglossian" optimism of the early Enlightenment and certainly deepening Kant's own temperamental pessimism. Yet despite (and perhaps because) of this pessimism and an almost gruesome fascination with what he was inclined to call the crucible of nature, Kant insisted that history could, and indeed, must be read as comedy (not farce)—if not for the individual, then for the species as a whole.

To these two difficulties—the moral unfairness of a progressive history, and its apparent conflict with what Kant elsewhere says is and can be strictly known of nature—might be added a third: a certain inconsistency that some scholars have discerned between earlier and later treatments of history during Kant's so-called critical period, leading them to treat an early critical work like the *Idea for a Universal History* (published, to be sure, when Kant was sixty, three years after the appearance of the first edition of the *Critique of Pure Reason*) as a less mature and in some sense precritical version of Kant's brief but significant accounts of history in later works like the *Critique of Judgment* (published in 1790). I will not have much to say here about this issue.[3] My own view is that the distinction between Kant's critical and precritical periods has been somewhat overdrawn and that much can be gained by viewing Kant's later works from the perspective of problems which occupied him—or so it is the burden of this book to show—throughout his philosophic career. In the present chapter I hope to suggest ways in which a more rounded, long-range view of Kant's interest in history can tease out, if not entirely remove, some of the more troubling aspects of those later works.

I. *Idea for a Universal History*

The *Idea for a Universal History from/with a Cosmopolitan Standpoint/Intention*[4] appeared in 1784 in a popular journal whose audience Kant could not have expected to have mastered the intricacies of the first *Critique*. And yet precisely because the *Idea* is a "popular" work, the link between it and his critical system as a whole remains unstated and, to that extent, all the more puzzling.

The occasion for the publication was the recent appearance in another journal of a notice by an unnamed scholar who had apparently visited Kant and reported the following:

A pet idea [*Lieblingsidee*] of Professor Kant is that the final purpose [*Endzweck*] of the human race is to achieve the most perfect
civic constitution, and he wishes that a philosophic historian
might undertake to give us a history of humanity from this point
of view, and to indicate to what extent humanity in various ages
has approached or drawn away from this final purpose, as well as
what, in order to achieve it, remains to be done.[5]

This pet idea — the German, *Lieblingsidee,* suggests a favorite or beloved — recalls Kant's exemplary discussion in the *Critique of Pure Reason* of
the "Platonic" idea of the perfect republic, which he defines as that constitution which allows "the greatest possible human freedom in accordance
with laws by which the freedom of each is made to be consistent with that
of all others."[6] An idea, according to the first *Critique,* is a spontaneous
projection of pure reason, a projection to which nothing in experience —
nothing that is empirically knowable — can be adequate, and yet which is
for all that no mere chimera or fantasy.[7] More specifically, a Kantian "idea"
is not an intuition to be contemplated (in which case the charge of fantasy
would stick) but a goal to be systematically and progressively approached.
An idea, in short, is essentially practical, grounded not, as traditional metaphysics would have it, in theoretical knowledge but rather, as German Idealists following Kant will insist, in freedom. The *Lieblingsidee* of the perfect
constitution replaces what Kant elsewhere calls his "first mistress" — the
metaphysical dream, with which he was once enamored, of comprehending the universe theoretically.

The occasion of Kant's essay, then, was the need to explain and perhaps
defend from misconstrual a pet idea that, as Kant knew, could well appear
in the most literal sense outlandish. Some years earlier he had written another "cosmopolitan history" which had achieved some notoriety. (Among
other things, it gave rise to what astronomers now call the Kant-Laplace
thesis of nebula formation. It also helped inspire Herder's *Ideas toward a
History of Humanity,* published in 1785.)[8] It is one of the fruitful ironies of
intellectual history that this work, publicly panned by Kant, yet crucial to
the development of nineteenth-century historicism, was written by Kant's
devoted former student. The title of Kant's earlier work — Kant at thirty-
one did not suffer from false modesty — was *Universal Natural History and
Theory of the Heavens;* and in it he sought to provide what Descartes and
Newton had for reasons of their own refrained from offering: a genetic
history, according to mechanical principles, of the universe in its entirety.

As we saw in chapter 3, this beautiful, bizarre, and difficult work was a
cosmopolitan effort in the most literal sense. For after sketching out the
mechanical principles by which the universe as we know it might have been
formed, a sketch that presupposed a sort of second Copernican revolution,

in which the Milky Way, traditionally conceived as a mantle encircling the earth, is reconfigured as an ellipse radiating outward from a central areola (a figure more in keeping, perhaps, with the "galactic" or milky connotations of its name). And after analogically extending this account of galactic formation to that of the universe as a whole, Kant went on to speculate about the relation between the suns and planets and the characteristics of their inhabitants (for although it would be dogmatic to assume that all heavenly bodies are inhabited, it would be unreasonable, according to Kant, not to assume that most are or might become so). To the physical constitution of the universe, infinite numbers of galaxies revolving about a central point, there corresponds a spiritual universe, infinite gradations of intelligence ascending upward toward God and downward toward that point where matter meets spirit and reason borders on unreason. While not literally ranking human beings lowest within this spectrum of spiritual life (Kant places human beings, along with Martians, somewhere near the middle), he does suggest us to be the most "degraded" because of all creatures we least achieve the end for which we were created.

That end, Kant at thirty-one believes, is to contemplate creation. To be sure, the Saturnians, who are made of finer stuff, can do a better job of it. For one thing, they live longer, being further from the sun, which both energizes and destroys the bodily machine. For another, being less dependent on gross matter, they think with greater agility and can thus more quickly unify or combine what we put together more haltingly and with greater pain and effort. Still, we are similarly advantaged in comparison with the slugs — the mental mollusks — of Venus and Mercury. What brings us down is not absolute but relative inability; where lower spirits are sunk in a material torpor from which they cannot arise, and where higher spirits painlessly transcend their bodily coils, we can escape the inertial pull of matter only by the greatest effort. The few willing to make that effort find noble release; the rest remain content to "suck sap, propagate their kind, and die," achieving awkwardly what lower creatures manage with greater decency and finesse. If Mercurians fail to transcend their vegetative condition, they do so without fault. Man's humiliation lies not in his inability but in his unwillingness to rise. Poised between the higher charms of contemplation and the lower ones of animal desire, man finds neither goal conclusively attractive. Within the natural order, man's "end" is uniquely indeterminate — a "freedom" that goes together with the burden of responsibility for his own failure.

All of this, of course, places Kant's own authorial efforts in the *Universal Natural History* in a most peculiar light; for his struggle to assume a truly cosmopolitan standpoint becomes the basis on which mankind — and with it the perfection of the whole, which man seems otherwise monstrously to violate — can be redeemed.

A final summary note: Kant's universal natural history, as we have seen, is timely in a special way. The unity of creation is unthinkable apart from the timeless divine schema or plan out of which creation temporally unfolds and in which each creature finds its ground or raison d'être. History is a never-ending story whose ending God only knows. Within this framework, man, along with all other created spirits, can only temporally approach as best he can God's immediate comprehension of the whole. In fulfilling this task, however, human beings are especially burdened. Located midway between wisdom and unreason, man finds his material and spiritual entelechies singularly out of sync. Man of all creatures seems least to realize his end because he alone lacks adequate time for the development of his higher capacities. The prospect of an eternal life, or at the very least, perpetual progress, arises from the palpable discrepancy between physical and spiritual perfection, the former obtainable by the individual, the latter, as Kant will much later put it in the *Idea for a Universal History,* only by the species.[9]

Rousseau's concept of a universal will becomes the basis, for Kant, of a humanized and moralized version of the divine schema of creation. The spiritual community that Kant once sought through intellection becomes newly accessible through the idea of a republican constitution of free and equal beings. That this constitution is, at least in Kant's original formulations, explicitly masculine serves only the more emphatically to remind us of the material problem that it addresses. Where Kant once condemned man for the "indeterminacy" of his nature, torn as he is between higher and lower principles of desire, he now exalts in human freedom. The problematic effort theoretically to transcend a metaphorically feminized nature — the exchanges of matter are figured by Kant in abysmally maternal terms — gives way in the face of a practical elevation to the moral world — a community of spirits beyond the flux of time and matter. The only question for Kant, writing in 1766, is how to translate that immediate but merely ideal elevation into real worldly terms — how, in other words, to give a wholly spiritual republic political weight and bite.

Kant's *Idea for a Universal History* situates itself in that *intermundia* or space between worlds toward which his early notes on Rousseau experimentally reach. A rational history, Kant insists, requires a plan. The problem of composing a *human* history is therefore unique. "Since men," he writes, "behave, on the whole, not just instinctively, like the brutes, nor yet like rational citizens of the world according to some agreed-on plan, no history of man conceived according to a plan seems possible, as it might be possible to have such a history of bees or beavers."

Kant thus calls for a philosophic history that will discover a "natural plan" for creatures who have no "plan of their own." He suggests that he is in part motivated in this effort by a certain "indignation" at the apparently idiotic and childish course of things human, which seem woven together from malice and folly. The eligibility of humanity for membership in a higher world cannot, it seems, wholly eclipse the repulsiveness of a species that (unlike the beavers and the bees) defies purposive conceptualization — an answer to the question "what is man?" (VIII:18; 42).[10]

Kant here seeks out a "guiding thread" (*Leitfaden*) for such a history, leaving it to nature to bring forth the man (*Mann*) in a position (*der im Stande ist*) to compose it. The one who achieves such a history would, like Kepler or Newton, succeed "in an unexpected way," a phrase that calls to mind Kant's later characterization of genius.[11]

The remainder of the work consists of nine theses, intended, perhaps, to recall the famous ninety-five theses of Luther, as well as the theses (and antitheses) of Kant's own *Critique of Pure Reason*. According to thesis 1, "*All natural capacities of a creature are destined to evolve completely to their natural end.*" Without such a principle, which is confirmed in the case of animals by outer and inner (*zergliedernde*, "anatomical") observation, we have a purposelessly playing, rather than lawful, nature, and unconsoling (*trostlos*) chance takes the place of reason's guiding thread.

In man, however (according to thesis 2), "*these natural capacities, insofar as they pertain to the use of reason, are destined (or determined) to develop fully only in the species.*" Man alone ("as the only rational creature on earth") achieves his destiny not in one life span but only over the endless course of generations. To observe an animal is to attribute to it a purposive cause — a goal toward which its parts seem to aim. In man alone, however, this rule is breached by virtue of the infinite reach of reason itself. Reason "acknowledges no limits to its projects," for it is itself the power to extend the rules and intentions (*Absichten*) to which its forces are applied beyond the limits of nature. The palpable discrepancy between the shortness of our individual life span and the time needed to develop all our faculties threatens to turn man alone into nature's childish "sport" (*Spiel* means "play," but also "freak").[12] The purposeless "play" of nature that Kant earlier feared is now connected with man's apparent freakishness or failure to conform to type. A sport of nature is, of course, an offspring differing in form from that of its parent; and man, by virtue of his very freedom, threatens the presumption of natural purposiveness on which judgment and all practical principles ultimately depend. But what does Kant mean by "judging"? Judgment, he elsewhere states, is the capacity to place the individual under a universal concept, as when we judge that this is a tree and that a desk. In the case of man, however, this task is uniquely problematic; for the very concept of humanity, if there can be said to be one at all, is, by virtue of man's freedom, indeterminate and open-ended. What from one point of view constitutes man's glory, from another makes him, in the most literal sense, a monster.

It is therefore necessary that man strive toward ("if only in the idea") that point in time at which we reach the level of development that conforms to nature's intention. The idea of history is the guiding thread that leads us out of the labyrinth of man's natural monstrousness — the ideal moment in which nature's leading strings give way to rational self-direction.[13]

To think this moment is to attribute to nature the will that, as Kant puts it in thesis 3, *"man himself bring forth everything that goes beyond the mechanical ordering of his animal existence, and that he should partake of no other happiness or perfection than that which he himself, free of instinct, has created by his own wisdom."* Man, in short, is to give birth to himself — all of himself, that is to say, that goes beyond mere physical existence. He is to "bring forth everything from himself" rather than being "guided by instinct." Nature is thus, a stepmother to man in the most literal sense: her harshness is linked to a lack of genuine kinship.[14]

Man overcomes the status of contempt in which his monstrousness places him by "working himself up" and thus making himself "worthy of life" itself. Man alone furnishes the *ground* (or sufficient reason) of his own existence (just what Kant's youthful metaphysics vainly sought) not physically, to be sure, but morally; for man alone of all known creatures can provide out of himself a reason why he ought to exist, and with it a justification or sufficient reason for the rest of creation.[15] Humanity is, as Kant will later say, the final purpose *of* nature and the ultimate purpose or reason *beyond* nature by which creation as such is justified.[16]

Man can so work himself up, however, only historically or as a species; individually, man is of nature born, and nature in the guise of death exacts its due. Hence the "strange" but "necessary" sacrifice of earlier generations (who, to be sure, labor unintentionally) for the sake of later ones — strange, inasmuch as history appears unjust, yet necessary, *if* one assumes that a "species of animals [born to die] should yet have reason." The discrepancy between the physical and spiritual entelechies of which Kant once complained — our inability as natural creatures to develop all the rational capacities of which we find ourselves capable — must be accepted as the fate of a mortal animal endowed with reason. Man's traditional *Bestimmung,* his scholastic definition as the rational animal, rings true *only* if it is interpreted historically.[17]

Man is born in order to give birth to himself. The means employed by nature to bring this development about is, according to thesis 4, the famous antagonism or "a-social sociability" that brings men, driven by vainglory, lust for power, and greed to conquer their natural laziness or torpor

(*Trägheit* also means "inertia"). (Thus, thesis 4: *"The means that nature employs to bring the development of all her disposition about* [zu Stand zu bringen] *is that of antagonism within society, insofar as in the end it is a cause of law-governed social order."*) Without these inclinations toward evil, man's other talents would remain hidden, and men, effortlessly content, would have no more value than the domestic animals they raise.[18] In such a case, the question of why there are men at all would remain unanswerable, as Kant insists is actually (almost) the case for such primitive peoples as the putatively happy but lazy Greenlanders and Tierra del Fuegians. Evil is thus preferable to natural goodness, and nature is to be thanked for freeing us of the need to thank her (VIII:20; 14. Cf. VIII:21; 16). (The paradoxical character of this remark reminds us that even as nature's stepchildren we remain her progeny.)

As a result, the first steps are taken from rudeness to culture by means of a dynamic relation between human forces of attraction and repulsion, that is, from men's desire to unite, as a state in which one feels "more [than] human" (*mehr als Mensch*), joined with a tendency, arising from well-grounded mutual suspicion, toward self-isolating individuation (*vereinzeln*).[19]

"*The greatest problem for the human species,*" according to thesis 5, "*to the solution of which we are naturally driven is the establishment of a universal civil society administering law or justice.*" In such a perfect civic constitution, in which there is mutual opposition among members, and at the same time the most exact determination of freedom and fixing of its limits so that it may be consistent with the freedom of others, all man's dispositions or aptitudes (*Anlagen*) can develop. To such a state of reciprocal limitation, Kant insists, men are naturally driven by their very love of boundless freedom. Civic union is thus a sort of enclosure or preserve in which wild growth gives way to cultivation, just as trees hemmed in together grow straight and tall through mutual competition for the sunlight, while those in isolated freedom put out branches at random.[20] Though made of crooked wood, man can be made to grow straight through the collective discipline of his own evil inclinations.[21] All culture and fine art, along with the finest social order, are the "fruits" of unsociableness — a deeper and, so to speak, unconscious artfulness by which man's natural seeds are to develop to perfection.

Kant's likening of civil society to an enclosure (the word also means "corral") recalls, however, the domesticated beasts, our similarity to which renders us contemptible. How does man, who is, as Kant states, in need of a master, become master of himself and thereby justify his own existence?[22] What is required is that man's merely private will be broken and required to conform to a universal law (that is, that he be forced to be free). Man can obtain a master, however, only from the human species;

hence his master will himself need a master. The Platonic problem of who is to rule is thus, according to thesis 6, *"the most difficult and the last to be solved by the human race."* Indeed, it is not fully solvable; for from such crooked wood as man is made of, "nothing perfectly straight or upright [*Gerade* also means "just"] can be built."

That it is the last problem to be solved follows also from the fact that it requires the coincidence of a proper concept of a possible constitution, great experience of the world course, and, most of all, the good will to accept that constitution—a coincidence of king, philosopher, and saint that will occur, if at all, "very late, and after many futile attempts" (VIII:23; [18]). Nature therefore requires us only to approximate this idea, so that the task (which is itself now designated as an idea), rather than its fulfillment (as Kant had earlier suggested), defines us somehow as a species.

Achieving that goal depends, according to thesis 7, on the solution of a problem involving the relation among states: *"The problem of achieving a perfect civil constitution is dependent on the problem of a lawful external relation among states, and without the latter cannot be solved"* (VIII:24; [18]). This result, which reason might have brought about from the beginning, nature achieves by means of the same unsociability and intolerance (*Unvertragsamkeit*) that drives individuals to enter a civil compact (*Vertrag*). In the ensuing devastation, (civic) bodies continually dissolve and reform, until such revolutions (like those from which our solar system arose) bring about a self-maintaining constitution. This tendency toward dynamic equilibrium presupposes (on the analogy of cosmic evolution) a purposive arrangement rather than blind chance. For to accept the latter would be to reduce nature to a lawless treadmill—a revolting eternal return of the same—and thus to renounce altogether the idea of progress, the hope that mankind is moving, by however secret an art, from worse to better.

That war (and its growing threat) ultimately leads to a system of stable peace is the lynchpin of Kant's hope. The same "a-social sociability" that forces men to form civil societies eventually compels the latter—after a course of devastating upheavals and revolutions—to enter into a federation in which the security of each is guaranteed and which maintains itself "automatically." Such a future condition is, we may reasonably believe, no less likely than the cosmic system that has evolved from analogous physical forces of attraction and repulsion:

> Whether we should expect that states, by an Epicurean concourse [*Zusammenlauf*] of efficient causes, should enter by accidental [*ungefähren*] collisions (like those of small material particles) into all kinds of formations which are again destroyed by new collisions, until they arrive *by accident* [von ungefähr] at a formation that can maintain itself in its form (a happy chance occurrence, that will hardly ever occur!); or whether we should more readily

assume that nature here follows a regular course, in leading our species gradually upwards from the lowest level of animality up to the highest level of humanity through an art that is man's own, though forced, and hence that nature develops man's original dispositions in an entirely regular manner within this apparently wild arrangement; or whether one should prefer that out of all this human activity and counteractivity in the large, nothing overall, or at least nothing wise, will emerge, that it will remain as it always has been, and that one would thus not be able to predict [*voraussagen*] whether the schism [*Zweitracht*] so natural to our species is not in the end preparing the way for a hell of evils to overtake us, however civilized our condition, in that it again nullifies this condition and all progress in culture made hitherto, through barbarous devastation (a fate one cannot stay [*nicht stehen kann*] under a rule of blind chance [*blind Ungefährs*] — which is, indeed, identical with lawless freedom — if one does not attribute to it [*ihr ... unterlegt*] a secret guiding thread of nature, a thread tied together [*geknüpften*] with wisdom). (VIII:25; [19–20])

These three questions approximately amount to yet another, or, in Kant's own language, "das läuft ungefähr auf die Frage hinaus" (which literally translates as "from these questions there approximately [with verbal echoes of "safely" and "unintentionally"] runs out"). Kant's use here of *laufen* and *ungefähr*, especially given the latter's multiple meanings,[23] brings his three cosmological alternatives to an ironic and self-reflexive conclusion. The course of his questions — which turn on the propriety of attributing intentionality to nature's course — itself approximately amounts (or, alternatively: without intention and yet safely runs out) to the question of "whether it is reasonable to assume that nature's order (*Naturanstalt*) is *purposive* in its parts and yet *without purposiveness* as a whole." The course of Kant's questioning itself leads, in a way that is inexact (and unintentional yet safe?), to a summary question in which both rationality and the purposiveness of nature's parts are already assumed. And yet if this is indeed the issue to which Kant's other questions amount, one is left somewhat perplexed, given the apparent lack of purposiveness in a rational *part* (the human one) that initiates Kant's inquiry and that his essay as a whole is meant to address.

Owing, perhaps, to that difficulty, Kant turns to partiality in another sense — the parts of the political whole, a system that is not without danger (*nicht ohne alle Gefahr*) and yet wholesome (*heilsam*).[24] Just as the state of savagery eventually forced individuals to enter into a civic condition, so the barbaric freedom of civil states

compels our species to discover a law of equilibrium for the opposition of many states towards one another, an opposition in itself
wholesome and that originates in freedom, and to introduce a
united power to give the former support, and thus also a cosmopolitan condition of public state security. This condition is not
without all danger, so that the forces of humanity do not go to
sleep, but also not without a principle of equality of reciprocal
action and reaction, so that they do not destroy one another.
(VIII:26; [20–21])

Like the cosmic system to which he explicitly compares it, Kant's cosmopolitan mechanism will be self-enforcing—a kind of second universe
which, unlike the first, is attuned to the requirements of moral culture. Yet:

Before taking this final step (the union of states), thus when it is
just past the halfway mark of its formation [*Ausbildung*], human
nature endures the hardest evils under the guise of outward welfare. . . . We are *cultivated* to a high degree through art and science. We are *civilized* to the point of excess. . . . But for us to consider ourselves *moralized* much is lacking. For while the idea of
morality already belongs to culture, the use of this idea, which
only extends to the simulacra of virtue in honor and outward propriety, constitutes mere civilization. So long as states apply all their
forces toward vain and violent aims of expansion [*Erweiterungsab-
sichten*], unceasingly obstructing [*hemmen*] the slow effort toward
the inner formation [*bilden*] of the way of thinking [*Denkungsart*]
of their citizens—even removing from them all support for this
aim—nothing from this way is to be expected. For the former
demands a long inner elaboration [*Bearbeitung*] of each commonwealth for the formation/education [*Bildung*] of its citizens. But
everything good that is not grafted onto a morally good mentality
[*Gesinnung*] is nothing but empty appearance and glittering misery. The human race will probably remain in this condition until
it has worked its way out of the chaotic state of its state relations
in the way I have described. (VIII:26; [21])

   The problem, then, is roughly this. Human history "according to a
plan" has started, *ex hypothesi*, to take shape. Human nature is just past the
midpoint of its formation. (Is Kant's own explication of the moral idea as
a system-constituting ground itself the midpoint?) That moral idea, Kant
says, already belongs to culture, but is used by states in ways leading to
only the simulacra of virtue. Hence the hardest evils lie ahead, evils consisting in states' unceasing obstruction of the formation/education of citizens.[25]
   How then is the education of citizens to go forward, barring a coinci-

dence of philosopher, king, and saint that is (almost) as unlikely as the emergence of self-maintaining order from Epicurean chaos?

Thesis 8 indicates a way out of this seeming impasse, if only by way of a hint that nature furthers reason's goal: "*One can in the large see the history of the human race as the fulfillment of a hidden plan of nature to bring about an inwardly — and for this purpose also outwardly — perfected constitution of states, as the only condition in which she can fully develop in humanity all her dispositions*" (VIII:27; [21]). Unlike the chiliastic expectations of revelation, the fulfillment of philosophy's goals can be hastened by awareness of the idea they are based on, this fact being sufficient to distinguish such goals from *schwärmerisch* illusions.

But distinguishing ideas from illusions is not enough; one must, it seems, also secure the thread by which the ideas of reason connect with nature. Or so one is lead to understand from Kant's claim that "it comes down only to this: whether experience discovers *something* of such a course of nature's intention."

What, then, of nature's intention does experience discover? Kant says (*Ich sage*): "a *little bit*" (*etwas* Weniges). This littleness is, to be sure, not unexpected; for "the circle of our course seems to take so long to complete, and mankind has covered so small a part in this aim [*Absicht*], that one can as little determine with certainty the shape of its course and the relation of the parts to the whole" as one can determine with certainty the path of our sun through the remainder of the fixed stars. And yet just as we can still conclude that such a solar path exists, we can conclude — given a systemicity analogous to the one we assume in making astronomical calculations — that mankind too follows an intentional trajectory. The difference, of course, is that the natural systemicity we are for purposes of astronomy *entitled* to assume is in the case of human history just what's at issue. Still, the fact that "human nature" cannot "be indifferent" to the most distant epochs in which our species treads, combined with the fact that we may in our own case (*in unserem Falle*) be able to accelerate this happy point in time for our descendants through our own rational organization (*Veranstaltung*), suggests a naturally supported, albeit ideal, closing of the circle by which the species is to be defined.[26] In any case, our natural inability to be indifferent to the certain future of our race (an inability heightened by our present awareness that we can consciously act to further a happy end) makes even "weak traces" (*Spuren*) "extremely important to us," so that the faintness of the track is, in effect, offset by its potential significance.

Kant discovers those traces in the relations among states, which find themselves in so artful/artificial (*künstlichen*)[27] a condition with respect to one another that none can neglect inner culture without losing power and influence over the rest. Given the combination of nature and art arrived at in the current moment, the selfish tendencies of rulers are no longer (or need no longer appear as) an implacable obstacle to the articulation of history according to an idea. First, the ambitious intentions of states tend all by themselves in such a condition to secure the "maintenance of nature's end." Beyond this, state power comes actually to *require* the freedom of citizens. For to hinder the citizen from doing what he will so long as it is consistent with the freedom of the rest "obstructs the vitality of ongoing business [*durchgängigen Betriebes*]"[28] and thus impedes "the forces of the whole." It follows that personal limitations (*Einschränkung*) (including restrictions on religion) grow ever weaker; and there thus gradually arises, with intermittent delusion and crankiness, *enlightenment,* a "great good that the human race must reap even from its rulers' self-aggrandizing intentions, if only they know their own advantage." At the same time, the sympathy (*Herzensantheil,* literally, "heart-sharing") enlightened persons feel for anything good they fully comprehend will gradually spread upwards to heads of state. In the meantime, rulers, even if they do not actively support education, find it in their own interest not to impede citizens' own efforts. And war itself, by virtue of a growing commercial interdependence that makes a tremor in one state felt by all the rest, becomes increasingly costly and hence unappealing to the very heads of state who formerly found it attractive (VIII:27–28; [22–23]).

The upshot of these remarks[29] is to suggest the emergence of "a great state body" (*großen Staatskörper*), the stirring of whose "members" (*Gliedern*) is already (nearly) visible:

> Although this state body is discernible for now only in very rough outline [*Entwurfe*], it seems as if, so to speak, a feeling is rising in all members for maintaining the whole: and this gives hope that after many revolutions . . . what nature has for its highest intention will at last come to pass — a universal cosmopolitan condition, as the womb [*Schooß*] in which all original dispositions of the human species will become developed. (VIII:28; [23])

It is as if, in human history's case, the revolution of the heavens gave rise — as it were, spontaneously — not just to a mechanism of dead nature but to a *living being;* a being, moreover, whose body is itself a *Schooß* or "womb" in which all the natural dispositions of mankind can develop. This womb is both the visible trace of history's unfolding and the site out of which humanity emerges, the only individual (so far as we know) of its kind — a child, so to speak, without a parent. In short, mankind (by virtue of this conceit) gives birth to itself, and in doing so secures — however paradoxically — an otherwise dubious natural affinity. The secret tie that binds nature and reason thus stands exposed or promises so to do to the extent that this is humanly conceivable.

Unlike Alexandre Kojève, the twentieth-century Hegelian who worried that the end of history—the universal rational state—would spell the end of human negativity, and thus the end of man, Kant sees it as the dawn of the first truly human, if not Saturnian, age. Prior to its emergence from that new and happier womb, mankind would presumably remain a sort of fetus, inwardly developing the organs of ethical culture that would allow it to be reborn at last as a fully determined species.[30] Mankind would at last transcend the monstrousness adherent to its hybrid status as an animal endowed with reason.

Kant's ninth and final thesis inserts the effort to sketch out a plan for human history into the very thing it seeks: *"a philosophic attempt to work out* [bearbeiten] *a universal history of the world according to a plan of nature that aims at a perfect civic union of the human species must be regarded as possible, and even as furthering this intention of nature"* (VIII:29; [23]).

The possible success of such an attempt is sufficiently established, it seems, by the attempt itself. For by so linking the observer and the observed, such an attempt is itself the sought-for trace of reason's natural embodiment and hence the strongest indication available that such a plan exists. Kant is thus able to establish that the philosophic effort to work out a planful history is not itself unreasonable.[31]

He is also to this extent able to defeat the apparent "strangeness" or "absurdity" of the design (*Anschlag*) of wishing to compose (*abfassen*) history—as distinguished from "romance" (*Roman*)—according to an idea. The *utility* of that idea, so long as we may assume that nature, even in the "play of human freedom," does not operate without a plan, distinguishes it decisively from an illusion, and this despite the fact that, unlike (other) rational ideas, the idea of history *is inseparable from* its own physical embodiment. Unlike other rational ideas, which belong to all rational beings, the idea of history, in other words, belongs peculiarly and especially to man.

But what exactly does it mean to assume that nature does not operate without a "final intention"? Is this to presume that nature acts intentionally? Or is it merely to reject the claim that intentionality on nature's part is lacking? (Might it be the case that nature does not operate either with intention or without it?) In any case, *if* we may make that assumption:

> And even though we are too near-sighted[32] to penetrate the secret mechanism of [nature's] organization [*Veranstalltung*], this idea may yet serve as a guiding thread to represent an otherwise planless *aggregate* of human actions as, at least in the main, a *system.* For if one starts out with Greek history—as that in which all earlier or contemporaneous histories are preserved, or at least must be authenticated [*beglaubigt*]; if one follows the influence of

Greek history on the formation and misformation of the state body of the Roman people, which swallowed the Greek state; again, if one follows down to our own times the influence of the Romans on the Barbarians, who destroyed the Roman state in turn; if one then adds episodically the state histories of other peoples, insofar as knowledge of them has gradually come down to us through these enlightened nations; one will then discover a regular course of improvement of state constitution in our part of the world/continent (which will probably one day legislate for all others). Further, one must always attend [*Acht hat*] only to the civil constitution and its laws, and to the relations among states, and notice how both, through the good that they impart, served to lift up peoples for a time (and with them also arts and sciences). But we should also attend to how their defects . . . led to their overthrow, but in such a way that a seed of enlightenment always remained over, developing further through each revolution. (VIII:29–30; [24])[33]

One would in this way, Kant believes, discover a

guiding thread that can serve not only for explaining the confused play of human things, or for political prophesying of future political alterations (a use to which human history merely as the disjointed effect of rule-less freedom has already been put!); rather, it would serve to open up a consoling prospect into the future (that we, without presupposing a plan of nature, cannot hope for), a prospect in which we are shown from afar how finally the human species works its way up to a condition in which all the germs that nature has placed in it can fully develop and its destiny be here on earth fulfilled.

In the case of humanity alone, the divine schema, to which we can otherwise, according to Kant's critical teaching, only figuratively appeal, becomes accessibly our own; and the figure of a perfect machine purposively united, by which we metaphorically — but only metaphorically — conceptualize all other living things is actualized in the earthly incarnation of a community of moral beings. In the case of humanity, too, the vexed "problem" of generation — how the intercourse of two living individuals can produce another — is, if not overcome, at least set aside; for as species in the determinate sense, humanity is one individual, whose "natural history" ceases at the moment in which men consciously unite, thereby becoming pregnant, so to speak, with their own future.

The discarded traditional ideal of knowledge as an apprehension of the inner essence or perfection of a thing is in this manner newly and uniquely revived. For in mankind alone knower and known are, or can be, one. Mankind unites through the idea of such a union that each member shares. It is in this crucial sense that mankind, unlike the race of dogs and horses, literally creates itself—not just as an aggregate of individual living beings but as a whole, a species that is not only worthy of membership in the cosmos (which the current state of affairs might lead us to doubt) but which also justifies the rest of creation. In humanity so conceived, Leibniz's question of sufficient reason—why is there something rather than nothing?—finds its only humanly adequate response.[34]

Man, one might be tempted to conclude, is a historical being. But Kant, unlike Hegel, does not go so far. For to the extent that history depends upon nature, whose ways we can interpret but not entirely control, progress remains a hope rather than a realized certainty. As moral being, man's full humanity is assured, albeit only in another world to come. As natural being, on the contrary, man's full humanity is merely an idea, distinguished from a fantasy or romance only by the fact that that idea, to the extent that it is propagated, can become a self-fulfilling prophecy.[35] This, and man's "natural" interest in the most distant epoch that our species may encounter, if only he can anticipate it with certainty, creates a sort of ideal union of mankind—a common humanity, so to speak, before the fact. Concern for the welfare of one's own progeny is displaced by a projection of self-interest (and vanity—Kant later asks princes to consider how they will be viewed by our descendants) onto infinity.

The result is an authenticated *Bildungsroman* whose hero is the learned (*gebildet*) public at large, a community of letters unbroken by the course of time. The authors of history—those who tell its tale—are thus in an important sense its subject matter as well. History, according to Kant, begins with the "first page" of Thucydides—written about and for the first people capable of perpetuating the story.[36] Only with the Greeks, in other words, does mankind achieve continuous self-awareness, a sort of communal equivalent of the transcendental unity of consciousness on which Kant pegs individual human identity. Once one accepts this collective consciousness, one has only to grant the survival and further development (however slight) of the "germ" of enlightenment in each subsequent political revolution, and perpetual progress is assured.[37] Add thesis 1—that all natural dispositions of a creature are destined or determined to evolve completely to their end—and the earthly fulfillment of the human race, however distant, becomes a certainty. This "consoling" prospect is at once Kant's "guiding thread" and his most important "motive ground," the "end" of history in both senses of the term. Man reconciled with nature is man literally remade: man as the mother of himself.

We are not, it seems, very far here from the "self-developing self-consciousness" of Hegel's "world spirit," the historical *Weltgeist* under whose wheels many a (mere) individual is crushed. But Kant is not Hegel. The "strangeness" of a history that holds the fate of some hostage to the well-being of others cannot be entirely suppressed. Kant's historical totalization of humanity thus remains incomplete. Man's historical evolution leads up to, but does not include, his full emancipation or rebirth, for which a new moral "grafting" (*pfropfen*) is required. The tension between nature and reason — and with it man's hybrid or bastard status, his failure to conform to type — cannot be fully resolved.

Thus Kant does not himself offer the consoling prospect of man's full development on earth, and with it nature's "completed rational intention," but only his "belief" (*Glaube*) that such a prospect is possible, and this despite the fact that without such a prospect, the history of the human race is not only a "constant reproach" to the putative wisdom embodied in the rest of nature, but actually forces us to "turn away our eyes" from nature in revulsion. His "idea of a world history" has, then, an a priori *Leitfaden* only "to a certain extent" (*gewissermaße*) (or alternatively, "only in a manner of speaking"). It would, Kant insists, be a misunderstanding of his intention (*Absicht*) to think that with that idea he would wish "to displace the working out [*Bearbeitung*] of history [*Historie*] proper, which is composed merely empirically." His idea of world history is rather

> only a thought [*Gedanke*][38] of what a philosophic head (who must also be very artful historically) might be able to attempt from another standpoint. Besides, the otherwise praiseworthy detail with which one now composes the history of one's time must naturally bring about concern as to how our remote descendants will cope with the burden of history that we bequeath to them some centuries from now. Doubtless, they will value the history of the oldest times, of which the original documents would have long disappeared, only from the view point of what interested them, namely, what peoples and governments have done to help or harm a cosmopolitan intention. To consider [look back on] this so as to direct the love of honor of heads of state and their servants to the only means by which their fame can spread to later ages: this can be a minor motive ground for attempting such a philosophic history. (VIII:30–31; [25–26])

Kant's own intention and the intention of world history mentioned in the title of his essay, then, both do and do not coincide. The announced goal of the essay — to "see whether we can succeed in finding a guiding thread" to human history according to a plan — issues in the discovery of a guiding thread, but one that only goes so far, and thus remains ambiguous at best. (Is a thread that leads Theseus only part way through the labyrinth better than none at all?) Kant's idea cannot authenticate itself historically. It is not, however, for all that, useless, for it supports the hope that nature will produce another, more historically artful philosophic head in which such an authentication might be accomplished. With that authentication, the composition of a human whole (articulated according to an idea of which each member was aware) would, it seems, also be achieved, but for the reliance of such composition on art rather than philosophy. Given that reliance, the articulation of human history—which is bound by a thread in which reason's *Leitfaden* and nature's "leading strings" (*Gängelband*) intertwine—must remain equivocal. In any case and in the meantime, Kant's own attempt overcomes blockages to human self-formation that are imposed by (otherwise) misguided states.

II. Culture and the "History of Pure Reason"

In the penultimate section of the *Critique of Pure Reason* Kant characterizes metaphysics as "the fulfillment [*Vollendung*] of the entire culture of human reason" (A/850 = B/878). Culture here evidently has a more inclusive meaning than at A/710 = B/738, where Kant distinguished culture from discipline, the former giving positive, the latter negative help to the development of talents, which already, he says, have "an impulse to externalize themselves." Since Kant includes the "discipline" (but not the "culture") of pure reason as one part of the "transcendental doctrine of method," and by implication, as one element (but not the whole) of metaphysics, one is left to wonder about the exact place of reason's culture in Kant's philosophic system. The puzzle is heightened by the fact that in the sentence following Kant's discussion at A/850, culture and discipline are implicitly equated.[39]

Any attempt to understand what Kant means here by the "entire culture of human reason" faces another difficulty: the path-breaking nature of his general use of the term "culture." As Allan Bloom and others have observed, Kant is a primary source of the modern notion of culture as a totality of human customs and practices, a usage sufficiently new that it does not appear in early nineteenth-century editions of Grimm's dictionary. The immediate provenance of the word is, apparently, French, from the Latin *cultus, cultivare*, which refers to habitation of a place (hence also to worship or devotion) and to the growing of crops.[40]

If one looks ahead to the *Critique of Judgment,* one finds "culture" defined as the cultivation (which includes both negative discipline and positive fostering of talent) of a sort of general hability, and thus as that "aim of man" which can also be called the "last end of nature." So understood, culture is the (vexed) point of juncture between what "nature can do for man" and "what man must do for himself"—in short, a bridge that passes over without abolishing the chasm dividing intellect and matter. But what, if culture ends where reason begins, is meant by the "fulfillment of reason's culture?" Is metaphysics the product of nature or of reason? Or can it be both?

Kant's association in the first *Critique* of metaphysics with the culture of reason follows on a division of metaphysics in accordance with "the originative [*ursprüngliche*] idea of philosophy":

> *Philosophy* is the system of all philosophic knowledge. We must take it objectively, if we are to understand by it the archetype [*Urbild*] for the judgment [*Beurteilung*] of all efforts at philosophizing, and for the judgment of each subjective philosophy, whose structure often is so manifold and alterable. Thus regarded, philosophy is a mere idea of a possible science, that is given to no one *in concreto,* but which, by many different ways, we seek to approach, until the one footpath [*Fußsteig*], very much overgrown, to be sure, through sensibility, is discovered, and the ectype [*Nachbild*], heretofore so abortive [*verfehlte*], arrives at likeness with the archetype insofar as it is permitted to man. Until then one can learn no philosophy, for where is it, who possesses it, and how shall we recognize it? One can only learn to philosophize, i.e., to exercise upon certain present attempts the talent of reason in accordance with its universal principles, yet always retaining the rights of reason to investigate, to confirm, or to reject these principles in their very sources. ([A/838 = B/866])

A division based on this idea is legislative and unalterable, distinguishing itself in this respect from one based on accidentally observed affinities. But how is philosophy's idea (which is given concretely only when achieved) discovered in the first place? By what criterion, as Hegel might say, is reason to recognize its own criterion (cf. A/844 = B/872)?

What makes such a division possible (and with it, metaphysics) is, above all, Kant having clearly distinguished for the first time the two elements of our knowledge, the a priori (which is fully in our power) and the a posteriori (which is only obtainable from experience) (A/843 = B/871). By virtue of this clarification, the idea of science, which is "as old as speculative human reason" and much labored upon, could at last be brought forth (*zu Stande bringen könnte*). To this distinction must be added the further contrast, "always in a manner felt" but never (before Kant) clearly defined, between philosophy and mathematics, that is, a priori knowledge based on concepts and a priori knowledge based on the construction of concepts. The result is an *articulatio* or organic whole, one that appears to arise through a *generatio aequivoca,* in the manner of lowly worms, but which in fact has its schema, "as its original [*ursprünglichen*] germ, in the sheer self-development of reason," by virtue of which each system is individually membered (*gegliedert*) and all organically united (A/835 = B/863).

Here then, is the philosophic idea, membered in accordance with the essential ends of human reason, yet in a manner to which Kant's own discoveries give new and, it seems, decisive access. Metaphysics, for its part, is that portion of philosophy which is to present pure a priori knowledge in its unity, a unity deriving from the common origination of such knowledge in reason.

Heretofore, scientific foundings were burdened by the (near) invisibility of that original articulation:

> No one attempts to establish [*zu Stande zu bringen*] a science unless he has an idea upon which to base it. However, in the working out of the science, the schema, nay even the definition that [the founder] first gave of the science, is very seldom adequate to his idea. For this idea lies hidden in reason, like a germ in which the parts are still undeveloped and barely recognizable to microscopic observation. Consequently . . . we must not explain and determine [sciences] according to the description given by their founder, but instead according to the idea which, out of the natural unity of the parts we have assembled, we find to be grounded in reason itself. For we shall then find that the founder and even his latest successors are groping for an idea which they have never succeeded in making clear to themselves, and that consequently they have not been able to determine the science's proper content, its articulation (systematic unity) and limits. ([A/834 = B/862])

Kant, on the other hand, is (or here claims to be) the *first founder* of a science to whom the germinal articulation is, as it were, *clearly visible*. Accordingly, his metaphysics articulates itself completely into (1) ontology, (2) rational physiology (the rational study of nature), (3) rational cosmology, and (4) rational theology (A/846 = B/874).

However, one erstwhile member—empirical psychology—is out of joint: even though empirical psychology is "completely banished [*verbannt*] and excluded" from metaphysics by the very idea, Kant permits it to remain "episodically," lest it be forced to settle where it has even less (*sic*) affinity: "Though [empirical psychology] is but a stranger [*Fremdling*], it has long been a resident, and we allow it to stay for some time longer, until it can set up an establishment of its own in a complete anthropology (pendant to the empirical science of nature)" ([A/848–49 = B/876–77]). Empirical psychology is thus at once wholly cut off from metaphysics and sufficiently familiar to merit temporary shelter. This peculiar status is not, perhaps, wholly unexpected; for empirical psychology is, in a sense, the black hole of Kant's philosophic universe, which, as will emerge, can account for everything but the origin of its own originating idea.[41]

Reason recognizes its idea only when it has become, or is on the verge of becoming, actual. Prior to that clarifying moment, the idea lies "hidden in our minds" and can only be discovered through the laborious and seemingly random "collection of materials" which proves only in retrospect to have been rational (A/835 = B/863). Prior to that moment, all knowledge, subjectively regarded, remains merely "historical," that is, "given from outside" and "in the form" in which it has been given. Prior to that moment, knowledge is not authentically one's own, for it does not arise *out* of (one's own) reason.

Thus, one who merely learns a system without producing its idea anew has merely a historical (*historisch*) knowledge, not true possession. Such a person "forms himself according to a foreign reason, but the imitative [*nachbildende*] faculty is not the productive one" ([A/836 = B/864]).

Once brought into focus, the idea of reason propagates itself, not by imposition from without, but by an awakening (such being Kant's general intent) of individual productive faculties. Such ideal propagation, unlike the natural sort, might seem to bypass matter entirely, except insofar as the latter plays the (minimal) role of furnishing a sensible medium of communication. And yet, strangely perhaps, Kant returns to nature and history in the last section of the *Critique,* a section entitled "The History [*Geschichte*] of Pure Reason."

Why, having just summarily dismissed history (as *Historie*), does he return to consider it (as *Geschichte*) and from what he calls the "transcendental standpoint" of the "nature of pure reason" — a standpoint that cannot help but appear, given the discussion preceding it, oxymoronic? For surely an investigation of the *nature* of reason (understood as in inquiry into the empirical cause[s] of reason) has just been excluded, or at best, given episodic asylum.

Earlier, Kant had insisted that the gathering of the great material that has been collected, or which can be obtained from the ruins of the past, into a system of human knowledge is not only possible but "would not be difficult" (A/835 = B/863). The title of the final section of his work stands to indicate not the completion of his system, but the "one remaining place that the future must fill in."

Kant contents himself with casting a merely "volatile [*flüchtige*] glance," from a merely transcendental standpoint — that of the "nature of reason" — on the entirety of past belaborings of the same, belaborings that freely present themselves to his eyes as structures, but structures only in ruins. That glance reveals a pattern of revolutions of which Kant here gives only a "volatile sketch" — that of a history of reason which implicitly includes his own self-educative journey.[42]

Out of the ruined methods of the past, he says, only the critical way lies open, a way that can, as one may judge, bring human reason complete satisfaction before the close of the century. Yet however close at hand, that satisfaction remains unconsummated, awaiting as it does the judgment of others to follow in Kant's footsteps.[43] In enjoining such collaboration Kant indicates, even as he strives to overcome, the one remaining gap in his architectonic as a self-propagating system. The future, and with it complete clarification of the idea, is not wholly in Kant's power.[44]

III. Conclusion

In his essay *What Is Enlightenment?* Kant dares mankind to "sever" its "leading strings." But what sort of guiding thread can replace those leading strings — nature's stepmotherly cord — without evicting us from nature entirely?[45] What Kant elsewhere calls the object of practical reason (or happiness conjoined with worthiness to be happy) does not here suffice; for while that object can deliver us into a moral world to come, it cannot determinately indicate the path we are to tread on earth.

In the end, Kant's idea of history does not and cannot answer the question with which it begins — that of how a species as *eingebildet* (the word means "conceited," but also "imaginary")[46] as ourselves is to be conceived at all. This failure points at once to the marginality and the centrality of history to Kant's project as a whole, whose three basic subjects of inquiry — what can I know? what ought I do? what may I hope? — reduce, as Kant elsewhere observes, to the single question: what is man?[47] It is, ultimately, Kant's insistence on human dignity, the absolute moral worth of every individual, that prevents, or saves, him from taking the Hegelian plunge, in which philosophy and history ultimately merge in the self-conceptualization of a spirit that is no longer, for that very reason, altogether human.[48]

We thus return to the simultaneous necessity and strangeness, by Kant's own account, of his historical idea. The necessity of that idea arises not so much from its moral utility, the spur to worldly action for which it is generally taken (though there is surely something to this), but from a deeper imperative on Kant's part: a desire, or need, to figure the relation between reason and unreason. The ensuing exercise in spontaneous generation (or what Herder called "spiritual self-birthing") escapes the charge of fantasy (of which Herder accused it) only by virtue of history's strangeness — the unrelievable tension between man as a progressive or "species-being" and the infinite value of the individual — a value that sets an absolute limit to both nature's and history's reach. It is this strangeness, I believe, that ultimately prevented Kant from writing a true philosophy of history, forcing him to rely instead on the pure postulates of practical reason — God and the immortality of the soul — to stave off the inertial despair that would otherwise weigh down our moral action.[49]

But Kant's insistence on human dignity, which he would like to be the final word, is itself both philosophically and historically entangled, bound up with his own lifelong effort to come to terms with nature's infinite fecundity—a fecundity that constantly threatens to swallow up again the progeny to which it gives rise. (Kant's humanity is itself, as Nietzsche might say, all too human.) It is this tangled root of Kantian thought that partially resurfaces in Heideggerian historicity and being toward death—that other great shaper, along with Hegelian spirit, of historical consciousness in the twentieth century.

It is today difficult—even more difficult than in Kant's time—to find consolation in the hope of perpetual progress, a hope that has been all but blasted by the totalizing politics to which Kant's idea of history indirectly contributed. Still, that Kant's call for philosophic history has born some bitter fruit should not be held entirely to his account. For like the antidotes which, according to Kant, nature conveniently places next to toxic mushrooms so that the species who consume them may survive, Kantian morality—and in particular his account of human rights—may well offer the best prospect of relief from the political afflictions for which his thought is also, in some sense, responsible. If this is so, Kant's idea of history may provide strangely redeeming comfort after all.

IV. Appendix: Kant and Herder on Nature and Freedom

In 1784 Herder published the first volume of his *Ideas on the Philosophy of the History of Mankind*. In the same year (the year in which his own *Idea for a Universal History* also appeared), Kant wrote the first of three reviews of Herder's work that were to end their already faltering friendship.[50]

Scholars have noted certain thematic similarities between Herder's *Ideas*[51] and Kant's early *Universal Natural History,* which Herder read in the early 1760s, around the time that he was attending lectures as Kant's student. This continuing allegiance to doctrines Kant had subsequently rejected may have contributed to the unmistakable tone of annoyance that pervades Kant's reviews and no doubt angered Herder. But a deeper source of Kant's hostility may lie in what must have struck him as a proximity on Herder's part, bordering on the perverse, to Kant's mature position as well.

Nowhere is this clearer than in Herder's "poetic" treatment of nature as the "maternal" source of human freedom. Kant, as we recall, says *almost* as much, but in a saving, if paradoxical, formulation that would have us thank nature only for not having to thank her. Herder's "Great Mother Nature," on the contrary, is not that from which we must emancipate ourselves (even if in doing so we develop germs somehow naturally implanted) but that to whose support—in bidding us to stand—we owe our rational awakening (*Ideas* III:6).

A number of telling passages from Herder's *Ideas* illuminate the issue dividing the philosopher and his former student. At I:18, for example, Herder presents as a model for human emulation the "phoenix of nature" who perpetually "lifts herself up," thus almost exactly reversing the import of the phoenix of nature in Kant's own earlier history. In keeping with this reversal, Herder (unlike Kant) figures air as unambiguously feminine; made pregnant [*beschwängert*] and dissolving, air seems to be "the mother of earth creatures, as much as of the earth itself, the universal vehicle of things, that draws them into its womb and drives them forth" (p. 54).This femininity is associated, in turn, with man's affinity with all other earthly creatures, who are, like him, a "ward of the air," making him "a brother, in the entire circle of his existence, to all earthly organisms" (p. 55).

In keeping with this sense of earthly kinship, the cycles of nature do not strike Herder with the repellent force that they evoked in Kant:

> Although we find the bowels [*Eingeweiden*] of the earth to be a chaos and ruin [*Trümmer*], because we are not able to survey the first construction of the whole, yet we still observe even in that which seems to us smallest and most raw, a determinate existence, a shape and construction according to eternal laws that no human will can change. We notice these laws and forms; their inner forces, however, we do not know; and that which one designates with universal terms, e.g., harmony, extension, and affinity, only familiarize us with outer relations, without leading us any closer to the inner being" [p. 65]. . . . Holy [*heilsame*] mother, how economical [*haushälterisch*] and compensating [*ersetzend*] is thy circle! All death is new life, putrefying decay itself prepares for health and fresh forces. (P. 66)

Man's middling natural status, for its part, is not man's misfortune (as in Kant's *Universal Natural History*), but his pride — a function of his possession of that commanding form (*Hauptbild*) in relation to which the anatomy and physiology of all other creatures of the earth are to be measured (p. 77). Thus Herder proclaims, "take joy in thy state [*Stand*], o man, study yourself, noble middle creature, in all that lives around thee [*um dich*]!"

Where Kant would sever nature's leading strings, Herder enjoins us to cleave to nature's fetters (*Fesseln*) as the very source of healthy love of one's own and spiritual vitality: "nature," he says, "binds our spirit from childhood with strong fetters, each to his own property [*Eigentum*]." Each loves his own, that is, "his own earth, for what property finally do we have other than this?" Each loves his own land, customs, language, wife, children, "not because they are the best in the world, but rather because they are preserved as ones own, and in loving them one loves oneself and one's own effort." Even the bird of passage finds rest and comfort in its own nest, and the roughest fatherland has often for the human stock the most drawing fetters for those accustomed to it (p. 26). Where Kant bases political community on a moral and juridical usurpation of the earth's "maternity" in bearing us, Herder urges a more direct (and, one might add, simplistic) political and psychological autochthony:

> Thus if we ask, where is man's fatherland? Where is the center [*Mittelpunkt*] of the earth? the answer could everywhere be: here, where thou standest [*stehest*]—be it near the icy pole or exactly under the burning mid-day sun. Wherever human beings could live, they do, and they could live almost everywhere. Since the great mother could and would not bring forth any eternal monotony [*Einerlei*] upon the earth, there was no other means but that she should make appear the most monstrous [*ungeheuerste*] variety [*Vielerlei*], and wove human beings from a material to stand this variety. (Pp. 52–53)

Where Kant claims to be a citizen, first and foremost, of the world, Herder enjoins us to stand in the place (as the song goes) where we are. The universal hability that for Kant makes man, prior to his juridical appropriation of the soil, a "stranger on earth" leads Herder to cling all the more firmly to the accidents of earthly deliverance.

Thus nature's fetters direct the drives of propagation, as Herder puts it, so that the young come into the world at a friendly time (p. 97).[52] Thus, too, the "beneficent mother love" with which nature "educates and actively accustoms each living creature to activities, thoughts and virtues, suited to the composure of its organization," a love Herder calls "beyond all expression." [N]o virtue," he continues, "no drive is in the human heart, whose analog one may not find here and there in the animal world, and to which the formative mother [*bildende Mutter*] thus organically accustoms the animal." Love of one's own, society, even a sort of republic, have their prior image (*Vorbild*) in animal activity, and he who regards animals as mere machines "sins against nature," including his own (p. 97).[53]

What essentially distinguishes man from the other animals is not, as Kant insists, his idea of freedom and concomitant practical transcendence of the rest of nature, but a "noble upright posture"—a posture that is itself the (partial) work of nature, who in so forming man made him, Herder claims, a fellow regent and creator (pp. 100–101).

> Maternally, she offered her final, most artful creation her hand and said: "stand up [*steh auf*] upon the earth! Left to thyself thou wouldst be an animal like the other animals; but through my particular help and love, goest thou upright, and becomest the God of animals." Let us on this holy work of art, the charitable act [*Wohlthat*] through which our race [*Geschlecht*] became a human race, gratefully cast a lingering glance; with amazement we shall see which new organization of forces began with the upright form [*Gestalt*] of humanity, and through it alone the human being became a human being.

In a similar vein, Herder presents reason as nature's maternal product, the "inner brain," or "workshop of ideas," a "womb" (*Gebärmutter*) that forms the fruit of thought:

> If everything is healthy and fresh, and allows the fruit not only the pertinent spirit and life warmth, but also commodious space, a fitting place of consecration, in which the feelings of sense and of the entire body are grasped by the invisible organic force that here weaves everything together, and, speaking metaphorically, is united in the *lucid point* called higher *consciousness:* then, if there arise outer circumstances of instruction and the arousal of ideas, the finely organized creature of reason is ready. (P. 108)[54]

The natural affinity of reason is likewise reflected in the structure and placement of the unborn child (nothing here about the ills, of which Kant complains, visited on the fetus by the mother's "unnatural" upright gait!),[55] a placement that reveals nature's special attention to the formation of the human brain, to which gravity brings an abundance of blood: "Already thus in mother love the human being is formed for the upright position and everything that depends upon it. . . . The human being is what he ought to be — and to this work all his parts — an upwardly striving tree,[56] crowned with the most beautiful crown of a *fine thought formation*" (p. 111).

Herder's praise of nature culminates in a celebration of mother love in a most literal sense, that is, breast-feeding, which not only provides infants "with the tenderest and finest nourishment," but also (to continue the Rousseauist line) gives rise to the paternal household — that "first human society," bound by "blood, confidence, and love," by which the wildest and most inhuman are tamed (p. 126, cf. 216). Kant and Herder, it seems, divide between them Rousseau's two-faced Eve, Kant fixing on woman as devious seductress, Herder on woman as self-forgetting nurse. The maternal tenderness that (as Philonenko notes)[57] Kant (strangely) omits in his adaptation of Rousseau's insight into woman's role, Herder exaggerates almost beyond recognition. For Herder, motherly devotion, not sexual enticement, is the affective means by which woman (and through her, nature) engages history. Man for Kant is not, as with Herder, first tamed or made peaceful by woman (in her capacity as mother nurse); rather it is woman (in her capacity as seductress) who first makes him warlike.

Hence, too, the striking absence in Herder of the complex sexual pessimism so marked in the anthropologies of Rousseau and Kant alike. Rousseau and Kant see in the tension between man's natural and civil puberty the source of his dual potential for degradation and sublimity. Herder, by way of contrast, recognizing as he does only a continuously upward growth, associates the arrival of physical maturity with a wholly commend-

able tendency toward youthful hope and *Schwärmerei* (p. 123), thus placing in a favorable light the very qualities Kant criticized in Herder, at a
time when the two were still on very friendly terms.[58]

But man, it emerges (in opposition to Herder's insistence on man's
earthly brotherhood), also has a spiritual parent—the divine father who
heads the household of the earth's economy (*Haushaltung*). Man, Herder
insists, is "created for freedom" and has no law on earth other than one he
lays out (*sich auflegt*) himself, for he would become the wildest creature if
he did not already recognize God's law in nature and, as a child, strive after
the perfection of the father. Where animals are born servants (*Knechte*) in
the great household of earth's economy, the true human being is free and
(or in the sense of being) obedient to the good and to love made manifest
by nature's laws. "If thou goest not willingly," say the wise, "thou must still
go, for the rule of nature does not alter itself on thy account" (p. 129).
Withal, freedom and the moral law never require for Herder the *break* with
matter on which, for Kant, human dignity ultimately rests. The spiritual
father that for Kant communicated ineffably (if at all) speaks for Herder in
the language of the earth itself. Speech is at once the seed or semen (*Samen*)
of reason, the "divine art of ideas," and the "mother of all arts" (p. 107).
Man's hybrid status as the child of earth and spirit poses for Herder no
special riddle.

Man's distinctness is reflected for Herder, as for the early Kant, in human
hopes for immortality (for we are "children of eternity)," a hope reinforced,
Herder claims, by the observable affinities of nature's outward forms (p.
131).[59] These ascending forms are to be regarded either as plays of nature
(*Spiele der Natur*)—"and understanding-rich nature never plays sense-
lessly"—or as indications of a realm of invisible forces that stand in the
same harmony and dense transition (*Übergang*) as that which we observe
in external forms (p. 132).

In enlarging upon human distinctiveness, Herder also invokes morality:
where the animal is led securely by instinct, which Herder calls the maternal gift (*Muttergabe*) of nature, man, as child in the highest father's house,
must learn that which pertains to humanity, a task he performs imperfectly
because along with the seed of understanding and virtue he also inherits
that of prejudice and evil customs (p. 143). Where animals depend wholly
on the earth, man has in him the seed of immortality, which requires another plant garden. Man is thus the juncture (*Mittelglied*) of two worlds
(p. 146). Ostrichlike, he for the most part swings his wings in vain, his
heavy body pulling him to the ground. Yet here as well, Herder claims,
organizing nature has exercised care and makes perfect what in our eyes
seems unformed. Only one more step may be needed before the immortal
spirit can breath freer air (p. 147). Thus earthly life keeps us, as it were, in

bonds (*Banden*). Leibniz's expression, according to which the soul is the "mirror of the world-all," contains perhaps a deeper truth, for forces of a world-all seem hidden in it and need only an organization or series of organizations to be activated.

And yet even here, where Herder's rhetoric seems most securely within the orbit of Kant's thought — at least its earlier versions — the two thinkers essentially diverge. For Herder, the "all goodly one," who "would not deny such organization," keeps the soul in leading strings (*er sie gängelt,* as in *Gängelband*) like a child. The soul, to whom even in its present fetters (*Fesseln*) space and time are "empty words," is thus gradually prepared for a wealth of growing enjoyment in the fancy (*Wahn*) of its own acquired (or self-earned) powers (p. 148). We should therefore take no trouble (*Mühe*) over the place and hour of our future existence, but rather enjoy our earthly life, regarding it as the school of suffering and joy through which we come of manly age (*Mannesalter*), a school in which man is held benevolently "in tether" by a higher power.

Herder, in short, insists on both reason's *immanence* and reason's *transcendence* — on man's *self-won freedom* and on his *original and ongoing dependence* — without acknowledging (and this for Kant is the matter's crux) that these positions stand in fundamental opposition.[60]

This contrast finds political expression in Kant and Herder's divergent approaches to the question of human individuality. If Herder is in one sense a celebrator of the particular and the individual (hence an early defender of "difference" against the hegemony of the "universal"), he is in another and deeper sense radically monistic. For Kant, true individuality is inseparable from the experience, grounded in the moral law, of man's division from himself, a division that is humanly defining. Political community, therefore, is neither a simple unity, nor simply natural. For Herder, who compares nations to plants, individuality is the product of continuity and finds its experiential basis in the natural efflorescence that is an aspect of our sympathetic connection with all living beings and/or the tie that binds us to a higher power.

Hence, too, Kant and Herder politically and personally freighted disagreement over happiness. For Herder, the "happiness of man is in all places an individual good," in the sense of being the "offspring of practice, tradition, and custom." Man, says Herder, is neither "susceptible of pure bliss" nor "capable of creating felicity for himself." Since each is conditioned to enjoy happiness in a different way, each must determine its content for himself. The idiosyncrasy of happiness, which for Kant constitutes its fatal "indeterminacy," does not lead Herder to reject happiness as man's final end. Kant's idea of a history that sacrifices the happiness of individuals to the progress of the species is from Herder's point of view an arrogant usurpation, in the name of a spurious "humanity," of the right of each to follow the dictates of his own heart—a substitution of the attainable happiness that is the true end of human nature for a Tantalus-like quest for the unreachable. (None of this, to be sure, stops Herder from speaking of historical progress, just as his insistence on the equal value of all cultures as efflorescences of nature does not stop him from insisting on the superiority of European culture to all others.) Hence the "Averroism" (or reification of an imaginary universal) of which he accuses Kant, to which Kant replies (after noting Herder's inconsistencies in this regard) that without a species to whose perpetual progress one can contribute, it would be better, happy or not (and who, faced with death, can be happy?), never to have been born. Kant's idea of history, in other words, aims to establish—out of freedom and yet within the natural world—a ground or reason for man's existence, a move that Herder derisively describes as spiritual "self-birthing" (pp. 225–26; 220–21).[61]

Kant and Herder's differences on the issue of man's dual world citizenship cast a useful light on cosmopolitan liberalism and romantic nationalism as divergent fragments of Rousseau's libertarian legacy. The relative immunity of Kantian politics to the excesses and temptations of its romantic cousins owes much to the anthropological perplexity that preempts, in Kant, an unproblematic "idea of history." Kant did not come away from his exchange with Herder unfazed, as the following chapters will attempt to show. Kant's later works are increasingly open to a variety of configurations of human unity—aesthetic, teleological, and architectonic. What never changes is his discomforting yet bracing insistence that the hybrid status of man—and with it, the abysmal separation of our natural and moral character—receive its due. On this insistence, as much as anything, hinges the distinction between romantic rhapsody (with all its dangerous charms) and the peculiar decencies of Kantian rigor.

8   Adventures of the Organism (I)

The following two chapters focus on the theme of generation in the *Critique of Judgment*. Attention to this theme, whose logical and structural dominance of the work is frequently overlooked, not only makes more accessible the underlying intention of the *Critique of Judgment* in relation to Kant's philosophic project as a whole; it also focuses regard on the tension in his work between assimilating mind and matter, and (more decisively) resisting such assimilation.[1]

The question of the possibility of generation, or the apparent, and apparently absurd, emergence of life and reason out of "dead matter" or "unreason," is a seminal expression of the problem raised by our contingency as individuals and as a species, and of our consequently ineluctable concern to discover how it is that we come to find ourselves in the world—to discover, that is, a sufficient ground for our own worldly existence. The overall strategy of the third *Critique* is to accept the ineluctability of this concern (with what threatens to dissolve the mind/matter boundary) as itself defining. The unanswerable question (how is generation possible?) is replaced by the answerable question (how is our *concept* of a living organism as the unity of matter and intention possible?) The result is an assimilation of reason and nature—but only subjectively or for man, hence in a way that secures rather than destroying the boundaries of the *Geschlecht*.[2]

Kant's argument, however, depends in turn on a new notion of nature as a whole (the so-called supersensible substrate), a notion that evades the conceptual requirements of ordinary cognition and to which aesthetic experience—with its openness to what Kant calls "aesthetic ideas" and other noncognitive "hints" of nature's purposiveness—also renders us peculiarly privy, that is, in a way that keeps consciousness at a safe step of reflective or self-limiting removal.

In thus pointing to the unity of reason and nature without ceasing, on a cognitive level, to deny it, the third *Critique* articulates, to the extent theoretically possible, the paradox of reason's (human) embodiment. In so doing, moreover, it offers a more satisfactory answer to the question "what is man?" than the monstrous image of a moral stem engrafted to crooked wood provided in *Idea for a Universal History*, or at least an answer more attuned to the wholeness of a creature, even a monstrous one—a wholeness implicit in the fact that it is, after all, alive.

I. Generation and the Problem of Race

It might seem to a reader of the first and second *Critiques,* that the problem of natural generation had been laid to rest. One is therefore surprised to discover, in turning to Kant's third and final *Critique,* that the problem survives — that, indeed, a full quarter of the work is devoted to little else. To be sure, a closer look at Kant's earlier works shows that the issue had never disappeared. Three essays spanning more than a decade — from 1775 to 1788 — take up the problem of generation in a way that touches, in the final essay, on a major theme of Kant's last *Critique,* reason's a priori "need."[3]

ON THE VARIOUS RACES OF MEN

The topic of these three essays is the concept of "Race" (*Rasse*). The first of these essays, *On the Various Races of Men,* was one of only two works that Kant published in the years separating the *Inaugural Dissertation* (1770) and the first edition of the *Critique of Pure Reason* (1781). (About the other, even briefer work — a review of Moscati's *On the Essential Corporeal Difference between Animals and Human Beings* — more anon.)[4]

The fact from which Kant's first essay on race proceeds is the existence of certain characteristics not belonging to the human species as such, but which are invariably inherited by offspring. Thus, to use Kant's own example, whereas brunette and blond parents may produce either brunette or blond children (who inherit the characteristic of only one parent), white and black parents invariably produce children of mixed color (who inherit the characteristics of both parents).[5]

What makes this invariable inheritance a puzzle is the problem it appears to raise for the definition of the human species. Kant approvingly cites Buffon's rule — that animals that can produce fertile offspring belong to the same physical *Gattung* — as a crucial advance over "scholastic" schemes of classification which rely on mere resemblance to establish a collective identity.[6] According to Buffon's concept, "all human beings of the wide earth belong to . . . the same natural Gattung, because, however great may be the differences in their shape [*Gestalt*], they consistently produce fertile offspring with one another" (II:429). Kant's gloss, however, is characteristically his own: what makes Buffon's rule important is the ground of necessary unity to which it points.

> For this unity of the natural Gattung [II:430], which is as great as that of the communally [*gemeinschaftliche*] valid force of reproduction, one can ascribe only to a single natural cause: namely, that all belong to the same stem [*Stamme*], from which they issue despite their diversity, or at least could have issued.

The problem is to reconcile community of natural origin with diversity of inheritance in the special case where it is invariable. That this is a problem follows from Kant's peculiar definition of a species. What unites a species, for Kant, is not merely the temporal succession of fertile generations (in which case the species would be a mere aggregate), but the invariable passing down, from one generation to the next, of a common seed. It is the invariability (and hence, implicitly, necessity) of this inheritance according to what Kant would later call a rule that marks the species as a real, rather than merely nominal, whole. In short, Kant's definition of a natural species is not merely descriptive, but "historical" (in the special sense of securing a collective identity over time) and hence "scientific."

The existence of half-breeds (*Halbschlagen*), which invariably inherit the characteristics of each parent, gives prima facie evidence, however, for the existence of different originating stems, as the only way that such invariable heredity can be explained. Buffon's basic argument for the unity of the human species — the universal "validity" of our genetic currency (an argument to which Kant adheres, he says, to avoid the gratuitous multiplication of causes) — must therefore be supplemented by an explanation of invariably inherited, or "racial," differences.

Kant finds his answer in the essential *Bestimmung* of the species "for every sort of climate and soil" (II:435). The original human germ contained *in potentia* all of the seeds out of which the various races developed. Racial differences emerged only with the dispersal of mankind to the various regions of the earth, whose specific conditions of soil and climate "occasion" the development of certain seeds (for example, short stature in frigid regions, where body heat must be conserved) along with the suppression of others. The suitability of each race for its region — a harmony that some wrongly take as proof of local creation — is thus subordinated to mankind's original determination: his (unique) suitability for anywhere on the planet.[7]

Kant's resort to teleology, however, is not so much positive (as if we had immediate insight into nature's purposes) as negative — a result of our inability otherwise to give a stable account of organic species. If invariably inherited characteristics were not derived from the original seed — if, that is to say, it were possible for anything "foreign" to enter the generative force — organisms might distance themselves further and further from the original stem. In such a case the distinction between degeneration and descent, and with it the very notion of a determinate species, would lose all meaning. Thus not only inherited changes that help an animal survive (like the second layer of feathers developed by certain birds), but also inherited changes whose purpose remains obscure, cannot be explained by chance or mechanical causes alone and must rather be considered preformed (*vorgebildet*) (II:435).

Kant divides variations *within* a race into *Spielarten,* which perpetuate themselves, albeit not in every generation, even if the population is "transplanted" to a different climate (for example, in the case of the white race, blue eyes); and *Varietäten,* or "family resemblances," which often but not always do so. As a consequence, a population that remains under the influence of a given soil and climate for many generations acquires a family stamp (*Schlag*), as with the Boethians, who differed from the Athenians owing to the differing humidity of their respective soils. (In a twist on traditional notions of "autochthony," national differences are occasioned by what is literally a people's "native ground.") The inbreeding of a hereditary nobility likewise produces an identifiable stamp; nevertheless, Kant rejects as counterproductive Maupertuis's eugenic suggestion that a "naturally noble" type of human being be bred for each geographic region, it being the mixture of good and bad that "sets the sleeping forces of humanity in play" and thus requires us to "develop all our talents and so approach the perfection of our *Bestimmung*" (II:431).

Of the four races "under which all the manifoldness of our *Gattung* can be grasped" Kant singles out dark-haired whites as the race that climate has least affected and which therefore most closely resembles the original stock. Kant risks his own "volatile conjecture" that the differing skin colors by which the races are primarily identified result from the different precipitants of dissolved iron left in the channels of dermal excretion by the action of varying proportions of heat and humidity on the blood. In the case of whites iron does not precipitate at all (owing to the especially moderate climate in which the race developed), leaving the channels free of obstruction and producing a vigor superior to that of other races.[8]

Once developed, racial characteristics are permanent, even when later migrations bring populations into climates for which they are not physically suited (as with the Gypsies in Europe). Thus the fact that similar climates are currently inhabited by different races does not disprove Kant's basic thesis. To know the ground of the manifoldness of human derivations, description of what now exists does not suffice. One must rather, he says, "dare [*wagen*] a history of nature, as a particular science, which may gradually go forth from opinions to knowledge" (II:443).

Kant's major publication of the seventies thus ends with a "daring" call for natural history, a particular science of the interaction between geology and human generation stretching backward toward the original germ in which the destiny of the species was deposited. Man as such is destined for everywhere, that is, for nowhere in particular, with race serving as a temporary resting point: an early and one time only concession to his animal dependence, until the art of survival achieves sufficient development to replace man's earlier reliance on biological adaptations. (In a later work, Kant suggests, on the basis of fossil evidence, that a younger earth underwent frequent, cataclysmic revolutions, an instability to which the species would have been vulnerable [and to which other species indeed succumbed] without the ability to disperse into all regions of the globe). Kant, indeed, speculates that new races might yet form if populations remained isolated in one region long enough, a circumstance that social intercourse (or the emergence of what we might call a world culture) now renders highly unlikely.

Two conclusions emerge. First, biological species are not mere aggregates, assembled (as Linnaeus would have it) solely on the basis of a subjectively perceived "likeness," but genuine wholes, united through the necessary passing down from one generation to another of characteristics deriving from a single germ. In the case of man, however, two facts seem to call into question the unity of the species so conceived: the existence of variations that are inherited, but not invariably (for example, blue eyes); and the existence of characteristics that are inherited invariably without belonging to the species as a whole (for example, dark skin). Both are reconcilable with a common origin, but only if man's *Bestimmung* is conceived, not only in terms of individual conformity to a determinate type, but also as a historical, and racially differentiated, process consisting both in the spreading of humanity throughout the globe and in open-ended awakening of our unlimited talents.

Definition [*Bestimmung*] of the Concept of a Human Race

Kant's second essay on race, published in 1785, defended the basic argument of the first, but this time with the explicit rationale of guiding the investigation of experience and thus satisfying a "need" that experience alone cannot meet. Once again, Kant takes his bearings from the existence of biological half-breeds, or *Bastarde* — offspring who inherit the differing, invariably inherited characteristics of both parents. A racial characteristic is thus one that, while not belonging to the species as a whole, is invariably inherited.[9]

Kant sets his discussion in the context of new empirical reports concerning the diversity of the human *Gattung*, reports that raise more questions than they answer (VIII:91). Some observers, insisting on the common origin of the human species as certified by Scripture, argue that human diversity is the effect of external factors such as heat and climate. Others, noting the invariable inheritance of certain group characteristics, argue for those groups' separate origins. Kant finds either alternative intolerable. Separate origins should be rejected because it multiplies causes unnecessarily, it being impossible to conceive how organisms of differing origin could be capable of fertile interbreeding (VIII:102). But the first alternative, which assumes the power of outer forces to modify the inner seed, is equally unthinkable.

Kant's first "maxim of reason," that causes not be multiplied unnecessarily (a maxim that militates against the hypothesis of multiple creations), is thus limited by a second, that species maintain themselves unchanged[10] (VIII:96). Concerning the second maxim, Kant is especially emphatic. To admit such changes would be tantamount to granting that the imagination of a pregnant woman can effect inheritable changes in a fetus, or that docked horses can pass on their shortened tails to their descendants:

> If the magic force of imagination, or the artfulness of man is given to have a capacity in animal bodies to alter the generative force itself . . . one would not know anymore from which original nature may have proceeded, or how much it might deviate from that original, and, since the human imagination knows no limits, into what grotesque forms of genuses and species it might finally degenerate/run wild. (VIII:97)

It is this consideration, it seems, above all, that moves him to adopt the following "grounding thesis," namely, "not to accept as valid any botching influence of imagination on the generative force of nature," nor "any ability of men to effect the old original of the genus." For if, he adds, "I were to allow even a single case of this kind it would be like making room for a single ghost story or tale of magic. The bounds [*Schranken*] of reason once penetrated [*durch brochen*], delusion presses through the same gap [*Lücke*] by the thousands."

The "hundreds of facts" against which Kant sets his maxim are no match for the delusional horde that would otherwise penetrate the bounds of reason. The (putative) power of maternal imagination typifies in an especially vivid way the breach that denial of the constancy of species effects — the "monstrous idea" of unbounded natural fertility from which reason, as Kant elsewhere states, "recoils" [*zurückbebt*] in "horror."[11] For fetus and researcher alike, imagination threatens monstrously to dissolve the boundaries upon which the identity of individual and species respectively depend. (The relation between imagination and natural fertility becomes explicit, as we shall see, in Kant's later treatment of genius.) In the face of this threat there is no recourse other than a resolve to "constancy," that is, adoption as one's grounding maxim, and in the face of all facts purportedly to the contrary, that nature conserves its species. In rejecting, on a priori grounds, such adventurous (*abenteuerlich*) glimpses one does not blind oneself to actual experience; for such glimpses bear the telltale sign of all such stories — an unwillingness to submit nature to experiment (VIII:97).[12]

Kant's concept of race thus steers a middle course between the Scylla of palingenesis and the Charybdis of miscegenation. Against those who, in supporting a single human origin, attribute invariably inherited differences to external causes, and those who explain such differences on the basis of multiple origins, Kant urges a third alternative: an account that reconciles a single origin with invariably inherited differences by appealing to the idea of an original, invariably inherited germ whose various *potentia* are differentially actualized. Without the assumption of such a germ, imagination threatens to give birth to monsters, either figuratively, in the brain of the researcher, or literally, in the germ of the maternally susceptible fetus.

KANT AND FORSTER

In 1786 Georg Forster published an attack on Kant's theory of race.[13] Forster, whose recent *Voyage Round the World*, an account of his travels with Captain Cooke, had won him instant celebrity, seems to have found the work of the sedentary philosopher particularly irksome. Forster rejected Kant's (Scripturally correct) insistence on human descent from a single pair on the basis of his own observations of the black inhabitants of Africa. Where Kant had defended his use of an a priori concept of race on the grounds that "one finds [in experience] what one needs only when one knows what one is seeking," Forster, the self-styled "empiricist," replies that Kant sees what he wishes to see rather than what is really there (p. 75). Forster thus called into question Kant's basic distinction between natural history and natural description. A history of the sort that Kant attempts is, he says, a science "for gods rather than men."

> Who has the ability to explain the family tree of even a single variety back to its *Gattung,* if it does not begin from another before our own eyes. Who has regarded the laboring earth in that far removed and wholly inconceivably veiled point in time when animals and plants issued forth from their source [*Schoβ*], in many myriads of multifariousness, without generation from their like, without seed housing, without womb? Who has counted the number of their original *Gattungen,* their autochthons? Who can tell us how many individuals of each shape, in wholly different regions of the world, arising . . . organized from sea fructifying slime, from their laboring mother? Who is so wise as to be able to teach us whether they roused themselves only once, in a single place, or one at a time, from entirely separate parts of the world, from organic forces emerging each time from the ocean's embrace? (P. 87)[14]

That the four races should have sprung from a single couple is as marvelous as the fable of Leda's egg, twinning itself so that each differing brother would also have a similar wife (p. 94). Forster does not choose lightly the figure of Leda (who mated with Zeus appearing as a swan). For Forster, mating between men and animals is not different in principle from mating between blacks and whites. Miscegenation is thus a kind of bestiality; the "nausea [*Eckel*] and revulsion [*Abschau*]" that it arouses in blacks and whites alike, at least where the voice (*Stimme*) of instinct has not been silenced, is comparable to the exclusive inclination of all other species for their own kind. Natural feeling overrides fertility as an indication of nature's boundaries. That men of different original stock should be able to interbreed (a possibility that Kant had called incomprehensible) is no more mysterious than that reindeer and bison are able to do so: either they are species that approach very closely each other's limits, or varieties of a single species, varieties that bear the stamp of the climate in which they arose (pp. 88–89). Classification on the basis of fertility is thus no less arbitrary than classification on the basis of other similarities, a fact which undercuts Kant's distinction between real and nominal species.

Finally, Forster argued, Kant's insistence on a single origin violated Kant's own principle of economy, it being easier to account for the existence of human beings throughout the world on the basis of their beginning in different places for which they were specially suited (of which black Africans are the preeminent example), than it is on the basis of a single pair, subject to all the vagaries of nature.[15]

The "Need" of Reason

Kant responded to Forster in *On the Use of Teleological Principles in Philosophy* (1788), which further clarifies the "need" mentioned in Kant's earlier essay. Kant had in the interim published a brief work, *What It Means to Orient Oneself in Thinking* (1786), in which the "need" of reason had played a central role.

In that work Kant drew an analogy between the subjective feeling that allows us to distinguish between right and left and hence to orient ourselves spatially even in a darkened room, and an analogous feeling that allows us to orient ourselves logically even where we are, so far as objects of experience are concerned, in "empty [*bloβ*] space" (VIII:136; [239–40]). What distinguishes a guided incursion into the supersensible from capricious (and delusional) wandering is the anchoring of the former in a feeling of "need" (*Bedürfnis*). The character of that need Kant describes as follows. In certain cases, it seems, reason requires us to render judgment even though in so doing we run up against the "limits of experience." Like the ability to differentiate between right and left, the need of reason is a "feeling of distinction within my own *subject*" that arises when reason's demand for satisfaction confronts the limits of experience (VIII:134; [238]). As a consequence of this (volatile) combination of constraint and will ("For reason will at last be satisfied" [VIII:136; (240)]), it becomes "necessary" to seek out a substitute for objective knowledge. The only option is to examine the concept "by which we would venture out beyond all possible experience," in full recognition of the fact that no objective intuition is available by which we might assure ourselves of its real possibility. By determining that such a concept is in any case not contradictory, we can at least bring the relation of such an object to objects of experience under a pure concept of reason, and while not making it sensible, make something supersensible suitable for the uses of experience.

The use Kant has in mind, from a theoretical perspective, has to do with our efforts to judge the "contingency" of things, above all when that contingency involves "purposiveness." Certain appearances (one thinks immediately of organic beings) present themselves in such a way that we cannot think their possibility without attributing their existence to an intelligent author. In such cases, reason's need authorizes us to assume the existence of such a first cause, even though it could never be for us an object of knowledge. Rational belief in the existence of an intelligent first cause is thus distinguished from "belief in ghosts" (and other *Träumerei*) by the suitability of the former for the uses of experience (especially as it involves organic life). The need of reason, at least where theory is concerned, arises from the perplexity with which we encounter living beings, whose existence we cannot deny, but whose possibility we cannot explain on the basis of objective experience alone.

It is, at bottom, this perplexity that, for Kant, guides our theoretical incursions into the supersensible realm. Not God (our "knowledge" of whom can never be other than a delusional "vision") but our need to believe in him (a need that our "drive for knowledge" makes palpable [VIII:139 n; (241 n)]) becomes the "compass" of the speculative soul. The subjective need that arises from the conflict between reason's demand and the limits of experience provides (like Kant's own beating heart, which permits him to tell left from right)[16] surer guidance than the visions that "nature's favored" mistake for genuine "illumination" (*Erleuchterung*). Our need to determine our own power of judgment "in the dark" is equivalent to our need to account for the contingency of (living) things — to explain to our own satisfaction how relations the basis of whose necessity we cannot grasp may never the less be lawful.

Reason's theoretical need is, to be sure, only hypothetical. Theoretically speaking, we need assume the existence of God only if we want to judge the first cause of everything contingent, especially as it concerns the order of actual (*wirklich*) ends situated in the world. Practically speaking, on the other hand, we *must* assume it, for otherwise the highest good and with it all virtue might be taken as a "mere ideal," lacking in objective reality.

Rational belief in the existence of God, understood both as intelligent creator and as supreme unconditioned good, thus opens up a new basis for the unification of theory and practice: the "guidepost" (*Wegweiser*) or compass by which the speculative thinker orients himself in his rational incursions (*Vernunftstreiferei*) into the field of supersensible objects is also one that enables a human being of healthy but common understanding "to trace a way fully appropriate to the entire end of his destination [*Bestimmung*] in both a theoretical and a practical *Absicht*" (VIII:142; [245]).[17]

Politically speaking, Kant's maxim/postulate of rational belief marks out the narrow way between *Freidenkerei* (whose lawless subjectivity is incompatible with the requirements of civic peace) and the doctrinal tyranny to which such freethinking ultimately leads, a way therefore authorized by reason's own maxim of "self-preservation." Freedom of thought must be limited by the law that reason sets itself. Without such self-restraint, "genius, in its bold impetus [*Schwung*], slips off the thread [*Faden*] by which reason otherwise steers it" and is finally checked by the external forces of exterior witness and tradition. In breaking its "fetters," reason must learn that it cannot adopt a maxim of independence from its own need, a maxim incompatible in its "unbelief" with genuine morality.[18]

Kant's *On the Use of Teleological Principles in Philosophy* takes as its point of departure the "need" of reason to resort to teleology in order to make up for the limitations of its theoretical investigation of nature, a need "analogous" to the one that authorizes our resort to a practical idea—that of the highest good—to compensate for the deficiencies of contemplative reason, which strives in vain to grasp the "Inbegriff" of nature (VIII:159).

In resorting to teleology of the former sort, reason seems to take its bearings, not from the characteristics of the object, but from its own needs and intentions (VIII:160). Constrained by the "double, reciprocally limiting interests" of theory and teleology, reason thus finds its own standpoint vis à vis the object peculiarly "ambiguous" (*zweideutig*). Kant undertakes to resolve (or at least mitigate) that ambiguity by explaining "in a manner not yet brought sufficiently to light" how one may make use of teleology without undermining the priority of theoretical investigation.

Forster's review furnishes Kant with an opportunity to remove earlier misunderstandings. His rejection of Kant's distinction between a description and a history of nature merely indicates his ignorance of what the latter involves. Precisely because, as Forster says, a history of the ultimate beginnings of species would be a "science of the gods," reason needs to assume an intentional creation by an intelligent cause—not, to be sure, as a matter of scientific cognition, but rather as marking out the limits of empirical explanation. The natural history Kant has in mind is no science of the gods, but a collection of "broken and wavering [*wankende*] hypotheses" guided by the idea of an intelligent cause. It is an attempt that is now (and may forever remain) more "sketch" than completed work, and yet for all that a science separate from and wholly heterogenous with a merely "descriptive system of nature" (VIII:163). Kant's history of nature can thus be seen as a second, critically authorized (but nonmoral) compensation for the failure of his early *Universal Natural History*.

Kant proceeds to offer one such fragment. He begins with a conceptual division into species, races, and varieties (characteristics not invariably inherited) — a "simple idea" which combines the "greatest diversity in generation" (a diversity serving an infinity of ends including, but not limited to, the early survival of the species) with the "greatest unity of derivation." The telos or end Kant has in view is not a model of perfection that each individual more or less successfully actualizes (as in scholastic schemes) — a teleology, in other words, based on the "form" or appearance of a certain type. Instead, Kant identifies the end with the *Bestimmung* or destiny of the species as a whole. Kant's use of teleology is thus intrinsically historical. What unites the species is not a common model of individual perfection but an inheritance designed to secure the progressive hability of the species for an infinite variety of ends. In such a scheme, "looks" (*Gestalt* or *eidos*) do not matter at all, except (as in the case of skin color) as a "sign" of this deeper original intention. In such a scheme as well, nature's "mistakes" (the "degenerations" of scholastic systems) have no place, implying as they do a breakdown in the constancy of the original germ.

The fact that people have different looks cannot in itself establish that they have different origins and thus belong to a different species (as Forster argues vis à vis blacks.) Given an ability to interbreed, even the greatest physical dissimilarity is no bar to the possibility of common derivation (for reason should not make use of many causes when it can make do with one). It is only armed with such presuppositions that the observer can read the signs of nature properly and thus distinguish merely nominal affinities based on physical resemblance from those that are "actual."[19]

Since Forster and Kant agree that invariably inherited characteristics must be traced to a common stem, that is, that they are not to be taken for a mere play of nature (*Naturspiel*) or the work of accidental impression (VIII:168), all that divides them, says Kant, is the question of whether there is one stem or several. Since both also agree that the origination of the first organic beings is humanly inexplicable, there is no recourse but to resolve the matter according to the principle of economy, one act of creation being more parsimonious than many. Given that original germ (created we know not how), no further, particular dispensation of nature need be assumed, each racial disposition developing by "chance" according to the patterns of settlement a given people happens to assume (VIII:173).

That such an origin *is* inexplicable (Kant now claims) follows from the very concept of an organized being, a concept that implies a material whole (*All*) whose parts serve each other reciprocally as ends and means. For human beings at least, such a system is only thinkable as a system of final causes, hence one whose possibility requires a teleological, rather than mechanical, mode of explanation (VIII:179).

Kant's "Unmanly Fear"

In his defense of Herder's *Ideas,* Karl Leonhard Reinhold had accused Kant of an "unmanly fear" in the face of the "monstrous" (to Kant's mind) suggestion that all life originated in a common womb. (Kant responded in the second installment of his review of Herder that the only horror he felt was the "horror vacuui" provoked by empty thought.) Forster repeated the charge of an "unmanly fear" on Kant's part (p. 84), this time in the context of the suggestion that blacks and whites, though physically capable of interbreeding, have different natural origins. In repeating Forster's charge, Kant sets it (out of context) alongside the pregnant image of an original womb that provoked his quarrel with Reinhold. Since Kant and Reinhold are now friends (Reinhold's recently published *Letters on Critical Philosophy* is praised in the final pages of Kant's essay), Kant's move seems all the more pointed:

> The earth in travail [*kreißende*] . . . that lets spring forth from the maternal womb fertilized by sea slime, all animals and plants not generated from their like, and which brings forth local generations thus grounded of organic species, to Africa their human beings (the Negro), to Asia theirs. . . . The affinity of all so derived and the imperceptible gradation in a natural chain of organic beings from human being to whale, . . . so on down (supposedly to moss and lichen), not only in a system of comparison but in a system of generation from a common stem—

There is, to be sure, "nothing here to make a naturalist recoil, as from a monster . . . (for it is a game [*Spiel*] that more than one has undertaken only to give it up when nothing came of it)."

> One is, however, driven back by the consideration that one imperceptibly strays from the fruitful soil of natural science to the wasteland of metaphysics. In this regard I know a not unmanly fear, a shrinking back from everything that relaxes reason from its first principles and allows it to wander about in limitless [*grenzlosen*] imaginings. (VIII:179–80)

The idea in question—no longer called "monstrous," or even "vacuous"—is still "repulsive," at least for one who wishes to preserve himself from nomadic wanderings through imagination's wasteland. The Herderian effort to uncover a fundamental force, mediating between matter and reason, is as doomed as the effort to reduce the several operations of the mind to the single operation of imagination, or—for in this case it amounts to the same thing — attribute our representation of the world to a single *Grundkraft* of the soul (VIII:180 n).

What Kant rejects is neither mechanism nor teleology in its place, but their intermingling in the guise of a so-called fundamental force. It is man's "hereditary defect" (*Erbfehler*) to know force only through experience (without which nothing is real for us) — experience either of the world, which operates according to mechanical causes, or of one's own understanding and will, which together can produce according to an idea (VIII:180–81). That living beings must be thought of in nonmechanical terms, that is, in terms of a cause acting according to an end (on the analogy of our own ability to produce a thing according to an idea), does not permit us to renounce this congenital legacy. The concept of a being's ability, as a special *Grundkraft,* to act "purposively," without itself (or its cause) purposing or intending it, is a power "without example in experience," hence, fully invented (*erdichtet*) and empty, "without the least guarantee that any object could correspond to it" (VIII:181–82). The concept of a fundamental force in Herder's (and Foster's) sense is thus equivalent to the empty and invented notion of "purposiveness without purpose" (the very formula, it should be noted, on which Kant's *Critique of Judgment* will later build). We are, then, to think of organic beings as having an intelligible cause, *not* because we know the alternative to be impossible (as Mendelssohn insisted), but to avoid fabricating (*erdichten*) a *Grundkraft*[20] (of which reason has no "need" and which saps our ability to make an effort) (VIII:182].[21]

Living beings, whose parts are each other's ends and means, instantiate the reciprocal interdependence of worldly community — a community that Kant's first "natural history" tried and failed to comprehend. Herder's "organic force" is in this respect equivalent to the world soul — the monstrous image of natural self-sufficiency — whose alternating attractiveness and repulsiveness fueled the ambiguous dynamics of that earlier attempt.

What is new in Kant's fear is the transposition of its focus from the self-fertilizing *Schoß* of nature to the wastelands of an imagination detached from the "fruitful soil" of natural science. To avoid the fate of the nomadic Gypsies and Creoles, who, having strayed from their native soil, are unable to get down to work (VIII:174 n), reason must tie itself to nature — not, to be sure, by a leading string, but rather by a tether one is at liberty, as Kant will later put it, to tighten or loosen at will.[22]

Science so conceived becomes a sort of "autochthony" of reason, which recoils in fruitful (hence not unmanly) fear from nomadic wanderings (*herumschweifern*) that yield no product. The wavering (*wankend*) hypotheses of Kant's own natural history are finally rooted in an appeal to scientific productivity by whose lights mankind's primitive determination into races is both comprehended and superseded. Henceforth, the determination of the species for all regions of the earth hinges not only on physiology but also on reason. Henceforth, the history of the species will be written in the character, not of race (by which mankind was enabled to survive the geological upheavals of the earliest ages), but variety (by which individuals show their suitability for an infinity of ends).[23]

In short, we are on the verge of that alliance between nature and reason developed in the *Critique of Judgment,* in which the mind finds new cause to presume upon nature's agreement with our purposes. To secure that alliance, however, it will be necessary to work out a different relationship between reason and imagination.

II. Purposiveness in the *Critique of Judgment*

Sometime between late December of 1787, when Kant wrote to Reinhold that he was completing a new work on teleology to be entitled the "Critique of Taste," and 1790, when the *Critique of Judgment* actually appeared, Kant evidently decided to divide his final critique into two parts, the "Critique of Aesthetic Judgment" (in which taste [or beauty] is marked off from spiritual feeling [or the sublime]) and the "Critique of Teleological Judgment." What led him to separate taste and teleology in this way (where he had previously linked them) is a matter of speculation. Comparison of his essay *What It Means to Orient Oneself in Thinking* (1786) and *On the Use of Teleological Principles in Philosophy* (1788), however, suggests at the very least the growing refinement during this period of his conception of living beings. Where the earlier essay spoke of a need to attribute an intelligent cause to "purposive" beings generally, the later essay explicitly links that need to assume a determinate cause of living beings. What remains to be accomplished between 1788 and 1790 is an appropriation of "purposiveness without purpose"—the very formula for fundamental force that Kant rejects, in *On the Use of Teleological Principles,* as entirely "invented" and "empty"—as the principle of taste itself.

Kant returns in the third *Critique* to the problem raised by the heterogeneity of mind and matter, a problem characteristically expressed in Kant's early work by a vacillating revulsion against nature's "blindness" on the one hand, and reason's "emptiness" on the other. Kant's early work sought refuge from blind nature in the fact or premise of nature's divinely implanted lawfulness, only to succumb to the suspicion that the claim to knowledge of God on which such refuge depended itself rested on empty illusion. Kant's first *Critique* approached the problem in a different way, by seeking to uncover the conditions of real knowledge, an approach summarized in the famous remark that "concepts without content are empty, intuitions without concepts blind."[24] Real knowledge, then, is neither blind nor empty—neither thoughtless, conceptless matter nor contentless, vacuous thought. In the first *Critique* it seemed sufficient to refer the lawfulness that characterizes such knowledge (whose production Kant likened to "epigenesis") to the transcendental unity of consciousness. Kant's third *Critique* represents a partial reprisal of the older approach, in which the lawfulness of nature as a whole, along with that of certain appearances within it, are once again referred to a grounding creative intelligence — not, to be sure, as a matter of real knowledge, but as "satisfying" a genuine, if strictly human, set of needs.

The basic notion here is of a nature we are constrained to regard as purposive, either in part or as a whole, even as we are constrained to deny to nature, either in part or as a whole, the intentionality (or ability to produce according to an idea) that such purposiveness seemingly implies. It is these opposing, if not contradictory, constraints and the "ambiguous" position to which they give rise that at least partially fuel Kant's new approaches to the "supersensible." Either through the moral "symbolism" of aesthetic judgment, or the "as if" of teleological judgment, nature is metaphorically transformed from a mere mechanism into a "veiled goddess" through whom might be glimpsed (could we, *per impossibile,* but lift her veil) the all-sufficiency of the divine idea. The peculiar satisfactions that this transformation involves for Kant go some way, I think, toward explaining, in ways I will describe below, the direction of a work whose basic structure has remained notoriously elusive.

Unity and Disunity in the *Critique of Judgment*

The peculiar standpoint from which the *Critique of Judgment* proceeds is indicated in the "First Introduction,"[25] which begins by dividing philosophy "insofar as it contains principles for the rational cognition of things through concepts" into the theoretical and the practical, the former concerned with concepts of *nature,* the latter with concepts of *freedom.* This twofold division, however, is countered by the "grounding" of the system of philosophy as a whole upon a single footing: the "system of higher cognitive powers" (that is, powers concerned with our ability to think); and this ground is in turn divided into three parts: understanding, judgment, and reason (XX:201; 391). The twofold is thus grounded in the threefold, the "cleft" separating nature and freedom (the space, as it were, dividing the two parts of the system of philosophy) corresponding to judgment (the part occupying the center of the system of the higher cognitive powers).

But the power of judgment (though forced to bear such systematic weight) lacks "independence" (*Selbstständigkeit*). As the faculty that subsumes the particular under the universal (or, as we later learn, searches out a universal for a given particular), judgment, unlike reason and understanding, yields no ideas or concepts of any object. What it does provide —

there being, so to speak, no other alternative — is a concept of things of nature "insofar as they conform [*richtet*] to our power of judgment," and hence "such a constitution [*Beschaffenheit*] of nature as we can form no concept of other than that its arrangement [*Einrichtung*] arranges [*richte*] itself according to our ability to subsume particular given laws under more universal laws not given" (XX:202; [392]). It is this arrangement that constitutes nature's "Zweckmässigkeit,"[26] or adaptation to our need to regard its empirical laws as constituting a systematic whole. Though the assumption of such empirical systemicity is not a requirement of experience as such, it *is* a requirement of judgment's seeking out of universals for given particulars, universals which might not exist for all we know on the basis of the categories of understanding. For the categories alone, which guarantee the possibility of objective knowledge, cannot assure us that the world of objects known is not so "infinitely diverse" in its laws and "so very heterogenous" in its forms as to render the very possibility, let alone necessity, of such a system "beyond our grasp."

What Kant seeks, then, is a way of conceiving the possibility of an aggregate of particular experiences as a system — a whole, united by an idea.[27] The conception of such a possibility is necessary, he insists, if judgment is to go about its work of searching out more general classes under which particulars can be subsumed. In setting to work, judgment needs to presume in advance that nature arranges itself in conformity with our end.[28] Such an end or idea, however, cannot be attributed to nature as objectively known. It must therefore be *assumed* (XX:204; 393),[29] not in such a fashion as might interfere with our empirical investigation of nature according to mechanical laws, but only as a subjective necessity of our own.

Kant's point is a somewhat subtle one: it is not that judgment needs assurance that it will, in fact, discover the higher laws it seeks. Rather, judgment needs, and makes for itself, a concept whereby it counters the otherwise disabling possibility (which understanding does not preclude) of nature's "foreignness" (*Fremdheit*). Judgment's concept thus functions as a kind of talisman, an idol fashioned by the mind, which escapes the charge of idol worship by never taking its image to be more than a reflection of the mind's own need.[30]

This concept, which arises "originally" (*ursprünglich*) from judgment, is that of "nature as art," that is, of the "technic of nature regarding its particular laws."[31] While this concept does not (like the categories) determine particular experiences, it does furnish a guiding thread (*Leitfaden*) (XX:204 n; [393 n]), without which we "could not hope to find our way" in the "labyrinth of the diversity of possible particular laws" (XX:214; [402]). Empirical laws might, for all the understanding knows, be so heterogenous "that we could never bring them under a common principle to the unity of kinship [*Verwandtschaft*]" (XX:209; [397]), rendering reflection "blind" and "haphazard" (XX:212; [401]). Even if judgment could, by merely groping about (*herumtappen*) among natural forms, manage to hit upon a harmony between particular laws, it would have to regard that harmony as utterly contingent (XX:210; 398), and so could not assure itself against the possibility of nature's "disturbing [*besorgliche*] boundless divergence [*Ungleichartigkiet*]" and "heterogeneity [*Heterogeneität*]" (XX:209; 398). It is against the disturbing possibility of this utter lack of affinity, both within nature and between her and ourselves, that judgment produces a concept of its own, a reflective principle that allows judgment to turn away from, and thus (temporarily) disregard, the otherwise "blinding" prospect of a diversity that knows no bounds.

The transcendental principle of judgment, then, concerns a lawfulness that is "contingent objectively but necessary subjectively" (XX:242–43; 432); or alternatively, it concerns laws that as empirical "are contingent as far as *our* understanding can see," yet as laws of *nature* must be regarded as necessary "by virtue of some principle of the unity of what is diverse, even though we do not know this principle."[32] It follows that empirical laws must be viewed "in terms of such unity as they would have if they too had been given by an understanding (even though not ours) so as to assist our cognitive powers by making possible a system of experience in terms of particular natural laws" (V:180; 19).

Judgment's need to proceed systematically leads it to regard nature "as if" it possessed a unity given by an understanding (though not our own) so as to make possible, to the purpose (*Behuf*) our cognitive faculties, a system of experience according to particular laws. It is not as if [*als wenn*] such an understanding "must in this way actually be assumed" (for this idea serves reflective, not determining judgment).

It is this discrepancy between determinacy and reflection that allows judgment to slip through an otherwise contradictory demand to regard nature "as if" it were grounded in an understanding without actually assuming it. (Were that distance [*per impossibile*] closed, the difference between human and divine intelligence would dissolve, and the understanding we regard only indirectly, through our reflection upon nature, would be indistinguishable from our own.)

In this way, judgment guides its own search, according to such maxims as "nature makes no leaps," maxims without whose application "we could make no [cognitive] progress" (V:186; [26]).[33]

In short, judgment produces an idea that is in nature, but not of it, an idea of the idea held by a divine understanding — an understanding, moreover, not assumed but only "reflectively" regarded, via experience. It is this reflective regard that transforms nature's otherwise disturbingly boundless heterogeneity into fit matter for cognitive progress, a heterogeneity, therefore, with which we can be "satisfied" (V:188; [28]). The implicit theme of judgment, whose search recalls both Perseus's slaying of the Gorgon and Plato's mirroring of the sun,[34] reflectively projects the idea of "nature as art." It thus transforms both the astonishing image of a self-sufficient nature and the blinding vision of the divine into the artful figure of a "veiled Goddess," an "Isis" whose "sublime" oracle ("I am all that is and was and will be, and none who would approach me dare lift my veil") both speaks and conceals. In this figure of a mother nature, so pointedly at odds in its "favoring" of our purposes with the niggardly "step-mother" of the *Groundwork,* the maternal and paternal principles that once divided themselves between matter and spirit find a new, if still only partial, reconciliation.[35]

"ART AS NATURE," "NATURE AS ART": KANT'S "CRITIQUE OF TASTE"

Taste was a major theme of Kant's early *Observations on the Feeling of the Beautiful and the Sublime* (1764) and played a prominent role in the *Remarks.* There taste essentially concerned the swings of mankind (for the most part worked out on the basis of the dynamic interaction of the sexes) from natural rudeness to artificial corruption, with a hopeful glance, on Kant's part, toward the future possibility of a healthy resting place between them (a resting place poised, as he put it, on a hair's breadth). The idea of an "aesthetic education of mankind" was, then, nothing new to Kant when he came at last to write his long promised "Critique of Taste," by now swollen to include not only an "appendix" on the sublime, but also an entire second part, almost as long as the "Critique of Taste" itself, largely devoted to the subject of natural generation.

Kant's general approach to taste derives inspiration from Rousseau's treatment of taste in book 4 of *Emile,* a treatment remarkable for its democratization of a subject more typically associated with aristocratic "connoisseurship."[36] In what Rousseau there calls "a kind of essay on true taste," he stresses not only the communicability of aesthetic pleasure, but also its (relative) universality and disinterestedness. "Taste," he says, is only the faculty of judging what pleases or displeases the greatest number. . . . we are not dealing here with what we love because it is useful to us or with what we hate because it harms us."[37]

Taste is thus politically important for Kant, not only as a historical vehicle of "socialization" toward genuine morality (a vehicle that remains, by Kant's own account, "very ambiguous" [V:298; 165]), but also as an externalization of the egalitarian reciprocity of the kingdom of ends. More than scientific or even juridical community, aesthetic community is one in which all can aspire to play an active role.[38] Thus too, Kant's deliberate devaluation of the stature of "genius," along with producers of art generally, in favor of their audience—an audience of which everyone, at least everyone willing to cultivate taste, is potentially a member.[39]

Taste, according to Kant, is the ability to judge the beautiful (V:203 n; 43 n) and has four moments, which include the following characteristics: (1) disinterestedness, (2) conceptless universal liking, (3) formal purposiveness, and (4) subjective necessity.

(1) Kant's treatment of beauty is remarkable—especially when we compare that treatment with his earlier writings—for its separation of beauty from charm (*Reiz*), which he here classifies with the sensually pleasurable (that is, the merely "agreeable"). Beautiful objects are those in which we take pleasure apart from any interest (either sensual or moral) in their actual existence. Feminine charm is no longer prototypical, as in Kant's early writings, of beauty generally. Indeed, given Kant's distinction in the *Critique of Judgment* between judgments of taste concerning nature and those concerning art, the example of feminine beauty seems particularly problematic. (Is the beautiful woman a product of nature or, as Kant's early writings would have it, a product of [her own] art? Or is she not rather both?)

(2) A judgment of taste is distinguished from judgments concerning the agreeable by the former's universality, albeit one that, lacking as it does a determinate concept, cannot (unlike theoretical or moral judgments) "compel assent." To call an object beautiful is to "believe oneself to have a universal voice" (*allgemeine Stimme*) (V:216; 59), or, as Kant later puts it, to judge from a sort of "common sense" (V:239; 89). Judgments of taste are therefore universal yet "free" and associated with our "favor" (*Gunst*) rather than inclination (*Neigung*) or respect (*Achtung*), which involve compulsion, albeit in differing ways (V:210; 52).

(3) The third characteristic of beauty—its formal purposiveness—is a purposiveness involving not the object as such but its relation to the subjective faculties of understanding and imagination thereby set in play. We call objects, acts, or states of mind "purposive," says Kant, when we can "explain and grasp them only if we assume that they are based on a causality according to purposes, i.e., on a will that would have so arranged them in accordance with the presentation of a certain rule" (V:220; 65). "Purposiveness without purpose" thus involves an assumption of intentional causation for the sake of our own understanding, but not an assertion that the thing in question actually has an intentional cause or that its existence isn't otherwise possible. This delicate distinction on which the formula of "purposiveness without purpose" rests is, indeed, in tension with his earlier treatment of purposiveness in the introduction, which specifically excluded even the "assumption" of an intentional cause. (Kant there spoke instead of a "regard" for the object "as if" it had been so produced.) "Purposiveness without purpose" defines our experience of "kinship" with nature,

yet in a manner that resists, through the explicit fictiveness of its device, the twin pitfalls of vitalism (or the confusion of matter and reason) and mysticism (or the confusion of truth and illusion).

In judgments of taste, we judge a liking to be universally communicable, even though it lacks a concept. Tasteful pleasure thus differs both from subjective enjoyment (which is not experienced as valid for everyone) and from cognition (which is valid for everyone precisely through its conceptual reference to an object). This liking, which we "judge to be the basis determining a judgment of taste," is the "form of purposiveness, in as much as we are conscious of it, in the presentation by which an object is *given* to us" (V:221; [66]). Subjective purposiveness emerges on the scene as the only way in which communicable pleasure can be accounted for. In judging an object beautiful, we feel our cognitive forces set in a self-quickening, self-reinforcing play—a harmony that liberates imagination from the laborious task of schematizing the concepts of understanding. "In judging the beautiful we present the *freedom* of the imagination (and hence of our power of sensibility) as harmonizing with the lawfulness of understanding" (V:354; [229]). What is purposive, then, is precisely that harmony—not the object as such, but the relation between our cognitive powers that its presentation evokes, a relation that we therefore experience as a kind of "common sense" possessed by all other (human) beings who share our manner of engagement with the sensible world.

(4) The fourth moment of the beautiful concerns the "necessity" of our liking. This necessity, which we think as merely exemplary, or as characterizing a rule we are unable to state (V:237; 85), makes aesthetic judgment valid for everyone, but only conditionally, on the assumption that the individual instance in question has in fact been correctly subsumed under a rule we cannot state. Our inability to state the rule to which judgments of taste implicitly defer means that though we require the assent of others in so judging, we cannot (as with ordinary cognition) count on it (V:237; 86).[40]

"Pure" or "free" judgments of taste do not combine with any concept of what an object is "to be," that is, with any idea of a thing's purpose or perfection.[41] Thus artifacts, and even natural products judged with reference to the kind of thing they are, can be adherent (*pulchritudo adhaerens*) but not free beauties (*pulchritudo vaga*). Flowers, for example, are free beauties, but only when one ignores their natural purpose as the "reproductive organs" of the plant (V:229; 76). Yet while taste lacks a determinate rule, it does have an idea or archetype, albeit one that everyone must "generate within himself" (V:232; 79). (The only aesthetic ideal, or presentation of an individual adequate to that idea, involves the expression of the moral in man himself, an expression that oversteps the bounds of aesthetic judgment proper.)

We are left with the impression (to be later qualified) that beauties in the most proper sense of the term are free beauties of nature, which, being furthest removed from any conceptual determination, give freest play to the purposive harmony of understanding and imagination (V:242; 93). (Imagination so employed is a productive originator of forms [V:240; 91].) In the case of the sublime, by way of contrast, purposiveness arises precisely from an (initial) lack of harmony, in this case between imagination and reason, one that gives unique (if paradoxical) expression to a human destiny altogether beyond empirical apprehension. If with beauty, imagination succeeds in effortlessly accommodating itself to understanding; with the sublime it succeeds only by failing, despite its utmost striving, to accommodate to reason.

Spirit Revisited: The Erotics of the Sublime

If independent natural beauty invites us, through its form, to regard nature as purposive for our judgment, the feeling of the sublime[42] (which Kant also calls spiritual feeling, or *Geistesgefühl* [XX:250; 440]) is usually aroused by nature's chaos, by her "wildest and most ruleless disarray and devastation," so long as it has magnitude and might. Thus, whereas the basis of beauty must be sought outside ourselves, the basis of the sublime lies entirely within, a fact that "completely separates" the idea of the sublime from that of purposiveness in nature and which turns the theory of the sublime into a mere appendix to the critique of taste.[43]

The mathematical sublime involves things that are "simply large [*schlechthin groß*]" (V:248; [103]), or large "in comparison with which everything else is small" (V:250; [105]). It therefore has no external measure, nor can anything in nature be sublime, since however large we may judge it to be, we can always judge it small by considering it in a different relation. What *is* sublime is the feeling aroused, in the aesthetic presentation of certain objects, by imagination striving to exceed the limits of its ability to comprehend aesthetically, that is, to take in the quantity in question in a single intuition.[44]

Aesthetic comprehension thus exhibits absolute magnitude "to the extent that the mind can take it in in one intuition." Imagination, one could say, succeeds by failing, making accessible (to judgment) through the peculiar character of its own effort an absolute greatness imagination cannot present directly.

Whence, then, the universal liking that attaches to the sublime, and how is it related to an awareness of the inadequacy of imagination in our estimation of magnitude?

Before answering this question, Kant draws our attention to the relation between imagination in its ordinary (mathematical) estimation of quantities which can proceed ad infinitum, and the mind in its attendance to the voice (*Stimme*) of reason, which demands totality for all given magnitudes, infinity not excepted. Reason, according to Kant, "invariably makes the infinite (in common reason's judgment) thought as *entirely given* (in its totality)" (V:254; [111]). The human mind would thus contradict itself did it not also have a supersensible power whose idea makes a given infinite thinkable. In Kant's words,

> That the given infinite *should be even thinkable* without contradiction, demands a supersensible power to that effect within the human mind. For only through it and its idea of a noumenon, which itself permits [*verstattet*] no intuition, but which underlies, as supersensible substrate,[45] the world intuition [*Weltanschauung*] as mere appearance, is a purely intellectual estimation of magnitude of the infinity of the sensible world entirely comprehended under a concept. (V:254–55; [111–12])

To be able to think the given infinite is man's special stamp — the passport, as it were, of his dual world-citizenship. But *can* man think the given infinite without contradiction? Is not the very attempt to do so "ambiguous" in the precise sense charted by Kant's earlier *Universal Natural History*?

Man can, Kant now replies, but only on the condition of his having a supersensible power to generate a special idea of nature as noumenon — an idea, it must particularly be noted, with the peculiar virtue of *conjoining intellect and nature without confusing mind and matter*. Even the power to *think* nature in this way "is large beyond any comparison even with the power of mathematical estimation — not, it is true, for a theoretical aim [*Absicht*] of our cognitive power, but still as an expansion [*Erweiterung*] of the mind that feels able to cross over the limits of sensibility with a different (practical) aim" (V:255; [112]).

The mind, in short, is itself enlarged "beyond comparison" through its power to generate an idea that combines intellect and nature without a (disturbing) violation of the barrier that separates matter and reason. This expansion of the mind is accomplished, or registered, as a feeling "of being able to cross over" the limits of sensibility — though only with an aim that is specifically noncognitive (and/or practical). The mind feels itself expanded, in other words, without seeing quite where it is going.

Having described the mind and *its* feeling of expansion, Kant is now ready to give an account of the sublime in nature. "Hence," he continues, "nature is sublime in those of its appearances whose intuition carries with it [*führt bei sich*] the idea of sublimity." This "carrying with"[46] sets up, as we shall see, a sort of resonance (or discordant harmony) between the feeling of the mind previously described and a structurally similar expansion of imagination, a resonance that explains the peculiar harmonics of the sublime as a vibratory "attunement" (*Stimmung*), registering a voice (*Stimme*) of reason that remains unseen.

All estimations of magnitude (*Größenschätzung*) involve a measure; in the case of the sublime, this measure is supplied directly by imagination, insofar as it is capable of assimilating something in a single intuition (V:251; 107). Thus, whereas in the mathematically determinate estimation of magnitude, there is no maximum, in the case of the aesthetic estimation of magnitude, such a maximum subjectively exists at the point at which imagination cannot further "expand" itself, that is, add to its apprehension without loosing as much as it gains. It is thus in the aesthetic rather than mathematical estimation of magnitude that intuition can "carry with it the idea of the infinite," and this only through imagination's effort "to perform a comprehension that surpasses its ability to encompass the progressive apprehension in a whole of intuition" (V:255; [112]). Kant's description of the sublime thus recapitulates that agonizing, yet strangely pleasurable, tension between perpetual progression and immediate apprehension that characterized his own early cosmological strivings, with the crucial difference that the feeling aroused is now attuned (as in *Geistestimmung;* see V:250; 106), not to the "unnameable" speech (*Sprache*) of God, but to the "voice [*Stimme*] of reason within" (V:254; 111).[47]

The feeling of the inadequacy of our capacity to attain to an idea that is a law for us is respect. But the idea of comprehending every appearance in the intuition of a whole *is* such a law, for reason knows no other universal measure. Thus the feeling aroused by the sublime, in which imagination shows both its inadequacy and its determination (*Bestimmung*) to make itself adequate to the idea, is that of respect for man's own vocation (*Bestimmung*), a respect that, by a (for once) permissible "subreption" is accorded to an object of nature (V:257; 114).

Kant likens the movement (*Bewegung*) of the sublime in its inception to a tremor (*Erschütterung*), that is, a "rapidly alternating repulsion from and attraction to one and the same object." That which is excessive (*überschwenglich*) for imagination (to which excess it is driven in apprehending the thing in intuition) is, "as it were, an abyss in which imagination fears to lose itself" (V:258; [115]). At the same time, what is excessive for imagination is conformable "to reason's law to give rise to such striving by the imagination." What was repulsive to mere sensibility therefore becomes attractive, and pain gives way to pleasurable discord.

The Kantian sublime thus returns us to that moment in the *Universal*

Natural History in which the mind, alternating between attraction and repulsion in its efforts to encompass nature progressively, attempts finally to swing (*schwingen*) itself into immediate community with the divine. In the case of the sublime, this double movement is replicated in the tension, exhibited by imagination, between the mathematical "boundlessness" of its ability to estimate magnitudes successively and the self-transcending "boundedness" shown in its effort, *per impossibile,* to take in infinity. What is involved in that effort is a "canceling of the conditions of time" so as to make "*simultaneity* intuitable," a cancellation (*Aufhebung*) that does violence (*Gewalt*) to "inner sense" and thus to subjectivity itself. And yet it is precisely this painful collapse into (what threatens to be) a single, subject-obliterating moment that is pleasurably "purposive for the whole Bestimmung of the mind," inasmuch as the subject discovers, "through his own inability [or impotence] [*Unvermögen*], the consciousness of an unlimited ability that is also his" (V:259; [116]).

The chasm that imagination fears is the collapse of temporal projection on which inner sense and with it finite consciousness itself depends.[48] It is thus—at least for finite consciousness—a kind of "little death," but also the supersensible source that Kant associates with reason. The "abyss as it were" celebrated in the sublime is thus the feared or anticipated collapse of one faculty into another; it is also a return to the traditional, hierarchical model of the soul (with reason in charge), but with this post-Rousseauian twist, namely that we do not experience reason directly but only as exhibited in feeling.

The apparently futile (hence purposeless) drive to render the successive as coexistent proves by virtue of its very compulsion a submission to law that can only be reason's own. The sublime is thus purposelessness rendered purposive, an exemplary answer to Kant's earlier question about the point of pointless longing.[49] The end of issueless desire is not only the self-testing necessary to progress in a being without determinate limits, but also the desire itself, given point in the pleasurable feeling of spiritual (self-) arousal (*Erweckung*] (V:260; 117).

In mathematical estimation of magnitude, the impossibility of arriving at an absolute totality arises from a limitless successive generation of numerical concepts. In aesthetic estimation, on the contrary, the impossibility in question is a nonconceptual or subjective one, in which imagination's "comprehension to a unity" (or degree thereof) must itself serves as measure.

"If a magnitude approaches the outermost dimensions [*Äußerste*] of our ability to comprehend in one intuition, and imagination still is commanded through numerical concepts (regarding which we are conscious of having an unbounded ability) to aesthetic comprehension in an even greater unity, so do we feel in our mind aesthetically confined in limits." In view, however, of the

> necessary expansion [*Erweiterung*] of imagination toward ade-quacy with that which in our rational ability is unbounded, namely the idea of the absolute whole, the displeasure is presented as purposive for the rational ideas and their arousal, and hence so is the unpurposiveness of imagination's ability [*Vermögen*]. (V:259–60; 116–17)

The discrepancy between imagination's limited capacity to intuit a suc-cession of presentations as an immediate unity, and its limitless capacity to expand progressively through the generation of numerical concepts, re-flectively reenacts the conflicting impulses of Kant's early *Universal Natural History*.[50] Imagination's incapacity or impotence (*Unvermögen*) is thus transformed into a purposive (albeit indeterminate or aimless) potency (*Vermögen*). To be driven beyond one's outermost is literal ecstasy, a step-ping outside of one's own skin.[51] And yet it is only the mind as a whole, not imagination, that finds itself in a position, as audience, to recognize the basis of this transformation (of which imagination itself remains oblivious (V:269; 129)).[52] In Kant's depiction of the mathematical sublime, imagi-nation becomes a quasi-hero, whose agonistics enact a drama of sacrifice and deliverance — a fiction that objectifies (to the extent that this is pos-sible) the mind's own discordant unity. The shudder of the sublime is thus a life-quickening alternative (despite or even because of its pain) to those "exhausting" fictional romances against which Kant earlier warns — repre-sentations of perfection that both distend and leave us flaccid.[53]

In all of this, it is the idea, as a *Zusammenfassung* in comparison with which all combination (*Fassung*) on the part of imagination is small, that is sublime or genuinely uplifting — an idea aesthetically exhibited in imagi-nation's conflicting tendencies to comprehend in an intuitive unity and to expand progressively via concepts into infinity. Wherever imagination finds itself forced to stop it also finds itself aware of a capacity to go on, a dis-junction that arouses in the mind the idea of that absolute whole in com-parison with which everything, including infinity itself, is small. The total-ity that is *merely* an idea (to which no experience can be adequate) thus gains, in the felt failure of imagination, a sort of proxy content and negative reality. Through the surrogacy of imagination, the mind feels itself both at a maximum and able to go boundlessly beyond it. Imagination schema-tizes, so to speak, the consummation of a longing in which the mind's force is infinitely extended rather than exhausted.[54]

The mathematically sublime involves an estimation of nature's magnitude as great beyond the ability of imagination to comprehend and yet as small in comparison with reason's idea. The dynamically sublime involves a judgment of nature's power (*Macht*) as superior to great obstacles and yet unable to do us violence (*Gewalt*). Judgment of the dynamically sublime therefore involves a presentation of something as "arousing fear," the only way to gauge *Macht* aesthetically (that is, nonconceptually) being by the magnitude of the obstacle (furnished in this case by our own resistance) such power can overcome. What we actually fear, however, cannot be conjoined with pleasure. The sublime therefore involves representation of a hypothetical fear—a representation of the utter futility (*Vergeblichkeit*) of a merely possible resistance on our part. That representation of such fearfulness is pleasurable has to do with the courage (*Muth*) it gives, in "lifting the soul's fortitude [*Seelenstärke*] above its usual middle range," that "we could be a match [*messen zu können*]" for nature's apparent omnipotence (*Allgewalt*). The sublime thus involves the discovery of a power of resistance on our part of a "wholly different sort" and reveals both an ability to judge ourselves "independent of nature" and a superiority (*Überlegenheit*) over nature that grounds a "self-preservation quite different in kind" from that which nature can endanger (V:261; [120]).

The dynamical sublime is thus bound up with admiration, or respect for that part of ourselves—humanity in our person—which stands above nature in our regard. By furnishing the opportunity to regard nature's force as small, that is, as unable to displace our highest principles, the sublime allows imagination to play hero. By feeling ourselves capable of upholding our highest principles, we feel ourselves upheld in a "self-preservation" wholly beyond the power of nature to reach. In uncovering "an ability to judge ourselves independent of nature" (V:261; 120–21) the sublime exhibits (*darstellen*) that very independence.

The pleasure of the sublime thus concerns man's vocation (*Bestimmung*), whose elevation (*Erhabenheit*) beyond nature it allows the mind to feel (V:262; 121). Against the charge that this principle is itself overly subtle (*vernünftelt*) and highflying (*überschwenglich*) (as such a conjunction of sensibility and reason might well seem), Kant counters with the observation of a man, who reveals, even in his most savage state, admiration for the person "who is not terrified . . . but promptly sets to work."[55] The empirically attested universality of such admiration certifies its a priori provenance.[56]

It would not be *überschwenglich* to say that everything hinges on this *Gefühl*, which translates both linguistically and structurally between the empirical and the moral, and so effects the *Übergang*, the negotiation of the "cleft" between the domains of the concepts of nature and freedom, of which Kant's introduction spoke. The systematic requirement that judgment serve as a *Mittelglied* or joint between understanding and reason

(V:176; 15) is fulfilled here, if anywhere, by a judgment turned Janus-like to understanding or reason, depending on whether the sublimity in question is mathematical or dynamical.[57]

The distinction between the mathematical and the dynamical sublime itself renders articulate judgment's jointure of the higher faculties. The appended "General Comment on the Exposition of Aesthetic Reflective Judgments," on the other hand, tends to pass over or blur that very distinction. The mathematical and the dynamical sublime are now each indifferently described as "an object (of nature) *whose representation determines the mind to think the inaccessibility of nature as an exhibition of ideas*" (V:268; [127]). When

> we expand our empirical power of representation (mathematical or dynamical) for the intuition of nature, reason invariably steps in, as a power of the independence of absolute totality, and brings forth a striving, albeit futile, of the mind to make representations of sense adequate to that totality. This striving, and the feeling of the inaccessibility of the idea through imagination, is itself an exhibition of the subjective purposiveness of our mind in its use of imagination for that supersensible vocation [*Bestimmung*], and it requires us subjectively to *think* nature itself in its totality, as an exhibition of something supersensible, without our being able to bring this exhibition *objectively* about [*zu Stande bringen*]. (V:268; [128])

Kant's description of the sublime now conflates the absolute magnitude formerly (uniquely) identified with the mathematical and the independence formerly (uniquely) identified with the dynamic. The inaccessibility of the idea to sense is figured or exhibited in the inaccessibility of nature as a whole, which we are therefore required to think as itself the exhibition of something supersensible. We are on the verge of that figurative divinization of nature to which Kant's reference to Isis alludes. The sublime lifts us above nature (or makes us feel so raised), even as we think nature as whole (or in its "inaccessibility") as portraying that which is equally uplifted. In this latter aspect, the sublime determines us to think that ultimate articulation — that of the divine idea and its world-historical actualization, i.e., what Kant in *On the Use of Teleological Principles* called the "Inbegriff" of nature. "We soon become aware [*inne werden*] that the unconditioned — hence absolute magnitude — which is after all demanded [*verlangt wird*] of the commonest reason, is wholly lacking in [or "goes from," the primary meaning of *abgehen*] nature in space and time" (V:268; [128]).

That which nature in space and time wholly lacks (or which "goes from" it) is a power of independence (*Vermögen der Independenz*) to which nature also (or literally) gives issuance.[58] It is this lack (or going from) that reminds (*erinnert*) us that we have to do only with an appearance of nature—a "mere exhibition of nature in itself"—which reason alone has "in the idea." Nature in herself is no blindly self-sufficient maw but reason's own. Nature exhibited is, as Kant later suggests, a goddess whose veil, could we but lift it, would reveal our own higher selves.[59]

This pleasing reflection, however, must be free of influence from any determining or teleological concepts—be they of worlds inhabited by rational beings, or of water vapor that impregnates the clouds for the benefit of earth,[60] or concepts of the purposes of our own bodily members (*Gliedmassen*). To let the harmony of those members with their ends influence aesthetic judgment would render it "impure," though (Kant adds) it is certainly a necessary condition of aesthetic pleasure that these members not conflict with such ends. (Monstrous deformities [or what Kant elsewhere calls *Misgeburthen*] are inconsistent with aesthetic pleasure; but it also follows, as we will later see, that the [unveiled] female shape [*Gestalt*] presents a peculiar problem for aesthetic judgment.)

Affects are mental agitations that temporarily "disable" reason (V:272; [132]). Enthusiasm (or the affect that may accompany the idea of the morally good) seems sublime, and many therefore say that "nothing great" can be accomplished/set right (*ausgerichtet*) without it.[61] In fact, however, enthusiasm, like any affect, is "blind" and thus incompatible with reason's free deliberation and determination toward an end.[62] The sublimity of enthusiasm, then, stems not from great accomplishment in the usual sense but rather resides in a straining (*Anspannung*) of our forces by ideas that impart a momentum (*Schwung*) to the mind greater and more permanent than any produced by sense (V:272; 132). (Unenthusiastic or affectless moral vigor [*Nachdrücklichkeit*], which pursues unwavering [*unwandelbaren*] principles, is more sublime and in a far superior sense; and it alone can be called "noble" [V:272; 133].)

The ambivalence of enthusiasm, given "swing" by moral ideas, and yet characterized by a "blindness" reason "cannot like," recalls Kant's efforts from the *Universal Natural History* onwards to distinguish the noble impetus of spiritual sublimity from the delusive attractions of *schwärmerisch* fanaticism. Kant now approaches the problem by distinguishing between enthusiastic and "noble" sublimity—a distinction whose "strangeness" (*Befremdheit*) he concedes. The difference between the enthusiastic and the noble sublime lies in what distinguishes a merely relative constancy of motion (that is, constancy in comparison with the duration of drives elicited by sensible representation) from motion genuinely "unwavering."[63] The falsely noble (or noble so called), on the other hand, makes the heart "languid" and "insensitive to the stern precept of duty" (V:273; 133). Affects, or "nature in us," are sublime whenever they are brave (*wacker*), that is to say, make us conscious of our "animus strenuus," as opposed to affects that are languid (*schmelzenden*), or melting (V:272; 133)).[64]

The sublime is thus generally associated with steadfast, upright, firm, and (in an at least relative sense) constant motion, as opposed to the wavering, melting affects of the beautiful, not to speak of the flaccidity (*Welkheit*) induced by romances and whining dramas. The difficulty is to know in what precisely this aesthetic impetuosity consists. If it were merely a matter of tempestuousness (*Stürmischkeit*) and strain, the agitation of the sublime would not differ in principle from the pleasure enjoyed by "Oriental voluptuaries" (*Wollüstlinge des Orients*) who allow their "joints" (*Gelenke*) to be "gently squeezed and bent" to experience the agreeable lassitude or limpness (*Mattigkeit*) that follows such vibration (*Rüttelung*) (V:274; 134).[65]

Kant's comparison of such inner strain and motion to an oriental massage makes explicit the erotic charge of the sublime, which differs from sensuous enjoyment through an oscillating emotion of attraction and repulsion — a vibration that does not finally succumb, as with the voluptuaries of the East, to limpness.[66] (The sublime thus becomes a sort of object lesson in how *not* to orient oneself in thinking.)[67]

Kant's lifelong interest in the sublime comes finally to this: whereas material desire implicates us in an exhausting cycle of "tension," "consummation," and "remission," ideal desire maintains itself by constantly rising, that is, by continually approaching a maximum (the idea) without ever reaching it.[68] The peculiarity of the sublime is that it is at once neither and both: like ideal desire the sublime maintains itself (relatively) constantly; like material desire it is linked with pleasure.[69]

I do not mean to suggest that the sublime is erotic in the usual sense — Kant's "emotional" version of, or substitute for, a dirty "movie." But the sublime as the *Critique of Judgment* defines it *is*, structurally speaking, a remarkable compromise between ideal and material desire. Kant is finally able definitively to distinguish (as his work from the *Universal Natural History* onward struggled to do) the weakening appeal of the (sexually) charming or exciting (*reizend*) (now only problematically associated with the beautiful) from the strengthening appeal of the sublime. The wavering, and ultimately deflating, attractions of sensuous desire, whose objects disgust once we are sated, contrast with the unwavering draw of the ideas, whose "ungroundable depth" is the source of their infinite capacity to uplift us. The notion of absolute totality, with its implicit negation of the conditions of finite consciousness, becomes distinguishable from death — hence unambiguously upholding — through our willingness to avert our eyes and thereby transform an otherwise dizzying alternation between rising and falling into a sublime or vibratory exhibition of our "supersensible" *Bestimmung*.[70]

It is for this reason that Kant singles out as "perhaps the most sublime passage in the lawbook of the Jews," the commandment:

> thou shalt not make unto thee any graven image, or any likeness of any thing that is in heaven, or on earth, or under the earth, etc. This commandment alone can explain the enthusiasm that the Jewish people in its civilized [*gesitteten*] era felt for their religion, when they compared themselves with other peoples, or that pride that Mohammedanism inspires [*einflöst*]. (V:274; [135])

The difference between a "pure, elevating, and merely negative exhibition of morality" on the one hand, and fanaticism (*Schwärmerei*) on the other, lies precisely in the latter's "*delusion* [Wahn] *of wanting to SEE something beyond all limits of sensibility,* i.e., to dream according to principles (go mad with reason)" (V:275; [135]; Kant's emphasis). (By guarding against wanting to see we protect ourselves from all "danger of fanaticism.")

To this delusive insistence on SEEING Kant contrasts the inscrutability (*Unerforschlichkeit*) of the idea of freedom, which entirely "cuts off the way" of any positive means of exhibition: for the moral law, which can sufficiently and originally determine us, does not even permit us to "look about" for another, external ground of determination (V:275; [136]). The *Unerforschlichkeit* of which Kant's *Universal Natural History* complained has been transformed from a "problem" of human determination (*Bestimmung*) into its only possible solution.[71]

"Art as Nature," "Nature as Art": The Problem of Womanly Beauty

In the "Analytic of the Sublime," Kant argued that pure aesthetic judgments concerning animate objects (including human beings) cannot be determined by any concepts of purposes or ends—for example, those ends "*for which* [the human shape] has all its members."[72] This blanket disallowance of teleological concepts determining, or even influencing, pure aesthetic judgments of the human body (except in the negative case, where contrariety to purpose renders things repulsive) also strongly suggests that such pure judgments are both possible and exemplary as expressions of the "power of judgment in its *freedom*" (that is, as the consequence of free mental activity sustained by imagination alone [V:271; (131)]). Earlier (in what Tonelli claims is a passage of more ancient composition), Kant argued that aesthetic judgments concerning human beauty are *always* adherent or "impure" rather than free: whereas flowers can be judged without reference to the (sexual) purposes of their parts, the same apparently does not apply to horses or human beings. The beauty of a human being (Kant there claims), including that of a man, woman, or child, presupposes a concept of perfection, or what that being is to be, and such beauty is therefore merely adherent (*adhaerens,* that is, attached) or dependent (*anhängend*) rather than free (*frei*) or wandering (*vagus*). A figure might, for example, be decorated with all sorts of curlicues, which would then be objects of aesthetic liking, *but* for the fact that that figure is a human face (as with primitive tattoos), a fact that renders those same curlicues unlikable. And the outline of a face might be likably pretty, *but* for the fact that it is to represent a man.

If the at least apparent inconsistency among these passages is not to be attributed to mere sloppiness, we are forced to find some other way of dealing with it. The question is, can we or can we not make pure — that is, free — aesthetic judgments concerning the human shape? Can we find (part of) a human being beautiful in the same way that we do a flower or designs *à la grecque?* And if not, in what does the purity (if purity there be) of an adherent judgment concerning the beautiful consist?

The importance of the question of human beauty to Kant's understanding of taste has not generally been remarked. (Even Eva Schaper, in her careful study of free and dependent beauty, for the most part sets human beauty aside.)[73] This is all the more striking, given Kant's identification, in the *Remarks* and notes written in ensuing years, of human (especially womanly) beauty both with charm (*Reiz*) (decisively distinguished, in the *Critique of Judgment,* from beauty) and with the artificial. In the case of woman preeminently, at least as she is presented in those notes, the distinction Kant later draws between natural beauty and artificial beauty (or fine art) is difficult if not impossible to draw. Women are, as it were, beautifully artful by nature. More "preformed" (*vorgebildet*) then men, they are therefore "less perfect but more art[ful]."[74] Woman is, so to speak, the original "technique of nature" (or its exemplar par excellence).[75]

Woman's natural art takes the form of a "refusal" that procures (*vermittelst*) the man. Without refusal, Kant adds in a note from the late seventies or early eighties, woman would have no charm and hence no influence. "Nature in regard to that which charms, refuses. makes itself scarce." Rivers of milk and honey (the *Schlaraffenland*) would soon be "unbearable."[76]

As a number of other reflections also suggest, Kant's understanding of the role of refusal differs from that of Rousseau (from whom Kant otherwise freely borrows) in its emphasis on the need to overcome man's natural sense of disgust. Woman's enemy is not man's natural indifference to sex (as with Rousseau) but rather his "delicacy." Refusal is nature's charming expedient against the repulsiveness of superfluity (a charm required, it must be said, by no other animal). Without the charm of refusal, superfluity, like the "faces of old women," is "disgusting."[77] Of all the pleasures associated with animal needs, moreover, only begetting leaves an unpleasant after sense (or "aftertaste").[78] Men are by nature not so much indifferent to sex (as with Rousseau) as repelled by it, at least in the aftermath.

Women naturally compensate for their weakness, not by eliciting men's amour propre (as with Rousseau), but by awakening men's capacity to project ideals which overwhelm the (natural) repulsiveness of satiety.[79]

Reflections on taste written between the late 1760s and early 1790s show Kant's various and repeated attempts to discover in the relation of the sexes (the social basis of taste) a movement toward ever greater *Gesellig-keit*, and with it a reconciliation of man's natural and supernatural destinies. A key question, on which Kant's efforts turn, is thus how to mediate sensual enjoyment on the one hand, and genuine morality on the other — or, to state the issue another way, how to define the relation between charm or excitement (*Reiz*) and beauty (*Schönheit*). Kant's conflicting answers to the latter question suggest the presence of a problem he did not find easy to resolve.[80]

Throughout the *Nachlaβ* reflections, Kant's efforts to discover in taste a "universally valid" or "communicable" pleasure go hand in hand with an attempt to distinguish enjoyment of beauty (particularly beauty in women) from the merely sensual. That female beauty should play as small (and inconsistent) a role in the *Critique of Judgment* as it does is therefore at once remarkable and, in a certain sense, to be expected. The stipulation that pure aesthetic judgments be disinterested, that is, that they not be based in any way on inclination (V:211; 54), rules out from the start any confusion of beauty with charm.[81] Charm is so far from contributing to beauty that it must rather be considered as an "alien" distraction, admitted out of indulgence when taste is still unpracticed.

Whether woman's beauty can itself be the object of purely aesthetic liking (that is, one not in any way dependent on a concept of what that object is "to be") is a further question, on which Kant comes down at least three ways. In the "Analytic of the Sublime," as we have seen, he suggests that woman's beauty can be such an object; only to insist, in the "Analytic of the Beautiful," that it cannot. All judgments of beauty concerning human beings, according to the latter passage, involve an ideal of beauty, which itself has two components: first, an average or "standard" idea, empirically arrived at through some unknowable "secret" of nature (such a standard varies from people to people and from race to race); second, an "ideal" that consists in the expression of the moral, an expression without which the ideal "would not be liked universally" (V:235; 83). This ideal, presumably the same for men and women alike, applies to human beings alone, because man alone has the purpose of his existence "within himself" (V:233; 81) and thus (unlike other animate objects that also are judged aesthetically in relation to purposes) furnishes to judgment a sufficiently determinate concept.

Kant's description of the aesthetic *ideal* of beauty for all human beings speaks to an earlier regard for male beauty as superior to female: whereas male beauty, as Kant once expressed himself, is "absolute," female beauty (in men's eyes at least) is relative to charm, so much so, indeed, that even female animals are beautiful in an inferior way.[82]

The "correctness" of the ideal of beauty, as Kant now understands it, is proven by "its not permitting any charm of sense to mingle with the liking for its object," even as it "makes us take a great [that is, moral] interest in it." But precisely this interest also proves that a judging by the ideal of beauty "is not a mere judgment of taste" (V:236; [84]).

The standard *idea* of beauty, on the other hand, is only one of academic correctness, as with the model of a horse or dog of a particular breed — the "image" on which "nature's technic was, as it were, intentionally based" (V:234; [83]). Here the relevancy of the specific humanity of the object of beauty drops away; and the judgment of a man or woman as beautiful is (presumably) in principle the same as a judgment concerning the conformation of a collie or a Saint Bernard.

A third answer occurs in the part of the *Critique of Judgment* devoted to beautiful or fine art (*schöne Kunst*). Kant distinguishes fine art both from the beautiful in nature and from art that is merely agreeable (or which "charms"), such as those arts associated with dinner entertainment and games (*Spiele*). (These agreeable arts thus concern activities which may, when carried out in an artless manner, lead to disgust.) Fine art is "a way of presenting that is purposive on its own, and that furthers, even though without a purpose, the culture of our mental forces for social communication [or "imparting"] [*geselligen Mittheilung*]" (V:306; [173]). Nature, Kant adds, "is beautiful [*schön*] if it also looks like art, and art can be called fine [*schön*] art only if we are conscious that it is art while yet it looks to us like nature" (V:306; 174). Or, to put the distinction another way, "a natural beauty is a *beautiful thing;* artistic beauty is a *beautiful presentation* [Vorstellung] of a thing" (V:311; 179). In judging beautiful art we take into account what the object represented is "to be," that is, its purpose, and hence its perfection (or the harmony of its manifold with that purpose).

Now when judging certain (animate) objects of nature (such as a "human being or a horse"), we also take a purpose into account, but in this case it is not what the representation is meant by the (human) artist to be, but an "objective" purpose. That is to say, we judge nature "no longer as it appears as art, but insofar as it actually *is* art (albeit of a superhuman kind)." Such judgments are no longer pure-aesthetic, no longer mere judgments of taste, because they presuppose a teleological judgment "that serves the aesthetic as foundation and condition, and which the latter must take into regard" (V:312; [179]). If we say, for example:

> this is a beautiful woman, we do in fact think nothing other than that nature beautifully presents in her shape [*Gestalt*] the purposes

of the female structure [*Bau*]; for in order to think the object in this way, through a logically conditioned aesthetic judgment, one must look beyond the mere form to a concept. (V:312; [180])

Here female beauty is judged, neither according to a standard idea of beauty, nor according to its ideal, but rather in relation to the purposes of the female *Bau,* just what (what we have called) Kant's first answer to the question of female beauty seemingly ruled out, namely a positive appeal to the "purposes" served by the body or its parts (as distinguished from the negative condition that their form not actually seem to conflict with such purposes). As to what it means for nature to "beautifully present" the purposes of a woman's bodily structure (let alone what exactly they are) Kant does not here purpose to say. That there is more than delicacy behind his reticence is suggested by remarks in the *Anthropology* concerning the purpose of women as distinguished from that of mankind simply (VII:305; 169).[83] Indeed, one could say that the difference between woman's natural purpose and the purpose of mankind generally (hence, between woman's beauty as a function of the purposes of her bodily structure, and woman's beauty as an expression of the final end of humanity) is precisely the issue on which the *Critique of Judgment* turns: how to "go over" the cleft separating nature and freedom without abolishing it entirely.

Immediately after citing the female *Bau* as an example of beauty in nature of a peculiar kind, Kant speaks of the superiority of fine art to natural beauty (including beauty in women?), a superiority that "indicates itself in this: that [fine art] beautifully describes things that in nature would be hateful (*häßlich*) or shocking (*mißfällig*). Thus:

> The furies, diseases, devastations of war, and so on, can, as instances of harm, still be described, or even presented in a painting, very beautifully; only one sort of hatefulness cannot be presented according to nature without obliterating [*zu Gründe zu richten*] . . . the beauty of art: namely, that which arouses disgust [*Ekel*]. For in that strange sensation, which rests on mere imagination, the object is presented as if it, so to speak, pressed enjoyment upon us, even though that is just what we strive against with force [*Gewalt*]; hence the artistic presentation of the object is no longer distinguished in our sensation from the nature of the object itself, so that it cannot possibly be considered beautiful. (V:312; [180])

What is remarkable about this passage, in addition to the fact that the "furies," mythic figures both female and hideous, are gratuitously included in a list of *natural* calamities, is the train of association that takes Kant from the female *Bau,* to the superiority of art, to the "furies" (and other "natural" devastations), to disgust, a sensation which rests on imagination alone, and yet which—collapsing the distinction between object and representation as it does — destroys the very possibility of art, or the beautiful presentation of nature.[84]

Female beauty is the missing centerpiece of Kant's critique of taste — the unacknowledged articulation of "art as nature" and "nature as art." It also remains, as the text before us suggests, an unresolved problem. Like the wife who becomes repulsive with age, disinterested pleasure and disgust cannot, in woman's case, be long kept apart.[85]

It is for this reason, perhaps, that female beauty plays as small, and inconsistent, an explicit role in the *Critique of Judgment* as it does, a fact at odds with the emphasis of many of his earlier notes. Beauty, for Kant, ultimately requires a screen that is, like Isis's veil, impregnable. Mortal woman's natural lie — her charming concealment of what "arouses low esteem" — does not do the trick, with Kant at least, of covering what needs covering. If Kant's account of the *Erhabene* represents what an indebted Freud might call a "sublimation" of libidinal energy, Kant's treatment of beauty has about it the whiff of the suppressed.[86]

Genius and Generation

At the heart of Kant's treatment of fine art stands the genius, the human conduit through whom "nature gives the rule to art." If in the case of certain animate beings, nature acts as artist directly, in the case of fine art, she bestows that gift as an endowment in the form of talent. Since talent, as an "inborn productive ability," itself belongs to nature, genius can be called an "innate mental disposition [*Gemüthsanlage*] (ingenium)" (V:307; [174]).[87]

Genius is a talent for producing something for which "no determinate rule," that is, no concept, can be given (V:307; 175). The first property of genius is thus *originality,* though such originality must be *exemplary* rather than nonsensical. The genius is also a power of generating *ideas;* though how he comes by these ideas is beyond his power to describe, and their production is likewise outside of his control (*Gewalt*). Thus he cannot plan out artistic productions in advance. Nor can he impart to others some reliable method by which they might produce similar objects. (Fine art, for Kant, is thus intrinsically unreproducible, and as such defines itself not only against science, but also against everything craftlike or mechanical.)[88]

Kant notes that the word "genius" derives from the Latin *genius:* "the protecting and guiding [*leitenden*] spirit given to a human being as his own at birth" (V:308; [175–76]). The crucial emphasis, as Kant makes clear in *Anthropology* (VII:225; 94), is on the "individuality" of this spirit. Whether the gift of such a spirit is part of, or in addition to, the act of birth, the myth does not say, leaving it open whether or not spirit and nature are ultimately one.[89] As such, the myth of genius speaks to Kant's earlier figure of a stepmotherly nature who in her endless generations "cares nothing" for the individual. The genius is, in a word, nature's "favorite" (*Günstling* [V:318; 187]).⁹⁰ The artist who has nothing but his genius (that is, nature?) to thank (*verdanken*) thus recalls a mankind who, in an earlier account, thanks nature only for having nothing for which to thank her.⁹¹

To the "originality" of genius Kant opposes the spirit of imitation, or what can be learned according to rules. Thus great scientific minds (such as Newton) are not geniuses, since "the greatest discoverer differs from the most arduous imitator and apprentice only in degree" (V:309; 177).⁹² But such originality has its downside too; inasmuch as scientists' talent lies in increasing knowledge and teaching it to others, it is far superior to genius, which has probably already reached its outermost limits. What is more, inasmuch as the genius cannot teach others to be geniuses, he is in a certain sense without issue, his skill (*Geschicklichkeit*) "dying with him" until "nature again endows someone in the same way."

The principle power of genius lies in spirit (*Geist*), which Kant defines (taking the word, he says, in its "aesthetic sense") as the "animating principle of the mind": "That through which this principle enlivens the soul, the stuff through which it thereto applies itself, is that which sets the forces of the mind purposively in swing [*Schwung*], i.e., such a play as maintains itself and strengthens those forces further" (VII:313; [182]).⁹³ In terms that recall both Kant's earliest work on "living force" and the stoical model of generation on which that work partly relied, Kant revives the (male) principle of enlivening, which stirs or sets in play the otherwise dormant powers of the soul.⁹⁴ Genius is, and arouses in others, a sort of self-motion (Kant later speaks of "autonomy") that is analogous to, though not identical with, moral freedom itself.

This principle Kant summarily identifies with the power to exhibit aesthetic ideas, by which he means representations of imagination that occasion much thought, but to which no determinate concept can be adequate — hence thoughts, like those that ended his *Universal Natural History,* that no language can make fully comprehensible (VII:314; 182). The ultimate source of the ideas is "productive" imagination, which is "very mighty in the creation [*Schaffung*] of, so to speak, another nature out of the stuff that it is actually given." This ability (which we often use simply to amuse ourselves) goes hand in hand with the freedom of imagination from laws of association by which it is bound in its empirical use, freedom that allows it to "work up," from materials acquired from empirical experience, that which "surpasses nature."

In art (especially poetry [*Dichtkunst*]) this power manifests itself to the fullest extent; for the poet ventures to give sensible expression to rational ideas (such as invisible beings) or, alternatively, strives to sensualize (*zu versinnlichen*) that which has example in experience (such as love or fame) but with a completeness that "emulates reason in reaching [toward] a maximum" (V:314; [183]). The poetic imagination achieves this by "creatively" prompting so much thought as to expand the concept "in an unlimited way" and thus sets the power of intellectual ideas (or reason) in motion by prompting the mind to think more than is actually contained in the representation before it. The special gift of the artist is to impart a similar momentum (*Schwung*) to the imaginations of his audience so that they too can think more, in an "undeveloped way," than can be contained in a determinate concept. Thus Frederick the Great gives life to the "rational idea of a cosmopolitan attitude" in his poetic conjunction of death with the experiences associated with a serene summer evening, while another poet links the "flowing" sun with the serenity of virtue (V:315–16; 184).[95]

That Kant should pick these complementary solar images (and only these) is itself remarkable, recalling the more fearsome (and peculiarly) female suns of his earlier and ambiguously "poetic" *Universal Natural History*. The assimilation of the spiritual center with the sun, an assimilation that Kant once rejected as "fanatical," is now acceptably vague; while the awful theme of death and rebirth, nature's fearsome phoenix, has been softened by association with the constancy of virtue. Even Epicurean lawlessness, the threat of nature unbound, has lost its earlier sting, in Kant's conception of aesthetic freedom—a freedom, as it were, beyond the law.[96] In short, Kant's theory of genius revives the "poetic" feeling of impetuosity leading to transcendent calm and accompanied by "unnameable" and "undeveloped" concepts, to which the *Universal Natural History* unsuccessfully appealed; only this time the explicitly poetic character of Kant's move frees it from the inertial drag to which his earlier, "scientific" attempt finally succumbed. As empirical observer man cannot, Kant now knows, evade the limits of the natural world. Man frees himself from nature aesthetically not (as in Kant's earlier effort) by attempting to encompass it conceptually, but, in a certain sense, by welcoming it within, that is, by giving himself over to a pleasurable but lawless "play" of feeling. In the universal validity (or communicability) of that pleasure lies the assurance that the outcome of such play is neither monstrosity nor madness but, as the resolution of the "antinomy of taste" would have it, the exhibition of a higher law.

Thus artists of genius (as distinguished from their followers) are permitted a certain latitude where monstrosity (*Mißgestalt*) is concerned: for it would be difficult to remove such misshapings without weakening the idea. "This courage [*Muth*] does honor [*Verdienst*] to genius alone," for whom a certain boldness (*Kühnheit*) and deviation (*Abweichung*) from the common rule is fitting, not because the defect (*Fehler*) is not a defect, but because a genius has a certain "privilege to allow it to remain" lest the inimitable element of his spiritual impetus (*Geistesschwung*) be disarmed by anxious caution (*ängstliche Behutsamkeit*) (V:318; [187]). Spiritual momentum, in short, requires a certain courageous tolerance for (otherwise deflating) defects.[97]

Genius, then, is that "happy relation" — "one that no science can teach us and that cannot be learned by any diligence" — to discover ideas for a given concept and hit upon an expression of these through which the so-affected mental attunement (*Gemüthstimmung*) accompanying a concept can be imparted (*mitgetheilt*) to others. And spirit "properly so-called" is the latter talent, which consists in the apprehension and uniting in a concept of imagination's "play" without constraint of rules, a concept that is at once "original" and "revealing of a new rule" that could not have been anticipated in advance (V:317; [185–86]).

Spirit aesthetically reenacts reason's primordial positing of *the* law, a positing synonymous with freedom in its original break with, and ascendance over, nature. Hence the peculiar aptness of the example — the figure of Isis — that Kant appends in a note to the section on "the powers of the mind that constitute genius": "Perhaps nothing more sublime has ever been said, nor any more sublime thought expressed, than that inscription above the temple of *Isis* (Mother Nature): 'I am all that is, that was, and that will be, and no mortal has lifted my veil.'"

The solar king embodied by Kant's earlier, official example is now answered by a queen of the night — sacred and thrilling, but no bar (despite the inscription) to the advance of science, whose "temple" is interchangeable with that of "mother nature" herself. In the *Critique of Pure Reason* Kant famously urged reason to break from "nature's leading strings" and "coerce" nature as one "compels a witness," that is, through principles of judgment based on "fixed laws" (B/xiii). Now, however, the emphasis is quite the other way, against constraint and in favor of a certain holy awe as the appropriate introduction to natural science.[98] This differing emphasis, though by no means an overturning of the first *Critique*'s basic orientation toward nature, does suggest a new spirit of accommodation. This accommodation is facilitated by two developments: first, Kant's break, in the *Critique of Practical Reason,* with his earlier efforts (for example, in part 3 of the *Groundwork of the Metaphysics of Morals*) to derive moral freedom from the spontaneity, or idea-projecting capacity, of reason.[99] Once that break is made, his figurative identification of freedom with an (antimaternal) severing of "leading strings" (an association especially strong in the relatively early *What Is Enlightenment?*) tends to recede, leaving in the foreground enlightenment's public and "pluralistic" components (as in the formula that appears in the official "appendix" ("On Methodology Concerning Taste") that concludes the "Critique of Aesthetic Judgment."[100] Second is Kant's "discovery," as reported in his letter to Reinhold dated December

31, 1987, of "a priori principles" for the faculty of pleasure and displeasure, principles later modified, it seems reasonable to surmise, by considerations partially recorded in the essay *On the Use of Teleological Principles in Philosophy* (1788) and discussed earlier in this chapter. Once the communicable pleasure that Kant had long associated with taste is construed as implying, or resting on, the satisfaction of an a priori "need," the purposiveness of nature for ends other than strictly moral also follows. Where Kant earlier spoke, half-ironically, of nature's purposive frustration of human satisfaction, he now finds himself authorized to assume natural purposiveness (that is, furtherance of human purposes) of a more positive sort, albeit one that remains merely "subjective."

But Kant's account of genius is by no means simply positive. Despite the seeming sufficiency of genius as initially described, he goes on to insist that the wings of genius be "severely clipped" by taste so as to render its products "lasting and universal" and so "fit for an ever advancing culture." In keeping with this fact, and despite his earlier claim that fine art is not possible without genius, he now states that if a choice must be made between genius and taste, the latter should prevail (V:319–20; [188–89]). What (artistic) genius sacrifices, it seems, in its spirited *Schwung* is a direct link with human progress.[101]

Originality, then, is not enough; it must be combined with taste (and the discipline that taste requires) if the rich "spiritual materials" originated by genius are to receive communicable artistic form. Generally speaking, the role of genius is to provide ideas, albeit ones that, unlike the ideas of reason, are merely aesthetic, or lacking in a determinate concept. If rational ideas are concepts to which no intuition can be adequate, aesthetic ideas are intuitions to which no concept can be adequate. Aesthetic ideas are like rational ideas in aiming at a maximum, and yet also counterparts (*Gegenstücke*) to those ideas. This lack of a determinate concept corresponds, for Kant, to the lack of deliberate purpose that we attribute to all products of fine art (V:344; 217). The work of fine art has, in addition to tasteful correctness, an "unstudied" aspect; it must (or must seem to) be a product of nature working through the artist, as it were unconsciously, rather than of his own deliberate intention. Thus the work of fine art blurs the line between the blind necessity of natural events and the conscious intentionality of human action.[102]

The genius is the mere vehicle of nature; but nature, for her part, has undergone a transformation, it being nature not as mere mechanism, but as supersensible substrate to whose agency the product of genius is ultimately referred. In placing himself in the hands of nature in this transmuted sense, the artist does not (as with the later Romantics) abandon himself to a force alien to reason. The spirit of Kant's genius does not turn demonic.[103]

Withal, there is something *limited* about the genius, which places him — at least for those engaged in scientific pursuits — beyond the reach of envy. And yet Kant elsewhere places within genius's ranks not only scientists (like the "epoch-making" Newton and Leibniz, whom the *Critique of Judgment* had specifically excluded) but also "the architectonic mind," a description that, with all due allowance for modesty (such genius is called a "subaltern" though "uncommon" sort), cannot but raise the thought that Kant means thusly to include himself.[104]

Notes from the late 1760s and 1770s supply further clues to the relation between genius (and its correlative, spirit) and philosophy itself.[105] On the one hand, Kant associates spirit with the "production ground of the ideas" (*Reflection* no. 933 [XV:414]) and an "original enlivening, that comes from ourselves and is not derived" (*Reflection* no. 934 [XV:415]). In such reflections, spirit is sometimes another name for freedom conceived as the power of reason to originate ideas.[106]

In keeping with this train of thought, one early note specifically links genius to philosophy and fine art, as distinguished from criticism and history (*Historie*), the latter of which constitute learnedness (*Reflection* no. 1781 [XVI:112]), while another calls genius the "vital inner principle of knowledge" (*Reflection* no. 1900 [XVI:152]). Sometimes, spirit and genius join with knowledge as distinguished from art.[107] In general, genius and spirit are associated with ideas, invention, and the new (see, for example, *Reflection* no. 4863 [XVIII:13], 949 [XV:420–21], 943 [XV:418], and 974 [XV:426]), as opposed to imitation, or rigid adherence to rules already laid down.

Kant's identification of genius and spirit with an "enlivening" principle sometimes approaches vitalism, that is, an assimilation of rational freedom, artistic production, and natural generation within the single category of "life." *Reflection* no. 6862 (XIX:183), for example, identifies freedom with "the original life," adding that what facilitates the "feeling of universal life" causes the pleasure of taste. Kant wonders, however, whether "we indeed feel ourselves in universal life" and concludes that the harmony of our feeling is therefore a merely formal one. Another note (*Reflection* no. 945 [XV:419]) calls spirit "all in all and all in every part," while another (no. 938 [XV:416]) states that "there is only one genius: the unity of the world-soul."[108]

Organism, in this context, provides the basis for a sort of intuitive knowledge that (somehow), by virtue of its unification of mind and body, steers clear of fanaticism. Thus:

That our soul without a body should intuit other things as spirit
is an overstepping of the limits of the given [*dati*]. For we know
the soul only as an object of inner sense and the body as the means
to outer sense. Our intuition is not mystical but physical; the
physical is not pneumatological but organic. (*Reflection* no. 4863
[1776–78] [XVIII:13])

Another reflection, however, speaks of the "life spirit" that appears to
be the peculiar principle of the unification of the soul and the body, one
that works by itself and on which the will has no influence — a principle,
moreover, that is peculiarly identified with imagination and certain "representations" (such as heart palpitations and blushing) that cannot be
brought forth at will. Kant here links spirit, not with reason, but rather
with imagination and the "affected [*angegriffenes*] heart" as the "ground of
commerce" between body and soul (*Reflection* no. 1033 [1773–78 (?)]
[XV:463]).

Kant's comparison of physical and intellectual generation provides one basis for a recurring metaphor of knowledge as a kind of "epigenesis" of
reason, a reduplicative, individuating repetition according to rules laid out
in an original or "germinal" idea.[109] According to one note from the early
seventies (no. 4851 [XVIII:8–10]), the difference between *Schwärmerei*
and Kant's own account lies in the difference between the notion of "innate
ideas" (*ideis connatus*) and that of an a priori conceptual epigenesis. In another, Kant distinguishes his own epigenetic procedure from the physical
influx of Locke and Aristotle, the intellectual intuition of Plato and Malebranche, and the "preformation system" of Crusius.[110]

The appeal to a principle of epigenesis carries over to the B edition of
the *Critique of Pure Reason* in a section devoted to a consideration of alternative ways of regarding the necessary agreement between experience and
our concepts of its objects ([B/165–68]). There are, Kant says, only two
ways of regarding such agreement: "Either experience makes possible these
concepts, or these concepts make possible experience." The first alternative,
however, cannot hold for the categories (nor for pure sensible intuition),
for being a priori and hence independent of experience, "the ascription to
them of an empirical origin would constitute a kind of generatio aequivoca." "Consequently," Kant concludes, "there remains only the other alternative, a system of the *epigenesis* of pure reason, so to speak: namely, that
the categories, from the side of the understanding, contain the grounds of
the possibility of all experience in general."

Kant proceeds to raise the possibility of a third alternative midway between the other two: namely, that the categories are neither "self-thought"
(*selbstgedacht*) nor derived (*geschöpft*) from experience, but rather "subjective dispositions (*Anlagen*), implanted in us, so to speak, with our exis-

tence, that are so arranged by our creator (*Urheber*) that their use exactly harmonizes (*stimmte*) with the laws of nature according to which experience proceeds (a kind of *Praeformations* = *System* of pure reason)." Kant rejects this third alternative not only because on such a hypothesis "one could foresee no end to how far one might carry the assumption of determined dispositions to future judgments," but also, and "decisively," because there would then be lacking in the categories the *necessity* "that belongs essentially to their concept." The concept of a cause, for example, "would be false" if it rested only "on an arbitrary [*beliebigen*] subjective necessity implanted in us, of connecting certain empirical representations according to such a rule of relation." "I would then not be able to say," he significantly continues, "that the effect is connected with the cause in the object (i.e., necessarily)," but only that I cannot think the representation other than as so bound, which is "just what the skeptic most desires." In such a case, the necessity in question could only be "felt," and one cannot dispute (*hadern*) with another over that which merely concerns the way in which the subject is organized (*organisirt ist*).[111]

Here, as in reflections recorded fifteen years earlier, epigenesis serves as a way of preserving the peculiar necessity that characterizes worldly experience. A preformation system gives the skeptics all that they could wish by failing to provide an adequate account of "objective" necessity. If the connectedness of our representations rested merely on the organization of our subject (hence on "feeling"), not only could we not foresee any end to the modifications that our judgment might undergo in the future, but also, and "decisively," we could give no account of the necessity inherent in the very concept of a category by which experience as such is made possible. To grasp that concept, Kant seems to want to say, is to oppose to dogmatist and skeptic, intellectualist and empiricist alike the real community or common world of experience that all sane men share when awake. To assume any other principle is to abandon that common world in which "dispute" over the particulars of experience is possible.[112]

In the "Critique of Aesthetic Judgment," on the other hand, Kant finds an alternative "middle way" in which feeling and necessity *are* reconciled, albeit merely "subjectively." Thus the "Dialectic of Aesthetic Judgment" turns precisely on the question of how a judgment lacking in a determinate concept (hence evading the net of the categories) can nevertheless be a matter for argument (as judgments concerning the merely agreeable are not.) Kant's "solution" replaces dispute (*disputiren*) (which requires a determinate concept) with conflict (*streiten*) (for which an indeterminate concept — that is, that of the "supersensible substrate of humanity" — is said to suffice) (V:337 ff.; 209 ff.). If one follows up the analogy, one could say that aesthetic judgment makes qualified room for the system of "individual preformation" that his earlier work rejects. In his elaboration of aesthetic taste — as distinguished from tastes of a more ambiguous and threatening kind — Kant comes closest to endorsing preformationism in the ordinary sense; preformationism, in other words, that isn't epigenesis by another name.[113]

The question of the origin of the ideas (and the role of genius in their origination) raised questions, for Kant, of a more disturbing order. The distinction between genius and *Schwärmerei* does not seem to be something concerning which Kant had an entirely consistent view. Thus he distinguishes in one note from the mid 1770s between "a genius for ideas" and a "talent for brainstorms [*Einfällen*]" (*Reflection* no. 969 [XV:425]); and he calls "heating [*Erhitzung*] through an idea" inspiration (*Begeisterung*), heating "without an idea" being fanatical (*schwarmend*) fire (no. 951 [XV:421]; cf. no. 950 [XV:421]); while elsewhere *Begeisterung* is itself the mark of fanaticism. In one passage, the *Schwärmer* is chided for lacking a graspable idea (no. 899 [XV:393]), in another for clinging to an idea too tenaciously (no. 921 [XV:406]). In some reflections, indeed, genius itself is suspect. Thus it is called one "disturbed [*gestörter*] whom others must first interpret. images instead of things. Creation craziness [*Schaftollheit*]" (no. 940 [1776–89] [XV:417]). With genius, "there is much illusion" (*Blendwerk*) (no. 791 [1772–78] [XV:346]).

In one extraordinary and belabored passage Kant compares — in a tone that combines a literally visceral sympathy with woman's lot with an equally visceral abhorrence — the trials of inspired genius with the noisy birth pangs of a pregnant housewife. (The sentence immediately preceding states, without apparent bearing on the ones that follow, that women have no sense of duty and are bound by no law.)

> An inspired [*begeistertes*] genius is {very}[114] always ungrateful, arrogant, unbridled and scornful. Just as the cackling of a hen must be endured because she has with lamentations [*Wehen*] laid us an egg, and as pregnant housewives commonly give many complaints to our ears because they must suffer inconvenience [*Beschwerlichkeit*] in order to give birth to a child, so is the genius pregnant from {ethereal} plastic nature also imperious, arrogant and sulky because {its danger with straining [*Anspannung*] of rupturing all tender tissues} is under difficult [*bescwherlichen*] {lamentations convulsions} ecstasies of imagination, under great danger to healthy reason, bears us [us and with strong lamentations] a (God =) child, a child that is so to speak lovely to contemplate [*anzuschauen*], but because it is of ethereal origin, dissolves in ether in an instant, after one has stripped off the shell of mystical language. *Its reproaches hit everything, because the inspired genius sees everything under it, since it has lifted itself up [*sich erhoben hat*] above the region of {all} the {thick} corporeal air, in which common plants of healthy reason grow. * (It never brings anything

about, but rather is inexhaustible with regard to many idols of reason, containing much that powerfully swarms about its eyes.) (No. 936 [1776–79] [XV:415–16])

Made pregnant by nature herself, the inspired genius (in fear of "rupturing tissues" more tender even than those of the tender sex) reverses the correct relation between former and informed.[115]

A final early passage bears mentioning in this regard. In one lengthy reflection from the seventies entitled "On Genius," Kant distinguishes between a *schwärmerisch* and enthusiastic genius, which has a "good head" and from which Kant can "really learn" because it has some connection with true ideas, and a "fantastic kind of writing" that is nothing more than a sort of alchemic fakery. As examples of the former he cites Rousseau and Plato; among the latter he cites the theosophists (whose ranks, according to Adickes's guess, include Hamann and Herder). Unlike the latter company, Rousseau is said to be a *Schwärmer* "worthy of respect," and Plato "swarms with ideas in general." From *schwärmerisch* genius, Kant notes, "I can really learn; for either its ground idea is according to reason, or the consequences are . . . unconcealed and uncover defects in fundamental principles . . . that through sly political investiture [*Einkleidung*] would only remain masked [*verdeckt*]" (no. 921, 921a [1775–78] [XV:406–8]).

As to whether the architectonic mind is or is not to be classified with spirit and genius is a question upon which Kant's reflections vacillate.[116] What is perhaps his final word appears in a reflection from the late eighties — around the time of the composition of the *Critique of Judgment:*

> To deal in a geniuslike [*geniemäßig*] way with deeply entangled [*verwickelte*] philosophic questions: this honor I entirely forego. I only undertake to work on these in a schoollike [*schulmäßig*] way. If herein the labor [*Arbeit*], which requires steady industry and care, succeeds, then it remains {to} true genius (not to those who undertake to make all from nothing), to bind [*verbinden*] to it the sublime impulse of spirit [*Geistesschwung*], and so set the use of dry/barren [*trocken*] principles in motion.
>
> Poetic art [*Dichtkunst*] is properly the enlivening of spirit. Eloquence, impregnated [*geschwängert*] through poetry, is true fluency [*Beredsamkeit*]; otherwise it is rhetoric or . . . [breaks off].
> (*Reflection* no. 990 [1785–89] [XV:435])

Why, then, Kant's belabored equivocation on the relation between philosophy and genius? Because on it turns, as he well knew, the ultimate status of reason's *Hauptidee,* the idea on which Kant's system as a whole depends and the history of philosophy begins and ends.[117]

As the first to formulate and propagate (intentionalize) that *Hauptidee,* Kant both completes the history of philosophy and inaugurates, he hopes, the true history of man.[118] But what of Kant's own natural history? Does not the (utterly contingent) fact of his own birth contaminate the idea's rational pedigree? Kant's *Idea for a Universal History* sketched the beginning of a (prematurely aborted) answer. The *Critique of Judgment* strikes out in a different direction, under the aegis of the indeterminate concept of a supersensible substrate (and the sting, perhaps, of Herder's accusations concerning spiritual self-birthing). Whereas in the *Idea for a Universal History* Kant looks to a(nother) genius to fulfill the task of composing a history of the human species, in the *Critique of Judgment* he seems to have arrived at a more satisfactory conception of his own historical position. Still, difficulties remain. If the source of the idea is to be construed as nature (albeit noumenal), the line separating philosophy from poetry threatens (again) to blur. If it is *not* nature, then the indeterminate concept of a supersensible substrate, on which Kant pins his hopes for systematic unity, begins to dim. To be other than nature's stepchild without becoming her favorite[119] is by no means the easiest labor that Kant sets himself in undertaking to philosophically assess the power to judge aesthetically.

9   Adventures of the Organism (II)

My discussion of the second part of the *Critique of Judgment* takes as its point of departure two apparently unrelated claims, one characterizing epigenesis (for the first time) as a sort of "preformation system," the other acknowledging the transmutation of species (for the first time) as a "daring adventure of reason," that is, a hypothesis neither absurd, empty, nor repulsive on its face. As we shall see, this qualified acceptance of doctrines Kant had previously opposed sheds useful light on his effort, in part 2 of the *Critique of Judgment,* to explain the possibility of our conceiving of a living being without commingling intellect and matter.

I. Nature and Intention

Kant begins part 2 by distinguishing the objective purposiveness of nature from that subjective purposiveness which is grounded in the universal idea of nature as *Inbegriff* (or sum) of the objects of sense (V:359; 235). Such an *Inbegriff,* which is implied by our assumption of nature's *subjective* purposiveness for the prehension (*Faβlichkeit*) of human judgment, does not in itself support our thinking of things in nature as *objectively* purposive, that is, as beings whose possibility we can understand only by regarding them as products of purposive (Kant does not go so far as to say "intentional") causality. To see that a thing is possible only as a purpose (the essential characteristic of the intrinsically purposive) implies that the form of a thing could not have arisen from mechanical laws alone, or, to put matters otherwise, "requires that even empirical cognition of this form in terms of its cause and effect presupposes concepts of reason" (V:370; 248).

Objective purposiveness, then, is a purposiveness that is thought as itself making possible the thing in which it is exhibited. Such a "nexus finalis" provides us a basis for understanding the object's possibility, on the "analogy" of our own purposive causality (that is, the technical causality that, as Kant puts it, "we meet in ourselves") (V:360; [237]). We understand the possibility of such things, in other words, by thinking of them as similar to products of human making, where the end held in view (for example, money, in the case of a building constructed for the purpose of collecting rent) constitutes the "cause" of the thing's existence. Since, however, no such intentional activity can be attributed to nature (which we do not assume to be intelligent), and since the purposes in question are not our own either (as is the case with products of human making), Kant opts for a third alternative, which utilizes the concept of such causality only regulatively, as a way of guiding our investigation of nature on the analogy of human *technai,* without attributing such causality to nature directly.[1] The regulative or reflective concept of objective purposiveness in nature is thus a way of attributing to nature something more than "blind mechanism" without going so far as to credit (*unterlegen*) it with causes that act intentionally.[2]

Such objective purposiveness is distinguished from its subjective counterpart by its intrinsic relation to a concept. As such, it may be merely formal (as with geometric figures generated by a rule "within me") or real (as with organisms — cases where I find order in a bounded *Inbegriff* of things "outside me") (V:364; 241–42).[3]

Experience leads judgment to the concept of objective purposiveness in nature wherever a relation of cause to effect can be "seen as lawful" only if we regard the cause's action to be based on the idea of the effect. Objective purposiveness, then, reconciles lawfulness with the manifest, and indeed, infinite contingency of a phenomenon judged on the basis of mechanical causation alone. A bird's wing, for example, insofar as we judge solely on the basis of mechanical causation, might have been formed in any number of ways, just as a rock takes precisely the form it does for reasons infinitely varied. But we attribute to the constitution of the wing, and not that of the rock (unless we take it for an artifact), a kind of lawfulness that is inseparable from the notion that the wing has been made for flight (or some similar use).[4]

What is required, then, is the notion of an alternate causality, which is both lawful (as all causality must be) and yet contingent with respect to the necessity of blind mechanism. Kant finds the requisite conjunction of contingency and lawfulness in an analogy with human making. Human artifacts are things whose possibility depends on the intentional activity of a rational will, which brings about lawfully, or according to a rule, that which would not otherwise occur according to the course of nature. Where something is cognized as a product of nature (rather than human will) and yet judged to be an end or purpose (a "natural purpose" [*Naturzweck*], in other words, if there does not, Kant adds, herein lie a contradiction), the causality in question can be "thought" [*gedacht*] without contradiction but not "conceived" (V:371; [249]). One can provisionally say that such a product is "both cause and effect of itself" (thus preempting, if not solving, what Kant might once have called the problem of "Adam's father"). It does so, moreover, in at least two different senses.

First, the natural product (Kant uses the example of a tree) generates (*zeugt*) its own kind (*Gattung*) and thus endlessly begets or produces (*erzeugt*) and is begotten by itself, preserving itself as a species.

Second, the tree begets itself individually through a process of growth that is generation (*Zeugung*), as Kant puts it, by a different name (V:371; 250). For the tree works upon the raw material of nature that it assimilates so as to endow that material with a species-proper quality (just as, we might add, pneuma or spirit, according to the Aristotelian account of generation, works upon unformed matter). An organism thus exhibits an originality (*Originalität*) in its separating and forming ability infinitely beyond human art when it attempts to put back together or give life to that which it dissects (*Zergliederung*).

Finally (Kant adds a third sense of self-generation, not previously mentioned), the organism reproduces itself not only specially and individually but also partially, inasmuch as each part depends reciprocally on (or mutually produces and is produced by) all the rest. In this respect an individual branch is no different, vis à vis the organism as a whole, than a scion of alien stock grafted to the stem of a particular plant: "even in one and the same tree, we may regard each branch or leaf as merely grafted [*gepfropft*] or inoculated [*oculirt*] onto another, as if [each were] an independent [*für sich selbst bestehenden*] tree that only attaches itself [*anhängt*] to another and nourishes itself parasitically" (V:371–72; [250]). Kant's striking depiction of organic parts as parasites, fetuslike in their attached or pendulous means of nourishment, contradicts his description elsewhere in the paragraph of the relation between parts and whole as one of mutual support. The depiction would thus seem wholly gratuitous (as well as inaccurate) did it not also call to mind Kant's earlier characterization of the human species (in the *Idea for a Universal History*) as essentially *gepfropft*.[5]

In regarding an organized being as a collection of mutually supportive grafts, Kant not only loosens the conceptual barriers between species (since every organism is, in a certain sense, a collection of [species-distinct] parasites), but also implicitly withdraws from his earlier conception, in the *Idea for a Universal History,* of the human species as uniquely defined by its engraftment. Inoculation, in other words, is no longer the defining attribute of man, a development that raises the hope that another, more satisfying definition of our species may be forthcoming.[6]

In any case, if each living thing is, as Kant now puts it, "cause and effect of itself" such that each part relates to every other part as do parasite and host (or embryo and parent), the problem of human freedom vis à vis nature can be seen in a new and less adversarial light. The agonistics of human self-emancipation are prefigured (one is tempted to say preformed) in the structure of the living organism. This is not, of course, to say that plants and animals are free in a moral sense; it is, however, to grant "life" a more central role than Kant was previously willing to concede.[7] The "former chambermates" above whom Kant once raised mankind's head have, at the organic level at least, been rejoined. Nature may not be the "Great Mother" rhapsodized by Herder (Kant prefers her as a Goddess), but neither is she—whose "marvelous" properties of self-healing, especially in the case of anomalous deformities, Kant notes—to be described (as in Kant's reviews of Herder) as altogether indifferent to the fate of individuals.

The conceptual basis of this new rapprochement lies in Kant's new understanding of the role of ideas in (our comprehension of) organic life. By virtue of this new understanding, Kant claims to be able not only to reconcile formal and efficient causal explanation, but even, in the case of biological phenomena, to elevate the former over the latter, without opening the floodgates of *schwärmerisch* illusion.

Kant's starting point is the concept of a natural purpose, a concept seemingly contradictory inasmuch as it appears to require that nature (which we "cannot think intelligent") act "intentionally," or on analogy with human art, the only sort of ideal causality with which we are directly familiar. The old problem of reconciling nature's intelligibility with its lack of intelligence (its radical "otherness" or externality vis à vis the inwardness of reason) reappears as a meditation on what it means for something to be living. Kant's preliminary answer—that such a thing is both cause and effect of itself—is now further refined. First, a natural *purpose* is "covered" (*befasst*) by a concept or idea determining everything a priori, such that the possibility of the parts depends on their relation to the whole. But (Kant continues) if we think a thing as possible only in this way, that is, as the product of a rational cause, distinct from a thing's matter (or parts), then we think of it merely as a work of art. We must therefore also think it possible (if it is a *natural* purpose) without the causality of concepts, that is, without a causality that implies rational agency. This latter condition is satisfied through the requirement that the parts "combine into the unity of a whole" because "they are reciprocally cause and effect of one another's form." For

> it is only in this way possible that the idea of the whole should conversely (reciprocally) determine the form and connection [*Verbindung*] of all parts, not as cause—for then the whole would be a product of art—but as the ground of knowledge [*Erkenntnisgrund*], for one who judges it, of the systematic unity of form and connection of everything manifold contained in the given matter. (V:373; [252])

The "idea," then, is the "ground" by or through which we judge or know the systematic unity of the whole. It is not the "formal" cause of that unity, separate from the matter thus informed (as with, say, the blueprint of a builder); rather, the idea is that on the basis of which we recognize matter as itself productive or able to both give form and receive it. A natural purpose is thought of as self-propagating (*sich fortpflanzend*); or alternatively — since each part may also be thought of as a tool (or organ) for all the rest — as self-organizing (*selbstorganisirend*) (V:374; [253]). From the perspective of traditional dichotomies, in which form is male and matter female, one could say that the idea "masculinizes" matter (or, better yet, renders matter hermaphroditic), endowing it with a "formative force"[8] (*sich bildende Kraft*) not distinguished (as is the case with art) from the "matter of the thing."

One says "far to little" in calling nature's self-organizing power "an analog of art," which implies the apartness of the artist and the work of art. One might, Kant adds, "step closer to this inscrutable property of nature if one called it an analog of life." "Then, however, one must endow matter as matter with a property (hylozoism) that contradicts its essence, or conjoin matter with a an alien principle (a soul) standing in community with it." The former is contradictory on its face; the latter either removes the product from (corporeal) nature or treats matter (to which soul is conjoined) as already organized, which explains nothing. The only strict conclusion is that the organization of nature has nothing analogous to any causality known to us (V:375; [254]).[9]

The ultimate inscrutability of life amounts to our inability either to reduce the self-organizing power of nature monistically (through a conflation of matter and life, the literal meaning of "hylozoism") or expand it dualistically (into a community between matter and soul). This inscrutability — the "veil," as it were, surrounding nature's nuptial bed — is, one hazards to guess, at once "sublime" and satisfying to Kant because it gives scope to the (masculine) expression of form within nature without insisting overscrupulously on understanding (seeing) how such expression is possible. It is enough to admit that such expression occurs, or rather, that we must judge it to occur (and to have occurred) wherever we are aware of organic life, as is the case with our own living bodies — for we too, as Kant notes, "belong to nature" (V:375; 254).

It is for this latter reason, I believe, that after insisting that "strictly speaking," the "organization of nature has nothing analogous to any causality known to us" (V:375; 254), Kant goes on to allow, on virtually the same page, "a remote [*entfernten*] analogy with our own causality concerning purposes generally" (V:375; 255). This analogy, he says, can guide (*leiten*) our investigation of organized beings and ponder their highest ground, "not for the purpose [*Behuf*] of knowing nature or its original cause," but rather "for the same practical power of reason [*Vernunftvermögen*] in us" by which he previously analogized the purposiveness of nature (V:375; [255]). This "organic" power of human artifice (or what Hegel will call labor) to bring about effects in nature through ideas is itself served by a consideration of natural purposes. We make use of an analogy with our own worldly or embodied efficacy, not only for the sake of investigating nature, but also for the sake (as we meditate upon nature's "Urgrund") of that very efficacy.

The reflective (*reflectirend*) solution of the problem of generation is thus doubly empowering, not only for our study (*Nachforschung*) of biological nature, a study that would otherwise lack guidance, but also as an enabling meditation or reflection (*Nachdenkung*) on origins.[10] In both of these senses, the regulative idea implicit in (and given "objective reality" by) organized beings supports, by a strategy of distancing indirection, man's worldly potency. This strategy of a gaze averted or — what amounts to the same thing — indefinitely put off releases the mind from an otherwise issueless preoccupation, as evinced in Kant's earlier work, with the particulars of procreation.[11]

There is, however, one sort of organization that can be more intimately known, albeit analogically: a certain human association (*Verbindung*), met with "more in the idea than in actuality." Kant speaks particularly of "a recently undertaken whole transformation [*Umbildung*] of a great people into a state, to which the term 'organization' was frequently and very aptly applied, not only to the establishment of magistrates, etc., but also for the entire body politic [*Staatskörpers*]" (V:375 n; 254 n). What renders "organization" here especially apt is the fact that each member exists in relation to the whole, "not only as a means, but also an end," so that "each member commonly effects [*mitwirkt*] the possibility of the whole," even as "the place and function of each is determined through that whole's idea." The ideal republic brought, so to speak, to life is an organic whole to whose inner workings we are uniquely privy, inasmuch as the idea in question is one that we as members intentionally share.[12] The establishment of a new social contract is thus the one case of "palingenesis" that Kant is willing critically to concede.[13]

Kant's analysis of organization calls to mind his discussion, in the *Critique of Pure Reason,* of the "organic" unity of reason, whose modes of knowledge (*Erkenntnisse*) "must not be permitted to be a mere rhapsody, but which must form a system" (A/832 = B/860). The idea underlying this unity is the "form of a whole — insofar as the concept determines *a priori* not only the scope of its manifold content, but also the positions which the parts occupy relatively to one another." The result is a unity that is not merely heaped up (*gehäuft; coacervatio*), but membered (*gegliedert; articulatio*) ([A/833 = B/861]). This memberment or articulation according to a germinal idea is, however, historically obscured: "Systems seem initially garbled [*verstümmelt*] like worms [*Gewürme*] through a *generatio aequivoca* from a mere confluence of assembled concepts, to become perfectly formed with time, even though they have all had their schema as the original germ in sheer self-developing reason" (A/835 = B/863). A *generatio aequivoca* is literally a generation that is "equivocal," that is, "equal" to generation in "name" only. (Earlier in the *Critique* Kant associates equivocal generation with an empirical origination [*per impossibile*] of the categories.) In so describing the necessarily historical development of philosophy as a system, Kant equates his own critical awakening with the moment in which the germ of the idea emerges (or becomes recognizable), transforming what had seemed to be a heaped up (or mutilated, as in *verstümmelt*) aggregate, wormlike in its approximation to dead matter, into a genuine organism that is also, for once, intellectually transparent. The system of philosophy is thus one membered whole in which we can ourselves participate "productively" — not, to be sure, as archetypal intellects ("philosophers" in the ideal sense) — but insofar as we ourselves "philosophize," that is, let knowledge "issue forth out of reason." (One who acquires knowledge from a "foreign reason," by way of contrast, is called merely the "plaster caste" of a living human, an image that transforms the traditional figure of the ectypal or receptive intellect into a sort of death mask [(A/836 = B/864)]).[14] Kant does not claim to *know* the whole (as Hegel will later do); he does, however, claim to "sketch" (*entwerfen*) it out in terms of the world-concept (*Weltbegriff*) taken in conjunction with the essential ends of human reason and thus fulfills at least one role he once reserved to a creative, world-projecting God.[15]

Kant, who himself brings the idea to light, and whose very life recapitulates (ontogenetically, as it were) the philosophic history that it completes, does not here stop to note his own crucial role in marking the transition from a merely "vocal generation" to the "self-development of reason."[16] Nothing more radically reveals the limits of reason's self-organizing power than the shear contingency of Kant's own birth. His life (and the natural history of reason that it organically inscribes) is at once part of and outside the system it makes possible.[17]

II. Organism and the System of Nature

In the case of relative (or extrinsic) purposiveness, something is regarded as useful or beneficial to a(nother) creature, as rivers are deemed to exist because they deposit soil suitable for the growth of certain plants. Such purposiveness, however, is viciously circular (each thing being conceivable as benefiting some creature or other) unless it can be related to that which is itself, or intrinsically, a natural purpose.

It might seem, on the basis of Kant's previous discussion, that nature as such is (or could be conceived as) an organism, each part of which reciprocally serves the others as both means and ends. This, however, Kant explicitly denies on the grounds that, unlike the parts of a living being, pieces of nature (unless they happen to be alive) *can* be explained in solely mechanical terms. Nothing forces us to link the possibility of a mountain or a river (as is the case with living organs) with purposive causality. To judge all parts of nature purposive vis à vis the whole, one would therefore have to know the final end or *scopus* of nature. This end, however, could not itself be part of or internal to nature (as is at least problematically the case with the end or purpose of a natural product). The extrinsic purposiveness of one being vis à vis another can never get beyond a round of circular hypotheses: the blade of grass that feeds the cow that feeds the man that feeds the vermin (see V:379; 259). We cannot arrive at a categorical purpose in this way, however, because we cannot say why human (or any other natural) beings should necessarily exist (a question that would not seem so easy to answer, Kant adds, if one had in mind what he elsewhere calls the "cattle-like" existence of New Hollanders or Tierra del Fuegians) (V:378; 258). What is required to escape that circle is a final or unconditioned end — an end that cannot, therefore, itself (or "in its entire species [*Gattung*]") be regarded as a natural product.

Man, in short — for he, as will shortly emerge, is the sought for categorical purpose — is not himself (or is not to be regarded) as a natural product, at least insofar as he is thought of as a species being (*Gattungswesen*), a proviso that presumably lifts up the otherwise contemptible del Fuegians. Still, the principle of nature's purposiveness as a whole (such that everything is good for something), a principle to which the idea of natural products directs us, has regulative value, for example, in suggesting to us that certain inner afflictions (like tapeworms [*Bandwürmer*] or bad dreams) are in fact conducive to health.[18]

But what "leads us necessarily," as Kant puts it, from the concept of an organism as a natural purpose to "the idea of all of nature as a system according to the rule of ends"? (V:378–79; [258]).[19] The same train of thought, it seems, that Kant himself followed in interpreting his childhood dream of drowning — an interpretation that reads the *fantasy* of drowning (or being swallowed up by the abyss) as a preventative against literal asphyxiation, and the abysmal image of nature's destructiveness as a sign of her life-quickening solicitude.

Such thoughts "entitle us" to "the idea of a great system of the ends of nature." On this basis, even beauty in nature, that is, "nature's harmony with the free play of our cognitive powers in the apprehension and judgment of her appearance," can be considered as an "objective purposiveness, of the whole of nature as a system that includes man as member" (*Glied*) (V:380; [260]). The "entertaining" (*unterhaltend*) and instructive consideration as natural of what seems in man's internal organization to be "un-natural" allows us to objectify our otherwise subjective judgment of the beautiful. Nature so construed becomes "lovable," even as we become her "favored." Contemplation of the beauty and charms of such a nature makes us "feel ennobled" — "exactly as if" she had erected and decorated her magnificent (*herrlich*) stage expressly with that intention (*ganz eigentlich in dieser Absicht*).

Thus objectified, judgment of the beautiful in nature articulates our own natural membership, and with it nature's systemicity — a systemicity that takes us to the brink of attributing intentionality to nature without actually doing so.[20] It also allows us to contemplate nature's charms and beauties nobly and with reverence — without disavowing interest or intrinsic relation to a concept.[21]

We are entitled, Kant concludes, to judge products of nature as belonging to nature as a system of purposes, even if organisms, both individually and collectively, do not require us to look beyond blind mechanism to explain their possibility. And this because "the idea of nature as a system" already "leads us beyond the sensible world" to unity of the supersensible, so that "we must judge the latter to be valid for nature as a whole just as much as it is valid for certain species of natural beings within it" (V:381; [261]).

Kant's reflection on the purposive character of that in nature (and especially our own inner organization) which seems counterpurposive leads, then, to the idea of nature as a whole as a system of purposes. This idea has the advantage over the divine schema — its precritical rival — of being thinkable by a mind that is itself *part* of nature. Intellect insinuates itself into nature, if only to the extent that one can genuinely regard oneself as nature's "member."[22]

The next section ("On the Principle of Teleology as a Principle Inherent in Natural Science") therefore quite properly turns to the relation between natural and divine purpose, and the boundary that separates scientific and theological teleology.

We must not consider unimportant whether the expression, purpose of nature, is exchanged with that of a divine purpose in the arrangement of nature, let alone whether the latter is passed off as more appropriate . . . on the ground that surely in the end we cannot get around deriving those purposive forms . . . from a wise author of the world. Rather we must carefully and modestly restrict ourselves to that expression that says only exactly as much as we know. For even before we inquire as to the cause of nature, we find in nature and in the course of her generation [*Erzeugung*] such products, products that are generated in her by known laws

of experience. Natural science must judge its objects in accordance
with such laws, and must therefore seek in nature their causality
according to the rule of purposes. Hence, natural science must
not overleap its boundary, in order to absorb, as an indigenous
[*einheimisches*] principle, something to whose concept no experience whatever can be adequate. (V:382; [262])

Kant therefore "abstracts entirely" from the (metaphysical) question of
whether "natural purposes are purposes *intentionally* or *unintentionally*," a
question whose very posing would constitute a "meddling [*Einmengung*]
in foreign business" (V:383; [263]). The very absurdity of attributing intentionality to lifeless matter assures against misunderstanding (that is,
mistaking determinate for reflective judgment) when we do so: in rightly
speaking of nature's parsimony, foresight, or benevolence we "do not make
nature into an intelligent [*verständig*] being (for that would be absurd);
nor are we so bold as to posit a different, intelligent being above nature as
its architect (for that would be presumptuous [*vermessen*])." Instead: "We
use these terms to designate a kind of causality in nature following the
analogy of our own causality in the technical use of reason, since that helps
us keep in view the rule we must follow in investigating certain products
of nature."

The vexed question of the intentionality of nature is thus set aside. Natural purposiveness is to be regarded neither as material nor as intellectual,
but as technical, on the analogy of our own use of reason in making
things.[23] This analogy, however, only extends so far, since natural organism
infinitely surpasses human art, while our judgments concerning extrinsic
purposiveness lack an exhibition of necessity adherent to the character of
things.[24]

Section 68 thus ends inconclusively. The appeal to a divine schema, to
be sure, is done in by its false modesty (V:384 n; 264 n). Still, its rival—the
idea of nature as an articulated organism—remains dialectically equivocal.

III. The "Antinomy of Teleological Judgment"

In sections that follow (nos. 69–78), Kant takes up that dialectic, which
consists in an antinomy between the thesis: "All production of material
things and their forms must be judged to be possible in terms of merely
mechanical laws"; and an antithesis: "Some production of material nature
cannot be judged to be possible in terms of merely mechanical laws . . . but
requires a different causal law—viz. that of final causes" (V:387; [267]).

The question posed by the antinomy comes down to this: not whether
we must judge organized beings in terms of the concept of final causes (a
principle Kant holds indubitable) but whether such final causality is objectively in nature, or merely a subjective principle of judgment (V:390;
270–71).

Now nothing concerning science or speculation requires us to decide this question, our very pursuit (*nachspüren*) of which therefore becomes significant, pointing to a "suspicion" (*Ahnung*) on the part of reason, or nature's "hint" (*Wink*), that we might reach beyond nature to a highest cause. First, however, Kant pauses to consider the question itself, that is, to find out where that "stranger" (*Fremdling*) in natural science—the concept of a natural purpose (*Naturzweck*)—may lead. Is, then, nature itself causally purposive (that is, purposive in an "objective" way), or do we merely use this concept to judge nature subjectively?

"ON THE VARIOUS SYSTEMS THAT CONCERN THE PURPOSIVENESS OF NATURE"

From objective maxims concerning natural purposiveness arise a variety of systems, which are dogmatic and mutually exclusive. (Subjective maxims, on the contrary, may be mutually compatible.) Such systems are either "idealistic" or "realistic," the former maintaining that all natural purposiveness is *unintentional,* the latter that such purposiveness, at least as it pertains to organized beings, is *intentional* (V:391; 272).

"Idealism of purposiveness," in turn, is either "causualistic" or "fatalistic." The former system—that of Democritus and Epicurus—refers the relation (*Beziehung*) of matter to the physical ground of its form, that is, to the laws of motion, and is so "manifestly absurd," according to Kant, as not to require further comment. The latter, associated with Spinoza, refers that relation to a hyperphysical ground of matter and, indeed, all of nature; unlike the first it is not patently absurd and is indeed difficult to refute because its concept of the original being (*Urwesen*) is unintelligible. According to the fatalistic principle, purposive connection in the world derives not from the *intention* of an original being, but from the necessity of its nature; hence it too is, in the special sense intended, idealistic.

"Realism of purposiveness," on the other hand, is either "physical" (that is, hylozoistic) or "hyperphysical" (that is, theistic). The former grounds purposes of nature on the analog of an intentionally acting power—the so-called life of matter—whether that power be in matter itself or due to a "world soul," that is, an "inner animating principle." The latter derives such purposes from the original ground (*Urgrund*) of the world-all, that is, an intelligent, originally living being that produces (*hervorbringen*) with intention (V:392; [273]).

All such dogmatic systems try to explain our teleological judgments about nature either (in the case of idealism) by denying the latter's truth or (in the case of realism) by promising to establish the possibility of nature through the idea of final causes.

Casualistic idealism fails because by reducing even mechanism to blind chance (V:393; 274), it explains nothing, not even our idealistic illusion of intention in production (*Erzeugung*). Fatalistic idealism, on the other hand, explains the *unity* of natural forms, but not *unity of purpose,* which requires a notion of *contingency* and which carries with it reference to a cause with understanding. It thus fails to explain the emergence of our idea of even so much as unintentional purposiveness.[25]

Realists, for their part, claim insight into a "special kind of causality" — that of an intentionally acting cause — or at least of insight into the latter's possibility, for one does not make the most daring (*gewagtesten*) hypothesis without assurance as to the possibility of its ground, assurance without which one could not be certain that one's concept of that basis had objective reality (V:394; 275). Here, however, realism fails. For living matter (as posited by one form of hylozoism) cannot even be thought, since the essential character of matter is lifelessness (in Latin, *inertia*).[26] Those, on the other hand, who regard matter not as life but as animated (and nature in its entirety therefore as an animal) merely argue in a circle.[27]

Theism, the other realistic alternative, introduces a genuine concept of intentionality and thus succeeds in rescuing purposiveness in nature from idealism; it cannot, however, prove (as it must) that the unity of purpose we find in matter could not result from mechanism (V:395; 276).

From this consideration of competing systems the following conclusion emerges: each system fails because it is unable to explain on the basis of its maxim how our *judgment* of an organic being is possible. Such judgment requires a concept of a thing as natural purpose, a concept "that subsumes nature under a causality only thinkable [by us] through reason." To use that concept dogmatically, we would have to be sure of its objective reality. In fact, however, such knowledge is in principle unavailable to us: not only don't we know whether or not things deemed natural purposes require for their production causality "of a very particular kind (requiring intention)"; we "*cannot even ask the question*" (V:396; [278], emphasis added).

We cannot do so, Kant adds, because the objective reality of the concept of a natural purpose is undemonstrable (*nicht erweislich ist*) by reason, and this because the concept contains both *natural necessity* and, at the same time, *contingency* of form relative to the mere laws of nature. Hence (if that conjunction is not to be contradictory): "[the concept] must contain not only a ground of the thing's possibility in nature, but also a ground of the possibility of this nature itself and of its relation to something that is not empirically knowable nature (but supersensible), and hence for us not knowable at all." Natural necessity and purposive contingency are logically compatible only if the possibility of the former is thought of as grounded in a nature whose supersensible status renders it unknowable.

We can save our selves from contradiction, in other words, only by substituting for the dogmatic question "how are natural products possible?" the critical or reflective question "how is the concept of a natural product thinkable?" But the movement of the argument suggests a deeper substitution as well, namely, for the forbidden "how do living beings [that is, how did I] originate?" the permitted "why am I so interested?" It is the latter, we recall, that constitutes the rational "suspicion" (or natural "hint") that guides Kant's underlying pursuit (*nachspüren*).

For the reasons given above, the concept of a natural purpose is not constitutive but only regulative or "problematic." Although we can think such a concept without contradiction, we "cannot derive [it] from experience, nor is it required to make experience possible" (V:397; 279).[28] The question of its objective reality therefore remains in principle undecidable. Even if (*per impossibile*) we had assurance as to the objective reality of a divine artist, we could not explain how we come to regard natural products as products *of nature*.

In making such a judgment one cannot help referring to a supreme understanding as world cause. This ground, however, cannot justify any objective assertion, since the concept of a natural purpose is not necessary for experience. One cannot establish the real possibility of an object conforming to the concept of a natural purpose (as with the categories). And the proof is that natural purpose forces us to combine natural necessity with a contingency of form, that is, a natural and a supernatural ground, the latter of which for us is, as such, unknowable, though not (unlike the notion of living matter) intrinsically contradictory or unthinkable.

Taken as a regulatory principle, intentionality in nature allows Kant to resolve the "antinomy" of teleological judgment by transforming what would otherwise be a palpable contradiction into a cipher for the ineluctability of human ignorance (what he earlier referred to as our congenital defect as a species [VIII:180–81]). Kant, in other words, is able to change a "dogmatic" debate over whether or not nature herself acts according to purposes (a question whose literal answer for him is clear) into the fruitful, critical undecidability of the question as to whether what seems to us to be so caused is in fact brought about mechanically or by a supernatural intelligence. The abysmal absurdity of an intelligent nature, which would, as such, erase the very distinction between reason and matter, is reduced to nature's *Wink* (or alternatively, reason's "suspicion") that there is more in heaven and earth than can be found in natural philosophy. The other explanation — in terms of a supernatural intelligence — which fails, when posed objectively, succeeds so long as it claims no more than a subjective necessity, rooted in the peculiar requirements of human cognition. Though not necessarily or knowably valid for other (higher) beings, the appeal to supernatural intelligence is "perfectly sufficient in every human intention [*in jeder menschlichen Absicht vollkommen genugthuend ist*]"

(V:397, 400; 280, 282). The totality of human intentions may thus itself be said to furnish sufficient ground for judging in accordance with the (subjective) idea of a world-grounding *Absicht*.

The key to dealing with the mystery of generation is to accept that mystery's human ineluctability—our ineradicable concern, and simultaneous inability, to know the ground of our own (along with every other organism's) possibility. Thus, where he once equivocated over the solubility of that mystery,[29] he is now bold: it is "absurd for human beings to attempt or even to hope that perhaps someday another Newton might arise who could explain to us, in terms of natural laws ordered by any intention, as much as the production [*Erzeugung*] of a blade of grass." Human insight must rather here be "absolutely denied" (V:400, 409; [282–83, 209]). Yet we also cannot absolutely rule out the possibility that the phenomena that we judge purposive might have a "hidden" natural, that is, mechanical ground.[30]

Hence only "this much is certain":

> If we are at any rate to judge according to that which we are be-grudged/permitted to see through our own nature [*was uns einzu-sehen durch unsere eigene Natur vergönnt is*] (subject to the conditions and limits of our reason), then we are absolutely unable to ground [*zum Grunde legen*] the possibility of those natural purposes other than in an intelligent being. (V:400; 283)

Such, at any rate, "is all that conforms[31] to our reflective maxim, and thus to a ground that, though only subjective, is to the human race [*Geschlecht*] inescapably attaching [*unnachlaßlich anhängenden*]" (V:401; [283]).

In short, reference to an intelligent cause attaches not to the object but to ourselves as knowers. To attempt to prove otherwise, that is, that *all* knowing beings are subject to the same necessary condition, would "entangle us in difficulties from which we could not extricate [*herauswickeln*] ourselves" (V:399; [282]). To be sure, not every difficulty is thus avoidable: viz., our "attachment" to the question of generation, an attachment we literally "cannot leave behind." Yet what is unavoidable need not be "inextricable": witness the attachment that in this case furnishes the ground by which we recognize ourselves as a *Geschlecht*. The need to refer the possibility of organisms (including ourselves) to an intentional cause marks and to that extent defines us specially. This much penetration of the principle "whereby nature make[s] the familiar universal laws specific" is, it seems, begrudged to us.

We can regard (*ansehen*) our own (and every other organism's) inner possibility only by tracing it to a divine intelligence, an intelligence *our* idea of which is not contradictory but whose *own* presentation of the whole is literally (for us at least) unthinkable. The impetuosity of Kant's early

Universal Natural History is in this way stabilized: the very ambiguity of that impetus—both toward and away from a self-consciousness-canceling presentation of the whole—becomes decipherable. The undecidability of whether the "trace" followed here is nature's "hint" or reason's "suspicion" proves "hermeneutically" (for man at least) determinative.

CONTINGENCY AND THE "PECULIARITY" OF HUMAN UNDERSTANDING

A defining characteristic of our species is thus itself rooted in the mystery of generation, or rather its mysteriousness to us, a mysteriousness that registers our specific difference from other kinds of intellect.[32] This mystery, however, is itself linked with that endemic heterogeneity of mental powers which enables us (as Kant observes in an "episodic" digression intended to provide matter [*Stoff*] for reflection [*Nachdenken*]) to distinguish between the possible and the actual (V:401; [283–84]). This distinction, which exists only for the human mind (or any finite mind that we are capable of conceiving) is merely subjective, according to Kant—bound up with our ability to distinguish between our thought of something (which we can entertain without that thing actually being present) and our positing of the thing itself as actual. Reason's "constant demand" that we assume an *Urgrund* in which the distinction between actual and possible does not arise is proof enough, Kant says, that this distinction does not adhere in things themselves.

For such an *Urgrund* or absolutely necessary being, to think would be to create ("I think, therefore it is!"). To such a being, no conception of contingency (or the merely possible) could ever arise. Hence, such a being would not distinguish between obligation and action—between a practical law that says what is possible through our doing, and a theoretical law that says what is actual through our doing. Nor (for the same reason) would it distinguish between natural mechanism and the technic of nature.

We can conceive of a being, in other words, in/to whom the whole as whole would be immediately (intuitively) present. "Such an understanding, as well as its representation of the whole, would contain no contingency in the connection of the parts, in order to make possible a determinate form of the whole" (V:407; [291]). We, on the other hand, cannot conceive the possibility of such a determinate form without connecting it to the idea of contingency, that is, of the *choice* of some being to whom it was open (on the analogy of human making) to do something else. That we require such contingency, and can make sense of the whole as a determinate form in no other way, is the "peculiarity" of human understanding that explains how the concept of a natural purpose is "possible for us" (V:405; 288. V:407; 291).[33] At the same time, however, Kant urges us to recognize that such an attribution of choice to the *Urgrund* is merely subjective, as is the concept of a natural purpose that it makes possible. The contingency, both in nature as a whole and in her individual products, that we refer "heuristically" (*heuristisch;* V:411; 295) to a creative being is in fact rooted not in the nature of things, but in the peculiarity of our nature (a peculiarity that is therefore itself "contingent" in the special sense of not being necessary to intelligence as such).

We cannot grasp the whole immediately. We can however, conceive the possibility of its form, albeit only on the basis of an intentional, and hence contingent, making, on the analogy of human art.

Kant's struggle to lay bare the relation between divine creation and natural production (and therewith the mystery of generation) is thus laid definitively to rest. The radical contingency of things, including one's own life, is not the sign of an inscrutable God (Who will be what He will be), nor of a chaotic, all-devouring nature, but the birthmark of a rational yet finite, or embodied, being. At the same time, the problem of "life," which seems to distinguish absolutely between mind and matter (whose very definition implies "lifelessness") even as it calls that distinction absolutely into question, is referred once and for all to the "supersensible substrate," where it can "wink" (and stimulate, perhaps, our own poetic gifts) without otherwise "disturbing" us. We are required by our nature to seek out the ground of purposive connection in a supersensible substrate, even as we are entirely cut off (*abgeschnitten*) from any possible insight into that substrate (V:410; 294).[34]

The crucial step of Kant's argument lies in the connection he draws between the "contingency" of human knowledge of the particular (a contingency that arises from the fact that we cannot derive such knowledge directly from the universal) and the "contingency" of purposive causation (a contingency that arises from the fact that all such causation, insofar as we are able to conceive it, conforms to the analogy of human art and thus involves a notion of the merely possible, as distinguished from the necessary and the actual).[35] By virtue of this connection and the peculiar humanness of contingency that it implies, Kant can at last reconcile mechanical and purposive causation (or, in the terms of his early work, natural production and divine creation) by leaving open the nature of the causality in which things have their ultimate ground. Since the very distinction between mechanical (or necessary) and purposive (or contingent) causation is a peculiarly human one, and since both mechanical and purposive causation have their ultimate basis in the supersensible, we are assured that it is at least possible that both these principles might be reconcilable in a common (*gemeinschaftlich*), higher principle, in a way we can indicate (*anzeigen*) but which is otherwise both indeterminate and incomprehensible to us (V:413; 298).

Kant thus finds a middle ground between a "mere mechanism" in which reason wanders "fantastically" among "chimeras" of natural powers, and a "mere teleology" that makes reason "rave" (*schwärmerisch*). (The threat of madness lies, revealingly enough, in both directions.) By virtue of such a common basis, mechanism and teleology stand in community (*Gemeinschaft*), though we cannot use that basis to explain how a natural product can derive from two such heterogenous principles (V:411–12; 296–97). In short, the lingering association of male and female with form and matter, respectively, is finally transcended by referring the two "heterogenous" principles of generation to the supersensible substrate, in which God and/or God's nature (the so-called *Inbegriff*) cohabit, as it were, hermaphroditically. (The heterogeneity of generation is no more or less mysterious than the heterogeneity of human understanding, whose peculiarity it is to think contingency.) We are driven by our nature to seek (*suchen*) the basis of generation in this common principle, even as we are "cut off" from gaining any insight (*Ansicht*) into such community (V:410; 294).[36] Indeed, the very indeterminacy of such community proves useful (or purposive) for scientific investigation, since it bestirs us to explain natural events mechanically "so far as we can" (and we cannot tell the limits of our ability in this regard), all the while keeping in mind that such investigation will always be inadequate (V:415; [300]).[37]

Almost as if he regretted the indeterminacy he has just allowed, Kant turns immediately in the appendix (the "Methodology of Teleological Judgment") to fix the boundaries of teleology vis à vis the (other) sciences. The place of teleology as a science cannot be "transitional," because a transition (*Übergang*) between sciences (in this case, natural science and theology) "articulates" or "organizes" the system without signifying (*bedeuten*) a place in it (just as the faculty of judgment articulates the system of philosophy without occupying a place in that system via its own special sort of knowledge) (V:416; [301]). Teleology, then, can have a place within the sciences, or articulate between them, but not both. And, indeed, it is the latter, merely "critical" (rather than doctrinal) role that, according to Kant, teleology "as a science" actually plays. The place "signified" by teleology (whose scientific credentials Kant affirms and denies almost in the same breath) is in this respect as elusive as that of judgment itself.

IV. Adventures of the Organism

We are finally in a position to consider Kant's "adventurous" hypothesis that all species might have their origin in a communal mother (*gemeinschaftliche Urmutter*), a claim similar to the one he rejected some years earlier (from the mouths of Reinhold and Forster) as empty or abhorrent. The hypothesis appears in the (disarming) context of a section entitled "On the

Necessary Subordination of the Principle of Mechanism to that of Teleology in Explaining a Thing Considered as a Natural Purpose" (V:417; [303]). By necessary subordination, Kant means that although we have unlimited authority to attempt to explain a natural product in mechanical terms (an attempt that is "reasonable" so long as there is hope of success), we also are forced to admit (on pain of otherwise working at a loss [*Verlust*]) the ultimate human insufficiency of that attempt. It is thus commendable (*rühmlich*) by means of comparative anatomy to go through the "great creation of organized beings," looking for something like a system regarding their principle of generation (*Erzeugung*); nor need we spiritlessly (*muthlos*) give up all claims to insight into nature (*Natureinsicht*) in this regard, even where such insight extends beyond the limits of judgment proper. The basis of this courage (*Muth*), without which a science of generation would be impossible, is the "common schema" shared by so many species, a schema suggestive of a single archetype and production from a communal *Urmutter,* for:

> The different animal genera gradually approach one another; from the genus in which the principle of ends seems to be borne out most, namely man, to the polyp, and from it even to mosses and lichens, and finally to the lowest stuff of nature noted by us — raw matter, from which . . . seems to stem all the technic of nature, that is to us so inconceivable in organized beings that we are required to think for it a different principle. (V:418–19; [304])

Noting the traces (*Spuren*) of nature's oldest revolutions, the *"archeologist* of nature" is free[38]

> to let the earth's womb [*Mutterschooβ*] emerge [*herausging*] from its state of chaos [like, so to speak, a large animal], and bear initially creatures of less-purposive form, with these forming others better adapted to their place of begetting [*Zeugungsplatze*] . . . until this womb [*Gebärmutter*] stiffened [or grew paralyzed: *erstarrt*], and ossified [or fossilized: *sich verknöchert*], limiting its birthings to determinate species that did not further degenerate, so that the diversity remained as it had been at the end of the operation of that fertile formative force. (V:419; [305])[39]

Punning on the recently discovered bones of extinguished species, Kant reads the earth itself as a petrified (or menopausal) record of her former self-producing fertility. (Earlier in the passage, Kant has the earth's womb emerging [phoenixlike] out of itself [that is, out of the chaos of the earth's ancient revolutions].)

The *crucial* point for Kant is that the "universal mother" must herself be conceived as purposively organized, hence as the tool of a (higher) intention. A family tree of the creation, from man to lichen (and even to rude matter) does not entail, as Kant had once supposed or feared, capitulation to a material—hence formless—all-sufficiency. Final causality still has a necessary, albeit regulative, role to play—that of making the possibility of a natural product (a being, that is to say, that is both lawful and contingent) "thinkable."

The derivation of all creatures from a common mother can be called, Kant notes, a "daring adventure of reason" (*gewagtes Abenteuer der Vernunft*)—one, indeed, that has probably occurred to (literally, "entered through the head" of) even the acutest researchers into nature. Since it is generation of the organized from the organized (though not of like from like), such production is not absurd (or "contradictory according to the a priori judgment of reason"), as is *generatio aequivoca,* or the generation of an organized being from the mechanism of raw matter.[40] Although it is not substantiated by a single example in experience, Kant does not reject the possibility of such an example out of hand, as he once refused to grant the possibility of even a single case (or "ghost story") of alteration of the fetal germ (for example, by the mother's imagination), on the grounds that to do so would open the floodgates to *Schwärmerei* and madness.[41]

Kant has, it seems, found a more satisfactory way to forestall the "penetration" of reason's boundaries: He is now open to the possibility that accidental changes might be found that are "taken up" into the generative force (*Zeugungskraft*) and become hereditary (V:420; 306). Only (he now adds) it is fitting (*füglich*) to *judge* such cases to be developments of dispositions originating with, and purposive for the self-preservation of, the species.[42] For if we abandon the principle that all hereditary changes are for a purpose (that is, preservation), we cannot know that any are, and the principle of teleology looses all reliability of application. Methodological concern with such reliability, and secondarily with self-preservation, neutralizes the invasion (for example, via motherly imagination) of the organism's generative force, an invasion that Kant had characterized, in his reviews of Herder, as an intolerable penetration [*durchbrechen*].[43]

Any change to which an individual is germinally subject can be presumed to be reasonable, that is, to favor the individual's survival or that of its kind. We are entitled to this presumption because the investigation of nature subjectively requires it—not because claiming otherwise would, "like admitting a ghost story," both figuratively and literally "unman" us.[44] (Kant can now put such hysteria behind him.)

If natural products are to be explained, however, mechanism must be conjoined (*beigesellen*) with, as well as subordinated to, the principle of teleology. And this even though such conjunction is, as Kant freely admits, beyond our grasp, requiring as it does a reconciliation of nature's universal lawfulness with her formal confinement (according to an idea) for which nature herself provides no basis (*Grund*) (V:421–22; 308). There are, as

Kant insists, two ways of characterizing the teleological generation of natural products: occasionalism and preestablished harmony. The first has the supreme cause on hand at each act of begetting, directly imposing a form, according to its idea, on a commingling matter. The second and, for Kant, preferred theory has the supreme cause imparting to the first products of its wisdom only the disposition (*Anlagen*) by means of which an organism produces another of its kind (V:422; 309). (The trouble with the first approach is that it denies to nature any role in production, and with it, any ability on our part to judge how such products are possible.)

For its part, preestablished harmony can precede by educt (individual preformation) or product (generic preformation, or epigenesis).[45] Epigenesis thus becomes a version of, rather than an alternative to, preformation or preestablished harmony.

Kant calls epigenetic preformation "virtual," linking it with an informing power (or *virtus*) traditionally (and linguistically) associated with maleness. For individual preformation, on the other hand, he uses the term "encapsulation" (*Einschachtelung; emboîtement*). *Schacht* means "tunnel" or "shaft"; and a *Schachtel* is a box.[46] Such (pejoratively) feminine associations are in keeping with Kant's implicit equation (at V:423; 310) of individual preformation with "ovism" rather than "animaculism" (or "spermatozoism"), the version of individual preformation favored by Leibniz.[47] Epigenesis thus becomes for Kant the "male" version, so to speak, of preformation theory—as distinguished from the "female" version (*emboîtement*), in which individuals are encased like Russian dolls.[48]

The implausibility of individual preformation is for Kant in part a function of the supernatural care that would be necessary on such terms to preserve the embryo from the destructiveness of nature. (The putative security of the womb within a womb within a womb is threatened by that greater womb which is the earth itself.) Kant's complicated attitude toward the security of the maternal womb is evident in the *Anthropology* (X:306; 169), where he justifies woman's characteristic lack of courage, and consequent moral deficiency, as a naturally purposive arrangement for the protection of the fetus (an arrangement, moreover, that allows woman to look in turn to the male for protection). Nature's indirection here (where weakness is strength) is the equivalent of those supernatural arrangements that would be required to preserve the ova of creation.

But the most telling evidence against individual preformation (as ovism) is the production of hybrids (*Bastarte*), which demonstrate by their existence the formative, as well as nutritive, contribution of both sexes.[49]

Kant also ridicules the individual preformationists for attributing monstrous births (*Mißgeburten*), which "cannot possibly be considered purposes of nature", to the sole (and "purposeless") purpose of causing *Anstoß* and "amazed dejection" to anatomists. Such monstrous "purposeless purposiveness" recalls the "purposiveness without purpose" of Kant's (monsterless) aesthetics. There is, indeed, something decidedly aesthetic about the individual preformationists' explanatory resort to the feelings of the observer, reminding one of the implicit link Kant earlier drew between aesthetic judgment and individual preformation. The superiority of Kant's own "preformation theory" is especially evident with respect to monsters and malformations (*Mißestalten*), which epigenesis permits, and toward which genius, as we recall, is granted a certain impetuous license.[50]

In short, Kant's reflective resolution of the problem of generation allows him to entertain the identity of intellect and nature without actually affirming it. Inasmuch as we discover in nature a form whose basis we cannot explain (that is, ourselves reproduce according to mechanical laws), we are compelled to attribute that form to an intelligent super-natural cause analogous to, though infinitely greater than, our own purposive causality. And yet, since we can form a conception of a supreme being for which the very distinction between mechanical and final causation would not arise, this model of super-natural causation must also be bracketed — qualified by the admission that the causation in question is one in which, for all we know, the difference between mechanism and teleology dissolves.[51] Kant's reflective strategy, in other words, lets him have it both ways, commingling nature and intention at a level of supersensible removal that preserves the barrier between intelligence and matter.

The a priori principle of reflective judgment seeks out a universal for the particular, a universal that is not already given or thought. With aesthetic judgment, this guided ignorance vis à vis the universal expressed itself as universal feeling without determinate concepts. In the case of teleological judgment, that ignorance expresses itself more directly and objectively in the indeterminacy of the supersensible, that is, the "veiled" character of nature her/itself.[52]

The attempt to systematize teleologically the extrinsic relation among organized beings presents a problem of a different sort — one, indeed, that in its own terms is ultimately insoluble. The prospect of such a system arises in the first place because the thought that something is an organized being is "difficult to separate" (for reasons described above) from the thought that it exists for some purpose, either as a means or as a final end (*Endzweck*) (V:426; [313]). So long, however, as we remain within nature, we only encounter beings conceivable as means in relation to the purposes represented by other organized beings. Man, to be sure, insofar as he is capable of having a *concept* of purposes and of using this reason "to turn an aggregate of purposively formed things into a system of ends," occupies

within this chain of reasons a very special place. This special status (as ultimate end [*letzte Zweck*]) does not, however, protect him from the circularity of that chain, which reduces him once again to the status of a means
(the fodder, as it were, of worms). (Man, as Kant here pointedly reminds
us, is no less subject to the destructive forces of nature than he is to her
productive ones. He does not, however, make the rhetorical claim [as in
earlier works] that nature is particularly grudging toward us as a species
[V:427; (314)].)

The impossibility of an intrinsic system of nature is demonstrated by the
history of the earth, whose manifest inhospitability to all her creatures is
(ironically) set beside her figuration as universal mother.

> If the natural beings on earth formed a purposively ordered
> whole, the first intentional arrangement would presumably have
> to be their place of habitation, the ground [*Boden*] and element
> on and in which they should have made their advance. But on a
> more exact knowledge of the character of this foundation [*Grund-
> lage*] of all organic generation, we find that it points to no causes
> other than ones effectual entirely without intention, causes more
> likely to destroy than they are to favor [*begünstigen*] generation,
> order and purpose. Land and sea not only contain memorials
> [*Denkmäler*] of ancient, mighty devastations, that long ago befell
> them and all creatures to be encountered on and in them; but even
> their entire structure [*Bauwerk*], the earth strata of one and the
> boundaries of the other, have entirely the look of a product of
> wild, all-powerful forces of a nature working in a state of chaos.
> The shape [*Gestalt*], structure and inclination [*Abhang*] of the land
> may now seem to be arranged to receive water from the air, to
> feed the water veins between diverse kinds of soil beds [*Erdschich-
> ten*] (for a variety of products). . . . but a closer examination re-
> veals them to be the effect of partly fiery, partly watery, irruptions,
> or of oceanic upheavals. Thus was the first production [*Erzeu-
> gung*] of this shape, along with, especially, its subsequent reforma-
> tions, which is encountered together with the submergence [*Un-
> tergang*] of its first organic products. If the place of habitation, the
> mother soil [*Mutterboden*] (of the land) and the womb/lap [*Mut-
> terschooβ*] (of the sea) for all these creatures gives no indication
> other than that of being produced by a wholly unintentional
> mechanism, how and with what right can we demand and assert
> that they have a different origin? As for man — even though a most
> exact examination of the remains of these natural devastations
> seems to prove (according to Camper's judgment) that he was not
> included in these revolutions — yet he is so dependent on these
> other creatures of the earth, that once one makes room for a uni-
> versal mechanism powerful over all the others, one must also re-
> gard man as comprehended under it, even though his understand-

ing may have been able to save him (at least for the most part) from its devastations. (V:427–28; [315–16])

This extraordinary passage summarizes the preoccupations of Kant's many earlier attempts at a universal natural history of creation. Kant's familiarly abysmal assimilation of womb and tomb sounds, however, a new note. The very existence of organized beings, as Kant goes on to argue, belies the reduction of nature's form to the principle governing a blind exchange of forces. Moreover, resolution of the antimony arising from our effort to explain the possibility of such beings holds forth the prospect of a reconciliation of mechanical and purposive causation by referring both to the "supersensible principle of nature." Nature "both without and within us" thus becomes a promise as well as a threat. And reason, for its part, insists on this referral, in order to find possible a lawful unity of appearances, albeit by means of a device (the highest cause as intentional being) that reason recognizes (as it were, in the same breath) as a fictional concession to human peculiarity (V:429; [316–17]).[53]

Since man can be reflectively, though not determinately, judged (for the permissible sake of being able to consider possible the lawful unity of appearances) to be the last end of nature, the next question becomes what it is in man that is an end, and how he is to further it through his connection (*Verknüpfung*) with nature. There are, according to Kant, two possible answers: happiness and culture. The first aim is not "abstracted" from nature, but a "wavering" (*schwankenden*) idea to which man tries to make his natural condition adequate, a task that is impossible, owing more to the "entanglement" of understanding with imagination and the senses, than to our impotence. Even if we restricted ourselves to the true natural needs shared by our entire species, or instead maximized our skill for realizing imagined ends, we would not be happy, since it "is not in man's nature . . . to be satisfied" (V:430; [318]).[54] But man's capacity to set himself purposes of his own (to attempt to realize his ideas, in other words) does qualify him as the last end of nature (in the appropriate regulative sense) and thus resolves at last the question of his destiny or determination (*Bestimmung*), but only on the condition that "he know how [*verstehe*] and have the will to give both nature and himself relation to an end, relation that can be independent of nature, self-sufficient and thus a final end" (V:431; [318]).

The last end of nature, on the other hand, can be discovered by separating out all that nature can do to prepare man for what he in turn must do to be a final end, as distinguished from those ends that nature can accomplish on her own. The latter sort taken together constitute the sum total (*Inbegriff*) of all human ends possible through nature outside or within us and is the "matter" which, if we make it our "whole" end, makes it impossible for us to "posit a final end for [our] existence." There thus remains only the "formal" and "subjective" condition of such ends, namely our aptitude (*Tauglichkeit*) for positing/setting ourselves ends in general, and (independent of nature in one's determination of ends) for using nature as a means according to the maxims of our free ends generally. Only this can align (*ausrichten*) nature with the intention (*Absicht*) of a final end lying outside of nature and therefore be regarded as her last end.

The bringing forth (*Hervorbringung*) of such aptitude in a rational being for preferences generally (hence in that being's freedom) is "culture," be it that of skill (*Geschicklichkeit*) or that of discipline (*Zucht*) (V:432; [319]. Culture, as distinguished from man's happiness, or from his status as the highest "tool" (*Werkzeug*) for ordering irrational nature outside him, is the sole entity that we have cause to call the last end of nature and thus the necessary condition of any judgment of the whole of nature as a teleological system.[55]

If we step back from the details of Kant's argument and compare its general direction with his earlier treatment of generation, the following scheme emerges: nature becomes organismlike to — and only to — the extent that man himself, in his capacity as *user* of nature (rather than as God's or nature's *tool*), enacts the form-giving role that had to be referred, at the level of organic life, to the supersensible substrate. Man himself, in other words, by virtue of a *Tauglichkeit* that "grows" in him with nature's help and yet without prejudice to his freedom, straddles the otherwise mysterious boundary between mechanism and intentional causation (alternatives that constitute, as we have seen, Kant's reworking of the traditional female and male principles of generation).

The trope of human self-generation thus takes a new and altogether more satisfying turn than was possible on the basis of Kant's earlier "idea" for a universal history. The womb of human history is now continuous with that of nature, whose guiding fetters/reins, provided to protect our animal characteristics, culture teaches us to "tighten or loosen" at will, thus postponing or averting the need for a permanent rupture (V:432; [319]). It is not that nature in herself has grown kinder (Kant's abandonment of his former attempts at an archaeology of human races suggests just the opposite), but that man can now simultaneously occupy (through a strategy of teleological "reflection") the dual roles of nature's child and nature's master (*Herr*). Freedom, in other words, has a new figuration, as manhood achieved not only by escaping nature (as in Kant's earlier insistence on severing "nature's leading strings"),[56] but also, strange as the image may seem, by cohabiting with her.[57]

This implicit recasting links in the most intimate of ways what is universal in Kant's thought, with what is most idiosyncratic. The inordinate concern exhibited by Kant in the face of the breakdown of traditional conceptions of generation, both metaphysical and physical, also helped show him a way out of what had become for thinkers of the eighteenth century attempting to define the relation between matter and reason a fundamental impasse.[58] His way out formed the basis of a variety of later movements, from speculative idealism and Naturphilosophie to the newly minted science of "biology." What distinguishes Kant's thought from these later developments is above all the rigor of his modesty (in both senses of the word), as shown in his "reflective" deference to the veil of nature.[59]

Such considerations may help explain a subtle shift in Kant's presentation of the relation between taste and morality, and with it the integrity of human history in general. The morally "preparatory" role that Kant now assigns the culture of taste (V:433; 321) (whose moral "ambiguity" he earlier touted [V:298; 265]) is connected with the way aesthetic experience "allows us to feel" our aptitude for higher ends, an allowance that presumably applies to Kant himself. He too, it seems reasonable to conclude, has been admitted by his own aesthetic reflection to an awareness of man's higher aptitude, an awareness linked, as the accompanying footnote suggests, to an economy of value in which man, by his own reluctance to be "born anew" to a life lived for the sake of mere enjoyment, gives value to the otherwise purposeless existence of nature.[60] (A disgust that overrides even the desire to live [or be born again] furnishes Kant with an aesthetic path from nature, with its endless chain of means, to a moral economy of final ends.)[61]

By means of this device, mankind itself comes to occupy the causal role traditionally reserved to God. "If things in nature need [*bedürfen*] a supreme cause that acts in terms of ends," that cause is to be found in man (in his capacity as a moral subject) and man alone (V:435; [323]).[62]

But man is supreme intentional cause only as a final end of nature, not as nature's creator. The "science" of teleology rests on a repudiation of the claim to comprehend how generation and/or creation is possible. The first subject of the "Methodology," the "negative influence" of teleology on natural science, thus leads to a second, the proper relation between teleology and theology (see V:417; 302).

V. Teleology and Theology

Physicotheology, which Kant defines as the inference of God's existence from purposes of nature that we recognize empirically, is one way of conceiving that relation (V:436; 324). Its claims are undermined, however, by the consideration earlier educed: although *we* cannot conceive of the possibility of a natural product other than as arising through an intentional cause, the existence of such a cause cannot be assumed absolutely.[63]

Physicotheology can therefore "prepare" for theology only if it is "propped up" by the "inescapable" judgment that without man as its final (moral) purpose, the entire universe, however purposively interrelated (or perfect, in the sense employed in Kant's *Universal Natural History*), would be a "wasteland" (*Wüste*). What makes this "estimation" possible is not theoretical knowledge but human "desire," albeit desire as the freedom of a good will, not that stemming from one's status as a member of nature (*Naturglied*) (V:442–43; [330–32]).[64]

By virtue of man's status as moral purpose of creation, and by virtue of it alone, we acquire a basis for regarding the world "as a whole that coheres in terms of ends," that is, as a "system of final causes." What would require omniscience to achieve theoretically — a determinate concept of a supreme intelligent cause — is ours practically through the notion of man (in his moral capacity) as sufficient reason for the world's existence (V:444; [333]).[65]

As to knowledge of the *existence* of such a cause, here too morality furnishes a practically adequate foundation, a moral proof of the existence of God that runs approximately as follows: The supreme ground of things that are contingent (that is, depend for their existence on a cause other than themselves) is to be sought either physically, in a supreme producing (*hervorbringend*) cause, or teleologically, in a final end for the sake of which that cause brings forth its products, assuming here that such a cause is intelligent, that is, capable of representing purposes. Now man (or any rational being) under moral laws is such a final end, the only one that we are capable of conceiving. (Man *actually* behaving according to the moral law cannot be that end, Kant adds, since we do not know if this is within God's power to assure. Such knowledge would require "insight both into the supersensible substrate of nature and into the identity of this substrate with what causality through freedom makes possible in the world" — insight, in other words, into that conjunction of nature and freedom to which the *Critique of Judgment* has repeatedly pointed and from which it has consistently veered [V:448 n; (338 n)].)

Now the moral law determines for us a final purpose toward which it obliges us to strive, namely the highest good achievable in the world through freedom, or happiness conjoined with worthiness to be happy. But we are unable to represent happiness and worthiness to be happy both as connected through mere natural causes and as conforming to the idea. The practical necessity, in other words, of such an end fails to harmonize with the theoretical concept of its possibility. We must therefore, Kant concludes, assume that God exists; for without this assumption we would have to give up our *aim* (*Beabsichtigung*) (V:451; 340).[66]

Unless we can convince ourselves that God exists, we must give up our aim, and with it, our privileged position as the informing purpose of creation. What is at stake is not the validity of the moral law (which even an atheist must acknowledge), but the law's ability to absolve man as a part of nature.

Hence the exemplary importance of someone like Spinoza, a "righteous man," who "reveres the law" and yet remains firmly persuaded that there is neither a God nor an afterlife.[67] How, Kant asks, will such a person judge his own inner determination (*Bestimmung*) to a purpose? On the one hand, he seeks no selfish advantage but only wants the good to which the moral law directs all his forces. And yet his striving is "limited," because he cannot expect nature to harmonize lawfully with that final purpose.

> Deceit, violence and envy will always be in vogue around him, even though he himself is honest, peaceful and benevolent. As for the other righteous people that he meets, no matter how worthy of happiness they may be, nature, which pays that no heed, will subject them, as she does all the other animals of the earth, to deprivation, disease, and untimely death. And they will stay subject to these evils always, until one wide grave swallows/entangles [*verschlingt*] them all (honest or not, it doesn't matter here), and throws them, who could believe themselves to be the final purpose of creation, back into the maw [*Schlund*] of the purposeless chaos of matter out of which they were drawn. (V:452; [342])

Such considerations would force a well-meaning person to give up as impossible the end that he, in following the moral law, had and ought to have "before his eyes." (Spinoza's moral deficiency is related to the lack in his system of nature [as earlier described] of an informing *Absicht*.) It is therefore incumbent on us all to assume the existence of God as moral author of the world, lest the moral law seem less worthy of respect by imposing on us an end whose possibility we are unable to conceive. The aim or vision by which we give form to and thereby withstand the maw of nature cannot, in the final analysis, independently sustain itself.

Against the familiar figure of the womb/tomb — the blind or eyeless mouth from which we are drawn and by which we are swallowed up — Kant sets the (male) effort to inform the whole through the sheer vision or aim (*Absicht*) of our own practical activity. Though we cannot create ourselves, we can, by acting according to the moral law, give God (if there is one) sufficient reason to create us. Yet even this is not enough. By itself, the idea that we set, and are obliged to set, before our eyes is no match for the discouraging image of nature as wasteland. In the end, Kant blinks, unable (without recourse to God)[68] to disabuse himself of the disabling thought that the idea of the highest good (Kant's reflective shield here against nature's blinding maw) is a chimera.[69]

Kant's moral teleology is thus burdened by a certain circularity: morality (that is, our "moral attitude") depends on our being able (unlike Spinoza) to judge ourselves the final end of nature; while our ability to judge our-selves the final end of nature depends upon morality. Beyond this difficulty, there remains the basic question as to why belief in God's existence is mor-ally necessary at all; that is, why the moral law as such, in keeping with the principle that "ought implies can," does not furnish adequate assurance of the possibility of actualizing the highest good, given that that end is not intrinsically (that is, logically) self-contradictory. Kant's final answer to this question suggests that what is ultimately at stake — the very possibility of "firm steadfastness" (*feste Beharrlichkeit*), as opposed to vacillation (*schwan-ken*) — runs deeper even than moral faith.[70] "Without moral faith the moral way of thinking lacks firm steadfastness, whenever it fails to fulfill theoreti-cal reason's demand for proof (of the possibility of morality's object), but vacillates between practical commands and theoretical doubts." This lack of firm steadfastness, itself a function of the theoretical/practical duality of reason, must be replaced by "reason grounded faith" that is "sufficient for reason's aim" (V:472; [366]). Through such faith or "free assent," reason becomes sufficient for its own *Absicht* or aim — and thus allays an other-wise disabling doubt that reason's idea is more or other than a chimera (*Hirngespinst*). It is, finally, our need to be constant with respect to that world-informing *Absicht* or idea — our need, in other words, to disregard (*ab-sehen*) the blind maw — that grounds moral faith.[71]

The problematic of the sublime thus returns with a new twist. Contrary to Kant's earlier suggestion, the steadfastness of the morally sublime re-mains vulnerable to the provocation of a nature without regard for human (moral) worth. To the renunciation of idolatry (no longer identified spe-cifically with the desire to see) must be added a positive, albeit merely prac-tical theology — a determinate concept of God as moral author of the world. This "determinate concept" is the mind's ultimate charm against the paralyzing vision of a nature without intention, a nature unable to return our gaze.

At the same time, the "mingling" of physical and moral teleology (the veiled goddess and the moral author of the world) is to be resisted (see V:462; 355. V:476; 371). Only on the basis of man's moral worth, a worth he gives himself, is a final purpose of nature conceivable to us. With or without traces (*Spuren*) of organization in the world, the moral proof of God's existence would be equally valid. The only merit of the so-called physicoteleological proof is that it "leads" the mind onto the way of ends and thus to an intelligent (*verständig*) world author, at which point "moral reference to purposes, and the idea of a moral author and legislator of the world, seems to develop on its own from this proof ground, though it is actually a pure addition [*Zugabe*]" rather than a "supplement" (V:478; [373]). Moral teleology *seems* to develop out of its physical basis and coun-terpart, whereas it is in fact sui generis. Reason, which here needs no instruction (*Anleitung*) from nature, finds the concept of freedom (and the moral ideas therein grounded) practically sufficient for postulating a determinate concept of the original being, and of nature, including our own existence, as a final end that conforms to laws of freedom (V:479; 374).

The *Critique of Judgment* thus ends as much on a note of disunity as of wholeness. The principles of nature and freedom are too "heterogenous" to yield a single, unifying proof (V:479; 374). Physicoteleology does not even "point to" the moral proof. And admiration for the beauty and sublimity of nature seems (but only *seems*) to affect the mind by arousing moral ideas (V:482 n; 377 n).

The crucial deficiency of the physicoteleological proof lies in its inability to supply a determinate concept of God.[72] All that investigation of nature can supply is a concept of God as a first, intelligent cause. But even this much is merely an analogical projection based on our own (merely human) doings in the world. Though we can think God as having the attributes we know in ourselves, we cannot properly attribute them to him (V:476; 371). Only the moral law, which enjoins an aim "impracticable for beings of sense," gives us license to attribute a determinate concept — hence reality — to God, albeit only in a practical regard. For without this concept, reason would be "at a loss" (*im bloßen*) with respect to the final aim (*Endabsicht*) (V:485; [380]).

The task of the *Universal Natural History* — to grasp the *Inbegriff* of nature — is finally achieved, supported by a command that makes the final aim of the creation our own. The moral necessity of this aim makes up for an impracticability (*Unausführbarkeit*) that would otherwise leave reason at a loss. In so doing, moreover, it gives the concept of God the determinacy requisite for knowledge (albeit of a moral sort) and thus allows us to enter at last into intellectual community with the divine (if only for the sake of a moral end).

What saves this vision of the whole from *Schwärmerei* is the stricture preventing the "commingling" (however appealing it may be to "sound common sense") of physics and theology. (The marriage, as it were, of the veiled goddess and the moral author of the world remains unconsummated.) Nature can only "give occasion" for the idea of a final end and thus "make feelable" (*fühlbar machen*) the "need" for a theology that would determine the concept of God sufficiently for the highest use of practical reason, without nature's being able to "bring forth" (Kant cannot resist a final put-down) such a theology on her own (V:485; [381]. Cf. V:478; 373).

And yet, if nature cannot arouse ideas, it can make feelable our need. In this feeling of need — to which Kant's treatment of the a priori principle of judgment gives both the first and final word — aesthetics and teleology, and with them judgment as a whole, find common ground.

10 Kant's Hypochondria: A Phenomenology of Spirit

Phenomenology is the natural history of alterations of the body contrary to nature.

Dr. Marcus Herz, *Grundrβ aller medicinischen Wissenschaften* (1782)[1]

The vicissitude of human affairs overturns whatever the daring genus of Iabetus[2] undertakes and spins it about (*vertigine*) in a restless whirlwind (*vortice*), allowing nothing man accomplishes to stand on a firm basis. So it is that neither in empires nor in peoples, nor in customs and the arts, whether the liberal or useful arts, is there any fixed place of character. Rather, everything revolves in an eternal vortex (*vertigine*) and is driven around in a circle (so that it will not settle down in an inert heap).

Everything whatsoever drags and is dragged around by the same things in turn. The only stayer and conserver is the author of a system, not a part of it.

Immanuel Kant (XV:951)

Between insanity and healthy {understanding} sense there is no clear division, for hypochondria fills out the middle.

Immanuel Kant (XV:218)

Kant's interest in his own health is legion. According to his friend and intimate, R. B. Jachmann, "perhaps no man who ever lived paid a more exact attention to his body and everything that affected it."[3] By contemporary report, Kant spoke openly and without embarrassment to friends about the most intimate details of his physical condition,[4] a topic on which his letters, when they deal with personal matters at all, almost invariably turn. His thorough acquaintance with the prevailing medical theories of his time, including the latest systems and discoveries, was, Wasianski reports, a direct result of his concern for his own health.[5] Unusually sensitive to external stimuli and physically weak, Kant was nevertheless "never sick," and was wont in later years to boast (for example, before going to sleep) that "there was never anyone so healthy as [him]self." Kant regarded his health, according to contemporary reports, both as the object of the experiments joyfully conducted on his own body and as an artistic masterpiece (or alternatively, as a gymnastic feat comparable to walking a tightrope).[6]

In this chapter I argue that Kant's peculiar attentiveness to his own bodily state — the consequence, by his own account, of a "disposition" (*Anlage*) to hypochondria — has a more intimate relation to his philosophic achievement than is generally supposed.[7] By virtue of that disposition, Kant was peculiarly inclined as a thinker, for reasons to be examined below, to see his way clear of a number of conflicts that had heretofore barred mankind's way to philosophic satisfaction.[8]

Etiologically considered, critical philosophy emerges as a kind of "dietetic" response to a condition that led Kant to ask at an early age, why exist at all? In a number of works written over the years, Kant presents philosophy as (among other things) a life preservative and means to health. That in the end, this medicine — in Kant's case at least — proved double-edged does not detract from the singular care that he devoted, over the course of a lifetime, to his philosophic "regimen."

According to his biographer, Jachmann, Kant regarded his health as a "masterpiece," a work of art, in other words, of the highest order. This self-portrayal of Kant as artist in the medium of his own body suggests both the curious ambivalence of his attitude toward nature (at a superficial level opposing his efforts, at a deeper one guiding them) and point of intersection between Kant's theory of world history (what Emile L. Fackenheim calls the irruption of freedom out of nature)[9] and his own personal biography. As the author of the critical system, Kant at once inaugurates the true emancipation of humanity and concludes (as he anticipates) the history of philosophy. The pivotal moment, as previous chapters have argued, in the emergence of that system is his reconfiguration of the intelligible world on the basis of moral freedom rather than theoretical knowledge. His discovery of the priority of moral freedom, a discovery prepared by his reading of Rousseau and earlier efforts to withstand the dispiriting attractions of nature, represents what is by Kant's later lights a nontemporal, nonspatial conversion literally out of this world. And yet it is also, as Kant's autobiographical remarks attest, quintessentially worldly, bound up with his attentiveness to his own bodily condition and a distinction between inner and outer sense he was disposed to find at once arresting and peculiarly elusive.

Like Kant's medical self-commentary, his equivocal self-designation as a genius underscores the complexity of his understanding of human emancipation as a rebellion against nature of which nature itself is in some sense the source. In the pages that follow, Kant's pursuit of health will reveal a similarly ambiguous effort to conform to nature by struggling against it.

Either by birth or owing to defects of his early (maternal) care,[10] Kant's bodily *Bau* destined him (as he believed) to a life of pain, as well as disposing him to madness and an early, self-inflicted death. That he instead lived long, and by his own account both cheerfully and well, Kant attributed both to his own courage and resolve, and to his heightened sensitivity to the indications of nature. The exaggerated attentiveness to inner (bodily) sense that is the first symptom of hypochondria became in this way not only a life-preserving preventative, but also, as I will argue below, a first step on the road to systematic science. Kant's hypochondriacal disposition and early efforts to orient himself take as their common point of reference his *beklemmende Herz*.[11]

According to contemporary accounts, Kant was of slight and delicate build, though with a large head and pleasant face of which the eyes — ethereally blue and clear — were especially arresting. Despite his father's occupation as a skilled saddle maker, Kant was apparently physically clumsy, as well as lacking in muscular strength and bulk. (According to Jachmann, he frequently joked that he had "no bottom [*Hintern*].")[12] Kant's shortness of stature provided, he believed, too little room for his intestines, predisposing him to wind and constipation. But his most disturbing deformity was a chest (*Brust*) so narrow and flat as to border on concavity. Owing to this narrowness, Kant's heart was, he claimed, forced up against the left side of his diaphragm, resulting in a steady feeling of painful discomfort that he identified as *Beklemmung* of the heart. To this *Herzbeklemmung* — a term that can mean both physical constriction of the heart (as in *angina pectoris*) and a more generalized sense of oppression or apprehension[13] — Kant attributed his disposition to hypochondria.

I. A Brief History of Hypochondria

Both hypochondria and melancholy,[14] with which it is historically associated, have their literal seat in the hypochondrium: the area containing the viscera directly below the costal cartilages or praecardia. According to Galenic theory, hypochondria arises from a dislocation upward to the heart of black humors (literally "vapors," or *Dünste*) originating in the spleen.[15] Hypochondria was also historically associated (for example, by Robert Burton)[16] with disturbances of the bowels and was sometimes treated (for example, by Thomas Sydenham) as a "male" version of hysteria, the latter traditionally thought to arise, as the name suggests, from a dysfunctional or "wandering" uterus.

The symptoms of hypochondria were variously thought to be abdominal discomfort, especially wind, fixation and heaviness of mind, and a general sense of foreboding and fantastic apprehension leading, in extreme cases, to suicide. That hypochondria was an occupational hazard of deep thinkers was a long-standing suspicion. Aristotle noted the susceptibility of poets, mathematicians, and philosophers to melancholy, a theme repeated in the works of, among others, Shakespeare and Milton. In the seventeenth and eighteenth centuries, this risk group expanded to include men of business, along with those subject to habits of unnatural luxury and refinement. As such, hypochondria became a sort of occupational hazard of civilization—one particularly associated, owing both to their commercial way of life and their bad weather, with the English.[17]

In the late seventeenth and eighteenth centuries, new medical theories came increasingly to compete with, though by no means entirely replace, the Galenic assumptions still widespread among medical practitioners. Generally speaking, these new theories divided along mechanist/animist lines. The first school, associated with the names of Hoffmann and Boerhaave, took its primary lead from the mechanical philosophy of Descartes.[18] The second, frequently associated with the name of Stahl, was more loosely inspired by the work of Paracelsus and the vitalism and plasticism of the Cambridge neo-Platonists.[19] Crucial to the emerging medical and social attitude toward hypochondria was a new emphasis, prevalent in both schools, on "irritability,"[20] understood either as a purely mechanical force, or as a supramechanical life principle. On either basis, hypochondria could be thought of less as a disorder of the humors than of the nerves, though in practice both sorts of explanations—absent the unified biological/medical paradigm that would not appear for another hundred years—tended to overlap.[21]

Hypochondria was especially associated with disturbances of the imagination during a century in which imagination was coming increasingly to be regarded, by philosophers and poets alike, as *the* seat of interaction between mind and matter.[22] Famous literary personalities who wrote about (and in some cases suffered from) hypochondria include Mandeville,[23] Swift, Boswell,[24] and Pope, and such German literary figures as Adam Bernd, whose autobiography appeared in 1738.[25] Thus identified with the ravings of diseased imagination, hypochondria was both fashionable and the frequent butt of satire, such as Butler's *Hudibras* (1663).

Hypochondria, in short, was of all recognized diseases that which most closely touched on the vexed question of the relation between mind and matter. This, combined with its prevalence, vagueness and diffusion of symptoms, and seeming intractability made it a magnet for medical dispute—a site in which the battle of the ancients and the moderns was still being staged, long after "Aristotely" had elsewhere fled the field.

A final note: one cannot help comparing hypochondriacal uneasiness (and uneasiness over that uneasiness) with the centrality of the concept of "uneasiness" in the philosophy of John Locke. One wonders if the general preoccupation with hypochondria in the eighteenth century was not in itself, at least in part, an exaggeration of certain Lockean themes, including the identification of rationality with a perpetual (and perpetually anxious) effort to relieve anxiety. In any event, it is striking that hypochondria should be associated *both* with the hyperrationality of scholars and men of business, *and* with the sort of popular religious fanaticism dismissively referred to by Locke and others as "enthusiasm." Lockean reason in extremis bears a curious (or uneasy) resemblance to unreason.

II. Kant on Hypochondria

INVESTIGATION CONCERNING DISEASES OF THE HEAD

Kant first discusses hypochondria in his *Investigation concerning Diseases of the Head* (1764), which appeared in Hamann's *Königsbergsche Gelehrte und Politische Zeitungen*.[26] Kant describes the condition in that rather sardonic essay as follows:

> The fantastic mental constitution is nowhere commoner than in hypochondria. The chimeras which this illness hatches do not properly deceive outer senses, but rather only make for the hypochondriac an illusion [*Blendwerk*] of the experience of his own state, either of the body or the soul, that is largely a mere crotchet [*Grille*].[27] The hypochondriac has an ill that, wherever it may have its main seat . . . wanders unsteadily throughout the diverse parts of the body. But it chiefly draws a melancholy vapor around the seat of the soul, to the extent that the patient has the illusion that he feels in himself almost every illness of which he has ever heard. He therefore speaks of nothing so happily as his indisposition, gladly reads medical texts, in which he everywhere encounters his own condition. . . . Because of the occurrence of such internal fantasies the images in his brain often acquire a strength and duration that burden him . . . so that his state is much like that of one deranged [*eines Verrückten*], only without the latter's necessity. (II:266)

Unlike derangement (*Verrückung*), a condition in which what one merely imagines is taken to exist in the external world, hypochondria involves an illusion of inner sense alone, whereby what one immediately feels concerning one's own state itself deceives. And unlike derangement, but like those half-waking dreams we can dispel at will, hypochondria is not "deeply rooted" and hence can go away, either spontaneously or as the result of medical intervention (II:266). Hypochondria is thus distinguished from genuine derangement or insanity by two things: its peculiar association with illusions that concern one's inner state—be it of the body or the soul—and its susceptibility to treatment.

Kant's account here of the difference between dreaming and insanity is also worth noting. Chimeras, he suggests, are present to normal minds both while asleep and while awake. When normal persons are awake, however, outer impressions drown out these illusions, which therefore have their "full strength" only in sleep, when the entrance to the soul of the livelier, outer impressions is "closed off." "It is thus," he says, "no wonder that dreams, while they last, are taken for true experiences of real things." In the deranged, these chimerical impressions are, for whatever reason, as strong as the normal impressions of outer sense, so that even a healthy reason, if it were subject to such chimerical impressions, would take them for real experiences. The deranged person can hence properly be said to "dream while awake." And because the testimony of the senses is stronger than the conclusions of reason, a deranged person cannot be cured by reasoning with him. A normal person finds himself in a similar condition when half awake, with the distinction that he can disperse such illusions at will, by drawing his mind out of its state of dispersal. In such a state "we dream only partially and have the chimeras in our power" (II:264–5).

One is led by Kant's account to wonder what else the hypochondriacal condition might have in common with this normal state of half-awakeness, since both—unlike derangement—are subject to willful control.[28]

DREAMS OF A SPIRIT SEER

Kant's essay *Dreams* (1766), itself an exercise in what might be called hypochondriacal wit, elaborates upon a theme that may well have been suggested to Kant by the passage from Butler's *Hudibras* to which Kant's essay alludes (II:348; 336).[29] So understood, *Dreams* not only *uses* hypochondria as a metaphor for metaphysical illusion, but (as we saw in chapter 5) *is itself* a sort of mental purgative, dispelling by means of ridicule Kant's own inspirational propensities.[30] When, as a result of this experiment, nothing is left, affectively speaking, besides "hope for the future," Kant is ready to commit himself morally, confident of being able to distinguish the enthusiasm without which nothing great can be accomplished in the world, as he put it in his earlier *Investigation,* from a dangerous—and from mankind's point of view potentially fatal—*Begeisterung.* Kant's moral turn, in short—at least as represented in *Dreams*—is a therapeutic option, both for himself and for the species, undertaken in the interest of (hope of) a future life.[31]

Kant's imaginary experiment upon himself in *Dreams* enacts, even as it comments upon, the connection between mind and matter with which hypochondriacs tend to be preoccupied. In making the experiment, moreover, Kant learns, viscerally as it were, the crucial lesson of the relativity and, unless care is taken, illusory character of inward sense. Far from giving immediate access to the real, our inner *Bilder* are only as valid as the external, phenomenal order, corroborated by the testimony of others, in which those images can be made to fit. If any inner state is privileged, it is moral feeling, purged of any claim to knowledge, not the impressions that — even in the case of touch, seemingly the most trustworthy of the senses — so readily give rise to delusive judgments, as with the hypochondriac "inspired" by his body's own windy movements.

Kant's experimental setup, a "secret philosophy" followed by a "common philosophy" or "antikaballa," prepares the stage for his later treatment of the history of philosophy as a continual struggle between intellectualist/noologist and sensualist/empiricist — a war culminating in, and ended by, his own founding of a genuinely philosophic science (see *Critique of Pure Reason* A/853 = B/881 ff.). It is therefore especially important to recognize that Kant's position in *Dreams* is not simply that of the antikabbalist, whose materialistic reduction, à la Butler, of enthusiasm to intestinal gas is itself, from Kant's own perspective, a literal reductio ad absurdum, purging in its effects, but no "truer" (or less "dogmatic") than the inspiration it replaces.[32] Instead, Kant in *Dreams* remains zetetically suspended, unwilling to decide whether to cut off or dissolve/untie the "metaphysical knot" that joins together body and soul (II:319; 307).[33]

In a letter to Mendelssohn,[34] written in response to Mendelssohn's generally supportive review of *Dreams,* Kant makes clear the underlying intentions of his essay. Undecided (*wiedersinnisch*) concerning the veracity of Swedenborg's visions, Kant is more concerned with the inflated (*aufgeblasen*) (and contagious) arrogance of fashionable metaphysics, which is so harmful to the true welfare of our species that it would be better to exterminate all imaginary insights than to permit bad metaphysics to continue. Kant therefore presents, not an organon (which would suit a healthy but uninstructed understanding), but a catarcticon to dispel the false insights of a corrupted reason. Along these lines, he has drawn certain conclusions that he was unable to spell out clearly in his published essay, concerning "how the soul is present in the world." The difficulty comes down to the old question of how the external relation of substances is to be understood and how it can be known. This relatedness entails, Kant believes, a combination of external efficacy and receptivity to external efficacy, of which the union of the soul with the human body is only a special case. Only experience, however, can tell us anything about such external efficacy; and the harmony of our own soul and body, which discloses an inner condition (thinking and willing) in "counter-relation" with an outer condition (of our own body), tells us nothing about how one substance outwardly affects and is affected by another. Hence one is led to wonder whether it is possible at all to determine these powers of spiritual substances (to affect and be affected by other substances) by means of a priori judgments.

Equally significantly, one is led, Kant says, to ask whether one can by means of rational inferences discover a "primitive force" or primary grounding relation between cause and effect (or as he put the question in his earlier essay, *Negative Quantities,* how one can conclude from the fact that something exists that something else exists [II:202; 239]). Kant's answer is that what he elsewhere calls real relations between substances can only be known via experience. It is, he concludes, impossible to determine by means of a priori judgments the external force of substances to affect and be affected by other substances. The existence of spirits can therefore neither be proven nor disproven. Kant concludes by voicing his suspicion that even *experiential* knowledge of how the soul is present in the world—and thus of birth (in a metaphysical sense), life, and death—is impossible, the whole matter falling beyond the limits of human reason and/or experience.

By calling his essay *Träumerei,* Kant implicitly identifies, on some level, with the spirit seers themselves.[35] As a state in between healthy reason and insanity, hypochondria is comparable to that dreamlike condition we experience upon awakening; it is also a condition which (like the controlled or half-wakeful experiment represented by Kant's essay, but unlike most dreams) can be canceled by an act of will. *Dreams* is thus a specific against hypochondria on at least two levels, "purging" reason metaphorically (a process in which mind and matter are themselves rhetorically inverted), even as it places knowledge of the body/soul connection beyond the bounds of reason, thereby blocking inquiry into an area of compelling, but ultimately morbid, fascination.[36]

THE 1770S

Kant did not publish much during the decade of the seventies. What evidence we have, however, by way of letters, notes, and one published review, suggests that the relation between mind and matter, in general, and hypochondria as a mental and physical distortion of that relation, in particular, were important areas of concern. To be sure, a letter to Marcus Herz, written toward the end of 1773 (X:145), announces that Kant will omit from his new course on anthropology the "subtle, and to [his] eyes, eternally fruitless investigation of the way in which bodily organs and thoughts stand in connection." His continuing correspondence with Herz, however, as well as personal notes and the review of Moscati, published later in the decade, demonstrate Kant's continuing interest in the topic.

Indications from the *Nachlaß*

Many notes from the *Nachlaß* dated around this period (and beyond) bear on the subject of hypochondria. One passage (dated around the late 1760s) lists, among diseases rooted in imagination, both hypochondria and *Schwärmerei,* and repeatedly wonders whether "we play with images, or images play with us," making much of the difference between representations that nature produces in us and those that we produce at will. That moral as well as physical mastery is at issue is suggested by Kant's inclusion of the example of woman, who "governs man by letting him imagine himself her master," and princes, who give their subjects an imaginary freedom (*Reflection* no. 313 [XV:122–23]). Both here and in several later passages Kant contrasts the benign play of imagination that we control, with malignant conditions in which nature plays with us. To lose control over that play is equivalent to madness (*Reflection* no. 335 [XV:132]): "no condition is more dangerous than that in which we tarry in the world of imagination until we so to speak lose ourselves there and cannot find the way back. Paradise of fools. One must never be outside oneself but rather always by oneself and awake." Intuitions must always adhere to conscious perception and harmonize with the condition of the world. He who, unawake, has representations, dreams. The wakeful dreamer who willingly exceeds the force of his spirit is a *Schwärmer.* Hypochondria, for its part, is related to involuntary distraction (*zerstreuen*) (*Reflection* no. 525 [XV:227]).

Not every benign involvement of imagination, however, need be consciously controlled. Dreaming, for example, is crucial to maintaining the vital connection between mind and body during sleep. As one note states, should dreaming cease, the connection between the vital spirit and the intestines would be interrupted, resulting in death. Elsewhere, Kant argues that dreams sustain the vital connection between the nervous energy of the brain and muscular contractions of the viscera. Kant, in other words, believed not only in the necessary continuity of mental activity (via dreaming), even in sleep, for animals as well as humans (a belief that Leibniz, among others, shared), but also in the peculiar relationship between that activity and certain vital bodily contractions, as if the mind needed to maintain, even in sleep, continual alertness lest bodily activity cease.[37] Kant's conviction may have gained additional support from his belief that he had once been saved from asphyxiation by a nightmare about drowning, an imaginary terror in this case preserving him from a real one.[38]

Other notes expand upon the connection, mediated by feeling and imagination, between the mind and the organs of involuntary motion, especially the heart and viscera (*Eingeweide*), as in Kant's treatment elsewhere of vertigo and nausea. Thus, *Reflection* no. 487 (XV:206–10) speaks of:

> Disease of the head. Free course of fantasy. Disease of the mind . . . : either crotchet [*Grillen*] disease or disturbed mind; in the first case, one knows that one does not possess oneself; in the second, one doesn't know it. In the first case, the cause is in the brain; in the second, in the bowels [*Eingeweide*]. In the first case one cannot cast one's fantasies out of one's (sense) mind. (*Reflection* no. 487 [XV:210])

In one note, Kant cites the strange case of a young man whose ulti-mately fatal attack of intestinal worms was eased by music.[39] In another, extraordinary note (*Reflection* no. 1033 [XV:463]), he approaches the question of mind/body commerce more directly. There are, he observes, "most inward bodily movements over which the will has no influence, but rather only certain representations that can stimulate [*reitzen*] our will." Turning pale, blushing, shivering, pounding of the heart "can not be pre-vented or brought about by choice." Rather, "imagination does all of this," imagination, "which is united with the body." Kant goes on to speculate that the vital spirit is a peculiar principle of the union of the soul with the body, a principle that works by itself and on which the will has no influ-ence. "Once this vital spirit is aroused, it involuntarily moves the thoughts, as well as the body. The heart is seized [*angegriffen*], and this is the ground of *commercii. enormon, incitens.*"[40]

This affecting, or gripping of the heart, in which "the ground of com-merce" between body and mind or soul consists, recalls both the tradi-tional understanding of the heart as the soul's bodily seat[41] and Kant's own *Herzbeklemmung*, that perpetual discomfort—at once an inner feeling and an impression of outer sense—that he could neither cause nor will away.

Review of Moscati's *On the Corporeally Essential Difference between the Structure of Animals and Humans*

Of the two brief essays that Kant published in the decade of the seventies, following the appearance of his *Dissertation* of 1770, one—the review of Moscati (1771)—bears intimately on the question of mind/body influence in general, and hypochondria in particular.[42] In that review, Kant attributes the causes of hypochondria, vertigo, and a host of other human ills to the inverted position—unique among mammals—of the human fetus and to the equally unnatural upright position of man's viscera after birth. Kant's discussion is sufficiently remarkable to deserve quoting at length.

> We are here returned, by an acute analyzer/dissector [*Zergliederer*] to natural man on all fours, to where the insightful *Rousseau* did not as a philosopher wish to arrive. Dr. *Moscati* proves that the upright gate of man is forced and contrary to nature; that he is, to be sure, so constructed as to be able to maintain and move himself in this way, but that if he makes it a necessity and his con-stant habit, discomforts and illnesses arise sufficient to prove that he has been misled by reason and imitation to diverge from the first, animal arrangement. Man in his innards is constructed no differently than all animals, which stand on four feet. When he stands upright, his viscera [*Eingeweide*], and especially the fetus of a pregnant person, have a pendulous [*herabhängende*] position and

half upside down placement . . . that causes deformities [*Mißge-staltungen*] and a host of illnesses. So, for example, the heart, since it is obliged to hang/be suspended, extends the blood vessels to which it is tied, [and] assumes a sloping position such that it rests against the diaphragm and slides against the left side with its point. This position is one in which man, i.e. adult man, is distinguished from all animals and which gives rise to an unavoidable inclination [*Hang*] to aneurisms, heart throbbing, narrow-chestedness, edema of the chest, etc. . . . By this upright posture of man, the mesenterium sinks, drawn from the load of the intestines, vertically underneath, and is elongated and weakened, preparing for a host of ruptures. In the portal artery, which has no valves, the blood must rise against the direction of gravity, moving slowly and more heavily . . . , from which spring hypochondria, hemorrhoids, etc., etc., not to mention the difficulty suffered in the course of blood, which from the vessels of the legs must again rise to the height of the heart, causing swelling, vericosity, etc., etc. The disadvantage of this vertical placement is especially visible in the pregnant, as regards the fruit as well as the mother. The child, placed on its head, receives the blood in very unequal proportions, the blood being driven in much higher amounts to the upper members, into the head and arms, such that both grow and extend in proportions wholly different than with all other animals. From the first influx arise hereditary dispositions to vertigo, stroke, headache and madness; from the rush of the blood to the arms and issue from the legs stem the remarkable disproportion virtually unknown in any other animal — that is, that the arms of the fruit are longer and the legs shorter than they would be in suitable relation, a situation that is, to be sure, improved after birth from the constant vertical position, but which shows that the fetus must earlier have suffered violence. The injuries of the two-footed mother are the gushing forth of the womb [*Gebärmut-ter*], untimely births, etc., etc., which, with an Iliad of other evils, arises from her upright position, and from which four-footed creatures are free. One could add to these fundamental proofs that our animal nature is properly four-footed. Among all four-footed animals there is not one that cannot swim, if it should accidentally fall into water. Man alone drowns, if he has not specially learned to swim. The cause is that he has given up the custom of going on all fours, for it is this movement through which he would maintain himself in the water without art and whereby all four-footed animals swim, even those to which water is repulsive. As paradoxical as this thesis of our Italian doctor may appear, it so attains in the hands of a so acute and philosophical dissector [*Zer-gliederers*] almost complete certainty. One thus sees: the first concern of nature was that man as an animal be preserved *for himself and his kind;* and in this regard that placement, *four-footedness,* was most appropriate for his inner construction, for the position of the fruit, and for preservation from danger; but in man there was also lain a seed of reason, whereby, if it should develop, he is determined/destined for *society,* and by means of which, he constantly accepts/assumes [*annimmt*], the position most suited [*geschickteste*] to it, namely the *two-footed one,* a position through which, on the one hand, he wins infinitely more than the animals, but whose accompanying inconveniences he must also accept, since they stem from the fact that he has lifted up his head [*Haupt*] so proudly above his old comrades [chambermates]. (II:423– 25)[43]

Heart palpitations, narrow-breastedness, and hypochondria are all consequences, according to this analysis, of a gait unnatural from the perspective of our animal survival, but appropriate to the development of the seed of reason. Some of these difficulties, indeed, would vanish (for example, the human tendency toward vertigo and insanity, and women's troubles with pregnancy) if women's posture remained horizontal. But this would hardly promote that process of "idealization" to which Kant entrusts the moral and aesthetic education of the species.

In his own *Anlagen* to hypochondria and vertigo, then, Kant can read the syncopated entelechies of our species—hybrid, as he will later put it, of both nature and reason.[44] Kant is thus a child of Iabetus in a specially emphatic way. Moscati's anatomical theodicy (which goes further than Rousseau's philosophy wished or dared) "justifies" Kant's own infirmities as the price that the species in general must pay for the development of reason. In doing so, however, it also gives Kant a more personal reason to be reconciled with these infirmities, which provide him with a privileged inner vantage point from which to observe the human condition—infirmities that provide, as we will see, a stimulating focus for his own emerging philosophical *Zergliederung.*

Kant and Marcus Herz

The personal bearing of Kant's physical ailments on his emerging philosophic project finds expression in his correspondence with Marcus Herz, a former student with whom Kant seems to have had, during this period of his life, uniquely close and significant relations.

It would not be an exaggeration to call Herz Kant's earliest influential exponent. Herz, originally from Berlin (where his father was a Torah scribe), came to Königsberg at the age of fifteen to work as a clerk. He attended Kant's lectures from 1766 until 1770, when he returned to Berlin. Here he became friendly with Mendelssohn and his circle, and, supported by David Friedlander, studied medicine at Halle, receiving a medical appointment in 1774 at the Berlin Jewish Hospital. Herz, whose skills as a physician were highly regarded, also kept up an active interest in philosophy and was among the first to promulgate Kant's thought widely. In 1770 Kant chose him as the "advocate" or public defender of his dissertation. In 1771, Herz published a book explaining Kant's ideas (*Betrachtung aus der spekulativen Weltweisheit*). In 1777, he began to lecture on philosophy and experimental physics in his home, where he was heard by important members of Berlin society, including the royal family and future emperor. In 1779, Herz married fifteen-year-old Henriette de Lemos, daughter of a Jewish physician from Hamburg. Henriette was soon to become an important literary and intellectual figure in her own right, making their home a center of enlightened intellectual Berlin life that attracted, among others, Mendelssohn, Maimon, Mirabau, Jean Paul Richter, Schleiermacher, and von Humboldt.[45]

The correspondence between Kant and Herz that I here consider extends from 1770 to 1781, a period during which Kant published little, and the critical system was actively taking shape. (Indeed, this correspondence is often treated as a principle source of knowledge about the development of Kant's thought during his crucial "silent decade.") In Kant's letters to Herz, extended commentaries on Kant's emerging system frequently appear side by side with requests for Herz's help — sometimes in his capacity as a physician, sometimes in his capacity as an intermediary with the outer intellectual world.[46]

Kant's peculiar intimacy with Herz during this time — he speaks in his letter of September 27, 1770 (X:99–102), of sharing in Herz's "language of the heart" (*Sprache des Herzens*) — was at once medical, intellectual, and social. Herz's letter of September 11, 1770, expressed his own devotion to his teacher in affective, almost clinical terms. The postal wagon delivering Kant's letters causes Herz unbroken and body-weakening shivers (*Erschütterungen*). The mere thought of Kant fills his soul with reverent (*ehrfurchtsvoll*) astonishment, so that he can only with great effort ready himself to gather up his distracted consciousness and set forth his thoughts. He has Kant alone to thank for turning him from the brutish path of prejudice followed by so many of his coreligionists (*Mitbrüder*). Without Kant, in short, Herz would "be nothing" (*ich wäre nichts*), despite the "complaint of hypochondriacal scholars" (*Klage hypochondrischer Gelehrte*) that our knowledge only increases our unhappiness. Herz continues with a description of his discussions of Kant's philosophy with Mendelssohn and an explanation of why he has not yet met with others, as Kant had apparently requested. He concludes with some medical advice (evidently solicited) concerning an unnamed "weakness" that Herz attributes to an excessive pedagogical burden but that Kant had linked to too much sitting combined with moving of the mouth (for other teachers in Königsberg, Herz notes, sit and talk for many hours without Kant's complaint [*klagen*]). Herz then asks for a more detailed description of Kant's "entire bodily state," offering to consult physicians on Kant's behalf, and adding that he would be happy to consider himself even the "smallest instrument" of Kant's well-being. One is left wondering who or what is the true subject of "hypochondriacal complaints," the so called "learned" — Herz (the shuddering and distracted devotee), or Kant himself.

Kant's letter to Herz dated June 7, 1771 (X:121–24), gives two reasons for his failure to reply to a previous letter. The first is delay in working out the plan of his book (to be entitled "The Limits of Sensibility and of Reason"). "Long experience has taught me," says Kant, "that insight into the matters we are intending cannot be compelled nor speeded up (*beschleunigt*) through straining" (X:122) (*beschleunigen* is, among other things, a medical term meaning to accelerate, as with a pulse or heartbeat). The second reason given is ill health, Kant adding that when his "stomach gradually comes to do its duty, [his] fingers will not delay in performing theirs." Kant ends by expressing his pleasure that Herz's treatise will be coming out before his own, and closes as Herz's "most sincerely sympathetic [*aufrichtigtheilnehmenden*] friend."[47]

Herz's letter of reply (July 9, 1771 [X:124–27]) was, if anything, more highly charged than that of September 1770. Herz speaks, for example, of his disgust (*Eckel*) with science and of the half-delivered ideas he was about to "strangle at birth" until Kant's letter pulled him back to levelheadedness in the nick of time.

Kant's lengthy letter of February 21, 1772, again apologizes for his silence, which he once again attributes to the burden of completing his book (which he now calls a "Critique of Pure Reason" and goes on to describe in considerable detail), combined with his continuing frailty of health. After extended comments on the progress of his work, Kant strives to meet an objection to Herz's recently published treatise in defense of Kant's views. This objection, which Kant calls the "most essential that can be raised against the doctrine," continues to insist on the privileged status of inner sense.[48] (The objection runs somewhat as follows: Changes are real according to the testimony of inner sense. But changes are possible only on the presupposition of time. Therefore time is something real, involved in the determination of the things in themselves.) Kant's answer to this criticism, which he does not here fully spell out, involves the recognition that changes registered in inner sense testify to the reality of change as an appearance. Kant ends by extending his greetings to Mendelssohn, Lambert, and Sulzer,[49] and closes as Herz's "constant friend."

Kant's letter to Herz dated towards the end of 1773 comments extensively on the progress of Herz's medical studies and on the improving, but by no means steady, condition of Kant's own health, an improvement that he attributes to better acquaintance with what doesn't suit him. Due to his sensitive nerves, all medicines are to him like poison. "Do study the great variety of natures," Kant advises, adding that "every physician who was not a philosopher" would upset Kant's constitution (literally, "throw it in a heap") (X:144). (This is also the letter in which Kant disavows all "subtle, and to [his] eyes, eternally fruitless investigation of the way in which bodily organs and thoughts stand in connection" [X:145].) Kant excuses the non-appearance of his promised "Critique" (which Herz had apparently vainly sought at the Leipzig book fair), calling Herz the one person to whom he can reveal his philosophic hopes without "being suspected of the most extreme vanity."

The next extant letter to Herz is dated November 24, 1776 (X:198–200; [86]). Kant expresses his pleasure upon news of the progress of Herz's medical practice, an activity he especially commends for the health that it bestows upon the practitioner, whose mind is nourished without being used up. In like manner, Kant adds, our greatest analysts (for example, Baumgarten, Mendelssohn, and Garve) playfully "spin out their brain nerves into the tenderest threads, and thereby make themselves extremely sensitive to every impression or tension" (X:198). In keeping with this theme, Kant congratulates Herz for his recently published book on taste. He goes on to speak of the progress of his own work (which now encompasses a "critique, discipline, canon, and architectonic of *pure reason*") as steady but slow — Kant having only recently overcome "the last hindrances" — and claims to look forward, health permitting, to its completion "next summer."

Kant's letter of the following summer (August 20, 1777 [X:211–14]; [87–91]), in which he thanks his former student for a copy of (yet another) publication, also brings out the parallel, implicit in earlier correspondence, between Kant's physical and mental condition. The mental and bodily obstacles with which he struggles seem to be both formally identical and factually interdependent.[50] On the one hand, Kant solicits Herz's help with an "insufficient evacuation" (associated, according to Kant, with the cardial wind that is the general cause of all his indispositions), a problem that is causing his "cloudiness of brain." Diuretics have not been able to remove the "impure stuff" (*grobe Unreinigkeiten*) and have only added to the weakness of his bowels.[51] On the other hand, Kant complains of an "obstacle" (*Stein im Wege*) to the completion of his "Critique of Pure Reason," namely the effort (*Bemühung*) to present it with full clarity. Kant nevertheless anticipates a winter completion.

In his letter to Herz dated the beginning of April 1778 (X:230–32), Kant seems to have accommodated himself to slowness of production on both scores. Turning down an invitation to leave Königsberg,[52] he admits to feeling something in the way of melancholy (*Schwermuth*) in thus denying wider scope to his chief aim and intention (*Absicht*), which lies in "spreading good mental attitudes, based on principles [*Grundsätze*], to the well disposed . . . and by this means, of giving the only purposive [*zweckmäßige*] direction to the cultivation of talents." Such, however, is the limit imposed by his "small share of life force." He is thus reconciled: all he has wished and received is a peaceful situation, varied between work, speculation, and social intercourse, where "[his] easily affected but carefree mind, and [his] still more capricious [*läunischer*] but never ill body, can be kept occupied without exhaustion." All change makes Kant anxious (*bange*). He chooses therefore to respect this instinct of his nature, so as to further draw out the thread that the Parcae have spun so thin and tender (X:231).[53] Like Socrates with his daimon, Kant respects this anxiety as a Godlike sign and calls upon the well-disposed Herz to protect him from outer disturbance. (The conduit, in other words, becomes a buffer.) The threads of Kant's fate are like sensitive nerves, easily affected, and yet for all that capable of a life-extending flexibility.

This spirit of resignation applies equally to Kant's medical condition, Kant now turning down the prescription he had once requested of Herz. Laxatives, it seems, only increase the obstruction. So long as evacuation occurs regularly, Kant "is healthy in [his] own manner, that is, weakly." As for his book, Kant (here too) will not allow anything to be forced out of him, since he expects to live long enough to complete his project in timely fashion, that is, health permitting, sometime the following summer.

The same resigned patience permeates his letter of August 28, 1778 (X:240–42; [89–90]); the promised work should be ready soon, and with a clarity of plan that will make it easy to understand, and that should facilitate sending the notes Herz had requested to aid in his own lectures. In any case, it will take time to retrieve them, since "everything that depends on the diligence and skill of [his] auditors is precarious." He will, however, speak to Kraus. Meanwhile, he is well, having accustomed himself for many years "to regard a very limited [*eingeschränktes*] wellbeing, that most people would complain of, as health" (X:241; [90]). Kant's efforts to communicate to a variety of people through Herz continue.[54]

Kant's letters of December 15, 1778, and January 1779 express pleasure in the success of Herz's lectures and distress over the "hypochondriacal" condition of Kraus (who bears the letter along with a copy of the requested notes). Kant hopes that Herz—whose "art doubtless contains remedies, and friendship more so"—can help Kraus (X:248). Kant's follow-up letter (February 4, 1779 [X:248]) admits to sharing in Kraus's "misology and misanthropy," which stem from, among other things, "impatience for results." A letter from Kraus soon thereafter (March 2, 1979) mentions the natural helps (good air, company, and diet) by which he means to cure himself (X:249).

There are no other extant letters to Herz until that of May 1, 1781 (X:266–67; [93–94]), in which Kant announces the immanent publication of the *Critique of Pure [reinen] Reason* and pays especially moving tribute to Herz, the "same insightful man who deigned to cultivate [Kant's] ideas" and "who penetrated [them] more deeply than anyone else." (Requests follow for help in distributing copies to various important persons.) A follow-up letter (May 11, 1781) betrays a certain uneasiness concerning the work's reception: Mendelssohn has set it aside, and Herz is busy with his own book. Kant nevertheless hopes that Herz, above all, will find time to read the *Critique:* Herz, who "as a student delighted [Kant] by grasping [his] ideas and thoughts more quickly and exactly than any of the others" and who is, it seems, best equipped to evaluate the worth of a work that "can bring about nothing other than a complete change of the way of thinking [*Denkungsart*] in this part of human knowledge that concerns us so intimately [*innigst*]" (X:269; [95]).

Here the intense correspondence between Kant and Herz comes to a close.[55] Herz was slow to respond to the *Critique.* Others complained of its obscurity; and no review appeared that year.[56] Whether owing to Kant's disappointment, or for some other reason, Herz, the student who had "penetrated [his] thought most deeply," no longer served Kant either as personal confidant or as principle link with the larger intellectual world. Thus ended Kant's peculiar intimacies with a student whose very name calls to mind the site of Kant's indisposition — the place where mind and matter are traditionally said to meet.[57]

Even as he decried as "fruitless" the effort to explain the mutual influence of mind and matter, Kant, as his letters to Herz reveal, was struggling to gain mastery over that influence. Herz, who served Kant uniquely during these years as confidant, conduit, and buffer, was a trusted (but also somehow alien) figure of mediation between the outer world and what was for Kant, both physically and intellectually, most intimately inward. Kant's most philosophically significant communication to Herz concerns, interestingly enough, the question of how a priori concepts, whose source is wholly inward, can convey knowledge of the outer world. In the same letter, Kant denies Lambert's claim that the temporality of inner sense applies to things in themselves. He thus implicitly differentiates sensual inwardness (the same sense that reports on our inner bodily state) from the more radical, unsensed inwardness of the pure ideas. Not least, Herz was the prototype of the philosopher/physician whose borderline activities Kant both endorsed and in his own way practiced. Though neither ever called Kant hypochondriacal,[58] their exchanges over Kraus implicitly extend the diagnosis (or something very much like it) to Kant himself. Hypochondriacal or not, during the years in which Kant's critical system was developing, he was also learning to accept his own constricted condition as a kind of health. On both the intellectual and physical fronts, images of straining and purgation give way to one of patient gestation, as trust in nature supplants artificial aids. The relieving catharsis for which Kant initially hopes comes to be resisted as a kind of premature birth, a forcing of Kant's product before it is fully formed into the public light. When, finally, the *Critique* appears, it is the more precociously prolific Herz, devoted to popularizing the concepts of the *Inaugural Dissertation* they worked out together, who isn't ready.

On Philosophers' Medicine of the Body

Notes written mostly in Latin by Kant sometime in the late 1780s in preparation for an academic address and collected under the title *On Philosophers' Medicine of the Body* offer a tantalizing, if textually inconclusive, glimpse at Kant's theoretical views concerning the relation between mind and body, as well as giving indirect hints as to his own philosophic diet.[59]

Philosopher's medicine of the body involves treatment of the body through the mind, both through diversionary tactics (such as conversation to divert the mind from meditations that impede digestion) and, especially, through imagination (XV:940; 228). The philosophic doctor will therefore turn his attention to the school of Stahl, rather than that of Hoffmann; for whereas the latter treats men and cattle in the same way, that is, mechanically, the former wants to treat man with due regard for the force of the human mind in curing diseases or bringing them to a head.[60]

Imagination is the principle of perception and motion, in both animals and human beings, by which things that are absent can "really exist" in the soul as if they were present. What distinguishes human imagination is its susceptibility to direction by the will or "deliberate intention," rather than — as is the case with animals — being set in play solely by impulses implanted by nature.[61] This difference accounts both for man's unique susceptibility to "black anxiety" and to the unique vulnerability of his heart to "profound assaults" from a wandering (*vagus*) imagination. Imagination, in other words, is both our undoing and our salvation. And its power of contagion — imagination, can, for example, spread convulsions through the sheer power of suggestion — gives the philosophically minded physician a peculiarly penetrating means of influencing the body (XV:944; 231).

The ticklish boundary between philosophy and medicine Kant resolves here as follows. The philosopher's special province is the use of mind to treat ills of the body, but only where the mind retains its throne. In cases where "imagination turns savage" (for example, fanaticism and hypochondria), the bodily care of a physician proper is required (XV:943; 230.

XV:947; 233). What Kant calls corporeal discipline, on the other hand, belongs properly to the philosopher, "not because he knows the body in a mechanical way, but because he knows it from experience" (XV:941; [229]).[62] As a consequence, he treats it according to the dictates of a companion rather than a harsh master, and so avoids the fate of Mendelssohn, whose aversion for the discomforts of satiety and its accompanying sense of fullness made him, as it were, intemperate in fasting.[63]

The mind's activity, then, can either augment or deplete the body's energy. Where the force of mental impulsion remains within the limits of a mind in control of itself, the body's force also increases, as with the lively conversation that promotes good digestion; if the mind loses control of itself, on the other hand, such impulsions violently assault and shake the vital principle.[64] Kant's philosophic regimen thus essentially consists in this: the mind's periodic release from concentrated attention on a single object,[65] through deliberate, albeit temporary, abandonment to a distracting play of images and/or affects, and all this to energize, and thereby promote, certain vital functions of the body.[66] In short, Kant's regimen is a deliberate and controlled surrender of mental self-direction, a way of using play by intentionally allowing oneself to be played with. One is in this context struck by Kant's designation, in the *Anthropology*, of earliest childhood (before the infant attains to a representation of itself as a unity, under the concept of an object) as the time of play (*Spielzeit*), the "happiest time of all" (VII:128; 10). As with the aesthetic experience of the beautiful, Kant's regimen represents a qualified return to that earliest *Spielzeit,* before self-consciousness and the force of resistance to the play of sense that such mental unity requires began to take their vital toll.[67]

Attention directed to oneself, on the other hand, is harmful; attention to the body causes illnesses, especially cramps, while:

> Attention . . . to the mind [also] weakens the body. the diary of one given to self-observation.[68] Hence the utility of not fixing one's attention, eventually sleep. This is a dispersion through dreams, hence there is motion without empirical (*figiertes*) self-consciousness. Conversation is internal motion with continual distractions. Reproaching oneself inwardly is very prejudicial to the body. Affects that pass away without any aftermath are helpful, longings are harmful. (XI:952; 237)

We will soon have reason to recall Kant's singular attentiveness to the curative effects of self-distraction.

THE *ANTHROPOLOGY*

(On Anthropology.) 1. The doctrine of soul health. 2. The doctrine of soul sickness. 3. Soul medicine . . . 4. The doctrine of soul signs. Thus always to proceed from human beings, not from a spiritual life principle that is sustaining for itself, but rather from the community of that principle with the body. (*Reflection* no. 159 [mid 1790s; XV:57])

This note, composed around the time that Kant published his *Anthropology from a Pragmatic Point of View*, suggests an intimate relationship between the topic of anthropology and that of philosophic medicine. Recognition that the vital spirit cannot be apprehended directly, but only in community with the body (as with the bodily "experience" that allows philosophers to practice a uniquely effectual sort of medicine), goes together with the intent to study man as species being (see VII:119; 3). To "proceed from men" is not only to assume a community of body and soul that cannot humanly be further reduced or analyzed. It is also to avoid the distinct risks to mental health that arise from self observation, or otherwise "eavesdropping" on one's own mental states. As such, pragmatic anthropology is itself a medicine of the soul, directing our attention away from morbid fixation on our own inner states (the characteristic vice of would-be psychologists and Platonizing enthusiasts alike) to the outer world and the ways of mankind at large.[69]

Hypochondria—the extreme version of a morbid preoccupation with inner sense—receives much discussion in the *Anthropology*, not only as one type of mental disease, but also as exemplifying in its most pathological form an error that the work as a whole means to prevent or remedy.

Hypochondria and the Power of Abstraction

Man, says Kant, is raised infinitely above all other earthly beings by his ability to represent "I," that is to say, by his possession of a "unity of consciousness through all the changes he can undergo" (VII:127; 9). Such unity of consciousness is inseparable from the threefold power of the understanding (taking this term in a general sense) to attend, to abstract, and to reflect, that is:

> 1) *the power of apprehending* [*Auffassungsvermögen*] (attentio) given representations to produce an intuition; 2) *the power of abstracting* [*Absonderungsvermögen*] (abstractio) what is common to several of these to produce a concept; and 3) *the power of reflection* [*Überlegungsvermögen*] (reflexio) to produce knowledge of an object. (VII:138; [19])

This threefold division, particularly as it applies to the power to abstract, is sufficiently germane to an understanding of the role of hypochondria in Kant's thought to be worth lingering over. As early as his essay *Negative Quantities*, Kant presents abstraction, not merely as an absence or diminution of attention, but as a real mental force in its own right. Abstraction thus requires genuine effort.[70] Notes from the *Nachlaß* echo this emphasis on abstraction and underlie its importance for an understanding of one essential ground of Kant's departure from Leibniz.[71]

Because they failed to distinguish concept and intuition, Leibniz and the Platonic school generally wrongly assumed that intellectual intuitions could be brought from obscurity to distinctness through greater attention alone.

> It was a great failing of the school of Leibniz and Wolff to locate *sensibility* merely in the indistinctness of representations, and *intellectuality* in their distinctness, and thereby posit a merely *formal* (logical) distinction of consciousness rather than a *real* (psychological) one, having to do not merely with the form of thought but also with its content. Their failing was, namely, locating sensibility in a mere lack (of clarity in our partial representations) and so in indistinctness, and the character of intellectual representation [*Verstandesvorstellung*] in distinctness, whereas sensibility is something very positive and an indispensable adjunct to intellectual representation in order to produce knowledge—But Leibniz was properly to blame for this. For, as a dependent of the Platonic school, he accepted inborn, pure intuitions of understanding, called ideas, which in the human mind are now only obscured, and which, when analyzed and illuminated by attention, alone give us knowledge as they are in themselves. (VII:140 n; [21 n])

In fact, however, human cognition also requires the faculty of abstraction, by virtue of which the mind is able to turn its attention away from immediate sensation and thus gain mastery over its representations (*animus sui compos*).[72] Kant's crucial teaching with respect to the duality of human cognition, requiring as it does both sensibility and understanding,[73] is thus inseparable, in his own view, from the recognition that attention is supplemented in man by an opposing power of abstraction.[74]

Kant's claims as to the necessary "real repugnance" between attention and abstraction is linked, in turn, with his analysis of hypochondria. Mental health requires the avoidance, through voluntary efforts of abstraction and attention, of the extremes of involuntary fixation and distraction. Distraction, the mental deficiency of not being fixated, can become confusion (VII:206–7; 77–78). But fixation can (also) lead to insanity, as in the case of hypochondria:

> The hypochondriacal illness consists in this: that certain internal physical sensations do not so much uncover a real evil present in the body as arouse concern, and human nature has the peculiar characteristic (not found in animals) that paying attention to certain *local impressions* makes us feel them more strongly or persis-

tently; on the other hand, when we achieve *abstraction,* either deliberately or through distracting occupations, they subside, and if our abstraction becomes habitual, cease completely. [Kant notes his own success in preventing such sensations from "breaking out into sickness."] (VII:212; [82])

Hypochondria is thus a quintessentially human disease, having its source in man's characteristic ability to focus deliberately on local impressions and thus objectify (that is, make into an object of thought) his own inner sensations. In the process, such points of focus can come to appear to be genuine external objects, as where the discomfort caused by intestinal wind is taken for the representation of a dangerous external event. Indeed, in the case of hypochondriacs, who literally make themselves sick, the imaginary becomes real.[75] The remedy against such sickness (a remedy of which Kant has himself made use) is furnished by the complementary power of abstraction, especially where its use can be made habitual. The true hypochondriac cannot help what he does, and yet, Kant suggests, he is himself responsible for being as he is. Childish, and the plaything of his moods, he refuses to be talked out of his imaginings. "Childish, anxious fear at thoughts of death nourishes this disease," and "He who doesn't look away with manly courage [*männlichem Muthe*] from these thoughts will never become properly happy with life [*wird des Lebens nie recht froh werden*]" (VII:213; [83]).

The ability to "look away," a power to which Kant attributes his own self-won health, is a deliberate or voluntary version of that ability to abstract whose peculiar character previous philosophy, to its detriment, ignored.[76] Kant's refutation of Leibniz (who attributed knowledge to attention alone) and Kant's victory over hypochondria are thus rooted in a common discovery that is itself linked to a distinct — if not idiosyncratic — bodily experience.[77] Without this experience, Kant might never have been brought to attend to what he here calls "a freedom of the power of judgment and self-power [*Eigenmacht*] of the mind" (VII:131; [13]), a faculty that previous philosophers had evidently missed.[78] So construed, Kant's "disposition to hypochondria" becomes not only an affliction but also a gift, a natural version of that self-induced state "bordering on madness" to which scientists sometimes dangerously submit themselves to investigate the nature of the mind and its appearances (VII:217; 86).[79]

Unlike these artificial states, Kant's experiments upon himself are undertaken in the name of health as well as science. He thus enjoys the intellectual benefits of his borderline condition without incurring the guilt of willingly endangering his sanity.

Hypochondria and Insanity

Another aspect of Kant's treatment of hypochondria in the *Anthropology* bears mentioning. Where he had once attempted to classify mental diseases scientifically, he now dismisses the effort as medically useless, since mental diseases are, once they "break out," essentially incurable (VII:214; 84). Kant does however distinguish between insanity (*gestörtes Gemüth*), and hypochondria (*Grillenkraft*) and other forms of mental illness, such as mood swings and melancholia, that "are still not insanity" (VII:202; 73. VII:213; [83]). In the latter case, the patient is still able to recognize that something is wrong, that is, that reason is unable to control itself and thus direct the course of thought by "stemming it" or "pushing it on." In the former case, thought takes an arbitrary course in which the distinction between a subjective and an objective rule entirely disappears (VII:202; 73–74).[80] The seed [*Keim*] of insanity, which is hereditary, develops (like that of reproduction) with puberty. (The incurability of insanity, once it "breaks forth," also calls to mind an analogous irreversibility of racial characteristics.) Whether the milder sort of mental illness might also be hereditary remains unclear, involving as it does the unanswered question of whether Kant's own disposition to hypochondria is innate (that is, a genuine *Keim*) or physically acquired (for example, from leading strings).

Manly courage (*Muth*) is required to turn from and thereby master the thoughts of death associated with hypochondriacal fixation on inner sense. (This remedy is thus, as he observes in another work, generally unavailable to women.) But Kant speaks implicitly of another remedy as well. The hypochondrist wrongly interprets his pain, enhanced by his own fixated attention, as a signal of external harm. This link between pain and harm is severed by the acknowledgement of the role of pain, both in maintaining life (for example, by stimulating "necessary motions") and in enabling us to feel it. "To feel alive, to enjoy ourselves, is the same as to feel ourselves constantly impelled to leave our present state," so that, as Kant adds, "pain is just as continually recurrent." Thus the "anxious oppression" (*ängstliche Beschwerlichkeit*) associated with boredom and the *horror vacuii*. The pressure (*Druck*) to leave the present moment and pass into the following one can grow so great (for example, with voluptuaries) that one decides to end one's life to avoid that "void of sensations," whose terrifying "presentiment of a slow death" is regarded as more painful than a quick breaking by fate of the thread of life (VII:233–34; [101–2]). Accordingly, pleasure, initially associated with whatever prompts one to maintain one's state, and pain, initially associated with whatever prompts one to leave one's state, change places. Although Kant first defines pleasure as the feeling of life being promoted and pain as the feeling of life being hindered, he immediately qualifies these definitions with the "medical" observation that (animal) life is in fact a continual play of the antagonism of one with the other (VII:231; 100). Accordingly, too much pleasure can lead to an early death (as with the bored voluptuaries), while pain, without which "inertia would set in," is necessary to life.[81] Health consists not in the continual promotion of vital force, but in slight inhibitions of that force alternating with slight advancements.

Kant's medical reflections thus have as their immediate affect a suspension of the simple association of pain and harm by which Mendelssohn, Kant's friend and fellow hypochondrist, was himself undone. Life proves to be an inherently dialectical condition in which getting all we want (Kant's formal definition of happiness) is as fatal as getting nothing at all. Life is thus intrinsically paradoxical, health consisting not in the steady enhancement of vital force, but in an unsteady equilibrium between too much and too little.

But the "profoundest and easiest salve (*Besänftigungsmittel*) for every pain is the thought . . . that life as such, considered in terms of our enjoyment . . . has no value of its own, and that it only has value according . . . to the ends to which we direct it." The value of life thus falls within our power, and "he who is anxiously concerned about losing his life will never be happy with it" (VII:239; [107]). These words, which echo his previous exhortation to manly courage, suggest not only his personal stake as a sufferer of chronic pain in such a remedy, but also the extent to which morality itself is ultimately for Kant a life-preserving medicine. The deepest and easiest remedy for pain (whose burden once led Kant to think of taking his own life) lies in the thought of our moral power to give life value. Kant's idea of history, especially as elaborated in the *Critique of Judgment*, provides an analogous remedy against cosmic "hypochondria" concerning the human fate (see VII:326; 187).

Melancholy and Manhood

Part 2 of the *Anthropology* (on what can be "known of the inner from the outer") takes up melancholy as a temperament observable to others (where part 1 took up hypochondria by considering the "inner and the outer," as it were, in tandem).

The four temperaments are natural "characteristics" which Kant distinguishes in terms of *feeling* and *activity,* and the heightening (intensio) or slackening (remissio) of the vital force. A sanguine temperament is generally preferable to the melancholy, inasmuch as change, so long as we are in control of it, strengthens the mind more than does dwelling on impressions. But one of phlegmatic temperament is most fortunate, having about him a deliberativeness that substitutes for wisdom (VII:287; 152–53).

Genuine character, on the other hand, is something that one makes for oneself (VII:294; 159), so that man's chief characteristic is the ability to acquire character (VII:329; 189). Character is also "originality in one's way of thinking" (VII:293; 158), the grounding of which is like a "new epoch" and a kind of "second birth" (*Wiedergeburt*) (VII:294; [159]). Character involves a firmness and steadfastness that cannot be gradually learned but is achieved all at once by (as it were) an explosion resulting from disgust or surfeit (*Überdruβ*) over the wavering state of instinct. Few have attempted this revolution before thirty, and none ground it firmly before forty. Character, whose only outer sign is truthfulness, involves an absolute unity of our principle of conduct, without which our efforts at self-improvement remain fragmentary, one impression vanishing while we are working on another (VII:294–95; 159–60).

Putting this together (and taking special note of the fact that the ages Kant mentions correspond to those at which he wrote the *Universal Natural History* and first encountered Rousseau, respectively), one is once again led to see Kant's moral transformation as the decisive (and definitively manly) overcoming of an earlier erotic ambiguity. This may help to explain why femininity, according to Kant, is difficult to unite with genuine character (VII:308; 171. Cf. II:232; 81).

Kant's treatment of temperament in the *Anthropology* can be usefully contrasted with his early discussion in *Observations on the Feeling of the Beautiful and the Sublime* (1764), in which he gives highest marks to the melancholy temperament, which he associates both with a feeling for the sublime and with a constancy deriving from principles. The melancholic person most easily throws off excessive feelings (whereas the phlegmatic's indifference stems from a lack of finer feeling). The melancholic is also relatively immune to the deceptive charms of the beautiful, and more concerned with satisfaction than with pleasure. In addition, he is resolute, earnest in friendship, and has a strong feeling for "the dignity of man." "He esteems himself, and regards a human being as a creature who deserves respect. He suffers no depraved submissiveness and breathes freedom in a noble breast." But he also judges himself and others strictly, and is not seldom weary (*überdrüssig*) of himself and the world.

In its degeneration, melancholy earnestness inclines toward dejection (*Schwermuth*), devotion toward *Schwärmerei*, and love of freedom toward enthusiasm. Insult and injustice incite vengefulness. Perversity of feeling and lack of enlightened reason lead him toward the adventitious (*das Abenteuerliche*), that is, inspirations and appearances. If his understanding is still weaker, he becomes a fantasist or crank (*Grillenfänger*) (II:220–22; [64–66]). It is not difficult to read in these remarks a strong autobiographical component.

What distinguishes this early encomium to melancholy from his more negative later treatments derives, at least in part, from Kant's assimilation in 1764 (a time when he had read Rousseau but was still much influenced by the British moralists) of aesthetic and moral feeling, an assimilation that the more deeply Rousseauian *Remarks* of 1766 already strives to overcome. Of secondary interest is the relative friendliness that Kant evinces in this early essay (in contrast with the remarks written two years later) toward marriage, and even toward a certain crudely natural sexuality, as well as toward the "engraftment" upon that sexuality of "the finest and most lively inclinations of human nature."

After protesting his unwillingness to analyze such matters in detail, "since in doing so the author always seems to depict his own inclination," Kant nevertheless proceeds (at some length) to contrast (to the former's advantage) a woman of "moving" (though still "charming") sublimity to one of "attractive" beauty, adding:

> One can perhaps according to these concepts understand some-thing of the various effects of the shapes of just such a woman on the taste of men. I do not concern myself with that in these impressions which relates too near to the sexual drive, and may be of a piece with that particular sensual illusion with which every-one's feeling bedecks itself, as beings outside the circle of fine taste; perhaps what M. Buffon speculates is correct, namely that the shape that makes the first impression, at a time when this drive is still new and begins to develop, remains the primitive form [*Ur-bild*] which in the future all female shapes must more or less follow if they are to be able to arouse the fantastical ardor through which a rather course inclination is compelled to choose among the vari-ous objects of a sex. (II:237; [89])

Still, Kant is less concerned with crudeness than with an overrefinement of sexual inclination (which "misses nature's mark"):

> Along with these observations, the following comment [*Anmer-kung*] presents itself entirely naturally. The entirely simple and crude feeling in sexual inclination leads quite directly to nature's great end [*Zwecke der Nature*], and in fulfilling her claims it is fitted to make the person himself happy without digression [*Umsch-weise*]; but because of its great universality it degenerates easily into excess [*Ausschweifung*] and dissoluteness. On the other hand, a very refined taste serves to take away the wildness of a tempestu-ous inclination, and although it limits this to few objects, to make it modest and decorous, such an inclination commonly misses [*verfehlt*] the great final intention [*große Endabsicht*] of nature. As it demands or expects more than nature commonly offers, it sel-dom takes care [*pflegt*] to make the person of such delicate feeling happy. The first disposition becomes uncouth, because it applies to all of a sex, the second overly subtle [*grüberlich*], because it actu-

ally applies to none, but is only occupied with an object that the enamored inclination creates in thought. . . . Hence arises the postponement and finally the full abandonment of the marital bond, or what is perhaps just as bad, a peevish regret after making a choice that does not fulfill the great expectations one has made. (II:238–39; [90–91])

It would seem from the text that Kant was to a certain extent troubled, at least during this period, by his own sexual fastidiousness—a fastidiousness linked, by his own account, to the peculiarities of his own maternal care. The extraordinary worthiness of Kant's mother[82] virtually guaranteed—the common nursery of nature being what it is—his later sexual unhappiness.[83] According to his biographers, Kant at least twice contemplated marriage, each time putting it off until the lady in question was no longer available.[84] In any case, Kant's subsequent discovery of the true ground of moral character, and consequent elevation of the phlegmatic temperament as its partial substitute, seems to have gone hand in hand with a decisive personal rejection, after a period of procrastination, of nature's "great final intention."[85]

On the Power of the Mind to Be Master over Its Morbid Feelings [Krankhafte Gefühle] through Sheer Resolution

In an essay published late in life, Kant takes up hypochondria once again.[86] The context is a general discussion of how to prevent disease and prolong life by wholly mental or "philosophic" means.[87] As we will see, Kant's self-immunization against hypochondria provides him with a general model for mastering disease, a model whose success is not without its ironic consequences. To state those consequences in their simplest form: Kant's philosophic cure-all (Allgemeinesmittel), precisely by preserving life beyond its natural boundaries (as established by the actuarial tables), now threatens him with a mindless, and hence valueless, existence. The rational resolve to overcome nature, if only temporarily, by mastering disease reduces in the end to a natural instinct that is contrary to reason. The contradictory character of nature, which drives simultaneously toward life and death, proves in the end to contaminate reason itself. Kant's final assault against that contamination succeeds, if at all, only by giving vent to it, that is, by expressing, in the very matter of his essay, the oppressive encroachments of his own mental debility.

The essay begins (Socratically enough) with an apology and a joke. Kant's reply to Hufeland comes more than a year after the latter's gift of his own book on prolonging life. Kant, it seems, procrastinates his answer in the same way that he puts off dying (VII:97; 175).[88] (Procrastination, which

Kant once took to be synonymous with living philosophically, has become, un-Socratically, a way of knowing how *not* to die.)

Hufeland had asked Kant what he thought of his moral approach to prolonging life. Kant responds by praising him in the highest terms: Hufeland not only has the skill to provide the means that reason prescribes to realize the ends of medical science, but "is also a legislative member of the body of doctors drawn from pure reason," who "has . . . the wisdom to prescribe what is also *duty* in itself." Hufeland, in other words, grounds medicine, which would otherwise be nothing more than a technical skill, in moral ends prescribed by reason itself. He thus gets past the difficulty, around which the essay otherwise revolves, concerning the value of life. Unless preservation of life is a rational end, medicine itself cannot be a science. Morally practical philosophy thus provides medicine, which would otherwise remain a mere fragmentary means, with a panacea (*Universalmittel*), a cure-all that, though it does not do everything for everyone (*nicht Allen für Alles hilft*), must be included in any prescription (VII:98; 175–77).

This panacea is the dietetic (*Diätetik*) or negative art (*Kunst*) of preventing disease, an art presupposing an "ability that only philosophy or its spirit can give." To this (philosophy or its spirit) pertains the highest dietetic task, contained in the theme from which the essay gets its title: "On the Power of the Human Mind to Be Master over Its Morbid Feelings through Sheer Firm Resolution." Kant's examples confirming the possibility of such a power are apparently derived from the same sort of self-observation that he elsewhere condemns.[89] Kant's excuse here is that he has discovered something worthwhile for everyone and yet which would not occur to others without his drawing their attention to it. The peculiarities of Kant's own inner life, along with his willingness to submit his discoveries to public judgment, make him the exception to the general rule against introspective self-experiment (VII:98; [177]).[90]

That the end of Kant's dietetic — prolonging life — presents a difficulty, however, immediately becomes apparent. What men wish for most ardently may not be worth the wishing. And yet our wish for a long life is unconditioned. Even a sick man who cries out for a death for which reason prompts him to wish is not to be believed: natural instinct wills that he live. Nature thus makes prolongation of life an unconditional end (even where suffering makes continuation of life irrational) (VII:99; 179).[91]

But prolonging life is an unconditional end in another sense as well: to live long is not only an instinct but also a duty in the judgment of reason. What reason on the one hand scorns (life at the price of suffering), it on the other hand demands. What makes living long a duty turns on Kant's peculiar reading of the biblical injunction to honor one's elders "so that one's days on the earth may be long and prosperous."[92] Where the Bible treats a long life as the reward of honoring one's parents, Kant makes living to an advanced age itself an act of merit. The duty of honoring the old is not a function of their frailty or their wisdom (not to mention their status as one's parents).[93] It instead follows from the sheer fact of their succeeding so long in eluding "the most humiliating [*demüthigendsten*] sentence that can be passed on a rational being" ("you are dust [*Erde*] and will return to dust"; Genesis 3:19).

Kant draws a verbal connection, missing in Luther's translation, between the earth on which one lives a long life and the earth to which mankind's mortality requires that he return. The sentence that condemns man in the Bible follows upon Adam's sin. In Kant's version, on the other hand, sin is specifically excluded: "if no shame has stained his life, that man [*Mann*] is to be honored who has lived long and so eluded the most humiliating sentence that can be passed on a rational being." The implication is that, at the very least, the sentence of mortality is unjust, so that to avoid it is a noble act. Or to put it more accurately, the sentence becomes unjust as soon as one finds the courage (*Muth*) to object.[94] Kant's version of the biblical "Kinderpflicht" is, then, indifferent to (human) generation. Mortality, the dispiriting sentence to return to the earth that one already is, can be deferred through a sort of noble procrastination (*Vertagung, procrastinatio*), thereby gaining one an exemplary "immortality, so to speak" (VII:99; 179).[95] (Kant, needless to say, ignores God's mitigating command to "be fruitful and multiply.")

Good health, on the other hand, is a lesser end, it always being uncertain whether it is in fact fulfilled. One can *feel* well and yet be ill, just as one can feel ill and yet be well. The uncertainty of health follows from the fact that while the cause of natural death is always illness, causality itself "cannot be felt."[96] If some (like Kant) are sickly without ever being sick, others feel well while harboring hidden seeds of death (VII:100; 181). Kant's hypochondriacal sickliness thus brings to light the discrepancy between objective fact and subjective feeling on which his critical epistemology also insists. Feeling, though infallible, cannot tell us what is objectively the case (for example, whether we are actually sick or well).[97]

Accordingly, Kant cautions the elderly against nursing or coddling themselves (*sich pflegen*): ease and comfort consume one's forces rather than conserving them, as many believe.[98] It is therefore best to perform as much physical labor as one can. Marriage, on the other hand (though it is, Kant admits, contrary to the state's interests to say so[99]), leads to an early grave.[100]

Instead of marriage, Kant proposes *philosophy*, even if it is in the nature of a game (*Spiel*), both as a means to ward off unpleasant feelings and as a nonconsuming mental stimulant (*Agitation des Gemüths*). Philosophizing even in play arouses "interest," which being independent of "outer accidents [*Zufälligkeiten*]" is "powerful and inward" and thus able to check stopping of the vital force.[101] Moreover, philosophizing in earnest, "whose interest is the whole end of reason (which is an absolute unity), brings with it a feeling of force, that can to a certain degree make good the weaknesses of age, through rational estimation of life's value." Through such *mental* stimulation of his forces, the philosopher (in contrast to the voluptuary) enjoys "a life rejuvenated and prolonged without exhaustion" (VII:102; 185). As we will see, however, this phoenixlike revival is not without unpleasant consequences.

The experiential basis of Kant's dietetic lies in his personal struggle against hypochondria—the "opposite," as he puts it, of the mind's power of self-mastery. Hypochondria is the weakness of "despondently [*muthlos*] abandoning oneself to morbid feelings . . . which lack a determinate object." It is a creature of fictive imagination, and a "sort of madness," at the "ground of which there may well lie pathological matter [*Krankheitstoff*] (wind or constipation [*Blähung oder Verstopfung*])," but which imagination misrepresents (*vorspiegelt*) as an impending evil. The only means of relief—to "be a man" (*sich selbst zu ermannen*) and master one's feeling—is, however, just what is here impossible. Only the tormented one himself could, by "putting the play of his thoughts on a diet," cancel the involuntary representations harassing him. If he could resolve to do this, however, he would not suffer from hypochondria, a "type of insanity [*Wahnsinn*]" that must therefore be regarded as incurable (VII:103–4; [187–89]).

A rational human being establishes no such hypochondria (*statuirt keine solche Hypochondrie*). Instead, when uneasiness develops, threatening to break out in *Grillen*, he asks himself whether that uneasiness has any object. If he finds no object, or one he can do nothing about, "he goes on, with this claim [*Anspruche*] of his inner feeling, about his daily business" and thereby "leaves his oppression [*Beklommenheit*] (which is then merely topical) in its place." The rational sufferer, in other words, leaves his discomfort on the surface, or alternatively, in his intestines.[102]

Thus localized, it can be abstracted from and thereby alienated, if only fictively or hypothetically ("as if" it did not actually concern him [*als ob sie ihm nichts anginge*]). Kant's seminal "discovery," which underlies not only his diet but also his critical epistemology, is this very power over attention. Kant makes what brought this power to *his* attention the subject of the following story.[103] "I have," he says,

> on account of my flat and narrow breast, that leaves little play room for my heart and lungs, a natural disposition to hypochondria, which in early years bordered almost on surfeit [*Überdruß*] of life. But the reflection [*Überlegung*] that the cause of this oppression of the heart [*Herzbeklemmung*] was merely mechanical

and not to be lifted, soon brought it about that I no longer turned myself to it, so that during the times when I felt myself oppressed in the breast, calm and lightness reigned in my head, in such a way that they did not fail even to communicate themselves in society, not according to alternating moods (as is the hypochondriacal custom [*pflegen*]), but intentionally and naturally. And since one becomes happier with life [*des Lebens mehr froh*] through what one does in using life freely than through enjoyment, spiritual labor [*Geistesarbeiten*] can set another sort of promoted vital feeling [*Lebensgefühl*] against checks [*Hemmungen*] which concern [*angehen*] only the body. The oppression has remained with me; for the cause lies in my bodily construction. But I have become master over that oppression's influence on my thoughts and actions, by the turning of my attention [*Abkehrung der Aufmerksamkeit*] from this feeling, as if it did not at all concern me [*als ob es mich gar nicht anginge*]. (VII:104; [189])[104]

Kant's ability to communicate his cheerfulness "intentionally and naturally" (*absichtlich und natürlich*) gives outer support to his otherwise internal semiotics. He is thus able to overcome—at least in part—the potentially fatal discrepancy between *being* healthy and merely *feeling* so.[105]

Kant's technique—avoidance of fixation through a resolute "turning of attention" or regulated distraction—applies to other morbid feelings such as insomnia (from which Kant sometimes suffered), a condition he describes as an unavailing "intention to go asleep."[106] The usual medical counsel—to drive all thoughts from one's head—is ineffective, since new thoughts immediately take their place. Kant's remedy, by way of contrast, is to turn attention toward another object (just as if, "with one's eyes shut, one were to turn them to a different place"). This tactic results in a kind of deliberate disorientation, an intentional confusion by which "one's consciousness of one's bodily (external) location is canceled, and a wholly different order sets in, an involuntary play of imagination that in a healthy condition is called dreaming" (VII:105; [191]). When even this fails (as has happened to Kant) and the brain is seized by a cramplike spasm, strenuous fixation on an arbitrary object (such as the name Cicero, which "has many associated representations") provides the "stoical" remedy.

Through such scrupulous attention to his diet, Kant claims to have overcome the limitations posed by a structural constriction that has weakened, and would otherwise have checked, his vital force.[107] That he elsewhere attributes such constriction to misguided childhood coddling (*pflegen* also means to "nurse") strengthens the Herderian bead on Kant as a man who would be mother to himself (or at least be his own nursery). Though his *Diätetik*[108] is by no means restricted to eating and drinking, the entire regimen is shot through with alimentary allusions. Air, for example, is "drunk" through the nose, and thought is the "food" of the philosopher's mind. Both figuratively and literally, Kant's dietetic plays the quasi-maternal role of controlling — with a documented meticulousness bordering on the exquisite — what goes in and out of him, from food (once a day only) and water (as little as possible); to air ("drunk" through the nose, in order, among other things, to husband laxative saliva); to thought itself (rationed to avoid eating or walking at the same time that one is thinking systematically, a practice said to bring on hypochondria and vertigo) (VII:107–12; 195–205).[109]

But Kant's prescription ends on a sour note. Not all cramplike seizures are susceptible to his universal remedy; indeed, in one crucial case — a seizure of epidemic catarrh accompanied by pressure of the head (*Kopfbedrückung*)[110] — resort to that remedy actually made things worse. As a result he now suffers from a condition that "disorganizes" him for "head work" and will cease only with his death (VII:112–13; [205]).

The dictum that "causality cannot be felt" comes home to roost: the art of controlled distraction that had heretofore protected Kant from outer contingencies has in the end made him the more vulnerable to mental contagion. The upshot is an oppressive spasm that for once cannot be mastered, for it involves his very power to organize his thinking.

Kant succumbs, as he had always feared, to outward contagion; he is done in by a misreading of his own feeling, that is, by bad semiotics. But he also suggests that his error was unavoidable, inasmuch as the oppressive seizure in this case affects the organ of the brain, and with it, the mind's power over attention and abstraction.[111] As a consequence, in this (unique) case, the remedy proves indistinguishable from the affliction. Kant cannot detach himself mentally (as he has always done before) from cramplike feelings because his mind itself is now in spasm. This condition,

> which accompanies and impedes thought, insofar as it is the holding fast of a concept (of the unity of representations connected in consciousness), produces the feeling of a spastic condition of the organ of thought (the brain). This feeling of pressure [*Druck*] does not truly weaken thought and reflection [*Nachdenken*] itself, or the memory of preceding thoughts; but [that] which[112] should secure in discourse (oral or written) the firm coherence of representations in their temporal sequence against distraction, [this] itself causes an involuntary spastic condition of the brain, as an incapacity to preserve the unity of consciousness of successively alternating representations. (VII:113; [207])

That which should secure the mind's coherence instead disrupts it, so that Kant is literally disoriented in thinking — compelled to ask, in media res, "where was I? where did I start/come from?" (*Wovon ging ich aus?*).

The chief symptom of Kant's illness is a deficit not so much of spirit (*Fehler des Geistes*) or memory alone but rather of "spirit's very presence to itself in [making] connection [*der Geistesgegenwart (im Verknüpfen)*]." This symptom goes especially hard with Kant, who as a "worker in the field of philosophy"—and unlike a mathematician—must "hold the object before him in the air" to be able to describe it not only partially but also within "the system of pure reason." "Hence it is not surprising [*verwundern*] that metaphysicians are invalided [*invalid wird*] sooner than scholars in other fields." The very activity—philosophizing systematically—that stimulates the life force "without exhaustion" also leads to premature public senility,[113] a condition Kant likens to a sort of living death:

> This explains how a person can boast of being healthy *for his age* though he must put himself on the sick list with regard to public business. For his *incapacity* [*Unvermögen*] prevents the use and therefore also the abuse and exhaustion of his vital force, and he confesses to living only on as it were a lower rung (as a vegetating being), i.e., being able to eat, walk and sleep, which is healthy for his animal existence. But with regard to his civil existence (in which he is pledged to engage in certain sorts of public business), he is sick, i.e. invalid. Thus this candidate for death does not contradict himself in the least. (VII:114; [209])

In the end, metaphysics proves more dangerously dispiriting than any human bride. If husbands die prematurely, metaphysicians lose what is arguably more valuable than life itself. Better to die at once than to vegetate indefinitely, thanks to a life of self-denial.[114]

The art of prolonging life "thus comes to this: that one is merely suffered [*gedultet*] by the living." The sufferer lives only by making others suffer and is in this respect "guilty" of self-contradiction. In short, the art that has prolonged Kant's life has also, and by the same universal means, removed his reason (moral and otherwise) for living:

> Why am I not willing to give place to the younger world struggling upward, and why, in order to live, do I curtail my accustomed enjoyments of life? Why do I prolong by renunciation an enfeebled life to an unaccustomed length, and confuse by my example the obituary list, which is reckoned on the average of those weaker by nature and their conjectural duration of life; and submit to my resolve all that one once called fate [*Schicksal*] (to which one submitted meekly [*demüthig*] and piously)?—this resolve which, in any case, will hardly be accepted as a universal dietetic rule by which reason exercises immediate healing force, and which will never supplant the therapeutic prescriptions of the pharmacist?" (VII:114; [209])

With these unanswered questions, in which Kant comes close to endorsing abasement (*Demüthigkeit*) over courage (*Muthigkeit*), the essay proper ends. Kant, it seems, cannot justify his resolution to go on. His art is no longer an exercise in reason (if ever it was) but an expression of that natural "life instinct" he earlier characterized — tellingly enough — as "unconditional." Nature, in short, laughs last. As Kant puts it in a late note:

> Illness from strength is properly a contradiction. For illness is inadequate capacity, whether animal or merely vegetative functions are at issue. Health is the lawful conformity [*Gesetzmäßigkeit*] of an organic being, by which it preserves itself in the same form by continually sloughing off its parts and replacing them. This lawfulness of the organic being and the alterations of vital force implies, with respect to organic nature as a whole, that the creature, after it has produced its like, mixes with inorganic matter, and only the species endures. Aging and dying. This is not illness, but the fulfillment of the function of the vital force. (*Reflection* no. 1538 [XV:964–65])[115]

Organic nature is a lawful contradiction, driving the individual to preserve itself even as it works to bring about the latter's dissolution. Through an artful regimen (which includes, but is not limited to, sexual abstinence) the individual may be able to defer the operation of that law, though not necessarily, as Kant's self-experiment ultimately reveals, at a level capable of justifying the effort. The very discovery, in other words, for which Kant here seeks public validation founders on his own invalid and invalidating example.

This invalidity, or inability to perform one's public business, conjoined with animal strength, is what the art of prolonging human life ultimately comes to, making one able to claim without self-contradiction that one is healthy, that is, for one's age, and yet sick. Kant's formula both for hypochondria and his own characteristic state of health — that he is sickly without being sick — thus comes back to haunt him. The self-experiment that Kant conducted early in life has heretofore served to compensate for an otherwise defective will to live. It has done so, first, by furnishing him with a technique to nullify — if not altogether lift — the feeling of oppression that once brought him to the verge of suicide.

Moreover, by drawing Kant's attention both to the duality of human cognition and to the distinction between causality and feeling, his self-experiment has also played a crucial role in a philosophic career culminating in a "system of reason" that places the *value* of life, man's "raison d'être," in his own power. Both directly and indirectly, then, Kant's rational diet, which is superficially a remedy for his defective will to live (or *Überdruß* for nature within him), can also be judged to be instinctual.

III. Conclusion

Kant discussed the workings of his body as freely as other people talk about their clothes. This quirky sense of bodily propriety went hand in hand with Kant's peculiar insight into the idealist illusion that consciousness, by virtue of its sheer inwardness, renders us privy to the truth. Consciousness is no more testimony (as Leibniz and Rousseau differently believed) to the inviolability of the soul than are the feelings of constriction with which wakefulness for Kant was inextricably connected, his *Herzbeklemmung* bringing home to him in an especially forceful way the strange relationship between worldly consciousness and the body with which such consciousness, by virtue of its virtual location, is reciprocally united. To be wakefully aware, for Kant, was to be mindful of a painful constriction associated with the very act of breathing. If we tend, naively, to regard our body as our home — a barrier and protector against the world's assaults — Kant was more inclined than most to recognize the involute duplicity of the body's function. By the same token, his self-cure — a deliberate withdrawal of attention from feelings of constrictive oppression — is also likely to have contributed to his philosophical awakening by alerting him to the peculiar duality of worldly cognition. Not degrees of attention alone (as Leibniz thought), but attention in dynamic tension with an opposing power of abstraction is necessary to explain the discursive, rather than immediately intuitive (or divine), character of human knowledge. The deliberate or willful version of this force of abstraction (which Kant was disposed, for reasons I have suggested, to notice and perfect) brings into the open that preconscious power of thought which, unlike reason's Godlike projection of ideas, reveals a strictly human sort of freedom (see XV:958). Though some have decried Kant's philosophic regimen as a pathological symptom of self-alienation (whatever this might mean), it is, I think, more plausible and useful to regard it as a source (like Newton's fabled encounter with the apple) of philosophic inspiration.

So construed, Kant's *Anlage* to hypochondria becomes a special sort of gift — an instance of that involuntary but benign play (or sport) of nature that is, as Kant elsewhere insists, a condition of genius. As he once related to Herz, the goddesses of birth spun Kant's threads so tender and fine that they are easily affected, but also as extendable as necessary to enable him to author a system that "[would] give the cultivation of talents purposive direction." In his last years, Kant was forced — or forced himself — to put that (grateful) expectation to a final test.

IV. Postscript: The *Opus Postumum* (A Last "Faraggo")

In the last years of Kant's life the link between the final end of nature and the *Absicht* of reason — a link that the *Critique of Judgment* attempted to articulate — came to seem, for a variety of reasons, more problematic. This experience of dissolution both intellectual and personal contributed, I believe, to Kant's renewed efforts to secure a ground against the "vortex," leading him to seek in world authorship the steady and steadying basis he was earlier content to rest upon the practical idea of freedom.[116] Hence the growing tension, in these last works, between the letter of Kant's thought, in which morality remains primary and systematic unity secondary, and the spirit.[117]

Kant devoted the final years of his productive life to a work never completed (and published as [part of] the *Opus postumum*). That work, whose general aim was to provide a "transition" from the metaphysical foundations of science to physics proper, exists in manuscript form as a series of fragmentary notes composed (it is generally believed) between 1796 and 1803, that is, during the period of Kant's physical decline,[118] beginning around the time of the seizure of which he complains in the essay *On the Power of the Mind.*[119]

Generally speaking, these notes advance Kant's aim in two ways: first, by expounding the idea of an all-penetrating fundamental stuff (which he calls ether or caloric) whose internal vibration (*Erschütterung; vibratio*) serves as the basis for the community of all moving forces encounterable in experience;[120] second, by presenting the human subject's consciousness of acting and being acted upon as itself entailing the knowable systemicity of nature. A late series of arguments — the so-called *Selbstsetzungslehre* — attempts to ground an even more inclusive and comprehensive systemicity in man's idea of himself as thinking "being in the world" who is enjoined by duty. By virtue of that mediating idea, God and the world, though "heterogenous" to the greatest possible extent, are brought into a reciprocal unity (or *universum*), and man can claim, with new reason, to be his own author.[121]

By his own account, Kant's motive in seeking to establish a "transition" from the "metaphysical foundation of natural science" to "physics" proper was to close a gap (*Lücke*) in his philosophic system.[122] The source of Kant's concern remains a matter of dispute among scholars.[123] Evidently, the regulative idea of nature's technique, put forward in the *Critique of Judgment* as a guide for the systematic study of nature, no longer seemed to Kant sufficient (if it ever had) to secure the systematic unity of natural science.[124]

One striking difference between the *Critique of Judgment* and the *Opus postumum* is the virtual disappearance in the latter of the "hypo-physical" sense of "nature" (nature as "supersensible substrate") that dominated the *Critique of Judgment.*[125] Accompanying this shift is a new insistence on the "place-holding" status of the thing in itself (which he now calls "a mere thought-thing [*Gedankending*]") (XXII:31–34; [173–75]). Kant, it seems, came to believe that systemicity in science was incompatible with even the qualified "heterogeneity" or "otherness" of nature recognized in the *Critique of Judgment*. It was, after all, precisely our inability in principle to exclude a radical lack of affinity between ourselves and nature that gave rise to the subjective "need" that (according to Kant's earlier work) establishes the a priority of judgment's principles. Instead, Kant now attempts to ground the scientific status of physics in an a priori intuition and/or idea of matter (and its self-specification) in the human subject's primary awareness of itself as worldly agent.

Crucial to this latter project is the inclusion of organized bodies (or living beings) in physics proper, in contrast to the teaching of the *Critique of Judgment*, not to speak of the earlier *Metaphysical Foundations of Natural Science*. Förster has suggested — persuasively, I believe — that it was at least in part Kant's discovery that the ponderability of matter requires a rigid body (that is, a machine, like the lever) for its measurement that enabled him to find a place in physics for living beings (or natural machines), thus allowing him to insert the human subject into nature, not only as observer, but also, and with equal primacy, as actor — a conscious natural machine[126] (observation, as Kant puts it, *and* experiment).[127]

This expansion of the domain of science to include organic beings was also crucially advanced by Kant's appreciation for breakthrough developments in the study of heat and chemistry, developments that he followed with the keenest interest. As Michael Friedman has documented, whereas Kant had doubted in the *Metaphysical Foundations of Natural Science* (1786) that the study of chemistry could ever constitute a science, the discoveries of Antoine Lavoisier and others encouraged in Kant a new optimism that such studies could become more than mere "empirical aggregates," that is, that they might have a genuinely philosophical foundation.[128]

A principle result of these theories was a new account of solids, vapors, and gasses, not as separate elements (as with the traditional division of the elements into air, fire, water, and earth), but as resulting from the combination of a given element with *caloric* (*Wärmstoff*) or "heat-stuff." According to Friedman, Kant's version of the new theories, as expressed in the earlier sections of the *Opus postumum*,

> is a kind of compromise between a mechanical theory of heat and a true caloric fluid theory: heat is not literally a fluid that flows from one body to another while maintaining a constant total quantity, it consists rather in vibrations communicated from one body to another — which vibrations, however, themselves subsist in a special matter or vehicle that can in turn combine chemically with other matters. (P. 292)

This notion of an eternally vibrating ether or caloric that both contains and penetrates all other matter(s) (XXI:380) allows Kant to address in a new way the old problem of "influxus physicus" by supporting the possibility of a complete penetration of one material substance by another without their merger—a fact that may go some way toward explaining Kant's new-found equanimity before the idea of heat-stuff as a *phenomenon substantiatum*. Kant's vibratory revision resists, however, one implication of the caloric theory in its purest form—the ability of the caloric as "menstruum" to dissolve as well as penetrate all other elements.

In Kant's efforts to combine a vibratory account of the ether with a caloric theory of the various states of matter (rigid [solid], liquid, vaporous, gaseous), rigidity proves to be (as Friedman indicates) the problematic case, requiring an ingenious solution (in terms of crystallization and friction). The question then becomes how to establish the necessity of such ether, one line of response looking to the need for physical (not merely mathematical) rigidity, if quantity of matter is to be measured.[129] Since (as Kant hopes it can be shown) such physical rigidity requires caloric for its possibility, the latter acquires a status as fundamental to experience as the concept of the quantity of matter (see, for example, XXII:138, 158; Friedman, pp. 297–98). Indeed, in some later sections Kant attempts to demonstrate that the concept of such an ether can fulfill in a constitutive way what the Ideal of the ens realisimum could accomplish (in the *Critique of Pure Reason*) only regulatively.[130]

Deduction of the representation, or alternatively the idea, of ether as a kind of "realized space" not only subordinates mathematics to metaphysics more completely than previously possible;[131] it also suggests how in the single and decisive case of the subject's knowledge of itself as object, thinking can furnish its own (real) content, if only by virtue of the fact that the mind encounters itself in a self-affective worldly engagement that its idea of the ether allows it to anticipate.[132] Only now does it become possible to regard transcendental philosophy as an act of genuine self-origination.[133]

Withal, Kant's critical modesty with regard to knowledge of organic beings remains intact: knowledge of how life is possible, he continues to insist, exceeds the limits of human understanding; did we not *experience* organized body (in the first instance, through immediate self-awareness) we could not guarantee the existence of anything real corresponding to the concept.[134] To be sure, Kant seems more willing than previously to entertain the possibility of something like a "world soul"; still, even his boldest suggestions to this effect continue to resist hylozoism as literally defined, that is, the attribution of life to matter.[135]

Still, Kant's approach to the study of the organic does undergo important changes. First, he no longer takes his central bearings (as in the "Critique of Teleological Judgment") from the question of how the concept of a natural product is thinkable: the experience of worldly engagement that formerly served as a mere adjunct to that question — an analog that makes possible the thinkability of organisms — now occupies center stage, bringing the concept of organic bodies within the sphere of natural science. (This change may help explain Kant's new willingness to entertain notions of a nonhylozoistic world soul. For he earlier rejected the latter, not on the grounds of its intrinsic absurdity, but because it cannot help explain the thinkability of a natural purpose. In the *Opus postumum,* on the other hand, the experience of worldly engagement, along with the deduction of the a priori idea of ether, opens up the prospect of a more radically complete philosophic systemicity than Kant had earlier thought necessary, or proper, to demand, a wholeness to which morality itself sometimes gives the appearance of serving as a [mere] means. It is not surprising, then, that the notion of a world soul seems more attractive, though even Kant's most positive statements in this direction, it must be said, stop short of unqualified endorsement.)[136]

To put matters another way, the question of how generation is possible (a question which includes that of our own origin) can be set aside in part because Kant discovers a more satisfying way to conceive self-origination than he had earlier thought possible. Man posits himself as self-originating — not only in the sense of being morally entitled to regard himself as noumenally free — but also in a sense that reaches to the (double) root of his status as an embodied rational being. Accordingly, autonomy is no longer limited to the noumenal realm, nor to be regarded principally from the standpoint of morality.[137]

But perhaps the most striking change, albeit one that has gone largely unremarked, is the new centrality accorded by Kant to themes of sickness and health, *medicine finding a place (for the first time) within the science of physics.*[138] How are we to understand this new emphasis?[139] Kant's continuing concern with "self-specification of nature," or the transition from matter (in the singular) to materials or bodies (in the plural), points to one possible answer.[140] The problem of specification, which Kant had never before been able adequately to address, receives new direction from his recognition of the centrality of *one* organized body — that is, our own — to our awareness of matter as a system of forces.[141] Partly on the basis of this clarification, Kant gropes toward a science of nature that proceeds "purposively" from transcendental foundations and thus presupposes "organism" at its very core.

All of this, however, requires that some connection be established between the "dead" or "living" force exhibited by inanimate bodies, and the "vital" force attributed to living organisms, a connection that is accessible — perhaps uniquely — in our own "feelings" of health and sickness, feelings from which one's "objective" engagement with the world cannot finally be divorced.[142] As Kant tentatively puts it:

> the *influence* of the subject *on its own self* makes possible synthetic a priori progress to empirical knowledge, as in the transition to physics . . . *indirectly* . . . ; and that objects of the subject's sensation (e.g., pressure, or traction, or tearing) are displayed *a priori*, as *a priori* moving forces, in a system—e.g. caloric (not merely matter), even *health*, etc. (XXII:465; 131; final emphasis added)

Other passages, indeed, directly link the feeling of health with the perception of heat—a link that reaches toward, without quite arriving at, the underlying experiential unity of physics as a system.

> Whether all human beings do not each instant sicken and continually convalesce, more or less, in as much as they thereby remain alive. The permanent state is death.
>
> The feeling of heat (life) of cold (death). Neither of these are materials [*Stoffe*] but only relations of forces. Air, light, heat; positive and negative electricity. (XXI:118)[143]

If the above suggestion is correct, we are in a better position to understand the peculiar and pervasive role of health and sickness in the *Opus postumum,* ranging from Kant's (relatively early) designation of medicine as the "fourth division of physics"[144] to his very late mention of his own "unendurable" suffering from cardial wind, suffering that seems to raise new questions about the difference between subjective and objective principles.[145]

In their basic import, most of these references identify health and sickness with the principle of life, such that to be an organism is to be implicated in a cycle of health, sickness, death, and (insofar as the species rather than the individual is concerned) regeneration.[146] One discussion is sufficiently representative—and comprehensive—to be worth quoting at length:

> The transition from the metaphysical foundations of natural science to physics as a *doctrinal system* requires principles of *a priori division* according to concepts; in which the question is whether this division, like the (mathematical) *division* of matter, extends to infinity or is atomistic. First division of matter into *materials* and *bodies.* The former are represented as elements, albeit formless; the latter as formative, and the molecules as formed. Bodies whose inner form can be thought as intentional (that is to say, as possible only according to a principle of purpose) are organic; and hence, must also be thought as rigid. They are machines—either *lifeless* (merely vegetative) or living, *animal*—for which indivisible unity of the moving principle (soul) is required; for an aggregate of sub-

stances cannot by itself found a purposive unity. Such a natural characteristic cannot belong *a priori* to the principle of the division; for in itself the possibility of an organic body is not something into which we have insight—we experience organic forces in our own body; and we come, by means of the analogy with them (with a part of their principle), to the concept of vegetation of the same, leaving aside the other part, namely animality. In both cases, the phenomenon of a species that preserves itself in space and time is the continuation of the genus and the exchange of death and life of individuals, an exchange between which sickness is the constant (*beständigen*) transition.—The original moving forces, however, presuppose a certain number of subjective forces effective from the empirical power of representation and determined for perception.

Subjective, indirect appearance (*Erscheinung*)—since the subject itself is an object of empirical knowledge and yet makes itself, at the same time, an object of experience in as much as, in effecting itself, it is the *phenomenon* of a phenomenon. (XXII:373; [118–19])[147]

Sickness as the transition between death and life marks the passage from one individual to another—a fungibility that Kant seems more willing to accept as a (necessary) aspect of the world's organization.[148] Indeed, Kant goes so far as to represent the bringing forth of new species (one from another) as a positive good, suggesting that the earth itself can be regarded as developing from a kind of seed (*Keim*) (XXII:241).[149]

Withal, there is one natural articulation to whose mysteriousness Kant repeatedly defers—that involving sexual reproduction. Why two sexes should be necessary to generation throughout the animal kingdom (and beyond) is a perplexity, it seems, beyond human solving, a perplexity marked by its intimate connection with the fatal exchange of individuals.[150] If the latter is more tolerable to Kant than previously, it is perhaps because sickness itself—as transition between death and life—has been inserted into the heart of transcendental philosophy.[151]

The *Opus postumum* culminates in what Kant entitles "Transcendental Philosophy's Highest Standpoint: God, the World, and the Thinking Being in the World (Man)," a standpoint from which man (or his "spirit") looks out, a veritable *cosmotheoros* (XXI:31–32; 235. See also XXI:41; 240). One recalls, however, an earlier passage, which speaks of "vertigo from a high standpoint" along with "seasickness" and "nostalgia" (*Heimweh*). The passage continues with a brief discussion of what sort of happiness is "*enviable*," and then asks "Whether one could wish to live forever, given all the changes to which fate must by itself lead." Kant concludes as follows:

On the male and the female in the entirety of nature up to the mosses. Milton

One part should not continue (*fortwähren*) without the other of its species. (XXI:348–49)

One wonders whether in the end Kant put that thought behind him.

11 Conclusion and Epilogue

The highest standpoint of transcendental philosophy is that
which unites God and the world synthetically, under one
principle, nature and freedom
Kant, Opus postumum (XXI:23)

Seeing is repulsive — like touch.
Kant, Opus postumum (XXI:24)

From the time of his earliest work, Kant's thought differs from that of his
contemporaries by virtue of his peculiar understanding of the requirements
of worldly consciousness. To opt, with Leibniz, for pure, monadic inwardness, with its putative assurances of the soul's immortality, is to relinquish the claim to be able to distinguish fact from fantasy — to opt, in other
words, for madness. Kant's peculiar insight and/or anxiety in this regard —
an insight that anticipates his later, critical insistence on the dependence of
the transcendental unity of consciousness on outer sense — has its personal
correlative in a heightened awareness of inward bodily constriction that
Kant associated with his own (tendency toward) hypochondria. By virtue
of this feeling, which externalizes that which is, in bodily terms at least,
most intimate, the relation between mind and body comes to Kant's attention as especially strange.

By virtue of a related insight, Kant is able to provide what his earliest
work describes as the first clarification (*Erklärung*) of the world, which
reconciles the substantial "inwardness" of individual substances à la Leibniz with the reality of their interaction à la Newton. The upshot is a model
of worldhood as reciprocal community, in which each member inwardly
determines and is determined by the others — others with which it (therefore) stands in a relation of external, or spatial, interconnection. But Kant
cannot secure the possibility of such community without recourse to God,
who grasps as an immediate totality what we can only know sequentially
and partially. To know the world as it is present to the Creator would be
to know things in their inwardness (as pure ideas) and thus escape the
round of external reciprocal dependence by which finite (human) knowledge is fatally burdened. Divine understanding thus provides the standard

against which finite intellection is measured and in relation to which the latter inevitably falls short. Still, the human mind strives, with greater or lesser impetus, to rise to that understanding, both metaphysically and historically, and in that striving registers its own (upward) nobility.

This spirit of nobility, however, is brought down by the following apparently insuperable dilemma. To the extent that we ourselves remain tied to the exchanges of matter by which spatiotemporal community is defined, the object of our striving (knowledge of the universe) is more repulsive than attractive. To the extent, on the other hand, that we seek to transcend that connection, we lose our hold on the only dependable touchstone of real knowledge available to us, and philosophy threatens to dissolve into fiction and/or fanaticism. The problem is all the more acute, given the abysmally maternal figuration of these spatiotemporal exchanges, out of which composite bodies (like our own) continually arise and perish. Philosophy, for Kant at this stage, is an assertion of spiritual virility — an alternative to a physical potency whose vertiginous entanglement in nature's exchanges renders it (paradoxically) unmanly. Kant's exercise in spiritual uplift threatens, however (for reasons elaborated above), to be self-defeating, a fact registered in the dizzying "unsteadiness" of the argument of Kant's *Universal Natural History*. Kant's effort to free himself from the attractions of the abyss is itself vertiginous.

Kant's reading of Rousseau in the early 1760s opened a way out of this impasse, above all by emphatically linking morality and manhood. In so doing, Rousseau provides Kant with the basis for a new, radically egalitarian (if nonfeminist) conception of nobility, as well as a new, morally real idea of spiritual community. The lack of a determining end that Kant formerly treated as man's special problem, he now reckons as the very basis of human dignity. Freedom is no longer our monstrous undoing as a species, but our glory. And morality stands ready to replace metaphysics (with its wavering erotics) as the vehicle of human nobility.

Rousseau contributes in several ways to Kant's discovery of a thread out of the labyrinth of man's own (monstrous) duality. First, Rousseau's model of the general will gives Kant the clue he needs to reconceive spiritual manhood on a moral, rather than metaphysical basis. Second, Rousseau's autoerotic treatment of the power of the human mind to love its own constructions lays a foundation for Kant's new conception of ideas as self-projected "ends of reason" ("totality" in theory, the "highest good" in practice). Stymied in its efforts theoretically to overcome the disorderly dualism of human consciousness, the mind discovers in its own systematic need a way to rectify itself without ceasing to extend itself. Third, Rousseau's treatment of the relation between the sexes (especially in *Emile*) sets the stage for Kant's later systematic reliance on the feminine in its various guises as a sort of "missing joint," defining by its very lack the juncture of the material and the intellectual.

Rousseau convinces Kant that the primary end of reason lies not in knowing nature (a task that is, as Kant already suspected or feared, beyond our powers) but in striving morally to reform and/or transcend it. Such "zetetic" suspension of a heretofore compelling desire to know calls, however, for a special sort of spiritual "cathartic." Kant finds the occasion for such catharsis in the work of Swedenborg, whose unwitting parody of Kant's own metaphysical leanings proves, in more ways than one, therapeutic. In the course of the exercise (*Dreams of a Spirit Seer*), with its witty identifications of spirit and wind, the pretensions of rational psychology (or pneumatololgy) are permanently deflated. The effect of Kant's farce is to destroy the lingering illusion that inner sense is privy to the substantial.

In distinguishing his own moral idea from Swedenborg's visions, Kant also takes a decisive step in the direction of his later transcendental aesthetics, with its insistence on the a priori spatiotemporality of experience. The moral law furnishes the only nontemporal, nonspatial world form that is humanly conceivable. Any claim to know the immaterial world theoretically (as opposed to thinking it practically) violates the fundamental conditions of wakefulness and/or sanity.

This redirection of metaphysical interest sets the stage for transcendental idealism by removing one motive for attempting to explain theoretically how commerce among substances is possible. Having put that goal aside, Kant is free to pursue a more satisfying approach to the question of how experience is possible, an answer that substitutes for a (divinely grounded) community of substances-in-themselves, a community (grounded in the human mind) of substances as appearances. At the same time, the destabilizing oscillation between stasis and expansion that characterized his earlier cosmologies finds dynamic resolution in Kant's critical distinction between the constitutive concept of community and the regulative principle of totality.

The character of intelligible community, morally understood, is laid out in detail in the *Groundwork of the Metaphysics of Morals*. The possibility of the world as a reciprocal community of substances (understood as things in themselves rather than appearances) can finally be grasped, albeit, only practically, as the self-subsistence of the individual is reconciled with its participation in a larger unity. This moral solution of the central problem of Kant's early thought paves the way, as I suggest, for Hegel's and Marx's later recognitive and monetary logics. That Kant does not, like they, collapse the metaphysical into the social and/or economic is, in part, a tribute (or so I claim) to his own brand of bodily wisdom.

The lingering problem of our definition or *Bestimmung* as a species Kant takes up, tentatively, in his *Idea for a Universal History,* and with greater assurance in the *Critique of Judgment*. What separates the two works, above all, is Kant's definitive abandonment, in the *Critique of Practical Reason*, of his earlier attempts to derive moral freedom from the spontaneity of reason. This radicalizing of his treatment of freedom makes possible a new, albeit subtle, rapprochement with nature. Hereafter, nature is no longer figured as a stepmother (as if freedom implied that we somehow give birth to ourselves), but as a veiled goddess. The for Kant peculiar horror of a self-subsistent (or lawless) nature is hereafter answered by "reflective" judgment and other strategies of indirection. By virtue of such strategies, man himself replaces the divine father—if only for purposes of satisfying a subjective "need" of reason—as the informing final cause of nature. Man's spiritual and moral paralysis thereby forestalled, Kant finds a way at last of "constantly rising." By thematizing the contingency of generation—a contingency that had left a gap in the articulation of Kant's system as a whole—Kant finds a way to bring his system, as he insists, to its completion.

In his final years, and in the context of his own declining powers, this conclusion underwent a partial reassessment, precipitated in part by discoveries in chemistry, meteorology, and medicine that suggest new ways of conceiving organized matter. In the wake of that reassessment, Kant comes closest to answering the question that initiated his career—how to comprehend the whole of which one is a part—and in so doing seems to find new reason to exist.

As early as his *Thoughts on the True Estimation of Living Forces* and *Physical Monadology,* Kant's argument takes inspiration from his own sense of bodily constriction. As a consequence, Leibniz's threefold correlation of body, force, and substance becomes, for Kant, a twofold correlation between outer appearance (the external relations of substances) and inner existence. The reality of interaction is explained by a model in which outer expansion and contraction correlates with inner changes in intensity—a model that anticipates, in its peculiar articulation of the relation between inwardness and outwardness, Kant's later ruminations on the phenomenology of hypochondria. So considered, these early works are youthful exercises in what he later calls "philosophic medicine," transforming his own feeling of oppression into a worldly testimony that does not threaten (appearances aside) the soul's inner integrity.

Kant associated that feeling of oppression, in the first instance, with the womb that bore him. (Since women also are of woman born, Kant's misogyny, as the above chapters have attempted to suggest, ought not be criticized as simply sexist.) Matter for Kant is a matrix bearable to imagine only as informed by something other than itself, be it the divine intellect or, after Kant gives up the attempt to theoretically rejoin his heavenly father, man's own understanding. Even after his critical awakening, mother nature in both benign and malignant guises (veiled goddess and Medusa head) remains for Kant a figure of peculiar enthrallment; hence his novel identification of enlightenment, not with the sun (ambiguously "feminine" for Kant) but with freedom, tellingly figured as the command or dare (*sapere aude!*) to sever nature's leading strings. Only near the end of his life did Kant begin to take a more positive and, at the same time, assertive view of matter and its self-organizing possibilities. In the face of new scientific discoveries, and of debilitating infirmities that defied Kant's own hard-won and previously successful personal regimen, barriers on which he had previously insisted between the mental and the physical began to fall. The result was not the devastating "penetration" against which he had so vigilantly guarded, but, ironically enough, an autarky more absolute than he had previously thought possible to achieve. Man comes to *"make himself,* so to speak"—the latter qualification indicating, however, both the essential difference between a creative God and a morally grounded, human "cosmotheoros," and the limits to which the unity of nature and reason can ultimately be pushed. Kant never ceased to insist on the "absurdity" of intelligent matter (however much that formula might seem defining of humanity)—a career-spanning sticking point that contributes to the characteristic rigor of his final work (along with its characteristic distinctness from a romanticism it frequently approaches).

In so characterizing Kant's thought I have no wish to diminish it. By his own reckoning, Kant's idiosyncrasies were a sort of (natural) gift, drawing his attention to that which the rest of us would tend, without his aid, to miss. What Kant noticed was the "strangeness"—bordering on the vertiginous—of the self as modernly conceived, a self somehow with matter but not of it. Where Plato identified philosophy with the higher eros of reason, ruling principle of the soul, Kant joined philosophy with manly courage—modern counterpart to that part of the soul which Plato called spiritedness or *thymos*. The result was a lifelong pursuit of permanent (spiritual and moral) "erectness": Kant's virilized "spirit" is both *thymos* and *eros*.

It is, moreover, by no means clear that later efforts to explain, or explain away, the problems to which Kant's lifework addresses itself have met with better theoretical and practical success. Kant's formulation of the philosophic task set the agenda for later thinkers such as Hegel and Heidegger, who took up his "sapere aude" without sharing fully in its moderating motivation. The sense of limitation, both physical and moral, that stopped Kant from embarking on their path makes him invaluable, I believe, as a modern guide to decent politics. Kant's juridical sublimation of the totalitarian imperative yields a communitarian formula for reconciling individuality and unity, a formula that is, from a liberal perspective, especially appealing. The Kantian individual conceives itself neither as a discrete atom nor as the creature of society but as moral substance that sustains itself in and only in reciprocal community. Mutuality, on such a view, is the flip side of what Emerson calls self-reliance, that virtue whose one-sided application in the name of "individualism" is as untenable, in the final analysis, as the single-minded (and illiberal) yearning for political unity.

Kant's attachment to liberal principles, then, does not rest on the usual conventional conceits, but follows, at least where *knowledge* of the self is concerned, upon a skepticism that is almost Nietzschean in its probity. Kant is in this respect the model for a number of recent thinkers who have tried (with less success) to reconcile liberal democracy with "postmodern" irony.

At the same time, it remains crucial from a Kantian perspective that self-respect not be reduced, in the Hegelian fashion, to mutual recognition (nor spirit to history, or humanity temporally collectivized). Without the moral law, and the transcendental freedom of the individual that it invokes, Kant's "ennobling of democracy" (to borrow Thomas Pangle's phrase) — the spiritual erection of humanity on the basis of its own idea — is unsupportable. Mutuality of respect is thus inseparable from that noumenal world, or kingdom of ends, participation in which is part and parcel of Kant's credo. Kant has shown, better than anyone else, what community without domination genuinely requires. That the "daring progeny of Iabetus" are also "children of the earth" goes, as is said, with the territory. Kant's lifelong effort to do justice to this dual provenance is not only exemplary, but also — and in a less democratic and more ancient sense — heroic.

Coda

Questions posed by Kant's own embodiment survived him in peculiar ways. Shortly after Kant's death in February of 1804, Professor W. G. Kelch of the University of Königsberg published a brief study entitled *Immanuel Kants Schädel: Ein Beytrag zu Galls Hirn- und Schädellehre* (On Kant's skull: a contribution to Gall's brain and skull science).[1] Then nearing the apex of its popularity, Gall's "craniology" aimed, in Kelch's words, at "spying out the human interior" through observation of external "magnitudes of genius." Kelch hoped that his results, based on personal examination of Kant's uncremated remains, would "make no small contribution" to a subsequent biography of Kant, or at the very least, help to "confirm" one. Kelch's work was translated and published in Holland in the same year, with an introduction by the well-known anatomist and specimen collector G. Vrolik.

Nearly eighty years later, Kant's skull was reexamined: in June of 1880, two professors of the medical faculty took advantage of restorative work being conducted on Kant's grave site to exhume his remains for anatomical study. (A painting commemorating the event, carried out in the presence of various dignitaries, was for many years in the possession of the Prussian Society of Antiquities.) Measuring the skull according to the methods of Paul Broca, the famous and recently deceased anatomist and anthropologist, the researchers concluded that it had harbored a brain significantly larger than that of the "average German male." Their report, accompanied by five carefully composed photographs, was ceremoniously deposited in the Archive for Anthropology, according to an edition of both works published in Königsberg in 1924.

It is easy to smile at Kelch's little book, which claims to locate Kant's "organs" of (among other things) "philosophic speculation," "religion or theosophy," and "love of truth." The second report, with its meticulous attention to issues of comparative racial anatomy, evinces the entrenched preoccupations of a later scientific age, preoccupations that are today more likely to inspire foreboding than condescension.

One hardly knows what Kant, who famously doubted that psychology could ever be a science, but who also reviewed Soemmering sympathetically, would have made of these investigations.[2]

Kant's burial site, unlike most of Königsberg/Kaliningrad, survived World War II and its immediate aftermath.[3] Newlyweds nowadays go directly to his tomb, rather than to Marx's statue, to pose for photographs.

Notes

Chapter Two

1. *Gedanken von der wahren Schätzung der lebendigen Kräfte und Beurtheilung der Beweise, deren sich Herr von Leibniz und andere Mechaniker in dieser Streitsache bedient haben, nebst einigen vorhergehenden Betrachtungen, welche die Kraft der Körper überhaupt betreffen.* (Thoughts on the true estimation of living forces and criticism of the proofs that Herr von Leibniz and other mechanists have used in this controversy, preceded by a few reflections concerning the force of bodies in general). Publication extended over three years, during which time Kant apparently continued to revise the manuscript.

2. The historical dispute over living force centered on the question of what is "conserved" when bodies interact. Descartes, who defined body as extension and motion as a change in position, argued that *motion* is conserved. The *measure* of this motion is mass multiplied by velocity (mv), a quantity that he understood to be preserved, not only in the case of individual events (for example, where two objects collide), but also for nature as a whole. Leibniz disputed this thesis by comparing the quantity of force exhibited by a four-pound ball falling one foot with that of a one-pound ball falling four feet. Mechanically speaking, an equal quantity of force is needed to raise a one-pound object four feet and a four-pound object one foot. And in each case the falling ball has enough force, discounting friction, to raise itself back to its original height. And yet according to Galileo's principles the ball falling four feet achieves twice the velocity of the ball falling one foot. The quantity of motion ($1 \times 2v$) exhibited by the one-pound ball is thus half that exhibited by the four-pound ball ($4 \times 1v$). Their respective quantities of moving force, on the other hand, are the same. Generalizing from this example, Leibniz argued that what is conserved in nature is not quantity of motion (mv) but quantity of force (mv^2). D'Alembert is generally credited with having provided the definitive solution — in effect, by showing the dispute to be, for all practical purposes, a merely verbal one. See Leibniz, *Essay on Dynamics*, prop. 7, translated in P. Costabel, *Leibniz and Dynamics*, trans. R. E. W. Maddison. For a general account of the dispute, see Irving I. Polonoff, *Force, Cosmos, Monads and Other Themes of Kant's Early Thought*, pp. 6–38.

3. See Ernst Cassirer, *Kant's Life and Thought*, trans. James Haden, p. 30. Jill Vance Buroker argues that D'Alembert's essay was not available to Kant until the 1750s, but that Kant may have been aware of the Boscovich solution, which appeared in 1745 and turned on the distinction between force applied during a given time and force applied through a given distance. See Buroker, *Space and Incongruence: The Origin of Kant's Idealism*, p. 39; and Carolyn Iltis, "D'Alembert and the *Vis Viva* Controversy," *Studies in the History and Philosophy of Science* 1: 135–44.

4. Polonoff, *Force*, p. 39.

5. Among its other weaknesses, Kant's work has a stylistic infelicity to which the peculiar circumstances of its publication may have contributed (see note 1 above). The few extensive discussions of *Living Forces* include Erich Adickes, *Kant als Naturforscher*, vol. 1, pp. 65–144; Jules Vuillemin, *Physique et métaphysique kantiennes*, pp. 232–54; Giorgio Tonelli, *Elementi metodologici e metafisici in Kant dal 1745 al 1768*, pp. 1–41; Michael Friedman, *Kant and the Exact Sciences*, pp. 1–34; and Polonoff, *Force*, pp. 39–62. The emphasis of Adickes, and to a lesser extent, Polonoff and Vuillemin, is largely on the scientific defects of Kant's views in comparison with the achievements of his contemporaries. Vuillemin is especially concerned with ways in which Kant's early views, despite their failings, anticipate his later dynamics.

On the general import of *Living Forces* for Kant's early thought, see also Alison Laywine, *Kant's Early Metaphysics and the Origins of the Critical Philosophy*. Regrettably, Laywine's original and insightful treatment of *Living Forces* (and other metaphysical works of Kant's early period) came to my attention while the present study was already in press.

6. The motto of the work is, as Cassirer notes, the following epigram from Seneca: "There is nothing more important than that we should not follow like sheep the herd that has gone before, going not where we should go but where the herd goes." Kant continues a few pages later with the following remarks:

> I am of the opinion [*Ich stehe in der Einbildung*] that it is sometimes useful to place a certain noble trust in one's own forces. Such confidence vivifies [*belebt*] all our exertions [*Bemühungen*] and imparts to them a certain impetus [*Schwung*] that is very favorable to the search for truth. If one is in condition to persuade oneself that one dares somewhat still to trust one's own view [*Betrachtung*], and that it might even be possible to catch a Master Leibniz in error, then one makes every effort [*so wendet man alles an*] to verify one's supposition [*Vermuthung*]. Even after one has gone astray a thousand times, the gain thereby accruing to knowledge of truth will still be much more considerable [*erheblicher*] than if one had only kept to the beaten path.
>
> Here I take my stand. [*Hierauf gründe ich mich.*] I have already indicated the road that I will take. I shall embark on my course [*Lauf*], and nothing shall hinder me from proceeding. (I:10)

Despite its Lutherian resonance ("Here I take my stand"), the spirit of the passage is less pious than impetuous.

7. Leibniz's words, quoted by Kant with special emphasis, are that "there is something besides extension in corporeal things and, indeed, prior to extension." Leibniz goes on to identify that something with "a natural force everywhere implanted by the Author of nature — a force that does not consist merely in a simple faculty such as that with which the Scholastics seem to have contented themselves but which is provided besides with a striving or effort [*conatus seu nisus*] which has its full effect unless impeded by a contrary striving." This force, Leibniz, insists, "sometimes appears to the senses" and "is to be understood, on rational grounds, as present everywhere in matter, even where it does not appear to sense." Such force "constitutes the inmost nature of the body, since it is the character of substance to

act, and extension means only the continuation or the diffusion of a striving and counterstriving already presupposed by it." It is thus "beside the point" that all corporeal action arises from motion, since motion, like time, taken in an exact sense "never exists," a whole not existing "if it has no coexisting parts." Leibniz concludes that "there is nothing real in motion itself except that momentaneous state which must consist of a force striving toward change. Whatever there is in corporeal nature besides the object of geometry, or extension, must be reduced to this force." Leibniz presents his teaching as an improved version of "the Peripatetic forms or entelechies" (*Specimen dynamicum*, in Leibniz, *Philosophical Papers and Letters*, trans. Leroy E. Loemker, pp. 712–13).

8. Activity is not striving (as Leibniz claimed) but the telos or end of striving. To act is not to *strive* to oppose an obstacle, but to do so *in fact* — not by changing an obstacle's position, that is, by moving it (for this would make action parasitic on motion), but by changing its "inner state" (I:18). As Michael Friedman notes (*Kant and the Exact Sciences*, p. 5 n), Kant's notion of active force has the distinct virtue of allowing for external influence upon the soul without supposing "that the soul is in motion or that bodies act on the soul by producing motions," suppositions, one could add, that give way in Kant's account by recourse to pressure, understood as the experience of acting and being acted upon, that is, as testimony to the immediate presence to the soul of something external.

9. See, in this regard, Friedman, *Kant and the Exact Sciences*. Friedman's excellent study traces Kant's lifelong effort to reconcile a mathematically based conception of space with a metaphysically based conception of substance. My own study aims to help explain why Kant found this effort, to which he repeatedly returned in the face of new difficulties, so compelling.

10. Kant's account of knowledge is reminiscent of certain Stoic theories with which he may well have been familiar. According to Chrysippus, for example, knowledge involves an inner "modification of the soul" brought about by pneumatic currents functioning as sensory "messengers" from the external world. As one fragment puts it, "A presentation [*phantasia*] is a modification coming about in the soul and revealing itself also as that which has caused it" (Hans von Arnim, *Stoicorum veterum fragmenta*, vol. 2, p. 54, quoted in Josiah B. Gould, *The Philosophy of Chrysippus*, p. 55). While the familiar modern dichotomy between inner mind and outer world is often attributed to Descartes, it has ample precedent in Stoic thought (cf. Richard Rorty's useful corrective in *The Mirror of Nature*, p. 51 n). As we will see below, there are other interesting similarities between Kant's argument in *Living Forces* and traditional Stoic doctrine.

11. Alexander Gottlieb Baumgarten may be the immediate source of this emphasis. As Gordon Treach notes, possibility for Baumgarten is a function not only of logical consistency but also of what he calls "representability." See *Metaphysica* (1739), sec. 8 (in Kant, *Erläuterungen zu A. G. Baumgartens Metaphysica* [XVII:24]). See also the translator's introduction in Kant, *The One Possible Basis for a Demonstration of the Existence of God*, trans. Gordon Treash, p. 35 n.

12. On the controversy surrounding the doctrine of physical influence, see Tonelli, *Elementi*, p. 14 ff. Kant's teacher, Martin Knutzen, attempting to conciliate the two sides of the controversy, attributed the changes in a substance to a force internal to the substance itself, but only insofar as it is "stimulated" by an external

influence. As Tonelli notes, Kant's position cannot be fully identified with any of his predecessors. As compared to Knutzen, Kant is closer to the preestablished harmony school inasmuch as he gives pressure priority over motion; at the same time he is also closer to the realists in as much as, in Tonelli's words, he does not reduce influence to a mere stimulus, whose function consists in "arousing" a force internal to the patient substance (p. 14). In its insistence *both* on the priority of pressure over motion *and* on the reality of external influence, Kant's theory is unique. See also Benno Erdmann, *Martin Knutzen und seine Zeit*. According to Erdmann (p. 143), Knutzen is the "sharp-sighted author" whose defense of "physical influence" Kant praises (I:21). Kant also follows Knutzen in resorting to the theory of physical influence to explain not only the relation between body and soul but also the union (*Zusammenhang*) of finite substances in general (Erdmann, p. 85). In so doing (says Erdmann), Knutzen moves beyond a superficial Wolffian dualism of body and soul toward a new kind of spiritual monism. According to Kant, Knutzen is hindered in securing the "complete triumph" of physical influence over preestablished harmony by his failure to "direct attention" to the priority of pressure over motion (I:20–21).

13. On Kant's concern with pressure in a more personal context, see chapter 10 below. Kant claimed to have a heightened sensitivity to certain pressures originating within his own body. On the experience of pressure as the "instinctive" source of modern physics, see also Ernst Mach, *The Science of Mechanics*, 2d ed, trans. Thomas J. McCormack. According to Mach, "the original incitation that prompted the enunciation of the principle [of action and reaction]" was unquestionably "of a purely instinctive nature." We know that we do not experience any resistance from a body until we seek to set it in motion. "The more swiftly we endeavor to hurl a heavy stone from us, the more our body is forced back by it. Pressure and counter-pressure go hand in hand." Mach speaks of "many instinctive perceptions" in the domain of statics involving "the equality of pressure and counter-pressure" (pp. 199–200). Kant's account of pressure differs from that of Mach in a subtle but crucial respect: the radical priority of pressure to motion.

14. Kant notes in the *Critique of Pure Reason* that for the (Latin) terms *definition*, *explanation*, *explication*, and *declaration*, German has only the one word: *Erklärung* (A/730 = B/758).

15. On scholastic discussions of the plurality of worlds, see Pierre Duhem, *Medieval Cosmology: Theories of Infinity, Place, Time, Void, and the Plurality of Worlds*, ed. and trans. Roger Ariew. As Duhem notes, Aristotle in *De caelo* raises the question of a plurality of worlds and answers it in the negative. He justifies his answer on the basis of two principles: first, that beings seek their natural place; and second, that another world would have to have the same substantial form (idea) as ours, for otherwise it would not be another "world" in any but a merely verbal sense. It follows that the elements of the second world, having the same substantial form as the first world, would seek the same natural place. Thus every element would seek to be in two places at once, which is an absurdity (Duhem, pp. 431–32). It is a necessary premise of Aristotle's argument that distance not effect this tendency. His argument, in other words, assumes that differences in the motions of simple bodies arise wholly from differences in their essential forms, and not from differences

stemming from relation — that is, that matters of proximity or remoteness "do not reach the substance" (Duhem, p. 437).

Aristotle also denies that anything bodily or changeable can exist beyond or outside the outer circle of the cosmos. Everything outside this circle occupies no place and, since time does not corrupt it, is eternal. For without change, there is no passage from possibility to actuality. Without movement, "time, the measure of movement, disappears." In so arguing, Aristotle both affirms the uniqueness of the earth and rejects the argument of the Orphic Hymns (later reaffirmed by Copernicus) according to which each star is its own world, containing both earth and water. Finally, weight, for Aristotle, is not the effect of an attraction emanating from the center of the world but an effect stemming from the substantial nature of the weighty body itself.

Prior to the condemnations of 1277, scholastic commentators recognized the challenge posed to Aristotle's position on the plurality of worlds by the Christian doctrine of divine omnipotence. Nevertheless, they generally supported Aristotle's position (see, for example, Aquinas, *Expositio . . . de caelo et mundo,* bk. 1, lect. 19, quoted in Duhem, pp. 448–49). After 1277, counterarguments based on divine omnipotence increasingly gained favor. Affirming the possibility of a plurality of worlds as a necessary consequence of the omnipotence of God's will, thinkers such as Oresme challenged the Aristotelian conception of natural place and returned instead to something like the theory of motion expounded in Plato's *Timaeus* (according to which natural movement is not the moment toward or away from the center of the earth, depending on whether a body is heavy or light, but rather "the movement by which a body attempts to rejoin the set of elements from which it was previously violently forced" [Duhem, p. 477]) — a theory compatible, as Aristotle's was not, with, among other things, a nonstationary or diurnally rotating earth.

Duhem's exposition is colored by his attempt to establish the theological roots of modern science and consequent downplaying of the degree to which that science represents a radical break with preceding thought. Nevertheless, he convincingly establishes the importance to medieval theology of the argument concerning the plurality of worlds and the at least partial continuity of such discourse with metaphysical and scientific controversies of the seventeenth and early eighteenth century. See also Hans Blumenberg, who links the common agreement of both nominalism and epicureanism as to the possibility of a plurality of worlds with their common opposition to the "metaphysical idea of the cosmos" (*The Legitimacy of the Modern Age,* trans. Robert M. Wallace, p. 156).

16. Kant's argument here concerning multiple worlds has the same effect in this respect as his later argument, partly inspired by Crusius, that God, as himself the source of all possibility, is not limited by possibility as a condition prior to his will. See chapter 3 below.

17. Leibniz, *Philosophical Papers,* p. 604.

18. See Leibniz's *New Essays on Human Understanding,* bk. 4, chap. 2, no. 14. *New Essays,* not published until 1765, was read by Kant around 1769. Kant was, however, familiar with a similar argument advanced by Wolff (see Wolff, *Ontologia,* para. 493; discussed in Lewis White Beck, *Early German Philosophy,* p. 266).

19. "Thus by no argument can it be demonstrated absolutely that bodies exist, nor is there anything to prevent certain well-ordered dreams from being the objects of our mind, which we judge to be true and which, because of their accord with each other, are equivalent *so far as practice is concerned* [emphasis added]. Nor is the argument which is popularly offered, that this makes God a deceiver, of great importance. . . . For what if our nature happened to be incapable of real phenomena? Then indeed God ought not so much to be blamed as thanked, for, since these phenomena could not be real, God would, by causing them at least to be in agreement, be providing us with something equally as valuable in all the practice of life" (Leibniz, *Philosophical Papers,* pp. 604–5).

20. Leibniz, "Letter to Arnauld" (1686), in *The Monadology and Other Philosophical Writings,* trans. Robert Latta, pp. 98–99 n.

21. For a fuller treatment of the relation between bodies and monads in Leibniz, see Catherine Wilson, *Leibniz's Metaphysics: A Historical and Comparative Study,* chap. 5.

22. Cf. Robert Latta, in Leibniz, *Monadology,* p. 99 n. As Latta notes, Leibniz's claim as to the merely aggregate nature of *materia secunda* is difficult to reconcile with his insistence that *phenomena bene fundata* hold together in a system.

23. On the problematic relation between actual and merely possible worlds in Leibniz, see Peter Fenves, "Antonomasia: Leibniz and the Baroque," *Modern Language Notes:* 448. Leibniz represents the continuum of possible worlds as a pyramid, with the actual world as its apex (*Theodicy,* no. 416). In that account, presented as the dream of one "Theodorus," the real world is distinguished from the merely possible worlds with which it is (otherwise) continuous by the "entrancing ecstasy" that it engenders in the dreamer. Kant, for reasons to be discussed below, finds such "mystical" conflation of knowledge and pleasurable enchantment especially disturbing.

24. Cf. Kant's *New Elucidation of the First Principles of Metaphysical Knowledge,* prop. 7, in which he claims that God's existence is prior "to the very possibility both of [Him]self and of all things" [I:395].

25. Cf. *The One Possible Basis* (II:110 ff., 232; 111 ff., 233).

26. Kant's argument intriguingly anticipates his critical distinction between the analytic a priori, which is necessarily true for all rational beings as such, and the synthetic a priori, which is true only for rational beings who share our form of temporal/spatial intuition (and thus share with us in experiencing the common world we call nature).

27. Kant's argument thus represents a kind of midpoint between the traditional ontological argument and Hegel's later dialectic of the concept (*Begriff*). World, for Kant here, is a concept that (uniquely) entails its own actuality. Cf. Hegel, *Lesser Logic,* no. 142: "*Actuality* is the unity, become immediate, of essence with existence, or of inward with outward."

28. As Tonelli points out, Kant's understanding of activity is particularly apt at rendering intelligible attraction (or action at a distance) (*Elementi,* pp. 7, 15).

29. Although possible, the existence of a plurality of worlds is not probable, Kant believes, unless each world-space has a different number of dimensions. For if different world-spaces had the same number of dimensions, one would be com-

pelled to wonder why God separated them, giving Creation less unity than it was capable of (I:25).

30. On this point see Vuillemin, *Physique et métaphysique*, p. 234: "Kant even imagines that the love of attraction governs the relations of excitations and sensations, of volitions and of actions. But behind this psycho-physical fantasy, there already is evidence of the fundamental theorem of the *Critique:* the identity of the conditions of the possibility of an object and of the conditions of possible experience." On Kant's further elaboration of this "psycho-physical fantasy," see chapter 3 below.

31. Leibniz, *Philosophical Papers*, p. 717.

32. Ibid., p. 724.

33. Ibid., p. 716.

34. Ibid., p. 712.

35. Ibid., pp. 733–34.

36. "*The complete or perfect concept of an individual substance involves all its predicates, past, present and future.* For certainly it is already true now that a future predicate will be a predicate in the future, and so it is contained in the concept of the thing. . . . It can be said that, speaking with metaphysical rigor, *no created substance exerts a metaphysical action or influence upon another.* For to say nothing of the fact that it cannot be explained how anything can pass over from one thing into the substance of another, it has already been shown that all the future states of each thing follow from its own concept. What we call causes are in metaphysical rigor only concomitant requisites" (Leibniz, *First Truths*, in *Philosophical Papers*, pp. 414–15). See also Richard S. Westfall, *Force in Newton's Physics: The Science of Dynamics in the Seventeenth Century*, p. 313: "the derivative force of a perfectly elastic body repeats on the phenomenal plane the autonomous unrolling of the primitive force of the individual monads which constitute ontological reality."

37. On the contrast between Leibniz and Kant here, see Vuillemin, *Physique et métaphysique*, p. 242 ff.

38. As Vuillemin notes, Kant's argument (perversely) understands the "effect" that is "equal" to the force as a metaphysical rather than an empirically observable event (as it is for Leibniz). Rather than providing a conveniently accessible measure of an in-itself hidden reality, Kantian "effect" *is* the hidden reality.

39. With living force, by way of contrast, "the substance strives to maintain itself in the same state." The external resistance must therefore have sufficient force to overcome that striving — force that Kant computes as the square of the body's velocity (I:30).

40. Paragraph 5 (from Kant's introduction) draws a similar implicit comparison between the activity of bodies and that of Kant himself. So construed, many of Kant's key metaphysical terms (*Anwendung, laufen,* and *Bemühung,* to name a few) become oddly self-reflexive. Lessing's witticism (which rests on the same comparison) is more literal (and less humorous) than it first seems.

41. Like activity in general, as earlier described, philosophy presents itself, this side of eternity, as a perhaps endless task — in both senses of endless.

42. Living force is to dead force, according to Leibniz, as the "infinite is to the finite." A body makes the transition from a state of rest (or striving to move) to a

state of motion through a series of continuous increments of dead force; dead is thus to living force as the "lines are to their elements in our differentials" (C. I. Gerhardt, *Die philosophischen Schriften von G. W. Leibniz,* vol. 2, p. 154; quoted in Polonoff, *Force,* pp. 17–18 n). It is with this implicit quantification of the relation between dead and living force that Kant principally takes issue:

> what is generally valid of a body that has been in motion for a long time must be valid too when that motion is just beginning. For a very small period of motion is not distinguishable from its beginning; or one can reasonably interchange them [as Leibniz in fact assumes]. From this I conclude: if a body generally has a living force when it has moved for a time (be it as short as one will), it must also have living force when it first begins to move. For it is one and the same whether it has just begun to move or has moved for an extremely short period of time. I thus conclude that the Leibnizian law of force estimation cannot be approved, since it leads to the absurdity that there is living force even at the starting point of motion. (I:37)

43. One component of the struggle between the Cartesians and the Leibnizians revolved around the question of whether the total quantity of force in the universe would decline without God's continual or periodic intervention. Leibniz had argued both for mv^2 and for related claims as to the perfect elasticity of bodies, partly on the grounds that it avoided the necessity of divine intervention admitted by Newton and his followers. Kant meets the assault on God's seemliness (*Anständigkeit*) in a different way, one that hearkens back to the origination of the universe. The first motions cannot have been produced by moving matter (for then they would not have been first), nor directly by God (for God, who spares himself as much activity as he can without drawback (*Nachteil*) to the world machine, made nature as active and effective as possible). The first motion must therefore have arisen from matter itself, since (as Kant's treatment of living force has presumably shown) body can bring about motion from matter previously at rest. But since motion originally arose in this way, it can be similarly maintained or replenished (I:60–61). Kant's argument anticipates several cosmological themes he will develop in his *Universal Natural History,* among them nature's self-sustaining generative power and the all-important need to grasp what he here calls the "plan [*Plan*] of nature."

44. *Intension* is not to be confused with *Intention,* which in German means "aim or plan."

45. He also refers to it as "external stimulus" (*äußerlichen Anreizung*) (I:148).

46. See Polonoff, *Force,* p. 55.

47. See Vuillemin, *Physique et métaphysique,* pp. 242–43.

48. Although, as Latta notes (Leibniz, *Monadology,* p. 221 n), Leibniz's principle of continuity in some ways suggests a different view.

49. Cf. Leibniz, *Monadology,* no. 8: "monads, if they had no qualities, would be indistinguishable from one another, since they do not differ in quantity." As Latta adds, the later Kant "would say they may differ in 'intensive quantity'" (p. 221 n). See *Critique of Pure Reason* A/166 = B/208 ff.; B/414 ff.

50. This openness bespeaks a vulnerability to which Leibniz's monads were purportedly immune. Leibniz derived monadic immortality from their simplicity or

lack of parts, arguing that what cannot be dissolved is necessarily immortal. Kant's quantification of monadic substance strikes a serious blow against Leibniz's argument. As Kant later puts it in the *Critique of Pure Reason* (B/214), the intensive quantity of (putative) soul/substance can diminish to zero; soul's lack of extensive quantity is thus no guarantee against its disappearance. In the *Physical Monadology*, by way of contrast, Kant argues that substance can be infinitely "compressed" (and its inner force thereby brought to a maximum of intensity) but not "dismembered."

Chapter Three

1. Cf., for example, Kant's *Metaphysical Foundations of Natural Science* (VI:565; 134).

2. *Allgemeine Naturgeschichte und Theorie des Himmels, oder Versuch von der Verfassung und dem mechanischen Ursprunge des ganzen Weltgebäudes nach Newtonischen Grundsätzen abgehandelt* (Universal natural history and theory of the heavens, or an essay on the constitution and mechanical origin of the entire world-structure considered according to Newtonian principles). Citations below refer to the Akademie edition, followed by references to the English translation by Stanley L. Jaki (Edinburgh: Scottish Academy Press, 1981). Jaki's distinctly unsympathetic translation has the virtue of completeness, unlike the better-known and in many ways more faithful W. Hastie translation.

3. These households seem to have been exceptionally liberal. The von Hülsens had recently been elevated to the rank of count for liberating their serfs. Kant is also thought to have served as a tutor in the household of the von Keyserlings, with whom he was on very friendly terms in later life. According to C. J. Kraus, Kant usually sat in the place of honor next to Countess von Keyserling, except when it was given as an act of courtesy to strangers. As Cassirer notes, Kant was apparently spared the humiliating experiences of other famous former tutors (such as Rousseau and Fichte). The Countess von Keyserling may well represent Kant's model of the intellectually cultivated woman, whom he later compares, not exactly to her favor, with the woman of simple and pious moral faith. In any case, it seems likely that Kant was comfortable in, and benefited from, his exposure to a refined milieu of which he had little previous experience, and reflected in his subsequent sobriquet "the elegant master" (Cassirer, *Kant's Life*, p. 33 ff.) For details concerning Kant's relations with the von Keyserlings, see Emil Fromm, *Das Kantbildnis der Gräfin Karoline Charlotte Amalia von Keyserling*, which includes a sketch of the young philosopher drawn by the countess.

4. Thus centeredness alone does not for Kant secure systemicity, which also requires "reciprocal connection in relation to a central point," as evinced by the confinement of the planets to a common plane from which "they are free to deviate as little as possible." It is tempting to see in this model an analogy with the Hobbesian constitution, mutually supported by a single sovereign and the (equally necessary and universal) reciprocal antagonism of its constituents.

5. Both here and in his later treatments of sublime terror, Kant associates the horror of death with earthquakes and whirlpools in which one is "swallowed up," that is, with images of the cataclysmic and abysmal. See especially his three essays

on the Lisbon earthquake of 1755 (I:417 ff.) and his letter to Frau von Trunk on the death of her son, a former student (II:37 ff.). On the theme of earthquakes, see Peter Fenves, *A Peculiar Fate: Kant and the Problem of World History*.

6. Kant's treatment here of the divine intellect anticipates his later understanding of the "archetypal intellect." The classic studies of the relation between Kant's early (dogmatic) and critical understandings of the divine mind are Heinz Heimsoeth's "Metaphysical Motives in the Development of Critical Idealism," in *Kant: Disputed Questions*, ed. Moltke S. Gram; the original German version appeared in *Kant-Studien* [1924]); *Studien zur Philosophie Immanuel Kants,* Kantstudien Ergänzungshefte 71; and Gerhard Krüger's *Philosophie und Moral in der Kantischen Kritik*. More recent studies include Henry Allison, *Kant's Transcendental Idealism: An Interpretation and Defense;* J. N. Findlay, *Kant and the Transcendental Object;* Robert B. Pippen, *Kant's Theory of Form: An Essay on the "Critique of Pure Reason";* and Ermanno Bencivenga, *Kant's Copernican Revolution.*

7. Cf. *On Fire* (I:371; 24). On use of the labyrinth/thread metaphor in Leibniz and his predecessors, see Catherine Wilson, *Leibniz's Metaphysics: A Historical and Comparative Study,* pp. 7 f.; and G. Hocke, *Die Welt als Labyrinth*. As I argue below, Kant's critical undertaking can be seen as an effort to "sever nature's leading strings" without prejudice to the emergence of another sort of guiding thread. For an alternative account of Kant's "heroism," see Hermann Schmitz, *Was wollte Kant?*

8. See, for example, his unfinished *Le monde, ou traité de la lumière.*

9. Cf. Descartes, *Le monde,* chap. 6.

10. *Commercium* in Latin means trade or intercourse. Both Wolff and Kant's teacher, Martin Knutzen, used *commercium* with reference to the relation between the body and the soul (see, for example, Knutzen, *Commentario philosophica de commercio mentis et corporis per influxum physicum explicando* [1735]). On the *commercium* of worldly substances, see Baumgarten, *Metaphysica,* para. 448; in Kant, XVII:119. In the *Critique of Pure Reason* Kant notes that the German word *Gemeinschaft* can mean either "communio" or "commercium," "community" as an a priori category of understanding referring to the latter (A/213 = B/260). On the role of "community" in the first *Critique,* see chapter 6 below.

11. On the character of the ancient constitution, see Harvey C. Mansfield, *Taming the Prince,* especially pp. 28–71, 210, 223; and "Hobbes and the Science of Indirect Government," *American Political Science Review* 65: 97–110.

12. This "commercial" model becomes explicit in Kant's later comparison of physical and moral/juridical community. See especially *The Metaphysics of Morals* (VI:232–33; [58]). Cf. Locke's characterization of the state of nature as a condition of equality "wherein all the power and jurisdiction is reciprocal." For one formulation of the classical alternative see Aristotle, *Politics* 1254a: "whatever is constituted out of a number of things — whether continuous or discrete — and becomes a single common thing always displays a ruling and a ruled element." Kant's idea of metaphysical totality is from the beginning affected by a peculiarly modern political analogy. The ancient conception of the hierarchically ordered regime (which permeated scholastic metaphysics) is largely replaced in Kant's thought by a model of reciprocal equality whose closest political analogue is market society.

13. Compare the "not unmanly fear" to which Kant confesses in his *On the Use of Teleological Principles in Philosophy* in the face of this very thought.

14. For Wolff, everything noncontradictory "is something," that is, has positive existence (*Philosophia prima*, no. 59). On the relation between Leibniz's and Wolff's versions of the principle, see John Edwin Gurr, *The Principle of Sufficient Reason in Some Scholastic Systems: 1750–1900*, pp. 11–50.

15. This insistence on the immediacy of divine intelligence over against the successive character of human thought reemerges in Kant's critical distinction between the archetypal (or wholly intuitive) and discursive intellects. The argument that God does not reason is anticipated by Crusius.

16. Cf. Hegel, *Science of Logic*, bk. 2, sec. 1.3.

17. That God exists is proven not (as with Descartes) by the "internal impossibility" of a concept of God that does not contain existence, but rather by the dependence upon the existence of God of possibility itself. God's existence is known by the actuality of his creatures.

18. On Kant's later development of this argument see *The One Possible Basis for a Demonstration of the Existence of God*, trans. Gordon Treash, pp. 9–39. Treash notes Kant's indebtedness to Baumgarten, for whom possibility is a matter of "representability" and not merely (as with Leibniz and Wolff) conceptual self-consistency or noncontradiction. What Kant later (for example, in his 1763 essay) calls "real" or "material" possibility here turns on the divine "idea" in which the mutual determinations of things, in their real and not merely logical compatibility, is thought. On Kant's early theological thought see also Pierre Laberge, *La théologie kantienne précritique*.

19. Cf. Kant's claim on virtually the next page that "nothing can be conceived *more certain* than the *certain*," just as "nothing can be conceived *truer* than the *true*," that is, that such superlatives are logically redundant (I:400; [22]).

20. Kant's God is *not* constrained, like that of Leibniz, by the extrinsic dictates of possibility, but by the "internal" claims of worth and worthiness. The strains arising from the attempt to conceive the world both as created (hence radically different from) and as worthy of (hence akin or similar to) its creator emerge with force in Kant's *Universal Natural History*.

21. From the Latin *ambigo*, meaning quarrel or contest. According to the *Oxford Latin Dictionary*, *ambiguus* signifies hesitancy or uncertainty as well as being of doubtful meaning or status, as with monsters of hybrid form and persons of uncertain sex.

22. According to the *Oxford Latin Dictionary*, *caecus* (literally "squinting" or "one-eyed") means "blind," but also "of impaired judgment," "lacking in light," and "mysterious or hidden." The term is a traditional epithet of Fortune.

23. *Necto*, meaning "to weave or bind," and, secondarily, "to entrap." A *nexus* is a binding — physical, legal, or familial. It can also designate the coils of a snake and, by extension, a knotty problem.

24. As John A. Reuscher notes, the words of Kant's first interlocutor recall a passage attributed by Gellius to Chrysippus (see *Attic Nights*, bk. 7, chap. 2, discussed in Lewis White Beck, ed., *Kant's Latin Writings*, p. 107). This is perhaps Kant's earliest treatment of the problem of imputability, which played so large a role in the emergence of his critical philosophy. Significantly, the determinacy in question here is not that of Newtonian mechanics but of Stoic fate. Chrysippus and his followers were unique among classical thinkers in ruling out any element

of contingency or chance in what they regarded as the necessary and eternal chain of causes. (Chrysippus's defense of determinacy was closely linked with his belief in the truth of divination.) Chrysippus was not unaware of the problem posed by his doctrine for moral imputability. At least one of his responses — that some causes, though fated, are "in our power" — is echoed in the answer that Kant here proposes, an answer that combines (not altogether consistently) a Stoic account of moral action emphasizing the resistance of the will to evil, with a "platonic" account that stresses the soul's "attraction" to the good. On Chrysippus's understanding of fate and moral responsibility, see Gould, *Philosophy of Chrysippus*, pp. 133–52.

25. Cf. Chrysippus II:974, 1000. According to Chrysippus, it is in our power to assent or not assent to a given "presentation" (*phantasia*) (for example, eating an unhealthy meal or having sexual relations with one's neighbor's wife), which as such constitutes a merely proximate cause of that assent. To illustrate, Chrysippus cites the example of a cylinder rolling down a slope. The initial force needed to get the cylinder rolling corresponds to the proximate cause, or presentation to the mind. The cylinder's own form, on the other hand, is responsible for its continued motion and corresponds to the original cause, which is within our power (though it too is ultimately fated). Chrysippus's explanatory metaphor bears an odd resemblance to Kant's early treatment of living force and its relation to the solicitation of external causes, suggesting, perhaps, that Stoic influence on Kant's early thought was more far-reaching than has generally been recognized.

26. This difficulty is later solved by Kant's discovery of the moral "idea," projected by reason itself, as a substitute for representation and its implicit passivity. On Kant's early moral criticism of Wolff's treatment of the will, see also Dieter Henrich, "Über Kants früheste Ethik," *Kantstudien* 54; and Joseph Schmucker, *Die Ursprünge der Ethik Kants in seinen vorkritischen Schriften und Reflexionen*.

27. On the crucial importance of this power to abstract, that is, turn one's attention "ad lubitum," see (I:408; 92) and chapter 10 below. According to Kant's *Anthropology from a Pragmatic Point of View*, the power to abstract indicates a "freedom of the power of thought" — a capacity to have "the condition of one's representations under one's control (*animus sui compos*)" (IX:131; 13).

28. Cf. a structurally similar formulation in the late essay *An Old Question Newly Raised: Is the Human Race [Geschlecht] Constantly Progressing?* (pt. 2 of the *Conflict of the Faculties*).

29. Kant's distinction between inner and outer determination undermines another Leibnizian principle: the claim that no two things in the universe are entirely alike (the so-called identity of indiscernibles). On Kant's account, two things "inwardly" identical can be numerically distinct. His argument here appeals to the nature of such homogeneous bodies as gold, whose primitive parts, to judge from their effects, act as one "in regard to the use and function they are designed to serve." God's purposes can be served, it seems, by the wholesale actions of a given kind, whose uniform effects experience enables us to observe. In keeping with this insight, Kant's principle of natural plenitude applies to *species* rather than *individuals* (as with Leibniz) and gives no assurance as to the necessity (or immortality) of individual substances. Cf. Kant's later argument concerning incongruent counterparts in *Concerning the Ultimate Ground of the Differentiation of Directions in Space,*

which yields a similar conclusion. The history of the argument is otherwise very thoroughly discussed by Buroker in *Space and Incongruence.*

30. This view is saved from what Kant calls "pernicious materialism" by the fact that the disembodied soul still "represents," albeit in a manner incapable of change, a state that Kant elsewhere associates with both horror and the sublime (see, for example, *Observations on the Feeling of the Beautiful and the Sublime* [II:209–10 n]). See also Kant's late essay *The End of All Things,* on the representation, "revolting" to imagination, of a point in time in which all change [*Veränderung*] (and with it time itself) ceases. "The whole of nature will, then, harden and, so to speak, become petrified: the last thought, the last feeling will remain in the thinking subject ever the same and without change [*Wechsel*]. For to a being that can become conscious of its existence and its quantity/magnitude [*Größe*] (as endurance/duration [*Dauer*]) only in time, such a life, if indeed it can be called life at all, must seem equivalent to [*gleich*] annihilation." It is owing to this, Kant adds, that the Bible presents the inhabitants of the other world, whether heaven or hell, as forever singing [*anstimmen*] the same song, be it their hallelujah, or tones of lamentation [*Jammertöne*], as indicating the whole lack [*gänzliche Mangel*] of change in their state (VIII:334–35; [78]).

One cannot experience one's own death, let alone experience it as painful; and yet it is natural for foolish and wise alike to fear death, Kants says, owing to an illusion from which we cannot free ourselves, for "it belongs to the nature of thinking, insofar as thinking is talking to and about oneself." Still, "fainting," which customarily follows "vertigo," is "a foretaste [*Vorspiel*] of death," whose appearance (the inhibition of all sensation) is "asphyxia." (Hence the special aptness of a constant and eternal note [singing without breathing in and out] to represent an otherwise unrepresentable spiritual presence.) See *Anthropology* (VI:166–67; [43–44]); we will have later occasion to discuss at greater length the peculiar relation in Kant's thought between fainting, feelings of suffocation, and the exaltation of reason.

31. From *aperio,* which connotes opening as well as disclosure or enlightenment.

32. As Friedman brings out (*Kant and the Exact Sciences,* pp. 11–13), Kant's account of interaction provides a basis for distinguishing between the necessary order of the material universe (which entails a creator God responsible for the "very essence of matter") and the contingent order evident in living beings (which requires only an artificer God or demiurge). The distinction between these two sorts of order is worked out more fully (and sharply) in *The One Possible Basis,* whose summary of Kant's earlier mechanical cosmology omits the latter's systematic treatment of "the inhabitants of the various planets."

33. Cf. Chrysippus's account of knowledge as involving "alteration" of the soul's state (rather than, in the manner of crude materialism, an impressing of its surface). Chrysippus too had difficulty explaining how the soul distinguishes between presentations (*phantasia*) that truly represent the outer world and false ones that deceive us (Gould, *Philosophy of Chrysippus,* pp. 52–53).

34. This issue is taken up in part 1 of Hegel's *Logic,* which largely occupies itself with offering an alternative (or postcritical) solution to problems posed in Kant's precritical works.

35. Cf. *Critique of Judgment*, sec. 40, in which Kant calls prejudice a kind of "heteronomy of reason" whose opposite is "enlightenment." In both his early and later works, Kant associates liberation from prejudice with the adoption of a universal standpoint. In the case of his early thought, this standpoint is an infinitely receding goal pointing toward communion with God's intellect; in his later thought it is achieved (or, in principle, achievable) through community with fellow (human) beings. Kant's negative assessment of prejudice is the flip side of his positive assessment of judgment (*Urteil*). His elevation of judgment (over, say "attention," the mental activity emphasized by Wolff) is characteristic of his earliest work and may reflect Crusius's influence (but cf. chap. 10 below). On the overall importance of judgment in Kant's thought, see Richard Velkley, *Freedom and the End of Reason: On the Moral Foundation of Kant's Critical Philosophy*, p. 122 ff.; and Fenves, *A Peculiar Fate*, p. 51 n.

36. Kant's terminology calls to mind his later *Conjectural [Muthmaßlicher] Beginning of Human History* as well as the seafaring metaphor of which Kant was generally fond. In a preliminary draft of the *Universal Natural History*, for example, he explicitly compares himself to Columbus (XXIII:11). A sort of nautical Moses, Kant here only glimpses the promised land, leaving it to others to enter it and claim it as their own. In his critical writings, by way of contrast, he himself has made land, and it is others who are shipwrecked on the sea of uncertainty. For Kant's use of the metaphor in a more cautious context, see *The One Possible Basis:*

> Without speaking of the modest desire of arriving at complete and clear concepts about so important an item of knowledge, a desire that an understanding accustomed to investigation cannot dismiss, it is yet to be hoped that acquisition of such knowledge would be able to illuminate many other points. To attain this end, however, one must risk/venture upon [*wagen auf*] the groundless abyss [*bodenlosen Abgrund*] of metaphysics. A dark ocean without shores and without lighthouses, where one must begin like a seafarer on an unknown sea. Such a one, as soon as he encounters land, examines his path and investigates whether some unnoticed sea current has not confused/entangled [*verwirrt*] his course despite all the care that the art of navigation can command. (II:65–66; [43–45])

37. Cf. *Critique of Pure Reason* (A/625 = B/653), where Kant, in stating the so-called physico-theological argument, makes a similar point: "There exists . . . a sublime and wise cause (or more than one), which must be the cause of the world not merely as a blindly working all-powerful nature, by *fecundity* [*blindwirkende allvermögende Natur durch Fruchtbarkeit*], but as intelligence, through *freedom*."

38. Kant confronts the "court" of orthodoxy with his own upright candor (*Freimutigkeit*).

39. The example of Jamaica's cooling afternoon breezes was a stalking horse, according to Adickes, for Wolffian optimists (*Kant als Naturforscher* 2:14). As will appear below, Kant's own interest in winds went further than even his *New Remarks toward an Explanation of the Theory of the Wind* (1756) suggests.

40. Or Epicurus's poetic student, Lucretius. *De rerum natura* was a favorite of Kant, who was able late in life to quote lengthy passages from memory (see William R. Shea, "Filled with Wonder: Kant's Cosmological Essay, *The Universal Natural History and Theory of the Heavens*," in *Kant's Philosophy of Physical Science*, ed. Robert

E. Butts, p. 116). Despite Kant's criticism of Epicurus, *De rerum natura* is a model for Kant's own work, which he implicitly characterizes as a kind of philosophic poetry.

41. For the history of Kant's equivocating answer to this question, see Fenves, *Peculiar Fate*, p. 29, and chapter 9 below. The peculiar puzzle for Kant is the *origin* of life, that is, generation. The reference to a caterpillar (*Raupe*) calls to mind Leibniz's comparison of the soul's survival of the "swoon" of death to the butterfly's emergence from its cocoon (see his *Letter to Arnauld* [1687] [*Philosophical Papers*, p. 531 ff.]). Compare Kant's later treatment of "the status of the soul after death" (*Vorlesungen über Metaphysik* [XXIV:768 ff.]). Kant seems to have held palingenesis — that is, the migration or metamorphosis of the soul after death to community with a new or transformed body — to be possible, metaphysically speaking, but not necessary. Hence the soul is not (as Leibniz claimed) immortal in the strong metaphysical sense, and conviction as to its continuation after death is a matter of faith or hope rather than knowledge. The deathly "swoon," or lapse into unconsciousness, which is for Leibniz a necessary (and hence unproblematic) state of psychic transition, is for Kant a condition from which we can hope, but not assume, we will awaken — hence (as we will see) a condition of peculiarly abysmal fascination. Annulment of community between body and soul (which Leibniz's account rules out in principle) is for Kant a subject-canceling moment that arouses both hope and dread.

42. Cf. Kant's later discussion of the "technique of nature," *Critique of Judgment*, nos. 72–74.

43. Kant thus begins as he will end (I:367; 196), with an appeal to the sight of the starry heavens — an appeal repeated in his famous coupling of the "starry heavens above us" and "the moral law within us" as dual sources of sublime wonder (*Critique of Practical Reason* [VI:162; 166]).

44. Kant learned of Wright's theory from an account in the journal *Freye Urtheile und Nachrichten zum Aufnehmen der Wissenschaften und der Historie überhaupt*. A version of that review appears in translation in W. Hastie's edition of the *Universal Natural History and Theory of the Heavens* (trans. W. Hastie, with a new introduction by Milton K. Munitz; originally published as *Kant's Cosmology*). The title of Wright's work is *An Original Theory or New Hypothesis of the Universe, Founded upon the Laws of Nature, and Solving by Mathematical Principles the General Phenomenon of the Visible Creation: and Particularly the Via Lactea.*

45. According to the *Oxford English Dictionary*, "Milky Way" was a conventional poetic figure in the seventeenth and early eighteenth centuries for the female bosom. The maternal associations of Kant's vision are enhanced in German by the comparison between the Milky Way (*Milchstraße*) or galaxy (from the Greek *galactia*, meaning "milk") and the sun (in German, a feminine noun). Conspicuously absent in Kant's borrowing from Wright is any reference to the latter's identification of the center of the Milky Way with God, or what Wright calls the "infinite paternal principle." It is, as we will see, crucial to Kant's argument that the galactic center *not* be associated (as Wright had done) with a paternal God.

46. See I:232–33; 90. The author is William Derham, whose *Astrotheology, or a Demonstration of the Being and Attributes of God, from a Survey of the Heavens* was translated in 1728 into German by J. A. Fabricius.

47. The lines from Pope's *Essay on Man* (in Barthold Heinrich Brockes's translation) with which part 2 begins omit the poet's reference to "the general good," perhaps because Kant defers until later the subject of final purposes—perhaps also because there is something overly facile in Pope's optimism, at least as it relates to man. Quotations from Pope's work that appear throughout the *Universal Natural History* avoid Pope's association of God with the physical center of the universe. Kant's preference for the theodicy of Pope over that of Leibniz is a theme of his early *Optimism* (1759).

48. The "Hobbesian" resonance here is, I think, deliberate. Hobbes also charts a conjectural history in which an ordered constitution emerges out of chaos. As a whole informed by the reciprocal connection of its members in relation to a common center, Kant's cosmic constitution is a structural analogue of the Hobbesian commonwealth (see note 11 above). Kant's understanding of the requirements of systemicity in the *Universal Natural History* can be usefully contrasted with his definition of a system in the *Critique of Pure Reason* as "the unity of the manifold modes of knowledge under one idea. This idea is the concept provided by reason of the form of a whole" [A/832 = B/860]. Hans Saner usefully highlights similarities between Kant's cosmological and political ideas but overlooks significant differences between Kant's early and later conceptions of commercial community (see *Kant's Political Thought*, trans. E. B. Ashton, p. 28 ff.; and chapter 6 below). Other studies, generally Marxist in orientation, of the relation between physical and political theories of the time include Gideon Freudenthal, *Atom and Individual in the Age of Newton*, trans. Peter McLaughlin; and Jon Elster, *Leibniz et la formation de l'esprit capitaliste*.

49. The principle is generally attributed to Maupertuis.

50. Hartmut and Gernot Böhme link Kant's force of repulsion with middle-class aversion for the lower orders (!) (see *Das Andere der Vernunft: Zur Entwicklung von Rationalitätsstrukturen am Beispiel Kants*, p. 90 ff.). Of greater interest for my argument is Kant's association of the force of repulsion with gaseous (or spiritous/spiritual) (*geistig*) matter. (The semantic distinction in English between "spiritual" and "spirituous" has no German equivalent.) For a discussion of Kant's later, highly irreverent treatment of the relation between spirit and gas see chapter 5 below. Kant continued throughout his life to regard repulsion as an essential force of matter (see, for example, his *Metaphysical Foundations of Natural Science* [VII:449; 43]).

51. See *Metaphysics of Morals* (VI:233; 58).

52. The questionableness of Kant's derivation of this repellent force, which he calls an "undisputable phenomenon of nature" and explicitly substitutes for the swing or "clinamen" of Epicurus, has been noted by critics. See, for example, Vuillemin, *Physique et métaphysique*, p. 110 ff.; and Shea, "Filled with Wonder," who persuasively argues that Kant's account of repulsion in the *Universal Natural History* is fundamentally at odds with a Newtonian explanation of orbital motion (p. 118). For a more satisfactory treatment of repulsive force, see Kant's *Physical Monadology, The One Possible Basis*, and the *Metaphysical Foundations of Natural Science*.

53. See Martin Heidegger, *The Metaphysical Foundations of Logic*, trans. Michael Heim, p. 116.

54. The figure of nature as a perfect artifact reappears in the *Critique of Judgment*,

in the context, however, of a more radical resignation to the "limits" of human reason. See, for example, no. 74.

55. The traditional problem of the "actual infinite" (whose reality Aristotle denied) is resolved for Kant by the fact that the series of changes that makes up the future is "already at once entirely present to the divine understanding."

56. Cf. Giordano Bruno, who asks, "why should we suppose the divine potency to be idle?" (see *Opera latine conscripta,* I, 1, p. 242 f.; and *Le opere italiane,* p. 360; quoted in Arthur Lovejoy, *The Great Chain of Being,* p. 117 ff.). As Lovejoy notes, the derivation of the infinity of the world from the infinity of its creator goes back at least as far as Plato's *Timaeus.* For a learned account of the medieval debate see Duhem, *Medieval Cosmology.* On Bruno's reliance on the principle of plenitude and anticipation of the principle of sufficient reason, see Alexandre Koyré, *From the Closed World to the Infinite Universe,* p. 39 ff.; see also Blumenberg, *Legitimacy,* p. 549 ff. As Blumenberg observes, Bruno conceives of the world as "exhausting" God's potency. Kant, we might add, is spared this conclusion by his progressive conception of creation: God's potency is "inexhaustible" inasmuch as cosmic history is unending (or — what comes for Kant to the same thing — is "exhausted" only at the end of time) (I:314; [154]).

57. Analogy leads us, as Kant adds, "in all such cases in which understanding lacks the thread of undeceptive proofs."

58. Cf. Kant's *On Whether the Earth Grows Old, Physically Considered* and his "adventurous" suggestion, in the *Critique of Judgment,* that nature's womb, once capable of generating new forms, has "ossified" (sec. 80).

59. Worlds fail for Kant but not nature as such, as is true in the original version of the poem by Joseph Addison, whose German translation, by Johann Christoph Gottsched, Kant here quotes from.

60. "[I]n Wohlgefallen sich auflösen" means both "to end in satisfaction" and, colloquially and humorously, "to come to nothing."

61. The Akademie edition has *Trümmern,* the Cassirer edition *Träumen.*

62. This foretaste of divine "community" (a substitute for nature's Milky Way?) contrasts with Kant's earlier pursuit of the galactic source. On its relation to Kant's later treatment of the community of taste, see chapter 8 below.

63. As noted by the eighteenth century philologist Johann Heinrich Voss, "sun" is feminine in the Germanic languages and masculine in Graeco-Roman and its derivatives, a difference that carries over, as might be expected, to mythology. Where the Greeks and Romans associated the sun with masculine gods (for example, Helios and Apollo), the Eddas of Norse legend identify it with a secondary female goddess, created by Odin, who is himself overshadowed by a more primal "bottomless deep" and "world of mist" bordered by a "land of light" (see Thomas Bulfinch, *The Age of Fable,* chap. 38). The relative weakness and inconstancy of the solar deity in Norse legend bears an obvious relationship to climate. (According to the *Oxford English Dictionary,* the English word for "sun" retained its original, feminine gender until the sixteenth century.)

64. That chapter 7 of Kant's essay should alone call for a "supplement" is as remarkable as the latter's title, which suggests a microcosmic inversion of the *Universal Natural History* as a whole. Kant himself describes the section as gratuitously

lengthy and elaborate in view of its stated purpose, to fill in a remaining gap in his otherwise "complete cosmology" — a fact pointing either to a larger gap than Kant is willing to admit or to another sort of purpose entirely. As I will suggest, Kant's interest in the workings of the sun borders on enthrallment.

65. These light and volatile (*flüchtig*) components are also "the most efficacious in maintaining the solar fire."

66. "[S]o zu sagen, aus sich selbst wirksam." Cf. Kant's characterization, in the *New Elucidation*, of the divine idea as an "efficacious representation." The "so to speak" saves Kant (barely) from the self-sufficiency of nature from which he earlier recoiled. Cf. Kant's *On Whether the Earth Grows Old*, in which he wonders whether the "life of nature" may not reveal a "universal *Weltgeist*," by which he means no "soul of the world" or other "immaterial force" but a subtle heat material that is everywhere effective, "that constitutes the active principle in the formations of nature, and that is, like a true Proteus, ready to assume all shapes and forms." Kant identifies this force with the "Spiritus Rector" of the chemists. (He seems to have especially in mind Hermann Boerhaave's *Elements of Chemistry*. Boerhaave, who is generally regarded as a mechanist, revived the alchemaic notion of a "Spiritus Rector," identifying it as a "vapor" or "volatile" spirit that constitutes the principle of life.) The boundary on which Kant insists (and continues to insist throughout his life) between matter and reason is here crucial to his conclusion that the gradual exhaustion of the earth's fertility does not imply a corresponding cooling of the "fire animating the human soul" (I:212–13) (cf. Aristotle, *Generation of Animals* 737a). On traditional sixteenth- and seventeenth-century associations of innate or animal heat with ether, the heat of the sun, and the starry sphere, see Everett Mendelsohn, *Heat and Life: The Development of the Theory of Animal Heat*, p. 24; and Charles Serrington, *The Endeavor of Jean Fernel*, pp. 38–40. On the theme of an aging earth's loss of fertility, see Lucretius, *De rerum natura* II:1134–74.

67. *Schlünde*, literally "maws," as in the "*Schlünde* of hell."

68. The material Kant has in mind is saltpeter, or sodium nitrate (cf. *On Fire* [I:382; 41]). The theme of respiration as a conserver of vital heat (either by fueling it or, alternatively, by cooling it and thus preventing premature exhaustion) goes back to Aristotle and Hippocrates (see, for example, Aristotle, *De respiratione*, 472 b–473 a). The experiments of Boyle and others, establishing the necessity of air (or some "nitrous" substance therein contained) to the process of combustion, competed at the beginning of the eighteenth century with still-current explanations of respiration as a venting of "excrementitious vapors." Both theories seem to be rhetorically at work in Kant's speculations concerning the solar fire. On the historical background see Mendelsohn, *Heat and Life*, pp. 8–66.

69. The term means both abomination and disgust.

70. Kant, who suffered from vertigo, claimed that he was overcome by a disabling dizziness whenever he attempted to travel by sea or land. In the *Anthropology*, he connects this dizziness (*Schwindel*) and its accompanying nausea with the class of dangers "that exist only in our idea": "If a plank is lying on the ground we can walk on it without reeling; but if it lies over a chasm or, for someone with really weak nerves, merely over a ditch, the empty apprehension of danger often becomes really dangerous." Seasickness, for its part, results from an alternating "sinking and being lifted up": "As it sinks, nature strives to raise itself (because sinking generally

carries the notion of danger with it); and its effort, which involves an upward motion of the stomach and intestines, is connected mechanically with the impulse to vomit—an impulse that is intensified when the patient looks out of the cabin window and gets alternating glimpses of sea and sky, which heightens even further the illusion that the seat is giving way under him" (VII:264; 131. 170; 46). (The patient involved is evidently Kant himself.) Kant here plays on the fact that *Schwindel* also means fraud or cheat (as in "swindle"). Dizziness is akin to the "not disagreeable" sensation of the gruesome (*Das Graüseln*)—hence at least indirectly to the sublime. In its own rise and fall, the argument of the *Universal Natural History* evinces a similarly dizzying assimilation of the agreeable and disagreeable.

71. Cf. *Critique of Judgment*, sec. 27:

> In presenting the sublime in nature the mind feels *agitated*, while in an aesthetic judgment about the beautiful in nature it is in *restful* contemplation. This agitation . . . can be compared with a vibration, i.e., with a rapid alteration of repulsion from, and attraction to, one and the same object. If a [thing] is excessive for the imagination . . . then [it] is, as it were, an abyss in which the imagination is afraid to lose itself. Yet at the same time, for reason's idea of the supersensible [this same thing] is not excessive but conforms to reason's law to give rise to such striving by the imagination. Hence [the thing] is now attractive to the same degree to which [formerly] it was repulsive.

Although Kant refers to the object's effect on imagination as initially repulsive, the cause of that repulsiveness—imagination's fear of losing itself—presupposes a prior state of attraction that somehow puts imagination (and with it, consciousness itself) in jeopardy.

72. The location of that "inextinguishable" and "priceless" center "toward which all parts aim with uniform sinking" Kant declines to judge. It is precisely here, of course, in the leap from part to whole (or from finitude to infinity), that his "thread of analogy" breaks down.

73. Attraction, for Kant, still presupposes an eliciting "object," be it material or divine. He has yet to work out the notion of an "idea" as a self-projection of reason, which will enable him to reconcile the eros of attraction with human independence (or nobility). Indeed, the break between Kant's precritical and critical thought can be located in the latter's identification of reason's vocation, not with the theoretical pursuit of the unconditioned "ground," but rather with the practical effort to realize an idea projected by reason itself. Critical philosophy, as we will see, repudiates the "abyss" of metaphysics, Kant's "first mistress," in favor of reason's own free projection. From the standpoint of critical philosophy, Kant's earlier distinction between the rational and physical points of attraction—between ground and abyss—becomes blurred or insignificant. What sustains the distinction between reason and matter is no longer a strained differentiation of rational and physical objects of desire, but the freedom of reason itself, knowledge of which is ultimately rooted in awareness of the moral law. Critical reason is not just erotic (to borrow Yirmiahu Yovel's helpful phrase), but autoerotic (see Yovel, *Kant and the Philosophy of History*, p. 15 ff). Reason's erotic reach is no longer elicited or "attracted" by some external object (as in classical/scholastic models of desire) but emanates instead from its own self-grounded or spontaneous activity. So conceived, desire sustains rather

than threatens the integrity of the self. Kant's eagerness to regard as "ideas of rea-son" what for Rousseau arguably remain projective illusions of imagination stems, in part, from their fortuitous resonance with an intellectual scaffolding that Kant had previously erected. But see *Emile,* trans. Allan Bloom, pp. 254–56, 329, 391, 447, 474, for indications that even for Rousseau ideas are more than illusory pro-jections: "The golden age is treated as a chimera. . . . What, then, would be re-quired to give it new birth? One single but impossible thing: to love it."

74. Nature's intrinsic orderliness thus offers the surest proof of God's existence. In his *One Possible Basis* (1763), by way of contrast, Kant characterizes the "cosmo-logical proof" as morally affecting but logically inconclusive, given our inability to comprehend nature as a whole (II:159 ff.). What is new is Kant's resigned accep-tance of man's inability to comprehend the universe as a totality, a limitation against which the argument of the *Universal Natural History* continually struggles.

75. That *we* should not be able to imagine, for example, for what specific pur-pose God made the planets of uniform density is for Kant here a sufficient reason to reject the claim that this was brought about by God's immediate action.

76. On extraterrestrial life as a common theme among eighteenth-century thinkers as diverse as Locke, Berkeley, Leibniz, and Wolff, see Michael J. Crowe, *The Extraterrestrial Life Debate, 1750–1900: The Idea of a Plurality of Worlds from Kant to Lowell.* Kant himself later makes joking reference to Fontenelle's *Entretiens sur la pluralité des mondes.* Other antecedents with whom Kant was undoubtedly familiar include Huygens's *Cosmotheoros* and Wolff's *Elementa matheseos universae,* in the third volume of which he describes in detail the bodily proportions of the inhabit-ants of Jupiter (!).

77. Despite their appearance as "free digressions of wit," Kant claims for his speculations "so well-grounded a probability that one can hardly deny them valid-ity" (I:351; [183]). They are saved from the "limitless" freedom of "poetry" and "fantasy" by the thread of "analogy": "one must admit that the distances of celestial bodies from the sun embody certain relationships, which in turn entail an essential influence on the various properties of thinking natures that are found there" (I:352; [183]). This is because "these natures' manner of acting and feeling is bound to the condition of the matter with which they are connected and depends on the measure of impressions which the world evokes in them according to the properties of the relation of their habitat to the center of attraction and heat." The vexed question of "influence" between body and soul is thus accommodated to (or "held in track by") the physical relation between sun and planets, a relation in which intensity of influence varies inversely with extension or distance from the center.

78. See (I:355; [286]): "Man is so created as to accept through that body that is the visible part of his being, the impression and stirrings that the world excites in him, a body whose material serves not only to impress upon the invisible spirit that inhabits it the first concepts of external objects, but also to repeat [*wiederholen*], to bind them together in inner activity: in short [the body] is indispensable to thought."

79. Identification of "fibers" as the basic components of living organisms is gen-erally credited to von Haller.

80. Cf. *Idea for a Universal History from a Cosmopolitan Standpoint,* second thesis.

81. Cf. *Conjectural Beginning of Human History* (VIII:116 n), in Hans Reiss, ed., *Kant's Political Writings,* 2d ed., p. 228 n; and chapter 4 below. Culture, in Kant's later view, presupposes a gap between man's physical and civil maturity (that is, between his ability to beget children and his ability to support them in a civilized condition).

82. The centrality of judgment to Kant's understanding of human thought is brought out even more forcefully in his *On the False Subtlety of the Four Syllogistic Figures.* On error and evil as consequences of "egoism," or the attitude of "being occupied with oneself as the whole world," see *Anthropology* (VII:130; 12). The opposite of egoism (metaphysical, aesthetic, and practical) is "pluralism," or the attitude of regarding and conducting oneself as a "citizen of the world." Cf. Kant's reference to the "most gruesome cloudburst" at I:303; [146].

83. Nowhere is the ambiguity of solar attraction more evident: heat is both life-sustaining source and universal solvent. Life-forms maintain a precarious balance between dissipation and congealment. The more rarefied a spirit's bodily matter, the further from the center it can thrive, and the more perfect it is (though no creature severs matter's cord entirely).

84. Cf. Kant's counsel in the *Anthropology* to (perpetually) defer sensual gratification:

> A continuous series of sense representations that *differ* in intensity, with each one stronger than the preceding one, has an *outer limit* [*Aüβerstes*] of *tension* [*intensio*]. As we approach this limit we are *stimulated;* when we go beyond it, we *relax* again [*remissio*]. But in the point that separates these two states lies the *consummation* [*Vollendung*] (*maximum*) of the sensation, which is followed by insensitivity and its consequent inertia [*Leblosigkeit*]. If we want to keep our power of sensing lively [*lebendig*], we must not begin with strong sensations (that make us insensitive toward those that follow); we must rather forego them at first and mete them out sparingly so that we can always climb higher. . . . Young man! Deny yourself gratifications (of entertainment, revelry, love and so forth), if not with the Stoic intention of giving them up completely, then with the refined Epicurean intention of having ever increasing enjoyment to look forward to. . . . Like everything ideal, consciousness of having control over your enjoyment is more fruitful and comprehensive than anything that is used up in gratifying the senses, and so deducted from the total quantity. (X:165; 42)

Man best conserves his "vital feeling" by so spending it as to mount perpetually towards (but never reach) fulfillment.

85. See, for example, Aristotle, *Generation of Animals,* 741a. Aristotle also connects the male contribution with final and formal causation. The Stoical distinction between active (male) and passive (female) matter has a similar effect. See Zeno I:85 (quoted in Gould, *Philosophy of Chrysippus,* p. 97).

86. This effort can here only be briefly touched on (see, for example, Bacon's early, and tellingly entitled, essay *The Masculine Birth of Time*). Thinkers as diverse as Harvey (an "ovist" who argued, putatively in defense of Aristotle, that sperm "ignites" egg within the uterus much as ideas are "conceived" within the brain) and Van Helmont (an intellectual precursor of the Cambridge Platonists, who attrib-

uted generation neither to formal nor efficient causation but rather to an internal archai or "seminal principle") contributed to the general controversy over generation, along with upholders of "panspermia" (such as Leibniz and Malebranche), who denied the possibility of generating life from lifeless matter. Leeuwenhoek's discovery of sperm played an important role in the emergence of Leibniz's monadology. (Leibniz once wrote, half jokingly, that Leeuwenhoek's theory restored the "male kind to its eminence" [*New Essays on Human Understanding*, trans. Peter Remnant and Jonathan Bennett, p. 316].) For a fuller discussion of the controversy, see Wilson, *Leibniz's Metaphysics*, p. 175 ff.; and Thomas Laqueur, *Making Sex: Body and Gender from the Greeks to Freud*, p. 146 ff. Laqueur's intriguing study of the rise to prominence, beginning in the mid to late eighteenth century, of a "two-sex" model of human anatomy underestimates Rousseau's revolutionary significance. Specifically, Laqueur fails to observe that for Rousseau, unlike the "liberal" thinkers with whom Laqueur assimilates him (pp. 198–200), women are distinguished not only by their natural modesty but also, and equally crucially, by their natural insatiability.

On the complex history of the ways in which generation has been understood, see Thomas S. Hall, *Ideas of Life and Matter: Studies in the History of General Physiology, 600 B.C.–1900 A.D.*, 2 vols.; and Howard B. Adelmann, *Marcello Malpighi and the Evolution of Embryology*, vols. 4 and 5. On specific efforts to safeguard the male formative principle see Jacques Roger, *Les sciences de la vie dans la pensée française du XVIIe siècle*, pp. 118, 124–25, 356–57. Even Descartes's mechanical embryology retains something of the traditional order of sexual rank: although both parents contribute equally to generation (a view shared by the ancient atomists), sex is determined by the fetus's relative robustness and concomitant power to resist contamination by excremental solids in the mother's blood. If the fetus is sufficiently robust, it will purge fewer liquids than solids, and the outcome will be male. Roger suggests that Descartes's recourse here to highly traditional views (in a work he was in any case moved to suppress) may be less than frank (p. 150).

87. See *Monadology*, nos. 69–78.

88. *Critique of Pure Reason* B/414 f.

89. Cf., for example, William Harvey's association of warmth with agility and cold with lethargy (*De motu locali animalium* [1627], ed. and trans. Gweneth Whitteridge, p. 103). Kant's contemporaries were struck by the care he took to regulate his own bodily temperature. His room, for example, was heated to a steady seventy-five degrees in winter and summer. Borowski also comments on Kant's habit of standing perfectly still on warm days to avoid perspiring (L. E. Borowski, R. B. Jachmann, and A. Ch. Wasianski, in *Immanuel Kant: Sein Leben in Darstellungen von Zeitgenossen*.

90. Kant may here be drawing on Boerhaave, who attributed the pathologies of aging to increased constriction and rigidity of the fibers that carry the body's vital fluids. Boerhaave linked other pathologies with the undue softness or weakness of such fibers. See also *On Whether the Earth Grows Old* (I:211).

91. I:366. The *Mittelstraße*, one could say, supplants the *Milchstraße* as Kant's point of reference.

92. Kant allows that our neighbors the Martians may suffer a similar fate.

93. Man, it seems, is the only rational being who must emancipate himself. It is not man's intellectual force (which is "mediocre") but his capacity to overcome his natural languor that raises him to (and perhaps beyond) the level of the beings whom nature has more happily endowed.

94. Cf. I:365; [194–95]. Having previously kept his speculations (*Mutmaßungen*) in track with the leading strings (*Leitfaden*) of physical analogy, Kant here permits himself a final diversion (*Ausschweifung*) into the "field of fantasy"; for, as he rhetorically asks, "Who shows us the limits where grounded probability leaves off and arbitrary fictions [*wilkürlichen Erdichtungen*] begin?" Kant's present "diversion" (like that into the Lucretian abyss from which he earlier swerved) thus calls into question precisely the boundary between fact and poetry that distinguishes his theory, according to his earlier insistence, from the "fanaticism" of Thomas Wright.

95. See especially I:365; [194–95].

96. On the distinctly erotic charge of infinity conceived as a maximum, see the text at chapter 8, note 68. Kant's critical "idealism" (as I will claim) draws psychic energy from certain structural homologies between the functioning of a mathematical limit and his preferred model of eros (or what he sometimes calls "ideal desire") as a longing that moves ever closer to without ever arriving at fulfillment. The relation of this preference to Kant's especially dismal views regarding the sexual economy will be discussed more fully in later chapters. It can by way of anticipation be said that what makes this posture of suspension possible for Kant (a posture that Fichte reduces to a "feeling" of obstacles to the will increasingly giving way, and that Hegel treats as contradictory) is twofold. It lies, first, in the content of the moral ought experienced as duty or obligation, an experience that at once demands perfection of the will, and — by virtue of the finitude to which duty testifies — precludes it, without thereby rendering our striving for perfection self-contradictory. (The very experience of guilt, one could say, sustains the dynamic suspension of reason between finitude and the infinite, a suspension that Hegel attacks as ultimately irrational.) A second ground of support for this posture of dynamic suspension in Kant is, as we will see, the alternative it offers to the natural expenditure of vital (sexual) energy, an alternative whose peculiar satisfactions go some way toward explaining the appeal of what is commonly called "sublimation" (cf. Hegel, *Logic*, pt. 1 of *The Encyclopaedia of the Philosophical Sciences*, trans. William Wallace, para. 94, p. 138).

97. We are thus left wondering whether nature is an open system or a closed one. The image of the universe as an infinitely expanding circle coexists uneasily with one of eternal recurrence, of pulsating expansion and contraction, in which nothing finally is gained or lost. Boundless potency seems to contradict the law of conservation. This basic tension between closure and expansion (a tension that cuts to the heart of the German Idealist notion of dynamic totality) will later be made much of by Marx, who treats it as symptomatic of the contradiction fundamental to the capitalist system between the circulation of value and its reproduction. However this may be, Kant here seems unable to settle upon a stable image for the structure of the universe as a whole, one that does justice both to the principle of infinite force or potency and the principle of conservation. Compare Kant's later

excitement over the concept of negative quantity and "real" as opposed to merely "logical" opposition. The idea of real opposition (for example, between positive and negative vector forces) makes it possible to reconcile infinite expansion of the amount of positive and negative force with the balanced equality implicit in the law of conservation. Each vector force may be as great in magnitude as one pleases; so long as they are equal, the result is zero (see his *Attempt to Introduce the Concept of Negative Quantities into Philosophy*). (The distinction between real and logical opposition is generally attributed to Hume.)

98. The spiritual point of attraction here identified with God is replaced in Kant's later thought by the "idea," conceived as a rational projection. Rousseau's suggestions concerning the autoerotic or projective character of human thought is thus, as we will see, decisive for Kant.

99. "Inertial force" is thus "living force" in a new guise, one that has been liberated from the dubious scheme of "vivification" but which retains its role as source of the essential heterogeneity of matter. On Kant's early treatment of inertia, see also Friedman, *Kant and the Exact Sciences*, p. 6.

100. Cf. *Metaphysical Foundations of Natural Science* (VI:524; 308 ff. VI:532; 90 f.) and *Opus postumum* (XXI:323; 399). See also Kant's depiction of fire, in *On Fire*, as a medium of perfect elasticity. Kant's notion in the *Opus postumum* of a perfectly elastic "ether" or *Warmstoff* filling what would otherwise be conceived as void is only his final effort in a lifelong attempt to account for the heterogeneity of matter without assuming empty space. According to the conception of matter first elucidated in the *Physical Monadology,* the boundaries by which the volume of a body is defined is never absolute (as would be the case for a Newtonian body in empty space) but always relative to the dynamic interplay of force between that body and those with which it interacts.

101. In this way Kant is also able to reconcile (or so he here believes) the existence of impenetrable elements with the existence of the so-called medium of ether, or fire matter [*Feurstoff*], by which every other element is affected or compressed, albeit without "penetration" in the proper sense. For an earlier effort in this direction, see his *On Fire*. (On his very late treatment of matter in conjunction with an "all-penetrating" ether, see chapter 10 below.)

102. See, for example, *Specimen dynamicum* (*Philosophical Papers* 2:722); as well as his early essay "First Truths" (*Philosophical Papers* 1:415), where he defends his assertion that nothing can exercise metaphysical influence on another thing, by citing the elastic impact whereby bodies recede from each other "by force of their own elasticity and not by any alien force."

103. Prop. 9. In Latin, *sentitur,* from *sentio,* the primary meaning of which is "to sense or feel" but which can also mean "to encounter," a usage applicable mainly to persons but also to things. In blurring the difference between a physical and mental encounter, Kant's usage skirts the very boundary that he is attempting to define.

104. On the relation between Kant's physical monadology and what he elsewhere describes as a heightened sensitivity on his part (bordering on morbidity) to feelings of bodily compression, see chapter 10 below.

105. Cf. Virgil, *Eclogues* viii.27.

Chapter Four

1. For a useful study of these notes (hereafter referred to as the *Remarks*) in relation to Kant's earlier ethical thought, see Schmucker, *Die Ursprünge,* pp. 173–256. Richard Velkley argues forcefully for the centrality of the *Remarks* to the development of Kant's thought as a whole (see *Freedom*). On Kant's indebtedness to Rousseau, see also Dieter Henrich, *Aesthetic Judgment and the Moral Image of the World: Studies in Kant,* pp. 3–28. For a detailed analysis of Kant's moral thought prior to the *Remarks,* see Dieter Henrich, "Hutcheson und Kant," *Kant-Studien* 49: 49–69; and "Über Kants früheste Ethik," pp. 404–31. See also the edited text with introduction and commentary by Marie Rischmüller, *Bemerkungen in den "Beobachtungen über das Gefühl des Schönen und Erhabenen".* Rischmüller provides helpful information concerning Kant's literary and philosophic sources. On the dating of Kant's reading of specific works of Rousseau, see Jean Ferrari, *Les sources français de la philosophie de Kant.*

None of this is to deny that other factors also affected the development of Kant's moral thought. Keith Ward draws attention to the youthful influence, both positive and negative, of Pietism (*The Development of Kant's View of Ethics,* pp. 3–5). On Kant and the Scottish Common Sense school, see Manfred Kuehn, *Scottish Common Sense in Germany, 1768–1800.* Among earlier scholars, Paul Menzer especially stressed the influence of the British Moralists — influence that Henrich, among others, somewhat discounts.

2. Frederick Beiser intriguingly suggests that Kant's earliest exposure to Rousseau may have come by way of J. G. Hamann, who had recently undergone a spiritual "conversion" following a series of financial and personal disasters, including a relationship (most likely homosexual) Hamann seems to have found particularly disturbing. C. Berens, a mutual friend, enlisted Kant's efforts in winning back Hamann's allegiance to the principles of the Enlightenment. As Beiser notes, Hamann's responses to Kant's attempts, which proved unavailing, ring a number of Rousseauian changes at a time when Kant himself seems still to have been unfamiliar with the celebrated Swiss author. Hamann went on to become a founding figure of the Sturm und Drang and exerted considerable influence on Kant's student, Johann Gottfried Herder. Hamann is generally credited with introducing Kant to Hume. Hamann's deepest modern affinities, however, were, by his own account, with Luther (see Frederick Beiser, *The Fate of Reason: German Philosophy from Kant to Fichte,* pp. 16–43). Despite their profound disagreements, Kant and Hamann remained on fairly warm personal terms. Kant later helped Hamann secure a livelihood and allowed his son to attend lectures for free. Hamann, for his part, refrained from publishing his own "Metacritique" of Kant's philosophy until after the latter's death (see Beck, *Early German Philosophy,* p. 378). Hamann published a critical review of Kant's *Observations on the Feeling of the Beautiful and the Sublime* in 1764.

3. The reference is to the theodicy presented in Pope's *Essay on Man.* Pope's theodicy is favorably compared to its Leibnizian counterpart in a series of unpublished notes on "optimism" (ca. 1753–54) (XVII:229–39). King Alfonso of Castile, having found the Ptolemeic system of the universe disturbingly irregular, is

supposed to have said, "If I had been the Creator of the world, I would have made it better" (quoted by Ernst Cassirer in *Rousseau, Kant, Goethe,* trans. James Guttmann et al., p. 18 n).

4. See XX:180: "in all moral definitions the expression *mediocritas* is very poor and undetermined, e.g., in *parsimonia* for it shows only that it is a degree whose size is not good without saying how great the good must be. This *mediocritas aurea* is an occult quality."

5. The answer is furnished, as will appear below, by two "touchstones" (*Probiersteine*) — two questions that serve as criteria for distinguishing the natural from the unnatural. The first asks "whether [what is at issue] conforms to that which man cannot alter"; the second asks "whether it can be common to all men, or enjoyed only by a few with the subjection of the rest." Thus, necessity (or what cannot be changed) and equality (or what can be shared) provide a determinate standard by virtue of which the variety of human experience can be brought to order.

6. See, for example, XX:175: "The doubt that I accept is not dogmatic but that of procrastination. Zetetic researcher. I would hear the grounds of both sides. It is curious [*wunderlich*] that one fears danger from this. Speculation is not a necessary thing. Knowledge in regard to the final things is surer. The method of doubt is useful to the extent that it preserves courage, not to speculate but to act according to sound understanding and sentiment. I seek the honor of Fabius Cunctator." Fabius Cunctator ("the procrastinator") was a Roman general whose delaying tactics defeated Hannibal. He was also (like Rousseau) the adoptive father/educator of one "Aemilius." (Perhaps Kant takes this to be the reason why Rousseau chose *Emile* as the title of his famous book on education.) A further connection between Fabius and Rousseau is suggested by Fabius's use of female rule to regulate wayward desire (see *Plutarch's Lives,* trans. John Dryden, p. 227).

7. This transformation goes together with a new respect for "common understanding" in matters intellectual as well as moral. The common understanding is to be the touchstone of logical judgment in the same way that the general will is to be touchstone of moral judgment (see, for example, XX:44, 49, 97, 165, 167.) The respective structures of the physical and moral worlds are isomorphic: in each case individual elements are interrelated by a common "ground of motion" [*Bewegungsgrund*]. But whereas the ground of physical force must ultimately be referred to an unknowable God, that of moral force can be referred directly to the human will. Kant continued to insist, in his critical period, on the obscurity surrounding the basis of physical force. As he puts it in the *Metaphysical Foundations of Natural Science,* the possibility of fundamental forces "can never be comprehended" (IV:524; 79).

8. *Universal Natural History* (I:366; [195]).

9. Cf. *Universal Natural History,* according to which man is of all creatures the one who "least achieves the end of his existence" (I:356; [187]).

10. See XX:47: "As little as I can jump to the planet Jupiter should I long to have properties proper only to such a planet." Kant's pride lies not in longing to be a seraph but in "only this — that I am a man."

11. Compare Rousseau, *Discourse on the Origins of Inequality,* in *The First and Second Discourses,* trans. Roger Masters, p. 114: "Nature commands every animal,

and the beast obeys. Man feels the same impetus, but he realizes that he is free to acquiesce or resist; and it is above all in the consciousness of this freedom that the spirituality of his soul is shown. For physics explains in some way the mechanism of the senses and the formation of ideas; but in the power of willing, or rather of choosing, and in the sentiment of this power are found only purely spiritual acts about which the laws of mechanics explain nothing." Noting, however, the "difficulties surrounding all these questions," Rousseau immediately substitutes for "consciousness of the freedom to acquiesce or resist" the metaphysically more modest notion of "perfectibility" as the distinctive human trait. Kant seems to take Rousseau's first word here as his final one.

12. Awareness of one's own identity in the face of temporal succession is an integral feature of human consciousness, one that distinguishes it qualitatively (and not merely, à la Leibniz, as a matter of degree) both from the momentary character of animal consciousness and the intuitive immediacy of divine awareness. Cf. Rousseau, whose natural man lives entirely for the moment (*Discourse on the Origins of Inequality*, p. 117 f.).

13. On the importance of this distinction for Kant's critical understanding of human consciousness, see chapter 9 below; see also Richard Velkley, "Kant on the Primacy and the Limits of Logic," *Graduate Faculty Journal* 2 (2): 147–62.

14. Cf. *Critique of Pure Reason* B/131–32.

15. See Kant's *Universal Natural History* (I:228; 86). Cf. Rousseau, *Discourse on the Origins of Inequality*, p. 140, where he speaks of "chance combination of several foreign causes which might never have arisen" and "different accidents" as factors without which man would have remained eternally in his primitive condition. Unlike Rousseau, Kant presents the emergence of civil society as a "providential" development that is both inevitable (given the psychological forces of attraction and repulsion) and morally necessary, since primitive man is not yet man in his moral perfection. Kant's later distinction between culture/history and the moral kingdom of ends is prefigured in the ambiguous relation in the *Remarks* between the forces of freedom and desire, and moral worldhood proper.

16. See XX:183: "Love of woman is exclusive with regard to other men according to the law of nature." Even the "purely carnal drive" can be exclusive in regard to its object.

17. See, for example, XX:68, 73.

18. See, for example, Kant's comments on the crudeness of pleasures associated with the feeling of need — that is, eating, drinking, sleep, and cohabitation. Kant singles out cohabitation as particularly course (*plump*), noting Juno's wrath toward Tiresias after he judged women superior with regard to it (XX:124).

19. See, for example, XX:137, 174, 167: "Woman loves less tenderly than man; otherwise she couldn't master him."

20. See, for example, XX:51, 55, 188–89: "Where there are many castles and great differences between men, everything is given over to taste; with republics it is otherwise."

21. See XX:55: "illusory good consists in one seeking only the opinion of the thing, and regarding the thing itself with indifference or even hate. The first illusion is that of honor. The second of greed. The latter loves only the opinion that one could have many goods of life through one's money without ever willing one in

earnest." See also XX:186: The man who pursues money for its own sake is like a young lover. "The young lover is happiest in the hope [of enjoyment]; and the day that brings his happiness [*Glück*] to the greatest height [*auch höchste Steig*] also causes it to founder [*brinkt es auch wieder zum Sinken*]. . . . All pleasures of life have their greatest charm in the pursuit. Possession is cold and the enthralled spirit [*Geist*] is transpired (sweated out/exhaled) [*ausdunstet*]." The (natural) sex act (and/ or its anticipation) is thus for Kant a metaphor for illusory good generally. The difference between sexual anticipation and avarice lies in the fact that sexual longing lends itself to artful "idealization" and with it to a "prolonged" pleasure superior in every respect to its "short and exhausting" natural consummation. Despite his general endorsement of nature over refinement, sex is one case for Kant in which artful refinement is clearly superior to nature. Thus Kant's distinction, in his description of sexual love, of the "most extreme" [*außerst*] happiness (which as an anticipation of the future can be indefinitely prolonged) and its "greatest height" (which brings about an immediate sinking back). In its ability to endure, the "ideal pleasure" to which unconsummated sexual longing can give rise escapes from the oscillating pattern of attraction and repulsion, appetite and satiety, that characterizes the natural sexual drive.

22. As the outward expression of esteem, honor, like money, has its proper use as a means, in this case as a means to self-preservation. This sort of honor Kant calls "true honor," as contrasted with the "delusional" honor, which treats the good opinion of others as an end in itself. Self-esteem is "inner honor," or alternatively, "pride" and "dignity" [*Würde*], which have nothing to do with "measuring oneself" against another (XX:130). Like self-esteem, true honor asks for no more than equality. Not to be despised is already honor; and he who does not esteem himself is worthy of contempt (XX:107, 163). Thus the worth of persons is equalized without being relativized. Each person is a self-subsistent source and object of worth, connected, by the law of equality, with every other object-source. Similarly, the pursuit of wealth is reasonable when directed to real enjoyment, but delusional when money itself becomes the goal while real enjoyment is indefinitely postponed (XX:55, 96, 130, 163).

23. XX:164: "Delusional honor stems for the most part from sexual inclination." Pretension (or the desire for honor in excess of equality) arises from the desire to secure freedom and from sexual inclination (XX:163). Whereas "self-love and self-esteem are not in themselves exclusive," love of woman "is exclusive with regard to other men according to the law of nature" (XX:183). Women are thus both the only naturally exclusive articles of (acquired) property and the first to furnish men with a ground for quarrel. What Kant will later call the asocial sociability of man is rooted in an inherently dialectical relation between the exclusivity of man's sexual claims and the promiscuity of his desire, a promiscuity aroused by woman herself (see, for example, XX:98, 68, 73). The instability of the original state of nature is rooted in sexual difference. Cf. Kant's letter to Schiller of March 30, 1795 (XII:10–11; 221), on the necessity of sexual difference as a "kind of chasm of thought."

24. Cf. *Reflection* no. 4138 (XVII:430): "Nature is good as a whole. 2. Good in each particular order that has its law. e.g. even the shortcomings [*Fehler*] of the female sex, where they are natural."

25. A third alternative, in which women inspire men to virtue "by ruling them domestically through goodness," is discussed below.

26. The connection between female liberty and social corruption is already thematic in Montesquieu, who makes female modesty and domestic retirement a condition of the virtuous republic. For Rousseau the connection is even more emphatic. Where Montesquieu links the ascendance of women with the decline of an independent nobility, Rousseau links it with (male) civil inequality as such. Kant differs from Montesquieu in his lower estimation of the nobility (whose social effect in Germany corresponds to that attributed by Montesquieu to the French monarchy); he differs from Rousseau in his higher estimation of the life of commerce. Kant's comments on the businesslike English, who combine industry with a kind of noble wildness, and who alone among the European nations continue to separate the sexes, are instructive in this regard (see XX:73–74, 103, 155). For both Kant and Rousseau, women (but not men) naturally desire to rule over others. See Joel Schwartz, *The Sexual Politics of Jean-Jacques Rousseau;* and Joan Landes, *Women and the Public Sphere in the Age of the French Revolution.*

27. See, for example, (XX:57, 136; 48): "many people have theology but not religion, except perhaps insofar as they are restrained from committing great offenses through the fear of hell."

28. See, for example, XX:38; 41:

The greatest concern of man is to know how to fulfill the place in creation belonging to him and rightly to understand what one must do to be a man [*Mensch*]. When, however, he learns to be acquainted with pleasures above or below himself, ones that flatter him but for which he is not organized and which conflict with the arrangement of the scheme that nature has measured him for; when he has learned to be acquainted with moral [*sittliche*] properties that glisten there, then he himself destroys the beautiful order of nature, only widening the spoilation. For he has abandoned [sunk from] his post; he did not sufficiently allow himself to be what he is determined to be; for having been cast out of the circle of humanity, he is nothing, and the gap that he creates spreads his own spoilation to neighboring members.

See also XX:175: "Speculation is not a necessary thing." Philosophy, however, becomes necessary to undo the damage caused by the unnatural expansion of desire.

29. Kant's earlier distinction in his essay *Negative Quantities* between stasis arising from a simple lack of motion and that arising from the equilibrium of real opposing forces provides the conceptual model: whereas natural tranquility depends upon an absence of feeling (and to this extent implies a lack of awareness), perfected tranquility allows for the soul's full presence to itself. See II:167 ff.; 207 ff.

30. As Kant sees it, the task of Rousseauian education is not to return man to a state of natural simplicity, but rather to restore man's self-sufficiency in the context of society by replacing natural simplicity with wise simplicity (XX:77). Thus Kant refuses to attribute to Rousseau a genuine desire to return to presocial nature (XX:175), while at the same time complaining that the education sketched out in *Emile,* dependent upon the lifelong devotion of a teacher to a single charge, fails to provide a model applicable to society as a whole. Rousseau rightly seeks to edu-

cate freely and to produce thereby a free man (XX:167). His error lies in failing to provide an education that can be purveyed wholesale.

31. The emergence of taste enhances, in turn, men's sexual choosiness: "taste does not depend on our needs. A man must already be socialized [*gesittet*] when he chooses a woman according to taste" (XX:29).

32. The tenderness of the nerves "is one of the controlling determinations of taste; for thereby is modified or limited the degree of contrast or affect, the rigidity [*Härte*] of sensations." Unity is in accord with ease to the extent that it is bound up with activity, which craves manifoldness (XX:125). Kant's description of the physiology of taste reserves to aesthetics a formal standard of perfection he previously applied to knowledge as such. Cf. his earlier descriptions in the *Universal Natural History* of the mental powers of the more happily endowed Saturnians, whose greater material refinement and organic "elasticity" enabled them to know more with less effort. In its active ease and serendipitous harmony, aesthetic experience (both in the *Remarks* and the later *Critique of Judgment*) preserves the traces of an earlier (Wolffian) cognitive ideal.

33. Kant's repetitive and sometimes contradictory notes on the subject suggest his indecision about the precise character of that "whole," and in particular, whether its members are to be regarded as true equals. See, for example, XX:73: "Concord [*Einigkeit*] is possible where either [member] can be a whole without the other, e.g. between two friends, and where neither is subordinated to the other. Concord can also exist in an exchange or contract. . . . But unity [*Einheit*] comes about when, in regard to needs as well as enjoyments, two together naturally constitute a whole. This is the case with man and wife. Still, unity is here bound up with equality. Man cannot enjoy any of life's pleasures without his wife and she cannot enjoy any necessities without her husband. This constitutes the difference in their character." Here reciprocally balanced difference is said to produce "equality together with unity" (as distinguished from the homogeneous equality of beings that are regarded as individually complete, an equality that produces only concord). Elsewhere, however, Kant notes that "concord is compatible with equality, but unity is not." And "since in marriage there must be unity, either the husband or the wife must govern [*regiren*] all." Moreover, it being the case that "either the inclinations of the husband or those of the wife must govern, the latter is the best" (XX:76). In his later *Anthropology* Kant adopts a formula according to which the husband governs while the wife reigns: "Who, then, should have supreme command in the household? . . . I would say, in the language of gallantry (but not without truth): the woman should *reign* and the man *govern;* for inclination reigns and understanding governs." The husband is like a sober minister to a monarch who thinks only of amusement (X:309–10; 172–73). On the quasi-natural complementarity of husband and wife, see Rousseau, *Emile,* trans. Allan Bloom, p. 406 f.

34. "Romanisch" can have either meaning.

35. On this crucial point, see *Emile,* pp. 358–60, 439–45; and Schwartz, *Sexual Politics.* Women's natural "modesty" corresponds in Rousseau to men's capacity to control their "limitless inclinations" through "self-command." Women's "virtue" (unlike that of men) is therefore always linked to a desire to rule over others.

36. The relevant passages are part of what seems to be a sketch for a projected

essay on "refined feeling and its origin." See also *Observations on the Feeling of the Beautiful and the Sublime,* in which Kant describes his subject as feelings of a "refined" sort, so called because one can enjoy them longer "without satiety or exhaustion" (II:208; 46). In some other passages in the *Remarks,* refinement is a term of disapprobation. See, for example, Kant's extended comments at XX:52.

37. Many passages link the ideal pleasure stimulated by (female) beauty with appearance and deception. See, for example, XX:61–62, 71: "the chief ground of enduring beauty is appearance. Greasepaint. A kind of falsehood that is as lovable as the truth." See also XX:139–40: woman's "refusal is a kind of beautiful untruth. . . . All things if they only become recognized for what they are have little that is agreeable in themselves; only through appearing to be other than they are do they elicit [*erheben*] feeling. All ideal pleasures are promoted through the art of appearance. If woman could always appear as she wished this artfulness would be very much to be preferred. The evil arises from the fact that the thing comes and the appearance disappears." And XX:167–68: "appearance is sometimes better than truth, for its pleasures are true pleasures. Greasepaint[;] when one recognizes it, the deception is over." Female beauty constitutes a kind of "permissible" deception (XX:133–34). See also in this regard Kant's comments on "moral taste," which he specifically associates with the desire to seem purer or more refined in sexual matters than one is, and (hence) with the perfection of social life (XX:48). Because it inclines toward imitation and appearance, moral taste (or alternatively, "taste in marriage") is inferior to moral principles, which are "lifted above" it (XX:51). Yet it is also the saving grace associated with the "new invention" — free intermingling of the sexes — whose upshot otherwise is wantonness (XX:188). As such, moral taste represents the "ambiguous" juncture (cf. XX:129) of aesthetic and moral realms whose distinctness the *Remarks* elsewhere affirms. (On the latter point, see note 58 below.)

38. Cf. Kant's *Conjectural Beginning of Human History* (VIII:113; 224): "[Sexual] *refusal* was the feat that brought about the passage from merely sensual to spiritual [*idealischen*] attractions. . . . In addition, there came a first hint at the development of man as a moral creature." Kant attributes the latter to (woman's) inclination to "conceal" from others "all that which might arouse low esteem." As in the *Remarks,* the transition from rude nature to morality (and its perfect honesty) turns on the "permissible" deception by which women make themselves seem more worthy than they are. As we will see, to the extent that she can teach virtue without herself being virtuous, woman solves what Kant later calls the "problem" of moral education.

39. Cf. *Emile,* pp. 476–79.

40. There are indications that Kant's interest in the subject may have been more than academic. See, for example, (XX:84, 120); cf. the flirtatious letter to Kant of one Frau Maria Charlotte Jacobi (1762), a beautiful and notorious young widow. Kant's contemporary biographer, L. E. Borowski, is supposed to have insisted, without naming names, that Kant twice fell in love and twice intended to marry. See Arsenij Gulyga, *Immanuel Kant,* translated from Russian to German by Sigrun Bielfeldt, pp. 75–77.

41. In a descriptive catalogue of the various senses, Kant observes that "the

sense of feeling in sexual pleasure [*Wollust*] is brief and exhausting, in the warmth of embraces short and sensitive [*empfindlich*]." In pain "the sense of feeling can endure a long time and be great." It can also "be easily mastered by the understanding (with the exception of the sexual inclination)" (XX:126).

42. Cf. *Universal Natural History* (I:366 ff.; 183 ff.).

43. Cf. Kant's later critical concern with reason's natural tendency toward "dialectical illusion": the entire "Transcendental Dialectic" of the *Critique of Pure Reason* (or roughly half of the entire work) is concerned with "exposing" this illusion and "taking precautions that we be not deceived" by its "tricks" and "entrap[ments]" (A/298 = B/354–55). Kant's critical treatment of philosophic illusion is distinguished from his treatment of illusion in the *Remarks* by (among other things) his critical insistence on the difference between "appearance" and "illusion." See, for example, *Critique of Pure Reason* A/293 = B/350.

Of interest in this regard is Kant's *Concerning Sensory Illusion and Poetic Fiction*, preparatory remarks for his disputation with Johann Gottlieb Kreutzfeld, a former student who had recently assumed a professorship in poetry (a post that Kant himself had once declined). Kant's text is especially noteworthy for its praise of both poetry's pure and joy-triggering illusions (comparable to optical illusions), by which the mind is not deceived but rather "plays"; and poetry's sensory deceptions (or "pious frauds"), by which the mind is "entrapped" and thereby "freed" of its submission to "irrational desire" (XV:908–11; 203–4). Both sorts of illusions are distinguished from conjuror's tricks, whose entrapping deceptions are genuinely despicable. See also Kant's gloss on Petrarch's refusal to marry Laura, lest his verses "lose all fire and beauty": "Because in matrimony there happens what Lucretius affirms of death: only then true words are elicited. The mask falls and reality remains" (XV:930–31; 212). Cf. Lucretius, *De rerum natura* III:57–58: and *Anthropology* (VII:180; 55), cited in Meerbote's notes to his translation.

44. That zetetic task is carried out in *Dreams of a Spirit Seer* (1766), discussed in chapter 5 below.

45. But the possibility of such an ethic obviously retains great appeal for Kant. An ethic based on tranquility of soul produces friendship rather than "enthusiasm," sympathy rather than "softheartedness," gentleness rather than ceremoniousness, desire rather than longing. The soul at rest is not inactive with respect to the body or to reason but only with respect to desires and pleasures.

46. Cf. *Critique of Pure Reason* (A/316 = B/373), which describes the "necessary idea" of a "perfect state" allowing "*the greatest possible human freedom* in accordance with laws *by which the freedom of each is made to be consistent with that of all others.*"

47. A similar analogy is made in *Dreams of a Spirit Seer.* But compare his letter to Moses Mendelssohn of April 8, 1766, in which he dismisses the comparison drawn in that work between "spiritual substance's actual influx and the force of universal gravitation," as "not to be taken seriously," that is, as "an example of how far one can go in philosophic fabrications . . . when there are no *data.*"

48. As in his earlier metaphysical works, worldhood ultimately requires that unity be mediated by a conscious universal, that is, what Hegel calls the "concept." The difference is that where Kant's once referred that unity to the creative intellect of God, it now resides directly in (the idea of) a universal will.

49. Man's experience of himself as a free being is rooted for Kant in his unwillingness to be mastered by "lawless" desire. Thus man's original fear of slavery (or mastery by the desires of others) is the primal equivalent of moral virtue proper (which consists in the mastery of one's own desires). Kant's insistence on an original human fear of slavery not only drastically reduces the distance between natural and social man (as Rousseau conceived it) but also highlights aversion to mastery by desire as *the* fundamental human experience. Kant posits in primal man an immediate "horror" at the submission of the will to lawless desire, even before he has encountered it in himself. The conscious self-motion or spontaneity that is the source of human independence derives its repulsive force, it seems, from this even more primary aversion.

50. On Rousseau's corresponding treatment of pity, see Clifford Orwin, "Rousseau and the Problem of Political Compassion," in *The Legacy of Rousseau,* ed. Nathan Tarcov and Clifford Orwin (forthcoming).

51. Benevolence is a "quiet inclination to regard another's happiness as the object of one's joy and also as a motive ground of one's action." Sympathy is an affect of benevolence toward the needy according to which we represent to ourselves what we have in our power to do to help. "It is thus often a chimera, because it is not always either in our power or in our will." The burgher "sympathizes with another burgher subjected by the prince. The nobleman with another nobleman but not with serfs" (XX:134–35).

52. See also XX:158: "No one if he is in need can represent to himself that if he were rich he would help every sufferer."

53. See, for example, XX:89: "The sweetness that we find in doing good to other men is an effect of the feeling of universal welfare that would occur in a state of freedom." The moral world is thus posited as both the *effect* of moral action and the *cause* of the pleasure we take in it.

54. See XX:147: moral goodness is a surplus of power stemming from renunciation; and XX:3: "self-esteem requires sacrifice."

55. Kant's unwillingness in *Dreams of a Spirit Seer* to foreclose the possibility of a spirit-world is based on the appeal of such a "hope" (II:349; 337). Nevertheless, Kant minimizes the positive role of religion in moral action (not least because "the subordination of morals to religion" is connected to "the subjugation of the people" [XX:153]). Religion ought to find its "touchstone" in natural morals (*Sittlichkeit*). Dread of eternal punishment "is not an immediate ground of morally good action," but only a "counterweight" against the charm of evil (XX:18). Kant, however, inclines more positively toward religiously based hope of reward in a future life, a hope that social man appears to need, at least on an interim basis: "the question must be posed as to how much the inner moral grounds of a man amount to. It may amount to enough that he is good without great effort when he is in a condition of freedom. But when other injustices or the compulsion of delusion [*Wahnes*] exercise control over him, then this inner morality lacks sufficient power. He must have religion, and encourage himself by means of the reward of a future life. Human nature is not capable of an immediate moral purity. If, however, purity is active in him supernaturally, then future reward no longer has the property of a motive ground" (XX:28).

56. Only when the moral world is posited as outside of time does its simultaneous status as the *goal* of our moral activity and the *efficient cause* of the pleasure we
take in it lose its contradictory character.

57. See, for example, XX:5, 113: love is either sensual/corporeal or moral/spiri-
tual. Love of women always includes something of the former.

58. See, for example, XX:49 f. for what appears to be a sketch for a new work
with clearly distinguished aesthetic and moral components: "Through the metaphysical foundations of aesthetics the variety of non-moral feelings are to become
known, through the foundations of the moral [*sittliche*] world the variety of moral
feelings are to become known, according to differences of sex, age, education, government, race and climate." (The Rischmüller edition of the *Remarks* [p. 42] has
"moral world-wisdom" in place of "moral world.")

59. A partial answer lies in the peculiar character of man's primordial aversion
to slavery, an aversion characterized by a noble "horror" that links it as much with
the aesthetic experience of the sublime as with moral feeling proper. This peculiarity is all the more remarkable, given Kant's efforts in the *Remarks* to distinguish between moral and aesthetic feeling (and so break decisively with the doctrine of his earlier *Observations*, in which [moral] virtue and the [aesthetic] experience of the sublime are explicitly identified). Kant's insistence on the autonomy of
moral experience over against the aesthetic is beset by the following dilemma: On
the one hand, to the extent that man's fear of slavery is deemed "natural," the autonomy of the moral over against the aesthetic becomes questionable. On the other
hand, to the extent that one insists upon the strict autonomy of the moral over
against the nonmoral, the realizability of moral worldhood becomes questionable.
But a moral goal incapable of realization is indistinguishable from moral delusion.
Kant's critical position differs from that of the *Remarks* (and escapes, perhaps, from
the above dilemma) by grounding moral obligation (and with it the distinction
between moral and nonmoral feeling) in an absolute "fact of reason." The realizability of the moral world (or the kingdom of ends on earth) becomes a secondary
question relating to moral encouragement, rather than a primary test of objective
moral validity.

60. See XX:208 on the "most perfect [moral] world" and the unresolved relation between its "natural" and "supernatural" versions.

61. Kant's conception of woman as nonvirtuous educator in virtue has crucial
importance for later German Idealist thought, anticipating as it does the latter's
central effort to work out a satisfactory mediation of nature and freedom (see, for
example, Fichte's *Science of Right*, "Supplement on Family Right," *Werke*, vol. 3, pp.
304–53; and Hegel, *Philosophy of Right*, secs. 158–72); on the latter point, see Susan Meld Shell, "A Determined Stand: Stand: Freedom and Security in Fichte's
Science of Right." For some recent feminist responses to this essentially Rousseauian
view of women, see, for example, Ursula Pia Jauch, *Immanuel Kant zur Geschlechterdifferenz: Aufklärische Vorteilskritik und bürgerliche Geschlechtsvormundschaft;* Susan
Mendus, "Kant: An Honest but Narrow-Minded Bourgeois?"; and Pauline
Kleingeld, "The Problematic Status of Gender-Neutral Language in the History of
Philosophy: The Case of Kant."

62. Cf. Hamann's "Review of Kant's *Critique of Pure Reason*" and "Metacritique
of the Purism of Reason," in *J. G. Hamann: A Study in Christian Existence*, by Ronald

Gregor Smith, pp. 207–21. At the time of Kant's early reading of Rousseau, Hamann had recently become a sort of religious mystic and avowed follower of Socrates. (A famous letter to Kant [July 27, 1759] is full of half-mocking references to "Sapphic" mutual love, with Kant and Hamann each playing "Socrates" to Berens's "Alcibiades.") Kant renounces the principle of attraction in both its male (or spiritual) and female (or physical) forms at the very moment that he discovers, via his study of Rousseau, an explicitly masculine model of moral community. Goethe, perhaps, had something like this in mind when he commended Kant's "immortal service" to morality, in "[bringing] us all back from that effeminacy in which we were wallowing" (see his letter to Chancellor von Müller, April 29, 1818; quoted in Cassirer, *Kant's Life,* p. 270).

It is tempting to speculate on the differences between Kant and Hamann—two extraordinary thinkers of similar "Pietist" background, who were near neighbors for much of their lives. In Rousseau, Kant seems to have found a way to celebrate the qualities of his own father (a "common laborer" whose "upright honesty" Kant always praised), albeit at the cost of renouncing earlier objects of attraction. In so doing he found himself able to vindicate rationally, and in the name of human freedom, a paternal virtue linked otherwise with a discredited and servile piety. (On the relation between servility and piety for Kant, see Cassirer, *Kant's Life,* pp. 12–24.) Hamann's peculiar (and in its own very different way, Rousseauian) reprisal of Luther, on the other hand, asserted itself through the (unlikely) vehicle of an emancipated (and arguably bisexual) sensuality. On the matter of Hamann's homosexuality, see Beiser, *Fate of Reason,* pp. 20, 26; and H. A. Salmony, *Hammans metakritische Philosophie,* pp. 75–84. As Hamann says in the *Socratic Memorabilia,* apropos of Socrates' "vice" (and to excuse, as Beiser speculates, Hamann's own recent "sins"): "one cannot feel friendship without a little sensuality" (*Werke* 2:68). For Kant's decidedly harsher views of homosexuality, see, for example, *Lectures on Ethics,* pp. 169–71.

63. See, for example, Kant's *Anthropology from a Pragmatic Point of View* (X:250; 117). Perhaps under the influence of Adam Smith, the social and economic "mercantilism" of the *Remarks* (in which the acquisition of wealth is a zero-sum game) gives way, in Kant's critical thought, to a more optimistic perspective on wealth-getting as an activity from which all can gain.

64. *Anthropology* (X:305, 310, 321; 169, 173, 183). In the end, however, moral progress is only distinguished from "chimera and illusion" by the "fact" that it can come to be—or be regarded as—a self-fulfilling prophecy. See *Conflict of the Faculties,* pt. 2.

65. *Anthropology* (X:325 ff.; [186 ff.]). See also *Conjectural Beginning of Human History* (VIII:116 n; 228 n). On the importance of the gap between natural and civil maturity in Kant and Rousseau see Allan Bloom, "Introduction," in Rousseau, *Emile,* p. 17.

66. *Anthropology* (X:327; 188).

67. Kant was responding to Wilhelm von Humboldt's "On Sexual Difference and Its Influence on Organic Nature," which Kant said he found "impossible to decipher." In the same letter, Kant praised Schiller's *Letters on the Aesthetic Education of Mankind* (which his own *Remarks* in some ways anticipates), calling it "splendid" (XII:10–11; 221).

Chapter Five

1. Kant may have especially in mind Wolff's reference to Schlaraffenland in his discussion of the principle of sufficient reason. ("Schlaraffenland," or "Land of the Lazy" — alternatively called the "Land of Cockaigne" — is a fabled country of fantastic luxury and ease, in which whatever is wished for immediately presents itself. Trees, for example, bear fruit on demand, and pigeons offer themselves in edible form whenever someone is hungry. *The Country of Cockaigne* is also the title of a famous medieval satire on monastic life.) According to Wolff, a world without the principle of sufficient reason would be as fabulous as that mythic country — a "kind of mythic existence where human willing takes the place of reasons for things" (see Gurr, *Principle of Sufficient Reason*, pp. 42–43). The difference between truth and the "world of dreams" exactly parallels the difference between a world in which there are reasons for things and one dictated by an omniscient human will. The tale shows us, according to Wolff, that in a world in which the human will furnishes the unique reason for what is and will be there would be no possibility or actuality external to man. But without a reason extrinsic to his will, man would have no reason to wish one side of a contradiction rather than another, thus making two contradictories simultaneously true. In such a world, nothing would happen; moreover, the principle of noncontradiction would be breached, destroying the distinction between truth and dreaming (see Wolff, *Philosophia prima*, no. 6). As Kant himself admits "with some humiliation," in investigating the veracity of ghost tales he has found the "nothing" one usually finds where one has nothing to seek/ has no business to be (*nichts zu suchen hat*) (II:318; 306).

2. Cf. Kant's later *Definition of the Concept of a Human Race:* "If the magic force of imagination, or the artfulness of man is given to have a capacity in animal bodies to alter the generative force itself . . . one would not know anymore from which original nature man has proceeded, or how much it might deviate from that original, and, since the human imagination knows no limits, into what grotesque forms of genuses and species it might finally run wild. . . . If I were to allow even a single case of this kind it would be like making room for a single ghost story or tale of magic. The bounds [*Schranken*] of reason once penetrated [*durch brochen*], delusion presses through the same gap [*Lücke*] by the thousands" (VIII:97). The essay is taken up in chapter 8 below.

3. Given the context, Kant may be playing here on *gebannten*, from *bannen*, meaning "to cast a spell over," "fascinate," or "exorcise."

4. Kant here assimilates rational spirits and those beings which (putatively) constitute the inner ground of animal life. He never makes clear in the essay how such beings differ from rational spirits (or "spirits in the proper sense"), that is, what is here meant by "reason."

5. Physical atoms, on the other hand, do unite into solid wholes. This does not necessarily mean that such atoms lack the sort of representational inwardness we ordinarily associate with the mental.

6. Kant distinguishes divine spirit as creator and sustainer of the universe from a spirit-substance that is part of it. The concept of a spiritual nature of the former sort is easy, says Kant, for it merely involves the negation of all properties of matter. The concept of a finite spirit-substance (like the human soul) that is supposed to

exist in union with matter, on the other hand, involves this difficulty: "that I am to think the union of the soul with a bodily being as a reciprocal whole, and yet am to cancel [*aufheben*] the only sort of [such] connection of which I know, a connection that takes place among material beings" (II:321 n; [309 n]). The concept of an embodied spirit-substance as here presented combines the thought of reciprocal community with the "cancellation" of that very thought. In short, conceiving of the human soul (or any other embodied spirit-substance) instantiates as worldly act the very juncture it cannot, quite, represent (see II:323; [311]).

7. Cf. Rousseau, *Emile*, p. 83.

8. On a similar dream experience that Kant credited with saving his life, see chapter 10 below.

9. This "difference" is apparently not a function of the latter's "freedom"; both kinds of immaterial beings, according to the account here, are capable of voluntary action. Reason *is* identified with a certain kind of "self-activity"; perhaps Kant means that while both animals and rational beings are capable of voluntary action (that is, possessed of *will*), rational beings alone are *conscious* of its object (that is, aware of an aim or end in view). Or perhaps it is simply that animals would and could not be startled by the abysmal thought earlier described.

10. Cf. Hermann Boerhaave, *Elemente chimiae,* vol. 1, p. 64: "alimenta plantarum radicibus externis, animalium internis, hauriuntur" (the nutriments of plants are absorbed by means of external roots, that of animals by internal roots).

11. Kant tentatively distinguishes between animals and plants in terms of the fact that a plant, whose tool of nourishment is "sunk into the element of its support," is adequately supported by forces external to itself.

12. Thus "in our most secret motives [which include the "strong law of obligation" and the "weaker one of benevolence"] we recognize that we are dependent on the *rule of the general will,* which confers upon the world of all thinking beings its *moral unity* and invests it with a systematic constitution." As such, moral feeling may be conceived as an effect produced by "universal reciprocal interaction" (II:335–36; [322–23]).

13. And all of this "in virtue of the connection between the private and the general will," that is, "between the unity and the wholeness of the spirit world," without which the discrepancy between the moral and physical relations of men on earth remains "strange" [*befremdlich*].

14. *Fruchtknoten,* it may be helpful to note, is the German word for ovary.

15. See II:336; 323.

16. The allusion to Tiresias hints faintly at the sexual roots of such madness. As Kant notes in the *Remarks,* Tiresias's transformation came about through his intimate sexual knowledge (of copulation from both ends, as it were) and subsequent punishment for violating female modesty. As Kant will later be at pains to insist, his interest in death (or transition from this world to the other) does not extend to birth (or the transition from the other world to this); about birth and propagation he claims to know, and to want to know, nothing. In any case, the androgynous Tiresias would seem to constitute the ultimate synthesis, uniting in a single substance the heterogenous forms of male and female. His knowledge is to this extent analogous with the interworldly translation about which Kant here hypothocates. The "charm" of Kant's spiritual image is already threatened by an under-

tow of the grotesque. On the sexual roots of madness see also the *Anthropology*, where Kant insists that "the seeds of madness develop [only] with the seeds of reproduction," there being "no such thing as a deranged child" (the latter phrase appears only in the first edition) (VII:217; 86).

17. On the continuing importance for Kant of daydreaming, that is, the transitional state midway between sleeping and waking, see chapter 10 below.

18. See his extended comments on Descartes's *ideas materiales* understood as the vibration or concussion (*Erschütterung oder Bebung*) of the nerve fiber or nerve spirit (*Nervengewebe oder Nervengeist*) of the brain. Such a material account (which associates sanity with rectified vibration) might "reasonably" explain mental disturbance but for the fact that it locates the focus imaginarius not outside the body but in the back of the eye itself, a difficulty Kant admits he cannot presently solve (II:345–46; [332–33]).

19. *Emile*, p. 270.

20. Cf. *Emile*, p. 273.

21. On the semantic ambiguity of "pneumatology" (whose conventional contemporary meanings included both "the doctrine of spiritual substances" and that branch of mechanics concerned with "the properties of air"), see, for example, Samuel Johnson's *Dictionary* and Diderot's and D'Alembert's *Encyclopédie*. Under *pneumatique* the latter has: "The science occupied with spirits and spiritual substances. The science of the properties of air and the laws obeyed by fluids in condensation, rarefaction, gravitation. Also: a technical explanation of the pneumatic machine, invented ca. 1654 by Otto de Guericke, Consul at Magdeburg" (quoted in Barbara Maria Stafford, *Body Criticism: Imaging the Unseen in Enlightenment Art and Medicine*, p. 417). On pneumatics and pneumatology, see also Simon Schaffer, "States of Mind: Enlightenment and Natural Philosophy," in G. S. Rousseau, ed., *The Languages of Psyche: Mind and Body in Enlightenment Thought*, pp. 263–73, 283; Marielene Putscher, *Pneuma, Spiritus, Geist;* and G. Cantor and M. J. S. Hodge, eds., *Conceptions of Ether: Studies in the History of Ether Theories, 1740–1900.*

22. Kant attributed his own "hypochondriacal tendency" to a narrow chest that caused constipation and made breathing painful, that is, maladies associated with a restriction of air or wind and an ensuing feeling "inside" his body of the pressure or resistance normally associated with "outer" experience. Hypochondria, in short, seems to arise from a disturbing modification of the normal bodily boundary between inwardness and outwardness. Kant elsewhere insists that he was able to cure himself from this and other diseases by deliberate withdrawal of attention from the offending sensation, much as, in *Dreams,* he withdraws attention from the (attractive) image of the spirit world with a counter-image calculated to repel.

23. See *Dreams of a Spirit-Seer Illustrated by Dreams of Metaphysics,* trans. E. F. Goerwitz, p. 84.

24. False philosophy as philosophy with "one eye missing" is a recurring theme for Kant (see, for example, *Anthropology* [VII:227; 95. 128; 10]). Cycloptic thinking is the opposite of pluralism in thinking, or the willingness to test one's judgment by the understanding of others. Use of parallaxis in ascertaining the position of the stars in relation to the earth is associated with the new astronomy, hence — by analogy — with Kant's own later "Copernican" revolution. Cf. Kant's later con-

cern with his failure to notice that he had lost vision in one eye, a failure that apparently persisted for several years (*Conflict of the Faculties* [VII:116 n; 212 n]).

25. Like the Latin *spiritus,* the Greek *pneuma* originally referred to breath or wind (cf. the Hebrew *ruah,* which also means both breath and soul). "Spirit," by Kant's rendering, has the secondary meaning of breath or wind that neither resists matter nor meets matter's resistance. Compressed or restricted breath—the primary focus of Kant's own "hypochondria"—is thus the opposite of spirit in the proper Kantian sense. Air, which we continually draw in and expel, vitally connects the intimacy of the body and the external world. As will be argued in chapter 10, the pathological distortion, in Kant's case, of the act of breathing gives him a kind of privileged insight into the uncanny relation between "material and immaterial nature." Concerning the general epistemological problem of conceiving "spirit" other than materially, see Rousseau, *Emile,* pp. 25–26: "The word *spirit* has no sense for anyone who has not philosophized. To the people and to children, a spirit is only a body. . . . That is why all the peoples of the world, without excepting the Jews, have made corporeal gods for themselves. . . . I admit that we are taught to say that God is everywhere, but we also believe that air is everywhere. And in its origin the word *spirit* itself signifies only breath or wind." The biblical locus classicus for the treatment of breath or spirit as the mediating link between God and man is Genesis 2:7: "And the Lord God formed man of the dust of the ground and breathed into his nostrils the breath of life; and man became a living soul."

On "spirit" in the Protestant tradition see the informative discussion by Alan M. Olson in *Hegel and the Spirit: Philosophy as Pneumatology.* Olson reads Hegel as a "speculative pneumatolog[ist]" for whom the mediation of *Geist* as energizing bond between mind and body is functionally identical with the work of Holy Spirit as Luther understood it (pp. 10–11). Olson traces (with some irony) the "pneumatology thesis" in Hegel studies to the satirical *Hegel-Spiel,* published by O. H. Gruppe in 1832. Gruppe entitled his play *Der Wind, oder eine ganz absolute Konstruction der Weltgeschichte durch Oberons Horn* (The wind, or an entirely absolute construction of world history through Oberon's horn). Hegel is portrayed as one Nuss Knackerschen (Little Nutcracker), who seeks to uncover the secrets of the Aristotelian *nous* (but whose name also plays on Hegel's own vaunted effort to "crack" the nut of truth). It seems unlikely, however, that Gruppe was "blissfully unaware" (as Olson and the play's modern editor, Heiner Höfener, assert) of the "larger implications" of aligning *Geist* with *Luft* and *Atmen.* Gruppe's work is, indeed, continuous here with a literary tradition reaching back at least as far as *Hudibras,* Butler's "pneumatological" satire. The broad antisemitism displayed by Gruppe's work (on which Olson remarks) replays on a low political level Kant's own (more high-minded) "antikabbalism." On the Kaballah's historical association with theosophy and Christian mysticism, see *Encyclopedia Judaica,* vol. 10, pp. 643–47.

26. Cf. the happy Saturnians of Kant's *Universal Natural History,* who accomplish more than we do with less effort and thus effectually live longer.

27. Kant's customary spelling, in this work, of "Swedenborg."

28. *Einräumen* means to yield to, but also to make place for something in a delimited space, as when one arranges furniture in a room. Cf. II:346; 333.

29. Cf. II:372; 358. See also Kant's *Announcement of the Program of His Lectures*

for the Winter Semester, 1765–1766 (II:312–13; 298–300). Kant's course on "physical, moral and political geography" undertakes to study the condition of states throughout the world, not as the accidental consequence of the deeds and fates of individuals, but as the product of "the reciprocal interaction" of physical and moral forces — the condition of states, in other words, "in relation to what is more constant," namely, "the nature of their products, customs, industry, trade and population." In place of political history as conventionally studied (an accidental sequence of battles, kings, etc.), Kant urges the utility of what today would probably be called historical political economy. Such a "reduction" of science is necessary, he claims, if we are to be able to attain that unity without which "all our knowledge is nothing but a fragmentary patchwork." In a sociable century, he asks, is one not permitted "to regard the stock which a multiplicity of entertaining, instructive, and easily understood knowledge offers for the maintenance of social intercourse [*Umganges*] as one of the benefits which it is not demeaning for science to have before its eyes?" Promotion of human *Umgang* through the teaching of "*physical, moral* and *political* geography" is presented in Kant's "announcement" as essentially related to the central, self-unifying aim of science.

On Kant's pioneering academic treatment of geography, see J. A. May, *Kant's Concept of Geography,* pp. 3–5. Kant regularly offered courses in geography from 1756 until the year before his retirement in 1797 — forty-eight times in all, a figure exceeded only by the number of courses that he offered in logic (fifty-four) and metaphysics (forty-nine).

Kant's *Announcement* refers implicitly at a number of points to Rousseau's *Emile* (consider, for example, Kant's desire to make "public education" conform "more to nature," his reliance on "utility," and his ascent from intuitive judgments based on the comparison of sensations, through the formation of concepts, to scientific knowledge of concepts as parts of a well-ordered whole [II:306; 291]). While it is true that Kant praises the British moralists for "penetrating the furthest" in the search for fundamental moral principles, his aim — to establish the respective perfections of primitive and wise innocence — could not be more Rousseauian.

30. The editors of the Cambridge translation speculate that *Undenkliche* here puns on *Unendliche.* Kant's other editors treat it as a slip of the pen.

31. This coincidence is thus the one thing about which Kant, without digressing (*Umschweif*), declares himself to be serious (II:359; 346). This declaration is followed by Kant's arrival (in the final pages of his essay) to its end/purpose (*Zweck*), namely "the writings of [his] hero," that is, by the resumption of a tone that is less than earnest.

32. Letter to Moses Mendelssohn, April 8, 1766 (X:69–73; 54–57).

33. "The deception of the senses . . . concerns the ultimate/first fundament of all our judgments, and if that foundation were defective [*unrichtig*], there is little that the rules of logic could do to remedy the situation!" (II:360–61; [347]). Kant distinguishes here between *Wahnsinn* (lunacy) and *Wahnwitz,* a derangement of reason that reason itself can guard against.

34. Cf. Kant's treatment in the *Critique of Pure Reason* of the Second and Third Analogies.

35. According to Swedenborg's "gigantic" fantasy, all spirit societies taken together present themselves under the appearance of a "Greatest Man."

36. The childishness of Swedenborg's figure in fact goes deeper than Kant's reference to grammar school memory tricks suggests. Swedenborg's is a vision that literally obscures the pivotal distinction between inner sense and outer, objective experience that Kant will later associate with the infant's acquisition of a sense of self (see *Anthropology* [VII:128 f.; 10 f.]).

37. In this broad allusion to Socratic midwifery, Kant lays aside his pet concern with life after death to touch on procreative themes, a subject about which he previously claimed to know and want to know nothing. In the current instance, curiosity (*Vorwitz*) combined with "fertility of imagination" are singled out as the qualities disposing one to mental miscarriage.

38. Virgil, *Aeneid*, bk. 2, lines 793–94; bk. 6, lines 701–2.

39. Cf. (II:369; [355]): Simplicity, if it is to be wise, must "know the dispensable, yes, even the impossible."

40. Cf. Rousseau's *Emile*, in which the tutor likewise wastes time to gain it and resorts to benevolent fraud in the name of utility.

41. That the agent of this engorgement is as much quasi-erotic fantasy as bad mental diet bears out the term's alimentary/sexual connotations. On Kant's extended treatment of the relation between resisting cramps and sound philosophizing, see chapter 10 below.

42. *Wurm, Schlang.*

43. *Stypsis* is a medical term denoting contraction of organic tissue and, secondarily, a therapeutic remedy that binds the stomach or bowels.

44. Cf. Plato, *Phaedo* 98d.

45. Concerning immortality, Kant concedes this much:

I am acquainted with alterations in myself as in a subject that lives: namely, thoughts, choice, etc., etc.; and because these determinations are of a different sort than all which, taken together, make up my concept of body, I fairly [*billigmaßig*] think myself an incorporeal and permanent being. [But] whether this being will also be able to think without connection with the body, can never be established by means of the empirically known nature of this being. . . . All judgments, such as those concerning how my soul moves my body, or how it now or in the future may relate to other beings like itself, can never be any more than fictions. (II:370; [357])

Such immortality as we are able "fairly" to assure ourselves does not extend to our ability to think, that is, to consciousness as we can (in this world) imagine or conceive it. Such (thoughtless) immortality is only thinkable as a sort of living death — a contradiction in terms that is itself the cancellation of thought. Anticipation of such an annihilation of the subject arouses in us, according to Kant, a special horror which, when accompanied by conscience (or something like it), defines the essence of the sublime. This consideration, I would suggest, is an important source of his peculiar satisfaction in the idea of moral community, an idea that (alone) permits us to look forward with hope. On the latter point, see Kant's discussion of "Carazon's Dream" in *Observations on the Feeling of the Beautiful and the Sublime* (II:209–10 n; 48–49 n). Cf. *Anthropology* (VII:167; 44).

46. Cf. *Critique of Pure Reason* A/5 = B/9.

47. Letter to Mendelssohn, February 7, 1766 (X:68).

48. *Abdrucken* (to print) literally means to express or squeeze out.

49. Letter to Mendelssohn, April 8, 1766. This admission occurs in the same paragraph as Kant's famous claim that "everything comes down to seeking out the *data* of the problem, how the soul is *present in the world,*" a paragraph that is for this reason alone worth quoting at some length:

> It suffices for my not inconsiderable pleasure to hear that my small and volatile essay will have the good luck to entice "Basic Reflections" from you on this point, and I regard it as useful enough if it can occasion deeper investigations in others. I am convinced that the point [*Punkt*] to which all these considerations/weighings [*Erwägungen*] refer [*beziehen*] will not escape you, a point I could have signalled more knowingly had I not allowed the work to be printed sheet by sheet, owing to which I could not always foresee what would lead to a better understanding of what was to follow, and owing to which certain explanations had to be left out, because they would have occurred in the wrong place. In my opinion, it all comes down to [*kommt alles darauf an*] seeking out the *data* to the problem of *how the soul is present in the world, to material natures as well as to ones other than of that sort.* One must thus find the force of outer efficacy and the receptivity to suffer externally from such a substance, of which union with the human body is only a special kind. . . . This investigation resolves itself into another, namely, whether one can by means of rational inferences discover a *primitive* force, that is the primary, fundamental relation of cause to effect; and since I am certain that this is impossible, it follows that if these forces are not given in experience, they can only be invented [*erdichtet*]. But this invention, a heuristic fiction or hypothesis, can never even be proved to be possible, and its thinkability (the appearance of which follows from the fact that no impossibility can be derived from the concept either) is a mere delusion [*Blendwerk*]. . . . My analogy between the actual ethical influx of spiritual natures and universal gravitation is not properly my serious opinion but an example of how far one can go in philosophic invention where *data* are lacking. . . . If, for the time being, we put aside arguments based on propriety [*Anständigkeit*] or on the divine purposes, and ask whether from our experience such knowledge of the soul is ever possible . . . we shall then see whether *birth* (in the metaphysical sense), *life,* and *death* are something we can ever understand [*einsehen*] through reason. (X:71–72; [55–57])

"Basic Reflections" evidently refers to Mendelssohn's *Phaedon,* published the following year. It is generally regarded as Mendelssohn's most important philosophic work.

50. Cf. Hegel, *Logic,* vol. 2, trans. W. H. Johnson and L. G. Struthers, p. 158.

51. See his letter to Mendelssohn, April 8, 1766 (X:71; 55). On "logic" as the "cathartic" of healthy reason, see *Reflection* no. 1589 (XVI:27), 1600 (XVI:22), 1579 (XVI:22), 1600 (XVI:31), and 1602 (XVI:31), dated problematically between the late 1760s and the mid 1770s (cf. *Critique of Pure Reason* A/53 = B/78). Among the various philosophical and historical associations of "catharsis" see Addison's reference in the *Spectator,* no. 502, to Plato's thematic treatment in the *Laws* of the cathartic properties of philosophy. A variant of "catharsis" (that is,

"catharan") is also a (derogatory) synonym for members of extreme religious sects (for example, the Puritans). Spanning in its historical meanings both the expelling and the infusing of false belief, the term "catharsis" straddles the issue on which Kant's and Mendelssohn's competing recuperations of Plato turn: namely, whether and in what way reason is a vehicle of genuine knowledge, especially as regards the question of the separability of soul and body.

Chapter Six

1. This, at least, is one likely construction. See, for example, *Reflection* no. 5037 (XVIII:69). On the importance of Kant's discovery of the ideality of space and time for the development of the critical philosophy, see Buroker, *Space and Incongruence*.

2. This is not to discount the many obstacles that Kant worked to overcome in the next decade, some of which will be considered in chapter 10 below.

3. "*Coordinates* are related to one another as complements to a whole. . . . the relationship is reciprocal and *homonymous,* so that any correlate is related to the other as both determining it and being determined by it. . . . This coordination is conceived of as *real* and objective, not as ideal and depending upon the subject's power of choice, by means of which any multiplicity whatsoever may be fashioned into a whole by a process of adding together at will. For by taking several things together, you achieve without difficulty a *whole of representation* but you do not, in virtue of that, arrive at the *representation* of a *whole*" (II:390; 380–81).

4. Although Kant's question (about the nature of worldhood) "concerns a problem which arises in accordance with reason, namely, how it is possible for several substances to coalesce into one thing, and upon what conditions it depends that this one thing is not a part of something else," nevertheless, "the force of the word 'world,' as it is found in common use, springs to mind of its own accord. For no one assigns *accidents* to a *world* as its parts, but only to its *state* as *determinations.* Hence, the so-called *egoistic* word, which is completely constituted by a unique simple substance together with its accidents, is not properly called a world, unless, perhaps, it is called an *imaginary* world. For the same reason, it is wrong to attribute to the world as a whole the series of successive things . . . as part of it" (II:389; 380). A third condition of worldhood — its exhaustiveness or totality — is taken up below.

5. How it is possible that a plurality of substances should be in reciprocal interaction with each other is a question (he now puts it) that only discursive understanding, not intuition, is capable of answering (II:407; 401). Cf. Kant's later refinement of the relation between community and totality and concomitant differentiation of understanding and reason.

6. Cf. *Physical Monadology* (I:473; 115. I:475; 116). The *Dissertation*'s emphasis on the differing ancestries of metaphysics and geometry develops Kant's earlier comparison of their combination to the mating of a griffin and a horse. For a very thorough consideration of the problem of the relation of metaphysics and geometry as a unifying theme in Kant's thought, see Friedman, *Kant and the Exact Sciences.* Cf. also the later, critically framed question of how synthetic a priori knowledge is possible, that is, how heterogenous sources can produce (by a process Kant calls "epigenesis") a unified product — and what distinguishes said product from an in-

terspecies hybrid or monstrosity. The problem of worldly cognition has this in common with that of sexual generation; namely, that it is just as mysterious how one species can have two sexes that combine to form offspring as it is how two mental faculties (through a similar process of "epigenesis") can combine to produce knowledge.

7. Although phenomena are semblances (species) rather than ideas of things "and express no internal or absolute quality of the objects, knowledge of them is nonetheless perfectly genuine knowledge," both because as sensual concepts they "bear witness to the presence of an object—which is opposed to idealism" and because they arise according to "common laws" (II:397; [389]). The problem of accounting for sensible knowledge (that is, knowledge of "phenomena") is referred to the coordination by a "certain natural law of the mind," representations whose form or species is derived from that coordinating activity rather than from the sensa themselves; for "objects do not strike the senses through their form or configuration." The role assigned in the *Critique of Pure Reason* to the "transcendental unity of apprehension" is here passed off to an otherwise unclarified "internal principle of the mind," in virtue of which the various factors in an object that affects the senses can "coalesce into some representational whole" in accordance with "stable and innate laws" (II:393; 384–85). I take Kant's later clarification of this process in terms of the transcendental principles of judgment underlying the unity of consciousness to be the major theoretical achievement of the subsequent decade.

It is true that the *Dissertation* is often read as committing Kant to a continuing dogmatic insistence on the possibility of noumenal knowledge of a theoretical as well as practical kind; but compare Richard Velkley's persuasive interpretation, which brings the *Dissertation* more closely in line on this score with Kant's later critical position. As Velkley points out, Kant neither denies, nor explicitly affirms, more than a "symbolic" theoretical knowledge of noumena or things in themselves (II:396; 389; see especially *Freedom*, pp. 130–35). For a different reading, see T. K. Seung, *Kant's Platonic Revolution in Moral and Political Philosophy*.

The problem of how to account for the determination of what Kant here calls "species" is arguably one that he was never able fully to resolve. Kant's critical approach is to refer the problem to the dark workings of the mind approachable (if at all) via empirical psychology. The issue is informatively discussed in Pippen, *Kant's Theory of Form*, and Bencivenga, *Kant's Copernican Revolution;* on Kant's predecessors see also Richard Aguila, *Representational Mind*. On Kant's late return to the problem in the *Critique of Judgment* and, even more ambitiously, in the *Opus postumum*, see chapters 8 and 10 below.

8. See his letter to Marcus Herz, February 21, 1772, in which Kant admits to having "passed over in silence" the question of how noumenal knowledge (that is, a representation that refers to an object without being affected by it) "can be possible" (X:130–31; 73).

9. Cf. Lewis White Beck's remark, in the introduction to his translation of the *Dissertation*, that although all the premises (for the impossibility of knowledge of things in themselves) were already stated in the *Dissertation*, "almost incredibly the obvious conclusion [was] not drawn" (*Kant's Latin Writings*, p. 138). But see (II:396–97; 389–90): "there is (for man) no *intuition* of things intellectual, but

only a *symbolic cognition*....For our minds, intuition is always passive, and is possible only so far as something is able to affect our senses."

10. Cf. *Reflection* no. 4108 (1769–70): "The true intelligible world is the moral world," whose formal principle is valid for every man (XVII:418).

11. Substances, that is, in the strong metaphysical sense. Cf. (II:409; [403–4]): The world requires a principle of possible interaction (*commercium*) among a plurality of substances, a principle that cannot be given by their mere existence if the connection among them is to be construed as real rather than merely "sympathetic"; hence, that connection must be referred to their "communal ground." Granted that "we can conclude from a given world to a sole cause of all its parts," Kants adds, if we could proceed the other way, "we would be able to argue from a given common cause of all things to their [necessary] interconnection." Kant admits, however, to being less clear on the latter point. At issue is the continuing problematic relation between the reality of the worldly connection and the dependence of that connection on the mind of God, a relation that remains, for minds that cannot think like God, opaque. Kant claims in the same passage that the form of the given world "bears witness to" (*testatur*) the presence of the cause of its matter (II:408; 403), the same term he uses to describe the inconclusive bearing of space and time on our knowledge of the universal connection of things (II:391; 381). Earlier, however, he argues that our knowledge of noumena is "symbolic" rather than intuitive.

12. II:409; 404. But compare Kant's avowedly "mystical" scholium, in which he briefly entertains (only to reject as insufficiently attuned to the "mediocrity" of the human mind) the "Malebranchian" view according to which worldly knowledge already testifies to the omnipresence of God as a sustaining "common cause" (II:409–10; [404–5]).

13. See, for example, *Reflection* no. 4984 (from the 1780s), and nos. 5985–88 (from the late 1770s or the 1780s): "The commercium of substances as phenomena in space makes no difficulty — the other is transcendent" (no. 5985). "In the sensible world space already permits a condition of commerce, and outer causality (influence) is not more difficult to grasp than the inner causality of immanent action. Causality does not allow itself to be grasped. But if we take substances as noumena (without space and time), we find everything isolated; it follows that instead of space a third substance must be thought, in which all might be able to stand in mutual commerce through physical influx" (no. 5988, ca. 1783–84). (Kant's late concern with the "ether" as an all-penetrating material substance would seem to follow up this very point.) Notes from this period also touch on the related question of the ground of commerce between body and soul. See, for example, Kant's comment to the effect that such commerce is "unthinkable" precisely because it cannot occur in space (the soul not being "an object of outer intuition") (*Reflection* no. 5984).

14. *Attempt to Introduce the Concept of Negative Quantities into Philosophy* (1763) (II:202–4; 239–41). (Hume is frequently credited with bringing to Kant's attention the distinction between logical and real opposition.) Paul Guyer, who rightly notes Kant's metaphysical suspicion of relation, in my opinion too quickly dismisses this as a mere prejudice (later removed by the relational logic of Frege and

Russell) (see his *Kant and the Claims of Knowledge,* p. 352). Relation is for Kant intrinsically problematic, owing not to confusion over what it means to consider something "absolutely," but to the necessarily "inward" metaphysical definition of a substance which follows from the infinite divisibility of space.

15. In Henry Allison's words, "transcendental idealism" functions as "the great divide in Kant's conception of the history of philosophy." As Allison notes, Kant calls "transcendental realism" the "common prejudice" (A/740 = B/768), referring to it as "common but fallacious presupposition of the absolute reality of appearances" (A/536 = B/564). "Indeed," Allison adds, "[Kant] goes so far as to assert that prior to the *Critique* the confusion was unavoidable, and even that "until the critical philosophy all philosophies are not distinguished in their essentials" (XX:287, 335). (See *Kant's Transcendental Idealism,* p. 16.)

16. Attention to the problem of substantival community also helps explain Kant's claim that things in themselves do not coexist in time and space, a claim that many scholars have found puzzling and/or misguided. (For an extended treatment of such worries, see, for example, Guyer, *Kant and the Claims of Knowledge,* pp. 350–69.) The implicit argument underlying Kant's claim is (if my general analysis is correct) that the possibility of spatiotemporal interaction among substances is *only* comprehensible *if* one understands "substance" in the peculiar "phenomenal" sense that the first *Critique* spells out. The notion of things in themselves coexisting in time and space is thus quite literally absurd. A corollary claim limiting spatiotemporal knowledge to embodied minds rules out Kant's earlier tactic of referring such a notion — however unthinkable by us — to the Divine Intelligence. The possibility of spatiotemporal community of substances-in-themselves is thinkable, according to his mature view, neither by us nor by God.

17. This, of course, is to pass over the various and deep complexities of the "Deduction" in its several versions. I wish here merely to indicate certain (neglected) lines of argument that inform Kant's overall intention.

18. The only addition "strictly so called" in the second edition is the "Refutation of Idealism," which Kant further amends in the preface at B/xxxix f. See also Allison, *Kant's Transcendental Idealism,* p. 26.

19. At A/376 ff., for example, Kant asserts that "empirical idealism, and its mistaken questionings as to the objective reality of our outer perceptions, is already sufficiently refuted, when it has been shown that outer perception yields immediate proof of something actual in space, and that this space, although in itself only a mere form of representations, has objective reality in relation to all outer appearances, which also are nothing else than mere representations. . . . If we treat outer objects as things in themselves, it is quite impossible to understand how we could arrive at knowledge of their reality outside us, since we have to rely merely on the representation which is in us." (On "physical influence" rightly understood, see also A/390 ff.) The reality in question here refers not to objects independent of the mind, but to that which is "connected with a perception according to empirical laws." See also A/372: "The transcendental idealist is, therefore, an empirical realist." To be sure, Kant's wording is notoriously ambiguous. See, for example, A/371–72, where he implies that appearances are "representations in us of the reality of which we are immediately conscious."

20. See chapter 10 below.

21. See Guyer, *Kant and the Claims of Knowledge*, p. 267. Scholars as diverse in orientation as Jonathan Bennett, *Kant's Analytic;* and Henry E. Allison, *Kant's Transcendental Idealism*, ignore it almost entirely. For two recent exceptions, see Guyer, pp. 267–76; and Thomas Powell, *Kant's Theory of Self-Consciousness*, pp. 188–90. As Guyer notes, earlier commentators such as Ernst Cassirer and H. J. Paton were more inclined to recognize the importance of the Third Analogy. For other, more broadly thematic treatments of the concept of community in the first *Critique*, see Lucien Goldmann, *Kant*, trans. Robert Black (originally *Mensch, Gemeinschaft, und Welt in der Philosophie Immanuel Kants*); and Hans Saner, *Kant's Political Thought*, trans. E. B. Ashton. Recent works emphasizing the importance of Kant's notion of community also include Friedman, *Kant and the Exact Sciences;* and Karl Ameriks, *Kant's Theory of Mind: An Analysis of the Paralogisms of Pure Reason*, and "The Critique of Metaphysics: Kant and Traditional Ontology," in *The Cambridge Companion to Kant*, ed. Paul Guyer.

22. See B/110–11: "the third category in each class always arises from the combination of the second category with the first. . . . Thus . . . *community* is the causality of substances reciprocally determining one another." See also *Prolegomena* (IV:326 n; 73 n). If the argument of the Third Analogy seems "perfunctory," it may be less because Kant was "exhausted" by the Second Analogy (as one recent commentator claims) than because the main points (for example, that real connection is only conceivable as a reciprocal determination of substances) were ones that Kant believed, by then, that he could take for granted.

23. The first edition has: "All appearances are, as regards their existence, subject a priori to rules governing their relation to one another in time" (A/177).

24. The categories of modality, which lack a single "principle," speak to the mutual bearing of those two sorts of connection. In substituting for a single "principle" the three "postulates of empirical thought," Kant brings home the fact that these categories have to do not with "enlarging the concept to which they are attached as predicates" but with "the relation of the concept to the faculty of knowledge" (A/218 f. = B/265 f.).

25. According to the A version: "Principle of community: All substances, insofar as they are coexistent, stand in thoroughgoing community (i.e., reciprocity with respect to one another)" (A/211).

26. For the bearing of this position on Kant's treatment of the sublime, see chapter 8, note 50.

27. I am here indebted to Guyer's reading. What makes an otherwise perplexing elision from the necessary reversibility of the order of perception to a principle of "reciprocal determination of substances" is, of course, Kant's prior finding (which here goes without saying) that a nonlogical relation of mutual necessity is not otherwise conceivable than in terms of common subjection to a principle of mutual interaction (*Wechselwirkung*).

28. This interpretation of transcendental idealism is consistent with a view of individual cognition as relatively loose. Any given cognition rests on a kind of (preconscious) guess — an effort, subject to revision, to fit a particular sensible manifold into the systematic pattern of experience. The absolute determinacy in principle of this pattern (as per the Analogies) is thus to be construed in some sense as "regulative" rather than "constitutive" (A/179 = B/222 ff.). What I recognize at a

distance as a man may prove at closer range to be a mailbox, a fact that in no way jeopardizes the systematic unity of experience. Thus, too, the importance, for Kant, of comparing our observations with those of others as a useful, and perhaps necessary, means of self-correction. (For a similar view of particular objective cognition in Kant, see Bencivenga, *Kant's Copernican Revolution,* p. 174 ff.) See also Kant, A/97: "If each representation were completely foreign to every other, standing apart in isolation, no such thing as knowledge would ever arise. For knowledge is a whole in which representations are compared and connected." To state the point another way, reality is not, *primarily* speaking, a property of individual objects (as many commentators assume) but of their interconnection. This fact partly answers Pippen's complaint that Kant's rejection of the traditional account of knowledge (as an intuitive "reception" of form) leaves him unable to explain the "directedness" of experience.

29. The possibility of experience, one could say, involves a synthesis of community *cum communio* (the mere "belonging together" of space or apperception) and community *cum commercium* (the dynamic interaction of a plurality of substances). See A/212 f. = B/260 f., where Kant also argues that substances that cannot interact could not be judged by us to coexist. Empty space, though not intrinsically impossible, cannot be for us a possible object of experience. (That our world space must therefore be completely filled by matter — albeit of a special kind — is a theme further developed in the *Opus postumum.*)

30. See also A/218 n = B/265 n.

31. See, for example, A/86–87 = B/119: a *deduction* must furnish a "certificate of birth quite other than that of descent from experience." The metaphor of "epigenesis" is further considered in chapter 7.

32. For a general treatment of this section, see Powell, *Kant's Theory of Self-Consciousness,* p. 174 ff. See also Ameriks, *Kant's Theory,* pp. 84–127. Ameriks draws very helpfully on the later *Vorlesungen über Metaphysik,* which speaks of community between soul and some substance "whose phenomenon is called body." How such community is constituted ("wie . . . deiser commercium beschaffen ist"), however, is something, according to Kant, "we know nothing [about]" (XXVIII:758).

33. Earlier, Kant asks "why are we compelled [erroneously] to ground a doctrine of the soul on mere principles of reason?" "Beyond all doubt," he answers, "pre-eminently for the purpose [*Absicht*] of securing our thinking self against the danger [*Gefahr*] of materialism." For this, however, as he immediately adds, the "rational concept of our thinking self" just given suffices: "For so much are we thus freed from any fear that taking away matter would cancel [*aufheben*] all thought and even the existence of thinking being, that it is on the contrary shown, that when the thinking subject is taken away, the entire corporeal world must likewise be taken away as nothing but the appearance in sensibility of our subject and a mode [Art] of its representations" ([A/383]). Kant's insistence that the goal of rational psychology can be legitimately accomplished, despite our ignorance (as Kant goes on to say) of whether the thinking self is permanent — or, indeed, whether it even exists independent of the aforementioned transcendental substratum — suggests that the above named danger lies, above all, in an apparent challenge to human self-sufficiency: that is, "the independent [*selbständige*] and permanent existence of my thinking nature through all possible changes [*Wechsel*] of my

condition [*Zustandes*]." Once the threat posed by materialism is "repelled" (by "free confession of my own ignorance"), nothing else prevents my "adhering" to (*mich . . . zu halten*) my (morally based) hope for an independent and continuing existence ([A/383–84]). Morality here provides the basis for an expectation, our "adherence" to which, one might say, figuratively overcomes the literal dependence experienced at its extreme in infancy. The condition of exposed dependence to which morality responds was physically addressed by Kant's extraordinary personal regimen. On that regimen as a sort of "self-nursing," see chapter 10 below.

34. See A/390.

35. See B/19 and *Prolegomena* (IV:302, 308, 350; 50, 65, 99).

36. See chapter 10 below.

37. See Patricia Kitcher, *Kant's Transcendental Psychology*, pp. 11–14.

38. Kant's example of a disjunctive judgment ("The world exists either through blind chance, or through inner necessity, or through an external cause") seems curiously apt.

39. For purposes of brevity, I pass over the conceptual role of community in defining the cosmological ideal, as already dealt with sufficiently.

40. As earlier noted, Kant's characterization of the *ens realisimum* as a kind of "storehouse" from which the realities of finite beings are drawn plays on the primary meaning of *res* as "wealth" or "property." The "realities" that determinate a substance are thus (in different but related senses) both God's properties and their own. As will be seen below, this characterization has direct bearing on Kant's understanding of the political community as commonwealth or res publica.

41. See Kant's *Lectures on Philosophical Theology* (XXVIII:1016; 47). According to Adickes the notes on which the *Lectures* is based are probably from Kant's first course of the same title, offered in 1783–84. They are thus roughly contemporaneous with the first edition of the *Critique*. Kant gives as an example "decisiveness" and "caution," both of which are "realities," but the compatibility of whose effects cannot be known analytically.

42. Cf. *Dissertation* (II:416; 412): "understanding *only notices an impossibility* if it is able to notice the simultaneous assertion of opposites about the same thing. . . . Thus, wherever such a condition is not satisfied, no judgment of impossibility is open to the human understanding."

43. The ideal can also be described as that concept which is (uniquely) self-determining (since it contains all possible determinations of reality), or as the idea "not merely *in concreto,* but *in individuo,*" since it is "determinable or even determined by the idea alone" (A/568; B/596). Thus certain practical ideas (for example, that of the most perfect human being), which serve as models for complete determinations of their copy, can be called ideals, albeit only in a moral sense. Such ideals serve as archetypes for the complete, but never fully actualized, determination of human action (cf. *Dissertation* [II:396; 388]). Norman Kemp Smith argues that Kant's use of the notion of an *ens realisimum* — even for regulatory purposes — is inconsistent with his earlier rejection of the Leibnizian/Wolffian claim that all realities can be combined, that is, that realities are always positive (A/272–74 = B/328–30) (*A Commentary to Kant's "Critique of Pure Reason"*, p. 525). But when Kant asserts that "all true negations are merely limitations," he means this only in a transcendental sense, that is, as it applies to things apart from their appearance in

space and time. For an excellent discussion on this point see Michael Wood, *Kant's Rational Theology*, p. 25 ff.; see also John Findlay, *Kant and the Transcendental Object*, pp. 229–31.

44. See also *Prolegomena* (IV:348–49; 96): In the case of the theological idea, reason "totally breaks with experience and from mere concepts of what constitutes the absolute completeness of a thing in general." Thus "the mere presupposition of a Being conceived, not in the series of experience yet for the purposes of experience, for the sake of comprehending its connection, order, and unity — in a word, the Idea — is more easily distinguished from the concept of the understanding here than in [the cases of the previous ideas]."

45. A/579 = B/607; see also *Lectures on Philosophical Theology* (XXVIII: 1093–95; 133–35). As Kant there makes clear, it is this commerce — or rather, the contradiction involved in thinking of the world as a whole consisting of necessary things — that first put human reason on the track of the notion (virtually unknown among the ancients) of creation ex nihilo, that is, of God as creator, not just architect, of the world.

46. Exceptions include Karl Ameriks, J. N. Findlay and, from a slightly older generation of scholars, Heinz Heimsoeth, Gerhard Krüger, and Lucien Goldmann.

47. IV:427; 95. See also (IV:408; 76): "unless we want to deny to the concept of morality all truth and all relation to a possible object, we cannot dispute that its law is of such widespread significance as to hold, not merely for men, but for *all rational beings as such* — not merely subject to contingent conditions and exceptions, but with *absolute necessity*."

48. Kant's formula insists upon the private or mutually exclusive character of rational beings (who, at least insofar as they are human, do not *directly* share in *all* of one another's ends) even as it joins them universally. Unlike some earlier (Christian) and later (socialist) versions of the communitarian ideal, Kant's "kingdom of ends" consistently resists dissolving the individual into the greater All. Cf. Goldmann, *Kant*, p. 53.

49. Traditionally, *dignitas* as a legal term referred to the majesty of office (especially regal office), that is, to qualities that bestow on it a kind of immortality. Cf. Kant's notes on Achenwall (IX:383–85) and Ernst H. Kantorowicz, *The King's Two Bodies: A Study in Medieval Political Theology*, p. 383 ff. According to Kantorowicz, the king's "dignity" (ultimately derived from that of Christ) conferred a "phoenix-like" power to rise from the dead, as expressed in the traditional formula, "The King is dead; long live the King."

50. *Reflections* from the late 1760s or early 1770s suggest that what initially attracted Kant to the idea of "moral personality" is at least in part the relief it offers from the otherwise disturbing "contingency" of human life. See, for example, nos. 4238 (XVII:472) and 4239 (XVII:473–74): Man's claim to eternity

> cannot depend on the contingent connection with the body; for that perfection, which can only spring from connection with corporeal things, can also not endure without them. . . . The enduring life of the soul is distinguished from its immortality. The first signifies that it will not die . . . the second, that it, naturally speaking, cannot die. The proof of the first is moral, the second metaphysical. The enduring life of the soul consists not in the endurance of its substance of remaining forces, but rather

in its personality [*Persönlichkeit*]. When it cannot anymore arrive at consciousness, it is like a tree that remains standing but can no longer drive sap. The physical aspect of this life is of no significance, because it pertains only to the contingent connection with the corporeal world, which is not our natural condition; but the moral world . . . hangs together with spiritual life, and because what is moral belongs to inner value [*Werth*] of the person, it is unextinguishable [*unauslöschlich*], in that happiness [*Glück*] and unhappiness, which belong merely to the transient/volatile [*flüchtige*] state, lose all value during their short span.* Therefore we must place little value in [*gringe schätzen*] this life. We would, however, have cause to value it highly if the physical aspect of it were the condition of the beginning of the metaphysical. The physical aspect of life therefore remains insignificant [*eine Kleinigkeit*]; birth and death are the beginning and end of a scene in which only morality is of importance [*erheblich*], and, to sure, only insofar as one does not act counter to it.

*(To be distressed over pain . . . is soft [*weichlich*] or foolish; but over assaults [*Vergehungen*]: decent [*anständig*] and praiseworthy. Thus the latter belongs to our person, insofar as we are spiritual beings.)

51. *Wechsel* preserves the original equivalence of the English words "change" and "exchange."

52. Substance and accident thus assume what Marx will later call the "commodity form," with substances corresponding to persons (who can buy and sell), and accidents corresponding to things (which can be bought and sold). Indeed, as far as the principle of action and reaction is concerned, the analogy goes even further: force or action serve, like money, as a perfectly liquid, yet constant, medium of [ex]change. (It is tempting to suspect that Newton (who served for many years as master of the mint) found the market/monetary metaphor helpful in his theoretical investigations. For differing arguments along these lines, see Freudenthal, *Atom and Individual;* and Elster, *Leibniz.* In any case, that Marx based his own philosophic "settling of accounts" on a similar analogy between force and money is surely one of the more poignant ironies of recent intellectual history. As the *Grundriße* and portions of *Capital* make clear, Marx's theory of surplus value grows out of the observation that workers under capitalism function (illicitly) both as persons and as things. This "contradiction" is, as Marx sees it, the genuine reality underlying Hegel's dialectical logic, itself an "ideal" version of capitalism. The problem posed by the dialectical relation — or identity and difference — of exchanger and exchanged (a problem highlighted by the ambiguity of *Weschsel* in German) constitutes a central theme of Hegel's *Logic.* Telling in this regard is Hamann's description of Kant as "Warden of the Mint," a reference to, among other things, Newton's position as royal mintmaster (discussed in Beiser, *Fate of Reason,* p. 26).

53. See also *Reflection* no. 5979 (XVIII:413–14). For variations on this theme, see *Reflection* no. 5086 (XVIII:83) and no. 5429 (XVIII:179), of indeterminate date: "Community (commercium) (the ground of which, communitas, consists in the fact that what is an alteration in one is an effect in all the others) is twofold. . . . The community of bodies can be understood according to phenomenal laws, the community of spirits only according to intellectual laws." In one relatively late reflection (no. 5943 [XVIII:397]), Kant associates noumenal commerce with "pre-

established harmony" (because it is coeval with the creation of the world) and phenomenal commerce with "physical influx."

54. See also IV:403; 71. Pure reverence (*Achtung*) has to do with what is owed to a will "whose value is above all else." Admittedly, this idea of the "absolute value of a mere will" is "so strange [*befremdlich*]" as to seem fantastic" (IV:394; [62]), an impression it is the overall business of the *Groundwork* to dispel.

55. *Vergreifen* also means "to misappropriate funds."

56. Thus (to make the analogy even more explicit) the kingdom of ends is said to make possible an intelligible world (*mundus intelligibilis*), or more literally: the intelligible world "is possible as a kingdom of ends" (IV:438; 106).

57. See (IV:439; [107]): "The essence [*Wesen*] of things does not alter [*sich ändert*] through its outer relations, and that which, without thought of the latter, alone constitutes the absolute value of man—according to this must man be judged—by whomever, though it be the highest being [*Wesen*]." Cf. *Reflection* no. 4349 (XVII:515–16) (from the 1770s): "we are given no other world than the sensible; . . . only the moral world [*Mundus moralis*] . . . is intelligible. . . . The rule of freedom a priori in a world in general constitutes the form of the intelligible world [*formam mundi intelligiblis*]. The intelligible world as an object of intuition is a mere (undetermined) idea; but as an object of the practical relation of our intelligence to intelligences in the world, and to God as its practical author [*Urheber*] it is a true concept and determinate idea: Civitas dei."

58. See Kant's characterization of an end in itself as one that does not have to be produced (which would make goodness of will relative to something else) but is self-existent (*selbstständig*). It is also the "ground for all maxims of action" (IV:438; 105).

59. A further question—how the moral law itself is possible—is taken up in part 3 without being adequately answered. In the *Critique of Pure Reason* Kant gives up the effort to derive the possibility of the moral law from something else (that is, rational "spontaneity") and instead treats it as an immediate (and unique) "fact of reason."

60. See VI:233; 58.

61. *Deduction* for Kant is originally a legal term designating the establishment of a right (see *Critique of Pure Reason* [A/84 = B/116]). Thus he refers to the "Transcendental Deduction" as "an explanation of the possession [*Besitz*] of pure knowledge" (A/87 = B/119).

62. See XXIII:314: The *Grundsatz* of original natural possession of the soil is: "I have an inborn right to be on the soil (to occupy a place on earth) on which nature or contingency [*Zufall*] (hence without my consent) has put [*gesetzt*] me."

63. See (XXIII:323–24). Cf. *Reflection* no. 7686 (XIX:490), from the 1770s: "The monarch who is despotic maintains the state as his inheritance (patrimonium); one who is patriotic maintains it as his fatherland. The land [*Land*] itself is a fraternization [*Verbrüderung*] out of a common [*gemeinschaftlichen*] father." Seen in this light, the juridical synthesis both incorporates and rationally subsumes our contingency as wards of the (maternal) earth.

64. Kant's juridical deduction concerns "apprehension" or "subsumption (of the merely contingent connection of the will to objects in space and time) under the intellectual concept of possession." Empirical possession thus involves "apprehen-

sion," or "subsumption under the intellectual concept of possession" (XXIII:308). For further attempts along these lines, see *Vorarbeiten zur Rechtslehre* (XXIII:273–336); see also Susan Meld Shell, *The Rights of Reason: A Study of Kant's Philosophy and Politics*, pp. 127–45.

65. Hegel's representation of the social or human world (the realized goal of the Kantian "ought," suitably modified) as spirit historically objectified can be understood as an extension of Kant's argument here — an extension, to be sure, that lacks Kant's modesty with respect to human finitude.

66. Fungibles are, typically, not only individually exchangeable but also materially homogenous. See, for example, Erskine's *Institutes* (as quoted in the *Oxford English Dictionary*): coin and grain are fungibles because one guinea or one bushel of sufficient merchantable wheat "precisely supplies the place of another."

67. Cf. Kant's assimilation of illicit sex and animal commerce (*fleischliche* or *viehische Beiwohnung*) (VI:359; 166; see also *Reflection* no. 1087 [XV:4831]). The person who engages in commerce with animals, however, is rightfully excluded from civil community.

68. Kant defines marriage as "union of two persons of different sexes for lifelong possession of each other's sexual properties" (VI:277; [96]), a reciprocal equality fully consistent with the husband's "mastery" over his wife, insofar as the latter rests on the husband's "naturally superior ability" to promote their common ends. Kant's treatment of marriage was considerably more egalitarian than contemporary legal practice. The Prussian legal code enacted in 1794, for example, gave husbands an explicit right to subject their wives to corporal punishment.

69. See also *Reflection* no. 7879 (XIX:543); and no. 7936 (XIX:560), which refers to marriage as the "first juridical action." Apart from marriage, "carnal [*fleischliche*] enjoyment is *cannibalistic* in principle (even if not always in its effect). Whether something is *consumed* by maw and teeth, or whether the woman is consumed by pregnancy and the perhaps fatal delivery resulting from it, or the man by exhaustion of his sexual capacity by the woman's frequent demands on it, the difference is merely in the manner of enjoyment. In this sort of use by each of the sexual organs of the other, each is actually a *consumable* thing (res fungibilis) with respect to the other" (VI:359–60; [166]). The Latin root (fungor) can also mean to "pay one's debt to nature," that is, "to die."

70. It has become customary in some quarters to dismiss Kant's treatment of sex as a symptom of his "alienation" from his own body. (Typical in this regard is Robin May Schott, *Cognition and Eros: A Critique of the Kantian Paradigm*.) Such views fail to take into account the degree to which their own (more or less relaxed) Freudian presuppositions themselves depend on Kantian insights and/or anxieties. If certain recent critics of Kant's treatment of sex suffer from an overly simple view of what constitutes psychic "health" (that is, the body is good, repression is bad), Camille Paglia's spirited effort to recover the dark side of human sexuality ends up presenting nature as so intractably "formless" that the very notion of health becomes meaningless (see her *Sexual Personae*). In the process, the phenomenon of life (which distinguishes itself from the lifeless precisely by its capacity to maintain *form*) recedes from view. Telling in this respect is the almost total absence, in Paglia's panoply of sexual types, of fathers, whom an older philosophic tradition associated with form immanent in nature. For Kant's own subtle understanding of or-

ganic form — an understanding that exerted a profound influence on figures such as Goethe and the later German Romantics — see chapters 8 and 9 below.

71. See also *Reflection* no. 7937 (XIX:560) and *Vorarbeiten* (XXIII:302). It is not always possible to determine from the text whether by "gemeinschaftliche Wille/Willkühr" Kant means *commercium* or *communio;* the analogy with the transcendental deduction, however, would suggest the interplay of both.

72. On community and equality, see, for example, *Reflection* no. 7542 (XIX:451) and no. 7548 (XIX:452), both from 1769–70. On the juridical state as *Gemeinschaft,* see also the slightly later *Reflection* no. 7681 and no. 7682 (XIX:488). On monarchy as organism, despotism as mechanism, see no. 7688 (XIX:491). On the need for three powers of the state to maintain equilibrium, see no. 7853 (XIX:535).

73. Cf. *Reflection* no. 8065 (XIX:600): an individual human being without juridical security is "only an accident," which can only exist as inherence; a "civil whole," on the other hand, "is substance."

74. One can hardly stress too much the importance of Kant's insistence that the source of national unity is *essentially* political and consensual, rather than involuntarily cultural and/or biological, as Herder and others were already claiming. Kant's deliberate correction of a tendency of the German language highlights the politically liberal character of his nationalism, along with its central point of divergence from nationalisms of a romantic and/or racist stripe.

On the Kantian state see also Ernest J. Weinrib, "Law as Idea of Reason," in Williams, *Essays on Kant's Political Philosophy;* and Wolfgang Kersting, *Wohlgeordnete Freiheit. Immanual Kants Rechts- und Staatsphilosophie.*

75. The state thus bears a certain analogy with the matrimonial condition, which also regulates the natural commerce of human beings. In both cases, lawful reciprocity transforms a commerce naturally destructive of the individual into a whole in which each individual is secured. The difference lies in the fact the marriage, which Kant elsewhere calls the "earliest juridical condition," upholds the individual — who remains susceptible to death in childbirth, etc. — only ideally.

76. See *Critique of Pure Reason* A/316–19 = B/372–76; and chapter 9 below.

77. The classic study is Kantorowicz, *King's Two Bodies.* See especially his discussion of the "Corpus Ecclesiae mysticum" and "Corpus Reipublicae mysticum" (chapter 5).

78. Cf. Kant, *Reflection* no. 1486 (XV:710): "Leviathan: a symbol of Hobbes for a state, the soul of which is the prince."

79. On *res* as "property," see note 40 above. According to the *Cambridge Latin Dictionary, publica* is a relatively late assimilation of *populus* (meaning multitude of people) and *pubes* (meaning adult men). In Kantian terms as well, to be a member of the public is bound up with coming of age (as a male), albeit in a civil rather than merely biological sense. Women, according to Kant, are incapable of civil maturity: they can be "parts," but not "members" [*Gliedern*] of the state. See (VI:314; 126); and *On the Common Saying: "This May Be True in Theory but It Does Not Apply in Practice"* (VIII:295 n; 78 n).

80. See (VI:261; 83): "Land (understood as all habitable ground) is to be regarded as the *substance* with respect to whatever is movable upon it, whereas the existence of the latter is to be regarded only as an *inherence.* Just as in a theoretical

sense accidents cannot exist apart from a substance, so in a practical sense no one can have what is movable on a piece of land as his own unless he is assumed to be already in rightful possession of the land." ("Reality" here approximates the sense of "real" in "real estate.") The juridical division of the substance of reality solves at a practical level the otherwise unanswerable question of how substance (in the strong metaphysical sense) resolves itself into substances.

81. Cf. Saner, *Kant's Political Thought*, pp. 27–28.

82. On the *Eintheilung* of the total sphere of reality in a theoretical sense, see *Critique of Pure Reason* A/576 = B/604.

83. Cf. the so-called right of necessity, which excuses juridically—but not morally—acts undertaken to preserve oneself that violate another's rights (VI:235; 60).

84. Kant later withdraws the suggestion that the French people committed formal regicide in executing Louis XIV: the people really acted out of fear and only resorted to formalities (*Formlichkeit*) against the eventuality that the state might revive and punish them. Their cover or disguise (*Bemäntelung*), however, "aborted" (*verunglückt*). Cf. Kant's characterization in the *Conflict of the Faculties* of Cromwell's republic as an "abortive monstrosity [*verunglückte Mißgebürt*]" (VII:92 n; [167 n]). It is, as he continues, "with these creations of states as with the creation of the world: no man was there, nor could he have been present at such, because he then would have had to have been his own creator." In the *Doctrine of Right* as well, Kant warns the people against inquiring "with any practical intention" into the origin of the state (VI:318; [129]), as if the generative mystery involved were in some way comparable to the sexual act. A completed "state product" (of a morally adequate sort) is a "sweet dream"; its perpetual approach, however, is a duty, not of the citizen, but of the head of state (*Staatsoberhaupts*). Only that person whose form-giving legislation resembles the creative act of God is permitted (and indeed morally required) to hold the generation of the state "intentionally" in view.

85. For a reading with a somewhat different emphasis, see Fenves, *Peculiar Fate*, p. 274 ff.

86. It is therefore more than can be conceived in terms of the "mechanism of nature."

87. VI:314–15; 126. See also *Theory and Practice* (VIII:294; [77–78]):

> The *independence (sibisufficientia)* of a member [*Gliedes*] of the common-wealth [*gemeinen Wesens*] as a citizen, i.e., a co-legislator, may be defined as follows. In the question of actual legislation, all who are free and equal under existing public laws may be considered equal, but not as regards the right to make these laws. . . . An individual will cannot legislate for a commonwealth. For this requires freedom, equality and *unity* of the will of *all* the members. And the prerequisite for unity, since it necessitates a general vote (if freedom and equality are both present), is independence. . . . Anyone who has the right to vote on this legislation is a *citizen* [*Bürger*] (*citoyen*, i.e. citizen of a state [*Staatsbürger*], not townsman [*Stadtbürger*] *bourgeois*). The only qualification required by a citizen apart from the natural one (not being a child or a woman) is that one be one's own master (sui iuris), and have some property (which can include any skill, trade, fine art or science) to support oneself [*sich ernährt*]; i.e., in cases where one must acquire from others in order to live, it be only by alien-

ating [*Veräußerung*] what is one's own, rather than through allowance given to another to make use of one's own forces, so that one serves, in the proper sense of the word, no one but the commonwealth.

Kant's notion that one who works under the direction of another is not fit for active citizenship is faintly echoed in Abraham Lincoln's hope that every American might have the opportunity to move up from working for another to self-employment. However economically archaic (neither Kant nor Lincoln seems to have fully foreseen the development of modern industry with its reliance on wage labor), their shared sentiment finds continuing resonance in the modern desire to (as we say) "be one's own boss." The point of relevance is that participation in a market economy per se does not provide, either intellectually or psychologically, the sort of independence necessary for liberal citizenship and perhaps best expressed in the Emersonian phrase "self-reliance."

88. Cf. *Reflection* no. 7686 (quoted in note 63 above); and (VI:343; 150), where Kant speaks of the republic as a sort of "intellectual" mother: "The human beings, who constitute a people [*Volk*], can be represented as native of the land [*Landeseingeborne*], according to the analogy of production from a common ancestral stem (congeniti), even though they are not. Yet in an intellectual and juridical sense, since they are born from a common mother (the republic), they constitute, so to speak, a family (gens, natio), whose members (citizens) are all of equally high birth [*ebenbürtig*], and do not mix with those who may live near them in a state of nature, whom they regard as inferior."

89. Kant's formulation is not, however, without historical precedent. Compare, for example, Nicholas Cusanus, according to whom the Prince becomes "father of the individual citizens" only insofar as he recognizes himself as "the creature of all his subjects collectively" (quoted in Kantorowicz, *King's Two Bodies*, p. 231).

90. See, for example, *Theory and Practice* (VIII:290–91; [74–75]):

a government might be erected on the principle of benevolence toward the people, as of a father toward his children, i.e., a *paternal* [väterliche] *government* (imperium paternale), in which the subjects would thus be unemancipated [*unmündige*] children. . . . This is the greatest despotism thinkable (a constitution that cancels all freedom of its subjects, so that they have no rights at all). A government that is not paternal, but *patriotic* [vaterländische] . . . is the only government thinkable for men capable of possessing rights, however benevolent the ruler. *Patriotic* [patriotische] is, namely, the way of thought, such that everyone in the state (not excepting the ruler) regards the common wealth as the maternal womb, or the land as the paternal soil, out of and from which he himself sprung, and which he must leave behind as a treasured pledge.

At the same time, the head of state is not merely a member [*Glied*] of the commonwealth, but its "creator or preserver" [*der Schöpfer oder Erhalter*].

91. For some historical precedents, see Kantorowicz, *King's Two Bodies*, pp. 390–94.

92. On traditional views of political sovereignty as the embodiment of an undying *corpus mysticum*, see Kantorowicz, *King's Two Bodies*, p. 231 ff.

93. In the case of cosmopolitan right this natural commerce — facilitated by a spheroid earth, whose continents are divided by traversable oceans — gives rise to

economic exchange, which eventually produces the international peace that right alone is powerless to secure. "For the *spirit of commerce* sooner or later takes hold of every people, and it cannot exist side by side with war." See *Perpetual Peace: A Philosophic Sketch* (VIII:368; 114). This universal community has already developed to such a point, Kant notes, that a violation of rights in *one* part of the earth is felt *everywhere* (VIII:360; 107–8).

94. This was the fate literally suffered by Kant's mother. See note 97 below.

95. Kant made a similar argument in the *Remarks,* where he links compassion with feminine good-heartedness.

96. Thus one has a duty to avoid cruel treatment of animals as a practice that dulls one's "shared feeling of their pain" and thus weakens "a natural predisposition that is very serviceable to morality" (VI:443; 238).

97. Compassion is generally linked in Kant's mind with women, and with contagion whether through physical proximity or through the imagination (hence too, with the putative influence — which Kant is at pains to discredit — of the maternal imagination on the fetus). (As we will later see, *Schwärmerei* — or the contagion of reason by imagination — finds its prototypical example, for Kant, in the belief that the fetus's "germ" can be influenced by the imagination of the mother.) Man emancipates himself both from the imaginary authority of others and from the womb of nature by an act of courage ("sapare aude") of which woman is seemingly incapable. In the *Anthropology,* Kant attributes woman's perpetual immaturity [*Unmündigkeit*], as well as her lack of moral character, to a natural cowardice that benefits the fetus she might be carrying (VII:305–6; 169]. Kant discounts, among other things, nature's possible stake in the willingness of mothers to risk their lives for the sake of children already born. There is perhaps a veiled complaint in all of this against Kant's beloved mother, whose sympathetic (and personally fatal) attentions to a lovesick female friend — when Kant was about thirteen — can hardly be called cowardly. Regina Kant's guilt lay, rather, in her failure to make the sort of calculus of moral cost and benefit Kant here enjoins; or perhaps in her (unnatural) valuation of the welfare of a friend over that of her own children.

98. On Kant's personal practices in this regard, see Thomas De Quincey, *The Last Days of Immanuel Kant,* in *The Works of Thomas de Quincey,* vol. 9, pp. 500–501.

99. Associates report Kant's frequent quoting of the saying (which he attributed to Aristotle) "friend, there are no friends." For an insightful discussion of the role of friendship in thinkers influenced by Kant, see Ronald Beiner, *Political Judgment,* pp. 119–28.

100. Cf. Friedrich Nietzsche, *Thus Spake Zarathustra,* pt. 1, "Zarathustra's Prologue," no. 6; and *The Antichrist,* aphorism no. 7: "Pity makes suffering contagious."

Chapter Seven

1. On Kant's treatment of history, see the insightful discussion by Patrick Riley, *Kant's Political Philosophy;* see also Bernard Yack, *The Longing for Total Revolution.* Yack's synoptic discussion of post-Kantian thought brings much needed attention to the influence of Kant on several waves of (silent) epigones. Other valuable works in English on Kant's treatment of history include Yovel, *Kant and the Philosophy of*

History; William A. Galston, *Kant and the Problem of History;* George Armstrong Kelly, *Idealism, Politics and History: Sources of Hegelian Thought;* William James Booth, *Interpreting the World: Kant's Philosophy of History and Politics;* Velkley, *Freedom;* Fenves, *Peculiar Fate;* and Emil L. Fackenheim, "Kant's Concept of History," *Kant-Studien* 48: 381–98. Alexis Philonenko, *La théorie kantienne de l'histoire,* draws useful attention to the bearing of the *Nachlaβ* of the 1770s on Kant's treatment of history. See also Monique Castillo, *Kant et l'avenir de la culture;* and Jean-Michel Muglioni, *La philosophie de l'histoire de Kant: Qu'est-ce que L'homme?*

2. Hannah Arendt, *Lectures on Kant's Political Philosophy,* ed. Ronald Beiner, p. 77. Arendt rightly emphasizes the "melancholy" implications of Kant's interest in history. Her treatment suffers, however, from a tendency to depreciate the importance of his explicit constitutional doctrine (which she incorrectly attributes only to his last writings, published after 1790); her own more "aesthetic" reconstruction of Kant's politics depends in no small measure on such a depreciation (see, for example, pp. 15, 72 ff.).

3. See, for example, Yovel, *Kant and the Philosophy of History,* p. 155. Yovel sees an inconsistency between the "dogmatic," merely political history of the *Idea for a Universal History* (in which progress is achieved "unconsciously"), and the cultural history of the *Critique of Judgment,* in which the highest moral good is to be consciously realized (p. 127 ff.). While agreeing with Yovel that these two works differ in important ways, I disagree with him about the nature of their divergence. As my reading will attempt to show, Kant in the *Idea for a Universal History* is already perfectly aware of the radical tension between a natural and a moral conceptualization of humanity. Far from ignoring the difficulty posed by the relation between nature and culture, Kant's essay takes that relation as its central problem. For a more detailed discussion of the *Idea for a Universal History* and the *Critique of Judgment* on this point, see chapter 9 below.

4. *Idee zu einer allgemeinen Geschichte in weltbürgerlicher Absicht. Absicht* can have either meaning.

5. The passage appeared in the twelfth issue of *Gothaische Gelehrte Zeitungen* (Feb. 11, 1784). Kant's essay was published in *Berlinische Monatsschrift* 4 (Nov. 11, 1784).

6. A/316 = B/373. Cf. Arendt, *Lectures on Kant's Political Philosophy,* p. 15.

7. Cf. A/570 = B/597.

8. The first part of Herder's *Ideen zur Philosophie der Geschichte der Menschheit* had opened with thinly veiled praise for his former teacher. Kant's three published reviews were (Herder felt) highly condescending. They certainly did not disguise their irritation with Herder's entire approach, one whose exuberant pursuit of "analogies" and failure to observe the boundary between nature and reason may well have reminded Kant of his own youthful essay on history, as Fenves remarks (*Peculiar Fate,* p. 181). That the title of Kant's 1784 essay speaks of an "idea" of history, where Herder's work speaks (plurally) of "ideas," already suggests the depth of their differences: where Herder glories in the sheer variety of natural and cultural forms, Kant insists on a single unifying thread as the only alternative to chaos. Interestingly enough, it is Kant (not Herder) who insists on the existence of different human "races," a fact that must be weighed in the balance in any attempt to compare their respective understandings of the unity of "humanity."

On Kant and Herder's complicated intellectual and personal relationship, see the appendix below; and Beiser, *Fate of Reason,* pp. 127–41. As Beiser observes, both Kant and Hamann opposed Herder's efforts to explain the mind in naturalistic terms.

A clue to the differing grounds on which Kant and Hamann oppose Herderian naturalism may be found in Hamann's telling claim that "the stamina and menstrua of our reason are revelation and tradition, which we make into our own property and transform into our powers and vital juices" (*Werke* III:39; quoted in Beiser, p. 140). Hamann's (sexually self-forgiving?) association of revelation and tradition with reason's male and female parts, respectively, contrasts with Kant's own association of reason with a self-elevating (and matter-free) virility. Measured by that standard, Herderian naturalism and Hamannian supernaturalism fall equally short.

Hamann's figure of speech bases itself on older alchemaic/religious themes (in which, for example, death is said to melt us down into a "menstruum" for the "chemistry" of the Resurrection to work upon). On the latter point, see Richard Whitlock, *Zootomia,* p. 406, as quoted in the *Oxford English Dictionary.* "Stamina" (literally, "threads") refers to the male sexual organs of a plant and more archaically to the "threads" spun by the Fates — hence to an organism's quantity of living force. "Menstruum," in Hamann's text, refers both to the female contribution to generation according to Aristotle and the so-called universal solvent of the alchemists.

9. In the *Universal Natural History,* Kant conceives of man's problem in terms of a struggle between spiritually and physically erotic forces of "attraction." The soul can philosophically "ascend" only by overcoming the physical machinery on which it also vitally depends. It is not just a case of "too soon old, too late smart," for our mental potency depends upon the very animal vitality that makes stupidity so tempting, a dilemma from which only the most mentally precocious can escape. Rousseau's *Emile* provides a more democratic remedy (which by Kant's own account turned him around) for the gap that separates man's physical and spiritual maturity.

10. So that, as Kant here puts it, "in the end, we do not know what sort of concept we should make of our species, so fanciful/imaginary in its pretensions" ("was man sich von unserer auf ihre Vorzüge so eingebildeten Gattung für einen Begriff machen soll").

11. See *Critique of Judgment* (V:307–20; 174–89). Kant here divides the labor (later ambiguously united in the genius) of seizing on the *Absicht* or idea and cognizing its worldly realization, the latter requiring more natural favor than Kant is willing or able at this point to claim. In calling for another Kepler or Newton, Kant also indirectly suggests the insufficiency of Rousseau, whom he once called the "Newton" of the moral world, and whom he once praised for discerning the "deeply hidden laws" that underlie the ever-shifting shapes of human affairs. Beyond the physical and moral laws of Newton and Rousseau, respectively, Kant seeks a third principle that would permit (*per impossibile*) a satisfactory conception of man as *Gattung,* or species, being.

12. On the biological meaning of *Spiel* (as in "play of nature"), see Jacob and Wilhelm Grimm, *Deutsches Wörterbuch.* Cf. Kant's own use of *Spielart* in *On the Various Races of Men* (II:430) to designate a genetic trait that does not invariably repeat in the next generation. Kant distinguishes the variations that distinguish two

races (for example, white and black skin) from varieties (or *Spielarten*) within a single race (for example, blond and brown hair). In the former case, interbreeding produces a blending, whereas in the latter case, the characteristic of a parent may not appear in the offspring (for example, a blond father and brunette mother having blond children). For a more detailed discussion of this point, see VIII:94 and chapter 8 below.

13. The "monster" at the center of the labyrinth of classical myth was itself, of course, the offspring of a mating between man and beast. The theme of the "labyrinth of nature" appears frequently in baroque thought (including that of Leibniz). Kant in his early works often recurs to the labyrinth image, along with that of Ariadne's thread, which he identifies in the *Universal Natural History* with both the mathematical infinite and the principle of "analogy." In the *Critique of Pure Reason,* by way of contrast, reason is said to provide its own "guiding thread" via the Ideas.

14. See *Groundwork of the Metaphysics of Morals* (IV:394; 62). At the same time, this very harshness is presented as beneficent.

15. Much of the essay is thus taken up with the question of our natural affinity or lack thereof.

16. Cf. *Critique of Judgment,* nos. 83–84.

17. Cf. Kant's later speculation, in a note to thesis 7, that inhabitants of other planets may fulfill their destinies within an individual lifetime.

18. See here Kant's reference to culture as the domain of man's "social value" (VIII:21; [15]), a phrase that recalls the threefold division of his practical economy (*Marktpreis, Affectionspreis,* and *Würde*) in the *Groundwork of the Metaphysics of Morals.*

19. The latter "mutual resistance" results from each acknowledging in himself a tendency to want things his own way ("nach seinem Sinne richten zu wollen"), while anticipating the same from others, hence in a misdirected (but in its own way just) intimation of equality.

The automaticity sometimes attributed by scholars to this transformative process is not borne out by the text, which speaks, more tentatively, of a "beginning" made of a "foundation" of a "kind of thinking" that can "in time" transform (*verwandeln*) natural dispositions into principles and so can "at last" (*endlich*) transform a pathologically enforced union into a moral whole (VIII:21; [15]). In any case, this passage (from the section following thesis 4) itself proves to be provisional, in light of Kant's later statements about "crooked wood" and the need for a new moral "engraftment."

20. Cf. the opening image of Rousseau's *Emile,* which compares man in society to a shrub "which chance has caused to be born in the middle of a path and that the passers-by soon cause to perish by bumping into it from all sides and bending it in every direction." Rousseau's call upon the would-be cultivator of souls to "erect an enclosure" around his charge is replaced, in Kant's account, by the self-regulating mechanism of a forest (albeit one whose "containment" seems to presuppose some sort of artifice). Rousseau's tutor is to give way (as Kant suggests in the *Anthropology*) to history (or Providence) as the solution to the otherwise insoluble problem of human education. The ultimate limits of that solution is suggested by the fact that where Rousseau attributes men's "crookedness" wholly to society (or "chance"), Kant insists it is inherent.

21. Cf. Ecclesiastes I:14–15.

22. The difficulty "which the very idea of this task lays before the eyes, is this: that man is an animal who, when he lives with others of his kind, requires a master," because "though as a rational creature he wishes a law to set limits on the freedom of all," his "animal inclination" leads him to exempt himself. The fundamental problem arising from man's dual character thus remains to be solved.

23. *Ungefähr,* which means both "accidental" and "safe" (hence "approximate," that is, close enough to avoid danger) is etymologically associated with "lack of danger or evil intention." Given that "blind accident" is for Kant synonymous with great danger, that is, a progress-annihilating fate, his argument itself inverts (as underscored by terminological repetition) the word's historically accreted meaning. That the world might be governed by an *evil* intention is precluded by Kant's association of reason with an ordering intentionality — an intentionality, therefore, whose goodness goes without saying. The greatest danger is not something like Descartes's "evil genius," but a question whose unanswerability would render us unable to predict (or "speak of before [the fact]") a progressive course for man. Even this fate can be averted (without answering the question) if we assume that nature's secret "thread" is itself "tied/knotted together with" wisdom, a figure whose vaguely umbilical suggestion leaves (purposefully?) obscure the character of the connection.

24. According to Grimm and Grimm (*Deutsches Wörterbuch*), *heilen,* primarily associated with "health," can also mean "to make whole."

25. The physiological metaphor of obstructed formation is both reinforced and countered by Kant's reference to "engraftment" onto a morally good *Gesinnung.* That *Gesinnung,* we may conclude, does not itself develop or grow from an amoral parent but is present from the start, a self-originating stock into which another species (animal man) is inserted, like a plant. The idea itself is unchanging. And yet the "idea in us," which is not present *to us* (that is, consciously acknowledged) from the start, involves *Bildung,* or education. (The "in itself," as Hegel will later put it, must become "for itself.") In any case, man's hybrid status (rational, animal, and vegetable) remains intact.

26. There are thus two circles at issue: mankind's actual completion of its course (and with it, the realization of our specieshood), and the ideal anticipation that Kant here attempts, an anticipation that allows us somehow to conceive our species, as it were, before the fact. Kant's essay is a continuing meditation on the meaning of man's hybrid and/or engrafted status, that is, on the problematic relation between freedom and nature that constitutes our humanity.

27. In an earlier note, Kant referred to man's very artificial (*künstlich*) role (as compared to what may go on on other planets) as a way of underscoring the fact that nature requires only approximation (*Annäherung*) to the idea. Man is "forced" by his asociability (itself born of his love of freedom) to discipline himself and thus develop through "compelled art" the seeds of nature (VIII:22, 23 n; [17, 18 n]). One could hardly find a more artful way to reconcile the dual provenance of man in freedom and nature.

28. *Durchgängig* is also a medical term meaning "permeable" or "unobstructed."

29. These remarks to a large extent anticipate the argument of *Perpetual Peace.* One important difference — Kant's reliance in the latter work on a growing league

of republics to provide a sort of critical mass — can be explained, at least in part, by the intervention of the French Revolution. *Perpetual Peace* was written in 1795, at the time of the Treaty of Basel, concluded after Napoleon's victory.

30. Cf. *Foedus amphictyonum* (VIII:24; 19), on which Kant may be punning. A *foedus amphictyonum* is literally a league of neighbors, or "those who dwell around," and consisted of cities in close proximity which engaged in peaceful intercourse.

31. Kant does not, however, actually work out such a history or even try to establish that the latter can be done. It is only the *attempt* to work out a philosophic history on whose possibility Kant here insists. All he means, or needs, to establish is the reasonableness of the attempt, as it were, of an attempt.

32. Alternately, "shortsighted." For a thoughtful treatment of Kant's problematic optimism, see Howard Williams, *Kant's Political Philosophy;* and "Kant's Optimism in His Political Theory," in *Essays on Kant's Political Philosophy,* ed. Howard Williams.

33. Germinal survival of repeated cataclysms is a major theme of Bonnet's *Palingénésie.* Cf. Kant's characterization in the *Doctrine of Right* of improvement of the constitution through revolution as a "palingenesis" rather than a "metamorphosis" (VI:340; 148).

34. On Kant's understanding of history in relation to the question of man's "ground" or lack thereof, see Fenves, *Peculiar Fate,* p. 35 ff.

35. On progress as a self-fulfilling prophecy, see Kant's later *An Old Question Newly Raised: Is the Human Race Constantly Progressing?*

36. Kant here cites, but also slightly misquotes, Hume. Thucydides takes issue on that first page with the Athenian myth of autochthony (or origination of a people from the earth). It is, according to Thucydides, precisely the sterility of Attic soil that accounts for Attica having "from great antiquity" been inhabited by the same people. Regions of richer soil, by way of contrast, experience perpetual "seditions" and "removals" of population. Thucydides notes that before the Trojan War, "nothing appears to have been done by the Greeks in common," and that before the time of Hellen, son of Deucalion (himself the supposed offspring of Prometheus and Pandora), there is not even a name for Greece (Hellas). The origin of the Greeks, at least insofar as it can be "conjured out of Homer," is thus itself political, arising from the fact that Hellen of Phthiotis and his sons, being powerful, were called in to aid other cities, who consequently began to "converse" with the former. Only with the Trojan War, however, did the Greeks enter into genuine joint action — a break with the "imbecility of former times." According to Thucydides, then, the entity Greece (Hellene) succeeds its name and is genuinely constituted only with the strength and correspondence consequent to the common military effort represented by the Trojan War. What makes the contemporary events that he records worth writing down is their unprecedented commotion and shattering of what that earlier war created. Although the most ancient things "cannot by any means clearly be discovered," he is persuaded, from what can be construed of times prior to the Trojan War, that the commotions of the past were not very great.

The first page of Thucydides thus incorporates a number of themes crucial to Kant's own historical idea — the essential darkness of the most ancient things; the dubiousness of traditional mythic accounts, including those of Athens (which hold, among other things, that Athenians sprang from the soil like grasshoppers); the importance of federative political origins, which are in principle knowable — in short, an almost critical methodological caution on Thucydides' part, when compared, say, with Herodotus, about whom Kant is here silent.

37. Cf. Kant's related treatment in the *Critique of Pure Reason* of reason's "architectonic" as the idea or "original germ" that underlies all true philosophy ([A/835 = B/863]; for an incisive discussion, see Yovel, *Kant and the Philosophy of History*, p. 236). Kant sets out this idea as an alternative to the principle of *generatio aequivoca* (or spontaneous generation of life from the non-living), which apparently governs earlier philosophic systems — systems that seem to be ordered, in this respect, like "lowly organisms" (*Gewürme*). "It is unfortunate," Kant notes, "that only after we have spent much time in the rhapsodic (*rhapsodistisch*) collection of materials at the suggestion of an idea lying hidden in our minds, and after we have, indeed, over a long period assembled the materials in a merely technical manner, does it first become possible for us to discern the idea in a clearer light, and to devise a whole architectonically in accordance with the ends of reason." The history of philosophy as a whole organized according to an idea is the history of the emergence of the germ of reason to full consciousness. As a later discussion of this section will make clear, the history of human reason is repeated (and retrospectively completed) phylogenetically, as it were, in Kant's own intellectual biography. His final history of reason retrospectively interprets the equivocations and confusions of his own earlier philosophic rhapsodies (and in particular, the *Universal Natural History*) as birth pangs. Man's philosophic self-generation combines the spirituality Kant earlier reserved to divine creation with the "historical" character that he associates with natural propagation (in the sense that bees and beavers have an evident "natural history"). As with Hegel, moreover, human history so conceived (that is, as the germ of reason actualized by becoming conscious of itself) is necessarily retrospective, a fact that crucially distinguishes it, in Kant's case, from the practical history of the human race (or history with a cosmopolitan, and not merely architectonic, intention), which necessarily looks toward the future. In this one respect, at least, Kant's essay on the idea of history is indistinguishable from what he dismissively calls "rhapsody." Or to put matters somewhat more accurately, it treads the line between philosophy and rhapsody, a line he elsewhere compares to that between dreaming and waking.

38. *Gedanke,* or "thought," has generally in Kant's work a further connotation of "emptiness," as in "mere thought." See, for example, his use of *Gedanke* in discussion of the Second Paralogism, where *Gedanke* refers to the mere thinking (as in the "I think" that accompanies all of our representations) from which dogmatists falsely infer the existence of the soul as simple substance (*Critique of Pure Reason* A/355 ff.). See also Kant's cognate use of *Gedankending* and *Gedankenswesen* in conjunction with the "Amphibole" of reason (A/292 = B/348) and reason's "natural dialectic" (see A/673 = B/701). In the latter case, *Gedankenswesen* (which Norman Kemp Smith translates as "thought-entities") are specifically *distinguished* from ideas. (For a thematic discussion of the problem of "emptiness" in Kant, see Martin Sommer, *Die Selbsterhaltung der Vernunft.*)

There is another meaning of *Gedanke* — as in *Gedankenstrich* (a dash or stroke which, as Keith Spalding puts it, "indicates that the writer falls silent and allows the reader to pursue his own thoughts" [*An Historical Dictionary of German Figurative*

Usage]) — which Kant may (also) have in mind when he states, by way of conclusion, that his idea of history is not intended to replace empirical inquiry (*Historie*), but is rather to be interpreted as "thought [*Gedanke*] of what a philosophic head . . . might be able to attempt from another standpoint." Kant's idea so construed is literally a dash — a speechless stroke inviting completion by another.

39. The "Transcendental Doctrine of Method" makes up part 2 of the *Critique of Pure Reason* (part 1, the "Transcendental Doctrine of Elements," is almost five times longer). Its four chapters include "Discipline," "Canon," "Architectonic," and "History of Pure Reason." The "Doctrine of Elements" includes the "Transcendental Aesthetic" and the "Transcendental Logic," itself divided between the "Transcendental Analytic" and the "Transcendental Dialectic," that is, virtually everything in the *Critique* usually understood to be of fundamental importance. It is thus somewhat surprising to be reminded that Kant puts *at least equal* systematic weight on part 2, as he makes clear in its initial paragraphs. Part 1 provided an estimate of the materials, and a determination of the sort of edifice, and for what height and strength of building they suffice, and all this "if we look upon the sum [*Inbegriff*] of all knowledge of pure speculative reason as an edifice for which we have at least the idea within ourselves." Part 1 also showed that although we had had in mind (*Sinn*) a tower that should reach to the heavens, the "supply of materials sufficed only for a dwelling house [*Wohnhause*], which is roomy enough for our business on the level of experience, and just high enough to overlook it." The "bold undertaking" that Kant/we had earlier planned must miscarry (*fehlschlagen*) owing to "lack of stuff," even without reckoning on the "confusion of languages" that gives rise to disputes over the plan to be followed and disperses workers over the world, where each builds according to his own design. Part 2, for its part, is concerned "less with the materials than with the plan [*Plan*]." Nevertheless, since we have been warned "not to venture at random upon a blind project which may be altogether beyond our capacities, and cannot yet well abstain from building a fixed abode [*festen Wohnsitzes*] for ourselves, we must plan our building in conformity with the material which is given to us," and which is also "appropriate to our needs." Part 2 concerns itself then, as Kant immediately adds, with determining "the formal conditions of a complete system of reason" ([A/707 = B/735]).

This governing description of the *Critique of Pure Reason* as a whole is remarkable for its assimilation of constructive, biological, and political figures in a single metaphor. The object, nothing less than completion of the system of pure reason, is here presented as a perfected version of Hobbes's famous Leviathan (itself modeled on the Tower of Babel), a human artifice that at once secures to man (and secures man to) a worldly home (see A/850 = B/878) and gives birth to ideas self-generated in reason's womb, which is, so to speak, self-bearing (*selbstgebärend*) without impregnation from experience (A/763 = B/791; A/765 = B/793] (self-criticism, in other words, as an immaculate conception).

Where dogmatists wander, and skeptics assume temporary posts, criticism aims at, and achieves, permanent settlement (A/761 = B/789). One is at the same time struck by Kant's emphasis on the political dimension of the self-development/generation of reason through self-criticism. Reason is not dictatorial but depends on freedom for its very existence: "its verdict is always simply the agreement of free citizens" (A/739 = B/707). Hence Kant's likening of criticism to a judicial proceeding in which reason, in its fragmentation among disputing schools, is presided over by reason as adjudicator—with its implicit reference to the question of how reason can be the source of discipline and yet discipline itself (see A/737 = B/765). What remains unclear is precisely how the transition from civil war among philosophic schools to civic peace occurs. Reason's title to judge itself depends on its consciousness of the idea; and yet reason's consciousness of the idea is presented as historically the outcome of the dispute itself.

The fundamental ambiguity of this founding moment, in which reason's own systemicity through the idea becomes known to it—the moment, in other words, that reason first recognizes itself as what, subjectively speaking, it is (see A/737 = B/765)—finds unique articulation in the life history of Kant himself. Kant's own life, in terms of that system, is at once infinitely contingent and hence unimportant (of himself, as we are elsewhere reminded, he "says nothing" [B/ii]), and pivotally vital.

It is helpful to compare in this regard Kant's approval of the polemical use of "pneumatology" as a "transcendental hypothesis" to combat the great "difficulty" of reconciling man's eternity with the conditions of his generation and birth: "The contingency [*Zufälligkeit*] of generation—which for human beings as for reason-less creatures, is dependent on occasion, and often indeed on maintenance/amusement [*Unterhalte*], on the moods and caprices of rulers, often indeed from vice—makes a great difficulty against the opinion as to the endurance of a creature stretching to eternity, given that its life has its beginning in circumstances so insignificant [*unerheblich*] and so entirely given over to our freedom" ([A/779–80 = B/807–8]). This is no great difficulty, according to Kant, as concerns the species, since accidents in the individual case are still subject to general law. So far as the individual is concerned, however, to expect such a formidable effect from such puny causes seems dubious (*bedenklich*). It is noteworthy that human freedom, otherwise identified with human transcendence, is here just what ("seemingly") calls that transcendence into question. Freedom as rational spontaneity and freedom as sexual choice divide between them the twin possibilities of sublimity (*das Erhabene*) and inconsequentiality (*Unerheblichkeit*). Completion of the history of the idea hinges, like its initiating moment in sexual refusal, on the resolution of this tension. That Kant later "sketches" but does not "complete" the last part of the "Transcendental Doctrine of Method" (the "History of Pure Reason") suggests that this tension remains unresolved, that is, that the "contingency" of generation remains disturbing in a way that even the self-articulating unity of reason does not (yet) altogether evade. The latter task must await Kant's reconsideration of the notion of contingency in the third *Critique* as the defining feature of human understanding (a reconsideration that will be taken up in chapter 9 below). On the importance of sexual refusal for the emergence of the idea, see *Conjectural Beginning of Human History* (VIII:113; 224).

40. Other sources include Cicero's characterization of philosophy as "cultura animi," or culture of the soul (*Tuscan Disputations* 2.5; cited in Rotenstreich as referred to below), as well, perhaps, as the Spanish *culterismo*, a literary movement originally associated with imitation of the classics and which later became proverbial for a sort of pompous refinement. The distinction between culture and civilization on which the *Idea for a Universal History* implicitly relies (see text at note 25

above) finds its most important philosophic source, however, in Rousseau's enlightenment critique. Rousseau's concomitant attempt to reconcile nature and history (or reason) lays the conceptual ground for "culture" in the modern sense — be it the essentially singular world culture elaborated in the *Critique of Judgment* or the multiple cultures of Herder's contemporaneous romantic nationalism.

For further accounts of the history of the modern notion of culture as it relates to Kant, see Richard Velkley, "The Tension in the Beautiful: On Culture in Rousseau and Other Thinkers," in *The Legacy of Rousseau*, ed. Clifford Orwin and Nathan Tarcov (forthcoming); and Nathan Rotenstreich, "Morality and Culture: A Note on Kant," *History of Philosophy Quarterly* 6, no. 3: 303–16.

41. Empirical psychology in the excluded sense would encompass rational physiology, understood not as the rational study of nature (mentioned above) but as the natural study of reason. For more on rational physiology in the latter sense, see chapter 10 below.

42. Kant recounts his past as that of a traveler seeking a lasting abode. In terms of the extended analogy that informs the first *Critique* as a whole, his alternating wanderings (dogmatism) and temporary resting places (skepticism) have been governed all along by a longing for permanent residence, a longing finally to be satisfied by the fruits of criticism. It is this longing, as he presents it here, that — as much as anything — consciously informs Kant's efforts from beginning to end (cf., in this regard, *Opus postumum* [XXII:53; XXI:348]). As Kant there suggests, the sublimity of the ideas (especially practical ideas) has about it a certain "wistfulness" (*Wehmuth*). Transcendental philosophy calls man back to his own "fatherland." Still, the spherical enclosure that Kant seems to have in mind as reason's enduring abode (or, at the very least, the "plan" of that abode: see, for example, A/762 = B/790) bears a curious resemblance to the womb from which man must emerge. For a somewhat different consideration of the theme of homelessness, see Richard Velkley, "The Homelessness of the Soul: Modern Reflections," presented at the annual meeting of the New England Political Science Association, April 1994.

43. Cf. Yovel, *Kant and the Philosophy of History*, p. 257.

44. Cf. Kant's "idea" of "the philosopher" as one whose title it would be "very vainglorious" for anyone to claim, that is, as the goal toward which all philosophizing, including his own, aspires (A/840 =B/868). Philosophy in this sense is an idea, "which nowhere exists *in concreto*, but to which, by many different paths, we endeavor to approximate, until the one true path, overgrown by the products of sensibility, has at last been discovered, and the image, hitherto so abortive, has achieved likeness to the archetype, so far as this is granted to man" (A/838 = B/866). Kant's achievement, in the terms of this formulation, would seem to lie in having discovered "the one true path." What is less clear is where he claims to stand in the consequent process by which the image of the philosopher is assimilated to the archetype, whose full realization would require complete carrying out (*per impossibile*) of man's theoretical and practical vocations, that is, man's complete theoretical and practical determination as a species. Hegel's later claim to "wisdom" is, to no small degree, a claim to have accomplished that very task.

Kant returned to the question of whether or not the history of philosophy is part of philosophy proper in his unpublished *Prize Essay on What Real Progress Metaphysics Has Made in Germany since the Time of Leibniz and Wolff* (1791) (see especially his

·suggestive preparatory remarks [XX:342–43]). The idea of philosophy glimpsed, finally, as a sketch of the history of pure reason is doubly volatile (A/852–53 = B/880–81). The culture of reason, and with it Kant's perpetual return to metaphysics, his "besevered [*entzweiten*] mistress" (B/878 = A/850), falls short of occupying that space in which the volatility of his system finds its ultimate seat. The history of pure reason is thus, in an especially intimate way, the story of Kant himself.

45. According to Spalding (*Historical Dictionary of German Figurative Usage*), *Leitfaden* and *Gängelband* were used in the eighteenth century as synonyms. The strings to which *What Is Enlightenment?* refers are held by an infantilizing political and ecclesiastical authority. In the *Critique of Pure Reason,* on the other hand, Kant speaks of reason's liberation from nature's leading strings. Following the experiments of Galileo, Torricelli, and Stahl, "a light broke upon all students of nature," who "learned that reason has insight only into that which it produces according to a plan of its own, and that it must not allow itself to be kept, as it were, in nature's leading strings" (B/xiii). Enlightenment is a self-emancipation that replaces a harness or leading string (with their suggestion both of a domestic animal and a toddler whose inability to walk on his own keeps him attached) with reason's own idea, which Kant repeatedly associates with the projection of a guiding thread. (On Kant's own experience with childhood leading strings, see chapter 10 below.)

The German Aufklärung (Enlightenment) is historically associated with motion from "obscure" to "clear" ideas, a movement that Wolff called the fundamental impetus of the soul. In Wolff's words: "The light in our souls makes our thoughts clear" (*Vernünftige Gedanken von Gott,* para. 203). See Beck, *Early German Philosophy,* p. 272. See also the thematics of light and darkness in such early Kantian works as the *New Elucidation* and the *Universal Natural History.* Kant's later treatment of "enlightenment" in the essay of that name plays on "*Erklärung*" not in the sense of "making light" but of "declaring" or "making public," as in the expression "[*etwas*] *für mündig erklären*" (declaring [someone] to be of age). What is usually translated as "self-imposed tutelage" (the opposite of enlightenment) is literally a failure to declare oneself to be an adult. In offering this definition, Kant radically if subtly transforms the primary meaning of the term from "making light" to "declaring oneself to be of age." Although Kant speaks of "daring to be wise" rather than political emancipation per se as the motto of the Enlightenment, the latter's sense is perhaps ultimately better expressed by the American "Declaration [*Erklärung*] of Independence" than by "science" as such.

On Rousseauian roots of the Kantian theme of "coming of age," see Susan Neiman, *The Unity of Reason: Rereading Rousseau,* pp. 199–204. On the mixed etymology of *Mündigkeit* — originally from the German *Munt,* meaning "mastery," but also drawing historically on *Munt,* or "mouth" — see Martin Sommer, *Identität im Übergang: Kant,* pp. 117–39. As Sommer notes, the latter development was encouraged by the association of the Latin *emancipatio* — a synonym historically for *Mündigkeit* — with emergence from "infancy," which literally denotes lack of speech (*in-fans*).

46. As in *Der eingebildete Kranke,* the title of the German translation of Moliere's *Imaginary Invalid.*

47. *Jäsche Logic* (IX:25; 538). On this Kantian question as a way of entry into

the thought of Fichte, see Didier Julia, *La question de l'homme et le fondement de la philosophie.*

48. Kantian "humanity," one could say, is both canceled and preserved in the irreducible "strangeness" of its history.

49. The problem here is precisely that of moral individuation: the fact that each must act in pursuit of an end that can only be attained with the cooperation of all the others, a cooperation beyond the power of any individual to assure. The idea of history partially — but only partially — relieves this problem, by making it at least thinkable that nature cooperates in this accomplishment.

50. The character of that dispute will be taken up in detail in chapter 8; here I consider only one aspect of their intellectual and personal falling out.

51. See Johann Gottfried Herder, *Ideen zur Philosophie der Geschichte der Menschheit.*

52. Cf. *Anthropology* (VI:268; 136).

53. For Kant, by way of contrast (as indicated in the passage from the *Anthropology* cited in the previous note), man's sense of justice both endangers him at birth and decisively distinguishes him from the rest of animal creation. By its tears, the newborn infant "immediately announces his claim to freedom (an idea that no other animal has)." According to Kant, the moral law proscribes the causing of needless pain in animals — not, however, because of their essential affinity with humans, but because such action tends to dull a feeling of shared pain that is useful to morality in one's relations with other men (see *Metaphysics of Morals* [VI:443; 238]).

54. If, on the other hand (Herder continues), essential parts are lacking, or grosser sap takes the place of finer in the brain, the radiating together of ideas cannot take place, and the creature remains the slave of sense. What is fatally lacking here, even from the perspective of Kant's early thought, is a recognition of the inseparability of nobility (in this case intellectual) from earthly transcendence. (The conceit linking womb and brain was given currency by Von Helmholt.)

55. On the latter point, see Kant's *Review of Moscoti* and chapter 10 below.

56. Cf. the competitive arboreal enclosure of Kant's *Idea for a Universal History.* Herder's conceit of the freely developing tree seems closer to the botanical image invoked at the beginning of Rousseau's *Emile;* the spirit of that work, however, leaves a very different impression. Rousseau's major point is to reveal how difficult it is to reconcile the force of nature with the requirements of society, a difficulty Herder gets round by treating societies as natural organisms that (unlike real plants and animals) can thrive without devouring their neighbors.

57. Philonenko, *La théorie kantienne de l'histoire,* p. 186.

58. See Kant's letter to Herder (May 9, 1768 [X:73-74]) in which he expresses the hope that Herder's "fertile spirit" will not be so much "driven by the warm movement of youthful feeling." Herder replies, in a tone of ironic modesty, that he is now idle, inasmuch as Lockean "uneasiness," the "mother" of so many undertakings, is mother in him of a paralyzed (or benumbed: *gelähmt*) quiet (letter to Kant, Nov. 1768 [X:75-79]). The calm that Kant praises as a philosophic antidote to the hyperfertility of mysticism is for Herder an unhealthy fruit of "motherly" restlessness.

59. Such a consideration supposedly "does all" (that is, everything one could

require) to satisfy the human desire for immortality, while establishing the perpetuity (*Fortdauer*) of the living forces of world-creation. No force, Herder says, can die (*untergehen*); for of such dying we have neither psychic concept nor natural example. As little as the atom can be destroyed, just as little if not more so can be destroyed the force that moves it. In a word, it is unthinkable that a nature all powerful and divine should annihilate a part of its own living activity (p. 132). As Kant observes, however, the power of such arguments in establishing *individual* immortality remains doubtful.

60. See, for example, Herder's claim that life, in whose ascending chain man serves as central link, suffers thereby no genuine break, our duality of essence being merely "apparent" (p. 146). Kant's complaint that Herder, despite fashionable anti-metaphysical intentions, "leaps off the tip of nature's *Leitfaden* into a metaphysical void," is here apropos. For an insightful account of Herder's relation to liberalism, see Fred Baumann, "Historicism," in *Confronting the Constitution,* ed. Allan Bloom.

61. Cf. Kant's dismissive reference to Herder's punning claim that reason (*Vernunft*) is merely something acquired (*Vernommenes*) (VIII:49; 205).

Chapter Eight

1. That Kant's resistance to assimilating mind and matter proves decisive is of no small political, as well as philosophical, significance, as Kant's debates with Herder already suggest. Kant's struggle with Herder reveals certain illiberally nationalist (or anti-individual) possibilities harbored within liberalism itself. Both Kant and Herder take nationalism's claims seriously within a fundamentally liberal framework. But whereas for Herder nature organically assures the mutual compatibility of national self-development and individual happiness, Kant argues (from Herder's point of view, illiberally), that man "has need of a [human] master," that is, that peace among nations can be secured and individual rights upheld only if we go beyond "what nature can do for us." Kant's peculiar combination of moral idealism and political realism (or what he elsewhere calls the innocence of the dove and the wisdom of the serpent) asserts itself in opposition to Herder's seductive (and from Kant's point of view absurd) dependence on an intending nature — dependence that is the very opposite of human "self-reliance." On the theme of self-reliance and Kant, see also Stanley Cavell, *Conditions Handsome and Unhandsome: The Constitution of Emersonian Perfection* [the Paul Carus Lectures].

2. A notable exception is Rudolph A. Makkreel, *Imagination and Interpretation in Kant.* See especially his informative treatment of the concept of life and its relation to imagination (pp. 88–107).

3. I therefore disagree with Beiser's claim in *The Fate of Reason* that the theory of teleology advanced in the third *Critique* "is in no way anticipated in earlier writings," an opinion that contributes to what is, I believe, an overestimation on Beiser's part of Herder's contribution to Kant's thought. For my own views concerning Kant's lesser, but still very real, debt to Herder, see the text at notes 20 and 118, and chapter 9 below.

4. That a previously prolific Kant should have seen fit, during this period, to publish an essay on human races (and to publish virtually nothing else) is in itself remarkable, as if the new thoughts struggling to be born somehow managed to

objectify themselves, so to speak, embryonically. Kant's review of Moscati is concerned with mental and physical effects of the human transition from four- to two-footedness, particularly as those effects bear on the fetus of a two-footed mother. Kant's review is thus also concerned with generation, here localized within the space out of which man "bravely lifts his head above his former comrades [literally, chamber-mates]" (II:425). On gestational aspects of Kant's intellectual struggles at this time, see his letter to his physician-friend and former student, Marcus Herz (Aug. 20, 1777), and chapter 10 below.

5. Kant consistently upheld the "epigenetic" view that offspring are the product of both parents, a view shared by Maupertuis and C. F. Wolff but denied by such prominent contemporary thinkers as von Haller and Boerhaave. (On the inadequacy of preformationism, see also *Reflection* no. 1256 [XV:553–54] and no. 4239 [XVII:473–74].) On the complexity of the issues involved in the dispute between epigenesis and preformationism, see Helmut Müller-Sievers, *Epigenesis,* and Hall, *Ideas of Life and Matter,* p. 382 ff. It must suffice here to note that thinkers as diverse as Aristotle, Epicurus, and Descartes also supported the view—albeit on widely divergent grounds—that both parents contribute to conception.

6. Cf. Aristotle, according to whom "many animals of different species are fertile with one another" (*Generation of Animals* 746a, 748a). For Aristotle, identity of form, not the ability to produce fertile offspring, marks a male and female as of one species.

Buffon eventually had to come to terms with the fact that members of what he had previously regarded as different species can produce fertile offspring—for example, sheep and goats. His response was to expand and to some extent historicize the notion of a species. For a fuller account of Buffon's treatment of the concept of a species, see Paul L. Farber, "Buffon and the Concept of Species," *Journal of the History of Biology* 5, no. 2: 259–84; and Peter J. Bowler, "Bonnet and Buffon: Theories of Generation and the Problem of Species," *Journal of the History of Biology* 6, no. 2: 259–81. On the role of necessity in Buffon's theory of the organic "moule," see Jacques Roger, "The Living World," in *The Ferment of Knowledge: Studies in the Historiography of Eighteenth-Century Science,* ed. G. S. Rousseau and Roy Porter, p. 280. For a helpful discussion of the scientific background, see also Peter McLaughlin, *Kant's Critique of Teleology in Biological Explanation.*

7. Cf. Herder's *On the Origin of Language.* As Beiser observes, human adaptability is the centerpiece of Herder's attempt to explain the origin of language in naturalistic terms (see *Fate of Reason,* pp. 130–35). The locus classicus of late eighteenth-century discussions of human adaptability and the origin of language is Rousseau's *Discourse on the Origin of Inequality,* which traces mankind to its putatively prerational, prelinguistic beginnings, even as it raises doubts as to whether we can ever really know how language first arose. Rousseau wrote an essay entitled *Dicourse on the Origin of Language* (which remained unpublished during his lifetime) in 1749. Kant's own account of the origins of the human race (the *Conjectural Beginning of Human History* [1786]) takes the existence of language explicitly for granted.

8. On related personal medical concerns on Kant's part, see Borowski, in Borowski, Jachmann, and Wasianski, *Immanuel Kant,* p. 53. The notion that racial differences are caused by differences in climate was popularized by Montesquieu.

9. Kant attributes black skin, not, as in his earlier essay, to precipitated iron, but

to the (alleged) ability of Negro blood to cope with a phlogiston-rich atmosphere (J. Priestly discovered "dephlogistonated air," or oxygen, in 1774). The adaptive properties associated with other skin colors remain obscure (VIII:103). Accordingly, Kant now believes, the original human stock is irrecoverable.

10. Compare Kant's central disagreement with Herder over whether reason is, as Herder punningly asserts, something merely "acquired" (*Vernommenes*) (*Review of Herder's "Ideas on the Philosophy of the History of Mankind,"* pt. 1 [VIII:49; 205]). See, also, his objection that reason, for Herder, is not an "inherent capacity of the human species," but an externally derived "original tradition" which man must thank—rather than himself—for all his progress toward wisdom (VIII:63; 218).

11. *Review of Herder's "Ideas"* (VIII:54; 210). Kant adds that it would be unjust to attribute such ideas to Herder, whose deficiency lies, rather, in providing an organizational ladder that is little more than a tautology, that is, does not genuinely lay claims leading to the "monstrous" idea from which reason rightly recoils. In the second installment of Kant's review (directed against Reinhold's recently published defense of Herder), he restates his earlier position (VIII:57; 212).

12. Kant's maxim, on the other hand, can guide experiments without being provable by them. His argument here anticipates his later treatment, in the *Critique of Judgment*, of purposiveness in organisms as a regulative idea.

The basis of Kant's insistence on the impossibility of externally induced changes in the fetal germ is not, on the face of things, obvious. Respectable empiricist contemporaries (such as Maupertuis), who denied that mothers could mark their developing fetuses with their thoughts, were nevertheless open to inheritance of acquired characteristics (such as docked tails) as an empirically testable hypothesis. Ancient assumptions, dating back to Hippocrates, about the ability of the maternal imagination to influence the fetus were revived by the Cambridge neo-Platonists and gained additional respectability from Malebranche's influential *Recherche de la vérité*. (On increasing opposition in the latter half of the eighteenth century to belief in the marking power of motherly imagination, see Roger, *Sciences,* p. 214 ff.)

In treating the (rationalist/spiritualist) assertion that the mother's imagination can influence her fetus, and the (empiricist/materialist) assertion that physically acquired characteristics can be inherited, as equivalent "absurdities," Kant stakes out a defense of reason's "boundaries" that echoes, in curious ways, the critical enterprise itself (see, for example, the "History of Pure Reason," *Critique of Pure Reason* A/852–56 = B/880–84; see also A/834–36 = B/802–64, and chapter 7 above). One is led to wonder whether Kant's understanding of reason is not itself partly shaped by the requirements of an assertion that resembles, in its seemingly unfounded "a priority," a related insistence on the impossibility of "living" matter.

13. See Georg Forster, *Noch etwas über die Menschenrassen,* vol. 2 of *Werke,* pp. 207–15. On the general circumstances of Kant's exchange with Forster, see John H. Zammito, *The Genesis of Kant's "Critique of Judgment",* pp. 207–15.

14. Cf. Zammito, *Genesis,* p. 210 ff.; and Lovejoy, "Kant and Evolution," in *Forerunners of Darwin,* ed. Bentley Glass, Owsei Temkin, and William L. Strauss, Jr., p. 196. Forster's point was that Kant's assumption of a single human origin exceeded human capacity as much as would a viewing of the earth in its "primordial labor." Hence, from Forster's standpoint, the need to stick with empirical observation, rather than reverting, as Kant had done, to a priori—and, in Forster's view,

theological — hypotheses. (The "observable" mutual aversion of blacks and whites to mating is thus a better guide to species barriers than definitions that arbitrarily define species in terms of common fertility.) I must therefore disagree with Zammito's claim that Forster attributed to Kant a belief in the transmutation of species. But Zammito is right to claim that Kant did not attribute such a view to Forster (as a puzzled Lovejoy insists).

15. Forster, politically liberal and an opponent of slavery, insisted that acceptance of his theory would not increase oppression of blacks by whites, because "kinship is more likely to increase than diminish the relish of the oppressor" (!). For a compelling account of less liberal uses to which the theory of multiple origins has more commonly been put, see Stephen Jay Gould, *The Mismeasurement of Man.*

16. See *Concerning the Ultimate Ground of the Differentiation of Directions in Space* (II:381; 369).

17. Kant finds his "polestar" within the subject, whose "striving toward freedom" (VIII:145; [248]) is, so to speak, heliotropic. On orienting oneself in the dark and its role in dispelling imaginary fears, see Rousseau, *Emile,* pp. 134–38. (According to De Quincey, *Last Days of Immanuel Kant,* Kant used a rope suspended between his bed and an adjoining room to find his way in the dark [504–5].)

18. On the controversy between Mendelssohn and Friedrich Heinrich Jacobi to which Kant's essay responds, see Beiser, *Fate of Reason,* p. 92 ff. Initially reluctant, Kant was finally induced to enter the fray by Jacobi's use of Kant's critique of metaphysics with a view to discrediting reason itself.

19. According to Kant, the nonuniversal characteristics of all other species are "racial," that is to say, subject to hybridization. The existence of varieties (or characteristics not invariably inherited) is unique to man and explicable only from a "higher standpoint," on the grounds that species devoid of reason, and having the value of "means only," are preformed by nature. Human beings, who are more unified in their ends, require less in the way of natural formation. Racial differentiation is thus a lingering sign of mankind's affinity with his animal comrades. One could say the same thing of women, who are, according to Kant, more "preformed" than men.

20. As an accompanying note makes clear, Kant's insistence on our ability to distinguish imaging (*Einbildung*) from other "effects of the mind" is emblematic of his general refusal to reduce the variety of effects to a single fundamental force (*Grundkraft*):

> The fundamental force to which [imaging] refers can not be designated otherwise than as imagination [*Einbildungskraft*]. Thus the fundamental forces of repulsion and attraction are classified under the title "moving forces." To explain the unity of substance many have believed it necessary to assume a single fundamental force, and have thought in giving diverse fundamental forces a common title to have discovered it. For example, they say that the single fundamental force of the soul is the force of representing the world [*Vorstellungskraft der Welt*]. It is just as if I were to say: the only fundamental force of matter is moving force, because repulsion and attraction both stand under the common concept of motion. However, one would well wish to know if the former can be deduced from the

latter; but that is impossible. For differences between inferior concepts can never be derived from superior concepts. And concerning the unity of substance, whose concept already seems to imply unity of fundamental force, the illusion rests on an incorrect definition of force. For this is not the ground that contains the reality of accidents (i.e., substance), but merely the relation between substance and accidents, insofar as this contains the ground of their reality. But many relations can be attributed to substance without injury to its unity. (VIII:180 n–181 n)

21. Labor, as Kant will later say, is the mark that distinguishes the philosopher from the *Schwärmer* (*On a Newly Arisen Superior Tone in Philosophy* [VIII:389 ff.; 51 ff.]); it is also the mark of our needful engagement of real forces, without which genius slips its leash.

22. See *Critique of Judgment* (V:432; 319). Cf. *On a Newly Arisen Superior Tone* (VIII:391; 54).

23. Kant's lengthy considerations of race in *On the Use of Teleological Principles* make no mention of the physical superiority of whites. Unpublished notes, however, suggest Kant's continuing conviction to that effect. In one particularly disturbing passage, Kant speculates that all other races will be exterminated/uprooted (*ausgerottet*), adding that the white race has been responsible for all mankind's "revolutions." He also registers his approval of the policy of the governor of Mexico disallowing (against the orders of the king of Spain) intermarriage between whites and Indians; from such intermingling, according to Kant, the better lose more than the worse gain. See XV:878–99 and an unpublished manuscript of Kant located at the University of Geneva and cited in Philonenko, *La théorie kantienne de l'histoire*, pp. 177–78.

In the "Critique of Teleological Judgment," Kant will not mention race at all; in the *Anthropology*, which takes up national and sexual character in great detail, racial character is mentioned only in passing, by way of a favorable reference to the work on that subject by Kant's admirer, Christoph Girtenner (VII:320–21; 182). (Girtenner's *Ueber das kantische Prinzip für die Naturgeschichte*, which applies Kant's concept of race to nonhuman species, takes as its motto Kant's call in his own essay on race for a daring "history of nature.") What removes race from the forefront of Kant's anthropological interest may be, in part, a new understanding of human history emphasizing the cultural advances introduced by European peoples. The concept of race reappears in Kant's reference to mankind itself as a "race" of rational being—a race distinguished from others by the ability of its members to dissimulate their thoughts, making "lying" the single "foul spot" on the human character (*Announcement of the Near Conclusion of a Treaty for Eternal Peace in Philosophy* [VIII:422; 93]).

24. *Critique of Pure Reason* A/51 = B/75.

25. Composition of the "First Introduction," which Kant did not publish with the *Critique of Judgment*, is dated by Tonelli prior to May 1789. According to Zammito, the "First Introduction" marks the "highpoint of Kant's confidence in the systemicity of his whole philosophy," a confidence from which he subsequently retreated owing to his apprehension of the danger of hylozoism associated with the work of Herder (*Genesis*, p. 6). As I argue below, however, this apprehension was nothing new for Kant; and in any case, his alleged confidence is even in the

"First Introduction" more restrained and nuanced than Zammito's gloss suggests. I am, however, in broad agreement with Zammito's claim that Kant's conflict with Herder played an important role in the overall development of the arguments advanced in the third *Critique* (a point particularly stressed by Beiser in *Fate of Reason*). As Zammito notes (p. 387 n), Kant later allowed the "First Introduction" to be published unedited and claimed that both versions were philosophically equivalent.

26. We call something purposive (*zweckmaeβig*), according to Kant, "if its existence seems to presuppose a presentation of that same thing" (XX:216; 404). Alternatively, purposiveness is a "lawfulness that the contingent may have insofar as it is contingent" (XX:217; [405]). What is at issue is how contingency (which implies a lack of necessity, that is, that things might be other than they are) and lawfulness (which implies necessity) are to be combined. Kant's answer — the "technique of nature" — takes its bearings from an analogy with the (human) experience of artful making: what is so produced follows by a kind of lawful necessity from a prior idea and yet remains contingent in the sense of owing its existence to a free act of will (see [V:183; 22–23], [XX:241; 430], and [V:184; 24]).

This model of contingent lawfulness can be fruitfully compared to the notion of a divine schema, which he once (similarly) invoked to account for the peculiar necessity of the world (a necessity irreducible to logic alone). Where that inseminating schema inspired a progress that was at best "ambiguous," the concept of a "technique of nature" is productively grounded in the mind's own requirements. The very failure of Kant's early cosmological attempt (and consequent inability constantly to rise) becomes the basis of a projected idea of nature with which (despite the still present possibility of boundless heterogeneity) we can be "satisfied."

A lengthy footnote included in the "First Introduction" and repeated almost verbatim in the published version draws the reader's attention to this comparison by speculating on the benefits of the human tendency to "vain longings." Such empty desires (nourished by "mystical presentations, similar to novels, of fanatical bliss"), which alternately "expand the heart and make it languid," "exhaust" the mind's forces and "allow it to relapse into consciousness of its impotence." Kant ends, however, on a positive note: "if we had to assure ourselves that we can in fact produce the object, before the presentation of it could determine us to apply our forces, our forces would presumably remain largely unused. . . . So nature has provided for the connection between the determination of our forces and the presentation of the object even before we know what ability we have, and it is often precisely this effort, which to that very mind seemed at first an empty wish, that produces that ability in the first place" (XX:231 n; [420 n]. Cf. V:178 n; 17 n). It is not difficult to read in these lines a reference to Kant's personal philosophic history. It remains strange, however, to find this tribute to the potency of empty ideas in a work whose enabling claim is our "need," if we are to set to work, on prior assurance of success. Kant's own history belies at least to this extent the claim on which its (putatively) successful completion rests.

27. See *Critique of Pure Reason* A/832 = B/860.

28. Judgment thus finds itself in a position analogous to that of practical reason, which, in order to go about *its* work (achieving the highest good) looks for assurance that nature conforms to our purposes sufficiently as not to render all moral

efforts nugatory. Why either faculty should need such strong assurance on this score is not made fully clear. (Paul Guyer, for example, argues that even without such assurance it is rational to proceed so long as the risk is otherwise worth taking [see *Kant and the Claims of Taste,* p. 50].) One explanation, in the case of judgment, would seem to be the peculiarly paralyzing "disturbance" produced, for Kant, by the prospect of a boundless diversity without the unifying mediation of the idea.

29. This formulation is later modified. See text below at note 32.

30. Cf. Bacon's criticism of the so-called idols of the mind.

31. Kant also speaks of a sort of "self-specification" on nature's part (XX:215; 403), an image that calls to mind his early referral of nature's differing kinds to God's inseminating idea. The concept of nature's technique, by way of contrast, leaves the character of that differentiation (Oedipally) vague ("determinable," one could say, without being "determined"). As we will see, Kant's completion of the "system of philosophy" rests partly on the (repressed) image of an (unholy) family trinity. On the determinable/determined distinction, see Werner S. Pluhar, "Translator's Introduction," in Kant, *Critique of Judgment,* p. xcvii ff.

32. Kant returns to the model of contingent lawfulness that guides his earliest cosmological efforts, albeit with the more "satisfying" grounding of the lawfulness in question on a subjective "need" on our part, rather than an ultimately inaccessible "divine schema." We are to this extent able to grasp the possibility of worldly totality — a possibility that is for us otherwise incomprehensible. So long as it can be linked to the requirements of scientific "progress," our disturbance before a nature devoid of reason gives us warrant to endow nature with (or regard it as if it were the product of) intelligence. Judgment's "need," grounded in the requirements of scientific progress, furnishes a means (where desire alone would not suffice) of overcoming the disturbance in question without succumbing to ghost stories.

33. Or alternatively (as Kant expresses it in the "First Introduction"), maxims without which judgment could not systematically rise from the particular to the more general. Generally speaking, the motivating "disturbance" of the "First Introduction" gives way, in the published version, to an emphasis on the requirements of cognitive progress in their own right. Cf. Kant's reference, in the latter version, to "dislike" (V:188; 27).

34. On reflection (*Reflexion*) as a preventative against blindness, see *On a Newly Arisen Superior Tone* (VIII:399; 63–64): "to look into the sun (the supersensible) without becoming blind is impossible. But to see, as the elder Plato did, this sun in *reflection* (of reason morally illuminating the soul) and, indeed, to do so sufficiently from a practical point of view is entirely possible." Kant goes on to ridicule certain "Neo-Platonists" (especially Johann Schlosser) who want to confuse us with feelings in order to hold us in suspense with the delusion of objective knowledge. Such "Platonizing philosophers" make the veil of Isis (which they admit they cannot lift) so "thin that one can *intimate* the goddess under this veil." "Precisely how thin is not said; presumably, just thick enough so that one can make the specter into whatever one wants. For otherwise it would be a vision that should definitely be avoided." Kant also counters Schlosser's charge that a "sublimating" critical philosophy is emasculating (*Entmannung*) with the counter-charge that in a priori principles practical reason feels "its otherwise never intimated strength,"

whereas in "falsely attributed empirical properties . . . reason is emasculated and lamed [*entmannet und gelähmt*]."

Kant also contrasts "theophany," which "makes an *idol* from Plato's Idea," with his own morally based "theology," which proceeding from reason's concepts "sets up an *Ideal*" (VIII:401 n; 67 n) (cf. *Anthropology* [VII:191–92; 65]). On Kant's repudiation of the desire to *see*, see the text at note 71 below. On the conflict between Kant and Schlosser, see the introduction and notes by Peter Fenves in *Raising the Tone of Philosophy*.

35. See (V:317 n; 185 n): "Perhaps nothing more sublime has ever been said, or a thought ever been expressed more sublimely, than in that inscription over the temple of Isis (Mother Nature) [*Mutter Natur*]: I am all that exists, and that has existed, and that will exist, and no mortal has lifted my veil." Kant continues by approvingly citing Segner's use of this idea in a vignette prefixed to his *Naturlehre* intended to "imbue the pupil who is to be led into the temple with the sacred thrill [*Schauer*] that should attune the mind to solemn attentiveness." The passage can be usefully compared with Kant's earlier identification of the "sublimest thought" with the all-sufficiency of God: "God is all-sufficient. What exists, be it possible or actual, is only something insofar as it is given through him. Human language can let the infinite thus speak to itself: I am from eternity to eternity, outside of me is nothing save what is something through me" (see *One Possible Basis* [II:151; 215]). The same identification of the sublimest thought and God's all-sufficiency recurs in the *Critique of Pure Reason*, though now in the profoundly unsettling context of an "unconditioned necessity" that constitutes "the true abyss of reason" (A/613 = B/641). In the third *Critique*, by way of contrast, the sublimest thought is emblematic of — and to this extent domesticated by — the domicile of science.

In Kant's late essay *On a Newly Arisen Superior Tone*, the gap between a feminine nature and a masculine God is further narrowed in the aesthetic figuring of the moral law itself as Isis: "the veiled goddess before whom we bend the knee, is the moral law within us, in its inviolate majesty" (VIII:405; 71). According to that late work, to be able to intimate the goddess (as Schlosser, Kant's putatively Platonic critic, claims to do) is an expression that "means nothing more than to be led to concepts of duty by moral *feeling* before one could have *clarified* the principles on which this feeling depends."

36. Kant's early *Observations on the Feeling of the Beautiful and the Sublime* already shows the influence of *Emile*. The importance of Rousseau for Kant's theory of taste is frequently overlooked. Generally speaking, among Kant's predecessors, rationalists (such as Baumgarten) stressed the universal quality of judgments of taste as a species of cognition, while empiricists (such as Hutcheson and Hume) argued for its noncognitive basis in feeling. Kant adapted something from each so as to assert that judgments of taste, while noncognitive, make universal, necessary claims and thus require an a priori principle. As Pluhar points out ("Translator's Introduction," p. li), as late as 1781 Kant was still denying the possibility of such a principle (A/21 n =B/35 n).

In the main, growing interest in the category of the aesthetic (as typified by the English expression "good taste") seems to have coincided with a rising educated middle class eager to appropriate for mankind generally prerogatives of refinement previously reserved to the aristocracy. Good taste avoids the twin pitfalls of grossness (associated with the naively unenlightened) and over-refined luxury (associated with aristocratic decadence). For Kant's own early ruminations on this theme, see chapter 4 above. One important contribution of Kant's *Critique of Judgment* is to secure for aesthetic feeling an autonomous (albeit noncognitive) stature, independent of and in a sense midway between empirical sensibility on the one hand, rational knowledge on the other. By way of contrast, Baumgarten (who is the first to use the term "aesthetic" in the modern sense) treats the aesthetic (*aesthaita*) as a species of "confused" or perceptual knowledge, as distinguished from what is known distinctly (*noaita*). See *Reflections on Poetry* (*Meditationes philosophicae de nonnullis ad poema pertinentibus*), trans. Karl Aschenbrenner and William B. Holther, p. 78.

37. "Taste," Rousseau continues, "is exercised only in regard to things which are neutral or which are at most of interest as entertainment, and not in regard to those things connected with our needs" (*Emile*, pp. 340, 354).

38. On the exclusion of women from active juridical participation, see *Theory and Practice* (VIII:295; 78). Even in the case of taste, Kant sometimes suggests that women are, properly speaking, more objects of judgment than judges themselves.

39. Kant's insistence on the universality of judgments of taste—a universality that implies their (potentially) universal availability—is another aspect of this democratization. In a similar vein, he distinguishes his own scholarly activity from such cultivation. Where Baumgarten still treats aesthetics as a science of perfection best appreciated (by implication) by the learned, Kant is careful to say at the outset that what he does with taste as a philosopher has nothing "with form[ing] and cultivat[ing] taste (since this will continue to proceed, as it has in the past, even if no such investigations are made)" (V:170; 7).

40. Pluhar and Guyer disagree as to whether the necessity in question is (quasi-)epistemological (as the deduction at section 38 suggests) or (quasi-)moral (as the solution of the antinomy of taste at section 57 seems to insist); and Kant's language is, indeed, ambiguous on this score. Clearer is the structural weight the necessity in question is meant to bear—connected as it is to an "intrinsic contingency"—in the "Critique of Taste" and with it the "system" of the critique of pure reason as a whole.

41. Cf. Baumgarten, who defines philosophical poetics as "the science guiding sensate discourse to perfection" (*Metaphysica*, para. 115).

42. The Kantian sublime was, until recently, a relatively neglected topic in Kant studies. Recent works include (among others) Donald W. Crawford, "The Place of the Sublime in Kant's Aesthetic Theory," in *The Philosophy of Immanuel Kant*, ed. Richard Kennington, pp. 161–83; Jean-François Lyotard, "Answering the Question: What is Postmodernism?" in *The Post-Modern Condition: A Report on Knowledge*, trans. G. Bennington and B. Massumi; Makkreel, *Imagination and Interpretation*, p. 67 ff.; John Sallis, *Spacings: Of Reason and Imagination in Texts of Kant, Fichte, Hegel*, p. 82 ff.; Paul Guyer, "The Beautiful and the Sublime," in *Kant and the Experience of Freedom*; Fenves, *Peculiar Fate*; and Ronald Beiner, "Kant, the Sublime, and Nature," in *Kant and Political Philosophy*, ed. Ronald Beiner and William James Booth.

43. On the genesis of the sections on the sublime, see Giorgio Tonelli, "La formazione del testo della *Kritik der Urteilskraft*," *Revue Internationale de Philosophie*

8: 423–48), who argues for the lateness of the composition of the "Analytic of Judgment," along with those parts of the "Deduction of Pure Aesthetic Judgments" (and virtually the entire "Dialectic of Aesthetic Judgment") which emphasize the moral purposiveness of taste rather than, as is the case with the earliest material, taste's claim to universal validity. Crawford suggests that this difference indicates a shift in the course of Kant's writing of the *Critique of Judgment* toward questions of teleology generally, a topic not included in Kant's original study of taste ("Place of the Sublime," p. 161 ff.; Tonelli, "Formazione del testo," pp. 423–48). See also Zammito, p. 275 ff., who argues strongly for the moral impetus behind the addition of the analysis of the sublime to Kant's "Critique of Aesthetic Judgment." As we shall see, it is important to keep equally in mind Kant's continuing insistence on the *distinction* between the aesthetic and moral sublime.

44. The sublime involves what Kant calls an aesthetic estimation of magnitude, which he defines as a subjective judgment that involves the intuition as a unity of a homogeneous multiplicity. As such, it includes both the successive apprehension (*Auffassung*) of a multitude and their comprehension (*Zusammenfassung*) in a single intuition. Even mathematical (objective) estimations of magnitude ultimately refer for their standard to some unity that is comprehended aesthetically. On the significance of this notion for Kant's theory of knowledge generally, see Makkreel, *Imagination and Interpretation,* p. 68 ff.

45. What Robert Paul Wolff has called "the last word in mixed metaphors" is, I believe, intentionally so — a verbal identification of the "way up and the way down" (to cite Heraclitus) that points to the collapse (as any exhibition of the transcendent must ultimately do) of spatial representation as such. See Wolff, *Kant's Theory of Mental Activity,* p. 224, n. 2; and Makkreel, *Imagination and Interpretation,* p. 81.

46. This "carrying with" is later characterized as a sort of arousal (*erwecken*). Alternatively, "the magnitude of a natural object which imagination fruitlessly applies all its ability to comprehend" is said to "lead the concept of nature to a supersensible substrate (which underlies both nature and our ability to think)." The peculiar pleasure of the sublime turns, at least in part, on the veil it casts over its own source of motivation, that is, on what Kant speaks of as "legitimate subreption."

47. Cf. Kant's treatment here of nebulous systems such as the Milky Way, which — despite their "boundlessness" for the imagination — become "vanishingly small" in comparison to reason's idea (V:256–57; [113–14]).

48. On the relation between aesthetic comprehension of a magnitude and death, compare the *Critique of Pure Reason* A/168 = B/210, with B/414–15: our ability to comprehend manyness as one is inextricably connected with awareness of the possibility of a *remissio* (or "elanguescence") of our power of consciousness to zero, hence with the unprovability of the soul's permanence ("Beharrlichkeit"). Cf. Makkreel, *Imagination and Interpretation,* pp. 75–76.

49. See above, n. 26; see also (XX:231–32 n; [420 n]):

It is . . . an important article for morality to warn us emphatically against such empty and fantastic desires, which are often nourished by romances and sometimes also by similar mystical presentations of superhuman perfections and fanatical bliss. But even the effect that such empty desires and longings, which [alternately] distend the heart and make it flaccid [*welk*], have on the mind, making it languid by exhausting its forces —

this effect sufficiently proves that these forces are indeed repeatedly tensed by presentations to actualize their object, only to equally often let the mind sink back in the consciousness of its inability [*Unvermögens*]. It is indeed a not unimportant problem of anthropology to investigate why nature has given us the predisposition [*Anlage*] for such fruitless expenditure of our forces as are empty wishes and longings (which certainly play a large role in human life). It seems to me here, as in all else, that nature has made wise provision. For if we had to assure ourselves that we can in fact produce the object, before the presentation of it could determine us to apply our forces, our forces would presumably remain largely unused. For usually we do not come to know what forces we have except by trying them out. So nature has provided for the connection between the determination of our forces and the presentation of the object even before we know what ability we have, and it is often precisely this effort, which to that very mind seemed an empty wish, that produces that ability in the first place. Now it lies to wisdom to set limits to this instinct, but wisdom will never succeed in, or even demand, that instinct's uprooting [*auszurotten*].

50. The pleasure of the sublime arises from the subjectively purposive standard that comes into play in an estimation that exceeds the power of imagination to exhibit a magnitude. With ordinary (logical) estimations of magnitude, imagination provides a schema for the standard or measure given by some numerical concept. In such cases, imagination proceeds sequentially, without obstruction or any compulsion to complete the series. With the aesthetic estimation of magnitude, by way of contrast, the measure imagination is called upon to schematize must comprehend infinity. If, however, the human mind is "even to be able to think without contradiction" such a whole (which simultaneously demands and precludes intuitability), it must have a supersensible power [*Vermögen*] whose idea of a noumenon alone makes possible the comprehension of the infinity of the sensible world, under a concept, in a purely intellectual estimation of magnitude. This noumenon does not "permit [*verstattet*] intuition," but underlies, as substrate, "the world intuition [*Weltanschauung*] as an appearance" (V:253–55; [110–11]). This "most important" observation on Kant's part concerning what can be thought without contradiction is worth lingering over. The liking that accompanies aesthetic estimations of magnitude rests, finally, on an idea that manages, by virtue of its indirection, to intellectualize nature without confounding mind and matter.

51. On sublimity, see Longinus, *On the Sublime [Peri Hupsous]*, trans. W. Hamilton Fyfe, p. 125. Longinus's influence on modern aesthetics begins with the appearance of Nicolas Boileau's French translation in 1674. The classic study of his influence is Samuel H. Monk, *The Sublime.*

52. As the schematizing faculty, imagination expresses a duplicity that recalls the ambiguity of spirit that Kant formerly assigned (via his own person) to philosophy. (Kant's alternate name for the sublime, it is here useful to recall, is "spirit feeling," or *Geistesgefühl.*)

53. Cf. the unqualifiedly feminine imagination that figures in Jean-François Lyotard's "family story of the sublime" (*Lessons on the Analytic of the Sublime*, trans. Elizabeth Rottenberg, p. 179).

54. Imagination thus stands in for the mind itself, whose power to *think* the given infinite via the idea of a noumenon of nature is *felt* without being more conclusively established. The mind can only think the given infinite (that is, think it without contradicting itself) by assuming (or feeling) in itself a power to generate an idea of noumenalized nature (or nature intuited) that it cannot intuit (or see) directly.

55. On the importance of "work" as an antidote to various sorts of *Schwärmerei*, see note 21 above.

56. Despite this universality, Kant goes on in the next section to insist on the dependence of the sublime on cultural preparation, that is, on the development of moral ideas. One in whom such ideas have not developed will find what "we call sublime" merely repellent. Whereas all men admire, and so feel moved by, human courage, only some can feel that admiration through the intermediation of the fearful in nature. Thus the necessity without which aesthetic judgment would remain "buried" (*begraben*) among feelings of pleasure and pain, and without which it could not be "lifted above" (*erheben*) empirical psychology into transcendental philosophy—this necessity must undergo the following qualification: that while we can demand taste (which involves understanding or the faculty of concepts) of everyone (just as we can expect to share with them a common objective world), we can demand (*ansinnen*) feeling (for the sublime) of them only on the subjective presupposition of "moral feeling in man." Feeling (that is, for the sublime) is thus the analogue of common sense, both of which we are "justified in assuming" with the added proviso that the development of moral ideas accompanies (he does not quite say "requires") historical cultivation. What lifts (*erhebt*) the sublime (*das Erhabene*) out of the grave of empirical feeling into transcendental philosophy is not the "empty epithet" of refinement (which Kant in his own early essay on the sublime once gave it) but a justified if not precisely reasonable demand (*Ansinn*) that everyone feel morally.

In designating by the generic "feeling" the sublime analogue of common sense, Kant abandons his early characterization of the sublime as well as the beautiful (II:209; 46) as "refined" feelings, just as he abandons his early tripartite division of the sublime into the noble, the terrifying, and the splendid (*prächtig*). Kant now distinguishes noble wonder from the shudder of the sublime and locates the sublimity of St. Peter's Church not in its simple frame and splendid distribution of metalwork, but in its overwhelming complexity. Nevertheless, what Kant once meant by refinement—either "enjoyment without satiety or exhaustion"; or "the presupposition of a sensitive soul, so to speak, which fits it for virtuous impulses"; or "an indication of talents and intellectual excellences"—has to do, so long as one understands "sensitivity" as a sort of self-affection, more with the sublime in his later sense than with the beautiful.

57. Kant insists in the introduction that judgment be not only a *Mitglied*, or member of the "family" of our higher faculties, but also a *Mittelglied*, a "middlejoint" or linking member between understanding and reason (V:177; [16]).

It is useful to recall that analysis or *Zergliederung* (literally, "dismemberment" or "disarticulation") of knowledge is for Kant not only different from its critical expansion (*Erweiterung*), but a major obstacle thereto: what keeps us, in the faulty building of our knowledge, from suspecting its foundations is the circumstance that the greatest part of reason's business consists in the analysis (*Zergliederung*) of the concepts which we already have of objects (*Critique of Pure Reason* A/5 = B/9). The charm (*Reiz*) of expanding our knowledge is so great that nothing short of contradiction can arrest our course, contradiction we can avoid so long as we are careful in our fabrications (*Erdichterungen*). Such "Platonic" fabrications, however, actually get us nowhere, failing, as they do, to meet any resistance "that might, as it were, serve as a support [*Unterlage*]" on which one "could take a stand" (*sich steifen*) from which one could apply one's forces in order to dislodge (*von der Stelle zu bringen*) understanding. The need for such a point of support is obscured by reason's customary lack of anxiety (*Besorgnis*), a lack attributable to its confusion of analytic and synthetic knowledge (a lack attributable, therefore, precisely to a failure of analysis) (A/6 = B/10). In the *Prolegomena* Kant makes a similar argument concerning the insufficiency of *Zergliederung* in the context of the necessity that metaphysics, if it is to be something other than a natural disposition to illusion, be germinally "preformed" in critique (IV:365, 368; 114, 117).

58. *Abgang* is synonymous with "abort" or "discharge." *Nature* (*natura*), it may be useful to recall, derives from *nascor* (to be born), and its primary Latin meaning is "condition of birth."

59. That is, the "substrate" that underlies "both nature and our power to think" (V:255; [112]).

60. The movement of Kant's *Universal Natural History* is, to this extent, not purely sublime in his later sense. It is noteworthy that Kant's critical discussion specifically insists on the aesthetic equivalence of water represented as a smooth surface and water represented in its turbulence (or as an "abyss threatening to engulf everything"), treating as one the twin images—mirror and abyss—between which the *Universal Natural History* vacillates. Freed from teleological determination, those images become, from the perspective of the aesthetic sublime, equivalents (see V:270; 130).

61. Kant says as much in his own essay *On Diseases of the Head* (II:267).

62. On the other hand, what reason "likes" is the moral law in its might, a might that expresses itself aesthetically only as sacrifice, albeit one that reveals in us an "ungroundable depth" of a power from which unforeseeable consequences extend (*erstrecken*). Reason, too, as aesthetically exhibited, has its blindness and its abyss in the ungroundableness of "inner freedom" itself.

63. In the *Anthropology*, by way of contrast, Kant attributes enthusiasm to reason and the appetitive power rather than to affect. Enthusiasm is now said to be the cause of affect (which is itself only "more or less" blind) and thus compatible with "reason holding the reins [*Zügel*]," as with—to cite Kant's own example—spiritual or political addresses that "exemplify" moral ideas so as to "enliven" the people's will. This political rehabilitation of enthusiasm (and in a lesser sense, sympathy) goes together with a corresponding devaluation of apathy (or *phlegma* in the moral sense) to the status of a mere "favor of fortune." What transforms feeling into an affect of the wrong sort is not the intensity of the former but a failure of "government" (*Regierung*), that is, a failure to compare that feeling with the totality of all the pleasures and displeasures that go with our state (as with a rich man distraught by the loss of a single treasured possession) (VII:252–54; [120–22]).

64. *Wackern,* which also connotes upright honesty, and standing one's ground,

is associated with *Wack*, a kind of rock or boulder; *animus strenuus*, a term for "vigor," is drawn from *Strenia*, a Roman goddess of health and good auspices.

65. Even if they did not indirectly influence our consciousness of a strength and resolve for the supersensible, the agitations of the sublime, Kant suggests, might still be a boon to mechanical health (V:273; 134). Here he seems to have in mind the theories of the controversial Scottish physician John Brown. In his *Elementa medicinae* Brown identified as the vital principle of all life a principle of "excitability" (*Reizbarkeit* in German) manifesting itself in a cycle of animation and exhaustion. According to Brown, health depends on the principle of excitability being kept in even supply throughout the body. Too little brings on loss of energy and debility (the so-called asthenic diseases), while too much stimulation brings the body to a degree of intensity (the sthenic diseases) that forbodes immanent, terminal depletion. Death is the result of "a perfect extinction of the excitement, either from a complete exhaustion or extreme abundance of excitement." See *Elements of Medicine*, translated by the author, revised and corrected with a biographical preface by Thomas Beddoes, 2 vols., vol. 1, p. 266; and Hermione de Almieda, *Romantic Medicine and John Keats*, p. 69 f. Brown's single principle of life, described as a "peculiar attractive and repulsive force," was touted by his followers (including Girtenner, whose work on races [1796] Kant praises in his *Anthropology*) as an advance over both William Cullen's reduction of life to nervous energy in various degrees of "excitement," and von Haller's distinction between the irritability and sensitivity of animals, and the mere productivity of plants. In collapsing the distinction between plantlike "productivity" and animal "excitement," Brunonianism also renders that productivity potentially more dangerous, a danger taken up by Kant and later assumed by various popular nineteenth-century theories associating "excessive" (sexual) excitement with (potentially fatal) nervous "exhaustion." On the broader implications of Kant's interest in contemporary medical theories, see chapter 10 below. Girtenner was also the author of *Memoires sur l'irritabilité, considerée comme le principe de vie dans la nature organisée*. See also Mendelsohn, *Heat and Life*, pp. 169–70; and Alexander Gode-von Aesch, *Natural Science and German Romanticism*, pp. 195–96. Kant elsewhere likens Brown's contribution to medicine to that of Lavoisier's to chemistry (*Doctrine of Virtue* [VI:207; 3]; see also *Anthropology* [VII:255; 123]).

66. Cf. Kant's approval (for purposes of empirical anthropology) of the opinions of Edmund Burke, who attributes the feeling of the sublime to agitations that, while painful in themselves, lead to a pleasurable and life-enhancing clearing of obstructions from the fibers. The beautiful, on the other hand, according to Burke, involves "the relaxing, slackening, and enervating of the body's fibers, and hence to a softening, dissolution, exhaustion, a fainting [*Hinsinken*], a dying [*Hinsterben*] and melting away [*Wegschmelzen*] with delight" (*Philosophical Enquiry into the Origin of Our Ideas of the Sublime and Beautiful*, pt. 4, secs. 7 and 19). Kant cites Christian Garve's translation. "Dying" does not appear in the original Burkean passage.

67. Cf. *Reflection* no. 765 (XV:333), no. 789 (XV:345), and XV:344 n–355 n: according to unpublished notes from the 1770s, northern Europeans exhibit greater "purity of thought" and greater affinity for conceptual clarity than the more sensual Oriental peoples. (The larger intellectual context, as Adickes notes, is almost certainly a critique of Hamann and Herder.)

68. See *Anthropology* (VII:165; 42. Reworded at VII:237; 105). Cf. *Reflection* no. 1484 (XV:697): "(rising). The end stings from this (through saving the best for last) . . . because it cannot be further obscured. end of the fable, the comedy of life"; and no. 584 (XV:251): "one must always be able to rise. hope."

In the *Metaphysics of Morals* Kant compares the "consuming" danger of such exhaustion in men, to the danger posed to women by childbirth (VI:359-60) (from which, at the time Kant wrote, as many as one woman in ten is said to have perished). On intercourse as weakening or exhausting the male, see Aristotle, *On the Generation of Animals* 725b ff. According to Aristotle's account of generation, the male furnishes "concocted" semen; the female, who has less vital heat, unconcocted. Thus "a boy [not yet capable of generation] is like a woman in form, and a woman is as it were an impotent male, for it is through a certain incapacity that the female is female, being incapable of concocting the nutriment in its last state into semen (728a). According to Aristotle, "the male contributes to generation the form and the efficient cause, while the female contributes the material" (729a). (The pleasure of intercourse is due to the emission not only of semen but also of a spiritus [pneuma], the coming together of which precedes the emission, a fact said to explain sexual pleasure in young boys and others incapable of fertile emission.) The male, in other words, furnishes the motion, and the female that which is moved, just as a bed comes into being from the carpenter and the wood, and a ball from the form and the wax (729b).

The disappearance, in the new mechanical science of Descartes and Newton, of formal causation as an explanatory principle, along with the collapsing, by that same science, of material and efficient causation, posed a special challenge to the essentially Aristotelian account of generation still widely prevalent, particularly with regard to that account's explanation of male superiority (which Aristotle assumed as a matter of course). To my knowledge, this consideration — crucial, I believe, to an understanding of romanticism and its peculiar ambivalence toward women as objects of both veneration and loathing — has not been adequately explored by scholars.

69. Cf. *Reflection* no. 1511 (XV:833): "all enjoyments must be able to increase [*steigen*] (consist only in prospect). Thus abstinence prepares for the greatest pleasures. . . . One must harden oneself [*sich abhärten*], in order not to become soft [*weichlich*]."

70. In the *Anthropology* Kant recommends an analogous looking away for the relief of nausea at sea: the illusion that "one's seat is giving way," accompanied by an impulse to vomit, is intensified, Kant notes, in a veiled autobiographical reference, when the patient "looks out of his cabin window and catches alternating glimpses of sea and sky" (VII:264; [131]. Cf. VII:170; 46).

71. Enthusiasm, on the other hand, Kant links with madness, or the (temporary) unbridling of imagination, as opposed to mania, imagination's deep-rooted and brooding [*brütend*] lack of rule.

72. Kant's exact words are as follows: "The same [Kant had just spoken of the heavens and the ocean] is to be said about the sublime and beautiful in the human shape [*Menschengestalt*], where we do not look back to concepts of the ends *for which* it has all its members, as determining grounds of judgment. And we must not allow harmony with those ends to influence our (then no longer pure) aesthetic

judgment, even though it is certainly a necessary condition of aesthetic liking that these members not conflict with these ends" (V:270; [130–31]).

73. Eva Schaper, *Studies in Kant's Aesthetics*.

74. See the following note from the early 1770s (*Reflection* no. 1260 [XV:555]): "With women everything is more preformed; thus they are more imperfect, but more art, thus (mechanical) advantage {trick/device [*Der Masch*]}, the man more power [*Gewalt*]. She is ripe early so she can reproduce early." *Masch,* which literally refers to a stitch or loop, hence also to a net or trap, is related (along with our mechanism and machine) to the Greek *maixos,* meaning "device." The mechanism (technique?) of nature is, in woman at least, equivalent to an entrapping loop. On woman as an example of "mechanical advantage," see also *Anthropology* (VII:303–4; 166–67).

75. See, for example, *Reflection* no. 735 (XV:324): "Sex in women. That belongs to what pleases by art." On woman's dress (*Putz*) as fine art, see no. 683 (XV:305). On woman as an "artful machine," see no. 1283 (XV:565, 567); on her disposition (*Anlage*) for art, see XV:581 and XV:794.

76. "Thus the female sex is refusing through an instinct. Because otherwise it would lose its charm and the influence it thereby procures [*vermittelst*]. But this is also the refusal of belovedness [*Holdigkeit*]. Making common. It is pride in her sex. Rivers of milk and honey would soon make both unbearable for both of us. The lotus land [*Schlaraffenland*]. . . . Every {pleasure} good humor is refusing. Virtue . . . thus increases the charm of beauty. But marriage is also the price that the sex places on itself. Charm will be esteemed, flattered, attended. Wanton [*buhlerische*] and virtuous refusal" (*Reflection* no. 985 [XV:430]).

77. See *Reflection* no. 1067 (XV:473):

What is disgust [*Abscheu*]? how is it distinguished from hate (as compared to unkindness) and contempt (as compared to self-contemnation)? as it were, a mixture of both. It approaches nausea [*Ekel*].Nauseating [*Ekel-haft*] is false wit, often repeated caprices, boring narrative, self-praise. Superfluity in feeding. very sweet or fatty. often all in one. grouse. The nauseating faces of old women. heathens [*heidegger*]. Precisely speaking, to the decay and excrement of the animal body generally. Nauseating diseases. Nausea makes one sated, and hunger banishes nausea.

78. *Reflection* no. 562 (XV:244). On the "masking" (*verdecken*) of the sexual act with a nobler *Absicht* to render it more "savory" (*schmakhafter*), see no. 6620 (XIX:114). See also Kant's notorious comparison of the sexual act to "cannibalism" (VI:359–60), no. 7600 (XIX:481); and chapter 6 above. No. 1087 (XV:483) compares the cannibalistic character of sexual enjoyment to a prince's liking for fat subjects: "We find something indecent [*Unanständiges*], not in the sexual inclination, but in intercourse and the enjoyment one person has in another." We "can in no way beautify [*verschönern*] the two sorts of evacuation, as we can with dining [*Mahlzeiten*], but the noble and the common must act the same way, and it shames us to share one and the same lot with animals." But the greatest reserve (*Zurückhalt-ung*) concerns "speaking about as well as observation [*Augenschein*] of sexual intercourse," and this because, even though it seems to be ordered for spiritual (moral) ends, "it is yet so physical" (like *Rinderbraten* [roast beef]). Cf. no. 7865

(XIX:540): "The use of one's sexual capacity is also an abuse (abusus) of the same. Thus there is always in this act something that devalues [*abwürden*] humanity."

79. Cf. *Conjectural Beginning of Human History* (VIII:112–13; [57]):

In the case of animals, sexual excitement [*Reiz*] is merely a matter of transient [*voruebergehenden*] . . . impulse. But man [*Der Mensch*] soon discovered that for him this attraction can be prolonged and even increased by means of the imagination — a power that carries on its business the more moderately, but also at the same time the more constantly and uniformly, the more its object *is removed from the senses*. By means of the imagination, he discovered, the surfeit [*Überdruβ*] was avoided which goes with the satiety of mere animal desire. . . . *Refusal* was the artful trick [*Kunststüeck*] that brought about the passage from merely sensual to idealistic excitements. . . . [It is unclear from the context whether the trickery is to be attributed to women or to nature.] In addition, there came a first hint [*Wink*] at the formation of man as a moral [*sittlichen*] creature. This came from the sense of decency [*Sittsamkeit*] — that is, an inclination to inspire others to respect through propriety, (concealment of all that might arouse low esteem). Here, by the way, is the proper basis of all sociability [*Geselligkeit*].

In effect, Kant collapses the historical account of the natural relation between the sexes as presented in Rousseau's *Discourse on the Origins of Inequality* with the idealized account presented in the courtship sections of *Emile*. Unlike Rousseau, Kant never attempts to derive men's sociality from a more primitive or natural state of solitude. At least insofar as the relation between the sexes is concerned, human beings, for him, are always social. On the greater delicacy of male (sexual) taste, see also *Anthropology* (VII:306; 170).

80. Compare, for example, the many passages (including the very early [by Adickes's reckoning] *Reflection* no. 639 and no. 640 [XV:639 ff.]) in which beauty (and taste) are *contrasted* with charm, with no. 733 (XV:334 f.), from the early 1770s, in which charm is associated with "fantastic" representations of ease and freedom from care, along with (and here beauty is perhaps included) an invitation to sexual enjoyment. In the same note, Kant associates taste, here distinguished from charm, with "communicated" pleasure, hence with a means of unifying humanity. But cf. the early no. 640 (XV:281): "the beautiful person pleases through her shape and charms through her sex"; and the somewhat later no. 843 (XV:375), which defines beauty as a *combination* of charm and dignity (*Würde*). See also no. 701 (XV:310 f.), in which charm is associated with honor (in a good sense); and no. 685 (XV:305), which distinguishes between ideal and corporeal charm. The following passage, however, perhaps best captures the sense of troubled ambivalence concerning the relation between beauty and charm conveyed by the *Reflections* as a whole: "Since sensual charm alone drives its wanton [*übermüthigen*] game [*Spiel*], mocks all fundamental principles, and turns the wise into fools (for the deceived man, even in the object of his inclination), the drive to fortify ideal charms and beauties of wit is not a thing of sentiment. These drive so deceptively as to lead us each time, in our paradisaical expectations, under the light, and make us the plaything [*Spielwerk*] of a child. One should that much the more turn one's wit

to noble sentiments and the rights of reason against the tyranny of this drive, so as to call it an illusion [*Blendwerk*] and teach it to obey virtue and the rules of happiness. There is also in the first no art" (no. 718 [XV:318]). See also XV:687: "Who searches [*forscht*] very far beneath beautiful appearance, loses belief in virtue (the enjoyments of the game)."

81. See, for example, (V:212; 55), (V:223; 69), and (V:299; 166). But cf. V:244; 95. See also (V:225; 71), which associates charm with the "matter" rather than the "form" of aesthetic liking.

82. *Reflection* no. 1301 (XV:572): Feminine beauty is only relative, male beauty is absolute. (See also *Logik Philippi* [XXIV:350], where Kant quotes Winkelman approvingly to the same effect.) "Thus all male animals are beautiful in our eyes, because they have no charm relative to our feeling. Women, when they speak with one another about beauty, have no concept of charm. I have also never seen them to be in harmony with men in this. Figure is all that pleases them; for men, at best the structure [*Bau*]. Men very much love the soul; women the body. They believe a soul to be good enough, so long as it comes under their power [*Gewalt*]." What women, according to this passage written in the middle to late seventies, see in one another — the figure bereft of *Reiz* — provides a sort of model for Kant's later understanding of the disinterestedness of taste.

83. Woman's natural purpose, as there described, is to preserve the species and to prepare (inspire?) others (men?) to be virtuous.

84. Disgust (*Abscheu*), according to the *Anthropology* (VII:157–58; 35–36), is a sensation physiologically akin to the sublime, that is, a feeling of vertiginous revulsion against nature. But nausea as such is *not* sublime; for if with the sublime, we feel ourselves transcendent over natural sensation; with nausea, it is sensation that has the victory, forcing enjoyment upon us, as it were, against our own will and through the vehicle of our own imagination. Nausea (*Ekel*) is a vital feeling related to smell and taste, the "chemical" senses that have to do not (as with touch) with the surface of things, but with consumption (*Genuβ*) and a most inward partaking (*innigste Einnehmung*). Nausea is the feeling associated with ridding ourselves by the shortest route of something dangerous that we have taken in. Because, however, there is also a sort of spiritual consumption (*Geistesgenuβ*), which consists in the communication (*Mittheilung*) of thoughts, the mind experiences an analogously "nauseous" feeling of inner sense associated, for example, with monotonous witticisms. The latter sort of nausea is thus the negative counterpart to aesthetic taste (which also has to do with spiritual *Mittheilung*), just as physical nausea is the negative counterpart of "taste" (*Geschmack*) in the primary sense related to the ingestion of food.

Kant also associates disgust and nausea with superfluity (*Überfluβ*) of enjoyment, or public indulgence (*Schwelgerei*), that is, with tasteless "luxuries" as distinguished from tasteful "luxus" (VII:249–50; 116). By his own account, Kant put great personal effort into the "agreeably artful" arrangement of dinner parties (for male friends), in which he frequently indulged, for reasons both intellectual and digestive — that is, into "spirit culture" in both senses of the term (VII:277 ff.; 143 ff. See also *On Philosopher's Medicine of the Body* [XV:949–50; 235]).

For all its seeming insignificance, Kant's treatment of nausea and disgust reaches to the heart, as it were, of his concern with the boundaries of the individual, an "anxiety of influence" in the most literal sense. Aesthetic taste, one could say, is a rehabilitated version of the *Mittheilung* (or mutual imparting) whose primary, consumptive forms, be they alimentary, respiratory, or sexual, are "dangerous to the animal." Kant's mother, it is useful to recall, died (or so he seems to have believed) after sharing the tainted spoon of a lovesick friend—a literal enactment of Kant's metaphorical identification, via imagination, of (mental) sympathy and (physical) contagion. For more on this episode, see chapter 10 below.

85. See *Blomberg Logic* (XXIV:48; 34): beauty lessens with the furthering of reason and clarity, as woman's beauty vanishes when you look at it under a microscope.

86. Compare the image on which Kant draws, as an afterthought, as it were, when contrasting entertaining and dishonest fiction: "to fabricate [*erdichten*]—knowingly to set forth what is not true as true, as in novels, where this is done only for entertainment.—But a fabrication [*Erdichtung*] given out as true is a lie. (Turpiter atrum desinit in piscem mulier formosa superne.) [A beautiful woman above ends foully in a black fish.] Horace [*Ars poetica*, l. 4 ff.]" (VII:247 n; 114 n). (The theme of artful dishonesty plays no part in the original text of Horace.) Cf. Kant's *Concerning Sensory Illusion and Poetic Fiction* (XV:908; 203).

87. The Latin term *ingenium* literally denotes something inborn. In the *Anthropology* (VII:225; 94) Kant also refers "genius" [*Genie*] to the Latin *genius* (literally, "the begetter"), which he defines as "individual spirit." According to the *Oxford Latin Dictionary*, the primary meaning of *genius* in classical Latin was "the male spirit of a *gens* existing during his lifetime in the head of the family, and subsequently in the divine or spiritual part of each individual." The *Oxford Classical Dictionary* defines *genius* as "the attendant spirit of every man, a sort of guardian angel, but originally his inborn power whose activities were apparently directed largely towards fostering the natural desires and their satisfaction. . . . Every male, bond or free, seems to have had a *genius,* in family cult only one *genius* was honored in each household, that of the *paterfamilias,* especially on the occasion of his marriage." (Grimm's *Lexicon* lists under *Genie* "Geburtsgeist" or "Geburtsengel" as a prevalent eighteenth-century meaning.) According to the *Oxford English Dictionary, genius* in the specific sense of extraordinary artistic or intellectual ability first came into use in England in the eighteenth century, later achieving even greater prominence in Germany, particularly in connection with the so-called Sturm und Drang period (also known as the *Genieperiod*). As Tonelli observes ("Kant's Early Theory of Genius: 1770–1779," *Journal of the History of Philosophy* 4: 109–31, 209–24), many of the attributes of genius as Kant describes it (for example, its intuitively creative character and its inimitability) were common currency. Kant seems, however, to have placed exceptional weight on the older, "generative" connotations of the term as well. Alexander Gerard, whose views on genius Kant calls "the best," speaks of it as an "impetuous" and "ecstatic" "heating," and also compares it to the manner in which a plant assimilates nourishment. See Gerard, *Essay on Genius,* pp. 63, 68; and Kant, *Menschenkunde oder philosophische Anthropologie,* ed. F. C. Starke, p. 233. For a general discussion of the notion of *genius* in the eighteenth century, see John Engell, *The Creative Imagination.*

88. Cf. Paul Valéry, *Pièces sur l'art,* quoted by Walter Benjamin, "Art in the Age of Mechanical Reproduction," in *Illuminations,* ed. Hannah Arendt, p. 217.

89. In the *Anthropology* Kant calls spirit the *"animating* principle in man" (VII:225; 93); the *Critique of Judgment* attributes the animating principle of the mind to spirit in an "aesthetic sense" (V:313; 181).

90. But cf. *Reflection* no. 1592 (XVII:797), according to which woman is nature's "favorite": one loves in woman, Kant continues, "the *depositarin* of nature." Cf. *Anthropology* (VII:306; 169).

91. See *Idea for a Universal History,* prop. 3.

92. Cf. the text at note 104.

93. On Kant's early identification of life with self-maintaining and expanding motion, see chapter 2 above. In the *Metaphysical Foundations of Natural Science* Kant defines life as "the capacity of a substance to determine itself from an internal principle, of a finite substance to determine itself to change, of a material substance to determine itself to motion or rest as change of its state" (IV:544; 105). He adds, however, that matter as such is lifeless, inasmuch as desire is the only internal principle of change that we know of, and inasmuch as the only determining grounds of desire that we know of (pleasure, pain, and will) do not belong to the representations of the external senses, representations that determine matter as matter.

94. See *Reflection* no. 933 (XV:414) (1776–78): "Spirit is not properly a particular talent, but an enlivening principle of all talents." (Kant speaks here of spirit with specific reference to males [*der Mann*].) See also no. 1509 (XV:826) (1780–84): "Spirit is what is properly creative, what enlivens because it is the unity (swing) from which all movement of the mind derives." Cited in Makkreel, *Imagination and Interpretation,* p. 97.

95. In the original poem by Withof, "goodness" appears in place of "virtue."

96. See the partial rehabilitation of Epicurus at (V:331; 201), but cf. (V:274; [139]): "It cannot even be denied that, as Epicurus maintained, *gratification* and *pain* are always of the body, whether they come from imagination or even from presentations of the understanding; for without feeling of the bodily organ, there would be mere consciousness of one's existence, without feeling of well-being or its opposite, i.e., of the promotion or obstruction of the life force. For the mind is in itself entirely life (the life principle itself), and hindrances or promotions of it must be sought outside the mind and yet within man himself, in the connection [*Verbindung*] with his body." On the vexed nature of this *Verbindung* (which both joins and separates matter and mind/life), see chapter 9 below.

For an interesting discussion of certain anticipations in Kant's *Critique of Judgment* of Dilthey's *Lebensphilosophie,* see Rudolf A. Makkreel, "The Feeling of Life: Some Kantian Sources of Life-Philosophy," *Dilthey-Jahrbuch für Philosophie und Geschichte der Geisteswissenschaften* 3: 83–104. Makkreel here leaves unexplored what is arguably for Kant the matter's heart: the relation between the aesthetic feeling of life, and the feeling of what Makkreel calls life in the biological sense.

97. Cf. *Reflection* no. 4138 (XVII:431).

98. On Kant's emphatic rejection of "play," see B/xxxvii.

99. In the second *Critique,* our knowledge that we are free follows from awareness of duty (or knowledge "that we ought"), that is, from a moral consciousness that "may be called a fact [*Factum*] of reason." In order, Kant continues, to regard without misunderstanding this law as given, one must note that it is not an empirical fact but the "sole fact [*Factum*] of pure reason, that thus announces itself as

originally law giving (sic volo, sic jubeo)" (V:31; [31]). On the relation between these two texts, see Onora O'Neill, *Constructions of Reason,* p. 64. Contrary to O'Neill's intriguing suggestion, Kant does not call freedom proper a *Factum* of reason. It is difficult to avoid the conclusion that as regards the *ratio cogniscendi* of freedom, the two texts are inconsistent. From the perspective of the second *Critique,* awareness of the moral law is the cause of our knowing that we are free; while freedom is the *ratio essendi,* the cause without which "the law would never have been encountered in us" (V:5 n; 4 n). See also Dieter Henrich, "The Concept of Moral Insight," in *The Unity of Reason,* ed. Richard Velkley, pp. 82-87.

100. On anticipations of that formula in the essay *What Is Enlightenment?* see O'Neill, *Constructions,* p. 32 ff.

101. But cf. *Reflection* no. 1509 (XV:826): "What is essential is spirit and judgment and belongs to genius in general."

102. Thus genius is "invisible"; see *Anthropology* (VII:225; 94).

103. Fine art's putative subservience to nature is, indeed, ultimately reversed: for the audience, at least, poetry "lets the mind feel its ability — free, spontaneous, and independent of natural determination — to contemplate and judge phenomenal nature according to aspects that nature on its own does not offer in experience" and thus "lets the mind feel its ability to use nature on behalf of and, as it were, as a schema of the supersensible" (V:326; 196-97). In the end it is "we who favor nature," rather than "nature who favors us."

104. Cf. *Critique of Pure Reason* A/832 = B/860: "By an architectonic I understand the art [*Kunst*] of system." See also *Anthropology* (VII:227; 95). As the inventor of the idea of philosophy as a system of "world wisdom," Kant could not avoid regarding himself as epoch-making. See also notes from the *Kolleghefte* associating philosophy with the science of genius (cited in Otto Schlapp, *Kants Lehre vom Genie und die Entstehung der "Kritik der Urteilskraft,"* pp. 125-26).

Elsewhere in the *Anthropology* genius is treated as applying peculiarly to imagination and the arts. There is also a kind of genius (*ingenium*) that Kant identifies (along Wolffian lines) with "motherwit," that is, with an ability to seek out the universal for the particular corresponding to judgment's ability to seek out the particular for the universal. The contrast between wit and judgment in this context is subsumed, within the framework of the *Critique of Judgment,* by judgment itself. As with a similar equivocation concerning the respective roles of genius and taste, Kant does not seem fully to have resolved the relation between judgment and wit.

105. On the wavering relation between genius and spirit in these notes, see Tonelli, "Kant's Early Theory of Genius," pp. 110-15.

106. See the very early *Reflection* no. 1654 (XVI:67-68): "spirit belongs to the discovery of that which lies at the ground of an idea, also with reason." See also no. 782 (XV:342): "Spiritual feeling consists in one experiencing one's share [*seinen Antheil . . . empfindet*] in an ideal whole," the latter being "the ground idea of reason." Such participation is specifically distinguished from sympathy [*Sympathie*], which derives "merely from the particular."

107. See, for example, *Reflection* no. 1880 and no. 1846 (XVI:147, 136): what understanding arouses belongs to spirit; what feeling arouses belongs to sense.

108. Tonelli's ingenious reconstruction of Kant's theory of genius as a kind of participation in the "world-soul" lays undue weight, in my opinion, on these two

(atypical) passages. The term "world-soul/spirit" does not, to my knowledge, appear in an unqualifiedly positive light anywhere else in the Kantian corpus, with the exception of a very early passage connecting the notion of a world-soul with a material "Spiritus Rector" (I:211) and with the highly qualified exception of certain sections of the *Opus postumum*, which will be taken up in chapter 10 below. On the connection between genius and creation, see also *Reflection* no. 753 and no. 754 (XV:329–30), from the early seventies, in which Kant calls "the original fertility of nature" the ground of the beautiful in art and likens genius to a wood "in which free and fertile nature propagates its empire," whereas art "is like a garden, in which all happens according to method and one is subjected to rules." Cf. no. 943 (XV:418), which likens the work of genius to a kind of new creation; and no. 761 (XV:332), which compares the idea itself (*Urbild*) as the "principle of rules" to a "creation of reason." A third set of notes designates philosophy—rather than mathematics, as Plato perhaps thought—as the "true motherland" of "ideas" but not of their "enlivening" (see nos. 942–43 [XV:418–19]). I differ, however, with Tonelli's reading of these passages, which draws a prematurely sharp distinction between poetic and philosophic genius (cf. "Kant's Early Theory of Genius," p. 126). On art as creation see also no. 959 (XV:423).

109. See *Critique of Pure Reason* B/166 f. and *Reflection* no. 4275 (VII:492), no. 4859 (VIII:12), and no. 4851 (XVIII:8–10). See also Wayne Waxman, *Kant's Model of the Mind*, pp. 250–51; and J. Wubnig, "The Epigenesis of Pure Reason," *Kant-Studien* 60: 147–52. Cf. A. C. Genova, "Kant's Epigenesis of Pure Reason," *Kant-Studien* 65: 259–73; and Hans Werner Ingensiep, "Die biologischen Analogien und die erkenntnistheoretischen Alternativen in Kants Kritik der reinen Vernunft B #27," *Kant-Studien* 85: 381–93. Ingensiep rightly warns against mistaking the "production of experience" in question for a spatiotemporal event. On Kant's use of "epigenesis" in the *Nachlaß*, see Günter Zöller, "Kant on the Generation of Metaphysical Knowledge," in *Kant: Analysen-Probleme-Kritik*, ed. Hariolf Oberer and Gerhard Seel. For some early moral experiments with the notion of epigenesis, see *Reflection* no. 6864, no. 6867, and no. 6916 (1776–78) (XIX:184, 186, 206).

110. *Reflection* no. 4275 (1770–71) (XVII:491–92) reads as follows:
Analysis of reason. principium contradictionis, identitatis; it gives objectively valid propositions.
Synthesis of reason: various laws (axiomata subreptitia), subjectively valid propositions.The conditions of our reason, which 1. knows objects only mediately and not through intuition, thus the *conditiones,* by means of which a cognition of something is possible, and the necessity of positing something *primitive* and without *conditiones.*
Sensual intuition (according to sensible form and matter) gives synthetic propositions that are objective. Crusius explained the real grounding principles [*grundsatze*] of reason according to the *systemate praeformationis* (according to subjective principles), Locke, like Aristotle, according to *influxu physico,* Plato and Malebranche from *intuitu intellectuali,* we according to *epigenesis* from the use of natural laws of reason.
(Common human understanding, sense of true and false, is *Qualitas occulta.*)
Antithesis: a method of reason, for discovering the opposition of sub-

jective laws, which, if by the subreptive vice they are taken for objective, is skepticism (in the objective sense); but if it is only a (critique of the subject) propaedeutic, is skeptical method. Toward the determination of the subjective laws of reason. Subjective antithesis.

111. Cf. Waxman, *Kant's Model of the Mind*, p. 251. Waxman's reading, in my view, fails to give sufficient weight to Kant's decisive rejection of this third way precisely on the grounds of its appeal to the principle of "organization."

112. For a compelling explication of this common world, see O'Neill, *Constructions*, pp. 28–50.

113. In the "Critique of Teleological Judgment," by way of contrast, Kant allows for what he calls "generic" preformation. See (V:422 ff.; 308 ff.) and chapter 9 below.

114. Curly brackets and asterisks here and elsewhere indicate bracketing and asterisks that appear in the Akademie edition.

115. *Reflection* no. 933 (1771–72) (XV:414), which speaks of spirit as the production ground (*Erzeugungsgrund*) of the ideas, also calls it the "enlivening of sensibility through [an] idea." The idea must first enliven understanding, and then sensibility. If it happens in reverse, it isn't inspiration (*Begeisterung*) but feverish heating. Spirit, in this context, is identified with the male (*der Mann,* just as [in the roughly contemporaneous passage quoted above] the inflated genius [who produces wind-eggs] is implicitly criticized for assuming the woman's part). Cf. Aristotle, *Generation of Animals:* "for the female is, as it were, a mutilated male, and the catamenia are semen, only not pure; for there is only one thing they have not in them, the principle of soul. For this reason, whenever a wind-egg is produced by any animal, the egg so forming has in it the parts of both sexes potentially, but has not the principle in question, so that it does not develop into a living creature, for this is introduced by the semen of the male" (737a). Kant may also have had in mind in the above quoted passage the "Luftgeisten" of the Theosophists (as per his own "Pneumatology"). The topos of the air-child dissolving into a mist of mystical speech calls to mind the famous "Euphorion" scene from Goethe's *Faust* II (1832): 9695 ff. A similar thought is expressed in the *Critique of Judgment* at (V:304; 171), where Kant speaks of the need to temper genius with mechanism and labor, lest *"spirit,* which in art must be *free* and which alone animates the work, would have no body at all and would evaporate [*verdunsten*] completely."

116. Cf., for example, *Reflection* no. 1847 (1776–78) (XVI:136): "genius is architectonic"; and no. 1815 (1770–78) (XVI:126), according to which the architectonic head judges only according to taste, not spirit.

117. For more reflections bearing on the relation between science and genius, see the relatively early *Reflection* no. 943 (1776–78) (XV:418) and no. 966 (1776–78) (XV:424), linking the genius and spirit of science to the discovery of new methods; and the relatively late no. 1510 (1780–84) (XV:826–28), linking Newton, Galileo, and Michelangelo. Genius, Kant there says, "is the source of the discovery of a science or art that isn't there yet." In a reflection that Adickes dates problematically around the time of the composition of the *Idea for a Universal History,* Kant calls for a genius to bind human history together with an idea (no. 1997 [XVI:188]). See also no. 2061, probably from the same period, calling one who "thinks for himself" rather than copying the thoughts of others "a head [ingen-

ium]." On the importance of the idea of reason to Kant's conception of philosophy as "world-wisdom," see Velkley, *Freedom,* p. 89–ff.

118. The pattern of that history charts the irruption, so to speak, into consciousness of the idea, transforming a previously natural and unintended (or merely "purposive") development into a purposeful project directed according to a conscious *plan.* See *Reflection* no. 1523 (XV:896): "One can also culturally progress blindly and without a plan, and nature has also not left this to our choice." When we are almost near the end, however, "a plan must be made." Compare, in this regard, no. 931: "Spirit seems to have no intention. It enlivens mechanism and is under no compulsion but free" (XV:413).

Like the artistic genius, Kant cannot explain how he arrived at his idea; unlike the artistic genius (but like a Leibniz or a Newton), he can impart the method inspired by the idea to others. On the intimate relation between ideas and the discovery of new methods, see *Reflection* no. 966 (XV:424) and no. 943 (XV:418): "a new idea presupposes an entirely new method." See also Onora O'Neill's very helpful discussion of the significance of Kant's "Transcendental Doctrine of Method" for his critical project as a whole (*Constructions,* pp. 13–27; and *Critique of Pure Reason* A/707 = B/735 ff.). There are, as it were, no rules for the discovery of ideas, which themselves give rules (and thereby inspire new methods).

On the problem of whether the idea is to be regarded as an "invention" or a "contingent discovery," see *Reflection* no. 949 (1776–78) (XV:420–21). The difficulty comes in uniting the natural emergence of the idea (according to what are presumably mechanical laws) and its causeless origin in (or along with) freedom. Owing to this difficulty, perhaps, Kant claims in one note to seek "not the physical causes of genius — for example, imagination, for those are not in our power," but merely the formal principle that gives "nature direction" (no. 960 [1776–78] [XV:423]).

Prior to the moment at which he became conscious of the idea, Kant was himself, it seems, the unconscious bearer of the *Anlage* of reason. (This, at any rate, he shares with the discomforting femininity of genius.) The natural irruption of freedom is inscribed — if anywhere — in Kant's own biography.

119. See (V:350; 224) and (V:219; 52). Cf. V:380; 260.

Chapter Nine

1. Kant's crucial appeal in the *Critique of Judgment* to purposive causality as we "encounter it in ourselves" anticipates the central role of human labor (or production according to a conscious plan) in Hegel and Marx. It would only be a slight exaggeration to say that the difference between Kant, on the one hand, and Hegel and Marx, on the other, lies in the fact that conscious production as a systematically unifying theme remains, for Kant, explicitly "problematic" (see V:360; 236).

On the bearing of this "encounter" on the (uniquely) human ability to distinguish between necessity and contingency, see the text at note 33 below. As Kant puts it here, objective teleological judgment furnishes "one more principle for bringing nature's appearances under rules where the causal laws of nature's mere mechanism are insufficient to allow us to do so" (V:360; [237]). It permits us, in other words, to reconcile contingency with lawfulness, not (as in Kant's earliest work) by a fanatical if "pardonable" appeal to "intellectual community with the origin of all beings" (V:363; [240–41]), but by drawing analogically on a sort of practical phenomenology or immediate experience similar to what Fichte will call "efficacy." The duality of mind and matter finds its ultimate, primary articulation in purposive causality (or realizing our objects) itself encountered as an object.

2. Seen in this light, Kant's discussion of Plato, in the treatment of "formal" objective purposiveness that follows, is especially instructive. Plato, according to Kant, was "overcome by enthusiasm" (*Begeisterung*) over the fact that "the original character of things" can be discovered apart from experience and that the mind "is able to derive the harmony of beings from their supersensible principle." It was this enthusiasm "that lifted Plato above empirical concepts to ideas that seemed explicable to him [and to a youthful Kant] only through an intellectual community with the origin of all beings." No wonder he turned those ignorant of geometry away, for what Anaxagoras inferred from objects of experience and their connection in terms of ends, Plato meant to derive "from the pure intuition dwelling within the human spirit [*Geist*]." As an alternative to Plato's mistaken appeal to heavenly fatherhood, Kant juxtaposes right admiration for nature "in our own reason." In short (and thanks to Kant's new concept of a "supersensible substrate"), the nature/reason breach can be closed without the sensible and intellectual contaminating each other. Human production according to ideas replaces both nonmaternal affiliation (as in Kant's youthful work) and metaphorical self-birthing (as in his writings of the early 1780s) as the seat of Kant's worldly *Erklärung*. Newly comfortable with "nature within," Kant now positions himself rhetorically, as we shall see, not as nature's stepson but as her consort. Kant has become, in some sense, a father.

3. In the case of formal objective purposiveness—for example, geometric figures—the basis of the regularity in question is immediately connected with the way I bound space according to an a priori rule. In the case of the materially (or really) purposive—for example, a flower garden—I recognize something as a *thing*, that is, a bounded *Inbegriff*, without being able to account for the unity it exhibits other than by appealing to a purpose. Why should a garden differ from a rock? Because I cannot take in the garden as the peculiar kind of whole it is without recognizing in its elements a unifying pattern or regularity distinguishable from the ordinary course of nature.

4. More accurately, as we shall see, we judge the wing both as means and end—both as for the sake of flight, and as that (among other things) for the sake of which the bird's other organs exist.

5. Kant also mentions "in passing," as among the "most marvelous" of characteristics of organized beings, the capacity to make good an accidental loss or, in the case of congenital defects or other deformities, to "form in an entirely new way . . . and so produce an anomalous creature" (V:372; 250–51). One wonders if this last example of nature "aiding herself" does not apply in an especially emphatic sense to man himself, whose "congenital defect" was earlier mentioned. The congenitally defective or deformed are no longer nature's defects, but on the contrary, instantiations of her vitality, a development in keeping with the newly benign (if veiled) image of nature that permeates the *Critique of Judgment* as a whole. (The existence of monsters [and worms whose parts when cut remain alive] were often cited by

opponents of preformation theory as proofs that living things do not simply "unfold" but are generated anew.)

6. Thus Kant says we can regard each branch or leaf (*Blatt*) of a tree as merely "inoculated or engrafted" (*oculiren* is from the Latin, meaning "to insert an eye or bud into"). Kant's tolerance for the idea of engraftment here seems at odds with his opposition elsewhere to the medical practice of vaccination against smallpox, that is, inoculation with "miasma" that is specifically "brutal." See *Metaphysics of Morals* (VI:424; 220), where Kant opposes "Pockeninoculation" as a sort of partial suicide inasmuch as it involves voluntary self-endangerment. According to Wasianski, Kant refused "very late" to use the common term *Schutzblattern* (literally, "protection pocks") with reference to vaccination, which he regarded as a kind of "familiarization" between mankind and animality whereby man might be inoculated with "brutality (in the physical sense)." He also feared that mingling the brutal miasma in human blood or lymph might communicate a human susceptibility to bovine epidemics or diseases (*Viehseuche*). Finally, he doubted, given the paucity of experiments, that vaccination actually protected against pox in humans (Borowski, Jachmann, and Wasianski, *Immanuel Kant,* p. 231). The passage is paraphrased by De Quincey, according to whom Kant "apprehended dangerous consequences from the absorption of a brutal miasma into the blood . . . , and at any rate . . . thought that as a guarantee against the variolous infection, it required a much longer probation" (p. 509). The practice of vaccination thus raises for Kant a double specter: both the fearful prospect of contagion generally, and an additional uncertainty arising from experimental destruction of nature's barrier against the intermingling of species.

One difference between medical inoculation and the engraftment that Kant entertains conceptually in the *Critique of Judgment* is the clear protection, in the latter case, of the engrafted. As Kant himself immediately adds, the leaves (which he has just described as "parasitic") sustain the tree producing them (V:372; 250). The relation, in other words, is both parasitic and, as we would say, symbiotic. On the general reception of vaccination in Europe and America, see Marc Shell, *Children of the Earth,* pp. 158–63.

7. Cf. Makkreel, "Feeling of Life," pp. 83–104; and *Imagination and Interpretation.* Makkreel usefully highlights the centrality of the theme of life in the *Critique of Judgment;* he leaves unexplored, however, what is arguably for Kant the matter's heart—the relation between the so-called aesthetic feeling of life and what Makkreel calls life in the biological sense.

8. A term that calls to mind the "formative drive" (*Bildungstrieb*) of Johann Friedrich Blumenbach, to whose work Kant later refers (V:424; 311).

9. Kant adds in a note that one can, conversely, "shed light, through an analogy with these direct natural purposes, on a certain connection [*Verbindung*] encountered more often in the idea than in actuality." Kant has in mind the sort of organization associated with a body politic (Staatskörper): "In speaking of the complete transformation [*Umbildung*] of a great people into a state, which took place recently, the word *organization* was frequently and very aptly used for the establishment of magistrates, etc., and even to the entire body politic. For each member [*Glied*] in such a whole should indeed be not merely a means, but also an end [*Zweck*]; and while each member contributes [*mitwirkt*] to the possibility of the

whole, each is determined in its place and function by the idea of the whole" (V:375 n; [254 n]).

One recognizes in this account (probably an allusion to the United States) the by now familiar contours of the Kantian "republic," here presented as an "enlightened" version of an otherwise inscrutable process of self-generation. Here, through an elucidating analogy that deflects Kant's disallowance of analogies, the problematic connection between life and matter can be set aside, contained, as it were, in and by each civic-bodily member, who consciously shares in the idea of the whole even as he makes possible through his cooperation (*mitwirken*) the idea's actualization (*Wirklichkeit*). The body politic is thus for Kant a uniquely accessible translation of natural production (its idea a human counterpart of the divine schema of creation).

10. Instructive in this regard are Kant's comments in the *Metaphysics of Morals* concerning the impossibility of "making a concept" of "the production of a being endowed with freedom through a physical operation." The right of children to parental support is therefore to be thought of as following from the parents having brought, through the act of procreation, the child into the world without his (prior) consent. (Procreation retains, to this extent, the scent of original sin — not, to be sure, against God but rather against personality itself, which must, so to speak, be compensated for the unchosen contingency of finding itself in the world; a status resembling what Heidegger will call Dasein's "thrownness.")

The problem, Kant goes on to note, is different from that arising from the concept of God's "creation of a free being"; for here the "contradiction" involved can be avoided by separating the concept of causality from the temporal condition and with it the chain of natural necessity that creation otherwise seemingly implies. The philosophic jurist, Kant adds, "if he reflects on the difficulty of the task" and "the necessity of solving it a way sufficient for principles of right" will not regard this investigation as "unnecessary [*grave*] musing [*Grübelei*]" that "loses itself in purposeless [*zwecklose*] obscurity" (VI:280–81 n; [98–99 n]).

11. Many thinkers at this time were, of course, concerned with the question of generation. See, for example, Roger, *Sciences de la vie;* Adelmann, *Marcello Malpighi;* and Jane M. Oppenheimer, *Essays in the History of Embryology and Biology.* Descartes's *L'homme et un traitté de la formation du foetus* is especially enlightening in this regard. Descartes, unlike the preformationists (be they spermatozists like Leibniz or ovists) emphasized the equal (albeit, wholly material) contribution of both sexes. Kant's approach, by way of contrast, combines a rejection of the spontaneous generation of life from matter alone (the position of both mechanists like Descartes and of many so-called vitalists) with an insistence (contrary to the claims of the preformationists) that both sexes contribute equally to the formation of the fetus. (Kant's conviction as to this equal contribution is obviously crucial to his concept of race, which makes no sense unless the child is assumed to inherit equally from both parents.) Kant's peculiar theory of "epigenesis" thus serves the essential conceptual function of reconciling the impossibility of equivocal generation (a notion he consistently finds absurd) with the equal and qualitatively homogenous contribution of both sexes. This homogenous contribution rules out the traditional, hierarchical account of generation (in terms of male form and female matter [Aristotle] or stronger male sperm and weaker female sperm [Galen]) that continued to find

favor in the seventeenth and eighteenth centuries. Harvey, for example, insisted, with Aristotle, that the female contribution to generation is the "vegetative soul," as distinguished from the "sensitive soul," contributed by the male. At the same time, Harvey also claimed, contrary to Aristotle, that all animals grow from eggs. Thus the formula on the frontispiece of his *Exercitationes:* "ex ovo omnia." The "neoterics," who, as their name suggests, broke openly with traditional medical Aristotelianism tended to attribute the efficient cause of generation to female heat. Most, however, continued to attribute the formal cause, in roughly the traditional sense, to male and female semen. (On the lingering influence of Aristotle and Galen, and for a useful summary of the range of respectable scientific positions in the early eighteenth century, see Roger, *Sciences de la vie,* pp. 118–25, 287–93.) Even Descartes's mechanical embryology retains something of the traditional order of sexual rank: although both parents contribute equally and in a purely material way to generation, sex is determined by the fetus's relative robustness and concomitant power to resist contamination by excremental solids in the mother's blood. If the fetus is sufficiently robust, it will purge fewer liquids than solids, and the outcome will be male. Roger suggests, however, that Descartes's recourse here to highly traditional views (in a work he was in any case moved to suppress) may be less than frank (p. 150). As Roger notes, the preformationism that dominated the first half of the eighteenth century was particularly attractive to mechanists eager to reconcile their teachings with traditional religious views concerning the "paternal presence" of God in nature. On the role of traditional views in ordinary medical practice, see also Barbara Duden, *The Woman beneath the Skin: A Doctor's Patients in Eighteenth-Century Germany.*

12. It thus satisfies the requirements, otherwise impossible to conceive, of intentionality *within* nature, or the divine schema (as per Kant's earlier lights) immanentized. For an elaboration on this point, see Hegel, *Philosophy of Right,* introduction, para. 24.

13. See his *Doctrine of Right* (VI:340; 111). For a general discussion of palingenesis, see *Vorlesungen über Metaphysik* (XXVIIII:768–70).

14. This extended organic treatment of the system of philosophy recalls Kant's earlier assertion that human judgment lacks a genuine "organon" (or tool) for the "production" of objective knowledge and must remain satisfied instead with a mere "canon" (or set of rules) and "cathartic" (A/53 = B/77; A/61 = B/85). (The *philosopher,* by way of contrast, who might be presumed to have just such an organon, is said to use human beings as "tools" [*Werkzeugen*] to further the essential ends of human reason [A/839 = B/867].) When taken in conjunction with his treatment of "organism," Kant's renunciation of a human organon of reason — an obvious reference both to the *Organon* of Aristotle and the *New Organon* of Bacon — seems calculated to show just where and how the human mind can be genuinely "productive." So understood, the entire first *Critique* becomes an exercise in philosophic midwifery — a canon and cathartic aimed at deflating false pregnancies even as it facilitates the issuing forth of knowledge that "originates" in human reason alone (see A/836 = B/864).

15. See the *Universal Natural History;* see also Yovel's helpful discussion of "weak" and "strong" versions of organic totality in *Kant and the Philosophy of History,* p. 227 ff.

16. Cf. O'Neill, *Constructions,* pp. 6–7. As O'Neill notes, the motto of the *Critique of Pure Reason,* taken from Bacon, begins "of ourself we say nothing." This double abjuring of self-reference only draws greater attention to the peculiarity of Kant's own personal role — simultaneously necessary and utterly contingent — in bringing the idea to light. See *Critique of Pure Reason* A/850 ff. = B/878 ff.; and chapter 7 above.

17. Cf. *Prolegomena* (IV:352 ff.; [101 ff.)]:

> So long as the cognition of reason is homogeneous [*gleichartig*], it can think no determinate bounds to that cognition. In mathematics and natural science, human reason to be sure recognizes limits, but not bounds. . . . But metaphysics leads us towards bounds through the dialectical attempts of pure reason (which are not undertaken arbitrarily or wantonly [*muthwilliger*] but driven thereto by the nature of reason itself); and the transcendental ideas, as they do not admit of evasion [*Umgang*] and yet never allow themselves to be realized, serve to point out to us actually [*wirklich*] not only the bounds of the use of pure reason, but also the way [*Art*] to determine them. And this is also the end and use of this natural tendency [*Naturanlage*] of our reason, which has given birth to [*ausgeboren*] metaphysics as its favored child [*Lieblingskind*], whose generation, like all others in the world, is not to be ascribed to approximate chance [*Zufalle*], but to an original seed [*Keim*] that is wisely organized for great ends. For metaphysics, in its fundamental features/urges, is, perhaps more than any other science, laid in us by nature herself, and cannot be considered the production of an arbitrary [*beliebigen*] choice, or a contingent enlargement from the progress of experience (from which it is entirely cut off).

Metaphysics is here presented not as mistress, but as child, born of (the heterogenous coupling of) a natural disposition and/or a wisely organized seed — and all of this in response, above all, to reason's irresistible and insatiable flight from the shear contingency and dependency of its thought insofar as it remains tied to principles of experience:

> Who does not see in the thoroughgoing contingency and dependency of all that one can only think and assume through principles of experience, the impossibility of remaining there; and who does not feel himself driven [*nothgedrungen*], in contempt of all commands not to lose oneself in transcendental ideas, to seek rest and satisfaction beyond all concepts that can be justified [*rechtfertigen*] through experience, in the concept of a being the possibility of which, according to the idea, can neither be understood nor contradicted, because it concerns a pure being of understanding, without which, however, reason must always remain unsatisfied. (IV:352; 100–101)

That being (namely, God) is a source compatible with human freedom, here (paradoxically) defined in terms of a *seeing* in shear contingency the impossibility of remaining in experience, and a *feeling* of being pressed/penetrated toward that which (could it but be justified) would bring rest and satisfaction. One is again reminded of Kant's earliest treatment of metaphysics as an impetuous swing toward union with the divine father (ambiguously fueled by spiritual repulsion that is both

412 NOTES TO PAGE 242

related and contrary to the blind fecundity of nature). Here, however, that leitmotif undergoes a curious inversion: metaphysics is now the child of nature, a child that leads us to the unevadable but also unrealizable idea of the father. The practically discernible purpose of so seemingly purposeless an urge is to lead us "as it were to the touch/contact [*Berührung*] of full space (experience) with empty space [or the void] (that of which we can know nothing, i.e., the noumena)." For "in all bounds" — as opposed to limits — "there is something positive." Having established the capacity of reason, not only to set limits for itself, but also to define its boundaries and thus make contact with "the void," the question becomes how our reason comports itself toward this coupling (*Verknüpfung*) of that which we know and that which we do not know and never will, a coupling that is actual (*wirklich*) and whose concept is determinate and can be brought to distinctness (IV:354; [102–3]). By reconfiguring the meeting of reason and unreason as a coupling of experience (or what we know) and the noumena (or what we do not know and never will), Kant's boundary image (*Sinnbild*) makes thinkable a heretofore wholly abhorrent contact with the void, a contact toward which a determinately bounded human reason is now able to comport [*sich verhalten;* literally, "retain"] itself.

Kant's effort in the *Prolegomena* ends by calling for a "tracking down" (*nachspüren*) of "the nature of reason" even "beyond its use in metaphysics into the general principles for making a systematic history of nature in general." Only by completing such a history, Kant implies, might the deeply hidden "nature of reason" be brought fully to light, a task that he, who "has made it his business to survey the whole field," can reasonably be expected to leave to others (IV:364, 364 n; [112, 113 n]). He thus here excuses himself from the task of laying bare the hidden unity of nature and reason, despite his profession of an "ever constant aim" of not procrastinating/letting slip (*versäumen*) anything that might bring to completion investigation into the nature of reason.

One major difference between the *Prolegomena* (completed in 1783, *prior* to the *Idea for a Universal History*) and the *Critique of Judgment* lies in the latter's abandonment of systematic natural history (and therewith the task of attempting a natural history of reason).

18. According to the *Anthropology* as well, dreams perform the crucial role of "exciting the vital force by emotional agitations related to happenings we invent involuntarily, while bodily movements based on choice — namely muscular movements — are suspended" (VII:175; 51). Without dreaming (that is, fantasy "playing with us while we are asleep") to keep the vital force active, the deepest sleep would bring on death. Kant later cites a corroborating experience remembered from his childhood:

> once when I was a boy, I went to bed tired out from play and, just as I was falling asleep, was suddenly awakened by a dream that I had fallen into water and was being carried around in a whirlpool, almost drowning. Soon afterwards I went back to sleep, this time more peacefully. Presumably the activity of the chest muscles in respiration, which is entirely voluntary, had slackened, and the failure to breathe properly inhibited the motion of the heart, which imagination had to set going again by a dream. — The same beneficial effect of dreaming is present in a so-called *nightmare* [Alpdrucken] (*incubus*); were it not for this frightful image of

an oppressing phantom [*drückenden Gespenst*], and the straining of every muscle to change our position, a lapse in blood circulation would soon bring life to an end. (VII:190; [63])

This remarkable passage, from a section entitled "On Involuntary Invention [*Dichtung*] in a State of Health," combines Kant's familiar *Grillen:* constricted circulation, oppression of the heart, and vertigo. It does so, however, in a way that interprets his own imaginative fixation on them as healthy and, indeed, life-sustaining, rather than morbid. The very emblem of nature's abysmal destructiveness becomes, through Kant's dream work, a sign of her benevolence, since difficulties and dangers stimulate the powers of the soul far more than happiness, that is, the "representation of having everything go as we wish." On the "providential" role of dreaming, see also *Conflict of the Faculties* (VII:106; 193) and chapter 10 below.

19. But cf. (V:398; 281), where Kant emphasizes the difference between individual natural products and the whole of nature, the latter of which "is not given us as organized (in the strictest sense of *organized*)."

20. We are, by Kant's conceit, both nature's audience and her playthings, "upheld" (*unterhalten*) as much by our own entertaining reflection as by the stage or platform (*Bühne*) on which she casts us.

21. Hence Kant's elimination here of the aesthetically crucial distinction between charm and beauty. Kant adds in a note that whereas, aesthetically speaking, we regard beautiful nature *with favor,* teleologically, we may regard nature as *favoring us* in wishing to further our culture by displaying so many beautiful shapes (*Gestalten*). Cf. in this regard Kant's distinction in part 1 between *empirical* interest in the beautiful (an interest concerned, above all, with physical adornment and which he calls the "beginning of civilization") and *intellectual* interest in the beautiful (an interest limited to beauty in nature) (V:296–303; 163–70). The latter, which Kant characterizes as "a, so to speak, voluptuousness [*Wollust*] for one's spirit [*Geist*] in a train of thought it cannot fully unravel," alone indicates a "morally good attitude," the disposition [*Anlagen*] to which, at least, such interest presupposes (V:300–301; [167]). "Spiritual voluptuousness" not only rhetorically conflates sublimity and sexual pleasure; it also bridges, or blurs, the distinction between a disposition for moral goodness and moral goodness proper (hence, between nature and freedom). In so doing, the phrase calls to mind a statement attributed to Kant by R. B. Jachmann: "I shall never forget my mother, for she implanted and nurtured in me the first seed of the good; and opened my heart to the influence of nature" (Borowski, Jachmann, and Wasianski, *Immanuel Kant,* p. 99 ff.). Kant's own mother (whose influence, as he acknowledged, inhibited his ability to love other women) is, it seems, the one woman who overcomes what Kant elsewhere calls the insoluble problem of human education. (For more on this point, see chapter 4 above.)

22. Kant's treatment of the purposiveness of nightmares (*Alpdrucken;* literally, that which weighs on one's breast) is in this regard especially instructive. His childhood dream of almost drowning, which he attributes to exhaustion after play, already suggests that the young Kant is somehow guilty or responsible for his bad experience. The vertiginous image that in other contexts arouses feelings of paralyzing horror is here transformed into a mobilizing emblem of deliverance — one, moreover, that redeems both nature and imagination, nature's most intimate men-

tal vehicle. In the process, Kant projects back onto nature his own revulsion against an infantilizing and smothering maternity. In interpreting his own revulsion as naturally purposive, that is, as (almost) intentional on nature's part, he gains, it seems, a kind of maternal forgiveness that allows nature to appear (for the first time) as genuinely lovable. With that forgiveness Kant comes as close as he ever does to endorsing normal (or nonsublimated) sexuality. Reflection upon nature's purposive (apparent) purposelessness renders *interested* pleasure in her beautiful *and* charming shapes consistent (as physical sex for Kant never is) with man's nobility.

In charting the extent of his rapprochement with nature in the third *Critique,* it is helpful to contrast Kant's dream depiction with his association, in earlier works (and especially those involved in his dispute with Herder), of human emancipation with the struggle to be born, that is, emerge from a confining womb in order to draw breath.

23. To be sure, organism, as an intrinsic purpose of nature, "infinitely surpasses all our ability to exhibit anything similar through art" (except, perhaps, in the case of the political organism, that is, the state).

24. Nightmares (which are, as it were, alien visitors that belong to our inner organization) stand at the juncture of these two sorts of natural purposiveness.

25. Spinoza reduces products to inherent accidents of the original being; he thus gives unity (which purposiveness requires) but not unity of purpose, which cannot be thought unless natural forms are also regarded as contingent. Without intentional cause, all unity is mere natural necessity. Or we can play the childish schoolman's game of calling everything that is a natural purpose, i.e., a thing that has in it what it takes to be what it is rather than something else (V:394; 275). What makes a natural purpose (in the Kantian sense) "special" is its combination of unity and contingency.

26. Cf. *Metaphysical Foundations of Natural Science* (IV:544; 106): "The possibility of a natural science proper rests entirely upon the law of inertia (along with the law of the permanence of substance.) The opposite of this, and the death of all natural philosophy, would be hylozoism." Kant continues with a comment that speaks directly to his early theory of living force: "From the concept of inertia as mere lifelessness there follows of itself the fact that inertia does not signify a positive effort of something to maintain its state. Only living things are called inert in this latter sense, inasmuch as they have a representation of another state which they abhor and strive against with all their power."

In the same section Kant defines life as "the capacity of a substance to determine itself to act from an internal principle, of a finite substance to determine itself to change, and of a material substance to determine itself to motion or rest as change of its state." "Now we know," he continues, "of no other internal principle of a substance to change its state but desire and no other internal activity whatever but thought, along with what depends upon such desire, namely, feeling of pleasure or displeasure, and appetite or will. But these determining grounds and actions do not at all belong to the representations of the external senses and hence also not to the determinations of matter as matter. Therefore, all matter as such is lifeless" (IV:544; 105).

27. Cf. *Dreams* (II:330; 317–18): "It will, perhaps, forever be impossible to determine with certainty how far and to which members of nature life extends, or

what those degrees of life, which border on the very edge of complete lifelessness, may be. *Hylozoism* animates everything, while *materialism,* when carefully considered, deprives everything of life."

28. Kant adds that the concept of a natural purpose (which cannot be abstracted from experience) is yet "empirically conditioned," that is, only possible on the basis of certain conditions given in experience (V:396; 278). The very considerable discussion in the literature of the validity of Kant's distinction between regulative and constitutive principles cannot here detain us; suffice it to say that moves toward their assimilation weaken a barrier Kant has a profound systematic interest in retaining.

29. Cf. *Universal Natural History* (I:230; 88).

30. Kant makes this possibility conditional on our discovery, somehow, of the principle in terms of which "nature makes the familiar general laws of nature specific." On the "self-specification" of nature, see chapter 8, note 31.

31. That is, "gemäß ist." Cf. the *Vermessenheit* (V:384 n; 264 n) involved in objective appeals to God's wisdom, as per Kant's own early experiments with the idea of a divine schema.

32. That is, from intellects that differ from us "qualitatively."

33. Kant thus succeeds where the previously mentioned "systems concerning the purposiveness of nature" failed. In claiming that those systems intended to explain how the concept of a natural purpose is possible, Kant exercises his facility for making explicit the intention implicit in an earlier work, that is, of understanding a thinker better than he understood himself. Cf. *Critique of Pure Reason* [A/314 = B/370], apropos of "idea" as understood by Plato: "I shall not engage here in any literary inquiry into the meaning which the sublime [*erhabene*] philosopher attached to the expression. I need only remark that it is by no means unusual . . . to find that we understand [an author] better than he has understood himself. As he has not sufficiently determined his concept, he has sometimes spoken, or even thought, in opposition to his own intention."

34. The supersensible substrate anticipates in this respect certain romantic theories of the "unconscious" as the seat of both physical reproduction and the divine. See, for example, Carl Gustav Carus, *Psyche: On the Development of the Soul,* pt. 1, "The Unconscious," with an introductory note by James Hillman and a précis of parts 2 and 3 by Murray Stein, p. 43 ff.

35. Kant identifies the contingency in the character of our understanding (a character that distinguishes it "from other possible understandings") with the contingency "we find quite naturally" in the particular. *Our* understanding, in other words, particularizes itself, that is, distinguishes itself from "other possible understandings, through its peculiarly discursive way of judging the particular, which always presents itself to us as one of any number of possible instances of the concept under which it is subsumed. "For through the universal [belonging to] our (human) understanding, nothing is determined." An understanding in the most universal sense of the term would be intuitive, that is, wholly spontaneous. "For such an understanding there would not be that contingency in the way nature's products harmonize with the understanding in terms of *particular* laws." "It is this contingency," Kant continues, "that makes it so difficult for our understanding to bring the manifold thereof to the unity of knowledge." This unity can come about

"only through the harmony of nature's characteristics and our power of concepts, a harmony that is very contingent."

To be able "at least to think the possibility of such a harmony" (which we present as contingent, that is, as possible only through a directed end), we must "think to ourselves a different understanding," an understanding to which we attribute no purpose, but through which "we can represent as necessary a harmony only thinkable by us through the connection-means of purposes." In short, Kant no longer identifies intentionality (or awareness of an aim) and intellect generally.

The intuitive intellect intuits the whole as a whole; hence "its presentation of the whole has no *contingency* in the combination of the parts in order to make possible a determinate form of the whole" (V:407; [291]). Our understanding, on the other hand, requires this contingency, because it moves from parts to whole; and, indeed, can regard a real whole of nature "only as effect as the concurrent motive forces of its parts." To think without contradiction (given the limits of our discursivity) the possibility of parts depending on the whole, we must present it *as a presentation,* that is, as a *purpose.* This attribution of purpose, however, is merely a consequence of the peculiar character of our own understanding, *not* a characteristic of things themselves.

That an archetypal intellect is possible need not be proved, but only that the contrast between it and our own (which "requires images"), and the contingency of the latter requirement, "leads us to the idea" of an archetypal intellect, an idea that does not itself contain any contradiction (V:408; [293]). (We cannot think, without contradiction, the thought that such an intellect would think. We *can* and *do,* however, think it *negatively* inasmuch as we present the discursivity of our own intellect as merely contingent.)

Kant finds a way at last to think "without contradiction" the formerly disabling notion of the schema of creation, a schema now reduced to the idea, as it were, of an idea. The price is a God who lacks consciousness in any sense we can conceive of. Consciousness is (at least contingently) bound up with *technai*—a peculiarly human way of being whose role anticipates that of Hegelian praxis and Heideggerian "projection" of "Dasein's" possibilities.

36. It nevertheless remains "of infinite concern" to reason not to let drop the "mechanism of nature." For even if there were allowed a "supreme architect" who either directly created the forms of nature as they have always been, or predetermined ones that keep developing in nature according to the same models, that allowance would yield us no insight; for "we do not know at all that being's way of acting or its ideas, which are supposed to contain the principles of the possibility of natural beings." We can therefore neither descend from God's supposed ideas to nature nor ascend from nature's forms to those ideas, an attempt that seduces reason into "poetic raving" in contravention of reason's highest vocation (*Bestimmung*), which lies precisely in preventing such raving (V:410; [295]).

37. Our only concept of the supersensible is the indeterminate one of a ground that makes possible our judgment of nature according to empirical laws (V:412; 297). Neither causal principle—one mechanical (and, in terms of Kant's early cosmology, natural or female), the other intentional (and, in terms of Kant's early cosmology, divine or male)—can replace the other. Their community is made

thinkable (albeit, "indeterminately") through the "reflective" subordination of the former to the latter (on which the possibility of empirical science subjectively depends—that is, for beings with our "peculiarity"). At the same time, Kant leaves open the possibility that the two types of production (*Erzeugung*) "might well be linked in the same ground," that is, that the differentiation and ranking of these two (sexual) types is strictly a function our own "contingency" (V:413; [298]).

38. The "free" assumption of actual kinship among the various species is, as Kant immediately goes on to say, the way we "must" conceive them, if their thoroughly coherent affinity "is to have a ground," a statement that goes a long way toward not only permitting but also endorsing a position he had previously strongly rejected.

39. Cf. *Universal Natural History* (I:318 ff.; 158 ff.).

40. Kant calls it instead *generatio univoca*, but *heteronyma*, as opposed to the *generatio univoca* and *homonyma* with which experience familiarizes us.

41. The subtlety of Kant's position on the transmutation of species has not generally been appreciated (see, for example, Lovejoy's barely disguised annoyance with Kant for failing to anticipate Darwin in "Kant and Evolution"). This lack of intellectual sympathy is related, I believe, to a general failure to recognize the centrality for Kant of the problem of generation to the question to which his lifework was in large measure devoted: how to comprehend the whole of which one is a part. Despite Darwin and later advances in the biological sciences, we are arguably no closer to answering this question than were thinkers in the eighteenth century. For a recent effort in that direction, see John McDowell, *Mind and World*.

42. Kant plays on *fügen*, meaning "to fit or join," and *Fügung*, a "dispensation or act of providence." In fitting ourselves to judge accidental changes as instances of natural and/or divine dispensation, we ourselves provide the system with its "joint" or articulating member.

43. *Zeugungskraft* means both "generative force" and "potency or virility." In the figure of the fetus cum philosopher, reason, preservation, and manhood face a common threat: thoughts which arise unbidden from a (therefore) alien source, here identified with the invasive imagination of the mother. It would not be altogether misleading to see in this most homely example of "influxus physicus" one ultimate source of Kant's efforts to secure the boundaries of reason.

44. Cf. *On a Newly Arisen Superior Tone* (VIII:400; 65–66).

45. Kant's earlier works on race already speak in various ways of the "preformation" of the fetal germ; only in the *Critique of Judgment*, however, are "epigenesis" and "preformation" terminologically linked, and the quarrel between preformationists and epigenecists thereby explicitly addressed.

On the intellectual and political significance of the preformationist-epigenesis controversy in the eighteenth century, and on Kant's relation to the earlier epigenetic theories of Maupertuis, Buffon, and Caspar Friedrich Wolff, see C. U. M. Smith, *The Problem of Life: An Essay in the Origins of Biological Thought*, pp. 262–80; and Shirley A. Roe, *Matter, Life and Generation*. especially stresses the relation of the conflict between preformationism and epigenesis to the larger struggle between Newtonianism and rationalism.) Kant differs from these earlier epigenetic thinkers (and from later constitutively teleological biologists whom he influenced) in his consistent refusal (shared by most preformationists) to entertain the possibility of spontaneous generation or to endow with explanatory force some intermediary "vital" or "organic" principle.

The direct bearing of Kant's resolution of the controversy on his lifelong effort to reconcile the insights of Newtonianism and rationalism may go some way toward explaining the profound effect of Kant on subsequent generations of biologists. On that effect especially in terms of Kant's relation to Johann Friedrich Blumenbach, whom Kant cites approvingly in the *Critique of Judgment,* see Timothy Lenoir, "Kant, Blumenbach, and Vital Materialism in German Biology," *Isis* 71:77–108; see also Roe, *Matter,* p. 151.

46. "Eine alte Schachtel" is proverbial for a repulsive old woman.

47. The "ova" in question were actually Graafian follicles; true mammalian ova were not discovered until 1837. By the mid-eighteenth century, ovism had become the predominant preformationist theory.

The ingenuity devoted by eighteenth-century thinkers to the question of generation is evident from such works as Maupertuis's *Earthly Venus.* Unlike the ovists and the animalculists, Maupertuis (following Aristotle and/or Galen) attributed generation to the mixture of both male and female seminal fluids, which combined, he speculated, in a manner resembling the "elective affinity" recently proposed by chemists. The role of the spermatozoa was to aid, by their motion, this process of admixture. Maupertuis's theory thus retains something of the ancient association of motion or efficient causality with the male contribution to generation.

Even ovism, according to which Eve contained within her body that of every human being that has existed or will ever exist, frequently assigned greater importance to the male, by attributing to him the crucial role of "vivifying" an otherwise lifeless body. For animalculists the female role was one of mere nurturance for a fully formed and already living human being.

48. Cf. *Reflection* no. 4239 (XVII:473) and no. 1256 (XV:556). The term *emboîtement,* also called *evolution,* could refer to either ovism or animalculism.

49. Maupertuis makes a similar argument in the *Earthly Venus.*

50. Monsters, hybrids, intestinal worms, and animals (such as hydra) capable of regenerating from parts — all themes that, as we have seen, feature with some prominence in Kant's writings — were important elements in the arsenal employed by eighteenth-century critics of (individual) preformationism.

51. See *On a Newly Arisen Superior Tone* (VIII:399 n; 64 n), where Kant asks, without answering, the question of whether the unavoidable concept of God as "the most real being of all" is to be thought of as the totality of all realities or as their ground.

52. Ibid. (VIII:399; 64).

53. Kant is now reconciled to the conventional identification of the term *natural history* with "the description of nature," reserving *archaeology of nature* for what he here calls the "literal" meaning of *natural history,* namely, an exposition of the earth's ancient state (V:428 n; 315 n). The systematizing function that Kant hopefully reserved in writings of the early 1780s to a future history — as opposed to mere description — of nature has been absorbed, as we will shortly see, by a history of human culture. As a consequence, the theory of race (Kant's natural history of man) loses its formerly pivotal status.

54. There is an at least verbal contradiction here. Kant appears to be arguing that even the satisfaction of our natural needs would fail, because of our inner nature, to satisfy us. The ambiguity lies in the status (natural or not?) of our inability or unwillingness to be satisfied, a formulation that calls to mind his characterization in *What It Means to Orient Oneself in Thinking* of the "need" that reason "appends to itself" (*an sich selbst anhängt*) ("for reason will at last be satisfied") (VIII:136; [240]). Even a perfectly beneficent nature (in an external sense) would not make us happy, due to nature within us, that is, to natural dispositions that are absurd (*[w]idersinnisch;* literally, "contrary to sense," a term that playfully undercuts their "naturalness," bringing them close to the "disposition" to freedom itself).

55. Cf. *Idea for a Universal History* (VIII:26; [21]): "We are to a high degree *cultivated* through art and science. We are *civilized* almost to excess in all sorts of social courtesies and proprieties. But to consider ourselves *moralized* — for that, much is still lacking." See also *Critique of Pure Reason* A/850 = B/878; and chapter 10 below.

56. Cf. *Critique of Pure Reason* B/xiii.

57. Or so man's contribution of nature's final cause suggests. Cf. Aristotle, *Generation of Animals* 715a–716a, 729a. Aristotle identifies the female principle with the material cause, and the male principle with the efficient and the formal cause. The latter, he notes, "we may regard as pretty much the same" as the final cause (715a).

Kant's (veiled) metaphor is anticipated by Bacon, as in his strikingly entitled "Masculine Birth of Time." On Kant's partial (moral) reprisal of Aristotle's understanding of form as essence, see *On a Newly Arisen Superior Tone* (VIII:404; 70).

58. On the early history of biology in the modern sense, see Eduard Farber, "Forces and Substances of Life," *Osiris* 11: 422–37. See also the conclusion of Roger's magisterial study of seventeenth- and eighteenth-century sciences of life in France:

> The study of living matter invincibly suggests the idea of an autonomous and poorly definable force. Analyses of a mechanistic sort seem to always leave aside what is essential, namely life. Man feels himself powerless against this universe, of which his body is nonetheless a part. For man does not conceive clearly what it does, and life rests outside his powers. By its manner of acting, it is estranged from man: it is internal spontaneity, it acts itself upon itself, while man remains exterior to his work. Aristotle compares male semen to a workman who gives form to matter without being in the matter. And this very human image expresses a profound need, namely of rendering life as a known and intelligible phenomenon. In a different way, Galenic "faculties," "archai," "plastic natures" — all such forces sent by God to work in living matter express the same need. It matters little that these divine works are unknowable. . . . They are at least conceivable, for these forces that work in matter are not matter. [Vitalism, on the other hand, is an abyss in which] man always risks having the sentiment of an abdication of the spirit, . . . of a renunciation or abandonment to natural forces, which confronts him as power or repose, but always in forgetfulness of self. . . . [Thus, Roger continues,] it is no longer through science and discursive thought that man can hope to ar-

rive at reality; it is through imagination, intuition, or instinct . . . that allows one to recognize and at times capture the forces of nature but without comprehending them. (*Sciences de la vie,* pp. 765–76)

Much of Kant's greatness, I would add, lies in his extraordinary alertness to related difficulties, combined with an extraordinary determination (motivated, in part, by that very awareness) to uphold the dignity of reason.

59. There is an important parallel here with Goethe, whose more erotically indulgent conception of "elective affinity" plays the similarly unifying role of reintegrating man into nature as an object of scientific study.

60. On the centrality of the theme of rebirth (*Wiedergeburt*) in Pietist thought, see M. Schmidt, *Wiedergeburt und neuer Mensch;* and Hans-Jürgen Schings, *Melancholie und Aufklärung: Melancholiker und ihre Kritiker in Erfahrungsseelenkunde und Literatur der 18. Jahrhundert*, pp. 75–76. (Cf. Kant, *Remarks* [XX:5].) For Kant's own views on religious (or "supernatural," as distinguished from "supersensuous") conceptions of rebirth, which he explicitly associates with Hamann, see the *Conflict of the Faculties* (VII:57–58; [104–5]). Kant there contrasts Pietist and Moravian appeals to the miraculous (*Wunder*) with what he calls the greatest (though nonmiraculous) wonder (*Bewunderung*), namely, the ascendancy of the "supersensible man in us." Since the supersensible in us is inconceivable though practical, those who regard it as supernatural — or brought about by the influence of "another, higher spirit" not within our power — are, according to Kant, to be "excused"; still, they are in this very defective (*fehlen*), for in their view the "effect of this power would not be our act or imputable to us," so that the power itself "would not be our own."

The "real solution [*ächte Auflösung*]" to the "problem of the new man" — one Pietist sectarians (such as Philipp Jacob Spener and August Hermann Francke) would resolve in "heart-crushing" grief, and Moravians (such as Nicolaus Zinzendorf) in "heart-melting" community with God — lies in "putting to use the idea of this power that dwells in us in a way we can't conceive," and in the "interpreting" (literally, the "laying out from the heart [*Ausherzlegung*]") of this idea from earliest youth (VII:59; [107]).

The problematic identity of the old and new man — the solution to what Kant once treated as the problem of Adam's father — is thus secured by the imputable personhood to which our practical awareness of the moral law uniquely attests. By virtue of that awareness, man knows himself to be, however incomprehensibly, both free and one. Between "soulless" orthodoxy and mystical or "reason-killing" sectarianism (hence, it seems, at the vexed juncture of reason and the principle of life) lies the true biblical teaching which reason "can develop out of itself" — the "spirit of Christ" that we make our own, or rather, since it is already "present in us," that we need only make "room" for.

Kant's discussion of the Pietist and Moravian would-be solutions to the problem of rebirth sheds further light on the distinction drawn here between a(n irrational) supernaturalism that melts or shatters the heart and a (rational) supersensualism that lays out and improves it. According to the Pietist hypothesis:

the separation of good and evil (of which nature is an amalgam) is a supernatural operation, a breaking and crushing of the heart in *repentance*, a grief (*maeror animi*) bordering on despair, which can, however, reach the necessary intensity only by the influence of a heavenly spirit. Man must himself beg for this grief, while grieving that he does not grieve sufficiently (so that the pain [*Leidsein*] cannot be driven completely from his heart). Now, as the late/blessed Hamann says, "This descent into the hell of self-knowledge paves the way to self-deification." In other words, when the fire of repentance has reached its height, there occurs a *break-through* [Durchbruch], and the regulus of the reborn gleams through the dross, which surrounds it without rendering it impure. . . . This radical change, therefore, begins with a *miracle* and ends with what we would ordinarily regard as natural, since *reason* prescribes it: namely, morally good conduct. But even in the highest flight of mystically inclined imagination, one cannot exempt man from doing anything himself, without making him a mere machine; and so what man has to do is *pray* fervently. . . . But since prayer, as they say, can be heard only if it is made in faith, and faith itself is an effect of grace . . . this view gets involved in a vicious circle.

The rationality of Kantian morality as here expressed lies in the latter's avoidance, through acknowledgment of the freedom to which conscience testifies, of the vicious circularity to which conceptions of guilt and salvation are otherwise exposed. The predication of this escape on an (otherwise ungrounded) insistence on the possibility of human agency—or our unwillingness to regard ourselves as mere machines—contrasts with the "slavery" and "gloomy fanaticism" associated with Kant's own early Pietist training. (On the latter point, see Cassirer, *Kant's Life,* pp. 15–19; on freedom as a specific against other sorts of heart-gripping misery, see chapter 10. Moral rebirth is also treated in *Religion within the Limits of Reason Alone* [VI:117–18; 108].) As Kant's gloss suggests, his entire difference with Hamann is summed up in the distinction between "rebirth" supernaturally and "rebirth" supersensuously conceived. Hamann's deliberately paradoxical acceptance of sexual "sin" (and comcomitant rejection of Kantian "purism") is the obverse of his piety. (On the latter point, see also Salmony, *Hammans metakritische Philosophie,* pp. 63–104.)

For a survey of the many references to rebirth in Kant's thought, see Hans-Georg Wittig, *Wiedergeburt als radikaler Gesinnungswandel.*

61. According to that note, human life assessed merely in terms of what we enjoy ("the natural purpose of the sum of all our inclinations") sinks below zero. For who, he goes on to ask, "would wish to begin [*antretten;* literally "step into"] life anew, either under the same conditions, or even according to a new, self-drafted plan, if it were devised merely for enjoyment?" To live such a life, whose content consists in "what we do (not just what we enjoy)," that is, according to the end nature "has with us," is still to live merely as a means to some "indeterminate last purpose." It is thus only the "value that we give our lives, not just through what we do, but through what we do purposively independent of nature," that can "give value to the existence of nature."

62. Cf. *Idea for a Universal History:* "For what is the use of praising and holding up for contemplation the glory and wisdom of creation in the non-rational realm of nature, if the very part—namely, the history of mankind— . . . that contains the purpose [*Zweck*] of the rest [of creation], is to remain an unceasing reproach to

everything else? If that spectacle forces us to turn away in revulsion, and, doubtful of ever finding any completed rational aim [*Absicht*] in it, reduces us to hoping for it only in another world?" (VIII:30; 25). By distinguishing between the final end (within nature) and the last end (beyond it), Kant accomplishes the task (the "justification of nature") his earlier essay leaves hanging.

63. V:437; 324–25. Kant adds that natural products might, for all we know, come about through an understanding that brings forth certain forms out of the necessity of its own nature, "by analogy with what is called artistic instinct in animals" (V:442; [330]). Intelligent causation for Kant implies not merely the intellectual substance of Spinoza, a substance analogous to the understanding possessed even by animals, but reason, that is to say, the capacity to act intentionally, or according to ideas, a capacity that is, in the final analysis, inseparable from freedom. (It is in this ultimate sense that the good or holy will, despite the fact that it wills as it must, is free.)

64. The "only thing which can give man's existence an absolute value, and by reference to which the existence of the world can have a *final purpose,* is the power of desire" (V:443; 332). The purpose of ethicotheology is to prevent our striving toward the universal highest cause from becoming flaccid (*ermatten zu lassen*) (V:446; 336).

65. Without this ethicotheology, physicotheology provides no more than "daemonology" (V:447; 336).

66. In requiring the assumption of God's existence as a necessary condition of our conceiving the possibility of the actualization of the highest good, Kant follows the pattern of his earlier treatment of organic beings, where positing the existence of something supersensible was a necessary condition of our conceiving the possibility of a natural product. In both cases, appeal to the transcendent overcomes a heteronomy that makes the possibility of unity otherwise inconceivable to us. What is different in the case of moral teleology is that man himself (in his moral striving) has the end in view. The world form furnished by moral teleology is like that of an organic being whose end (for once) stands visible before us.

67. On the example of Spinoza, see Booth, *Interpreting the World.*

68. On other versions of the moral argument for God's existence, see Lewis White Beck, *A Commentary on the Critique of Practical Reason,* p. 272 ff.

69. Kant uses "Chimera" throughout his work as a synonym for fantasy or illusion. The chimera (literally, "she-goat") was, according to ancient mythology, a fire-breathing female monster, part lion, part serpent, and part goat. She was slain by Bellerophon astride the winged horse Pegasus.

70. Kant lists as a principle benefit of moral teleology its guarding of rational psychology from the twin pitfalls of materialism and an "expansive" pneumatology. What remains of rational psychology, apart from morally based faith in the immortality of the soul, is "an anthropology of the inner sense," or empirical knowledge "of our thinking self *in life*" (V:461; 353). (On the systematic importance of this anthropology, see chapter 10 below.) If, on the other hand, we opine about pure spirits in the material universe, spirits that think without bodies, we engage in fiction (*dichten*) (V:467; 361).

71. *Absehen* means both "to aim at" and "to disregard."

72. Cf. *Critique of Pure Reason* A/576 = B/604: "This ideal [of the *ens realisi-*

mum] is . . . the only true ideal of which human reason is capable. For only in this one case is a concept of a thing — a concept which is in itself universal — completely determined in and through itself, and known as the representation of an individual."

Chapter Ten

1. M. Herz, *Grundriß aller medicinischen Wissenschaften*, p. 232. Herz classifies phenomenology under the study of pathology.

2. Iabetus in Greek mythology was son of heaven and earth; the name is also associated with Noah's son Jeptha. The universalistic implications of Kant's statement contrast with Luther's description of the German people in particular as the descendants of Aschkenaz, Japhet's first-born son (Arno Borst, *Der Turmbau von Babel: Geschichte der Meinungen über Ursprung und Vielfalt der Sprachen und Völker*, vol. 2, p. 1065). Luther's follower Simon Musaeus called Germany "Japhet's Geschlecht," which becomes through Luther "another Jerusalem to the world" (see Borst, pp. 1065, 1196, 1225–26).

3. Borowski, Jachmann, and Wasianski, *Immanuel Kant*, p. 194. For a recent discussion of the philosophic bearing of Kant's health, see Ben-Ami Scharfstein, *The Philosophers: Their Lives and the Nature of Their Thought*, pp. 209–30.

4. Jachmann in Borowski, Jachmann, and Wasianski, *Immanuel Kant*, pp. 186–87.

5. Ibid., p. 231.

6. See Borowski, Jachmann, and Wasianski, *Immanuel Kant*, pp. 184–87, 195, 207 (Jachmann); p. 227 (Wasianski); pp. 52–53 (Borowski). See also Kant's letter to Marcus Herz, beginning of April 1778 (X:231).

7. Other studies of Kant's medical preoccupations in the context of his thought in general include Böhme and Böhme, *Das Andere der Vernunft;* and Robert E. Butts, *Kant and the Double Government Methodology*. The locus classicus is Hans Vaihinger, "Kant als melancholiker," *Kant-Studien* 2. See also Mary J. Gregor's very interesting suggestion that "the development of Kant's philosophical position can almost be charted . . . by his handling of the question whether it is meaningful to talk about the location of the soul and its influence on the body" (in Beck, *Kant's Latin Writings*, p. 241 n).

It is interesting in this regard to compare Hegel, who calls "every disease" a "hypochondria of the organism, in which the latter disdains the outer world which sickens it" (see *Philosophy of Nature* [pt. 2 of the *Encyclopaedia of the Philosophical Sciences*], trans. A. V. Miller, p. 438). Hegel's entire treatment of disease is an elaboration of this point. As Jacques Derrida observes, Hegel's discussion of disease situates itself at the point of transition between the science of nature and the science of spirit (see, especially, *Glas*, trans. John P. Leavey, Jr., and Richard Rand [Lincoln: University of Nebraska Press, 1986]; and *Of Spirit: Heidegger and the Question*, trans. Geoffrey Bennington and Rachel Bowlby, p. 99).

8. See *Critique of Pure Reason* A/853–56 = B/881–84.

9. Fackenheim, "Kant's Concept of History."

10. On the use of harnesses and leading strings in childhood as a cause of painful narrow-breastedness in an unnamed "writer," see *Pedagogy* (IX:461). According

to D. Friedrich Rink, who edited the *Pedagogy,* Kant attributed his narrow-breastedness to inheritance from his mother, whom he physically resembled (see Rink, *Ansichten aus Immanuel Kant's Legen,* p. 13).

11. See *Concerning the Ultimate Ground of the Differentiation of Directions in Space* (1768) (II:380–81; [369]). See also *What It Means to Orient Oneself in Thinking* (VIII:135; [239]). According to Kant, one can orient oneself "simply by the feeling of difference between [one's] two sides, the right and the left." This feeling is evoked by the practical experience of greater power and skill on the part of the right side of the body, and, perhaps, by that of greater sensitivity on the left. It is also evinced, Kant says, by "the perceptible beating of the heart — whenever it contracts, the tip of the heart touch[ing] the left side of the chest with an oblique movement." Our ability to distinguish between left and right bears centrally on Kant's dispute with Leibniz vis à vis the nature of space. On the systematic importance of this ability, see also Hoke Robinson, "Kant on Embodiment," in *Minds, Ideas, and Objects: Essays on the Theory of Representation in Modern Philosophy,* ed. Phillip D. Cummins and Guenter Zoeller, pp. 337–39. On moral dimensions of the distinction between right and left, see *Announcement of the Near Conclusion of a Treaty for Eternal Peace in Philosophy* (VIII:415 n; 85 n).

12. Borowski, Jachmann, and Wasianski, *Immanuel Kant,* p. 210.

13. *Herzbeklemmung* is a German translation, it seems, of *angina pectoris. Angina* is from a Latin word meaning "to choke or strangle." Eighteenth-century medical dictionaries identify *angina pectoris* as a painful paroxysm or constriction of the heart, accompanied by a sense of suffocation and fear of impending death. According to Grimm and Grimm, *Deutsches Wörterbuch* (1854), *Herzbeklemmung* is also used in a more strictly literary sense (for example, by Schelling, von Humboldt, and Goethe) to denote a state of being seized with a powerful feeling of anxiety or foreboding.

14. For a fuller treatment of the history of hypochondria and melancholy, see Ilza Veith, *Hysteria: History of a Disease;* Susan Baur, *Hypochondria: Woeful Imaginings;* and E. Fischer-Homberger, *Hypochondrie.* On the general social context, see G. S. Rousseau, ed., *The Languages of Psyche: Mind and Body in Enlightenment Thought;* G. S. Rousseau, "Psychology," in Rousseau and Porter, *Ferment of Knowledge,* pp. 143–210; and Sander Gilman et al., *Hysteria beyond Freud.* See also Wolf Lepenies, *Melancholy and Society,* trans. Jeremy Gaines and Doris Jones. Lepenies treats hypochondria and utopian longing as related symptoms of the political frustrations experienced by certain social classes during this period.

Hypochondria (plural of *hypochondrium*) referred originally to those parts of the abdomen lying immediately under the ribs and to either side of the epigastric region (hence to the liver, spleen, and surrounding organs). It was apparently in England that *hypochondria* first came to signify a particular disease (associated with the hypochondriac regions). The *Oxford English Dictionary* cites as an early example of that usage Dryden's (1668) reference to melancholy as "a tincture of the hypochondria."

15. Melancholy takes its name from one of these humors, the so-called black chole or bile. Excessive quantities of black bile were thought to poison the blood.

16. An extraordinary compendium of historical thinking about melancholy is Burton's *Anatomy of Melancholy* (1621). Burton divides the disease into "head mel-

ancholy" and "windy or hypochondriacal melancholy," the former produced by, for example, too much study and/or blows to the head, but also by "fumes arising from the stomach, etc." Causes of the latter include "default of spleene, belly, bowels, stomach . . . etc." Symptoms of melancholy include "vertigo, much wit, headache, binding, much waking, winde, rumbling in the guts, pain in the left side, palpitations, troublesome dreams, heaviness of heart," and "continuall feare, sorrow, sulpition, discontent, superfluous cares . . . [and] anxiety" (pp. 128–29). *Humors* he defines as "a liquid or fluent part of the Body . . . for the preservation of it." Blood "is a hot, sweet, temperate, red humour, prepared in the *Meseraicke* veins. . . . And from it *Spirits* are first begotten in the heart, which afterwards by the *Arteries* are communicated to the other parts." Spirit, on the other hand, "is a most subtile vapour, which is expressed from the *Blood,* & the instrument of the soule," that is, "a common tye or *medium* betwixt the body and the soule, such as some would have it; or as *Paracelsus,* a fourth soule of itselfe." The source of the spirits, both vital and animal, is the heart, which Burton describes as "the seat and fountaine of life" and "Organ of all passions and affections." In keeping with the ancient association of the soul with the heart, Burton calls the heart the body's king, the brain serving (merely) as a "privy Councellour, and Chancellour" (p. 131). Also noteworthy is his division of the "inner senses" into common sense, fantasy, and memory. Common sense is the "judge or Moderator of the rest, by whom we discerne all differences of objects." "*Phantasie,* or Imagination . . . is an inner sense, which doth more fully examine the Species perceaved by common sense, of things present or absent, and keepes them longer, recalling them to mind againe, or making [infinite] new of his owne. In time of sleepe, this faculty is free, & many times conceaves strange, stupend, absurd shapes, as in sicke men we commonly observe. . . . In *Melancholy* men this faculty is most Powerful and strong . . . producing many monstrous and prodigious things" (pp. 139–40).

Kant would have known Burton, if not directly, then certainly through Laurence Sterne, whose "whimsical talent" Kant praises in the *Anthropology* (VII:235; 104. See also [VII:204; 75] and *Pedagogy* [IX:469]). Burton's familiarity with traditional medical opinion gives his work special value as a broad indication of the conventional background in and against which eighteenth-century medical opinion moved. Like the works of other literary hypochondrists, Burton's exhaustive study is intended as a self-curative.

17. See George Cheyne's influential *The English Malady.* Cheyne claimed that as many as one-third of his countrymen suffered from hypochondria, among whose symptoms he seems to have included mental suffering incident to gout, scurvy, consumption, and other ailments. As Baur points out (*Hypochondria,* p. 27), this national identification of the disease went together with its democratization.

18. Friedrich Hoffmann (1660–1742) and Hermann Boerhaave (1668–1738). According to Mary J. Gregor's helpful summary, for Hoffmann, life consists in perceptible movement, particularly of the heart and blood, and health involves a state of partial tonic contraction. The body is like a hydraulic machine utilizing an etherlike fluid "finer than all other matter, but not exactly spirit, soul or mind," a fluid that is distributed throughout the nerves. Hoffmann is one source of the medical theory according to which disease results from either too much or too little fluid, imbalances that cause either spasm or atonia. Georg Ernest Stahl (1660–

1754), on the other hand, held that the human body is by itself a "lifeless machine" whose vital principle is the soul, "which builds the organism, maintains, moves, and controls it, [and] preserves it from disintegration, decay, deterioration." The soul affects the body by making the nerves vibrate. Disease is a result of the errant activities of the soul, which spontaneously tries to correct its error, for example, through sweats and fever. Stahl was a strong believer in nature's self-healing powers (and was thus a forerunner of "homeopathy"). See Gregor, in Beck, *Kant's Latin Writings,* pp. 221–23. Kant finds something to like and dislike about each school: as he notes in *Dreams,* Stahl's "organic" account "is often closer to the truth" despite the fact that Hoffmann and Boerhaave "follow a more philosophical method." As for the influence of immaterial forces, "it can at most be known that it is there, but . . . never how it takes place or how far it extends." As Gregor notes, this equivocation anticipates his later account of the scientific investigation of life in the *Critique of Judgment.* On Kant's association in the *Opus postumum* of vital force with ethereal vibration, see the text at note [120] below.

19. On key issues dividing the two schools, Kant remained, by his own account, agnostic.

20. Or, following von Haller, "irritability" and "sensitivity."

21. Thus the characteristic therapies of the time — "purging" and bloodletting — which were both intended to release blood and other substances contaminated by, or productive of, bad humors. (Especially prior to Harvey's discovery of the circulation of blood, bloodletting was localized to that region of the body thought to be affected by the humoral disturbance.) As late as 1766, the English physician John Hill could attribute hypochondria to "thick and glutinous blood" that has "too long stagnated in the spleen" (see John Hill, *Hypochondriasis: A Practical Treatise,* with an introduction by G. S. Rousseau, p. 2). Robert James's *Medical Dictionary* (1743–45), on the other hand, defines hypochondria as a "spasmodic-flatulent disorder of the *Primae Viae,* that is, of the stomach and intestines, arising from an inversion or perversion of their peristaltic motion . . . disturbing the whole oeconomy of the functions."

22. Johnson's *Dictionary,* for example, defines *hypochondriacal* as "melancholy; disordered in the imagination." Kant himself in an early work classifies hypochondria, along with mental derangement (*Verrückung*) and insanity (*Wahnwitz*), among "diseases of the head." A chief symptom of hypochondria was a tendency to imagine oneself subject to nonexistent diseases — hence its primary identification with disturbances of the imagination, as in Moliere's famous *Imaginary Invalid.* Not until well into the nineteenth century, however, did our current understanding of "hypochondria" as primarily a mental (or moral) disorder come into prominence. See, in this regard, the treatise by the French clinician Jean-Pierre Falret, *De l'hypochondrie et du suicide,* which declares "the most usual causes" of hypochondria to be "moral and intellectual" (quoted in Baur, *Hypochondria,* p. 28).

23. See Bernard Mandeville (1670–1733), *A Treatise of the Hypochondriack and Histerick Passions, Vulgarly Call'd the Hypo in Men and Vapours in Women.* Mandeville champions the way of "experiment and observation" against both the theories of the "learned Galenist" and those of the "Modern Physician." Mandeville's own theories, which he claims to be based on observation, revolve around the capacity of

the stomach to ferment the animal spirits (p. 125 ff.) and an apprehension against too much "marital lust" as tending to exhaust those spirits (p. 145).

24. See James Boswell, *The Hypochondriack* (seventy essays appearing in the *London Magazine*), ed. Margery Bailey. Boswell, who calls himself a hypochondriac "from former sufferings," intends by his essays "to divert Hypochondriacks of every degree, from dwelling on their uneasiness" (I:109). See also I:142: "Nothing characterizes a Hypochondriack more peculiarly than irresolution, or the want of power over his own mind." Boswell claims to be driven to metaphysical speculations concerning the relation between body and soul (I:143) in lieu of describing his own symptoms, to which he feels a strange aversion. On fears as to the incurability of madness, see II:238 ff.

25. The eighteenth century has, not without reason, been called the hypochondriacal century. Other prominent German works on hypochondria include treatises by J. U. Bilguer (1767) and E. Platner (1798). A journal entitled *Der Hypochondrist, eine holsteinische Wochenschrift* appeared in 1762. On the German sources, see Böhme and Böhme, *Das Andere der Vernunft*, pp. 387–423; and E. Fischer-Homberger, *Hypochondrie*.

On the specific German Pietist background, in which "spiritual melancholy" (*tristitia spiritualis*) and "self-observation" (similar to that practiced by Adam Bernd) are celebrated as virtues, see Schings, *Melancholie*. The flavor of Bernd's autobiographical work is suggested by its full title, *Eigene Lebens-Beschreibung, samt einer Aufrichtegen Entdeckung, und deutlichen Beschreibung einer der größten, obwol großen Theils noch unbekannten Leibes-und Gemüths-Plage, welche Gott zuweilen über die Welt-Kinder, und auch wohl über seine Eigene Kinder verhänget* (Personal life description, together with a sincere discovery and clear description of one of the largest, though as yet unknown physical and emotional ailments which God has imposed on the world's children, and certainly on his own children). It seems fair to conclude that for many in Germany, melancholy retained an emphatically positive spiritual resonance, owing to Pietism's promotion of *tristitia spiritualis* and the "duty of mourning" (*Trauergebot*) as preconditions of Christian "rebirth," and to such (related) literary traditions as the baroque "mourning play" (*Trauerspiel*). As Schings suggests, this resonance, which Hamann (himself a professed "hypochondriac") did much to enhance, contributed to Romantic criticism of the Enlightenment. That Kant's struggle against hypochondria is also directed, in part, against aspects of his own early Pietist training is clear from a passage from *Conflict of the Faculties* (VII:57–59; 104–7 [quoted in chap. 9, n. 60]), a passage which, not incidentally, takes Hamann specifically to task.

26. According to Borowski, Kant originally intended to comment in his essay on a certain "adventurer" or "goat prophet" named Jan Komarnicki, who wandered the outskirts of Königsberg accompanied by a wild boy (Borowski, Jachmann, and Wasianski, *Immanuel Kant*, pp. 95–96; see also Butts, *Kant and the Double Government Methodology*, pp. 308–9 n). Concerning the pair, Kant elsewhere observed that the child might well be the perfect specimen sought by an experimental moralist who did not dismiss the propositions of Rousseau as mere chimera (*Hirngespinste*) (II:488–89). Kant's comments suggest that he wrote his brief study of mental diseases around the same time that he first became deeply interested in Rousseau. One

428 NOTES TO PAGES 268-69

obvious area of concern for Kant at this time was the relation between religious fanaticism, madness, and a laudable moral "enthusiasm" that he associates with Rousseau. In Kant's opening remarks in the essay on diseases of the head, Rousseau's poor reception among the "doctors of the Sorbonne" exemplifies the inability of the supposedly learned to recognize true wisdom when they see it. As we saw in an earlier chapter, Kant credited Rousseau with teaching him the distinction between such wisdom and fanatical illusion. The trick, he suggests in his comments on the adventurer Komarnicki, lies, at least in part, in having eyes "that like to discover raw nature." It is certainly remarkable, Kant adds, that the little naked savage, apparently reared in the raw to endure cheerfully the hardships of nature, and displaying none of the embarrassment that comes either from serfdom or the discipline of refinement, should find himself in the company of such an "inspired faunus." Perhaps Kant believed that the older man was so out of this world as hardly to affect his otherwise "natural" companion.

In his *Investigation concerning Diseases of the Head*, Kant also takes up *Schwärmerei*, which he calls an illusion of the "greatest danger" to mankind, and which he distinguishes from the innocuous fantasy associated with moral feeling, and that "enthusiasm" without which "nothing great in the world has been done." Rousseau, he says, is a fantasist, but not a *Schwärmer*.

27. From the Latin *gryllus* (and Greek *gryllos*), meaning "grasshopper or cricket." *Grylli* were also caricatures, or grotesque composites. See Stafford, *Body Criticism*, p. 270; and Duncan G. N. Barker, "*Grylli, Verstand und Unsinn* in Classical Glyptics."

28. Kant here classifies derangement as an inversion (*Verkehrtheit*) of the concepts of experience, as distinguished from lunacy (*Wahnsinn*), a disorder in the judgment of experience, and dementia (*Wahnwitz*), an inversion of reason itself. (He will later dismiss all such efforts at classification as pointless, owing to the incurability of insanity.) On Kant's account of insanity generally, see Butts's extensive discussion in *Kant and the Double Government Methodology*, especially pp. 282–318. According to Butts, this essay is the first published work of Kant in which the term *Schwärmerei* appears. As Butts notes, Kant's emphasis here on the importance of outer sense to offset a wayward imagination is Humean in flavor; one could add that it is also Rousseauian. Insanity, Kant also insists, can be accompanied by genius (II:268).

29. Quoted in the original English, that passage reads:

As *wind* in th'*Hypocondries* pend / Is but a blast if downward sent; / But if it upwards chance to fly / Becomes new *Light* and *Prophecy*: / So when your Speculations tend / Above their just and useful end: / Although they promise strange and great / *Discoveries* of things far fet, / They are but idle dreams and fancies / And savour strongly of the *Ganzas*. (Pt. 2, canto 3, lines 772–81)

Kant was no doubt familiar with the pungent German translation, entitled *Samuel Butlers Hudibras, ein satyrisches Gedicht wider die Schwärmer und Independenten zur Zeit Carls des Ersten, in neun Gesängen* and published in Leipzig in 1765, one year prior to the appearance of *Dreams*. "Ganzas" refers to the birds that carry the hero to the moon in Bishop Godwin's romance, *The Man in the Moon, or a Discourse of a*

Voyage thither by Domingo Gonzales. For a fuller discussion of Kant's essay, see chapter 5 above.

30. On various contemporary usages of "pneumatology" (and their tendency to blur physical/mental boundaries), see Stafford, *Body Criticism,* pp. 417–28. Stafford's rich and instructive discussion of this and other medical and aesthetic themes is marred by insufficient attention to the consideration of the issues at stake by the most serious thinkers of the period. Rousseau and Kant, for example, are (virtually) ignored; and yet these are arguably the figures who respectively address—most rigorously and with the greatest influence on subsequent eras—the centrality of sensibility, and the delineation of the relation between mind and matter. Her effort to open, through "metaphorology," a "wider and truly cross-disciplinary horizon onto the past and future" is partly betrayed by partisan suspicion of philosophy's (protextualist?) claims, an over-reliance on conventional accounts of the history of philosophy, and a tendency to dismiss the often considerable influence of philosophers on the "visual arts" (for example, Greuze's heavy debt to Rousseau). Metaphorology, she believes, "permits us to rethink, reformulate, and perhaps even constructively reshape the abiding yet changing problem of the relation of image to text, imagination to reason, and body to soul." The question of what metaphor *is* (or what the "reason" or "science" of metaphor might mean) is, however, not only avoided; it cannot, given her starting point, even arise.

31. For a later version of this argument, see *Metaphysics of Morals* (VI:484–85; 273).

32. Cf. Kant's comments in the *Anthropology* (VII:235; 103–4) to the effect that Butler's wit puts things topsy-turvy, giving us the pleasure of turning them right. Such whimsical (*launichten*) talent, Kant here insists, is to be distinguished from the capricious (*launisch,* deriving from lunatic [*lunatisch*]) disposition, that is, a natural tendency to imaginary joy and grief that he elsewhere associates with hypochondria. On Butler's wit making things seem more contemptible than they are, see VII:222; 91.

33. *Knoten* means both "knot" and "node" or "ganglion"; and the primary meaning of *untie* (*auflösen*) is "dissolve." On the association of nerve ganglia with soul/body interaction, see note 64 below.

34. Apr. 8, 1776 (X:69–73; 54–57).

35. See in this regard his letter to Mendelssohn, Feb. 7, 1766 (X:68), noting that he has sent Mendelssohn "some *Dreams*." Airy metaphysicians succumb to "dreams of reason," as Kant puts it, where spirit seers succumb to those of "sensation."

36. As Kant later puts it, he who thinks too much about death (or birth, for that matter) will never enjoy life. See the text at note 75 below.

37. Cf. his reference, in *Philosophers' Medicine of the Body,* to dreams as "guards" (XV:948; 234).

38. See, for example, *Anthropology* (VII:175; 51. And VII:190–91; 63–64). See also *Conflict of the Faculties* (VII:106; 193. Cf. *Reflection* no. 395 [XV:158]). Concerning the nightmare about drowning that Kant believed saved his life, see chapter 9 above. Kant's justification of nightmares figures in his attempt to present nature as a kind of organism.

39. On this case see also *Reflection* no. 295 [XV:111–13] (of uncertain date), in which Kant says that the worms were "stunned by music," an effect he attributes to the intestines, the only organs of the body constantly filled with air, vibrating sympathetically like stretched strings or drums. Wondering if comparable effects might be discerned with color and light, Kant notes that all effects of sense extend to the bowels, and that all sensations of feeling (pleasure and pain) seem to extend there first. Cf. Stahl's notion that the soul communicates to the body by making the nerves vibrate.

40. On the history of these terms, see Gregor, in Beck, *Kant's Latin Writings* (p. 238 n), and the editors of the Akademie edition. H. D. Gaubius, who composed two lectures on the relation between mind and body (*Sermones II academici de regimine mentis, quod medicorum est* [1747, 1763]), uses the Hippocratic terms *enormon* or *impetum faciens* to designate the principle of life. Cf. XV:940, where Kant associates vital force with the *impetum faciens*. Gaubius understands the *impetum faciens* to belong to the body rather than the mind. For Kant, both here and in that earlier passage, the question is not so much whether to locate it in the body or the mind (a central point of dispute between the mechanist Hoffmann and the vitalist Stahl), as how to understand its relation with the will.

41. Stahl, for example, located in the heart the relation between *anima* and soul. See Farber, "Forces," p. 428.

42. The other, an essay on human races, is itself not unconcerned with the former question.

43. For an extended discussion of the review in relation to the problem of human uprightness, see Fenves, *Peculiar Fate*, p. 151 ff.

The question of man's natural posture arises in Rousseau's *Discourse on the Origins of Inequality* in the context of a discussion of man's possible descent from four-footed animals, a discussion in which Rousseau calls for (among other things) further research in comparative anatomy (*The First and Second Discourses,* ed. Robert D. Masters, pp. 104–5). Cf. Aristotle's claim that man stands on two feet because "his nature and essence is divine" (*Parts of Animals* 686a), quoted by Masters in his informative note (p. 235 n).

Kant's review of Peter Moscati's essay appeared anonymously in the *Königsbergische Gelehrte und Politische Zeitungen* (Aug. 23, 1771).

44. See, for example, Kant's discussion of man's essential "inoculation" in *Idea for a Universal History;* cf. his later rejection of the identification of freedom with the ability to choose for *and against* the moral law, on the grounds that it is a hybrid definition (*definitio hybrida* or *Bastarderklärung*) (*Metaphysics of Morals* [VI:227; 52]).

45. It was at the Herzs' home that Dorothea Mendelssohn (Veit) met Frederich von Schlegel, and Rachel Varnhagen (Levin) met Varnhagen von Ense. For a brief but informative discussion of Kant's relation to Herz, see Lewis White Beck, *Studies in the Philosophy of Kant,* pp. 54–60.

In addition to his early exposition of Kant's philosophy, Herz's publications include a treatise on taste (*Versuch ueber den Schmack and die Ursachen seiner Verschiedenheit* [1776]), a treatise on vertigo (*Versuch ueber den Schwindel* [1786]), *Letters to Physicians* (*Briefe an Aerzte*) (1777–84), and *Grundriß aller medicinischen Wissenschaften* (1782).

Herz's continuing interest in Judaism is reflected in other writings which or may not have been known to Kant, including an English translation, published on the urging of Mendelssohn, of Manasseh Ben Israel's *Vindiciae Judaeorum*. He also wrote a dialogue (*Freimuetige Kaffegespraeche zweier juedischer Juschauerinnen ueber den Juden Pinkus* (1772) and, according to recent evidence, translated the "Prayer of the Jewish Physician," attributed to Maimonides, from Hebrew to German. The Herz salon represents the commingling of Christian and Jewish intellectual cultures in Germany at what was perhaps its friendliest and most fruitful. Despite this ease of intercourse, some members of the circle went on to promulgate versions of antisemitism. Henriette Herz herself converted to Christianity in 1817, following the death of her mother, at the urging of Schleiermacher. Despite Kant's warmth towards Herz (and Mendelssohn) and scrupulous politeness towards them in matters pertaining to their religion, Kant's attitude toward Judaism and Jews was not exactly positive. See, for example, his depiction in the *Anthropology* of the Jews as a "nation of cheaters" (VII:205 n; 77 n); and, on a more personal and trivial, but perhaps no less revealing, note, his privately expressed annoyance with a certain Jewish painter for portraying him with a "Jewish nose." Kant is, however, careful in the *Anthropology* to attribute this propensity to economic and political ("constitutional") factors, rather than to traits that are biologically inherited.

46. Kant's reliance on Herz's medical skill is already evident in the first extant letter between them (Aug. 31, 1770 [X:95]). On Kant's early use of Herz as intermediary, see, for example, Kant's letter to J. H. Lambert (Sept. 2, 1770), which Herz delivered to Lambert along with a copy of Kant's *Dissertation*. In that letter, Kant described Herz, the respondent of the *Dissertation,* as "a capable Jewish student of mine," commending him to Lambert as a "young man of excellent character, very industrious and capable, who adheres to and profits from every piece of good advice" (X:96–99). See also the letter from Moses Mendelssohn dated December 25, 1770 (X:113–16; [67–70]). Mendelssohn praises Herz (who Mendelssohn says he sees nearly every day), whose natural gifts ("a clear understanding, gentle heart, moderated imagination, and a certain subtlety of spirit which seems natural to his nation") have had, he says, the good fortune of Kant's instruction. See also Kant's letter to Herz (Sept. 27, 1770 [X:102]) asking him, among other things, for help with communications to Lambert, Sulzer, and the Minister, along with other channels (*Canäle*).

47. Kant's language is all the more striking, given the fact that, as Cassirer notes, Kant did not use terms like "friend" lightly (see *Kant's Life,* 122–23).

48. The author seems to have been Lambert.

49. Lambert was a well-known mathematician and scientific author with whom Kant kept up an important early correspondence. Johann Georg Sulzer, a member of the Berlin Academy of Sciences, wrote on aesthetics. Kant sent all three men copies of his *Dissertation;* their written responses appear in volume 10 of the Akademie edition.

50. The analogy is anticipated in Kant's earlier social pleasantries, which, among other things, liken Mendelssohn to a rare dish:

Today Mr. Mendelssohn, your worthy friend and mine (for so I flatter myself), is departing. To have a man like him in constant and intimate intercourse [*Umgange*] in Königsberg, a man of such gentle temperament, good spirits [*Laune*] and enlightenment [*hellem Kopfe*] — how that would give my soul the nourishment that it has lacked so completely here, a nourishment I miss more and more as I grow older. For as far as bodily nourishment goes, as you well know, I hardly worry about that and am quite content with my share of earthly goods. I fear I did not make full use of my one opportunity to enjoy [*genießen*] this rare man. . . . The day before yesterday he honored me by attending two of my lectures, taking potluck [*fortune du pot*], so to speak, since the table was not set for such a distinguished guest. . . . Please help me to maintain my friendship with this worthy man. (X:211; [87])

51. Kant prefers, in this regard, laxative purges to diuretics, an aversion to "excessive" consumption and excretion of water that his later medical commentaries also evince.

52. He had been invited to assume a prestigious academic post in Berlin.

53. The Parcae were Roman goddesses of birth, often assimilated with the Fates or Moira.

54. The conversation concerning lecture notes continues in the very friendly letters to Herz (Oct. 20, 1778 [X:242–43; 90–91]) and from Herz (Nov. 24, 1778 [X:243–45; (92–93)]), Kant especially commending Herz for his activity, and Herz expanding warmly (Kant is "constantly at the center of Herz's head and heart") upon his growing and influential circle of auditors. The able Kraus, whose help Kant anticipates, is the exception, he says, among note-taking students, who generally heap up piles of notes without distinguishing the important from the unimportant, and with whom in any case Kant has little "private acquaintance" (*Privatbekantschaft*). (There is, however, some difficulty with Kraus, who is apparently troubled in some way.)

55. There is no record of any further correspondence until 1785. A letter to Herz dated prior to November 25, 1785 (X:424–25) thanks him for the gift of his recent *Letters to Physicians* and solicits medical help for a friend. Herz's very warm response (Nov. 25, 1785 [X:456–57]) complains of the special burdens for spirit and body of the practical medical life, especially where the practitioner tries to be guided by reason. (Kant sends a brief but very friendly response on Dec. 2, 1785.)

Herz also mentions that he is working on an essay on vertigo, which he further describes in a letter sent on February 27, 1786. He once expressed the main idea of that essay in a conversation with Kant. "You see, dearest sir," he adds, "that I am not entirely disloyal to you, that I am much more a deserter who still wears your uniform and who, while associating with other (not hostile) powers, still seeks to adopt your service. Or, to express myself less Prussianly, I enjoy wandering around the border towns of both countries, philosophy and medicine, and it gives me joy when I can make suggestions and arrangements for their common government" (X:431; 120). Herz takes up in the same letter the controversy concerning Mendelssohn's death, a controversy that Kant's reply (Apr. 7, 1786 [X:442–43; 123–24]) attempts to minimize. (It seems unlikely that Herz found Kant's efforts on behalf of their common friend wholly adequate.)

Further extant correspondence (one letter [from Kant] in 1787, three [two from Kant] in 1789, and one [from Herz] in 1797) is cordial and in some ways wistful. See, for example, (XI:48; 150), where Kant notes Herz's "noble" gratitude — unusual, as Kant puts it, among his students; and (XII:225–26; 248), where Herz regrets that he is not a great doctor who might be called to Königsberg to embrace Kant before "one or the other of us leaves this earth."

56. On the general reaction to the *Critique*, see Beiser, *Fate of Reason*, p. 172. Beiser suggests that Herz remained loyal, for some time, to the *Dissertation*.

57. The name "Marcus Herz" suggests a phrase meaning "attend or mark the heart." On turning attention *from* the heart as a dietetic remedy, see below. I am indebted to Peter Fenves for drawing my attention to the literal meaning of Herz's name.

58. On Kant's later understanding, hypochondria was an incurable disease; his achievement lay in preventing a mere *tendency* from actually breaking forth. There is, however, something not a little paradoxical about Kant's vigilance (fueled by perpetual anxiety?) against the emergence of a disease whose chief symptom is perpetual anxiety.

59. For a description of the probable circumstances surrounding the address, see Gregor's introduction to her translation in Beck, *Kant's Latin Writings*, pp. 217–43. As the editor of the Akademie edition notes, the title is partly taken from H. D. Gaubius's *De regimine corporus quot philosophorum est*.

On "philosophic medicine" as a general theme in such thinkers as Bacon, Locke, and La Mettrie, see Schings, *Melancholie*, pp. 11–40; and the "Introductory Monograph" by Aram Vartanian in Julien Offray de La Mettrie, *La Mettrie's l'Homme Machine: A Study in the Origins of an Idea*. Where Kant's Pietist and empiricist predecessors tend to reduce hypochondria to spirit (in an immaterial sense) or matter, respectively, Kant's "philosophic medicine" insists on the essential indeterminacy of the phenomenon.

60. Kant does not, however, make any claims to expertise regarding the relative merits of the schools' respective teachings concerning the actual *causes* of healing (XV:245; 232).

61. Kant adds a note here concerning "affectus ganglia."

62. And this because the philosopher is one who turns his soul (anima) to things for the sake of cultivating reason, even as he despises everything merely sensual (or pertaining "to the lotus"). For the body that is burdened with yesterday's vices weighs down the mind "and presses a bit of the divine breath to the earth" (Kant repeats the allusion at XV:950; 235). The quotation, from Horace (*Satires* 2.2.77–79), was, as Gregor notes, a favorite of Kant's. Cf. (XV:952; 236): "Scorning the charms [*Reitze*] of life is the means of preserving it. This is not the apathy of indifference, but of even temper [*Gleichmüthigkeit*], bound up with all earnestness in duty, with frigidity [*Kaltsinn*] in enjoyment."

63. Like Kant, Mendelssohn suffered from hypochondriacal propensities (expressed in his dislike of feeling full), to which Mendelssohn, according to Kant, responded inappropriately and ultimately fatally. Kant attributed Mendelssohn's death, for which Kant might otherwise be thought to bear some indirect responsibility, exclusively to regimen that went wrong by confusing pain (that is, the uncomfortable fullness that follows eating) and harm. Mendelssohn succumbed, in other words, to a sort of hedonistic asceticism, or "excessive temperance." See (XV:950; 235–36): Wisdom does not require us to cheat our genius, in a "stepmotherly" way (*nouercae*), as Mendelssohn cheated his, owing to his unwillingness

to put up with the uncomfortable sense of fullness that follows a good meal. For details concerning the famous dispute with Jacobi that many thought precipitated Mendelssohn's death, see Beiser, *Fate of Reason*, pp. 92–108; and Beck, *Early German Philosophy*, pp. 353–60.

64. Attempting to explain the capacity of violent mental affects to harm the body, Kant mentions the views of a "certain English doctor," according to whom the mind's impetus in such a case "breaks through the barriers, called the ganglia of the nerves, that restrain motions of the will from affecting the vital organs" (XV:949; [235]). Cf. (XV:947; 233), where Kant calls "first in rank what nourishing and saving nature contributes to bodily health through the mind when a healthy man is in his normal state, as distinguished from that preternatural influx when affects break through the barriers by which nature strives to keep the mind from interfering with the vital motions."

The English doctor, according to the editors of the Akademie edition, was J. Johnstone, whose *Essay on the Use of the Ganglions of the Nerves* (1771) was translated into German in 1787 under the title *Versuch über den Nutzen der Nervenknoten*. According to Johnstone, these ganglia, inserted as barriers between the will and the vital organs, function both as "little brains" and as "sources and storehouses of nervous energy," and are the reason why we cannot, for example, stop the movement of our hearts by merely wishing to. Johnstone puts forward the ganglia as a special proof of God's providence, since otherwise we would kill ourselves in moments of despondency, anger, or illness, and the human race would soon become extinct. Johnstone published an earlier version of his theory in English in 1765. A. Monro (whose advice concerning the dropsy Kant mentions in one of his letters to Herz) published a critique, a German version of which appeared in 1787. Dreams, for Kant, serve an equivalently "providential" function by maintaining, through the perpetual activity of imagination even during sleep, the vital link between the nervous energy proceeding from the brain and the muscular power of the viscera. See *Conflict of the Faculties* (VII:106; 193).

65. Or "gluttony" in thinking; cf. XV:942; 229.

66. Kant's main example here of such controlled abandonment to play is the philosophically legislated consumption of food: "It is not only when the mind is free from care . . . that it aids the vital functions of the body, but also when it is stirred up, at dinner, by the sport and jests of conversation—when, to enliven the gathering, the guests enter into a contest, and the enthusiasm and exertion of the conversationalists rises to the limits of an affect. To what extent this happens is experienced every day by those who feast together: they can eat liberally and consume with impunity twice the amount of food they could safely eat if they were alone" (XV:949; 235). On special dangers that eating alone poses to philosophers, see VII:279–80; 145.

67. Kant also attributes consciousness without self-consciousness to the lower animals. See, for example, his letter to Herz, May 26, 1789 (XI:52; 153–54).

68. The Akademie edition editors speculate that Kant may have in mind Lavater's *Geheimes Tagebuch. Von einem Beobachter seiner selbst* and perhaps also von Haller's *Tagebuch*.

69. On this point, see Gregor's introduction in Beck, *Kant's Latin Writings*, p. 217 ff. The two parts of the *Anthropology* respectively address themselves to "dis-

cerning man's inner self as well as his outer" and "discerning man's inner self from his outer."

70. "It costs a real effort [*Anstrengung*] to eradicate an amusing representation that incites us to laughter, if we wish to concentrate our minds on something serious. Every abstraction is simply the canceling [*Aufhebung*] of certain clear representations; the purpose of the cancellation is normally to ensure that what remains is that much more clearly represented. But everybody knows how much effort that demands. *Abstraction* [Abstraction] can therefore be called *negative attention*. In other words, abstraction can be called a genuine doing and action which is opposed to the action by means of which the representation is rendered clear; the combination of the two yields zero, or the lack of a clear representation. For otherwise, if it were a negation and a lack absolutely, it would not require any more expenditure of force than is required not to know something, for not knowing something never needs a ground" (II:190-91; [228]). For a contrary view, see Baumgarten's *Psychologia empirica,* reprinted (with Kant's comments) in vol. 2 of the Akademie edition of Kant's works (II:35-37).

For Crusius on abstraction, see *Weg zur Gewißheit und Zuverlässigkeit der menschlichen Erkenntnis,* para. 93-97, in *Die philosophische Hauptwerke,* ed. G. Tonelli, vol. 3, pp. 164-72. Although Crusius attaches great importance to the power of abstraction (which he identifies with analysis, or the power to separate [*Absonderung*], and hence with judgment), he does not treat it as a power of negative attention (in the Kantian manner) or link it specifically with mental freedom.

71. See XV:34-37 (Kant's notes on Baumgarten's *Psychologica empirica*) and XV:58-63. *Reflection* no. 160 specifically mentions abstraction as conducive to mental health; hypochondria, on the other hand, is a disorder involving the power of attention. Adickes adds the following note, from a manuscript in the Royal Berlin Library: "Abstraction seems to be something arbitrary [*willkürlich*]; but it is a real work and effort. If one did not have it in one's power to abstract, imagination would run its course like a torrent [*Strom*]" (XV:59 n). See also no. 164 (XV:61): "Abstraction is more difficult than attention, because the drive to attention is natural. Still, compelled and long attention . . . wounds the brain." And see no. 168 (XV:62): "Through willful attention and abstraction we have the mind (our condition) in our power." These notes, mainly from the 1770s, are consistent in flavor with his comments in the *Anthropology,* suggesting that his view of the importance of abstraction remained fairly consistent over a long period.

See also in this regard the *Dissertation* of 1770 (II:394-95; 386-87), which links recognition of the dual provenance of human knowledge with acknowledgement of the peculiar character of abstraction as a leaving behind (rather than, as the term is usually taken to imply, a removal of the essence of): properly speaking, one "abstracts from something," rather than "abstracting something from". Rational concepts (forerunners of what Kant will later call the Categories) are here said to be "acquired" inasmuch as they are "abstracted from laws inherent in the mind" through attention to the mind's actions on the occasion of an experience. They are thus products of abstraction in a double sense. For what is perhaps Kant's earliest consideration of abstraction as an active power of the mind, see *New Elucidation* (I:403; 27) and chapter 3 above.

72. This power is especially evident in the striving (for example, on awakening?)

"to become conscious of one's representations" and necessarily involves more than lack or failure of attention (which is mere distraction). Kant cites the man who might have made a good match if only he could have "abstracted" from the woman's missing tooth, an example of the sort of morbid fascination (where attraction is inseparable from [sexual] repulsion) that prevents a man from doing what is properly in his own interest. Assuming that Kant's distaste for sex played a role in his own decision not to marry, the "missing tooth" can easily be read as standing for another sort of female lack. As Kant elsewhere suggests, women should be mouthless (*unmündig*). Kant was himself prone, for example, while lecturing, to become fixated on trivial items (such as an auditor's missing button), a tendency he used his power of abstraction actively to combat.

73. On the relation between this cognitive duality and Kant's understanding of human finitude, see Dieter Henrich, "The Unity of Subjectivity," in *The Unity of Reason,* ed. Richard Velkley, pp. 17–54. As Henrich notes, Kant was not the first to insist on a plurality of cognitive faculties, an old tradition that finds a modern representative in John Locke (p. 24). What is new in Kant, for Henrich, is the attempt to explain the unity of mind in a way that does justice to the plurality of mental faculties, an attempt that culminates in the claim (among others) that the "I" around which "we can only revolve in a perpetual circle" (A/346 = B/404) cannot get outside itself and reach the ground of its own possibility" (p. 30). Kant's recognition of the inaccessibility of the "common root" (if any) between sensibility and understanding, an insight that decisively distinguishes him from the German Idealists and Heidegger, is the key, in Henrich's view, to Kant's understanding of the peculiarly "discursive" character of human cognition.

One could add that Kant's "renunciation" of an answer, and acceptance of the "necessity of such a renunciation" (which, as Henrich notes, "did not come easy to Kant"), is inseparable from the problem of (sexual) generation generally. See, for example, *Anthropology* (VII:177; 53): "Understanding and sensibility, for all their dissimilarity, join together [*verschwistern sich;* literally "become brother and sister"] of themselves, to the effectuation of our knowledge, as if one had its origin from the other or both from a common stem; which, however, cannot be, or at least, it is inconceivable to us how the heterogenous [*Ungleichartige*] could sprout from one and the same root" (also cited in Henrich, p. 32). Kant goes on to ask in the accompanying note "why it is that all organic beings we know beget their kind only by the union of two sexes." Kant's amazement (concerning a sexual division that he specifically relates to the "material of our earth") reminds one of his amazement concerning the unity of the subject (see Henrich, p. 31).

One is led to wonder whether there is not a deeper experiential connection between Kant's "amazed" renunciation of any claim to insight into a "common root" (of the respective dualisms of knowledge, force, propagation) and his discovery concerning the power of abstraction (directed, in the first instance, against natural "attraction"). One suggestion: the feeling of suffocating pressure (or of being "swallowed up") that is, for Kant, coeval with repulsion (or the capacity to repel oneself) from maternal enclosure. In any event, it is noteworthy that Kant depicts human emancipation as a self-birthing, not in the sense of self-generation (which is strictly speaking inconceivable) but as a "voluntary" exit from the womb, in which freedom is, paradoxically enough, the condition of its own possibility. (Compare in this regard Heidegger, *Being and Time,* trans. John Macquarrie and Edward Robinson, p. 424 ff. [sec. 72 ff.].) On "amazement" (*Erstaunen*) as a state of uncertainty as to whether one is sleeping or awake, see *Anthropology* (VII:261; 128. And VII:177; 52).

74. On the early role of abstraction, see chapter 3 above. See also, for example, the *Dohna Logic* (XXIV:702; 440): "[consciousness of representation, or apperception] is the faculty of representation in relation to an object . . . which in the case of apprehension is still not present at all, but instead is, as it were, produced {grasped}. In the thought that man can say, I think — there lies exceptionally much. *Consciousness* of our concepts is always hard." Cf. the *Blomberg Logic* (XXIV:136; 107). See also (XXIV:252–54; 201–3): it is through a process of (nonarbitrary, nonfabricating) abstraction that one forms empirical concepts (as distinguished from a priori ideas). Kant adds: "Hypochondriacs are very much subject to nonarbitrary fabrication. . . . If man can subject everything to choice, then he is the most perfect of all beings, and hence arbitrary fabrication will often be very useful to him, too." Human perfection is here associated with the ability to control fully one's power of abstraction, an ability that is the antithesis of hypochondria. See also the *Vienna Logic* (XXIV:907; 351. XXIV:909; 352–53). Kant associates abstraction (in contrast with comparison and reflection) with negative effort and moral refinement. Cf. the *Jäsche Logic* (IX:94–95; 592–93). Abstraction is not a power to produce but to "leave out" — a power, in other words, to release oneself from that to which one is naturally or intuitively called upon to attend (that is, that by which one is naturally attracted). See, for example, *Dohna Logic* (XXIV:754; ca. 487) and *Jäsche Logic* (IX:45; 554): to abstract from that in a cognition which does not conform to our purpose is praiseworthy.

Involuntary nonfabricating abstraction lies at the heart of that hidden activity of the mind by which empirical concepts are somehow produced; voluntary (fabricating and nonfabricating) abstraction is crucial to the mind's ability to direct itself according to a conscious aim. Hypochondria (or involuntary, fabricating abstraction) is thus, logically speaking, the diseased meeting ground between the healthy conscious and unconscious versions of a power that is quintessentially human.

75. Hypochondria is in this respect like vertigo, which also has the potential for transforming imaginary evils into real ones (as when imagining one is about to fall leads one to fall).

76. Cf., in this regard, *Critique of Pure Reason* A/843 ff. = B/871 ff. Previous philosophers are there accused of having not adequately distinguished that which is "in our power completely *a priori*," and that which is obtainable via experience. Likewise, they have not adequately distinguished (within the area of the a priori) the metaphysical and the mathematical. As a result they failed in the task of developing the idea of their science. Kant does not, to my knowledge, anywhere directly discuss the bearing of his discovery of the importance of abstraction on his later clarification of the distinction between the a priori and the a posteriori (and between metaphysics and mathematics). It is, however, clear that the power to abstract has considerable bearing on his treatment of the Second and Third Analogies, which turns on the distinction between mental changes we experience as subject to our control and those which we experience as ordered independently of our will.

77. See *Conflict of the Faculties* (VII:104; 188).

78. So construed, Kant's innovation lies in combining an (anti-Leibnizian) awareness of the plurality of the powers of the mind with a (Leibnizian) appreciation of its unity. On this point, see Henrich, "Unity of Subjectivity."

79. Cf. (VII:220; [89]), where Kant defines a talent or natural gift as an "excellence of the means of knowledge that depends not on the instruction, but on the natural disposition [*Anlage*] of the subject."

80. The common characteristic of insanity is "loss of *common sense* (*sensus communus*) and substitution of *logical private sense* (*sensus privatus*)." To refuse to attend to the criterion of what others judge is to abandon oneself to a play of thought in which one thinks and acts, not in a common world, but a world of one's own, "as in dreaming" (VII:219; 88–89). On others' understanding as the *criterion veritatis externum* (external criterion of truth), see also VII:128; 10.

81. Kant adds here that if the vital force is continually promoted beyond its proper level, "what could follow but swift death in the face of joy?" The idea here seems to be the Brunonian one that every organism has its own proper quantity of vital force (in Kant's case, as he elsewhere notes, a rather meager one). Thus too much stimulus as well as too little can be fatal. On the importance to Kant of the medical doctrines of John Brown, see note 139 below.

82. See, for example, Jachmann, in Borowski, Jachmann, and Wasianski, *Immanuel Kant*, pp. 162–63.

83. To be sure, Kant's own hypochondria bespeaks a heightened sense of bodily interiority that borders on the feminine. We have already noted the customary association, in contemporary medical discussions, of hypochondria and hysteria. In an unpublished note, Kant suggests that swooning is for women what vertigo is for men (*Reflection* no. 134 [XV:19]). The difference, it would seem, lies in the fact that women (hysterics) actually lose consciousness, whereas men (hypochondriacs) undergo a kind of limit experience that embraces the extremes of consciousness and unconsciousness. What (most) women lack is, precisely, sublimity, that is to say, the capacity to represent in and for consciousness the incongruity of reason and unreason. (See also *Anthropology* [VII:166; 44].)

Cf., in this regard, Sarah Kofman, *Le respect des femmes*. Like many thinkers heavily indebted to Freud, Kofman takes a certain "materialism" for granted. It has been the burden of my analysis to suggest that the ambiguous relation between "mind" and "matter" is, for Kant, precisely what is at issue. Cf. also Lewis Feuer, "Lawless Sensations and Categorical Defenses: The Unconscious Sources of Kant's Philosophy," in C. Hanly and M. Lazerowitz, eds., *Psychoanalysis and Philosophy*. Feuer treats Kant's rejection of empiricism as ipso facto pathological.

84. See Karl Vorländer, *Der Mann und das Werk*, vol. 1, pp. 131, 192–93; and J. H. W. Stuckenberg, *The Life of Immanuel Kant*, pp. 189–91. Cf. Kant's comment late in life that when he could have used a wife he lacked means of supporting one, and when he had means, he no longer needed one (Vorländer, p. 194).

85. Cf. chapter 4 above.

Kant's discussion of the noble and aesthetic sublime in the *Critique of Judgment* treats the phlegmatic temperament somewhat less favorably. In general, Kant seems to have wanted sublimity in a woman without being able, quite, to reconcile that quality with femininity. (Cf. in this regard his discussion, in the *Remarks*, of the woman who perfectly unites beauty and sublimity.)

86. That essay, part 3 of the *Conflict of the Faculties*, was written in January 1798 and published independently in C. W. Hufeland's *Journal of Practical Pharmacology and Surgery*. Part 1, "On the Conflict between the Philosophical and Theological Faculties," was written in 1794, but Kant deferred publication to avoid censorship problems. Part 2, "On the Conflict between the Philosophical and Juridical Faculties" (or *An Old Question Newly Raised: Is the Human Race Constantly Progressing?*), was written in 1797. Kant does not seem to have thought of publishing the three essays together until sometime in 1798.

87. On the relation between philosophy and medicine seen from the other side, see Kant's *Announcement of the Near Conclusion of a Treaty for Eternal Peace in Philosophy*, which discusses the "physical causes" and "effect" of "human philosophy," and in which he compares the function of the natural "pressure" (*Drang*) to philosophize, to the function of the soul in pigs — given, as Chrysippus says, in place of salt to prevent their rotting. Philosophy, accordingly, is nature's way of preventing reason from "rotting alive" (VIII:413–14; 83–85). Since, human health "is an incessant cycle of illness and convalescence, it has not yet come to terms with the mere *diet* of practical reason (a gymnastics of reason, so to speak) in order to maintain the balance that is called health and that hovers on the tip of a hair; rather, philosophy must act (therapeutically) as a *remedy* (*materia medica*) for whose use, then, dispensaries and doctors . . . are required."

Kant's extended analogy proceeds in a way that combines two areas of increasing personal concern — continuing public opposition to his system, and his failing mental strength. The question he poses is whether an elusive philosophic peace (which he had claimed in the *Critique of Pure Reason* to conclude) is reconcilable with reason's natural well-being. Kant's answer manages to locate the cause of mental health in the very philosophic opposition he might otherwise be expected to find irksome. (He is thus able to declare, like the Stoic self-experimenter whom Kant here cites, that "pain is nothing evil.") Honest opposition that arises from misunderstanding can, if properly "policed," be counted on (like transcendental illusion) to keep the fighting spirit of reason alive. Kant thus finds a silver lining in the "cloud" of his declining public powers — or would, but for the presence of dishonest opposition, or lying (*Lüge*), which he concedes to be the "speck of rot in human nature." (Against the latter cloud there remains, if nothing else, the consolations of *Hudibras* [see Kant's Letter to J. C. C. Keisewetter, XII:258; 252].) See also XVIII:79 f. (*Reflection* no. 5073): "the critique of pure reason [is] a preservative against a sickness of reason the germ of which lies in our own nature." This sickness is "the opposite of the inclination (homesickness) that connects us to our fatherland — that is, [such sickness] is a longing to lose ourselves outside our circle and to relate to other worlds."

88. On the history of the essay, see the notes of the Akademie editors and those included in Gregor's translation. Hufeland sent his *Makrobiotik, oder die Kunst, das menschliche Leben zu verlängen* to Kant in December 1796. Kant replied with a letter of thanks, in which he noted his agreement with Hufeland's "bold but soul-elevating [*seelenerhabene*] idea of the power of man's moral disposition to animate even the physical element in him." Remarking that Hufeland had managed to put systematically what Kant had learned only in a fragmentary way, he indicated his intention to write an essay on his own regimen (*Diet*) (XII:148).

89. Kant's essay could thus be described as a (for once) permissible exercise in "egoism." On egoism and pluralism, see, for example, *Anthropology* (VII:128–34; 10–15); cf. O'Neill, *Constructions,* pp. 6–27. On society as a remedy for hypochondria (or overreliance on inner sense) see *Reflection* no. 1506 (XV:813).

90. Kant's exact words are as follows:

My examples confirming the possibility of this proposition [*Ausspruchs*] cannot be drawn from other people's experiences, but, first, only from what I have experienced in myself [*an mir selbst angestellten*], for they come from introspection [*Selbstbewußtsein*], and only afterwards can I ask others whether they have not noticed the same thing in themselves. I see myself thus forced [*Ich sehe mich also genöthigt*] to talk about myself [*mein Ich laut werden zu lassen;* literally, allow my "I" to become loud]; and although this would betray lack of modesty in a dogmatic treatise, it is excusable if it concerns not common experience, but rather an inner experiment or observation, which I had to make on myself before submitting to the consideration of others something that would not of itself occur to everyone unless he were led to it.

He adds in a note: "In dogmatic-practical treatises, for example, the sort of self-observation that is directed to duties incumbent on everyone, the pulpit-lecturer [*Kanzelredner*] speaks in terms of 'we,' not 'I.' But in the description of private feelings (the confessions that a patient gives to his doctor), or his personal experience as such, he must speak in terms of 'I.'" Kant leaves open which sort of discourse — medical confessional or personal story — his own here most resembles.

91. In Kant's words, "man's [wish for long life] is unconditioned [*unbedingt*]."

92. See Exodus 20:12; Luther's translation reads "Du sollst deinen Vater und deine Mutter ehren, wie dir der Herr, dein Gott, geboten hat, auf dass du lange lebest und dir's wohlgehe in dem Lande, das dir der Herr, dein Gott, geben wird." In Kant's version, "old age" (*Alter*) replaces "father" and "mother," and *Erde* replaces *Land,* God's giving of which is entirely omitted.

93. Kant's reference here to Nestor's age is a graceful (and ironic) allusion to Hufeland's earlier description of Kant as "the most honor worthy Nestor of our time." See Karl Vorländer's notes to the Akademie edition (VII:341).

94. Kant's use of *Mann,* where *Mensch* might otherwise be expected, reinforces the feminine associations of *Erde:* the honor due old age is, it seems, a peculiarly male prerogative.

95. Cf. Kant's own "exemplary" status, as discussed above. As we will see, however, that example, he believes, is one that few if any will follow.

96. Cf. *Critique of Pure Reason* B/168; and *Opus postumum* (XXII:99). Kant's famous answer to Hume concerning the nature of causality finds confirmation in the discrepancy between feeling well and being so.

97. The discrepancy between feeling and being as it relates to one's own bodily condition also bears on the human ability to act contrary to instinct. See, for example, *Conjectural Beginning of Human History* (VIII:111; 223).

98. Kant makes one exception to his general warning against heat: the abdomen should be kept warm to aid the intestines, which "must carry non-fluid matter so far" (VII:101; [183]).

99. On the state's interest in increasing population as a means of conducting

war, see chapter 6 above. That a ruler's destruction of his subjects in war is a sort of cannibalism is a recurrent theme in Kant's thought. Concern for problems of overpopulation and illegitimacy—not underpopulation—seems to motivate his own suggestion in the *Metaphysics of Morals* that a special tax be levied on bachelors.

100. Kant's argument jumps here (as if by a process of association?) from warmth, sleep, and coddling oneself (*sich pflegen*), to sexual activity. Presumably the latter is at once a self-indulgence and an unhealthy sort of labor. Cf. his description of bed as the "nest of many illnesses" (VII:101; [183]). Hufeland in his *Makrobiotik* had argued against *premature* sexual activity on the grounds that it draws off from a fixed quantity of vital force energy still needed for growth. As his own notes indicate, however, he did not, like Kant, believe that sexual activity generally (and therefore marriage) impedes longevity. Hufeland's influential essay no doubt contributed to nineteenth-century attitudes toward "vital energy" (intellectual and procreative) as a fixed sum needing husbanding.

101. For those less able mentally, Kant advises carefree puttering as a preventative against "dying from boredom."

102. Cf. Kant's distinction between *hypochondria vaga* and *hypochondria intestinalis* (or "topisch") (VII:103 n; 187 n). That which is corporeally most inward is medically outward or on the surface.

103. As in his earlier conjunction of medical and religious themes (through the rather humorous juxtaposition of what a pulpit orator says to his audience and what he may with propriety "confess" [or "take off/unburden himself of"] before his doctor), Kant's story combines the physical intimacies of a medical report with the hortatory quality of a tale of personal (in this case, secular) salvation. His publication here of what is most private or peculiar to himself would seem to represent the most excusable instance of such an act—one that allows the "I" to literally "become loud" (or sound) without canceling reason's universal *Stimme*. Kant, in other words, can, without breach of modesty, permissibly raise his own tone of voice—unlike the snobbish *Schwärmer* whose "newly raised tone" he elsewhere dismisses as *Adeptensprache*. See, for example, *On a Newly Arisen Superior Tone* (VIII:405 n; 72 n).

104. It is interesting to note, in this regard, Kant's comparison, in the *Prolegomena*, of precritical metaphysics to breathing foul air (*unreine Lust*), and skepticism to attempting not to breath. A "critique of pure reason," Kant continues, "must therefore be attempted . . . because there is no other way of supplying this pressing need [*dringenden Bedürfniss*] which is more than mere thirst for knowledge [*Wißbegierde*]" (IV:367; [116]). See also Yovel, *Kant and the Philosophy of History*, pp. 256–57. Critical philosophy is thus implicitly likened to a therapeutic means—a purgation of foul air that permits an otherwise intolerably positioned spirit to breath freely. The "irresistible law of necessity" that forces the emergence of critical philosophy is like that which forces us to breath, whatever the danger attendant on our doing so. One is reminded of Kant's claim to have been saved from death by a dream that he was drowning, an experience involving an intolerable conflict between the need to breath and willful suppression of that need. Critical philosophy is to the "human spirit" as was awakening from that dream (or emerging from any place whose foul air suffocates), a generative association that Kant's call for a rebirth (*Wiedergeburt*) of metaphysics explicitly invokes; a rebirth, moreover,

for which the present moment of "dissolution of all previous [partisan] connections" is said to be "most dangerous for the author but most favorable for the science."

105. Cf. Kant's claim in *Metaphysical Foundations of Natural Science* (IV:471; 8) that empirical psychology can, even less than chemistry, become a science. On later modifications of that view, see the text at note 128 below. On the special role of cheerfulness (*Fröhlichkeit*), see Kant's "Ethical Ascetics" in *Metaphysics of Morals* (VI:484–85; [273–74]):

> The rules for the exercise of virtue (exercitiorum virtuitis) aim at two attunements of mind [*Gemüthstimmungen*] in the fulfillment of its duties — stout [*wackern*] and cheerful (animus strenuus et hilaris). . . . The culture of virtue, i.e., moral ascetics, has in regard to the principles of vigorous, spirited [*muthigen*] and stout exercise of virtue, the saying of the stoics: accustom yourself *to put up* with the contingent [*zufälligen*] evils of life and *do without* its superfluous pleasures. . . . This is a kind of diet of human beings to preserve their health morally. Health, however, is only a negative kind of wellbeing; it cannot itself be felt. Something must be added to it, something that affords agreeable enjoyment of life, and yet is only moral. This is the ever-cheerful heart [*jederzeit fröhliche Herz*] according to the idea of the virtuous Epicurus. . . . The . . . discipline that a person practices on himself can only become meritorious and exemplary through the cheerfulness [*Frohsinn*] that accompanies it.

106. This perfectly ordinary condition, involving as it does the conscious willing of unconsciousness, is not without its paradoxes. On related problems surrounding awakening, see below.

107. Kant's aversion to constriction is suggested by his practice, as reported by De Quincey, of holding up his hose by a peculiar contrivance of his own devising, for the purpose of avoiding the circulatory obstruction caused by ordinary garters.

108. *Diet* from the Latin *dicta*, meaning "spoken rules," denotes a regimen or general way of conducting one's life; the term acquired very early, however, a preponderant reference to eating.

109. Such untimeliness in thinking (*Unzeit im Denken*) was perhaps in Nietzsche's mind when he called his un-Kantian, but in its own way therapeutic, early work *Untimely Thoughts* (*Unzeitgemäße Betrachtungen*).

According to Kant, the practice of reading or reflecting while dining alone "diverts vital force from the stomach," while walking and thinking at the same time places a similarly exhausting double demand on one's vital force. The remedy is to let one's imagination roam and to walk freely so that the exchange of objects prevent one's attention from becoming fixed (VII:109; 199). On the dangers of dining alone, especially if one is a philosopher, see VII:280; 145.

110. Kant refers to an illness that the *Copenhagen Newspaper* "described, about a year ago" (but that Kant says he himself came down with a year earlier), as an "epidemic of catarrh accompanied by *pressure of the head.*" Kant adds that he thinks it may be a kind of gout "that has to some extent penetrated the brain." A letter to Garve (Sept. 21, 1798 [XII:256–58; 250–52]) describes the seizure as having occurred "about a year and a half ago." Despite the slight discrepancy in dates, it seems likely that Kant became ill sometime during 1796. Kant seems to have associ-

ated the contagion with peculiar weather conditions (or "electricity of the air"). See, for example, *Opus postumum* (XXI:89); letter to Samuel Thomas Soemmering (Aug. 4, 1800 [XII:321]); and letter to Johann Benjamin Erhard (Dec. 20, 1799 [XII:296]). On Kant's subsequent extreme concern to protect himself from such conditions, see Jachmann, in Borowski, Jachmann, and Wasianski, *Immanuel Kant*, pp. 187–88; and Wasianski, pp. 281–82. On the mediating role of electricity as addressed by earlier figures such as Priestly and the vitalist Paul-Joseph Barthez, see Stafford, *Body Criticism*, pp. 414–26.

111. Kant's earlier attack of gout, which also involved a cramplike seizure of the brain, had its primary seat elsewhere, as Kant concluded from the redness of his toes (VII:107, 195). For a more optimistic account of the salutary effect of spasms for Kant, see Lyotard, "Judiciousness in Dispute, or Kant after Marx," in *The Lyotard Reader*, ed. Andrew Benjamin, pp. 324–59.

112. As Gregor notes, the grammatical subject is here unclear, an indication, perhaps, of the indistinguishability of that which would (ordinarily) act to relieve the oppression and the oppression itself. To put it another way, the organ that controls abstraction and attention (pulling and pushing) is itself, owing to Kant's affliction, in spasm, thus undermining the distinction — crucial to Kant's philosophic therapeutics — between intentional and involuntary distraction.

113. See Cassirer, *Kant's Life*, p. 410. According to Cassirer, Kant gave up lecturing in the summer of 1796 and in the same year declined the post of rector on the grounds of increasing feebleness. He vigorously protested, however, when an attempt was made two years later to restrict his public functioning in the university senate.

114. See Kant's comment here that "some people must devote [*widmet*] themselves entirely to metaphysics, since otherwise there would be no philosophy at all." Like marriage, metaphysics in the end proves to be a public service but a private sacrifice. (According to Grimm and Grimm, *Deutsches Wörterbuch*, *widmet* carries the archaic meaning of "to wed or marry.")

115. Cf. Gregor, translator's introduction in Kant, *Conflict of the Faculties*, p. xxiii. The context is a reflection comparing "the art of statecraft and that of medicine." Just as one has been recently compelled to "spin the threads of political science sooner from the duties of subjects than from the rights of citizens," so too "sicknesses have been driven off from physiology, so that not this but (pathology and) the clinic constitutes the beginning of medical science." The cause is that those who are well "don't feel themselves to be so, because it is mere consciousness of life, and only resistance to it arouses force to opposition. It is thus no wonder that Brown begins with the classification of illnesses." Kant goes on to classify the three acts of vital force as: (1) acts of labor (*Arbeiten*), (2) enjoyments, and (3) acts of vegetation. The latter may in turn be conducted with complaint, with pleasure, or with indifference with regard to feeling. In the last case the vital force operates merely mechanically, without the subject's intention (*Beabsichtigung*).

116. Cf. *Announcement of the Near Conclusion of a Treaty for Eternal Peace in Philosophy* (VIII:417; 88).

117. It is, however, the letter that Kant continues to want to lean on; cf. VII:115 n; 211 n. See also his "Declaration concerning Fichte's *Wissenschaftslehre*,"

in which Kant announces, following a sharp criticism of Fichte, that "critical philosophy must in spite of this feel convinced of its irresistible propensity [*Tendenz*] to satisfy reason from a theoretical as well as moral, practical viewpoint [*Absicht*], convinced that no change of opinions, no touching up or reconstruction into some other form, is in store for it; convinced that the system of the *Critique,* resting on a fully secured foundation, is held fast forever, and also [convinced] that it will be indispensable for the highest ends of mankind in all future ages" (Aug. 7, 1799 [XII:371; (254)]). It would not be the least irony of his waning years if in publicly denouncing Fichte (for "meaning one thing and saying another"), Kant was himself guilty of duplicity.

118. Concerning Kant's unhappiness over his declining powers, see his letter to Christian Garve, who was at the time suffering from a painful malignant tumor of the face:

> The description of your physical suffering affected me deeply. . . . But I wonder whether the lot that has befallen me . . . would not, if you were to put yourself in my place, feel even more painful. For I am as paralyzed [*gelähmt*] for mental labor [*Geistarbeit*], though physically reasonably well. I see before me the unpaid bill of my uncompleted philosophy, even as I am aware, both as regards ends and means, that it is capable of being completed—a Tantalus-like pain that yet isn't hopeless. The task, with which I now busy myself, is the "transition from the metaphysical foundations of natural science to physics." It must be completed lest there remain a gap [*Lücke*] in the system of critical philosophy. The claims of reason for this will not let up: nor consciousness of the capacity, but their satisfaction is put off, if not through complete paralysis of my vital force, then through its increasing limitation [*Hemmungen*], in a way that is to the highest degree insufferable [*Ungedult*]. My healthiness . . . is not that of a scholar but a vegetable." (Sept. 21, 1798 [XII:257; (251)])

Cassirer speaks of Kant's painful feeling of "a total end to his counting for anything in matters concerning *all* of philosophy" (*Kant's Life,* p. 410).

119. I do not thereby mean to imply that these fragments are to be regarded as the product of Kant's "senility" in any crude sense; a long-held belief to that effect (a belief that no doubt contributed to what has until recently been an almost total neglect of the *Opus postumum* in the scholarship) has recently been laid definitively to rest by the seminal work of Eckart Förster, Burkhard Tuschling, and Michael Friedman, to which my reading is indebted. There is nonetheless a certain poignant irony in Kant's having had to leave in so inconclusive a state his final— and in some ways most ambitious—effort to resolve fragments (or *farrago*—a term that literally denotes the forage fed to cattle) into a systematic whole. *Farrago* often appears in the *Opus postumum* as a synonym for aggregate or fragmentary collection: see (XXI:114), (XXI:484), (XXI:478), (XXI:615), (XXII:172), (XXII:474), and (XXII:486). On the further posthumous fragmentation of the manuscript, see Förster's very helpful discussion in his introduction to the *Opus postumum.*

120. Kant's description of the ether as a "continual excitation of world matter" and as a kind of "inner vibration" or "tremor" (see, for example, XXI:310) calls to

mind his account of the sublime in the *Critique of Judgment*, as well as the less satisfactory spiritual "oscillations" of the *Universal Natural History*.

All matter must have repulsive forces because otherwise it would fill no space; but attractive force must also be attributed to it, because otherwise it would disperse itself into the infinity of space — in both cases space would be empty. Consequently, one can think of such alternating [*wechsel-nde*] impacts and counter-impacts [as happening] from the beginning of the world, as a trembling (oscillating, vibrating) motion of the matter that fills the whole space world, includes within itself all bodies, and is both elastic and at the same time attractive to itself. These pulsations constitute a living force, and never allow dead force through mere pressure and counter-pressure (i.e., absolute rest in the innermost of matter) to occur.

And XXI:504: "All touch is repulsion [*Abstoβung*]. The beginning of repulsion is the shock [*Stoss*]. Repulsion continually exchanging with the attraction of matter is tremulous motion (. . . internal oscillation). This, as the motion of an original, fluid material, is heat." That this "all penetrating matter" has a spiritual affinity lacking in Kant's earlier concept of "all penetrating attraction" is suggested by one of his names for ethereal agitation — *Schwungsbewegung*, or "impetuous motion" (see, for example, XXI:591).

On Kant's association of ether with Euler's theory of pulsation (*pulsus*), see Förster, introduction to *Opus postumum;* and Louis Guillermit, *L'elucidation critique du jugement de goût selon Kant*, pp. 143–47. See also *Critique of Judgment* (V:224; 70).

121. For a persuasive reconstruction of the development of Kant's argument, see Förster's introduction to the *Opus postumum*.

122. See his letter to G. C. C. Kiesewetter, October 19, 1798 (XII:258–59; 252): "The state my health is that of an old man, free from illness, but nevertheless an invalid, a man above all who is superannuated for the performance of any official or public service, who nevertheless feels a little bit of strength still within him to complete the work at hand; with that work the task of the critical philosophy will be completed and a gap that now stands open will be filled. I want to make the *transition* from the metaphysical foundations of natural science to physics into an actual branch of natural philosophy, one that must not be left out of the system."

In an earlier letter to Christian Garve (Sept. 21, 1798 [XII:256–58; (250–51)]), Kant similarly speaks of the transition as something he must complete lest a gap remain in the critical philosophy. Reason, he continues, will not give up its demands for this; neither can the awareness of the possibility be extinguished; but the satisfaction of this demand is maddeningly postponed, if not by the total paralysis of his vital powers [*Lebenskraft*] then by their ever increasing obstruction [*Hemmungen*]. Not altogether by accident, Kant's final effort to complete his system — an effort rooted in the subject's knowledge of itself as an active agent of force — is contemporaneous with his own experience of diminished capacity in that regard.

123. Much debate has been waged over the status of this gap. One thing that is clear is Kant's eagerness to complete the "transition" which he described in private as the "keystone" of his system (Jachmann, in Borowski, Jachmann, and Wasianski,

Immanuel Kant, p. 124). In 1795 Humboldt reported to Schiller, on the basis of information received from Memel, that Kant was still carrying a monstrous load of ideas in his head, which he still intended to work out, so that he reckoned his life span more in accordance with the size of that stock of ideas than by the normal probabilities. See Humboldt to Schiller, *Briefwechsel,* ed. A. Leitzmann, as cited in Cassirer, *Kant's Life,* p. 409. Evidently, Kant's calculation on this score preceded his epidemic attack (which his letter to Garve places sometime near the beginning of 1796.) One is compelled to wonder whether Kant's conviction as to the existence of a "gap" in his system was not partly the outcome of a new appreciation, brought on by his own declining powers, for what he strikingly refers to as the "tyranny" of nature.

124. Förster makes a persuasive case for Kant having first thought of composing a transition from the metaphysical foundations of natural science to physics sometime between 1787 and 1790. Still, the fact that Kant writes in the preface to the *Critique of Judgment* (1790), "With this . . . I bring my entire critical undertaking to a close," suggests that only later did he come to view that transitional project as the closing of a gap that threatened the integrity of his system. (Cf. the account by one of his intimates that Kant regarded the manuscript as "his chief work, a chef d'oeuvre," and "an (absolute) whole completing his system.") See J. G. Hasse, *Letzte Äußerungen Kants von einem seiner Tischgenossen,* p. 22, quoted in Förster, introduction to *Opus postumum,* pp. xvi–xvii.

Förster points to Kant's discovery of a certain circularity in his earlier account of material density as one source of this reorientation. And Michael Friedman, in *Kant and the Exact Sciences,* has shown the importance of new developments in chemistry — developments Kant followed with the greatest interest — in promoting his systematic ambitions. One wonders, however, if Kant's Tantalus-like efforts to secure gap-free systemicity did not also owe something to his growing sense of inner fragmentation — a loss of that spiritual self-presence, or ability through an idea to hold everything "as a whole" before the mind, on which he prided himself and which was, for Kant, the characteristic mark of the philosopher. Kant's claim that he compensated for this loss "by writing" is perhaps particularly significant in this regard, given the dazzling profusion of unfinished text Kant left behind.

125. For one exception, see the following very early passage, which follows a reference to "nature as an art" and is accompanied by the title "Of the Whole of Nature in Space and Time": "In the investigation of nature, human reason is not content to pass from metaphysics to physics; there lies in it a fruitless, but not inglorious instinct to transcend even the latter, to exalt [*schwärm*] in a hyperphysics, and to create for itself a whole of nature of still greater extent, namely, in an idea world, according to projections [*Entwürfen*] directed toward moral ends, so that God and the immortality of the soul alone (the former as *natura naturans,* the latter as *natura naturata*) could entirely encompass our desire for knowledge of nature in general" (XXI:404–5; [17]). On the other hand, Kant in earlier sections of the *Opus postumum* tries to define the transition from metaphysics to physics in terms of a "tendency" (or "natural indication [*Hinweisung*] of reason toward an end") on the part of the metaphysical foundations of natural science toward physics (see, for

example, XXII:166), almost as if critical philosophy were itself an organic being endowed with reason.

126. See, for example, XXII:356, XXII:308, XXII:494, and XXII:481: The concept of an organic body (that contains a principle of life) already presupposes experience; for without this the mere idea of the former would be an empty concept (without example). But man has in himself an example thereof, an understanding that contains moving force and determines a body according to laws.

127. See, for example, XXII:50; but cf. XXI:89.

128. See Friedman, *Kant and the Exact Sciences*, p. 264 ff. Friedman documents the replacement in Kant's late work of Stahl's "phlogistonic" theory with the new chemistry of Lavoisier. Cf., in this regard, *Critique of Pure Reason* (1787) (B/xii–xiii), with *Anthropology* (1798) (VII:326) and *Metaphysics of Morals* (1797) (VI:207; 36), which refers to Lavoisier's establishment of "one chemistry" (a passage, I would add, in which Kant speaks with similar approval of Brown vis à vis medicine). As Friedman convincingly argues, Lavoisier's "revolution" in chemistry would have most likely seemed to Kant to consist in an integration of two earlier developments — the "pneumatic" chemistry associated with Priestly (among others), and the new research into heat associated with Joseph Black and Johan Carl Wilcke — with traditional analytic chemistry and metallurgy associated with Boerhaave, Becher, and Stahl, the key being "Lavoisier's oxygen theory of combustion and acidity" (p. 267; see also H. Guerlac, *Lavoisier: The Crucial Year;* and "Chemistry as a Branch of Physics: Laplace's Collaboration with Lavoisier," in *Historical Studies in the Physical Sciences* 7: 193–276).

Black's special contribution was a theory of latent heat that made it tempting to regard heat as a material substance in its own right (not just motion or vibration of ordinary matter) — a material substance capable of combining chemically with other substances in a such a way as to change them to the liquid or (newly discovered) gaseous state (Friedman, p. 270). Of special interest for our purposes is Lavoisier's notion (as expressed in an article in German by J. S. T.Gehler) that rigidity and fluidity are not essential properties of a substance, but the result of the chemical combination of a substance with heat. Gases, according to this reasoning, are to be understood as solutions in heat-element or caloric (Friedman, pp. 277–78).

129. Another approach to the problem of rigidity emerges from Kant's comments of 1795 on Samuel Thomas Soemmering's *Über das Organ der Seele* (XII:30–35). Although Kant continues to insist on the absurdity involved in attempting to find a spatial location for the soul, he is clearly taken with Soemmering's anatomical research into the importance of the water contained in the cavern of the brain (*Gehirnhöhle*) as a material condition for the unity of all sense representations in the mind. According to Soemmering, the only matter that qualifies as a *sensorium commune* is this liquid, which "on the one hand separates the nerve bundles ending in it so that the accompanying sensations do not become mixed, while on the other hand effecting among them a thorough going community." The difficulty, Kant continues, is that "water, being a liquid, cannot properly be conceived as organized. But without organization, i.e., without parts that are purposive and persistent in their form, no matter can serve as immediate organ of the soul." Liquid is the sort

of matter whose parts "the smallest force" can move from their former place, a property that "seems to contradict" the concept of an organized matter, which one thinks of as a machine (thus as rigid), capable of resisting the displacement of its parts (hence also the alteration of its inner configuration).

The difficulty, Kant suggests, might be resolved if instead of a *mechanical* organization one proposed a *dynamical* organization, based on chemical principles and thus compatible with the liquidity of such material. Just as the mathematical division of a space and the matter it contains (for example, the brain cavity and its encompassed water) can be carried on to infinity, so too can a chemical or dynamic division (separation of different reciprocally dissolved kinds in a matter) be carried on infinitely or indefinitely. Pure water, only recently thought to be an element, can now be separated through pneumatic experiments into two different kinds of air. Each of these kinds of air has in it, in addition to its basis, the caloric, which can itself, perhaps, be further decomposed (*zersetzen*) by nature into light-stuff and other materials, light into various colors, etc. Then, too, what an immense multiplicity of partly volatile substances plants are able to produce from common water, speculatively — through continual decomposition and recombination. One can thus represent the nerve ends finding in the cerebral water a variety of substances capable of making them receptive to the sensible world and, reciprocally, able to act upon it.

If, then, one accepts the hypothesis that the mind in empirical thought, that is, in the dissolving and composition of given sensible representations, is supported by a capacity of the nerves to decompose, each in its particular way, the brain water into elementary substances, and thus, through the release of one or another of these, to let play various sensations (for example, light, through the optic nerve, sound through the auditory nerve, etc.) in such a way that, after the stimulus ceases, the stuff at once recombines; then we could say such water "is continually becoming organized without ever being so." One would thus arrive at what one aimed at with persistent organization, namely the collective unity of all sensible representations in a common organ, but only made comprehensible according to its chemical analysis. (This, of course, does not solve the problem as Haller defined it: namely identification of the unity of the common sense organ with the unity of self-consciousness, a task that is absurd inasmuch as it involves representing the soul's "seat" as a local presence.)

Kant's suggestion, in short, is a new conception of material organization — not wholly dependent on rigidity — that approximates to a degree whose possibility is not otherwise thinkable the structure of consciousness itself. That suggestion is expanded in an unpublished draft (XIII:398–414), in which he compares the reordering of the cerebral water following stimulation to the reorganization (according to "laws of vitality") that occurs when we awaken out of sleep, and which he also links to an explanation of insanity and the production of hybrids.

Kant's attentions to Soemmering may be related to a contemporaneous interest in Franz Joseph Gall's craniology, as reported by Karl Reusch, Gall's student and a frequent dinner guest in Kant's later years. On the latter point, see *Opus postumum* (XXI:80); and notes to the Cambridge University Press translation (p. 284).

130. See Friedman, *Kant and the Exact Sciences*, pp. 308–9. Representation of the ether has what Friedman usefully calls collective, as well as distributive, univer-

sality. The author delineates a number of other attempts, all of which, he argues, end in failure (as Kant himself may or may not have recognized). Friedman explicitly excludes from his consideration Kant's extensive treatment of life and the organic.

131. See (XXII:78; 186–87): Mathematics is "indirectly founded" through philosophy. See also his comments concerning the mating of metaphysics' horse and mathematics' griffin (XXII:490. XXI:208; 63).

132. See Eckart Förster's expanded account of the role of the "ether proofs" in effecting this transition, in Förster, ed., *Kant's Transcendental Deductions,* pp. 223 ff. As he shows, the ether proofs allow Kant to move from consciousness of oneself as a self-moving machine (whose possibility is not further derivable) to the notion of an a priori concept of moving forces that our experience of motion (and in the first instance, our own motion) presupposes (see, for example, XXI:490). For a different view as to the status of the *ether,* see Friedman, *Kant and the Exact Sciences,* especially p. 305 n. (Friedman's alternative view, which places greater weight on ether's constitutive role, does not effect the matter at hand.)

133. See (XXI:78; 245): "Transcendental philosophy is the act of consciousness whereby the subject becomes the originator [*Urheber*] of itself and, thereby, also of the whole object of technical-practical and moral-practical reason in one system — ordering all things in God, as in one system." But cf. (XXI:404–5; 17), quoted in note 125 above. Evidently, Kant came to set more store by that instinct (or *Tendenz*), moving in the process from the guiding notion of a hypernature (or supersensible substrate) to an idea of matter that not only grounds the possibility of experience as a whole, but also, by virtue of its a priority — or purposiveness *for* experience — helps to certify man's world authorship. Cf. (XXII:449–50; 167): the proposition "I am to myself an object of the intuition and thought of the manifold of the intuition of myself" is "a synthetic a priori proposition into whose possibility I cannot inquire." This same proposition is said to be the principle of transcendental philosophy, "which answers the problem: How are synthetic propositions a priori possible?"

See also XXI:93–94: "Transcendental philosophy is the capacity of the self-determining subject to constitute itself as *given* in intuition, through the systematic complex of ideas which, a priori, make the thoroughgoing determination of the subject as object (its existence) into a problem. To make *oneself,* as it were." And XXI:152: "The formal [*Formale*] of the exhibition of the absolute whole of all beings in a system of them according to the principle of reason determining itself not only analytically but also synthetically is not God as being in the world but rather the pure idea of self construction like the pure intelligence of the subject itself. — The highest intelligence. The highest seeing; imagination and fantasy are not the same."

134. See, for example, (XX:383; [120]):

physics has as its object things whose cognition is only possible through experience, that is, such objects, whose concept, idea, or even fiction, as being without any reality (though also without internal contradiction), have no guarantee for their possibility, which they can only have from experience [for example, the concept of organized body]. . . . Nevertheless, since man can represent not only a feeling of his own body, but also a sensible presentation, combined with understanding, of his own form, abstracting from this object and thus in a universal concept, he can recognize himself by experience in something that would otherwise have to be rejected from his concepts as an empty fantasy. — Thus there are sense objects (even) whose possibility is only thinkable through actuality.

See also (XX:481; [137]): "The possibility of an organic body cannot be proved or postulated; but it is still a fact. To know oneself in experience as an organic body. N B *The concept of an immediately and primitively moving material* (CALORIC). The concept of organic bodies (which contain a vital principle) already presupposes experience: for without it, even the mere idea of organic bodies would be an empty concept (without example). But man has an example of the former in himself, [that is] of an understanding that contains moving forces, which determine a body according to laws."

135. See (XX:546 ff.; [84 ff.]), where Kant insists that the concept of an organic being requires more than matter, i.e., that it requires what he calls "a world soul, as it were," and this (in part) because "under no circumstances can it be a property of matter to have an *intention,* since it is the absolute unity of a subject which *connects* the manifold in one consciousness." At (XX:504; [148]), he admits world soul "to make purposive generation thinkable (not explicable)," but world soul only as "anima bruta," not thinking being or "spiritus." See also (XX:38; 177):

Spontaneity and receptivity with reaction at the same time.

(Not organized matter, for that is a contradiction, but organic body.)

Of the necessity of spiritual forces for the sake of organic bodies and even organic systems; because one must attribute an understanding to their cause in whicn the subject is thought of as a simple being (of the sort which matter or an element of matter cannot be).

At (XX:507; 149) Kant argues that matter being infinitely divisible, the principle underlying the possibility of organic body cannot be material, which isn't to say that one is allowed to assume that this cause is "a soul inherent in the body" or "a world-soul belonging to the aggregate of matter in general." In other words, he here reaffirms that we attribute an intelligent cause to organized bodies only on the basis of an "analogy." But cf. (XXI:137): "The world is an animal: but its soul is not God"; and (XXI:570): "as to whether [the immaterial basis of organic being] (a world soul, so to speak) is an understanding or only the effects of a capacity analogous to understanding, is a judgment outside the limits of our insight." See also XXII:114.

136. On possible connections with Schelling's *Von der Weltseele, eine Hypothese der höheren Physik zur Erklärung des allgemeinen Organismus,* see Förster, in the Cambridge University Press translation of *Opus postumum,* p. 274 n.

137. See, for example, XXI:100: "Tr.[anscendental] Ph.[ilosophy] is the self creation (autonomy) of theoretical/speculative and moral/practical reason"; for other uses of autonomy in a nonmoral context, see also (XXII:78; 186–87) and (XXII:447; 165). *Autonomy* is also used to describe the creation of ideas. See (XXI:79; 246), (XXI:81; 248), and XXI:156: "The final end of all knowledge is to recognize oneself in the highest practical reason." Transcendental philosophy is

also called the "self-creation (autocracy) of ideas to a complete system of the objects of pure reason" (XXI:84; 249–50). See also (XXII:129–30; 209): "The subject of the categorical imperative in me is an object which deserves to be obeyed: an object of adoration. . . . The idea of a being which would be its own originator [*Urheber*], would be the original being, and a product (not an educt) of pure practical reason. — The concept of it (the subject) is identical with it (the object) and transcendent [*überschwenglich*] without being contradictory." In general, the *Opus postumum* stresses God's role as moral legislator within us, as distinguished from his role as creator. (Indeed, as moral being, man cannot be created [XXI:65].)

138. See, for example, XXII:379, XXI:57, XXI:100, XXI:131, and XXI:134; see also his reference to systematic science at XXI:478 as a "physiologia generalis."

139. One contributing factor was undoubtedly Kant's interest in the theories of John Brown (1735–88), which seemed to offer a principle on which the rational division of medicine might be based. According to Brown, life is a "forced state" caused by stimuli or "exciting powers"; these, in turn, consisting either in external stimuli (heat, nourishment, etc.) or internal stimuli (muscular contraction and the force exercised by the brain). Death is a function either of too little stimulation or too much, and health a result both of stimulus and of the organism's predisposition to stimulation. Brown's classification (based on a principle of dynamic equilibrium) into sthenic and asthenic diseases seemed to Kant "irreproachable" as far as its systematic form was concerned, though he was less taken with Brown's empirical findings (see the *Metaphysics of Morals*, where Kant calls Brown's "the only principle for systematically classifying diseases" (VI:207; [36]. And *Reflection* no. 1539 [XV:963]). See Gregor's helpful introduction to her translation of *On Philosophers' Medicine of the Body*, in Beck, *Kant's Latin Writings*, p. 224. Brown's system, which was highly controversial in its day, is one source of the still popular use of "tonics" as a "stimulus" to health, a technique that Kant employed (in moderation) but that apparently killed their inventor (who is supposed to have died of an overdose of opium and whiskey).

140. See, for example, XXI:83; 249.

141. See, for example, XXII:481: "The possibility of an organic body cannot be proved or postulated, but it is still a fact — to recognize oneself in experience as an organic body." (The discussion concludes with a definitive rejection of atomism.)

142. See in this regard XXI:612: "Analogy between the Newtonian gravitational system — the autom/organization system — the Brunonian system of health and the — intellectual or supersensual system of mentality [*Seelichkeits System*]. On the difference between living force and vital force — The latter analogy with the Brunonian system of vital force [of] organized bodies, for organized matter is nothing." See also XXI:89, XXI:100, and XXI:118.

143. Yet another series of passages inserts this link between the feeling of heat and the caloric within zoonomy as a whole, which Kant divides according to its concern with (1) "nerve force" as the Brunonian principle of excitability; (2) "muscle force" as the Hallerian principle of irritability; (3) both forces in continual active and reactive play: an all-penetrating, all-moving substance of which heat is a phenomenon; and (4) an immaterial "organization force" in space and time consisting in efficacy according to ends (XXII:300–301). See also

XXII:100. To be sure, Kant is careful elsewhere to distinguish the subjective *feeling* of heat from the caloric as objective basis of experience (see, for example, XXI:109–10).

144. XXII:299–300; [103]. This fourth division is also associated with force of will (*Willenskraft*) and "assigns the creature, as intelligence, to the moving forces of nature." Kant continues: "These belong all together in the field of physics, in which there are no laws of freedom, but which contains all forces that self-initiate the motion of matter—not just those that continue motion. The skillful initiator [*Kunsturheber*] of these motions for the preservation of vital force is also called a *physician* (town or country doctor [as opposed to *Medizin*]), and his branch of the study of nature is called zoonomy." Here and elsewhere, Kant plays on the connection between "physics" and "physician" (*Physiker*), the term by which practicing medical doctors are colloquially known (see, for example, XXII:407; 122). Like the philosophically engaged subject, the physician is referred to as an *Urheber* or originator; and the two are, indeed, involved in parallel projects, especially insofar as the physician strives to keep himself alive. See also XXI:102: "Practical medicine also belongs to physics; and its greatest service is to be one, a hippocratic medicine, which grounds itself on experiences which should be called perceptions and yet is only one."

145. XXI:3–4 and XXI:6. Cf. XXI:158.

146. XXII:499; 144–45: a living body contains a principle of animal or vegetative life, which seems to include "a healthy, sick or dying state, and regeneration—not, indeed, of the same individual but of a body which preserves the species, from similar materials, through intercourse of two sexes." See also (XXII:406–7; 122): "In physics, however, . . . there must be included thought entities . . . as problematic, for the division of possible moving forces of matter; these are thought as so constituted that they *cannot* be thought *otherwise* than through experience. Of this kind are organic bodies, every part of which is there for the sake of the other, and whose existence can *only* be thought in a system of purposes (which must have an immaterial cause); of which the perception by man of his own organs furnishes the example. (Darwin's *Zoonomia*, Cullen, Brown, who are called physicians. . . .)"

147. See also XXII:379: "The transition to physics also stems from the human doctrine of health and sickness; thus [the term] town and country physicians [*Physiker*]. The doctrine of experience of moving forces of matter presupposes all around a priori principles."

148. See (XXI:212–13; 65–66) (dated 1798):

One must also think of a world organization as of a unified body, in which no forms disappear without bringing forth other better ones. . . . The idea of organic bodies is *indirectly* contained a priori in that of a composite of moving forces, in which the concept of a real *whole* necessarily precedes that of its parts—which can only be thought by the concept of a combination according to *purposes*. Regarded *directly*, it is a mechanism which can be known only empirically. . . . How can we include such bodies with such moving forces in the general classification, according to *a priori* principles? Because man is conscious of himself as a self-moving machine, without being able to further understand such a possibility, he can . . . introduce *a priori* organic-moving forces of bodies into the classification of bodies in general. . . . He [must], however, generalize the concept of vital force and of the excitability of matter in his own self by the faculty of desire. . . . By the same principle, the emergence of the organism of matter and its organization as a system for the needs of different *species,* becomes possible, from the vegetable kingdom to the animal kingdom (at which point *desires,* as true *vital* forces of bodily substances, first arise). One species is made for the other (the goose for the fox, the stag for the wolf), according to the differences between the races — indeed, perhaps, according to different primordial forms, now vanished. . . . Eventually, our all-producing globe itself (as an organic body which has emerged from chaos), completed this purpose in the mechanism of nature. To set a beginning or an end to this process, however, wholly exceeds the bounds of human reason [being, as Kant later puts it, "entirely hidden from our spying gaze." Kant does, however, exclude man from the now vanished forms destroyed by revolutions in the earth's lap (*Schooβ*)].

Elsewhere, this inability to set the beginning or the end overturns the alarming (*Besorgnis*) "horror of annihilation" in the face of the stasis that would eventually overtake the motion of the ether (XXI:519). Cf. (XX:549 n; 85–86 n), where Kant presents as "not [yet] to be thought" that "there are to be discovered, in the strata of the earth . . . examples of former kinds of animals and plants (now extinct) — proofs of previous (now alien) products of our living, fertile [*gebärenden*] globe," and, generally speaking, that the totality of species (man not excepted) "require each other" so as to point towards "a world organization (to unknown ends) of the galaxy itself."

149. On the theme of "earth revolutions," see also XXI:214 f. and XXI:567. At XXII:210 Kant distinguishes between living and vivifying force, the latter of which, in a separate world-system (and its generation), "is perhaps the cause of *plants* and *animals.*" Kant seems persuaded in these early passages that one can form such hypotheses "without transgressing the limits, determined a priori, of the transition to physics, or mixing into the material part of it." And this because although things are established only problematically, the "concept of a *system* of the moving forces of matter requires . . . the concept of an *animated* matter — which we at least think a priori . . . (without demanding — or surreptitiously assuming — a reality for it)" (XXI:184; 60).

150. See, for example, (XXII:494–95; [142]), where after speaking of "vital force in excitability" and of motion in the brain, the heart, the lung; and after listing (1) the object in pure a priori intuition, (2) in appearance (of oneself), (3) in perception or empirical intuition, (4) in experience, Kant adds: "Organic creatures have not just a life but also a vital feeling which is eroded [*aufreibt*] through intercourse [*Begattung*] and for insects through exhaustion. Amazing [*wundersam*] that no organic beings propagate without two sexes." See also XXII:99–100, XXI:346, XXI:349, XXI:568, XXI:571 (the latter two also mention Milton and/ or his doctrine of "male light"), and XXII:499. Cf. Kant's attempt at (XX:546 ff.; 84 ff.) to divorce the a priori concept of an organic body from its empirically sexual means of propagation.

151. See especially XXI:89, XXI:100, and XXI:118.

Coda

1. Dr. Wilhelm Gottlieb Kelch, "Privatlehrer der Medicin und Profector am anatomischen Theater zu Königsberg," reprinted from the edition of 1804 and expanded with a frontispiece of the exhumation of Kant's skull and five skull photographs, with accompanying remarks by Karl Kupffer and Fritz Bessel Hagen, July 1880.

2. See also *Opus postumum* (XXI:80) and notes to the Cambridge University Press translation, p. 284. According to Gall's student Karl Reusch, Kant was eager to hear about the latest developments in craniology and galvanism. Unlike Kant, who evidently found something in both sorts of studies appealing, Hegel rejected phrenology while embracing galvanism (which he associated with maternal/fetal influence) (see, for example, *Phenomenology of Spirit*, nos. 310–46; the *Philosophy of Nature*, no. 333; and the *Philosophy of Mind*, no. 405).

3. Amos Elon, "The Nowhere City," *New York Review of Books*.

Works Cited

Works by Kant

In citing the *Critique of Pure Reason,* I refer, as is customary, to the pagination of the original "A" (1781) and "B" (1787) editions. All other references to Kant's work cite the volume and page number of the Akademie edition (*Kants Gesammelte Schriften,* ed. Königliche Preußische (later Deutsche) Akademie der Wissenschaften [Berlin: Walter de Gruyter, 1902–)]. Wherever possible, such references are followed by the page number of an available English translation (preceded by a semicolon), as listed alphabetically below. In cases where my own translation differs, wholly or in part, from the translation cited, page references to the latter are placed in brackets.

Announcement of the Near Conclusion of a Treaty for Eternal Peace in Philosophy. Trans. Peter Fenves. In Peter Fenves, ed., *Raising the Tone of Philosophy: Late Essays by Immanuel Kant, Transformative Critique by Jacques Derrida.* Baltimore: Johns Hopkins University Press, 1993.

Announcement of the Programme of his Lectures for the Winter Semester (1765–66). Trans. David Walford and Ralf Meerbote. In *Theoretical Philosophy, 1755–1770* (The Cambridge Edition of the Works of Immanuel Kant). Ed. David Walford and Ralf Meerbote. Cambridge: Cambridge University Press, 1992.

Answer to the Question: What is Enlightenment? Trans. H. B. Nisbet. In *Kant's Political Writings,* 2d ed. Ed. with an introduction and notes by Hans Reiss. Cambridge: Cambridge University Press, 1970.

Anthropology from a Pragmatic Point of View. Trans. with an introduction and notes by Mary J. Gregor. The Hague: Nijhoff, 1974.

An Attempt at Some Reflections on Optimism. Trans. David Walford and Ralf Meerbote. In *Theoretical Philosophy, 1755–1770* (The Cambridge Edition of the Works of Immanuel Kant). Ed. David Walford and Ralf Meerbote. Cambridge: Cambridge University Press, 1992.

Attempt to Introduce the Concept of Negative Magnitudes into Philosophy. Trans. David Walford and Ralf Meerbote. In *Theoretical Philosophy, 1755–1770* (The Cambridge Edition of the Works of Immanuel Kant). Ed. David Walford and Ralf Meerbote. Cambridge: Cambridge University Press, 1992.

The Blomberg Logic. Trans. J. Michael Young. In *Lectures on Logic* (The Cambridge Edition of the Works of Immanuel Kant). Trans. and ed. J. Michael Young. Cambridge: Cambridge University Press, 1992.

Concerning Sensory Illusion and Poetic Fiction. Trans. Ralf Meerbote. In *Kant's Latin Writings: Translations, Commentaries and Notes.* Ed. Lewis White Beck in collaboration with Mary J. Gregor. New York: Lang, 1986.

Concerning the Ultimate Ground of the Differentiation of Directions in Space. Trans. David Walford and Ralf Meerbote, in *Theoretical Philosophy, 1755–1770* (The Cambridge Edition of the Works of Immanuel Kant). Ed. David Walford and Ralf Meerbote. Cambridge: Cambridge University Press, 1992.

The Conflict of the Faculties. Trans. with an introduction by Mary J. Gregor. New York: Abaris, 1979.

Conjectures on the Beginning of Human History. Trans. H. B. Nisbet. In *Kant's Political Writings*, 2d ed. Ed. with an introduction and notes by Hans Reiss. Cambridge: Cambridge University Press, 1970.

Critique of Judgment (including the *First Introduction*). Trans. with an introduction by Werner S. Pluhar. Indianapolis: Hackett, 1987.

Critique of Practical Reason. Trans. with an introduction by Lewis White Beck. Indianapolis: Bobbs-Merrill, 1956.

Critique of Pure Reason. Trans. Norman Kemp Smith. London: Macmillan, 1929; 2d impression with corrections 1933.

The Dohna-Wundlacken Logic. Trans. J. Michael Young. In *Lectures on Logic* (The Cambridge Edition of the Works of Immanuel Kant). Trans. and ed. J. Michael Young. Cambridge: Cambridge University Press, 1992.

Dreams of a Spirit-Seer Elucidated by Dreams of Metaphysics. Trans. David Walford and Ralf Meerbote. In *Theoretical Philosophy, 1755–1770* (The Cambridge Edition of the Works of Immanuel Kant). Ed. David Walford and Ralf Meerbote. Cambridge: Cambridge University Press, 1992.

The End of All Things. Trans. Robert E. Anchor. In *On History.* Ed. and introduction by Lewis White Beck. Indianapolis: Bobbs-Merrill, 1963.

The False Subtlety of the Four Syllogistic Figures. Trans. David Walford and Ralf Meerbote. In *Theoretical Philosophy, 1755–1770* (The Cambridge Edition of the Works of Immanuel Kant) Ed. David Walford and Ralf Meerbote. Cambridge: Cambridge University Press, 1992.

Groundwork of the Metaphysics of Morals. Trans. and analyzed by H. J. Paton. New York: Harper and Row, 1964.

Idea for a Universal History from a Cosmopolitan Point of View. Trans. Lewis White Beck. In *On History.* Ed. and introduction by Lewis White Beck. Indianapolis: Bobbs-Merrill, 1963.

The Jäsche Logic. Trans. J. Michael Young. In *Lectures on Logic* (The Cambridge Edition of the Works of Immanuel Kant). Trans. and ed. J. Michael Young. Cambridge: Cambridge University Press, 1992.

Lectures on Ethics. Trans. Louis Infield, with a foreword by Lewis White Beck. New York: Harper and Row, 1963.

Lectures on Philosophical Theology. Trans. Allen W. Wood and Gertrude M. Clark, with introduction and notes by Allen W. Wood. Ithaca: Cornell University Press, 1978.

Metaphysical Foundations of Natural Science. Trans. with introduction and essay by James Ellington. Indianapolis: Bobbs-Merrill, 1970.

The Metaphysics of Morals. Trans. with introduction and notes by Mary Gregor. Cambridge: Cambridge University Press, 1991.

A New Exposition of the First Principles of Metaphysical Knowledge. Trans. John A. Reuscher. In *Kant's Latin Writings: Translations, Commentaries and Notes.* Ed. Lewis White Beck in collaboration with Mary J. Gregor. New York: Lang, 1986.

Observations on the Feeling of the Beautiful and the Sublime. Trans. J. T. Goldthwaite. Berkeley and Los Angeles: University of California Press, 1965.

On a Newly Arisen Superior Tone in Philosophy. Trans. Peter Fenves. In Peter Fenves, ed., *Raising the Tone of Philosophy: Late Essays by Immanuel Kant, Transformative Critique by Jacques Derrida.* Baltimore: Johns Hopkins University Press, 1993.

On Philosophers' Medicine of the Body. Trans. Mary J. Gregor. In *Kant's Latin Writings: Translations, Commentaries and Notes.* Ed. Lewis White Beck in collaboration with Mary J. Gregor. New York: Lang, 1986.

On the Form and Principles of the Sensible and the Intelligible World (*Inaugural Dissertation*). Trans. David Walford and Ralf Meerbote, in *Theoretical Philosophy, 1755–1770* (The Cambridge Edition of the Works of Immanuel Kant). Ed. David Walford and Ralf Meerbote. Cambridge: Cambridge University Press, 1992.

The One Possible Basis for a Demonstration of the Existence of God. Trans. Gordon Treash. New York: Abaris, 1979.

On the Common Saying "This May be True in Theory, but it does not Apply in Practice." Trans. H. B. Nisbet, in *Kant's Political Writings,* 2d ed. Ed. with an introduction and notes by Hans Reiss. Cambridge: Cambridge University Press, 1970.

Opus postumum (The Cambridge Edition of the Works of Immanuel Kant). Ed. with an introduction and notes by Eckart Förster, trans. Eckart Förster and Michael Rosen. Cambridge: Cambridge University Press, 1993.

Perpetual Peace: A Philosophic Sketch. Trans. H. B. Nisbet, in *Kant's Political Writings,* 2d ed. Ed. with an introduction and notes by Hans Reiss. Cambridge: Cambridge University Press, 1970.

Philosophical Correspondence: 1759–99. Trans. Arnulf Zweig. Chicago: University of Chicago Press, 1967.

Prolegomena to Any Future Metaphysics. Trans. with an introduction by Lewis White Beck. Indianapolis: Bobbs-Merrill, 1950.

Reviews of Herder's Ideas on the Philosophy of the History of Mankind. Trans. H. B. Nisbet, in *Kant's Political Writings,* 2d ed. Ed. with an introduction and notes by Hans Reiss. Cambridge: Cambridge University Press, 1970.

Succinct Exposition of some Meditations on Fire. Trans. Lewis White Beck, in *Kant's Latin Writings: Translations, Commentaries and Notes.* Ed. Lewis White Beck in collaboration with Mary J. Gregor. New York: Lang, 1986.

Universal Natural History and Theory of the Heavens. Trans. with an introduction by Stanley Jaki. Edinburgh: Scottish Academy Press, 1981 .

The Use in Natural Philosophy of Metaphysics Combined with Geometry. Part I. Physical Monadology. Trans. Lewis White Beck, in *Kant's Latin Writings: Translations, Commentaries and Notes.* Ed. Lewis White Beck in collaboration with Mary J. Gregor. New York: Lang, 1986.

The Vienna Logic. Trans. J. Michael Young. In *Lectures on Logic* (The Cambridge Edition of the Works of Immanuel Kant). Trans. and ed. J. Michael Young. Cambridge: Cambridge University Press, 1992.

What is Orientation in Thinking? Trans. H. B. Nisbet, in *Kant's Political Writings,* 2d ed. Ed. with an introduction and notes by Hans Reiss. Cambridge: Cambridge University Press, 1970.

Works by Others

Addison, Joseph, and Sir Richard Steele. *The Spectator.* Ed. Donald F. Bond. Oxford: Clarendon Press, 1965.

Adelmann, Howard B. *Marcello Malpighi and the Evolution of Embryology.* Vols. 4 and 5. Ithaca: Cornell University Press, 1966.

Adickes, Erich. *Kant als Naturforscher.* 2 vols. Berlin: De Gruyter, 1924.

Allison, Henry. *Kant's Transcendental Idealism: An Interpretation and Defense.* New Haven: Yale University Press, 1983.

Almieda, Hermione de. *Romantic Medicine and John Keats.* New York and Oxford: Oxford University Press, 1991.

Ameriks, Karl. "The Critique of Metaphysics: Kant and Traditional Ontology." In Paul Guyer, ed., *The Cambridge Companion to Kant.* Cambridge: Cambridge University Press, 1992.

———. *Kant's Theory of Mind: An Analysis of the Paralogisms of Pure Reason.* Oxford: Clarendon Press, 1982.

Aquila, Richard E. *Representational Mind: A Study of Kant's Theory of Knowledge.* Bloomington: Indiana University Press, 1983.

Arendt, Hannah. *Lectures on Kant's Political Philosophy.* Ed. Ronald Beiner. Chicago: University of Chicago Press, 1982.

Aristotle. *Generation of Animals.* In *The Works of Aristotle Translated into English,* vol. 5. Ed. J. A. Smith and W. D. Ross. Oxford: Oxford University Press, 1912.

———. *Politics.* Trans. Carnes Lord. Chicago: University of Chicaco Press, 1984.

Bacon, Francis. *The Masculine Birth of Time.* In Benjamin Farrington, ed., *The Philosophy of Francis Bacon: An Essay on its Development from 1603 to 1609, with New Translations of Fundamental Texts.* Chicago: University of Chicago Press, 1964.

Barker, Duncan G. N. "*Grylli, Verstand und Unsinn* in Classical Glyptics." M.A. thesis, University of Chicago, 1989.

Baumann, Fred. "Historicism." In Allan Bloom, ed., *Confronting the Constitution,* 284–313. Washington, D.C.: American Enterprise Institute Press, 1990.

Baumgarten, Alexander Gottlieb. *Aesthetica.* Rpt., Hildesheim: Georg Olms Verlagsbuchlandlung, 1961.

———. *Metaphysica.* 4th ed., 1757; also in *Kants Gesammelte Schriften,* vol. 18, ed. Königliche Preußische (later Deutsche) Akademie der Wissenschaften. Berlin: Walter de Gruyter, 1902–.

———. *Reflections on Poetry.* Trans. Karl Aschenbrenner and William B. Holther. Berkeley and Los Angeles: University of California Press, 1954.

Baur, Susan. *Hypochondria: Woeful Imaginings.* Berkeley and Los Angeles: University of California Press, 1988.

Beck, Lewis White. *Early German Philosophy.* Cambridge, Mass.: Harvard University Press, 1969.

———. *A Commentary on the Critique of Practical Reason.* Chicago: University of Chicago Press, 1969.

———. *Studies in the Philosophy of Kant.* Indianapolis: Bobbs-Merrill, 1965.

Beiner, Ronald. "Kant, the Sublime, and Nature." In Ronald Beiner and William James Booth, eds., *Kant and Political Philosophy*, 276–88. New Haven: Yale University Press, 1993.

———. *Political Judgment*. London: Methuen, 1984.

Beiser, Frederick. *The Fate of Reason: German Philosophy from Kant to Fichte*. Cambridge, Mass.: Harvard University Press, 1987.

Bencivenga, Ermanno. *Kant's Copernican Revolution*. London and New York: Oxford University Press, 1987.

Benjamin, Walter. *Illuminations*. Ed. Hannah Arendt. New York: Schocken, 1968.

Bennett, Jonathan. *Kant's Analytic*. Cambridge: Cambridge University Press, 1966.

Blumenberg, Hans. *The Legitimacy of the Modern Age*. Trans. Robert M. Wallace. Cambridge, Mass., and London: MIT Press, 1985.

Boerhaave, Hermann. *Elemente chimiae*. Paris, 1724.

Böhme, Hartmut, and Gernot Böhme. *Das Andere der Vernunft: Zur Entwicklung von Rationalitätsstrukturen am Beispiel Kants*. Frankfurt am Main: Suhrkamp, 1983.

Bonnet, Charles. *La Palingénésie philosophique, ou idées sur l'état passé et sur l'état futur des êtres vivans*. 2 vols. Geneva: Chez Caude Philibert et Barthelmi Chirol, 1769.

Booth, William James. *Interpreting the World: Kant's Philosophy of History and Politics*. London, Toronto and Buffalo: University of Toronto Press, 1986.

Borowski, Ludwig Ernst. "Darstellung des Lebens und Charakters Immanuel Kants." In F. Gross, ed., *Immanuel Kant, Sein Leben in Darstellungen von Zeitgenossen*, Darmstadt: Wissenshcaftliche Buchgesellschaft, 1980.

Borst, Arno. *Der Turmbau von Babel: Geschichte der Meinungen über Ursprung und Vielfalt der Sprachen und Völker*, vol. 2. Stuttgart: A. Hiersemann, 1957.

Boswell, James. *The Hypochondriack* (seventy essays appearing in the *London Magazine*, Nov. 1777 to Aug. 1783). Ed. Margery Bailey. Stanford: Stanford University Press, 1928.

Bowler, Peter J. "Bonnet and Buffon: Theories of Generation and the Problem of Species." *Journal of the History of Biology* 6, no. 2 (fall 1973): 259–81.

Brown, John. *Elements of Medicine*. Translated by the author, revised and corrected with a biographical preface by Thomas Beddoes, 2 vols. London: J. Johnson, 1795.

Bruno, Giordano. *Le opere italiane*. 2 vols. 2 ed. Ed. Giordano Bruno and Giovanni Gentile. Naples: Bibliopolis, 1991; originally published 1879–91.

———. *Opera latine conscripta*. 3 vols. Ed. Francesco Fiorentino and Felice Tocco. Stuttgart: F. Frommann, 1962; originally published 1879.

Bulfinch, Thomas. *The Age of Fable*. Boston: Tilton, 1855.

Burke, Edmund. *Philosophic Enquiry into the Origin of Our Ideas of the Sublime and the Beautiful*. Trans. into German by Christian Garve. Riga: Hartknoch, 1773.

Buroker, Jill Vance. *Space and Incongruence: The Origin of Kant's Idealism*. Dordrecht, Boston and London: D. Reidel, 1981.

Burton, Robert. *The Anatomy of Melancholy*. Ed. Floyd Dell and Paul Jordan Smith. New York: Tudor, 1927; originally published 1651.

Butts, Robert E. *Kant and the Double Government Methodology*. Dordrecht: D. Reidel, 1986.

Cantor, G. N., and M. J. S. Hodge, eds. *Conceptions of Ether: Studies in the History of Ether Theories, 1740–1900*. Cambridge: Cambridge University Press, 1980.

Carus, Carl Gustav. *Psyche: On the Development of the Soul: Part I, "The Unconscious."* With an introductory note by James Hillman. Ed. Murray Stein. Dallas: Spring Publications, 1970.

Cassirer, Ernst. *Kant's Life and Thought.* Trans. James Haden New Haven and London: Yale University Press, 1981.

———. *Rousseau, Kant, Goethe.* Trans. James Guttmann et al. Princeton: Princeton University Press, 1945.

Castillo, Monique. *Kant et l'avenir de la culture.* Paris: Presses Universitaires de France, 1990.

Cavell, Stanley. *Conditions Handsome and Unhandsome: The Constitution of Emersonian Perfection.* Chicago: University of Chicago Press, 1988.

Cheyne, George. *The English Malady: or, A Treatise of Nervous Diseases of All Kinds.* London: Strahan and Leake, 1733.

Costabel, P. *Leibniz and Dynamics.* Trans. R. E. W. Maddison. London: Methuen, 1973.

Crawford, Donald W. "The Place of the Sublime in Kant's Aesthetic Theory." In Richard Kennington, ed., *The Philosophy of Immanuel Kant,* 161–83. Washington, D.C.: Catholic University of America Press, 1985.

Crowe, Michael J. *The Extraterrestrial Life Debate, 1750–1900: The Idea of a Plurality of Worlds from Kant to Lowell.* Cambridge: Cambridge University Press, 1986.

Crusius, C. A. *Weg zur Gewißheit und Zuverlässigkeit der menschlichen Erkenntnis.* In *Die philosophische Hauptwerke,* vol. 3. Ed. G. Tonelli, Hildesheim: Georg Olms Verlagsbuchhandlung, 1965.

Darwin, Erasmus. *Zoonomia; or, The Laws of Organic Life.* 2 vols. London: J. Johnson, 1796.

De Quincey, Thomas. *The Last Days of Immanuel Kant.* In *The Works of Thomas de Quincey,* Fireside Edition, vol. 9, 491–552. Cambridge, Mass.: Houghton Mifflin, 1877.

Derrida, Jacques. *Glas.* Trans. John P. Leavey, Jr. Lincoln and London: University of Nebraska Press, 1984.

———. *Of Spirit: Heidegger and the Question.* Trans. Geoffrey Bennington and Rachel Bowlby. Chicago: University of Chicago Press, 1989.

Descartes, René. *Le Monde, ou Traité de la lumière.* Trans. Michael Sean Mahoney. New York: Abaris Books, 1979.

———. *Oeuvres des Descartes.* Ed. C. Adams and P. Tannery. Paris: Le Cerf, 1902–.

———. *The Philosophical Writings of Descartes.* Trans. John Cottingham, Robert Stoothoff, and Dugald Murdoch. Cambridge: Cambridge University Press, 1985.

Diderot, Denis, ed. *Encyclopédie, ou Dictionnaire raisonné des sciences, des arts, et des métiers.* Lausanne and Berne, 1782.

Duden, Barbara. *The Woman beneath the Skin: A Doctor's Patients in Eighteenth-Century Germany.* Cambridge, Mass.: Harvard University Press, 1991.

Duhem, Pierre. *Medieval Cosmology: Theories of Infinity, Place, Time, Void, and the Plurality of Worlds.* Trans. Roger Ariew. Chicago and London: University of Chicago Press, 1987.

Elster, Jon. *Leibniz et la formation de l'esprit capitaliste.* Paris: Aubier, 1975.

Encyclopedia Judaica. Jerusalem: Keter Publishing, 1984?.

Engell, John. *The Creative Imagination*. Cambridge, Mass.: Harvard University Press, 1981.

Erdmann, Benno. *Martin Knutzen und seine Zeit*. Leipzig: Verlag von Leopold Voss, 1876.

Fackenheim, Emil L. "Kant's Concept of History." *Kant-Studien* 48 (1957): 381–98.

Falret, Jean-Pierre. *De l'hypochondrie et du suicide*. Paris: Croullebois, 1822.

Farber, Eduard. "Forces and Substances of Life." *Osiris* 11 (1954): 422–37.

Farber, Paul L. "Buffon and the Concept of Species." *Journal of the History of Biology* 5, no. 2 (fall 1972): 259–84.

Fenves, Peter. "Antonomasia: Leibniz and the Baroque." *Modern Language Notes* 105 (April 1990): 432–52.

———. *A Peculiar Fate: Kant and the Problem of World History*. Ithaca: Cornell University Press, 1990.

Ferrari, Jean. *Les sources français de la philosophie de Kant*. Paris: Librairie Klincksieck, 1979.

Feuer, Lewis. "Lawless Sensations and Categorical Defenses: The Unconscious Sources of Kant's Philosophy." In C. Hanly and M. Lazerowitz, eds., *Psychoanalysis and Philosophy*. New York: International Universities Press, 1970.

Fichte, Johann Gottlieb. *Grundlage des Naturrechts nach Principien der Wissenschaftslehre*. In Immanuel Hermann Fichte, ed., *Fichtes Werke*, vol. 3. Berlin: Walter de Gruyter, 1971.

Findlay, J. N. *Kant and the Transcendental Object*. Oxford: Clarendon Press, 1981.

Fischer-Homberger, E. *Hypochondrie*. Bern and Stuttgart: Huber, 1970.

Fontenelle, Bernard le Bovier de. *Entretiens sur la pluralité des mondes*. Ed. Robert Shackleton. Oxford: Oxford University Press, 1955.

Förster, Eckart, ed. *Kant's Transcendental Deductions*. Stanford: Stanford University Press, 1989.

Forster, Georg. *Werke*. Frankfurt am Main: Insel-Verlag, 1969.

Freudenthal, Gideon. *Atom and Individual in the Age of Newton*. Trans. Peter McLaughlin. Dordrecht: D. Reidel, 1986.

Friedman, Michael. *Kant and the Exact Sciences*. Cambridge: Harvard University Press, 1992.

Fromm, Emil. *Das Kantbildnis der Gräfin Karoline Charlotte Amalia von Keyserling*. Hamburg: Leopold Voss, 1924.

Galston, William A. *Kant and the Problem of History*. Chicago: University of Chicago Press, 1975.

Genova, A. C. "Kant's Epigenesis of Pure Reason." *Kant-Studien* 65 (1974): 259–73.

Gerard, Alexander. *Essay on Genius*. London: W. Strahan, 1774.

Gilman, Sander, Helen King, Roy Porter, G. S. Rousseau, and Elaine Showalter, eds. *Hysteria beyond Freud*. Berkeley: University of California Press, 1993.

Girtenner, C. D. *Ueber das kantische Prinzip für die Naturgeschichte*. Göttingen: Wandenhoek und Ruprecht, 1796.

Gode-von Aesch, Alexander. *Natural Science and German Romanticism*. New York: Columbia University Press, 1941.

Goerwitz, E. F., trans. *Dreams of a Spirit-Seer Illustrated by Dreams of Metaphysics,* by Immanuel Kant. London and New York: F. Sewall, 1900.

Goldmann, Lucien. *Kant.* Trans. Robert Black. London: New Left Books, 1971. Originally *Mensch, Gemeinschaft, und Welt in der Philosophie Immanuel Kants.* Zurich: Europa-Verlag, 1945.

Gould, Josiah B. *The Philosophy of Chrysippus.* Leiden: Brill, 1970.

Gould, Stephen Jay. *The Mismeasurement of Man.* New York: Norton, 1981.

Grimm, Jacob, and Wilhelm Grimm, eds. *Deutsches Wörterbuch.* Leibzig: Verlag von S. Hirzel, 1854.

Guerlac, H. "Chemistry as a Branch of Physics: Laplace's Collaboration with Lavoisier." *Historical Studies in the Physical Sciences* 7 (1976): 193–276.

———. *Lavoisier: The Crucial Year.* Ithaca: Cornell University Press,1961.

Guillermit, Louis. *L'elucidation critique du jugement de goût selon Kant.* Paris: Editions du Centre National de la Recherche Scientifique, 1986.

Gulyga, Arsenij. *Immanuel Kant.* Trans. from Russian to German by Sigrun Bielfeldt. Frankfurt am Main: Suhrkamp Verlag, 1985.

Gurr, John Edwin. *The Principle of Sufficient Reason in Some Scholastic Systems: 1750–1900.* Milwaukee: Marquette University Press, 1959.

Guyer, Paul. *Kant and the Experience of Freedom.* Cambridge: Cambridge University Press, 1993.

———. *Kant and the Claims of Taste.* Cambridge, Mass.: Harvard University Press, 1979.

———. *Kant and the Claims of Knowledge.* Cambridge: Cambridge University Press, 1987.

Hall, Thomas S. *Ideas of Life and Matter: Studies in the History of General Physiology, 600 B.C.–1900 A.D.* 2 vols. Chicago: University of Chicago Press, 1969.

Hamann, J. G. "Metacritique of the Purism of Reason." In *J. G. Hamann: A Study in Christian Existence,* by Ronald Gregor Smith. New York: Harper Brothers, 1960.

———. *Sämtliche Werke, Historisch-Kritische Ausgabe.* Ed. J. Nadler. Vienna: Herder, 1949–51.

Harvey, William. *De motu locali animalium.* Trans. Gweneth Whitteridge. Cambridge: Cambridge University Press, 1959.

Hasse, J. G. *Letzte Äußerungen Kants von einem seiner Tischgenossen.* Königsberg: Friedrich Nikilovius, 1804.

Hastie, W., trans. *Kant's Cosmogony [Universal Natural History and Theory of the Heavens].* Glasgow, 1900. Rpt., Ann Arbor: University of Michigan Press, 1969.

Hegel, G. F. W. *Logic,* pt. 1 of *The Encyclopaedia of the Philosophical Sciences.* Trans. William Wallace. Oxford: Oxford University Press, 1975.

———. *Science of Logic,* vol. 2. Trans. W. H. Johnson and L. G. Struthers. London: Allen and Unwin, 1929.

———. *Philosophy of Right.* Trans. T. M. Knox. Oxford: Clarendon Press, 1942.

———. *Philosophy of Nature* [pt. 2 of the *Encyclopaedia of the Philosophical Sciences* (1830)]. Trans. A. V. Miller. Oxford: Clarendon Press, 1970.

Heidegger, Martin. *Being and Time.* Trans. John Macquarrie and Edward Robinson. New York: Harper and Row, 1962.

————. *The Metaphysical Foundations of Logic*. Trans. Michael Heim. Bloomington: Indiana University Press, 1984.

Heimsoeth, Heinz. "Metaphysical Motives in the Development of Critical Idealism." In Moltke S. Gram, ed., *Kant: Disputed Questions,* 194–236. Chicago: Quadrangle Books, 1967.

————. *Studien zur Philosophie Immanul Kants.* Cologne: Kölner-Universitätsverlag, 1956.

Henrich, Dieter. *Aesthetic Judgment and the Moral Image of the World: Studies in Kant.* Stanford: Stanford University Press, 1992.

————. *The Unity of Reason* Ed. Richard Velkley. Cambridge, Mass.: Harvard University Press, 1994.

————. "Hutcheson und Kant." *Kant-Studien* 49 (1957–58): 49–69.

————. "On the Unity of Subjectivity." In *The Unity of Reason,* 17–54.

————. "Über Kants früheste Ethik." *Kant-Studien* 54 (1963): 404–31.

Herder, J. G. *Ideen zur Philosophie der Geschichte der Menschheit.* Darmstadt: Joseph Melzer Verlag, 1966.

Herz, M. *Grundriß aller medicinischen Wissenschaften.* Berlin: Christian Friedrich Voss und Sohn, 1782.

Hill, John. *Hypochondriasis: A Practical Treatise on the Nature and Cure of that Disorder, Commonly Called the Hyp and the Hypo.* London, 1766. Rpt., ed. G. S. Rousseau. Los Angeles: Clarke Memorial Library, 1969.

Hobbes, Thomas. *Leviathan.* Ed. C. B. MacPherson. Harmondsworth: Penquin, 1968.

Hocke, G. *Die Welt als Labyrinth.* Hamburg: Rowohlt, 1957.

Horace. *The Epistles and Art of Poetry.* Trans. Philip Francis. London: A. Millar, 1749.

Hume, David. *The Philosophical Works of David Hume.* Ed. T. H. Greene and T. H. Grose. 1886. Rpt. Darmstadt: Scientia, 1964.

Iltis, Carolyn. "D'Alembert and the *Vis Viva* Controversy." *Studies in the History and Philosophy of Science* 1 (1970): 135–44.

Ingensiep, Hans Werner. "Die biologischen Analogien und die erkenntnistheoretischen Alternativen in Kants Critik der reinen Vernunft B #27." *Kant-Studien* 85 (1994): 381–93.

Jachmann, R. B. "Immanuel Kant geschildert in Briefen an einen Freund." In Borowski, Jachmann, and Wasianski, *Immanuel Kant.*

James, Robert. *A Medicinal Dictionary.* London: T. Osborne, 1743–45.

Jauch, Ursula Pia. *Immanuel Kant zur Geschlechterdifferenz: Aufklärische Vorteilskritik und bürgerliche Geschlechtsvormundschaft.* Vienna: Passagen Verlag, 1988.

Julia, Didier. *La question de l'homme et le fondement de la philosophie.* Paris: Aubier, 1964.

Kant, Immanuel. *Bemerkungen in den "Beobachtungen über das Gefühl des Schönen und Erhabenen,"* ed. Marie Rischmüller. Hamburg: Felix Meiner Verlag, 1991.

Kantorowicz, Ernst H. *The King's Two Bodies: A Study in Medieval Political Theology.* Princeton: Princeton University Press, 1957.

Kelly, George Armstrong. *Idealism, Politics and History: Sources of Hegelian Thought.* Cambridge: Cambridge University Press, 1969.

Kersting, Wolfgang. *Wohlgeordnete Freiheit. Immanual Kants Rechts- und Staatsphilosophie.* Berlin: W. de Gruyter, 1984.

Kitcher, Patricia. *Kant's Transcendental Psychology.* Oxford: Oxford University Press, 1990.

Kleingeld, Pauline. "The Problematic Status of Gender-Neutral Language in the History of Philosophy: The Case of Kant." *Philosophical Forum* 25, no. 2 (Winter 1993): 134–50.

Kofman, Sarah. *Le respect des femmes.* Paris: Galilée, 1982.

Koyré, Alexandre. *From the Closed World to the Infinite Universe.* Baltimore: Johns Hopkins University Press, 1957.

Krüger, Gerhard. *Philosophie und Moral in der Kantischen Kritik.* Tübingen: Paul Siebeck, 1931.

Kuehn, Manfred. *Scottish Common Sense in Germany, 1768–1800.* Kingston and Montreal: McGill-Queens University Press, 1987.

Laberge, Pierre. *La théologie kantienne précritique.* Ottawa: Université d'Ottawa, 1973.

La Mettrie, Julien Offray de. *La Mettrie's L'Homme Machine: A Study in the Origins of an Idea.* Ed. Aram Vartanian. Princeton: Princeton University Press, 1960.

Landes, Joan. *Women and the Public Sphere in the Age of the French Revolution.* Ithaca: Cornell University Press, 1989.

Laqueur, Thomas. *Making Sex: Body and Gender from the Greeks to Freud.* Cambridge: Harvard University Press, 1990.

Laywine, Alison. *Kant's Early Metaphysics and the Origins of the Critical Philosophy.* Atascadero, Calif.: Ridgeway Publishing, 1993.

Leibniz, Gottfried Wilhelm. *Essays on Human Understanding.* Trans. Peter Remnant and Jonathan Bennett. Cambridge: Cambridge University Press, 1981.

———. *The Monadology and Other Philosophical Writings.* Trans. Robert Latta. London: Oxford University Press, 1898.

———. *New Essays on Human Understanding.* Trans. Peter Remnant and Jonathan Bennett. Cambridge: Cambridge University Press, 1981.

———. *Philosophical Papers and Letters.* 2 vols. Trans. Leroy E. Loemker. Chicago: University of Chicago Press, 1956.

———. *Theodicy.* Ed. Austin Ferrar. La Salle, Ill.: Open Court, 1985.

Lenoir, Timothy. "Kant, Blumenbach, and Vital Materialism in German Biology." *Isis* 71:77–108.

Lepenies, Wolf. *Melancholy and Society.* Trans. Jeremy Gaines and Doris Jones. Cambridge, Mass.: Harvard University Press, 1992.

Longinus. *On the Sublime.* Trans. W. Hamilton Fyfe. Cambridge: Harvard University Press, 1939.

Lovejoy, Arthur. *The Great Chain of Being: A Study of the History of an Idea.* Cambridge, Mass.: Harvard University Press, 1936.

———. "Kant and Evolution." In Bentley Glass, Owsei Temkin, and William L. Strauss, Jr., eds., *Forerunners of Darwin,* 173–206. Baltimore: Johns Hopkins University Press, 1959.

Lucretius. *De Rerum Natura.* Trans. Cyril Bailey. Oxford: Clarendon Press, 1947.

Lyotard, Jean-François. "Judiciousness in Dispute, or Kant after Marx." *The Lyotard Reader,* ed. Andrew Benjamin. Oxford: Blackwell, 1989.

———. "Answering the Question: What is Postmodernism?" *The Post-Modern Condition: A Report on Knowledge*. Trans. G. Bennington and B. Massumi. Minneapolis: University of Minnesota Press, 1974.

———. *Lessons on the Analytic of the Sublime*, trans. Elizabeth Rottenberg. Stanford: Stanford University Press, 1994.

Mach, Ernst. *The Science of Mechanics*. 2d ed. Trans. Thomas J. McCormack. Chicago: Open Court, 1893.

Makkreel, Rudolf A. "The Feeling of Life: Some Kantian Sources of Life-Philosophy." *Dilthey-Jahrbuch für Philosophie und Geschichte der Geisteswissenschaften* 3 (1985): 83–104.

———. *Imagination and Interpretation in Kant*. Chicago: University of Chicago Press, 1990.

Mandeville, Bernard. *A Treatise of the Hypochondriack and Histerick Passions, Vulgarly Call'd the Hypo in Men and Vapours in Women*. London: Dryden Leach, 1711.

Mansfield, Harvey C. "Hobbes and the Science of Indirect Government." *American Political Science Review* 65 (1971): 97–110.

———. *Taming the Prince*. New York: Free Press, 1989.

Maupertuis, Pierre-Louis Moreau. *The Earthly Venus*. Trans. Somone Brangier Boas. New York and London: Johnson Reprint, 1966.

May, J. A. *Kant's Concept of Geography*. Toronto: University of Toronto Press, 1970.

McDowell, John. *Mind and World*. Cambridge: Harvard University Press, 1994.

McLaughlin, Peter. *Kant's Critique of Teleology in Biological Explanation*. Lewiston, N.Y.: Edwin Mellen Press, 1990.

Mendelsohn, Everett. *Heat and Life: The Development of the Theory of Animal Heat*. Cambridge, Mass.: Harvard University Press, 1964.

Mendus, Susan. "Kant: An Honest but Narrow-Minded Bourgeois?" In Howard Williams, ed., *Kant's Political Philosophy*, 166–90.

Monk, Samuel H. *The Sublime*. Ann Arbor: University of Michigan Press, 1960.

Muglioni, Jean-Michel. *La philosophie de l'histoire de Kant: Qu'est-ce que L'homme?* Paris: Presses Universitaires de France, 1993.

Müller-Sievers, Helmut. *Epigenesis: Naturphilosophie im Sprachdenken Wilhelm von Humboldts*. Paderborn: Ferdinand Schöningh, 1993.

Neiman, Susan. *The Unity of Reason: Rereading Rousseau*. Oxford: Oxford University Press, 1994.

O'Neill, Onora. *Constructions of Reason*. Cambridge: Cambridge University Press, 1989.

Olson, Alan M. in *Hegel and the Spirit: Philosophy as Pneumatology*. Princeton: Princeton University Press, 1992.

Oppenheimer, Jane M. *Essays in the History of Embryology and Biology*. Cambridge: MIT Press, 1967.

Orwin, Clifford. "Rousseau and the Problem of Political Compassion." In Nathan Tarcov and Clifford Orwin, eds., *The Legacy of Rousseau* (forthcoming).

Paglia, Camille. *Sexual Personae: Art and Decadence from Nefertiti to Emily Dickenson*. New Haven: Yale University Press, 1990.

Pangle, Thomas L. *The Ennobling of Democracy: The Challenge of the Postmodern Age*. Baltimore: Johns Hopkins University Press, 1992.

Philonenko, Alexis. *La théorie kantienne de l'histoire*. Paris: Vrin, 1986.

Pippen, Robert B. *Kant's Theory of Form: An Essay on the "Critique of Pure Reason."* New Haven: Yale University Press, 1982.

Plutarch. *Lives.* Trans. John Dryden. New York: Modern Library, 1932.

Polonoff, Irving I. *Force, Cosmos, Monads and Other Themes of Kant's Early Thought.* Bonn: Bouvier Verlag Herbert Grundmann, 1973.

Powell, Thomas. *Kant's Theory of Self-Consciousness.* Oxford: Oxford University Press, 1990.

Putscher, Marielene. *Pneuma, Spiritus, Geist.* Weisbaden: Steiner, 1973.

Rorty, Richard. *The Mirror of Nature.* Princeton: Princeton University Press, 1979.

Riley, Patrick. *Kant's Political Philosophy.* Totowa, N.J.: Rowman and Littlefield, 1983.

Rink, D. Friedrich. *Ansichten aus Immanuel Kant's Legen.* Königsberg: Göbbels und Unzer, 1805.

Robinson, Hoke. "Kant on Embodiment." In Phillip D. Cummins and Guenter Zoeller, eds., *Minds, Ideas, and Objects: Essays on the Theory of Representation in Modern Philosophy,* pp. 337–39. Atascadero, Calif.: Ridgeview Publishing, 1992.

Roe, Shirley A. *Matter, Life, and Generation.* Cambridge: Cambridge University Press, 1981.

Roger, Jacques. "The Living World." In G. S. Rousseau and Roy Porter, eds., *The Ferment of Knowledge,* 255–84.

———. *Les sciences de la vie dans la pensée française du XVIIe siècle.* Paris: Armand Colin, 1963.

Rotenstreich, Nathan. "Morality and Culture: A Note on Kant," *History of Philosophy Quarterly* 6, no. 3 (July 1989): 303–16.

Rousseau, Jean-Jacques. *The First and Second Discourses.* Trans. Roger Masters. New York: St. Martin's Press, 1964.

———. *Emile.* Trans. Allan Bloom. New York: Basic Books, 1979.

Rousseau, G. S. "Psychology." In G. S. Rousseau and Roy Porter, eds., *The Ferment of Knowledge,* 143–210.

Rousseau, G. S., ed. *The Languages of Psyche: Mind and Body in Enlightenment Thought.* Berkeley: University of California Press, 1990.

Rousseau, G. S., and Roy Porter, eds. *The Ferment of Knowledge: Studies in the Historiography of Eighteenth-Century Science.* Cambridge: Cambridge University Press, 1980.

Sallis, John. *Spacings: Of Reason and Imagination in Texts of Kant, Fichte, Hegel.* Chicago: University of Chicago Press, 1987.

Salmony, H. A. *Hamanns metakritische Philosophie.* Basel: Evangelischer Verlag, 1958.

Saner, Hans. *Kant's Political Thought.* Trans. E. B. Ashton. Chicago: University of Chicago Press, 1973.

Schaffer, Simon. "States of Mind: Enlightenment and Natural Philosophy." In G. S. Rousseau, ed., *The Languages of Psyche: Mind and Body in Enlightenment Thought,* 233–290.

Schaper, Eva. *Studies in Kant's Aesthetics.* Edinburgh: Edinburgh University Press, 1979.

Scharfstein, Ben-Ami. *The Philosophers: Their Lives and the Nature of Their Thought.* Oxford: Oxford University Press, 1980.

Schings, Hans-Jürgen. *Melancholie und Aufklärung: Melancholiker und ihre Kritiker in Erfahrungsseelenkunde und Literature der 18. Jahrhundert.* Stuttgart: J. B. Metzler, 1977.

Schlapp, Otto. *Kants Lehre vom Genie und die Entstehung der "Kritik der Urteilskraft."* Göttingen: Vandenhoeck und Ruprecht, 1901.

Schmidt, M. *Wiedergeburt und neuer Mensch.* Witten: Luther Verlag, 1969.

Schmitz, Hermann. *Was wollte Kant?* Bonn: Bouvier Verlag, 1989.

Schmucker, Joseph. *Die Ursprünge der Ethik Kants in seinen vorkritischen Schriften und Reflexionen.* Meisenheim: Anton Hain, 1961.

Schott, Robin May. *Cognition and Eros: A Critique of the Kantian Paradigm.* Boston: Beacon Press Books, 1988.

Schwartz, Joel. *The Sexual Politics of Jean-Jacques Rousseau.* Chicago: University of Chicago Press, 1984.

Serrington, Charles. *The Endeavor of Jean Fernel.* Cambridge: Cambridge University Press, 1946.

Seung, T. K. *Kant's Platonic Revolution in Moral and Political Philosophy.* Baltimore: Johns Hopkins University Press, 1994.

Shea, William R. "Filled with Wonder: Kant's Cosmological Essay, *The Universal Natural History and Theory of the Heavens.*" In Robert E. Butts, ed., *Kant's Philosophy of Physical Science,* 95–126. Dordrecht: D. Reidel, 1986.

Shell, Marc. *Children of the Earth.* New York: Oxford University Press, 1993.

Shell, Susan Meld. "A Determined Stand: Freedom and Security in Fichte's *Science of Right.*" *Polity* 25 (1992): 95–121.

———. *The Rights of Reason: A Study of Kant's Philosophy and Politics.* Toronto, London and Buffalo: University of Toronto Press, 1980.

Smith, C. U. M. *The Problem of Life: An Essay in the Origins of Biological Thought.* London: Macmillan, 1976.

Smith, Norman Kemp. *A Commentary to Kant's "Critique of Pure Reason."* New York: Humanities Press, 1962.

Sommer, Martin. *Die Selbsterhaltung der Vernunft.* Stuttgart: Fromman-Holzbook, 1977.

———. *Identität im Übergang: Kant.* Frankfurt am Main: Suhrkamp, 1988.

Spalding, Keith. *An Historical Dictionary of German Figurative Usage.* Oxford: Blackwell, 1952–.

Stafford, Barbara Maria. *Body Criticism: Imaging the Unseen in Enlightenment Art and Medicine.* Cambridge: M.I.T. Press, 1992.

Stuckenberg, J. H. W. *The Life of Immanuel Kant.* London: Macmillan, 1882.

Thucydides. *History of the Peloponnesian War.* Trans. Thomas Hobbes. New Brunswick, N.J.: Rutgers University Press, 1975.

Tonelli, Giorgio. "Kant's Early Theory of Genius, 1770–1779." *Journal of the History of Philosophy* 4 (1966): 109–31, 209–24.

———. "La formazione del testo della *Kritik der Urteilskraft.*" *Revue Internationale de Philosophie* 8 (1954): 423–48.

———. *Elementi metodologici e metafisici in Kant dal 1745 al 1768.* Torino: Edizioni di "Filosofia," 1959.

Vaihinger, Hans. "Kant als melancholiker." *Kant-Studien* 2 (1898): 139–41.

Veith, Ilza. *Hysteria: History of a Disease.* Chicago: University of Chicago Press, 1965.

Velkley, Richard. "Kant on the Primacy and the Limits of Logic." *Graduate Faculty Journal* 2 (2): 147–62.

———. "The Tension in the Beautiful: On Culture in Rousseau and Other Thinkers." In Clifford Orwin and Nathan Tarcov, eds., *The Legacy of Rousseau* (forthcoming).

———. *Freedom and the End of Reason: On the Moral Foundation of Kant's Critical Philosophy.* Chicago: University of Chicago Press, 1989.

Von Haller, Albrecht. *Tagebuch seiner Beobachtungen über Schriftsteller und über sich selbst.* Ed. Johann Georg Heinzmann. Bern, 1787. Rpt., Frankfurt am Main: Athenäum, 1971.

Vorländer, Karl. *Der Mann und das Werk.* 2 vols. Leipzig: Felix Meiner, 1924.

Vuillemin, Jules. *Physique et métaphysique kantiennes.* Paris: Presses Universitaires de France, 1955.

Ward, Keith. *The Development of Kant's View of Ethics.* Oxford: Blackwell, 1972.

Wasianski, A. Ch. "Immanuel Kant in seinen letzten Lebensjahren." In Borowski, Jachmann und Wasianski, *Immanuel Kant.* Waxman, Wayne. *Kant's Model of the Mind: A New Interpretation of Transcendental Idealism.* Oxford: Oxford University Press, 1991.

Waxman, Wayne. *Kant's Model of the Mind: A New Interpretation.* New York and Oxford: Oxford University Press, 1991.

Weinrib, Ernest. "Law as an Idea of Reason," In Howard Williams, ed., *Essays on Kant's Political Philosophy,* 15–49.

Westfall, Richard S. *Force in Newton's Physics: The Science of Dynamics in the Seventeenth Century.* London: MacDonald, 1971.

Williams, Howard. "Kant's Optimism in His Political Theory." *Essays on Kant's Political Philosophy,* 1–14. Chicago: University of Chicago Press, 1992.

———. *Kant's Political Philosophy.* Oxford: Oxford University Press, 1983.

Wilson, Catherine. *Leibniz's Metaphysics: A Historical and Comparative Study.* Princeton: Princeton University Press, 1989.

Wittig, Hans-Georg. *Wiedergeburt als radikaler Gesinnungswandel.* Heidelberg: Quelle und Meyer, 1970.

Wolff, Christian. *Gesammelte Werke.* Ed. H. W. Arndt et al. Hildesheim: Olms, 1965.

Wolff, Robert Paul, *Kant's Theory of Mental Activity.* Cambridge, Mass.: Harvard University Press, 1963.

Wood, Michael. *Kant's Rational Theology.* Ithaca: Cornell University Press, 1978.

Wubnig, J. "The Epigenesis of Pure Reason." *Kant-Studien* 60 (1968–69): 147–52.

Yack, Bernard. *The Longing for Total Revolution.* Princeton: Princeton University Press, 1986.

Yovel, Yirmiahu. *Kant and the Philosophy of History.* Princeton: Princeton University Press, 1980.

Zammito, John. H. *The Genesis of Kant's "Critique of Judgment."* Chicago: University of Chicago Press, 1992.

Zöller, Günter. "Kant on the Generation of Metaphysical Knowledge." In Hariolf Operer and Gerhard Seel, eds., *Kant: Analysen-Probleme-Kritik.* Würzberg: Königshausen & Neumann, 1988.

Index

288, 307–8, 323n.3, 333–34n.73, 335–36n.86, 338n.98, 340–41nn.6, 11, 12, 15, 343nn.26, 30, 347nn.49, 50, 348–49n.62, 353–54nn.25, 29, 355n.40, 373nn.9, 11, 374n.20, 379–80n.40, 382n.56, 384n.7, 386n.17, 390n.36, 391n.37, 427–28n.26, 428n.28, 429n.30, 430n.43; on *amour propre*, 86–87, 220–21; difference from Kant, 83, 86, 399n.79; *Emile*, 4, 5, 115, 207, 382n.56, 343–44n.30, 344nn.33–34, 382n.56, 390n.36; influence of, 81–82, 288; Kant's early reading of, 81–83, 92; on natural man, 273, 275; as Newton of the moral world, 81–84; *Social Contract*, 4, 5; on taste, 207; on wholeness, 155; on woman, 186, 220–21, 335–36n.86. *See also* education; hypochondria

Sallis, John, 391n.42
Salmony, H. A., 348–49n.62, 420–21n.60
Saner, Hans, 330n.48, 361n.21, 369n.81
Schaffer, Simon, 352n.21
Schaper, Eva, 220, 398n.73
Scharfstein, Ben-Ami, 423n.3
Schelling, F.W.J., 450n.136
Schiller, Friedrich von, 104, 349n.67
Schings, Hans-Jürgen, 420–21n.60, 427n.25
Schlosser, Johann, 389n.34
Schmidt, M., 420–21n.60
Schmitz, Hermann, 324n.7
Schmucker, Joseph, 326n.26, 339n.1
Schott, Robin May, 367n.70
Schwartz, Joel, 343n.26, 244n.35
self-birthing, 174–75, 176, 182, 189, 234, 258, 294, 302, 407n.2, 413–14n.22, 436n.73
self-esteem, 86–87, 95, 101
Serrington, Charles, 332n.66
Seung, T. K., 358n.7
sexual inclination, 152–53, 367n.69, 398n.78; idealization of, 95–96, 289–90. *See also* generation, sexual
Shakespeare, William, 267
Shea, William R., 328n.40, 330n.52
Shell, Marc, 408n.6
Shell, Susan Meld, 366–67n.64
simplicity, 86, 88, 90–91, 93, 98–99, 107, 121, 132
skill (*Geschicklichkeit*), 53, 225, 257–58
sleep, 110, 113, 294; transition from to

wakefulness, 122, 269, 271. *See also* dreaming
Smith, Adam, 349n.63
Smith, C.U.M., 417–18n.45
Smith, Norman Kemp, 363n.43, 377n.38
Socrates, 97, 123, 130, 279, 290
Soemmering, Samuel Thomas, 447–48n.129
Sommer, Martin, 377n.38, 381n.45
soul, 4, 14, 15, 69, 75; relation of to body, 108–10; position of in world, 15, 125–26, 128, 131, 356n.49; presence of in world, 31, 72–73, 270–71; tranquility of, 97, 101–2
space: divisibility of, 76–77; ideality of, 127, 133, 134; imaginary, 124; inner and outer, 126; Kant's early views on, 21–22, 77–79; Leibniz's treatment of, 13, 76–77
Spalding, Keith, 377–78n.38
species, 62, 69, 191–99, 200, 203, 237, 302; origin of, 251–53, 304; transmutation of, 235, 253–55; unity of, 192, 194, 200
spirit, 6, 42, 108, 131, 207, 229–30, 283, 296, 353n.25; definition of, 107, 229–30, 310; and matter, 111, 237, 350–51n.6; as principle of genius, 225, 229–30; Rousseau on, 353n.25; as union of soul and body, 273; and wind, 308. See also *Dreams of a Spirit Seer*
Stafford, Barbara Maria, 442–43n.110, 428n.27, 429n.30
Stahl, Georg Ernst, 267, 281, 425n.18, 430nn.40–41
state, form of, 154; heads of, 156, 173, 177; as organism, 154–55, 157, 173, 240, 368n.72. *See also* constitution
Sterne, Laurence, 424–25n.16
stoicism, 39–40, 317n.10, 325–26nn.24–25; views on generation, 69; views on knowledge, 317n.10
Stuckenberg, J.H.W., 438n.84
sublimation, 337n.96
sublime, the, 49, 61, 62, 227, 332–33n.70, 262, 394n.56; attractive-repulsive forces and, 333n.71; dynamical, 61, 215–19; eroticism of, 218; mathematical, 210–15; and moral feeling, 295n.56, 348n.59; movement of, 212–13, 218–19; in nature, 395n.60; pleasure of, 393n.50, 396n.66
succession, principle of, 43, 138